Using the *Teach Yourself* in 24 Hours Series

Welcome to the *Teach Yourself in 24 Hours* series! You're probably thinking, "What, they want me to stay up all night and learn this stuff?" Well, no, not exactly. This series introduces a new way to teach you about exciting new products: 24 one-hour lessons, designed to keep your interest and keep you learning. Because the learning process is broken into small units, you will not be overwhelmed by the complexity of some of the new technologies that are emerging in today's market. Each hourly lesson has a number of special items, some old, some new, to help you along.

Minutes

The first 10 minutes of each hour list the topics and skills that you will learn about by the time you finish the hour. You will know exactly what the hour will bring, with no surprises.

Minutes

Twenty minutes into the lesson, you will have been introduced to many of the newest features of the software application. In the constantly evolving computer arena, knowing everything a program can do will aid you enormously now and in the future.

Minutes

Before 30 minutes have passed, you will have l[...] least one useful task. Many of these tasks take a [...] the newest features of the application. These tasks use a hands-on approach, telling you exactly which menus and commands you need to use to accomplish the goal. This approach is found in each lesson of the *24 Hours* series.

Minutes

You will see after 40 minutes that many of the tools you have come to expect from the *Teach Yourself* series are found in the *24 Hours* series as well. Notes and Tips offer special tricks of the trade to make your work faster and more productive. Warnings help you avoid those nasty time-consuming errors.

Minutes

By the time you're 50 minutes in, you'll probably run across terms you haven't seen before. Never before has technology thrown so many new words and acronyms into the language, and the New Terms elements found in this series will carefully explain each and every one of them.

Minutes

At the end of the hour, you may still have questions that need answered. You know the kind—questions on skills or tasks that come up every day for you, but that weren't directly addressed during the lesson. That's where the Q&A section can help. By answering the most frequently asked questions about the topics discussed in the hour, Q&A not only answers your specific question, it provides a succinct review of all that you have learned in the hour.

Teach
Yourself
UNIX

in 24 Hours

Teach Yourself
UNIX
in 24 Hours

Dave Taylor
James C. Armstrong, Jr.

SAMS
PUBLISHING

201 West 103rd Street
Indianapolis, Indiana 46290

Decimilli accipitrae Raptor Regina.—JA

To the newest light of my life: Ashley Elizabeth.—DT

Copyright © 1997 by Sams Publishing
FIRST EDITION

International Standard Book Number: 0-672-31107-0

Library of Congress Catalog Card Number: 97-66198

2000 99 98 97   4 3 2

Interpretation of the printing code: the rightmost double-digit number is the year of the book's printing; the rightmost single-digit, the number of the book's printing. For example, a printing code of 97-1 shows that the first printing of the book occurred in 1997.

Composed in AGaramond and MCPdigital by Macmillan Computer Publishing

Printed in the United States of America

President, Sams Publishng Richard K. Swadley
Publishing Manager Dean Miller
Director of Editorial Services Cindy Morrow
Director of Marketing Kelli Spencer
Product Marketing Manager Wendy Gilbride
Assistant Marketing Managers Jen Pock, Rachel Wolfe

Acquisitions Editor
Grace M. Buechlein

Development Editor
Brian-Kent Proffitt

Production Editor
Kristi Hart

Indexer
Greg Pearson

Technical Reviewer
Raj Mangal

Editorial Coordinators
Mandi Rouell
Katie Wise

Technical Edit Coordinator
Lynette Quinn

Resource Coordinator
Deborah Frisby

Editorial Assistants
Carol Ackerman
Andi Richter
Rhonda Tinch-Mize

Cover Designer
Tim Amrhein

Book Designer
Gary Adair

Copy Writer
David Reichwein

Production Team Supervisors
Brad Chinn
Charlotte Clapp

Production
Brad Lenser
Chris Livengood
Gene Redding
Janet Seib

Overview

		Introduction	xvi
Hour	1	What Is this UNIX Stuff?	1
	2	Getting onto the System and Using the Command Line	21
	3	Moving About the File System	43
	4	Listing Files and Managing Disk Usage	63
	5	Ownership and Permissions	87
	6	Creating, Moving, Renaming, and Deleting Files and Directories	113
	7	Looking into Files	127
	8	Filters and Piping	145
	9	Wildcards and Regular Expressions	161
	10	Power Filters and File Redirection	187
	11	An Introduction to the vi Editor	199
	12	Advanced vi Tricks, Tools, and Techniques	245
	13	An Overview of the emacs Editor	281
	14	Introduction to Command Shells	305
	15	Getting the Most Out of the C Shell	323
	16	Basic Shell Programming	347
	17	Job Control	361
	18	Printing in the UNIX Environment	379
	19	Searching for Information and Files	397
	20	Communicating with Others	407
	21	Using Netscape To See the World Wide Web	425
	22	Internet E-Mail, Netnews, and IRC	443
	23	Using telnet and ftp	479
	24	Programming in C for UNIX	509
		Glossary	531
		Index	541

Contents

Hour 1 What Is This UNIX Stuff?   **1**

    Goals for This Hour 1

    What Is UNIX? 2

    A Brief History of UNIX 3

        The C Programming Language 4

        UNIX Becomes Popular 5

    What's All This About Multiuser Systems? 5

    Cracking Open the Shell 6

    Getting Help 7

        Task 1.1: Man Pages, UNIX Online Reference 7

        Task 1.2: Other Ways to Find Help in UNIX 14

    Summary 17

    Workshop 17

        Key Terms 17

        Questions 18

        Preview of the Next Hour 19

2 Getting onto the System and Using the Command Line   **21**

    Goals for This Hour 21

        Task 2.1: Logging In and Out of the System 22

        Task 2.2: Changing Passwords with `passwd` 25

        Task 2.3: Picking a Secure Password 26

        Task 2.4: Who Are You? 28

        Task 2.5: Finding Out What Other Users Are Logged

          in to the System 30

        Task 2.6: What Is Everyone Doing on the Computer? 31

        Task 2.7: Checking the Current Date and Time 33

        Task 2.8: Looking at a Calendar 33

    Simple Math with UNIX 36

        Task 2.9: Using the `bc` Infix Calculator 36

        Task 2.10: Using the `dc` Postfix Calculator 38

    Summary 40

    Workshop 40

        Key Terms 40

        Questions 41

        Preview of the Next Hour 41

3 Moving About the File System   **43**

    Goals for This Hour 43

    What a Hierarchical File System Is All About 44

        Task 3.1: The UNIX File System Organization 45

        The `bin` Directory 46

The dev Directory 47

The etc Directory 47

The lib Directory 47

The lost+found Directory 48

The mnt and sys Directories 48

The tmp Directory 48

The usr Directory 48

Other Miscellaneous Stuff at the Top Level 49

How Mac and PC File Systems Differ from the UNIX File System 50

Directory Separator Characters 50

The Difference Between Relative and Absolute Filenames 51

Task 3.2: Hidden Files in UNIX 52

Task 3.3: The Special Directories "." and ".." 55

Task 3.4: The env Command 56

Task 3.5: PATH and HOME 57

Task 3.6: Find Where You Are with pwd 58

Task 3.7: Move to Another Location with cd 58

Summary 60

Workshop 60

Key Terms 60

Questions 62

Preview of the Next Hour 62

4   Listing Files and Managing Disk Usage   63

Goals for This Hour 63

The ls Command 64

Task 4.1: All About the ls Command 64

Task 4.2: Having ls Tell You More 65

Task 4.3: Combining Flags 68

Task 4.4: Listing Directories Without Changing Location 69

Special ls Command Flags 71

Task 4.5: Changing the Sort Order in ls 71

Task 4.6: Listing Directory Trees Recursively in ls 73

Task 4.7: Long Listing Format in ls 74

Permissions Strings 74

Task 4.8: Long Listing Format for Directories in ls 75

Task 4.9: Creating Files with the touch Command 78

Task 4.10: Check Disk-Space Usage with du 79

Task 4.11: Check Available Disk Space with df 82

Task 4.12: Shrink Big Files with the compress Program 83

Summary 84

Workshop 84

Key Terms 84

Questions 85

Preview of the Next Hour 85

5   Ownership and Permissions   87

Goals for This Hour 87
    Task 5.1: Understand File Permissions Settings 88
    Task 5.2: Directory Permissions Settings 93
    Task 5.3: Modify File and Directory Permissions with `chmod` 96
    Task 5.4: Set New File Permissions with `chmod` 98
    Task 5.5: Calculating Numeric Permissions Strings 102
    Task 5.6: Establish Default File and Directory Permissions
    with the `umask` Command 104
    Task 5.7: Identify Owner and Group for Any File or Directory 107
    Task 5.8: Change the Owner of a File or Directory 108
    Task 5.9: Change the Group of a File or Directory 109
Summary 110
Workshop 110
    Key Terms 110
    Questions 111
    Preview of the Next Hour 111

**6   Creating, Moving, Renaming, and Deleting Files
      and Directories   113**

Goals for This Hour 113
    Task 6.1: Creating New Directories Using `mkdir` 114
    Task 6.2: Copying Files to New Locations Using `cp` 116
    Task 6.3: Moving Files to New Locations Using `mv` 118
    Task 6.4: Renaming Files with `mv` 119
    Task 6.5: Removing Directories with `rmdir` 120
    Task 6.6: Removing Files Using `rm` 121
    Task 6.7: Minimizing the Danger of the `rm` Command 123
Summary 125
Workshop 125
    Key Terms 125
    Questions 126
    Preview of the Next Hour 126

7   Looking into Files   127

Goals for This Hour 127
    Task 7.1: Using `file` to Identify File Types 128
    Task 7.2: Exploring UNIX Directories with `file` 130
    Task 7.3: Peeking at the First Few Lines with `head` 133
    Task 7.4: Viewing the Last Few Lines with `tail` 135
    Task 7.5: Viewing the Contents of Files with `cat` 136
    Task 7.6: Viewing Larger Files with `more` 139
Summary 143
Workshop 143
    Key Terms 143
    Questions 144
    Preview of the Next Hour 144

8   Filters and Piping   **145**

  Goals for This Hour 145
    Task 8.1: The Secrets of File Redirection 146
    Task 8.2: Counting Words and Lines Using wc 147
    Task 8.3: Removing Extraneous Lines Using uniq 149
    Task 8.4: Sorting Information in a File Using sort 150
    Task 8.5: Number Lines in Files Using cat -n and nl 153
    Task 8.6: Cool nl Tricks and Capabilities 154
  Summary 157
  Workshop 158
    Key Terms 158
    Questions 158
    Preview of the Next Hour 159

9   Wildcards and Regular Expressions   **161**

  Goals for This Hour 161
    Task 9.1: Filename Wildcards 162
    Task 9.2: Advanced Filename Wildcards 164
    Task 9.3: Creating Sophisticated Regular Expressions 167
    Task 9.4: Searching Files Using grep 172
    Task 9.5: For Complex Expressions, Try egrep 175
    Task 9.6: Searching for Multiple Patterns at Once with fgrep 176
    Task 9.7: Changing Things En Route with sed 179
  Summary 185
  Workshop 185
    Key Terms 185
    Questions 185
    Preview of the Next Hour 186

10   Power Filters and File Redirection   **187**

  Goals for This Hour 187
    Task 10.1: The Wild and Weird awk Command 188
    Task 10.2: Re-routing the Pipeline with tee 196
  Summary 197
  Workshop 197
    Questions 197
    Preview of the Next Hour 198

11   An Introduction to the vi Editor   **199**

  Goals for This Hour 200
    Task 11.1: How To Start and Quit vi 200
    Task 11.2: Simple Cursor Motion in vi 205
    Task 11.3: Moving by Words and Pages 208
    Task 11.4: Inserting Text into the File Using i, a, o, and 0 212
    Task 11.5: Deleting Text 220
    Task 11.6: Searching Within a File 229
    Task 11.7: How To Start vi Correctly 234
    Task 11.8: The Colon Commands in vi 236

Summary 242
Workshop 243
    Key Terms 243
    Questions 244
    Preview of the Next Hour 244

12   Advanced vi Tricks, Tools, and Techniques   245

Goals for This Hour 245
    Task 12.1: The Change and Replace Commands 246
    Task 12.2: Numeric Repeat Prefixes 253
    Task 12.3: Numbering Lines in the File 255
    Task 12.4: Search and Replace 257
    Task 12.5: Mapping Keys with the :map Command 260
    Task 12.6: Moving Sentences and Paragraphs 266
    Task 12.7: Access UNIX with ! 270
Summary of vi Commands 278
Summary 279
Workshop 279
    Key Terms 279
    Questions 279
    Preview of the Next Hour 280

13   An Overview of the emacs Editor   281

Goals for This Hour 281
    Task 13.1: Launching emacs and Inserting Text 282
    Task 13.2: How To Move Around in a File 285
    Task 13.3: How To Delete Characters and Words 289
    Task 13.4: Search and Replace in emacs 294
    Task 13.5: Using the emacs Tutorial and Help System 297
    Task 13.6: Working with Other Files 299
Summary 303
Workshop 303
    Key Terms 303
    Questions 303
    Preview of the Next Hour 304

14   Introduction to Command Shells   305

Goals for This Hour 305
    Task 14.1: What Shells Are Available? 306
    Task 14.2: Identifying Your Shell 309
    Task 14.3: How To Choose a New Shell 310
    Task 14.4: Learning the Shell Environment 313
    Task 14.5: Exploring csh Configuration Files 317
Summary 321
Workshop 321
    Key Terms 321
    Questions 321
    Preview of the Next Hour 322

15   Getting the Most Out of the C Shell   323

Goals for This Hour 323
   Task 15.1: The C Shell and Korn Shell History Mechanisms 324
   Task 15.2: Using History to Cut Down on Typing 327
   Task 15.3: Command Aliases 333
   Task 15.4: Some Power Aliases 335
   Task 15.5: Setting Custom Prompts 338
   Task 15.6: Creating Simple Shell Scripts 340
Summary 344
Workshop 344
   Key Terms 344
   Questions 344
   Preview of the Next Hour 345

16   Basic Shell Programming   347

Goals for This Hour 347
   Task 16.1: Shell Variables 348
   Task 16.2: Shell Arithmetic 350
   Task 16.3: Comparison Functions 351
   Task 16.4: Conditional Expressions 355
   Task 16.5: Looping expressions 357
Summary 359
Workshop 359
   Key Terms 360
   Questions 360
   Preview of the Next Hour 360

17   Job Control   361

Goals for This Hour 361
   Task 17.1: Job Control in the Shell: Stopping Jobs 362
   Task 17.2: Foreground/Background and UNIX Programs 365
   Task 17.3: Finding Out What Tasks Are Running 368
   Task 17.4: Terminating Processes with `kill` 374
Summary 377
Workshop 377
   Key Terms 377
   Questions 378
   Preview of the Next Hour 378

18   Printing in the UNIX Environment   379

Goals for This Hour 379
   Task 18.1: Find Local Printers with `printers` 380
   Task 18.2: Printing Files with `lpr` or `lp` 384
   Task 18.3: Formatting Print Jobs with `pr` 387
   Task 18.4: Working with the Print Queue.. 391

Summary 394
Workshop 394
   Key Terms 395
   Questions 395
   Preview of the Next Hour 395

19 Searching for Information and Files   **397**
Goals for This Hour 397
   Task 19.1: The find Command and Its Weird Options 398
   Task 19.2: Using find with xargs 403
Summary 405
Workshop 405
   Questions 405
   Preview of the Next Hour 406

20 Communicating with Others   **407**
Goals for This Hour 407
   Task 20.1: Enabling Messages Using mesg 408
   Task 20.2: Writing to Other Users with write 409
   Task 20.3: Reading Electronic Mail with mailx 411
   Task 20.4: Sending Mail with mailx 417
   Task 20.5: The Smarter Electronic Mail Alternative, elm 420
Summary 423
Workshop 423
   Key Terms 424
   Questions 424
   Preview of the Next Hour 424

21 Using Netscape To See the World Wide Web   **425**
Goals for This Hour 425
Introduction to the Internet 426
   Task 21.1: Starting Your Browser 427
   Task 21.2: Finding Some Sites 432
   Task 21.3: Customizing Your Browser 437
Summary 440
Workshop 440
   Key Terms 440
   Questions 441
   Preview of the Next Hour 441

22 Internet E-Mail, Netnews, and IRC   **443**
Goals for This Hour 443
   Task 22.1: Sending E-Mail to Internet Users 444
   Task 22.2: Talking with Remote Internet Users 446
   Task 22.3: Searching Databases with WAIS 449
   Task 22.4: Having the Whole World with gopher 454

Task 22.5: Visiting Libraries Around the World 460
Task 22.6: All the News That's Fit or Otherwise 466
Workshop 477
Key Terms 477
Questions 477
Preview of the Next Hour 478

23   Using `telnet` and `ftp`   479

Goals for This Hour 479
Task 23.1: Connecting to Remote Internet Sites............................. 480
Task 23.2: Copying Files from Other Internet Sites 483
Task 23.3: Finding Archives with `archie` 493
Task 23.4: A Few Interesting `telnet` Sites 499
Workshop 507
Key Terms 507
Questions 507
Preview of the Next Hour 507

24   Programming in C for UNIX   509

Goals for This Hour 509
Task 24.1: Your First Program 510
Task 24.2: Basic Data Types and Operators 512
Task 24.3: Conditional Statements 517
Task 24.4: Looping Statements 520
Task 24.5: Functions 521
Task 24.6: Arrays 523
Task 24.7: Pointers 524
Task 24.8: Structures 526
Summary 528
Where To Go Next 528
Workshop 529
Key Terms 529
Questions 530

Glossary   531

Index   541

About the Authors

Dave Taylor

Dave Taylor is President and Chief Technical Officer of The Internet Mall, Inc., (`http://www.internetmall.com`), the largest online shopping site in the world. He has been involved with UNIX and the Internet since 1980, having created the popular Elm Mail System and Embot mail autoresponder. A prolific author, he has been published over 1,000 times, and his most recent books include the best-selling *Creating Cool HTML 3.2 Web Pages* and *The Internet Business Guide*. Dave has a weekly intranet column in *InfoWorld* and a Web/CGI programming column in *LOGIN*.

Previous positions include being a Research Scientist at HP Laboratories and Senior Reviews Editor of *SunWorld* magazine. He also has contributed software to the official 4.4 release of Berkeley UNIX (BSD), and his programs are found in all versions of Linux and other popular UNIX variants.

Dave has a Bachelor's degree in Computer Science (U.C.S.D., 1984) and a Master's degree in Education (Purdue, 1995), and he teaches evening courses in San Jose State University's Professional Development Program. His official home page on the Web is `http://www.intuitive.com/taylor`, and his e-mail address for the last decade has been `taylor@intuitive.com`.

James C. Armstrong, Jr.

James C. Armstrong, Jr., is the Director of Engineering at The Internet Mall, Inc., a San Jose, California-based firm, dedicated to making Web-based commerce a turnkey operation. James has nearly 15 years of professional experience with UNIX software products and has worked for Bell Labs, Sun, and Tandem Computers in the past. He is also an 18-year veteran of the Internet and its predecessors; his first contact was as a college student, exchanging electronic mail with his father at AT&T.

James has a Bachelor's degree in Computer Science from Duke University and has done some graduate study at the University of St. Andrews in Scotland. James is an avid naturalist and environmentalist and has traveled the world to photograph the beauty of nature.

Tell Us What You Think!

As a reader, you are the most important critic and commentator of our books. We value your opinion and want to know what we're doing right, what we could do better, what areas you'd like to see us publish in, and any other words of wisdom you're willing to pass our way. You can help us make strong books that meet your needs and give you the computer guidance you require.

Do you have access to CompuServe or the World Wide Web? Then check out our CompuServe forum by typing GO SAMS at any prompt. If you prefer the World Wide Web, check out our site at http://www.mcp.com.

JUST A MINUTE

> If you have a technical question about this book, call the technical support line at 317-581-4669.

As the team leader of the group that created this book, I welcome your comments. You can fax, e-mail, or write me directly to let me know what you did or didn't like about this book—as well as what we can do to make our books stronger. Here's the information:

Fax: 317-581-4669

E-mail: opsys_mgr@sams.mcp.com

Mail: Dean Miller
          Comments Department
          Sams Publishing
          201 W. 103rd Street
          Indianapolis, IN 46290

Introduction

Welcome to *Teach Yourself UNIX in 24 Hours*! This book has been designed so it is helpful for both beginning users and those with previous UNIX experience. This text is helpful as a guide, as well as a tutorial. The reader of this book is assumed to be intelligent, but no familiarity with UNIX is expected.

Does Each Chapter Take an Hour?

You can learn the concepts in each of the 24 chapters in one hour. If you want to experiment with what you learn in each chapter, you may take longer than an hour. However, all the concepts presented here are straightforward. If you are familiar with Windows applications, you will be able to progress more quickly through it.

How To Use This Book

This book is designed to teach you topics in one-hour sessions. All the books in the Sams *Teach Yourself* series enable you to start working and become productive with the product as quickly as possible. This book will do that for you!

Each hour, or session, starts with an overview of the topic to inform you what to expect in each lesson. The overview helps you determine the nature of the lesson and whether the lesson is relevant to your needs.

Main Section

Each lesson has a main section that discusses the lesson topic in a clear, concise manner by breaking the topic down into logical component parts and explaining each component clearly.

Interspersed in each lesson are special elements, called Just a Minutes, Time Savers, and Cautions, that provide additional information.

JUST A MINUTE

Just a Minutes are designed to clarify the concept that is being discussed. It elaborates on the subject, and if you are comfortable with your understanding of the subject, you can bypass them without danger.

TIME SAVER

Time Savers inform you of tricks or elements that are easily missed by most computer users. You can skip them, but often Time Savers show you an easier way to do a task.

CAUTION

A Caution deserves at least as much attention as a Time Saver because Cautions point out a problematic element of the topic being discussed. Ignoring the information contained in the Caution could have adverse effects on the task at hand. These are the most important special elements in this book.

Tasks

This book offers another special element called a Task. These step-by-step exercises are designed to quickly walk you through the most important skills you can learn in UNIX. Each Task has three parts—Description, Action, and Summary.

Workshops

The Workshop section at the end of each lesson provides Key Terms and Questions that reinforce concepts you learned in the lesson and help you apply them in new situations. You can skip this section, but it is advised that you go through the exercises to see how the concepts can be applied to other common tasks. The Key Terms also are compiled in one alphabetized list in the Glossary at the end of the book.

Hour 1

What Is This UNIX Stuff?

Welcome to *Teach Yourself UNIX in 24 Hours!* This hour starts you toward becoming a UNIX expert. Our goal for the first hour is to introduce you to some UNIX history and to teach you where to go for help online.

Goals for This Hour

In the first hour, you learn

- ☐ The history of UNIX
- ☐ Why it's called UNIX
- ☐ What multiuser systems are all about
- ☐ The difference between UNIX and other operating systems
- ☐ About command-line interpreters and how users interact with UNIX
- ☐ How to use man pages, UNIX's online reference material
- ☐ Other ways to find help in UNIX

What Is UNIX?

UNIX is a computer operating system, a control program that works with users to run programs, manage resources, and communicate with other computer systems. Several people can use a UNIX computer at the same time; hence UNIX is called a *multiuser* system. Any of these users can also run multiple programs at the same time; hence UNIX is called *multitasking*. Because UNIX is such a pastiche—a patchwork of development—it's a lot more than just an operating system. UNIX has more than 250 individual commands. These range from simple commands—for copying a file, for example—to the quite complex: those used in high-speed networking, file revision management, and software development.

Most notably, UNIX is a multichoice system. As an example, UNIX has three different primary command-line-based user interfaces (in UNIX, the command-line user interface is called a *shell*): The three choices are the Bourne shell, C shell, and Korn shell. Often, soon after you learn to accomplish a task with a particular command, you discover there's a second or third way to do that task. This is simultaneously the greatest strength of UNIX and a source of frustration for both new and current users.

Why is having all this choice such a big deal? Think about why Microsoft MS-DOS and the Apple Macintosh interfaces are considered so easy to use. Both are designed to give the user less power. Both have dramatically fewer commands and precious little overlap in commands: You can't use copy to list your files in DOS, and you can't drag a Mac file icon around to duplicate it in its own directory. The advantage to these interfaces is that, in either system, you can learn the one-and-only way to do a task and be confident that you're as sophisticated in doing that task as is the next person. It's easy. It's quick to learn. It's exactly how the experts do it, too.

UNIX, by contrast, is much more like a spoken language, with commands acting as verbs, command options (which you learn about later in this lesson) acting as adjectives, and the more complex commands acting akin to sentences. How you do a specific task can, therefore, be completely different from how your UNIX-expert friend does the same task. Worse, some specific commands in UNIX have many different versions, partly because of the variations from different UNIX vendors. (You've heard of these variations and vendors, I'll bet: UNIXWare from Novell, Solaris from Sun, SCO from Santa Cruz, System V Release 4 (pronounce that "system five release four" or, to sound like an ace, "ess-vee-are-four"), and BSD UNIX (pronounced "bee-ess-dee") from University of California at Berkeley are the primary players. Each is a little different from the other.) Another contributor to the sprawl of modern UNIX is the energy of the UNIX programming community; plenty of UNIX users decide to write a new version of a command in order to solve slightly different problems, thus spawning many versions of a command.

1

JUST A MINUTE

I must admit that I, too, am guilty of rewriting a variety of UNIX commands, including those for an electronic mail system, a simple line-oriented editor, a text formatter, a programming language interpreter, calendar manager, and even slightly different versions of the file-listing command ls and the remove-files command rm. As a programmer, I found that trying to duplicate the functionality of a particular command or utility was a wonderful way to learn more about UNIX and programming.

Given the multichoice nature of UNIX, I promise to teach you the most popular UNIX commands, and, if there are alternatives, I will teach you about those, too. The goal of this book is for you to learn UNIX and to be able to work alongside long-time UNIX folk as a peer, sharing your expertise with them and continuing to learn about the system and its commands from them and other sources.

A Brief History of UNIX

To understand why the UNIX operating system has so many commands and why it's not only the premier multiuser, multitasking operating system, but also the most successful and the most powerful multichoice system for computers, you'll have to travel back in time. You'll need to learn where UNIX was designed, what were the goals of the original programmers, and what has happened to UNIX in the subsequent decades.

Unlike DOS, Windows, OS/2, the Macintosh, VMS, MVS, and just about any other operating system, UNIX was designed by a couple of programmers as a fun project, and it evolved through the efforts of hundreds of programmers, each of whom was exploring his or her own ideas of particular aspects of OS design and user interaction. In this regard, UNIX is not like other operating systems, needless to say!

It all started back in the late 1960s in a dark and stormy laboratory deep in the recesses of the American Telephone and Telegraph (AT&T) corporate facility in New Jersey. Working with the Massachusetts Institute of Technology, AT&T Bell Labs was codeveloping a massive, monolithic operating system called Multics. On the Bell Labs team were Ken Thompson, Dennis Ritchie, Brian Kernighan, and other people in the Computer Science Research Group who would prove to be key contributors to the new UNIX operating system.

When 1969 rolled around, Bell Labs was becoming increasingly disillusioned with Multics, an overly slow and expensive system that ran on General Electric mainframe computers that themselves were expensive to run and rapidly becoming obsolete. The problem was that Thompson and the group really liked the capabilities Multics offered, particularly the individual-user environment and multiple-user aspects.

In that same year, Thompson wrote a computer game called Space Travel, first on Multics, then on the GECOS (GE computer operating system). The game was a simulation of the movement of the major bodies of the Solar System, with the player guiding a ship, observing the scenery, and attempting to land on the various planets and moons. The game wasn't much fun on the GE computer, however, because performance was jerky and irregular, and, more importantly, it cost almost $100 in computing time for each game.

In his quest to improve the game, Thompson found a little-used Digital Equipment Corporation PDP-7, and with some help from Ritchie, he rewrote the game for the PDP-7. Development was done on the GE mainframe and hand-carried to the PDP-7 on paper tape.

Once he'd explored some of the capabilities of the PDP-7, Thompson couldn't resist building on the game, starting with an implementation of an earlier file system he'd designed, then adding processes, simple file utilities (cp, mv), and a command interpreter that he called a "shell." It wasn't until the following year that the newly created system acquired its name, UNIX, which Brian Kernighan suggested as a pun on Multics.

The Thompson file system was built around the low-level concept of *i-nodes*—linked blocks of information that together comprise the contents of a file or program—kept in a big list called the *i-list*, subdirectories, and special types of files that described devices and acted as the actual device driver for user interaction. What was missing in this earliest form of UNIX was *pathnames*. No slash (/) was present, and subdirectories were referenced through a confusing combination of file links that proved too complex, causing users to stop using subdirectories. Another limitation in this early version was that directories couldn't be added while the system was running and had to be added to the preload configuration.

In 1970, Thompson's group requested and received a Digital PDP-11 system for the purpose of creating a system for editing and formatting text. It was such an early unit that the first disk did not arrive at Bell Labs until four months after the CPU showed up. The first important program on UNIX was the text-formatting program roff, which—keep with me now—was inspired by McIlroy's BCPL program on Multics, which in turn had been inspired by an earlier program called runoff on the CTSS operating system.

The initial customer was the Patent Department inside the Labs, a group that needed a system for preparing patent applications. There, UNIX was a dramatic success, and it didn't take long for others inside Bell Labs to begin clamoring for their own UNIX computer systems.

The C Programming Language

That's where UNIX came from. What about C, the programming language that is integral to the system?

1

In 1969, the original UNIX had a very-low-level assembly language compiler available for writing programs; all the PDP-7 work was done in this primitive language. Just before the PDP-11 arrived, McIlroy ported a language called TMG to the PDP-7, which Thompson then tried to use to write a FORTRAN compiler. That didn't work, and instead he produced a language called B. Two years later, in 1971, Ritchie created the first version of a new programming language based on B, a language he called C. By 1973, the entire UNIX system had been rewritten in C for portability and speed.

UNIX Becomes Popular

In the 1970s, AT&T hadn't yet been split up into the many regional operating companies known today, and the company was prohibited from selling the new UNIX system. Hoping for the best, Bell Labs distributed UNIX to colleges and universities for a nominal charge. These institutions also were happily buying the inexpensive and powerful PDP-11 computer systems—a perfect match. Before long, UNIX was the research and software-development operating system of choice.

The UNIX of today is not, however, the product of a couple of inspired programmers at Bell Labs. Many other organizations and institutions contributed significant additions to the system as it evolved from its early beginnings and grew into the monster it is today. Most important were the C shell, TCP/IP networking, vi editor, Berkeley Fast File System, and sendmail electronic-mail-routing software from the Computer Science Research Group of the University of California at Berkeley. Also important were the early versions of UUCP and Usenet from the University of Maryland, Delaware, and from Duke University. After dropping Multics development completely, MIT didn't come into the UNIX picture until the early 1980s, when it developed the X Window System as part of its successful Athena project. Ten years and four releases later, X is the predominant windowing system standard on all UNIX systems, and it is the basis of Motif, OpenWindows, and Open Desktop.

Gradually, big corporations have become directly involved with the evolutionary process, notably Hewlett-Packard, Sun Microsystems, and Digital Equipment Corporation. Little companies have started to get into the action too, with UNIX available from Apple for the Macintosh and from IBM for PCs, RISC-based workstations, and new PowerPC computers.

Today, UNIX runs on all sizes of computers, from humble PC laptops, to powerful desktop-visualization workstations, and even to supercomputers that require special cooling fluids to prevent them from burning up while working. It's a long way from Space Travel, a game that, ironically, isn't part of UNIX anymore.

What's All This About Multiuser Systems?

Among the many *multi* words you learned earlier was one that directly concerns how you interact with the computer, multiuser. The goal of a multiuser system is for all users to feel as though they've each been given their own personal computer, their own individual UNIX system, although they actually are working within a large system. To accomplish this, each user is given an *account*—usually based on the person's last name, initials, or another unique naming scheme—and a home directory, the default place where his or her files are saved. This leads to a bit of a puzzle: When you're working on the system, how does the system know that you're you? What's to stop someone else from masquerading as you, going into your files, prying into private letters, altering memos, or worse?

On a Macintosh or PC, anyone can walk up to your computer when you're not around, flip the power switch, and pry, and you can't do much about it. You can add some security software, but security isn't a fundamental part of the system, which results in an awkward fit between system and software. For a computer sitting on your desk in your office, though, that's okay; the system is not a shared multiuser system, so verifying who you are when you turn on the computer isn't critical.

But UNIX is a system designed for multiple users, so it is very important that the system can confirm your identity in a manner that precludes others from masquerading as you. As a result, all accounts have passwords associated with them—like a PIN for a bank card, keep it a secret!—and, when you use your password in combination with your account, the computer can be pretty sure that you are who you're claiming to be. For obvious reasons, when you're done using the computer, you always should remember to end your session, or, in effect, to turn off your virtual personal computer when you're done.

In the next hour, you learn your first UNIX commands. At the top of the list are commands to log in to the system, enter your password, and change your password to be memorable and highly secure.

Cracking Open the Shell

Another unusual feature of UNIX systems, especially for those of you who come from either the Macintosh or the Windows environments, is that UNIX is designed to be a command–line-based system rather than a more graphically based (picture-oriented) system. That's a mixed blessing. It makes UNIX harder to learn, but the system is considerably more powerful than fiddling with a mouse to drag little pictures about on the screen.

There are graphical interfaces to UNIX, built within the X Window System environment. Notable ones are Motif, Open Windows, and Open Desktop. Even with the best of these, however, the command-line heart of UNIX still shines through, and in my experience, it's impossible really to use all the power that UNIX offers without turning to a shell.

If you're used to writing letters to your friends and family or even mere shopping lists, you won't have any problem with a command-line interface: It's a command program that you tell what to do. When you type specific instructions and press the Return key, the computer leaps into action and immediately performs whatever command you've specified.

1

> Throughout this book, I refer to pressing the Return key, but your keyboard
> may have this key labeled as "Enter" or marked with a left-pointing,
> specially shaped arrow. These all mean the same thing.

In Windows, you might move a file from one folder to another by opening the folder, opening the destination folder, fiddling around for a while to be sure that you can see both of them on the screen at the same time, and then clicking and dragging the specific file from one place to the other. In UNIX it's much easier. Typing in the following simple command does the trick:

```
cp folder1/file folder2
```

It automatically ensures the file has the same name in the destination directory, too.

This might not seem much of a boon, but imagine the situation where you want to move all files with names that start with the word project or end with the suffix .c (C program files). This could be quite tricky and could take a lot of patience with a graphical interface. UNIX, however, makes it easy:

```
cp project* *.c folder2
```

Soon you not only will understand this command, but you also will be able to compose your own examples!

Getting Help

Throughout this book, the focus is on the most important and valuable flags and options for the commands covered. That's all well and good, but how do you find out about the other alternatives that might actually work better for your use? That's where the UNIX "man" pages come in. You will learn how to browse them to find the information desired.

Task 1.1: Man Pages, UNIX Online Reference

DESCRIPTION   It's not news to you that UNIX is a very complex operating system, with hundreds of commands that can be combined to execute thousands of possible actions. Most commands have a considerable number of options, and all seem to have some subtlety or other that it's important to know. But how do you figure all this out? You need to look up commands in the UNIX online documentation set. Containing purely reference materials, the UNIX *man pages* (*man* is short for *manual*) cover every command available.

To search for a man page, enter man followed by the name of the command to find. Many sites also have a table of contents for the man pages (it's called a whatis database, for obscure historical reasons.) You can use the all-important -k flag for keyword searches, to find the name of a command if you know what it should do but you just can't remember what it's called.

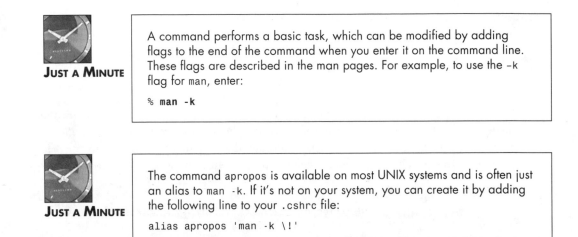

JUST A MINUTE

A command performs a basic task, which can be modified by adding flags to the end of the command when you enter it on the command line. These flags are described in the man pages. For example, to use the -k flag for man, enter:

```
% man -k
```

JUST A MINUTE

The command apropos is available on most UNIX systems and is often just an alias to man -k. If it's not on your system, you can create it by adding the following line to your .cshrc file:

```
alias apropos 'man -k \!'
```

The UNIX man pages are organized into nine sections, as shown in Table 1.1. This table is organized for System V, but it generally holds true for Berkeley systems, too, with these few changes: BSD has I/O and special files in Section 4, administrative files in Section 5, and miscellaneous files in Section 7. Some BSD systems also split user commands into further categories: Section 1C for intersystem communications and Section 1G for commands used primarily for graphics and computer-aided design.

Table 1.1. System V UNIX man page organization.

Section	Category
1	User commands
1M	System maintenance commands
2	System calls
3	Library routines
4	Administrative files
5	Miscellaneous
6	Games
7	I/O and special files
8	Administrative commands

ACTION

1. The mkdir man page is succinct and exemplary:

   ```
   % man mkdir

   MKDIR(1)                DYNIX Programmer's Manual              MKDIR(1)

   NAME
        mkdir - make a directory

   SYNOPSIS
        mkdir dirname ...

   DESCRIPTION
        Mkdir creates specified directories in mode 777. Standard
        entries, `.', for the directory itself, and `..' for its
        parent, are made automatically.

        Mkdir requires write permission in the parent directory.

   SEE ALSO
        rmdir(1)

   Revision 1.4.2.2 88/08/13                                           1
   %
   ```

JUST A MINUTE

> Notice in the example, that in the first line, the command itself is in
> boldface type, but everything else is not bold. Throughout this book,
> whenever an example contains both user input and UNIX output, the user
> input will be bold so that you can spot easily what you are supposed to
> enter.

The very first line of the output tells me that it's found the mkdir command in
Section 1 (user commands) of the man pages, with the middle phrase, DYNIX
Programmer's Manual, indicating that I'm running on a version of UNIX called
DYNIX. The NAME section always details the name of the command and a one-line
summary of what it does. SYNOPSIS explains how to use the command, including all
possible command flags and options.

DESCRIPTION is where all the meaningful information is, and it can run on for
dozens of pages, explaining how complex commands like csh or vi work. SEE ALSO
suggests other commands that are related in some way. The Revision line at the
bottom is different on each version of man, and it indicates the last time, presumably, that this document was revised.

2. The same man page from a Sun workstation is quite different:

```
% man mkdir
MKDIR(1)                        USER COMMANDS                        MKDIR(1)

NAME
     mkdir - make a directory

SYNOPSIS
     mkdir [ -p ] dirname...

DESCRIPTION
     mkdir creates directories.  Standard entries, `.',  for  the
     directory itself, and `..' for its parent, are made automat-
     ically.

     The -p flag allows missing parent directories to be  created
     as needed.

     With the exception of the set-gid bit, the current umask(2V)
     setting  determines  the  mode  in  which  directories  are
     created.  The new directory inherits the set-gid bit of  the
     parent  directory.  Modes may be modified after creation by
     using chmod(1V).

     mkdir requires write permission in the parent directory.

SEE ALSO
     chmod(1V), rm(1), mkdir(2V), umask(2V)

Sun Release 4.1    Last change: 22 August 1989                          1
%
```

Notice that there's a new flag in this version of mkdir, the -p flag. More importantly, note that the flag is shown in square brackets within the SYNOPSIS section. By convention, square brackets in this section mean that the flag is optional. You can see that the engineers at Sun have a very different idea about what other commands might be worth viewing!

3. One thing I always forget on Sun systems is the command that lets me format a floppy disk. That's exactly where the apropos command comes in handy:

```
% apropos floppy
fd (4S)                        - disk driver for Floppy Disk Controllers
%
```

That's not quite what I want, unfortunately. Because it's in Section 4 (note that the word in parentheses is 4S, not 1), this document will describe the disk driver rather than any command to work with floppy disks.

I can look up the disk command instead:

```
% man -k disk
acctdisk, acctdusg, accton, acctwtmp (8)    - overview of accounting and
➥miscellaneous accounting commands
add_client (8)                 - create a diskless network bootable NFS client on
```

1

```
→a server
chargefee, ckpacct, dodisk, lastlogin, monacct, nulladm, prctmp, prdaily,
→prtacct, runacct, shutacct, startup, turnacct (8) - shell procedures for
→accounting
client (8)                  - add or remove diskless Sun386i systems
df (1V)                     - report free disk space on file systems
diskusg (8)                 - generate disk accounting data by user
dkctl (8)                   - control special disk operations
dkinfo (8)                  - report information about a disk's geometry and
→partitioning
dkio (4S)                   - generic disk control operations
du (1L)                     - summarize disk usage
du (1V)                     - display the number of disk blocks used per
→directory or file
fastboot, fasthalt (8)      - reboot/halt the system while disabling disk
→checking
fd (4S)                     - disk driver for Floppy Disk Controllers
fdformat (1)                - format diskettes for use with SunOS
format (8S)                 - disk partitioning and maintenance utility
fsync (2)                   - synchronize a file's in-core state with that
→on disk
fusage (8)                  - RFS disk access profiler
id (4S)                     - disk driver for IPI disk controllers
installboot (8S)            - install bootblocks in a disk partition
pnpboot, pnp.s386 (8C)      - pnp diskless boot service
quota (1)                   - display a user's disk quota and usage
quotactl (2)                - manipulate disk quotas
root (4S)                   - pseudo-driver for Sun386i root disk
sd (4S)                     - driver for SCSI disk devices
sync (1)                    - update the super block; force changed blocks
→to the disk
xd (4S)                     - Disk driver for Xylogics 7053 SMD Disk
→Controller
xy (4S)                     - Disk driver for Xylogics 450 and 451 SMD Disk
→Controllers
%
```

JUST A MINUTE

Notice the → character at the beginning of some of the lines in this example. This character does not appear on your screen. It's a typographical convention used in the book because the number of characters that can be displayed by UNIX on a line of your screen is greater than the number of characters that can appear (legibly) on a line in this book. The → indicates that the text following it is actually part of the preceding line on your screen.

This yields quite a few choices! To trim the list down to just those that are in Section 1 (the user commands section), I use grep:

```
% man -k disk ¦ grep '(1'
df (1V)                     - report free disk space on file systems
du (1L)                     - summarize disk usage
```

```
du (1V)                      - display the number of disk blocks used per
➥directory or file
fdformat (1)                 - format diskettes for use with SunOS
quota (1)                    - display a user's disk quota and usage
sync (1)                     - update the super block; force changed blocks
➥to the disk
%
```

That's better! The command I was looking for is `fdformat`.

4. To learn a single snippet of information about a UNIX command, you can check to see if your system has the `whatis` utility. You can even ask it to describe itself (a bit of a philosophical conundrum):

```
% whatis whatis
whatis (1)                   - display a one-line summary about a keyword
%
```

In fact, this is the line from the NAME section of the relevant man page. The `whatis` command is different from the `apropos` command because it considers only command names rather than all words in the command description line:

```
% whatis cd
cd (1)                       - change working directory
%
```

Now see what `apropos` does:

```
% apropos cd
bcd, ppt (6)                 - convert to antique media
cd (1)                       - change working directory
cdplayer (6)                 - CD-ROM audio demo program
cdromio (4S)                 - CDROM control operations
draw, bdraw, cdraw (6)       - interactive graphics drawing
fcdcmd, fcd (1)              - change client's current working directory in
➥the FSP database
getacinfo, getacdir, getacflg, getacmin, setac, endac (3)    - get audit
➥ control file information
ipallocd (8C)                - Ethernet-to-IP address allocator
mp, madd, msub, mult, mdiv, mcmp, min, mout, pow, gcd, rpow, itom, xtom,
➥mtox, mfree (3X)            - multiple precision integer arithmetic
rexecd, in.rexecd (8C)       - remote execution server
sccs-cdc, cdc (1)            - change the delta commentary of an SCCS delta
sr (4S)                      - driver for CDROM SCSI controller
termios, tcgetattr, tcsetattr, tcsendbreak, tcdrain, tcflush, tcflow,
➥cfgetospeed, cfgetispeed, cfsetispeed, cfsetospeed (3V) - get and
➥set terminal attributes, line control, get and set baud rate, get
➥and set terminal foreground process group ID
tin, rtin, cdtin, tind (1)  - A threaded Netnews reader
uid_allocd, gid_allocd (8C) - UID and GID allocator daemons
%
```

5. One problem with `man` is that it really isn't too sophisticated. As you can see in the example in step 4, `apropos` (which, recall, is `man -k`) lists a line more than once if more than one man page match the specified pattern. You can create your own `apropos` alias to improve the command:

1

```
% alias apropos _man -k \!* ¦ uniq_
% apropos cd
bcd, ppt (6)              - convert to antique media
cd (1)                    - change working directory
cdplayer (6)              - CD-ROM audio demo program
cdromio (4S)              - CDROM control operations
draw, bdraw, cdraw (6)    - interactive graphics drawing
fcdcmd, fcd (1)           - change client's current working directory
➥in the FSP database
getacinfo, getacdir, getacflg, getacmin, setac, endac (3)    - get audit
➥control file information
ipallocd (8C)             - Ethernet-to-IP address allocator
mp, madd, msub, mult, mdiv, mcmp, min, mout, pow, gcd, rpow, itom, xtom,
➥mtox, mfree (3X)        - multiple precision integer arithmetic
rexecd, in.rexecd (8C)    - remote execution server
sccs-cdc, cdc (1)         - change the delta commentary of an SCCS delta
sr (4S)                   - driver for CDROM SCSI controller
termios, tcgetattr, tcsetattr, tcsendbreak, tcdrain, tcflush, tcflow,
➥cfgetospeed, cfgetispeed, cfsetispeed, cfsetospeed (3V) - get and set
➥terminal attributes, line control, get and set baud rate, get
➥and set terminal foreground process group ID
tin, rtin, cdtin, tind (1)   - A threaded Netnews reader
uid_allocd, gid_allocd (8C) - UID and GID allocator daemons
%
```

That's better, but I'd like to have the command tell me about only user commands because I don't care much about file formats, games, or miscellaneous commands when I'm looking for a command. I'll try this:

```
% alias apropos _man -k \!* ¦ uniq ¦ grep 1_
% apropos cd
cd (1)                    - change working directory
fcdcmd, fcd (1)           - change client's current working directory
➥in the FSP database
sccs-cdc, cdc (1)         - change the delta commentary of an SCCS delta
tin, rtin, cdtin, tind (1)  - A threaded Netnews reader
%
```

That's much better.

6. I'd like to look up one more command—sort—before I'm done here.

```
% man sort

SORT(1)              DYNIX Programmer's Manual              SORT(1)

NAME
     sort - sort or merge files

SYNOPSIS
     sort [ -mubdfinrtx ] [ +pos1 [ -pos2 ] ] ... [ -o name ]
          [ -T directory ] [ name ] ...

DESCRIPTION
     Sort sorts lines of all the named files together and writes
     the result on the standard output.  The name `-' means the
     standard input.  If no input files are named, the standard
     input is sorted.
```

```
    The default sort key is an entire line.  Default ordering is
    lexicographic by bytes in machine collating sequence.  The
    ordering is affected globally by the following options, one
    or more of which may appear.

    b    Ignore leading blanks (spaces and tabs) in field com-
--More--  _
```

On almost every system, the man command feeds output through the more program so that information won't scroll by faster than you can read it. You also can save the output of a man command to a file if you'd like to study the information in detail. To save this particular manual entry to the file sort.manpage, you could use man sort > sort.manpage.

Notice in the sort man page that there are many options to the sort command (certainly more than discussed in this book). As you learn UNIX, if you find areas about which you'd like more information, or if you need a capability that doesn't seem to be available, check the man page. There just might be a flag for what you seek.

JUST A MINUTE

You can obtain lots of valuable information by reading the introduction to each section of the man pages. Use man 1 intro to read the introduction to Section 1, for example.

If your version of man doesn't stop at the bottom of each page, you can remedy the situation using alias man 'man \!* ¦ more'.

SUMMARY UNIX was one of the very first operating systems to include online documentation. The man pages are an invaluable reference. Most of them are poorly written, unfortunately, and precious few include examples of actual usage. However, as a quick reminder of flags and options, or as an easy way to find out the capabilities of a command, man is great. I encourage you to explore the man pages and perhaps even read the man page on the man command itself.

Task 1.2: Other Ways to Find Help in UNIX

DESCRIPTION The man pages are really the best way to learn about what's going on with UNIX commands, but some alternatives also can prove helpful. Some systems have a help command. Many UNIX utilities make information available with the -h or -? flag, too. Finally, one trick you can try is to feed a set of gibberish flags to a command, which sometimes generates an error and a helpful message reminding you what possible options the command accepts.

ACTION

1. At the University Tech Computing Center, the support team has installed a `help` command:

```
% help
Look in a printed manual, if you can, for general help. You should have
someone show you some things and then read one of the tutorial papers
(e.g., UNIX for Beginners or An Introduction to the C Shell) to get
started. Printed manuals covering all aspects of Unix are on sale at the
bookstore.

Most of the material in the printed manuals is also available online
via "man" and similar commands; for instance:

apropos keyword - lists commands relevant to keyword
whatis filename - lists commands involving filename
man command - prints out the manual entry for a command
help command - prints out the pocket guide entry for a command
➥are helpful; other basic commands are:
cat - display a file on the screen
date - print the date and time
du - summarize disk space usage
edit - text editor (beginner)
ex - text editor (intermediate)
finger - user information lookup program
learn - interactive self-paced tutorial on Unix
--More(40%)-- _
```

Your system might have something similar.

2. Some commands offer helpful output if you specify the `-h` flag:

```
% ls -h
usage: ls [ -acdfgilqrstu1ACLFR ] name ...
%
```

Then again, others don't:

```
% ls -h
Global.Software    Mail/        Src/        history.usenet.Z
Interactive.Unix   News/        bin/        testme
%
```

A few commands offer lots of output when you use the `-h` flag:

```
% elm -h
Possible Starting Arguments for ELM program:
arg     Meaning
-a      Arrow - use the arrow pointer regardless
-c      Checkalias - check the given aliases only
-dn     Debug - set debug level to 'n'
-fx     Folder - read folder 'x' rather than incoming mailbox
-h      Help - give this list of options
```

```
-k        Keypad - enable HP 2622 terminal keyboard
-K        Keypad&softkeys - enable use of softkeys + "-k"
-m        Menu - Turn off menu, using more of the screen
-sx       Subject 'x' - for batchmailing
-V        Enable sendmail voyeur mode.
-v        Print out ELM version information.
-w        Supress warning messages...
-z        Zero - don't enter ELM if no mail is pending
%
```

Unfortunately, there isn't a command flag common to all UNIX utilities that lists the possible command flags.

3. Sometimes you can obtain help from a program by incurring its wrath. You can specify a set of flags that are impossible, unavailable, or just plain puzzling. I always use -xyz because they're uncommon flags:

```
% man -xyz
man: unknown option '-x', use '-h' for help
```

Okay, I'll try it:

```
% man -h
man: usage [-S ¦ -t ¦ -w] [-ac] [-m path] [-M path] [section] pages
man: usage -k [-ac] [-m path] [-M path] [section] keywords
man: usage -f [-ac] [-m path] [-M path] [section] names
man: usage -h
man: usage -V
a          display all manpages for names
c          cat (rather than page) manual pages
f          find whatis entries for pages by these names
names      names to search for in whatis
h          print this help message
k          find whatis entries by keywords
keywords   keywords to search for in whatis
m path     add to the standard man path directories
M path     override standard man path directories
S          display only SYNOPSIS section of pages
t          find the source (rather than the formatted page)
V          show version information
w          only output which pages we would display
section    section for the manual to search
pages      pages to locate
%
```

For every command that does something marginally helpful, there are a half-dozen commands that give useless, and amusingly different, output for these flags:

```
% bc -xyz
unrecognizable argument
% cal -xyz
Bad argument
% file -xyz
-xyz:   No such file or directory
% grep -xyz
grep: unknown flag
%
```

You can't rely on programs to be helpful about themselves, but you can rely on the man page being available for just about everything on the system.

SUMMARY As much as I'd like to tell you that there is a wide variety of useful and interesting information available within UNIX on the commands therein, in reality, UNIX has man pages but precious little else. Furthermore, some commands installed locally might not even have man page entries, which leaves you to puzzle out how they work. If you encounter commands that are undocumented, I recommend that you ask your system administrator or vendor what's going on and why there's no further information on the program.

Some vendors are addressing this problem in innovative, if somewhat limited, ways. Sun Microsystems, for example, offers its complete documentation set, including all tutorials, user guides, and man pages, on a single CD-ROM. AnswerBook, as it's called, is helpful but has some limitations, not the least of which is that you must have a CD-ROM drive and keep the disk in the drive at all times.

Summary

In this first hour, the goal was for you to learn a bit about what UNIX is, where it came from, and how it differs from other operating systems that you might have used in the past. You also learned about the need for security on a multiuser system and how a password helps maintain that security, so that your files are never read, altered, or removed by anyone but yourself.

You also learned what a command shell, or command-line interpreter, is all about, how it differs from graphically oriented interface systems like the Macintosh and Windows, and how it's not only easy to use, but considerably more powerful than dragging-and-dropping little pictures.

Finally, you learned about getting help on UNIX. Although there aren't many options, you do have the manual pages available to you, as well as the command-line arguments and `apropos`.

Workshop

The Workshop summarizes the key terms you learned and poses some questions about the topics presented in this chapter. It also provides you with a preview of what you will learn in the next hour.

Key Terms

account This is the official one-word name by which the UNIX system knows you. Mine is `taylor`.

arguments   Not any type of domestic dispute, arguments are the set of options and filenames specified to UNIX commands. When you use a command such as vi test.c, all words other than the command name itself (vi) are arguments, or parameters to the program.

i-list   See **i-node**.

i-node   The UNIX file system is like a huge notebook full of sheets of information. Each file is like an index tab, indicating where the file starts in the notebook and how many sheets are used. The tabs are called i-nodes, and the list of tabs (the index to the notebook) is the i-list.

command   Each program in UNIX is also known as a command: the two words are interchangeable.

man page   Each standard UNIX command comes with some basic online documentation that describes its function. This online documentation for a command is called a man page. Usually, the man page lists the command-line flags and some error conditions.

multitasking   A multitasking computer is one that actually can run more than one program, or task, at a time. By contrast, most personal computers lock you into a single program that you must exit before you launch another.

multiuser   Computers intended to have more than a single person working on them simultaneously are designed to support multiple users, hence the term *multiuser*. By contrast, personal computers are almost always single-user because someone else can't be running a program or editing a file while you are using the computer for your own work.

pathname   UNIX is split into a wide variety of different directories and subdirectories, often across multiple hard disks and even multiple computers. So that the system needn't search laboriously through the entire mess each time you request a program, the set of directories you reference are stored as your search path, and the location of any specific command is known as its *pathname*.

shell   To interact with UNIX, you type in commands to the command-line interpreter, which is known in UNIX as the *shell*, or *command shell*. It's the underlying environment in which you work with the UNIX system.

Questions

Each hour concludes with a set of questions for you to contemplate. Here's a warning up front: Not all of the questions have a definitive answer. After all, you are learning about a multichoice operating system!

1. Name the three *multi* concepts that are at the heart of UNIX's power.
2. Is UNIX more like a grid of streets, letting you pick your route from point A to point B, or a directed highway with only one option? How does this compare with other systems you've used?

1

3. Systems that support multiple users always ask you to say who you are when you begin using the system. What's the most important thing to remember when you're done using the system?

4. If you're used to graphical interfaces, try to think of a few tasks that you feel are more easily accomplished by moving icons than by typing commands. Write those tasks on a separate paper, and in a few days, pull that paper out and see if you still feel that way.

5. Think of a few instances in which you needed to give a person written instructions. Was that easier than giving spoken instructions or drawing a picture? Was it harder?

Preview of the Next Hour

In the next hour, you learn how to log in to the system at the login prompt (login:), how to log out of the system, how to use the passwd command to change your password, how to use the id command to find out who the computer thinks you are, and lots more!

Hour 2

Getting onto the System and Using the Command Line

This is the second hour of UNIX lessons, so it's time you logged in to the system and tried some commands. This hour focuses on teaching you the basics of interacting with your UNIX machine.

Goals for This Hour

In this hour, you learn how to

☐ Log in and log out of the system

☐ Change passwords with `passwd`

☐ Choose a memorable and secure password

☐ Find out who the computer thinks you are

☐ Find out who else is on the system

☐ Find out what everyone is doing on the system

☐ Check the current date and time

☐ Look at a month and year calendar

☐ Perform some simple calculations with UNIX

This hour introduces a lot of commands, so it's very important that you have a UNIX system available on which you can work through all examples. Most examples have been taken from a Sun workstation running Solaris, a variant of UNIX System V Release 4, and have been double-checked on a BSD-based system. Any variance between the two is noted, and if you have a UNIX system available, odds are good that it's based on either AT&T System V or Berkeley UNIX.

Task 2.1: Logging In and Out of the System

DESCRIPTION Because UNIX is a multiuser system, you need to start by finding a terminal, computer, or other way to access the system. I use a Macintosh and a modem to dial up various systems by telephone. You might have a similar approach, or you might have a terminal directly connected to the UNIX computer on your desk or in your office, or you might have the UNIX system itself on your desk. Regardless of how you connect to your UNIX system, the first thing you'll see on the screen is this:

```
4.3BSD DYNIX (mentor.utech.edu) 5:38pm on Fri, 7 Feb 1997
login:
```

The first line indicates what variant of UNIX the system is running (DYNIX is UNIX on Sequent computers), the actual name of the computer system, and the current date and time. The second line is asking for your login, your account name.

ACTION

1. Connect your terminal or PC to the UNIX system until the point where you see a login prompt (`login:`) on your screen similar to that in the preceding example. Use the phone and modem to dial up the computer if you need to.

   It would be nice if computers could keep track of us users by simply using our full names so that I could enter `Dave Taylor` at the login prompt. Alas, like the Internal Revenue Service, Department of Motor Vehicles, and many other agencies, UNIX—rather than using names—assigns each user a unique identifier. This identifier is called an *account name*, has eight characters or fewer, and is usually based on the first or last name, although it can be any combination of letters and numbers. I have two account names, or logins, on the systems I use: `taylor` and, on another machine where someone already had that account name, `dataylor`.

2. You should know your account name on the UNIX system. Perhaps your account name is on a paper with your initial password, both assigned by the UNIX system administrator. If you do not have this information, you need to track it down before you can go further. Some accounts might not have an initial password; that means that you won't have to enter one the first time you log in to the system. In a few minutes, you will learn how you can give yourself the password of your choice by using a UNIX command called passwd.

3. At the login prompt, enter your account name. Be particularly careful to use all lowercase letters unless specified otherwise by your administrator.

```
login: taylor
Password:
```

Once you've entered your account name, the system moves the cursor to the next line and prompts you for your password. When you enter your password, the system won't echo it (that is, won't display it) on the screen. That's okay. Lack of an echo doesn't mean anything is broken; instead, this is a security measure to ensure that even if people are looking over your shoulder, they can't learn your secret password by watching your screen.

4. If you enter either your login or your password incorrectly, the system complains with an error message:

```
login: taylor
Password:
Login incorrect
login:
```

CAUTION

Most systems give you three or four attempts to get both your login and password correct, so try again. Don't forget to enter your account name at the login prompt each time.

5. Once you've successfully entered your account name and password, you are shown some information about the system, some news for users, and an indication of whether you have electronic mail. The specifics will vary, but here's an example of what I see when I log in to my account:

```
login: taylor
Password:
Last login: Fri Feb 7 17:00:23 on ttyAe
You have mail.
%
```

JUST A MINUTE

> The percent sign is UNIX's way of telling you that it's ready for you to
> enter some commands. The percent sign is the equivalent of an enlisted
> soldier saluting and saying, "Ready for duty!" or an employee saying,
> "What shall I do now, boss?"

Your system might be configured so that you have some slightly different prompt
here. The possibilities include a $ for the Korn or Bourne shells, your current
location in the file system, the current time, the command-index number (which
you'll learn about when you learn how to teach the UNIX command-line interpreter to adapt to your work style, rather than vice versa), and the name of the
computer system itself. Here are some examples:

```
[/users/taylor] :
(mentor) 33 :
taylor@mentor %
```

Your prompt might not look exactly like any of these, but it has one unique
characteristic: it is at the beginning of the line that your cursor sits on, and it
reappears each time you've completed working with any UNIX program.

6. At this point, you're ready to enter your first UNIX command—exit—to sign off
   from the computer system. Try it. On my system, entering exit shuts down all my
   programs and hangs up the telephone connection. On other systems, it returns the
   login prompt. Many UNIX systems offer a pithy quote as you leave, too.

```
% exit
He who hesitates is lost.
4.3BSD DYNIX (mentor.utech.edu) 5:38pm on Fri, 7 Feb 1993
login:
```

CAUTION

> UNIX is *case-sensitive*, so the exit command is not the same as EXIT. If
> you enter a command all in uppercase, the system won't find it and
> instead will respond with the complaint command not found.

7. If you have a direct connection to the computer, odds are very good that logging
   out causes the system to prompt for another account name, enabling the next
   person to use the system. If you dialed up the system with a modem, you probably
   will see something more like the following example. After being disconnected,
   you'll be able to shut down your computer.

```
% exit
Did you lose your keys again?

DISCONNECTED
```

SUMMARY At this point, you've overcome the toughest part of UNIX. You have an account, know the password, logged in to the system, and entered a simple command telling the computer what you want to do, and the computer has done it!

Task 2.2: Changing Passwords with `passwd`

DESCRIPTION Having logged in to a UNIX system, you can clearly see that there are many differences between UNIX and a PA or Macintosh personal computer. Certainly the style of interaction is different. With UNIX, the keyboard becomes the exclusive method of instructing the computer what to do, and the mouse sits idle, waiting for something to happen.

One of the greatest differences is that UNIX is a multiuser system, as you learned in the previous hour. As you learn more about UNIX, you'll find that this characteristic has an impact on a variety of tasks and commands. The next UNIX command you learn is one that exists because of the multiuser nature of UNIX: `passwd`.

With the `passwd` command, you can change the password associated with your individual account name. As with the personal identification number (PIN) for your automated-teller machine, the value of your password is directly related to how secret it remains.

CAUTION

UNIX is careful about the whole process of changing passwords. It requires you to enter your current password to prove you're really you. Imagine that you are at a computer center and have to leave the room to make a quick phone call. Without much effort, a prankster could lean over and quickly change your password to something you wouldn't know. That's why you should log out if you're not going to be near your system, and that's also why passwords are never echoed in UNIX.

ACTION

1. Consider what happens when I use the `passwd` command to change the password associated with my account:

```
% passwd
Changing password for taylor.
Old password:
New passwd:
Retype new passwd:
%
```

2. Notice that I never received any visual confirmation that the password I actually entered was the same as the password I thought I entered. This is not as dangerous as it seems, though, because if I had made any typographical errors, the password I

entered the second time (when the system said `Retype new passwd:`) wouldn't have matched the first. In a no-match situation, the system would have warned me that the information I supplied was inconsistent:

```
% passwd
Changing password for taylor.
Old password:
New passwd:
Retype new passwd:
Mismatch - password unchanged.
%
```

SUMMARY Once you change the password, don't forget it. To reset it to a known value if you don't know the current password requires the assistance of a system administrator or other operator. Renumbering your password can be a catch-22, though: you don't want to write down the password because that reduces its secrecy, but you don't want to forget it, either. You want to be sure that you pick a good password, too, as described in Task 2.3.

Task 2.3: Picking a Secure Password

DESCRIPTION If you're an aficionado of old movies, you are familiar with the thrillers in which the hoods break into an office and spin the dial on the safe a few times, snicker a bit about how the boss shouldn't have chosen his daughter's birthday as the combination, and crank open the safe. (If you're really familiar with the genre, you recall films in which the criminals rifle through the desk drawers and find the combination of the safe taped to the underside of a drawer as a fail-safe—or a failed safe, as the case may be.) The moral is that you always should choose good secret passwords or combinations and keep them secure.

For computers, security is tougher because, in less than an hour, a fast computer system can test all the words in an English dictionary against your account password. If your password is *kitten* or, worse yet, your account name, any semi-competent bad guy could be in your account and messing with your files in no time.

Many of the more modern UNIX systems have some *heuristics*, or smarts, built in to the `passwd` command; the heuristics check to determine whether what you've entered is reasonably secure.

The tests performed typically answer these questions:

☐ Is the proposed password at least six characters long? (A longer password is more secure.)

☐ Does it have both digits and letters? (A mix of both is better.)

☐ Does it mix upper- and lowercase letters? (A mix is better.)

☐ Is it in the online dictionary? (You should avoid common words.)

☐ Is it a name or word associated with the account? (`Dave` would be a bad password for my account `taylor` because my full name on the system is Dave Taylor.)

2

Some versions of the `passwd` program are more sophisticated, and some less, but generally these questions offer a good guideline for picking a secure password.

ACTION

1. An easy way to choose memorable and secure passwords is to think of them as small sentences rather than as a single word with some characters surrounding it. If you're a fan of Alexander Dumas and The Three Musketeers, then "All for one and one for all!" is a familiar cry, but it's also the basis for a couple of great passwords. Easily remembered derivations might be `all4one` or `one4all`.

2. If you've been in the service, you might have the U.S. Army jingle stuck in your head: "Be All You Can Be" would make a great password, `ballucanb`. You might have a self-referential password: `account4me` or `MySekrit` would work. If you're ex-Vice President Dan Quayle, `1Potatoe` could be a memorable choice (`potatoe` by itself wouldn't be particularly secure because it lacks digits and lacks uppercase letters, and because it's a simple variation on a word in the online dictionary).

3. Another way to choose passwords is to find acronyms that have special meaning to you. Don't choose simple ones—remember, short ones aren't going to be secure. But, if you have always heard that "Real programmers don't eat quiche!" then `Rpdeq!` could be a complex password that you'll easily remember.

4. Many systems you use every day require numeric passwords to verify your identity, including the automated-teller machine (with its PIN number), government agencies (with the Social Security number), and the Department of Motor Vehicles (your driver's license number or vehicle license). Each of these actually is a poor UNIX password: it's too easy for someone to find out your license number or Social Security number.

JUST A MINUTE

The important thing is that you come up with a strategy of your own for choosing a password that is both memorable and secure. Then, keep the password in your head rather than write it down.

SUMMARY Why be so paranoid? For a small UNIX system that will sit on your desk in your office and won't have any other users, a high level of concern for security is, to be honest, unnecessary. As with driving a car, though, it's never too early to learn good habits. Any system that has dial-up access or direct-computer-network access—you might need to use such a system—is a likely target for delinquents who relish the intellectual challenge of breaking into an account and altering and destroying files and programs purely for amusement.

The best way to avoid trouble is to develop good security habits now when you're first learning about UNIX—learn how to recognize what makes a good, secure password; pick one for your account; and keep it a secret.

If you ever need to let someone else use your account for a short time, remember that you can use the passwd command to change your secure password to something less secure. Then, you can let that person use the account, and, when he or she is done, you can change the password back to your original password.

With that in mind, log in again to your UNIX system now, and try changing your password. First, change it to easy and see if the program warns you that easy is too short or otherwise a poor choice. Then, try entering two different secret passwords to see if the program notices the difference. Finally, pick a good password, using the preceding guidelines and suggestions, and change your account password to be more secure.

Task 2.4: Who Are You?

DESCRIPTION While you're logged in to the system, you can learn a few more UNIX commands, including a couple that can answer a philosophical conundrum that has bothered men and women of thought for thousands of years: Who am I?

ACTION

1. The easiest way to find out "who you are" is to enter the whoami command:

```
% whoami
taylor
%
```

Try it on your system. The command lists the account name associated with the current login.

2. Ninety-nine percent of the commands you type with UNIX don't change if you modify the punctuation and spacing. With whoami, however, adding spaces to transform the statement into proper English—that is, entering who am i—dramatically changes the result. On my system, I get the following results:

```
% who am i
mentor.utech.edu!taylor     ttyp4   Feb 8 14:34
%
```

This tells me quite a bit about my identity on the computer, including the name of the computer itself, my account name, and where and when I logged in. Try the command on your system and see what results you get.

In this example, mentor is a *hostname*—the name of the computer I am logged in to—and utech.edu is the full *domain name*—the address of mentor. The exclamation point (!) separates the domain name from my account name, taylor. The `ttyp4` (pronounced "tee-tee-why-pea-four") is the current communication line I'm using to access `mentor`, and `5 October` at `2:34pm` is when I logged in to `mentor` today.

JUST A MINUTE

> UNIX is full of oddities that are based on historical precedent. One is "tty" to describe a computer or terminal line. This comes from the earliest UNIX systems in which Digital Equipment Corporation teletypewriters would be hooked up as interactive devices. The teletypewriters quickly received the nickname "tty," and all these years later, when people wouldn't dream of hooking up a teletypewriter, the line is still known as a tty line.

2

3. One of the most dramatic influences UNIX systems have had on the computing community is the propensity for users to work together on a network, hooked up by telephone lines and modems (the predominant method until the middle to late 1980s) or by high-speed network connections to the Internet (a more common type of connection today). Regardless of the connection, however, you can see that each computer needs a unique identifier to distinguish it from others on the network. In the early days of UNIX, systems had unique hostnames, but as hundreds of systems have grown into the tens-of-thousands, that proved to be an unworkable solution.

4. The alternative was what's called a "domain-based naming scheme," where systems are assigned unique names within specific subsets of the overall network. Consider the output that was shown in instruction 2, for example:

```
mentor.utech.edu!taylor     ttyp4    Feb 11 14:34
```

The computer I use is within the `.edu` domain (read the hostname and domain—`mentor.utech.edu`—from right to left), meaning that the computer is located at an educational institute. Then, within the educational institute subset of the network, `utech` is a unique descriptor, and, therefore, if other UTech universities existed, they couldn't use the same top-level domain name. Finally, `mentor` is the name of the computer itself.

5. Like learning to read addresses on envelopes, learning how to read domain names can unlock a lot of information about a computer and its location. For example, `lib.stanford.edu` is the library computer at Stanford University, and `ccgate.infoworld.com` tells you that the computer is at InfoWorld, a commercial computer site, and that its hostname is `ccgate`. You learn more about this a few hours down the road when you learn how to use electronic mail to communicate with people throughout the Internet.

6. Another way to find out who you are in UNIX is the `id` command. The purpose of this command is to tell you what group or groups you're in and the numeric identifier for your account name (known as your *user ID number* or *user ID*). Enter `id` and see what you get. I get the following result:

```
% id
uid=211(taylor)  gid=50(users0) groups=50(users0)
%
```

JUST A MINUTE

> If you enter `id`, and the computer returns a different result or indicates that you need to specify a filename, don't panic. On many Berkeley-derived systems, the `id` command is used to obtain low-level information about files.

7. In this example, you can see that my account name is `taylor` and that the numeric equivalent, the user ID, is `211`. (Here it's abbreviated as `uid`—pronounce it "you-eye-dee" to sound like a UNIX expert.) Just as the account name is unique on a system, so also is the user ID. Fortunately, you rarely, if ever, need to know these numbers, so focus on the account name and group name.

8. Next, you can see that my group ID (or `gid`) is `50`, and that group number `50` is known as the `users0` group. Finally, `users0` is the only group to which I belong.

On another system, I am a member of two different groups:

```
% id
uid=103(taylor) gid=10(staff) groups=10(staff),44(ftp)
%
```

Although I have the same account name on this system (`taylor`), you can see that my user ID and group ID are both different from the earlier example. Note also that I'm a member of two groups: the `staff` group, with a group ID of `10`, and the `ftp` group, with a group ID of `44`.

SUMMARY Later, you learn how to set protection modes on your files so that people in your group can read your files, but those not in your group are barred from access. You've now learned a couple of different ways to have UNIX give you some information about your account.

Task 2.5: Finding Out What Other Users Are Logged in to the System

DESCRIPTION The next philosophical puzzle that you can solve with UNIX is "Who else is there?" The answer, however, is rather restricted, limited to only those people currently logged in to the computer at the same time. Three commands are available to get you this information, based on how much you'd like to learn about the other users: users, who, and w.

ACTION

1. The simplest of the commands is the users command, which lists the account names of all people using the system:

```
% users
david mark taylor
%
```

2. In this example, david and mark are also logged in to the system with me. Try this on your computer and see what other users—if any—are logged in to your computer system.

3. A command that you've encountered earlier in this hour can be used to find out who is logged on to the system, what line they're on, and how long they've been logged in. That command is who:

```
% who
taylor    ttyp0    Oct  8 14:10    (limbo)
david     ttyp2    Oct  4 09:08    (calliope)
mark      ttyp4    Oct  8 12:09    (dent)
%
```

Here, you can see that three people are logged in, taylor (me), david, and mark. Further, you can now see that david is logged in by connection ttyp2 and has been connected since October 4 at 9:08 a.m. He is connected from a system called calliope. You can see that mark has been connected since just after noon on October 8 on line ttyp4 and is coming from a computer called dent. Note that I have been logged in since 14:10, which is 24-hour time for 2:10 p.m. UNIX doesn't always indicate a.m. or p.m.

SUMMARY The user and who commands can inform you who is using the system at any particular moment, but how do you find out what they're doing?

Task 2.6: What Is Everyone Doing on the Computer?

DESCRIPTION To find out what everyone else is doing, there's a third command, w, that serves as a combination of "Who are they?" and "What are they doing?"

ACTION

1. Consider the following output from the w command:

```
% w
2:12pm  up 7 days,  5:28,  3 users, load average: 0.33, 0.33, 0.02
User     tty        login@  idle    JCPU    PCPU  what
taylor   ttyp0      2:10pm                   2          w
david    ttyp2      Mon 9am 2:11    2:04    1:13  xfax
mark     ttyp4      12:09pm 2:03                  -csh
%
```

This is a much more complex command, offering more information than either
users or who. Notice that the output is broken into different areas. The first line
summarizes the status of the system and, rather cryptically, the number of programs that the computer is running at one time. Finally, for each user, the output
indicates the user name, the tty, when the user logged in to the system, how long
it's been since the user has done anything (in minutes and seconds), the combined
CPU time of all jobs the user has run, and the amount of CPU time taken by the
current job. The last field tells you what you wanted to know in the first place:
what are the users doing?

In this example, the current time is 2:12 p.m., and the system has been up for 7
days, 5 hours, and 28 minutes. Currently 3 users are logged in, and the system is
very quiet, with an average of 0.33 jobs submitted (or programs started) in the last
minute; 0.33, on average, in the last 5 minutes; and 0.02 jobs in the last 15
minutes.

User taylor is the only user actively using the computer (that is, who has no idle
time) and is using the w command. User david is running a program called xfax,
which has gone for quite a while without any input from the user (2 hours and 11
minutes of idle time). The program already has used 1 minute and 13 seconds of
CPU time, and overall, david has used over 2 minutes of CPU time. User mark has
a C shell running, -csh. (The leading dash indicates that this is the program that
the computer launched automatically when mark logged in. This is akin to how the
system automatically launched the Finder on a Macintosh on startup.) User mark
hasn't actually done anything yet: notice there is no accumulated computer time
for that account.

2. Now it's your turn. Try the w command on your system and see what kind of
output you get. Try to interpret all the information based on the explanation here.
One thing is certain: your account should have the w command listed as what
you're doing.

On a multiuser UNIX system, the w command gives you a quick and easy way to see what's going on.

Task 2.7: Checking the Current Date and Time

DESCRIPTION You've learned how to orient yourself on a UNIX system, and you are able now to figure out who you are, who else is on the system, and what everyone is doing. What about the current time and date?

ACTION

1. Logic suggests that `time` shows the current time, and `date` the current date; but this is UNIX, and logic doesn't always apply. In fact, consider what happens when I enter `time` on my system:

    ```
    % time
    14.5u 17.0s 29:13 1% 172+217io 160pf+1w
    %
    ```

    The output is cryptic to the extreme and definitely not what you're interested in finding out. Instead, the program is showing how much user time, system time, and CPU time has been used by the command interpreter itself, broken down by input/output operations and more. This is not something I've ever used in 15 years of working with UNIX.

2. Well, `time` didn't work, so what about `date`?

    ```
    % date
    Tue  Oct 5 15:03:41 EST 1993
    %
    ```

    That's more like it!

3. Try the `date` command on your computer and see if the output agrees with your watch.

 How do you think `date` keeps track of the time and date when you've turned the computer off? Does the computer know the correct time if you unplug it for a few hours? (I hope so. Almost all computers today have little batteries inside for just this purpose.)

Task 2.8: Looking at a Calendar

DESCRIPTION Another useful utility in UNIX is the `cal` command, which shows a simple calendar for the month or year specified.

ACTION

1. To confirm that 5 October 1993 is a Tuesday, turn to your computer and enter `cal 10 93`. You should see the following:

```
% cal 10 93
    October 93
 S  M Tu  W Th  F  S
          1  2  3  4  5
 6  7  8  9 10 11 12
13 14 15 16 17 18 19
20 21 22 23 24 25 26
27 28 29 30 31
%
```

2. If you look closely, you'll find that there's a bit of a problem here. October 5 is shown as a Saturday rather than a Tuesday as expected.

   The reason is that `cal` can list any year from A.D. 0. In fact, what you have on your screen is how the month of October would have looked in A.D. 93, 1900 years ago.

JUST A MINUTE

> This is a bit misleading because Western society uses the Julian calendar, adopted in 1752. Before that, the program should really list Gregorian-format monthly calendars, but it can't, so don't use this as a historical reference for ascertaining what day of the week the Emperor Hadrian was born.

3. To find out the information that you want, you'll need to specify to the `cal` program both the month and full year:

```
% cal 10 1993
    October 1993
 S  M Tu  W Th  F  S
                1  2
 3  4  5  6  7  8  9
10 11 12 13 14 15 16
17 18 19 20 21 22 23
24 25 26 27 28 29 30
31
%
```

   This is correct. The 5th of October in 1993 is indeed a Tuesday. On some systems, `cal` has no intelligent default action, so entering `cal` doesn't simply list the monthly calendar for the current month. Later you'll learn how to write a simple shell script to do just that. For now, turn to your system and enter `cal` to see what happens.

4. My favorite example of the `cal` program is to ask for the year 1752, the year when the Western calendar switched from Gregorian to Julian. Note particularly the month of September, during which the switch actually occurred.

```
% cal 1752
                                 1752
          Jan                    Feb                    Mar
 S  M Tu  W Th  F  S    S  M Tu  W Th  F  S    S  M Tu  W Th  F  S
          1  2  3  4                      1    1  2  3  4  5  6  7
 5  6  7  8  9 10 11    2  3  4  5  6  7  8    8  9 10 11 12 13 14
12 13 14 15 16 17 18    9 10 11 12 13 14 15   15 16 17 18 19 20 21
19 20 21 22 23 24 25   16 17 18 19 20 21 22   22 23 24 25 26 27 28
26 27 28 29 30 31      23 24 25 26 27 28 29   29 30 31
          Apr                    May                    Jun
 S  M Tu  W Th  F  S    S  M Tu  W Th  F  S    S  M Tu  W Th  F  S
          1  2  3  4                   1  2             1  2  3  4  5  6
 5  6  7  8  9 10 11    3  4  5  6  7  8  9    7  8  9 10 11 12 13
12 13 14 15 16 17 18   10 11 12 13 14 15 16   14 15 16 17 18 19 20
19 20 21 22 23 24 25   17 18 19 20 21 22 23   21 22 23 24 25 26 27
26 27 28 29 30         24 25 26 27 28 29 30   28 29 30
                       31
          Jul                    Aug                    Sep
 S  M Tu  W Th  F  S    S  M Tu  W Th  F  S    S  M Tu  W Th  F  S
          1  2  3  4                      1          1  2 14 15 16
 5  6  7  8  9 10 11    2  3  4  5  6  7  8   17 18 19 20 21 22 23
12 13 14 15 16 17 18    9 10 11 12 13 14 15   24 25 26 27 28 29 30
19 20 21 22 23 24 25   16 17 18 19 20 21 22
26 27 28 29 30 31      23 24 25 26 27 28 29
                       30 31
          Oct                    Nov                    Dec
 S  M Tu  W Th  F  S    S  M Tu  W Th  F  S    S  M Tu  W Th  F  S
 1  2  3  4  5  6  7             1  2  3  4                   1  2
 8  9 10 11 12 13 14    5  6  7  8  9 10 11    3  4  5  6  7  8  9
15 16 17 18 19 20 21   12 13 14 15 16 17 18   10 11 12 13 14 15 16
22 23 24 25 26 27 28   19 20 21 22 23 24 25   17 18 19 20 21 22 23
29 30 31               26 27 28 29 30         24 25 26 27 28 29 30
                                              31
%
```

SUMMARY You can experiment with `cal` and easily find out fun information—for example, what day of the week you or your parents were born. If you're curious about whether Christmas 1999 is on a weekend, `cal` can answer that question, too.

When you used `cal`, you entered the name of the command and then some additional information to indicate the exact action you desired. You tried both `cal 10 93` and `cal 10 1993`. In UNIX parlance, the first word is the command, and the subsequent words are *arguments* or options to the command. A special class of options are those that begin with a single dash, called *flags*, and you'll learn about those starting in the next hour.

Simple Math with UNIX

Having both an internal wall clock and an internal calendar, UNIX seems to have much of what you need in an office. One piece that's missing now, however, is a simple desktop calculator. UNIX offers two different types of calculator, although neither rightly can be called simple.

Mathematicians talk about *infix* and *postfix* notation as two different ways to write an expression, the former having the operation embedded in the operators, and the latter having all the operators listed, followed by the operation required. Table 2.1 lists some examples of a mathematical expression in both formats.

Table 2.1. Comparing infix and postfix notation.

Infix	Postfix
75*0.85	75 0.85 *
(37*1.334)+44	37 1.334 * 44 +
cos(3.45)/4	3.45 cos 4 /

You're probably familiar with the infix notation, which is the form used in math textbooks throughout the world. Lots of calculators can work this way, too; you'd press the keys 1 + 1 = to find out that 1 plus 1 equals 2.

Some calculators offer the postfix alternative, also known as (reverse) Polish notation, invented by Polish mathematician and logician Jan Lukasiewicz. Notably, for many years Hewlett-Packard has been making calculators that work with RPN notation. On an HP calculator, you'd press the keys 1 Enter 1 + to find out that 1 plus 1 equals 2.

Notice that, although parentheses were required in the second equation in the table when using infix notation, parentheses weren't necessary to force a specific order of evaluation with postfix. Remember that in math you always work from the inside of the parentheses outward, so (3 * 4) + 8 is solved by multiplying 3 by 4, then adding 8, and that process is exactly what RPN mimics.

UNIX offers two calculator programs, one with infix notation and one with postfix notation.

Task 2.9: Using the bc Infix Calculator

DESCRIPTION   The first calculator to learn is bc, the UNIX infix-notation calculator.

2

ACTION

1. To use the infix calculator, enter the following command:

```
% bc
```

Nothing happens—no prompt, nothing. The reason is that bc, like its RPN cousin dc, waits for you to enter commands. The quit command lets you leave the program. You can see how it works by seeing how I solve the first and second mathematical equations of Table 2.1:

```
% bc
75 * 0.85
63.75
(37*1.334)+44
93.358
quit
%
```

2. Unfortunately, bc is, in many ways, a typical UNIX command. Consider what happens when I enter help, hoping for some clue on how to use the bc program:

```
% bc
help
syntax error on line 1, teletype
```

3. This is not very helpful. If you get stuck in a command, there are two surefire ways to escape. Control-d (holding down the Control—also called Ctrl—key on your keyboard and simultaneously pressing the d key) indicates that you have no further input, which often causes programs to quit. If that fails, Control-c kills the program, that is, forces it to quit immediately.

   The bc command has a number of powerful and useful options, as shown in Table 2.2.

Table 2.2. Helpful bc commands.

Notation	Description of Function
sqrt(n)	Square root of n
%	Remainder
^	To the power of (3^5 is 3 to the power of 5)
s(n)	Sine(n)
c(n)	Cosine(n)
e(n)	Exponential(n)
l(n)	Log(n)

4. If you wanted to calculate the sine of 4.5243 to the third power, you could do it with bc. You need to be sure, however, that the system knows you're working with higher math functions by specifying the command flag `-l math` (or, in some cases, just `-l`):

```
% bc -l math
s ( 4.5243 ^ 3 )
-.99770433540886100879
quit
%
```

 SUMMARY If you try this on your calculator, you probably won't get a result quite as precise as this. The bc and dc commands both work with extended precision, allowing for highly accurate results.

Task 2.10: Using the dc Postfix Calculator

DESCRIPTION By contrast, the dc command works with the postfix notation, and each number or operation must be on its own line. Further, the result of an operation isn't automatically shown; you have to enter p to see the most recently calculated result.

ACTION

1. To use dc for the calculations shown previously, enter the following characters shown in bold. The result follows each completed entry.

```
% dc
75
0.85
*
p
63.75
37
1.334
*
44
+
p
93.358
quit
%
```

2. The set of commands available in dc are different because dc addresses a different set of mathematical equations. The dc command is particularly useful if you need to work in a non-decimal base. (For example, some older computer systems worked in octal, a base-8 numbering system. The number 210 in octal, therefore, represents 2 * 8 * 8 + 1 * 8 + 0, or 136 in decimal.) Table 2.3 summarizes some of the most useful commands available in dc.

Table 2.3. Helpful commands in dc.

Notation	Description of Function
v	Square root
i	Set radix (numeric base) for input
o	Set radix for output
p	Print top of stack
f	All values in the stack are printed

3. For example, I used dc to verify that 210 (octal) is indeed equal to 136 (decimal):

```
% dc
8
i
210
p
136
```

SUMMARY With a little work, you can use different numeric bases within the bc program, so unless you're really used to the RPN notation, it's probably best to remember the bc command when you think of doing some quick calculations in UNIX.

JUST A MINUTE

I find both bc and dc ridiculously difficult to use, so I keep a small hand-held calculator by my computer. For just about any task, simply using the calculator is faster than remembering the notational oddities of either UNIX calculator program. Your mileage may vary, of course.

If you run the X Window System, the UNIX graphical interface, there are several calculator programs that look exactly like a hand-held calculator.

If you're old enough, you'll remember the early 1980s as the time when IBM introduced the PC and the industry was going wild, predicting that within a few years every home would have a PC and that everyone would use PCs for balancing checkbooks and keeping track of recipes. Fifteen years later, few people in fact use computers as part of their cooking ritual, although checkbook balancing programs are amazingly popular. The point is that some tasks can be done by computer but are sometimes best accomplished through more traditional means. If you have a calculator and are comfortable using it, the calculator is probably a better solution than learning how to work with bc to add a few numbers.

There are definitely situations where having the computer add the numbers for you is quite beneficial—particularly when there are a lot of them—but if you're like me, you rarely encounter that situation.

Summary

This hour focused on giving you the skills required to log in to a UNIX system, figure out who you are and what groups you're in, change your password, and log out again. You also learned how to list the other users of the system, find out what UNIX commands they're using, check the date and time, and even show a calendar view of almost any month or year in history. Finally, you learned some of the power of two similar UNIX utilities, bc and dc, the two UNIX desktop calculators.

Workshop

The Workshop summarizes the key terms you learned and poses some questions about the topics presented in this chapter. It also provides you with a preview of what you will learn in the next hour.

Key Terms

account name   This is the official one-word name by which the UNIX system knows you: mine is taylor. (See also **account** in Hour 1.)

domain name   UNIX systems on the Internet, or any other network, are assigned a domain within which they exist. This is typically the company (for example, sun.com for Sun Microsystems) or institution (for example, lsu.edu for Louisiana State University). The domain name is always the entire host address, except the host name itself. (See also **host name**.)

flags   Arguments given to a UNIX command that are intended to alter its behavior are called *flags*. They're always prefaced by a single dash. As an example, the command line ls -l /tmp has ls as the command itself, -l as the flag to the command, and /tmp as the argument.

heuristic   A set of well-defined steps or a procedure for accomplishing a specific task.

host name   UNIX computers all have unique names assigned by the local administration team. The computers I use are limbo, well, netcom, and mentor, for example. Enter hostname to see what your system is called.

login   A synonym for account name, this also can refer to the actual process of connecting to the UNIX system and entering your account name and password to your account.

user ID   A synonym for account name.

Questions

1. Why can't you have the same account name as another user? How about user ID? Can you have the same uid as someone else on the system?

2. Which of the following are good passwords, based on the guidelines you've learned in this hour?

foobar	4myMUM	Blk&Blu
234334	Laurie	Hi!
2cool.	rolyat	j j kim

3. Are the results of the two commands who am i and whoami different? If so, explain how. Which do you think you'd rather use when you're on a new computer?

4. List the three UNIX commands to find out who is logged on to the system. Talk about the differences between the commands.

5. One of the commands in the answer to question 4 indicates how long the system has been running (in the example, it'd been running for seven days). What value do you think there is for keeping track of this information?

6. If you can figure out what other people are doing on the computer, they can figure out what you're doing, too. Does that bother you?

7. What day of the week were you born? What day of the week is July 4, 1997? For that matter, what day of the week was July 4, 1776?

8. Solve the following mathematical equations using both dc and bc, and then explain which command you prefer.

454 * 3.84	sin(3.1415)
log(2.45)+log(3)	2^16

Preview of the Next Hour

The next hour focuses on the UNIX hierarchical file system. You learn about how the system is organized, how it differs from Macintosh and DOS hierarchical file systems, the difference between "relative" and "absolute" filenames, and what the mysterious "." and ".." directories are. You also learn about the env, pwd, and cd commands, and the HOME and PATH environment variables.

Hour 3

Moving About the File System

This third hour focuses on the UNIX hierarchical file system. You learn about how the system is organized, how it differs from the Macintosh and DOS hierarchical file systems, the difference between "relative" and "absolute" filenames, and what the mysterious "." and ".." directories are. You also learn about the env, pwd, and cd commands and the HOME and PATH environment variables.

Goals for This Hour

In this hour, you learn

- [ ] What a hierarchical file system is all about
- [ ] How the UNIX file system is organized
- [ ] How Mac and PC file systems differ from UNIX
- [ ] The difference between relative and absolute filenames
- [ ] About hidden files in UNIX
- [ ] About the special directories "." and ".."

☐ The env command

☐ About user environment variables, PATH and HOME

☐ How to find where you are with pwd

☐ How to move to another location with cd

The previous hour introduced a plethora of UNIX commands, but this hour takes a more theoretical approach, focusing on the UNIX file system, how it's organized, and how you can navigate it. This hour focuses on the environment that tags along with you as you move about, particularly the HOME and PATH variables. After that is explained, you learn about the env command as an easy way to show environment variables, and you learn the pwd and cd pair of commands for moving about directly.

What a Hierarchical File System Is All About

In a nutshell, a hierarchy is a system organized by graded categorization. A familiar example is the organizational structure of a company, where workers report to supervisors and supervisors report to middle managers. Middle managers, in turn, report to senior managers, and senior managers report to vice-presidents, who report to the president of the company. Graphically, this hierarchy looks like Figure 3.1.

Figure 3.1.

A typical organizational hierarchy.

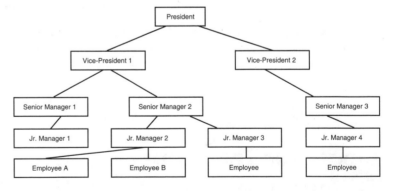

You've doubtless seen this type of illustration before, and you know that a higher position indicates more control. Each position is controlled by the next highest position or row. The president is top dog of the organization, but each subsequent manager is also in control of his or her own small fiefdom.

To understand how a file system can have a similar organization, simply imagine each of the managers in the illustration as a "file folder" and each of the employees as a piece of paper, filed in a particular folder. Open any file cabinet, and you probably see things organized this way: filed papers are placed in labeled folders, and often these folders are filed in groups under specific topics. The drawer might then have a specific label to distinguish it from other drawers in the cabinet, and so on.

That's exactly what a hierarchical file system is all about. You want to have your files located in the most appropriate place in the file system, whether at the very top, in a folder, or in a nested series of folders. With careful usage, a hierarchical file system can contain hundreds or thousands of files and still allow users to find any individual file quickly.

On my computer, the chapters of this book are organized in a hierarchical fashion, as shown in Figure 3.2.

Figure 3.2.

File organization for the chapters of Teach Yourself UNIX in 24 Hours.

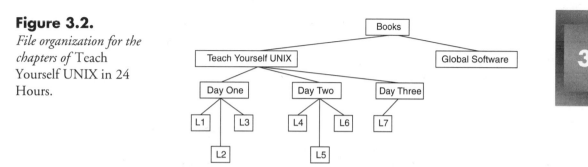

Task 3.1: The UNIX File System Organization

DESCRIPTION A key concept enabling the UNIX hierarchical file system to be so effective is that anything that is not a folder is a file. Programs are files in UNIX, device drivers are files, documents and spreadsheets are files, your keyboard is represented as a file, your display is a file, and even your tty line and mouse are files.

What this means is that as UNIX has developed, it has avoided becoming an ungainly mess. UNIX does not have hundreds of cryptic files stuck at the top (this is still a problem in DOS) or tucked away in confusing folders within the System Folder (as with the Macintosh).

The top level of the UNIX file structure (/) is known as the *root* directory or *slash* directory, and it always has a certain set of subdirectories, including bin, dev, etc, lib, mnt, tmp, and usr. There can be a lot more, however. Listing 3.1 shows files found at the top level of the mentor file system (the system I work on). Typical UNIX directories are shown followed by a slash in the listing.

```
AA           boot      flags/        rf/           userb/     var/
OLD/         core      gendynix      stand/        userc/
archive/     dev/      lib/          sys/          users/
ats/         diag/     lost+found/   tftpboot/     usere/
backup/      dynix     mnt/          tmp/          users/
bin/         etc/      net/          usera/        usr/
```

You can obtain a listing of the files and directories in your own top-level directory by using the ls -C -F / command. (You'll learn all about the ls command in the next hour. For now, just be sure that you enter exactly what's shown in the example.)

On a different computer system, here's what I see when I enter that command:

```
% ls -C -F /
Mail/          export/        public/
News/          home/          reviews/
add_swap/      kadb*          sbin/
apps/          layout         sys@
archives/      lib@           tftpboot/
bin@           lost+found/    tmp/
boot           mnt/           usr/
cdrom/         net/           utilities/
chess/         news/          var/
dev/           nntpserver     vmunix*
etc/           pcfs/
```

In this example, any filename that ends with a slash (/) is a folder (UNIX calls these *directories*). Any filename that ends with an asterisk (*) is a program. Anything ending with an at sign (@) is a *symbolic link*, and everything else is a normal, plain file.

As you can see from these two examples, and as you'll immediately find when you try the command yourself, there is much variation in how different UNIX systems organize the top-level directory. There are some directories and files in common, and once you start examining the contents of specific directories, you'll find that hundreds of programs and files always show up in the same place from UNIX to UNIX.

It's as if you were working as a file clerk at a new law firm. Although this firm might have a specific approach to filing information, the approach may be similar to the filing system of other firms where you have worked in the past. If you know the underlying organization, you can quickly pick up the specifics of a particular organization.

ACTION Try the command ls -C -F / on your computer system, and identify, as previously explained, each of the directories in your resultant listing.

SUMMARY The output of the ls command shows the files and directories in the top level of your system. Next, you learn what they are.

The bin Directory

In UNIX parlance, programs are considered *executables* because users can execute them. (In this case, *execute* is a synonym for *run*, not an indication that you get to wander about murdering innocent applications!) When the program has been compiled (usually from a C listing), it is translated into what's called a *binary* format. Add the two together, and you have a common UNIX description for an application—an executable binary.

3

It's no surprise that the original UNIX developers decided to have a directory labeled "binaries" to store all the executable programs on the system. Remember the primitive teletypewriter discussed in the last hour? Having a slow system to talk with the computer had many ramifications that you might not expect. The single most obvious one was that everything became quite concise. There were no lengthy words like binaries or listfiles, but rather succinct abbreviations: bin and ls are, respectively, the UNIX equivalents.

The bin directory is where all the executable binaries were kept in early UNIX. Over time, as more and more executables were added to UNIX, having all the executables in one place proved unmanageable, and the bin directory split into multiple parts (/bin, /sbin, /usr/bin).

The dev Directory

Among the most important portions of any computer are its device drivers. Without them, you wouldn't have any information on your screen (the information arrives courtesy of the display device driver). You wouldn't be able to enter information (the information is read and given to the system by the keyboard device driver), and you wouldn't be able to use your floppy disk drive (managed by the floppy device driver).

Earlier, you learned how almost anything in UNIX is considered a file in the file system, and the dev directory is an example. All device drivers—often numbering into the hundreds—are stored as separate files in the standard UNIX dev (devices) directory. Pronounce this directory name "dev," not "dee-ee-vee."

The etc Directory

UNIX administration can be quite complex, involving management of user accounts, the file system, security, device drivers, hardware configurations, and more. To help, UNIX designates the etc directory as the storage place for all administrative files and information.

Pronounce the directory name either "ee-tea-sea", "et-sea," or "etcetera." All three pronunciations are common.

The lib Directory

Like your neighborhood community, UNIX has a central storage place for function and procedural libraries. These specific executables are included with specific programs, allowing programs to offer features and capabilities otherwise unavailable. The idea is that if programs want to include certain features, they can reference just the shared copy of that utility in the UNIX library rather than having a new, unique copy.

In the previous hour, when you were exploring the dc calculator, you used the command dc -l math to access trigonometric functions. The -l math was to let dc know that you wanted to include the functions available through the math library, stored in the lib directory.

Many of the more recent UNIX systems also support what's called *dynamic linking*, where the library of functions is included on-the-fly as you start up the program. The wrinkle is that instead of the library reference being resolved when the program is created, it's resolved only when you actually run the program itself.

Pronounce the directory name "libe" or "lib" (to rhyme with the word *bib*).

The `lost+found` Directory

With multiple users running many different programs simultaneously, it's been a challenge over the years to develop a file system that can remain synchronized with the activity of the computer. Various parts of the UNIX *kernel*—the brains of the system—help with this problem. When files are recovered after any sort of problem or failure, they are placed here, in the `lost+found` directory, if the kernel cannot ascertain the proper location in the file system. This directory should be empty almost all the time.

This directory is commonly pronounced "lost and found" rather than "lost plus found."

The `mnt` and `sys` Directories

The `mnt` (pronounced "em-en-tea") and `sys` (pronounced "sis") directories also are safely ignored by UNIX users. The `mnt` directory is intended to be a common place to mount external media—hard disks, removable cartridge drives, and so on—in UNIX. On many systems, though not all, `sys` contains files indicating the system configuration.

The `tmp` Directory

A directory that you can't ignore, the `tmp` directory—say "temp"—is used by many of the programs in UNIX as a temporary file-storage space. If you're editing a file, for example, the program makes a copy of the file and saves it in `tmp`, and you work directly with that, saving the new file back to your original file only when you've completed your work.

On most systems, `tmp` ends up littered with various files and executables left by programs that don't remove their own temporary files. On one system I use, it's not uncommon to find 10–30 megabytes of files wasting space here.

Even so, if you're manipulating files or working with copies of files, `tmp` is the best place to keep the temporary copies of files. Indeed, on some UNIX workstations, `tmp` actually can be the fastest device on the computer, allowing for dramatic performance improvements over working with files directly in your home directory.

The `usr` Directory

Finally, the last of the standard directories at the top level of the UNIX file system hierarchy is the `usr`—pronounced "user"—directory. Originally, this directory was intended to be the central storage place for all user-related commands. Today, however, many companies have their own interpretation, and there's no telling what you'll find in this directory.

3

Standard practice is that /usr contains UNIX operating system binaries.

Other Miscellaneous Stuff at the Top Level

Besides all the directories previously listed, a number of other directories and files commonly occur in UNIX systems. Some files might have slight variations in name on your computer, so when you compare your listing to the following files and directories, be alert for possible alternative spellings.

A file you must have to bring up UNIX at all is one usually called unix or vmunix, or named after the specific version of UNIX on the computer. The file contains the actual UNIX operating system. The file must have a specific name and must be found at the top level of the file system. Hand-in-hand with the operating system is another file called boot, which helps during initial startup of the hardware.

Notice on one of the previous listings that the files boot and dynix appear. (DYNIX is the name of the particular variant of UNIX used on Sequent computers.) By comparison, the listing from the Sun Microsystems workstation shows boot and vmunix as the two files.

Another directory that you might find in your own top-level listing is diag—pronounced "dye-ag"—which acts as a storehouse for diagnostic and maintenance programs. If you have any programs within this directory, it's best not to try them out without proper training!

The *home directory*, also sometimes called *users*, is a central place for organizing all files unique to a specific user. Listing this directory is usually an easy way to find out what accounts are on the system, too, because by convention each individual account directory is named after the user's account name. On one system I use, my account is taylor, and my individual account directory is also called taylor. Home directories are always created by the system administrator.

The net directory, if set up correctly, is a handy shortcut for accessing other computers on your network.

The tftpboot directory is a relatively new feature of UNIX. The letters stand for "trivial file transfer protocol boot." Don't let the name confuse you, though; this directory contains versions of the kernel suitable for X Window System-based terminals and diskless workstations to run UNIX.

Some UNIX systems have directories named for specific types of peripherals that can be attached. On the Sun workstation, you can see examples with the directories cdrom and pcfs. The former is for a CD-ROM drive and the latter for DOS-format floppy disks.

There are many more directories in UNIX, but this will give you an idea of how things are organized.

How Mac and PC File Systems Differ from the UNIX File System

Although the specific information is certainly different, some parallels do exist between the hierarchical file system structures of the UNIX and the Macintosh systems.

For example, on the Macintosh, folders are distinguished by their icons. The common folders you'll find on all Macs include System Folder and Trash. Within the system folder, all Macs have a variety of system-related files, including Finder, System, and Clipboard. Folders include Extensions, Preferences, and Control Panels.

By comparison, DOS requires few files be present for the system to be usable: command.com must be present, and autoexec.bat and config.sys usually are present. Most DOS systems have all the commands neatly tucked into the \DOS directory on the system, but sometimes these commands appear at the very top level.

Directory Separator Characters

If you look at the organizational chart presented earlier in this hour, you can see that employees are identified simply as "employee" where possible. Because each has a unique path upwards to the president, each has a unique identifier if all components of the path upward are specified.

For example, the rightmost of the four employees could be described as "Employee managed by Jr. Manager 4, managed by Senior Manager 3, managed by Vice-President 2, managed by the President." Using a single character, instead of "managed by," can considerably shorten the description: Employee/Jr. Manager 4/Senior Manager 3/Vice-President 2/ President. Now consider the same path specified from the very top of the organization downward: President/Vice-President 2/Senior Manager 3/Jr. Manager 4/Employee.

Because only one person is at the top, that person can be safely dropped from the path without losing the uniqueness of the descriptor: /Vice-President 2/Senior Manager 3/Jr. Manager 4/ Employee.

In this example, the / (pronounce it "slash") is serving as a *directory separator character*, a convenient shorthand to indicate different directories in a path.

The idea of using a single character isn't unique to UNIX, but using the slash is unusual. On the Macintosh, the system uses a colon to separate directories in a pathname. (Next time you're on a Mac, try saving a file called test:file and see what happens.) DOS uses a backslash: \DOS indicates the DOS directory at the top level of DOS. The characters /tmp indicate the tmp directory at the top level of the UNIX file system, and :Apps is a folder called Apps at the top of the Macintosh file system.

3

On the Macintosh, you rarely encounter the directory delineator because the system has a completely graphical interface. Windows also offers a similar level of freedom from having to worry about much of this complexity, although you'll still need to remember whether "A:" is your floppy disk or hard disk drive.

The Difference Between Relative and Absolute Filenames

Specifying the location of a file in a hierarchy to ensure that the filename is unique is known in UNIX parlance as specifying its *absolute filename*. That is, regardless of where you are within the file system, the absolute filename always specifies a particular file. By contrast, relative filenames are not unique descriptors.

To understand, consider the files shown in Figure 3.3.

Figure 3.3.

A simple hierarchy of files.

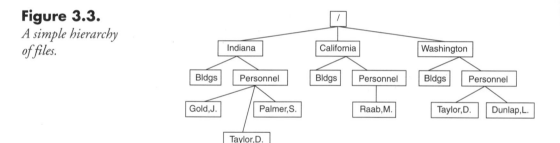

If you are currently looking at the information in the Indiana directory, Bldgs uniquely describes one file: the Bldgs file in the Indiana directory. That same name, however, refers to a different file if you are in the California or Washington directories. Similarly, the directory Personnel leaves you with three possible choices until you also specify which state you're interested in.

As a possible scenario, imagine you're reading through the Bldgs file for Washington and some people come into your office, interrupting your work. After a few minutes of talk, they comment about an entry in the Bldgs file in California. You turn to your UNIX system and bring up the Bldgs file, and it's the wrong file. Why? You're still in the Washington directory.

These problems arise because of the lack of specificity of *relative filenames*. Relative filenames describe files that are referenced relative to an assumed position in the file system. In Figure 3.3, even Personnel/Taylor,D. isn't unique because that can be found in both Indiana and Washington.

To avoid these problems, you can apply the technique you learned earlier, specifying all elements of the directory path from the top down. To look at the Bldgs file for California, you could simply specify /California/Bldgs. To check the Taylor,D. employee in Indiana, you'd use /Indiana/Personnel/Taylor,D., which is different, you'll notice, from the employee /Washington/Personnel/Taylor,D..

Learning the difference between these two notations is crucial to surviving the complexity of a hierarchical file system used with UNIX. Without it, you'll spend half your time verifying that you are where you think you are, or, worse, not moving about at all, not taking advantage of the organizational capabilities.

If you're ever in doubt as to where you are or what file you're working with in UNIX, simply specify its absolute filename. You always can differentiate between the two by looking at the very first character: If it's a slash, you've got an absolute filename (because the filename is rooted to the very top level of the file system). If you don't have a slash as the first character, the filename's a relative filename.

Earlier I told you that in the home directory at the top level of UNIX, I have a home directory called taylor. In absolute filename terms, I'd properly say that I have /home/taylor as a unique directory.

JUST A MINUTE

> To add to the confusion, most UNIX people don't pronounce the slashes, particularly if the first component of the filename is a well-known directory. I would pronounce /home/taylor as "home taylor," but I would usually pronounce /newt/awk/test as "slash newt awk test." When in doubt, pronounce the slash.

As you learn more about UNIX, particularly about how to navigate in the file system, you'll find that a clear understanding of the difference between a relative and absolute filename proves invaluable. The rule of thumb is that if a filename begins with /, it's absolute.

Task 3.2: Hidden Files in UNIX

DESCRIPTION   One of the best aspects of living in an area for a long time, frequenting the same shops and visiting the same restaurants, is that the people who work at each place learn your name and preferences. Many UNIX applications can perform the same trick, remembering your preferred style of interaction, what files you last worked with, which lines you've edited, and more, through *preference files*.

On the Macintosh, because it's a single-user system, there's a folder within the System Folder called Preferences, which is a central storage place for preference files, organized by application. On my Macintosh, for example, I have about 30 different preference files in this directory, enabling me to teach programs one time the defaults I prefer.

UNIX needs to support many users at once, so UNIX preference files can't be stored in a central spot in the file system. Otherwise, how would the system distinguish between your preferences and those of your colleagues? To avoid this problem, all UNIX applications store their preference files in your home directory.

Programs want to be able to keep their own internal preferences and status stored in your directory, but these aren't for you to work with or alter. If you use DOS, you're probably familiar with how the DOS operating system solves this problem: Certain files are hidden and do not show up when you use DIR to list files in a directory.

Macintosh people don't realize it, but the Macintosh also has lots of hidden files. On the topmost level of the Macintosh file system, for example, the following files are present, albeit hidden from normal display: AppleShare PDS, Deleted File Record, Desktop, Desktop DB, and Desktop DF. Displaying hidden files on the Macintosh is very difficult, as it is with DOS.

Fortunately, the UNIX rule for hiding files is much easier than that for either the Mac or PC. No secret status flag reminds the system not to display the file when listing directories. Instead, the rule is simple, any filename starting with a dot. These files are called *dot files*.

| A *hidden file* is any file with a dot as the first character of the filename. |

JUST A MINUTE

If the filename or directory name begins with a dot, it won't show up in normal listings of that directory. If the filename or directory name has any other character as the first character of the name, it lists normally.

ACTION

1. Knowing that, turn to your computer and enter the ls command to list all the files and directories in your home directory.

```
% ls -C -F
Archives/       Mail/        RUMORS.18Sept  mailing.lists
InfoWorld/      News/        bin/           newlists
LISTS           OWL/         iecc.list      src/
%
```

2. You can see that I have 12 items in my own directory, seven directories (the directory names have a slash as the last character, remember) and five files. Files have minimal rules for naming, too. Avoid slashes, spaces, and tabs, and you'll be fine.

3. Without an explicit direction to the contrary, UNIX is going to let the hidden files remain hidden. To add the hidden files to the listing, you just need to add a -a flag to the command. Turn to your computer and try this command to see what hidden files are present in your directory. These are my results:

```
% ls -a
./             .gopherrc      .oldnewsrc     .sig        RUMORS.18Sep
../            .history*      .plan          Archives/   bin/
.Agenda        .info          .pnewsexpert   InfoWorld/  iecc.list
.aconfigrc     .letter        .report        LISTS       mail.lists
.article       .login         .rm-timestamp  Mail/       newlists
.cshrc         .mailrc        .rnlast        News/       src/
.elm/          .newsrc        .rnsoft        OWL/
%
```

Many dot files tend to follow the format of a dot, followed by the name of the program that owns the file, with rc as the suffix. In my directory, you can see six dot files that follow this convention: .aconfigrc, .cshrc, .gopherrc, .mailrc, .newsrc, and .oldnewsrc.

SUMMARY Because of the particular rules of hidden files in UNIX, they are often called dot files, and you can see that I have 23 dot files and directories in my directory.

JUST A MINUTE

The rc suffix tells you that this file is a configuration file for that particular utility. For instance, .cshrc is the configuration file for the C shell and is executed every time the C shell (/bin/csh) is executed. You can define aliases for C shell commands and a special search path, for example.

JUST A MINUTE

Because it's important to convey the specific filename of a dot file, pronunciation is a little different than elsewhere in UNIX. The name .gopherrc would be spoken as "dot gopher are sea," and .mailrc would be "dot mail are sea." If you can't pronounce the program name, odds are good that no one else can either, so .cshrc is "dot sea ess aitch are sea."

Other programs create a bunch of different dot files and try to retain a consistent naming scheme. You can see that .rnlast and .rnsoft are both from the rn program, but it's difficult to know simply from the filenames that .article, .letter, .newsrc, .oldnewsrc, and .pnewsexpert are all also referenced by the rn program. Recognizing this problem, some application authors designed their applications to create a dot directory, with all preference files neatly tucked into that one spot. The elm program does that with its .elm hidden directory.

3

Some files are directly named after the programs that use them: the `.Agenda` file is used by the agenda program, and `.info` is used by the info program. Those almost have a rule of their own, but it's impossible to distinguish them from `.login`, from the `sh` program; `.plan` from the `finger` program; `.rm-timestamp` from a custom program of my own; and I frankly have no idea what program created the `.report` file!

This should give you an idea of the various ways that UNIX programs name and use hidden files. As an exercise, list all the dot files in your home directory and try to extract the name of the program that probably created the file. Check by looking in the index of this book to see if a program by that name exists. If you can't figure out which programs created which files, you're not alone. Keep the list handy; refer to it as you learn more about UNIX while exploring *Teach Yourself UNIX in 24 Hours*, and by the time you're done, you'll know exactly how to find out which programs created which dot files.

Task 3.3: The Special Directories "." and ".."

DESCRIPTION There are two dot directories I haven't mentioned, although they show up in my listing and most certainly show up in your listing, too. They are dot and dot dot ("." and ".."), and they're shorthand directory names that can be terrifically convenient.

The *dot* directory is shorthand for the current location in the directory hierarchy; the *dot-dot* directory moves you up one level, to the parent directory.

Consider again the list of files shown in Figure 3.3. If you were looking at the files in the `California Personnel` directory (best specified as `/California/Personnel`) and wanted to check quickly an entry in the `Bldgs` file for `California`, either you'd have to use the absolute filename and enter the lengthy ls `/California/Bldgs`, or, with the new shorthand directories, you could enter ls `../Bldgs`.

As directories move ever deeper into the directory hierarchy, the dot-dot notation can save you much typing time. For example, what if the different states and related files were all located in my home directory `/home/taylor`, in a new directory called `business`? In that case, the absolute filename for employee `Raab,M.` in California would be `/home/taylor/business/California/Personnel/Raab,M.`, which is unwieldy and an awful lot to type if you want to hop up one level and check on the `buildings` database in `Indiana`!

You can use more than one dot-dot notation in a filename, too, so if you're looking at the `Raab,M.` file and want to check on `Dunlap,L.`, you could save typing in the full filename by instead using `../../../Washington/Personnel/Dunlap,L.`. Look at Figure 3.3 to see how that would work, tracing back one level for each dot-dot in the filename.

This explains why the dot-dot shorthand is helpful, but what about the single-dot notation that simply specifies the current directory?

I haven't stated it explicitly yet, but you've probably figured out that one ramification of the UNIX file system organization, combined with its capability to place applications anywhere in the file system, is that the system needs some way to know where to look for particular applications. Just as if you were looking for something in a public library, in UNIX, having an understanding of its organization and a strategy for searching is imperative for success and speed.

UNIX uses an ordered list of directories called a *search path* for this purpose. The search path typically lists five or six different directories on the system where the computer checks for any application you request.

The question arises: What happens if your own personal copy of an application has the same name as a standard system application? The answer is that the system always finds the standard application first, if its directory is listed earlier in the search path.

To avoid this pitfall, you need to use the dot notation, forcing the system to look in the current directory rather than search for the application. If you wanted your own version of the `ls` command, for example, you'd need to enter `./ls` to ensure that UNIX uses your version rather than the standard version.

Action

1. Enter `./ls` on your computer and watch what happens.
2. Enter `ls` without the dot notation, and notice how the computer searches through various directories in the search path, finds the `ls` program, and executes it, automatically.

Summary When you learn about `cd later in the book`, you also will learn other uses of the dot-dot directory, but the greatest value of the dot directory is that you can use it to force the system to look in the current directory and nowhere else for any file specified.

Task 3.4: The `env` Command

Description You've learned a lot of the foundations of the UNIX file system and how applications remember your preferences through hidden dot files. There's another way, however, that the system remembers specifics about you, and that's through your *user environment*. The user environment is a collection of specially named variables that have specific values.

ACTION

1. To view your environment, you can use the env command. Here's what I see when I enter the env command on my system:

```
% env
HOME=/users/taylor
SHELL=/bin/csh
TERM=vt100
PATH=/users/taylor/bin:/bin:/usr/bin:/usr/ucb:/usr/local/bin:
➥/usr/unsup/bin:.
MAIL=/usr/spool/mail/taylor
LOGNAME=taylor
TZ=EST5
%
```

SUMMARY Try it yourself and compare your values with mine. You might find that you have more defined in your environment than I do because your UNIX system uses your environment to keep track of more information.

JUST A MINUTE

Many UNIX systems offer the printenv command instead of env. If you enter env and the system complains that it can't find the env command, try using printenv instead. All examples here work with either env or printenv.

Task 3.5: PATH and HOME

DESCRIPTION The two most important values in your environment are the name of your home directory (HOME) and your search path (PATH). Your home directory (as it's known) is the name of the directory that you always begin your UNIX session within.

The PATH environment variable lists the set of directories, in left-to-right order, that the system searches to find commands and applications you request. You can see from the example that my search path tells the computer to start looking in the /users/taylor/bin directory, then sequentially try /bin, /usr/bin, /usr/ucb, /usr/local/bin, /usr/unsup/bin, and . before concluding that it can't find the requested command. Without a PATH, the shell wouldn't be able to find any of the many, many UNIX commands: As a minimum, you always should have /bin and /usr/bin.

ACTION

1. You can use the echo command to list specific environment variables, too. Enter echo $PATH and echo $HOME. When I do so, I get the following results:

```
% echo $PATH
/users/taylor/bin:/bin:/usr/bin:/usr/ucb:/usr/local/bin:/usr/unsup/bin:.
% echo $HOME
/users/taylor
%
```

Your PATH value is probably similar, although certainly not identical, to mine, and your HOME is /home/*accountname* or similar (*accountname* is your account name).

Task 3.6: Find Where You Are with pwd

DESCRIPTION So far you've learned a lot about how the file system works but not much about how to move around in the file system. With any trip, the first and most important step is to find out your current location—that is the directory in which you are currently working. In UNIX, the command pwd tells you the present *working directory*.

ACTION

1. Enter pwd. The output should be identical to the output you saw when you entered env HOME because you're still in your home directory.

```
% env HOME
/users/taylor
% pwd
/users/taylor
%
```

SUMMARY Think of pwd as a compass, always capable of telling you where you are. It also tells you the names of all directories above you because it always lists your current location as an absolute directory name.

Task 3.7: Move to Another Location with cd

DESCRIPTION The other half of the dynamic duo is the cd command, which is used to change directories. The format of this command is simple, too: cd *new-directory* (where *new-directory* is the name of the new directory you want).

ACTION

1. Try moving to the very top level of the file system and entering pwd to see if the computer agrees that you've moved.

```
% cd /
% pwd
/
%
```

2. Notice that cd doesn't produce any output. Many UNIX commands operate silently like this, unless an error is encountered. The system then indicates the problem. You can see what an error looks like by trying to change your location to a nonexistent directory. Try the /taylor directory to see what happens!

```
% cd /taylor
/taylor: No such file or directory
%
```

3. Enter cd without specifying a directory. What happens? I get the following result:

```
% cd
% pwd
/users/taylor
%
```

4. Here's where the HOME environment variable comes into play. Without any directory specified, cd moves you back to your home directory automatically. If you get lost, it's a fast shorthand way to move to a known location without fuss.

   Remember the dot-dot notation for moving up a level in the directory hierarchy? Here's where it also proves exceptionally useful. Use the cd command without any arguments to move to your home directory, then use pwd to ensure that's where you've ended up.

5. Now, move up one level by using cd .. and check the results with pwd:

```
% cd
% pwd
/users/taylor
% cd ..
% pwd
/users
%
```

6. Use the `ls -C -F` command to list all the directories contained at this point in the file system. Beware, though; on large systems, this directory could easily have hundreds of different directories. On one system I use, there are almost 550 different directories one level above my home directory in the file system!

```
% ls -C -F
armstrong/   christine/   guest/     laura/    matthewm/   shane/
bruce/       david/       higgins/   mac/      rank/       taylor/
cedric/      green/       kane/      mark/     shalini/    vicki/
%
```

SUMMARY Try using a combination of `cd` and `pwd` to move about your file system, and remember that without any arguments, `cd` always zips you right back to your home directory.

Summary

This hour has focused on the UNIX hierarchical file system. You've learned the organization of a hierarchical file system, how UNIX differs from Macintosh and DOS systems, and how UNIX remembers preferences with its hidden dot files. This hour has also explained the difference between relative and absolute filenames, and you've learned about the "." and ".." directories. You've learned three new commands too: `env` to list your current environment, `cd` to change directories, and `pwd` to find out your present working directory location.

Workshop

The Workshop summarizes the key terms you learned and poses some questions about the topics presented in this chapter. It also provides you with a preview of what you will learn in the next hour.

Key Terms

absolute filename Any filename that begins with a leading slash (/); these always uniquely describe a single file in the file system.

binary A file format that is intended for the computer to work with directly rather than for humans to peruse. See also **executable**.

device driver All peripherals attached to the computer are called devices in UNIX, and each has a control program always associated with it, called a *device driver*. Examples are the device drivers for the display, keyboard, mouse, and all hard disks.

directory A type of UNIX file used to group other files. Files and directories can be placed inside other directories, to build a hierarchical system.

directory separator character   On a hierarchical file system, there must be some way to specify which items are directories and which is the actual filename itself. This becomes particularly true when you're working with absolute filenames. In UNIX, the directory separator character is the slash (/), so a filename like /tmp/testme is easily interpreted as a file called testme in a directory called tmp.

dot   A shorthand notation for the current directory.

dot-dot   A shorthand notation for the directory one level higher up in the hierarchical file system from the current location.

dot file   A configuration file used by one or more programs. These files are called dot files because the first letter of the filename is a dot, as in .profile or .login. Because they're dot files, the ls command doesn't list them by default, making them also hidden files in UNIX. See also **hidden file**.

dynamic linking   Although most UNIX systems require all necessary utilities and library routines (such as the routines for reading information from the keyboard and displaying it to the screen) to be plugged into a program when it's built (known in UNIX parlance as *static linking*), some of the more sophisticated systems can delay this inclusion until you actually need to run the program. In this case, the utilities and libraries are linked when you start the program, and this is called *dynamic linking*.

executable   A file that has been set up so that UNIX can run it as a program. This is also shorthand for a binary file. You also sometimes see the phrase *binary executable*, which is the same thing! See also **binary**.

hidden file   By default, the UNIX file-listing command ls shows only files whose first letter isn't a dot (that is, those files that aren't dot files). All dot files, therefore, are hidden files, and you can safely ignore them without any problems. Later, you learn how to view these hidden files. See also **dot file**.

home directory   This is your private directory, and is also where you start out when you log in to the system.

kernel   The underlying core of the UNIX operating system itself. This is akin to the concrete foundation under a modern skyscraper.

preference file   These are what dot files (hidden files) really are: They contain your individual preferences for many of the UNIX commands you use.

relative filename   Any filename that does not begin with a slash (/) is a filename whose exact meaning depends on where you are in the file system. For example, the file test might exist in both your home directory and in the root directory; /test is an absolute filename and leaves no question which version is being used, but test could refer to either copy, depending on your current directory.

root directory   The directory at the very top of the file system hierarchy, also known as *slash*.

search path   A list of directories used to find a command. When a user enters a command ls, the shell looks in each directory in the search path to find a file ls, either until it is found or the list is exhausted.

slash   The root directory.

symbolic link   A file that contains a pointer to another file rather than contents of its own. This can also be a directory that points to another directory rather than having files of its own. A useful way to have multiple names for a single program or allow multiple people to share a single copy of a file.

user environment   A set of values that describe the user's current location and modify the behavior of commands.

working directory   The directory where the user is working.

Questions

1. Can you think of information you work with daily that's organized in a hierarchical fashion? Is a public library organized hierarchically?

2. Which of the following files are hidden files and directories according to UNIX?
   ```
   .test    hide-me    ,test    .cshrc
   ../      .dot.      dot      .HiMom
   ```

3. What programs most likely created the following dot files and dot directories?
   ```
   .cshrc      .rnsoft      .exrc       .print
   .tmp334     .excel/      .letter     .vi-expert
   ```

4. In the following list, circle the items that are absolute filenames:
   ```
   /Personnel/Taylor,D.
   /home/taylor/business/California
   ../..
   Recipe:Gazpacho
   ```

5. Using the list of directories found on all UNIX systems (/bin, /dev, /etc, /lib, /lost+found, /mnt, /sys, /tmp, /usr), use cd and pwd to double-check that they are all present on your own UNIX machine.

Preview of the Next Hour

In the next hour, you learn about the ls command that you've been using, including a further discussion of command flags. The command touch enables you to create your own files, and du and df help you learn how much disk space is used and how much is available, respectively. You also learn how to use two valuable if somewhat esoteric UNIX commands, compress and crypt, which help you minimize your disk-space usage and ensure absolute security for special files.

3

Hour 4

Listing Files and Managing Disk Usage

This hour introduces you to the ls command, one of the most commonly used commands in UNIX. The discussion includes over a dozen different command options, or flags. You also learn how to use the touch command to create files, how to use the du command to see how much disk space you're using, and how to use the df command to see how much disk space is available. Finally, the compress command can help you minimize your disk-space usage, particularly on files you're not using very often.

Goals for This Hour

In this hour, you learn

- [ ] All about the ls command
- [ ] About special ls command flags
- [ ] How to create files with touch
- [ ] How to check disk-space usage with du
- [ ] How to check available disk space with df
- [ ] How to shrink big files with compress

Your first hours focused on some of the basic UNIX commands, particularly those for interacting with the system to accomplish common tasks. In this hour, you expand that knowledge by analyzing characteristics of the system you're using, and you learn a raft of commands that let you create your own UNIX workspace. You also learn more about the UNIX file system and how UNIX interprets command lines. In addition to the cd and pwd commands that you learned in the preceding hour, you learn how to use ls to wander in the file system and see what files are kept where.

Unlike the DOS and Macintosh operating systems, information about the UNIX system is often difficult to obtain. In this hour, you learn easy ways to ascertain how much disk space you're using, with the du command. You also learn how to interpret the oft-confusing output of the df command, which enables you to see instantly how much total disk space is available on your UNIX system.

This hour concludes with a discussion of the compress command, which enables you to shrink the size of any file or set of files.

The ls Command

This section introduces you to the ls command, which enables you to wander in the file system and see what files are kept where.

Task 4.1: All About the ls Command

DESCRIPTION   From the examples in the previous hour, you've already figured out that the command used to list files and directories in UNIX is the ls command.

All operating systems have a similar command, a way to see what's in the current location. In DOS, for example, you're no doubt familiar with the DIR command. DOS also has command flags, which are denoted by a leading slash before the specific option. For example, DIR /W produces a directory listing in wide-display format. The DIR command has quite a few other options and capabilities.

Listing the files in a directory is a pretty simple task, so why all the different options? You've already seen some examples, including ls -a, which lists hidden dot files. The answer is that there are many different ways to look at files and directories, as you will learn.

ACTION

1. The best way to learn what ls can do is to go ahead and use it. Turn to your computer, log in to your account, and try each command as it's explained.

4

2. The most basic use of ls is to list files. The command ls lists all the files and
directories in the present working directory (recall that you can check what
directory you're in with the pwd command at any time).

```
% ls
Archives        Mail            RUMORS.18Sept  mailing.lists
InfoWorld       News            bin             newels
LISTS           OWL             iecc.list       src
```

Notice that the files are sorted alphabetically from top to bottom, left to right. This
is the default, known as *column-first order* because it sorts downward, then across.
You should also note how things are sorted in UNIX: The system differentiates
between uppercase and lowercase letters, unlike DOS. (The Macintosh remembers
whether you use uppercase or lowercase letters for naming files, but it can't
distinguish between them internally. Try it. Name one file TEST and another file
test the next time you're using a Macintosh.)

JUST A MINUTE

Some of the UNIX versions available for the PC—notably SCO and
INTERACTIVE UNIX—have an ls that behaves slightly differently and may
list all files in a single column rather than in multiple columns. If your PC
does this, you can use the -C flag to ls to force multiple columns.

SUMMARY It's important that you always remember to type UNIX commands in lowercase
letters, unless you know that the particular command is actually uppercase; remember
that UNIX treats Archives and archives as different filenames. Also, avoid entering your
account name in uppercase when you log in. UNIX has some old compatibility features that
make using the system much more difficult if you use an all-uppercase login. If you ever
accidentally log in with all uppercase, log out and try again in lowercase.

Task 4.2: Having ls **Tell You More**

DESCRIPTION Without options, the ls command offers relatively little information. Questions you
might still have about your directory include: How big are the files? Which are files,
and which are directories? How old are they? What hidden files do you have?

ACTION

1. Start by entering ls -s to indicate file sizes:

```
% ls -s
total 403
    1 Archives      1 Mail      5 RUMORS.18Sept  280 mailing.lists
    1 InfoWorld     1 News      1 bin              2 newels
  108 LISTS         1 OWL       4 iecc.list        1 src
```

2. To ascertain the size of each file or directory listed, you can use the -s flag to ls. The size indicated is the number of kilobytes, rounded upward, for each file. The first line of the listing also indicates the total amount of disk space used, in kilobytes, for the contents of this directory. The summary number does not, however, include the contents of any subdirectories, so it's deceptively small.

JUST A MINUTE

> A kilobyte is 1,024 bytes of information, a byte being a single character. The preceding paragraph, for example, contains slightly more than 400 characters. UNIX works in units of a *block* of information, which, depending on which version of UNIX you're using, is either 1 kilobyte or 512 bytes. Most UNIX systems now work with a 1-kilobyte block.

3. Here is a further definition of what occurs when you use the -s flag: ls indicates the number of blocks each file or directory occupies. You then can use simple calculations to convert blocks into bytes. For example, the ls command indicates that the LISTS file in my home directory occupies 108 blocks. A quick calculation of block size multiplied by the number of blocks reveals the actual file size, in bytes, of LISTS, as shown here:

```
% bc
1024 * 108
110592
quit
%
```

Based on these results of the bc command, you can see that the file is 110,592 bytes in size. You can estimate size by multiplying the number of blocks by 1,000. Be aware, however, that in large files, the difference between 1,000 and 1,024 is significant enough to introduce an error into your calculation. As an example, I have a file that's more than three megabytes in size (a megabyte is 1,024 kilobytes, which is 1,024 bytes, so a megabyte is $1,024 \times 1,024$, or 1,048,576 bytes):

```
% ls -s bigfile
3648 bigfile
```

4. The file actually occupies 3,727,360 bytes. If I estimated its size by multiplying the number of blocks by 1,000 (which equals 3,648,000 bytes), I'd have underestimated its size by 79,360 bytes. (Remember, blocks $\times$ 1,000 is an easy estimate!)

JUST A MINUTE

> The last example reveals something else about the ls command. You can specify individual files or directories you're interested in viewing and avoid having to see all files and directories in your current location.

4

5. You can specify as many files or directories as you like, and separate them by spaces:

```
% ls -s LISTS iecc.list newels
  108 LISTS          4 iecc.list     2 newels
```

In the previous hour, you learned that UNIX identifies each file that begins with a dot (.) as a hidden file. Your home directory is probably littered with dot files, which retain preferences, status information, and other data. To list these hidden files, use the -a flag to ls:

```
% ls -a
.                .gopherrc       .oldnewsrc      .sig            RUMORS.18Sept
..               .history        .plan           Archives        bin
.Agenda          .info           .pnewsexpert    InfoWorld       iecc.list
.aconfigrc       .letter         .report         LISTS           mailing.lists
.article         .login          .rm-timestamp   Mail            newels
.cshrc           .mailrc         .rnlast         News            src
.elm             .newsrc         .rnsoft         OWL
```

You can see that this directory contains more dot files than regular files and directories. That's not uncommon in a UNIX home directory. However, it's rare to find any dot files other than the standard dot and dot-dot directories (those are in every directory in the entire file system) in directories other than your home directory.

6. You used another flag to the ls command—the -F flag—in the previous hour. Do you remember what it does?

```
% ls -F
Archives/        Mail/           RUMORS.18Sept   mailing.lists
InfoWorld@       News/           bin/            newels
LISTS            OWL/            iecc.list       src/
```

Adding the -F flag to ls appends suffixes to certain filenames so that you can ascertain more easily what types of files they are. Three different suffixes can be added, as shown in Table 4.1.

Table 4.1. Filename suffixes appended by ls -F.

Suffix	Example	Meaning
/	Mail/	Mail is a directory.
*	prog*	prog is an executable program.
@	bin@	bin is a symbolic link to another file or directory.

7. If you're familiar with the Macintosh and have used either System 7.0 or 7.1, you may recall the new feature that enables the user to create and use an alias. An alias is a file that does not contain information, but acts, instead, as a pointer to the actual information files. Aliases can exist either for specific files or for folders.

UNIX has offered a similar feature for many years, which in UNIX jargon is called a *symbolic link*. A symbolic link, such as bin in Table 4.1, contains the name of another file or directory rather than any contents of its own. If you could peek inside, it might look like bin = @/usr/bin. Every time someone tries to look at bin, the system shows the contents of /usr/bin instead.

You'll learn more about symbolic links and how they help you organize your files a bit later in the book. For now, just remember that if you see an @ after a filename, it's a link to another spot in the file system.

8. A useful flag for ls (one that might not be available in your version of UNIX) is the -m flag. This flag outputs the files as a comma-separated list. If there are many files, -m can be a quick and easy way to see what's available.

```
% ls -m
Archives, InfoWorld, LISTS, Mail, News, OWL, RUMORS.18Sept,
bin, iecc.list, mailing.lists, newels, src
```

SUMMARY Sometime you might want to list each of your files on a separate line, perhaps for a printout you want to annotate. You've seen that the -C flag forces recalcitrant versions of ls to output in multiple columns. Unfortunately, the opposite behavior isn't obtained using a lowercase c. (UNIX should be so consistent!) Instead, use the -1 flag to indicate that you want one column of output. Try it.

Task 4.3: Combining Flags

DESCRIPTION The different flags you've learned so far are summarized in Table 4.2.

Table 4.2. Some useful flags to ls.

Flag	Meaning
-a	List all files, including any dot files.
-F	Indicate file types; / = directory, * = executable.
-m	Show files as a comma-separated list.
-s	Show size of files, in blocks (typically, 1 block = 1,024 bytes).
-C	Force multiple-column output on listings.
-1	Force single-column output on listings.

What if you want a list, generated with the -F conventions, that simultaneously shows you all files and indicates their types?

4

ACTION

1. Combining flags in UNIX is easy. All you have to do is run them together in a sequence of characters, and prefix the whole thing with a dash:

```
% ls -aF
./               .gopherrc       .oldnewsrc      .sig
➥RUMORS.18Sept
../              .history*       .plan           Archives/
➥bin/
.Agenda          .info           .pnewsexpert    InfoWorld/
➥iecc.list
.aconfigrc       .letter         .report         LISTS
➥mailing.lists
.article         .login          .rm-timestamp   Mail/
➥newels
.cshrc           .mailrc         .rnlast         News/
➥src/
.elm/            .newsrc         .rnsoft         OWL/
```

2. Sometimes it's more convenient to keep all the flags separate. This is fine, as long as each flag is prefixed by its own dash:

```
% ls -s -F
total 403
    1 Archives/    1 Mail/       5 RUMORS.18Sept   280 mailing.lists
    1 InfoWorld/   1 News/       1 bin/              2 newels
  108 LISTS        1 OWL/        4 iecc.list         1 src/
```

3. Try some of these combinations on your own computer. Also try to list a flag more than once (for example, ls -sss -s), or list flags in different orders.

SUMMARY Very few UNIX commands care about the order in which flags are listed. Because it's the presence or absence of a flag that's important, listing a flag more than once doesn't make any difference.

Task 4.4: Listing Directories Without Changing Location

DESCRIPTION Every time I try to do any research in the library, I find myself spending hours and hours there, but it seems to me that I do less research than I think I should. That's because most of my time is for the tasks between the specifics of my research: finding the location of the next book, and finding the book itself.

If ls constrained you to listing only the directory that you were in, it would hobble you in a similar way. Using only ls would slow you down dramatically and force you to use cd to move around each time.

Instead, just as you can specify certain files by using ls, you can specify certain directories you're interested in viewing.

ACTION

1. Try this yourself. List /usr on your system:

```
% ls -F /usr
5bin/           diag/           lddrv/          share/          ucbinclude@
5include/       dict/           lib/            source/         ucblib@
5lib/           etc/            local/          spool@          xpg2bin/
acc/            export/         lost+found/     src@            xpg2include/
acctlog*        games/          man@            stand@          xpg2lib/
adm@            hack/           mdec@           sys@
bin/            hosts/          old/            system/
boot@           include/        pub@            tmp@
demo/           kvm/            sccs/           ucb/
```

You probably have different files and directories listed in your own /usr directory. Remember, @ files are symbolic links in the listing, too.

2. You can also specify more than one directory:

```
% ls /usr/local /home/taylor
/home/taylor:
Global.Software    Mail/          Src/                    history.usenet.Z
Interactive.Unix   News/          bin/
/usr/local/:
T/              emacs/          ftp/            lists/          motd~
admin/          emacs-18.59/    gnubin/         lost+found/     netcom/
bin/            etc/            include/        man/            policy/
cat/            faq/            info/           menu/           src/
doc/            forms/          lib/            motd            tmp/
```

In this example, the ls command also sorted the directories before listing them. I specified that I wanted to see /usr/local and then /home/taylor, but it presented the directories in opposite order.

JUST A MINUTE

> I've never been able to figure out how ls sorts directories when you ask for more than one to be listed—it's not an alphabetical listing. Consider it a mystery. Remember that if you must have the output in a specific order, you can use the ls command twice in a row.

3. Here's where the dot-dot shorthand can come in handy. Try it yourself:

```
% ls -m ..
armstrong, bruce, cedric, christine, david, green,
guest, higgins, james, kane, laura, mac, mark,
patrickb, rank, shalini, shane, taylor, vicki
```

If you were down one branch of the file system and wanted to look at some files down another branch, you could easily find yourself using the command ls ../Indiana/Personnel or ls -s ../../source.

4

4. There's a problem here, however. You've seen that you can specify filenames to look at those files, and directory names to look at the contents of those directories, but what if you're interested in the directory itself, not in its contents? I might want to list just two directories—not the contents, just the files themselves, as shown here:

```
% ls -F
Archives/       Mail/           RUMORS.18Sept  mailing.lists
InfoWorld/      News/           bin/           newlists
LISTS           OWL/            iecc.list      src/
% ls -s LISTS Mail newlists
 108 LISTS              2 newlists
Mail:
total 705
   8 cennamo     27 ean_houts     4 kcs      21 mark     7 sartin
  28 dan_sommer   2 gordon_haight 34 lehman   5 raf       3 shelf
  14 decc        48 harrism      64 mac       7 rock     20 steve
   3 druby       14 james        92 mailbox   5 rustle   18 tai
```

5. The problem is that ls doesn't know that you want to look at Mail unless you tell it not to look inside the directories specified. The command flag needed is -d, which forces ls to list directories rather than their contents. The same ls command, but with the -d flag, has dramatically different output:

```
% ls -ds LISTS Mail newlists
 108 LISTS            1 Mail/        2 newlists
```

Try some of these flags on your own system, and watch how they work together.

SUMMARY To list a file or directory, you can specify it to ls. Directories, however, reveal their contents, unless you also include the -d flag.

Special ls Command Flags

It should be becoming clear to you that UNIX is the ultimate toolbox. Even some of the simplest commands have dozens of different options. On one system I use, ls has more than 20 different flags.

Task 4.5: Changing the Sort Order in ls

DESCRIPTION What if you wanted to look at files, but wanted them to show up in a directory sorting order different from the default (that is, column-first order)? How could you change the sort order in ls?

ACTION

1. The -x flag sorts across, listing the output in columns, or first-row order (entries are sorted across, then down):

```
% ls -a
.                    .elm              .plan              Global.Software
..                   .forward          .pnewsexpert       Interactive.Unix
.Pnews.header        .ircmotd          .rnlast            Mail
.accinfo             .login            .rnlock            News
.article             .logout           .rnsoft            Src
.cshrc               .newsrc           .sig               bin
.delgroups           .oldnewsrc        .tin               history.usenet.Z
% ls -x -a
.                    ..                .Pnews.header      .accinfo
.article             .cshrc            .delgroups         .elm
.forward             .ircmotd          .login             .logout
.newsrc              .oldnewsrc        .plan              .pnewsexpert
.rnlast              .rnlock           .rnsoft            .sig
.tin                 Global.Software   Interactive.Unix   Mail
News                 Src               bin                history.usenet.Z
```

2. There are even more ways to sort files in ls. If you want to sort by most-recently-accessed to least-recently-accessed, you use the -t flag:

    ```
    % ls -a -t
    ./                   ../               .rnlock            .cshrc
    .newsrc              News/             .rnlast            .sig
    .oldnewsrc           .tin/             .rnsoft            .plan
    .article             .ircmotd          Interactive.Unix   Mail/
    .elm/                .delgroups        .accinfo*          .Pnews.header*
    .forward             .login            Src/               .pnewsexpert
    history.usenet.Z     bin/              Global.Software    .logout
    ```

    From this output, you can see that the most recently accessed files are .newsrc and .oldnewsrc, and that it's been quite a while since .logout was touched. Try using the -t flag on your system to see which files you've been accessing and which you haven't.

3. So far, you know three different approaches to sorting files within the ls command: column-first order, row-first order, and most-recently-accessed-first order. But there are more options in ls than just these three; the -r flag reverses any sorting order.

    ```
    % ls
    Global.Software      Mail/             Src/               history.usenet.Z
    Interactive.Unix     News/             bin/
    % ls -r
    history.usenet.Z     Src/              Mail/              Global.Software
    bin/                 News/             Interactive.Unix
    ```

4. Things may become confusing when you combine some of these flags. Try to list the contents of the directory that is one level above the current directory, sorted so the most-recently-accessed file is last in the list. At the same time, indicate which items are directories and the size of each file.

    ```
    % ls -r -t -F -s ..
    total 150
        2 bruce/     2 rank/       2 kane/        14 higgins/
    ```

4

```
2 laura/       2 christine/   2 shane/       6 mac/
2 cedric       2 peggy/       4 patrickb/   10 mark/
2 james@       4 taylor/      4 green/       6 armstrong/
2 vicki/       2 guest/       6 shalini/     4 david/
```

SUMMARY A better, easier way to type the previous command would be to bundle flags into the single argument `ls -rtFs ..`, which would work just as well, and you'd look like an expert!

Task 4.6: Listing Directory Trees Recursively in `ls`

DESCRIPTION In case things aren't yet complicated enough with `ls`, two more important, valuable flags are available. One is the `-R` flag, which causes `ls` to list recursively directories below the current or specified directory. If you think of listing files as a numbered set of steps, recursion is simply adding a step—the rule is if this file is a directory, list it, too—to the list.

ACTION

1. When I use the `-R` flag, here's what I see:

```
% ls -R
Global.Software    Mail/    Src/    history.usenet.Z
Interactive.Unix   News/    bin/
Mail:
Folders/  Netnews/
Mail/Folders:
mail.sent  mailbox    steinman    tucker
Mail/Netnews:
postings
News:
uptodate  volts
Src:
sum-up.c
bin:
Pnews*    punt*    submit*
```

Try it yourself.

Notice that `ls` lists the current directory and then alphabetically lists the contents of all subdirectories. Notice also that the `Mail` directory has two directories within it and that those are also listed here.

SUMMARY Viewing all files and directories below a certain point in the file system can be a valuable way to look for files (although you'll soon learn better tools for finding files). If you aren't careful, though, you may get hundreds or thousands of lines of information streaming across your screen. Do not enter a command like `ls -R /` unless you have time to sit and watch information fly past.

If you try to list the contents of a directory when you don't have permission to access the information, ls warns you with an error message:

```
% ls ../marv
../marv unreadable
```

Now ask for a recursive listing, with indications of file type and size, of the directory /etc, and see what's there. The listing will include many files and subdirectories, but they should be easy to wade through due to all the notations ls uses to indicate files and directories.

Task 4.7: Long Listing Format in ls

Description You've seen how to estimate the size of a file by using the -s flag to find the number of blocks it occupies. To find the exact size of a file in bytes, you need to use the -l flag. (Use a lowercase letter L. The numeral 1 produces single-column output, as you've already learned.)

Action

1. The first long listing shows information for the LISTS file.

   ```
   % ls -l LISTS
   -rw-------  1 taylor      106020 Oct  8 15:17 LISTS
   ```

   The output is explained in Figure 4.1.

Figure 4.1.
The meaning of the -l output for a file.

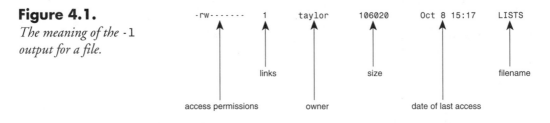

Summary For each file and directory in the UNIX file system, the owner, size, name, number of other files pointing to it (links), and access permissions are recorded. The creation, modification, and access times and dates are also recorded for each file. The modification time is the default time used for the -t sorting option and listed by the ls long format.

Permissions Strings

Interpreting permissions strings is a complex issue because UNIX has a sophisticated security model for individual files. Security revolves around three different types of users: the owner of the file, the group of which that the file is a part, and everyone else.

The first character of the permissions string, identified in Figure 4.1 as *access permissions*, indicates the kind of file. The two most common values are d for directories and - for regular files. Be aware that there are many other file types that you'll rarely, if ever, see.

The following nine characters in the permissions string indicate what type of access is allowed for different users. From left to right, these characters show what access is allowed for the owner of the file, the group that owns the file, and everyone else.

Figure 4.2 shows how to break down the permissions string for the LISTS file into individual components.

Figure 4.2.

Reading access permissions for LISTS.

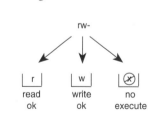

file type   owner   group   everyone else

Each permissions string is identically composed of three components—permission for reading, writing, and execution—as shown in Figure 4.3.

Figure 4.3.

Elements of a permissions string.

rw-

r		w		⊗
read	write	no
ok	ok	execute

Armed with this information—specifically, knowing that a - character means that the specific permission is denied—you can see that ls shows that the owner of the file, taylor, as illustrated in Figure 4.1, has read and write permission. Nobody else either in taylor's group or in any other group has permission to view, edit, or run the file.

Earlier you learned that just about everything in UNIX ends up as a file in the file system, whether it's an application, a device driver, or a directory. The system keeps track of whether a file is executable because that's one way it knows whether LISTS is the name of a file or the name of an application.

Task 4.8: Long Listing Format for Directories in ls

 The long form of a directory listing is almost identical to a file listing, but the permissions string is interpreted in a very different manner.

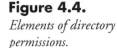

1. Here is an example of a long directory listing:

```
% ls -l -d Example
drwxr-x---  2 taylor        1024 Sep 30 10:50 Example/
```

Remember that you must have both read and execute permission for a directory. If you have either read or execute permission but not both, the directory will not be usable (as though you had neither permission). Write permission, of course, enables the user to alter the contents of the directory or add new files to the directory.

2. The Example directory breaks down for interpretation as shown in Figure 4.4.

Figure 4.4.

Elements of directory permissions.

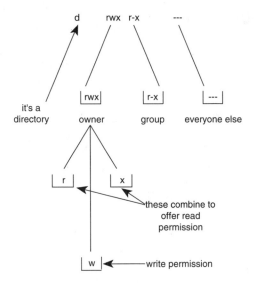

JUST A MINUTE

I've never understood the nuances of a directory with read but not execute permission, or vice versa, and explanations from other people have never proven to be correct. It's okay, though, because I've never seen a directory on a UNIX system that was anything other than ---, r-x, or rwx.

3. Now try using the -l flag yourself. Move to your home directory, and enter ls -l as shown here:

```
% ls -l
total 403
drwx------  2 taylor         512 Sep 30 10:38 Archives/
drwx------  3 taylor         512 Oct  1 08:23 InfoWorld/
```

```
-rw-------    1 taylor      106020 Oct  8 15:17 LISTS
drwx------    2 taylor        1024 Sep 30 10:50 Mail/
drwx------    2 taylor         512 Oct  6 09:36 News/
drwx------    2 taylor         512 Sep 30 10:51 OWL/
-rw-------    1 taylor        4643 Sep 20 10:49 RUMORS.18Sept
drwx------    2 taylor         512 Oct  1 09:53 bin/
-rw-------    1 taylor        3843 Oct  6 18:02 iecc.list
-rw-rw----    1 taylor      280232 Oct  6 09:57 mailing.lists
-rw-rw----    1 taylor        1031 Oct  7 15:44 newlists
drwx------    2 taylor         512 Sep 14 22:14 src/
```

The size of a directory is usually in increments of 512 bytes. The second field, the "link," is an interesting and little-known value when a directory is being listed. Instead of counting up the number of other files that point to the file, (that is, the number of files that have a link to the current file), the second field indicates the number of directories that are contained in that specific directory. Remember, all directories have dot and dot-dot, so the minimum value is always 2.

4. Consider the following example:

```
% ls -Fa
./              .gopherrc       .oldnewsrc      .sig            OWL/
../             .history*       .plan           Archives/
➥RUMORS.18Sept
.Agenda         .info           .pnewsexpert    Cancelled.mail  bin/
.aconfigrc      .letter         .report         InfoWorld/      iecc.list
.article        .login          .rm-timestamp   LISTS
➥mailing.lists
.cshrc          .mailrc         .rnlast         Mail/           newlists
.elm/           .newsrc         .rnsoft         News/           src/
% ls -ld .
drwx------ 10 taylor         1024 Oct 10 16:00 ./
```

5. Try entering ls -ld. and see if it correctly identifies the number of directories in your home directory. Move to other directories and see whether the listing agrees with your own count of directories.

SUMMARY The output from the ls -l command is unquestionably complex and packed with information. Interpretation of permissions strings is an important part of understanding and being able to use UNIX, and more explanation is offered in subsequent hours.

Table 4.3 summarizes the many different command flags for ls that you have learned in this hour.

Table 4.3. Summary of command flags for ls.

Flag	Meaning
-1	Force single-column output on listings.
-a	List all files, including any dot files.
-C	Force multiple-column output on listings.

continues

Table 4.3. continued

Flag	Meaning
-d	List directories rather than their contents.
-F	Indicate file types; / = directory, * = executable.
-l	Generate a long listing of files and directories.
-m	Show files as a comma-separated list.
-r	Reverse the order of any file sorting.
-R	Recursively show directories and their contents.
-s	Show size of files, in blocks (typically 1 block = 1,024 bytes).
-t	Sort output in most-recently-modified order.
-x	Sort output in row-first order.

Without doubt, ls is one of the most powerful and, therefore, also one of the most confusing commands in UNIX. The best way for you to learn how all the flags work together is to experiment with different combinations.

Task 4.9: Creating Files with the touch Command

DESCRIPTION At this point, you have a variety of UNIX tools that help you move through the file system and learn about specific files. The touch command is the first command that helps you create new files on the system, independent of any program other than the shell itself. This can prove very helpful for organizing a new collection of files, for example.

The main reason that touch is used in UNIX is to force the last-modified time of a file to be updated, as the following example demonstrates.

```
% ls -l iecc.list
-rw------- 1 taylor        3843 Oct  6 18:02 iecc.list
% touch iecc.list
% ls -l iecc.list
-rw------- 1 taylor        3843 Oct 10 16:22 iecc.list
```

Because the touch command changes modification times of files, anything that sorts files based on modification time will, of course, alter the position of that file when the file is altered by touch.

ACTION

1. Consider the following output:
```
% ls -t
mailing.lists    LISTS         News/         OWL/          src/
Cancelled.mail   newlists      bin/          Mail/
RUMORS.18Sept    iecc.list     InfoWorld/    Archives/
```

4

```
% touch iecc.list
% ls -t
iecc.list        RUMORS.18Sept    News/          OWL/            src/
mailing.lists    LISTS            bin/           Mail/
Cancelled.mail   newlists         InfoWorld/     Archives/
```

You probably will not use touch for this purpose very often.

2. If you try to use the touch command on a file that doesn't exist, the program creates the file:

```
% ls
Archives/        LISTS            OWL/           iecc.list       src/
Cancelled.mail   Mail/            RUMORS.18Sept  mailing.lists
InfoWorld/       News/            bin/           newlists
% touch new.file
% ls
Archives/        LISTS            OWL/           iecc.list       newlists
Cancelled.mail   Mail/            RUMORS.18Sept  mailing.lists   src/
InfoWorld/       News/            bin/           new.file
% ls -l new.file
-rw-rw----  1 taylor         0 Oct 10 16:28 new.file
```

The new file has zero bytes, as can be seen by the ls -l output. Notice that by default the files are created with read and write permission for the user and anyone in the user's group. You learn in another hour how to determine, by using the umask command, your own default permission for files.

SUMMARY You won't need touch very often, but it's valuable to know.

Task 4.10: Check Disk-Space Usage with du

DESCRIPTION One advantage that the DOS and Macintosh systems have over UNIX is they make it easy to find out how much disk space you're using and how much remains available. On a Macintosh, viewing folders by size shows disk space used, and the top-right corner of any Finder window shows available space. In DOS it's even easier; both items are listed at the end of the output from a DIR command:

```
C> DIR .BAT
 Volume in drive C is MS-DOS_5
 Volume Serial Number is 197A-A8D7
 Directory of C:\
AUTOEXEC BAT       142 02-28-93    8:19p
CSH      BAT        36 12-22-92    3:01p
        2 file(s)            178 bytes
                        5120000 bytes free
```

In this DOS example, you can see that the files listed take up 178 bytes, and that there are 5,120,000 bytes (about 5 megabytes, or 5MB) available on the hard drive.

Like a close-mouthed police informant, UNIX never volunteers any information, so you need to learn two new commands. The du, disk usage, command is used to find out how much disk space is used; the df, disk free, command is used to find out how much space is available.

ACTION

1. The du command lists the size, in kilobytes, of all directories at or below the current point in the file system.

```
% du
11        ./OWL
38        ./.elm
20        ./Archives
14        ./InfoWorld/PIMS
28        ./InfoWorld
710       ./Mail
191       ./News
25        ./bin
35        ./src
1627      .
```

Notice that du went two levels deep to find the InfoWorld/PIMS subdirectory, adding its size to the size indicated for the InfoWorld directory. At the very end, it lists 1,627KB as the size of the dot directory—the current directory. As you know, 1,024KB kilobytes is a megabyte. Through division, you'll find that the InfoWorld directory is taking up 1.5MB of disk space.

2. If you are interested in only the grand total, you can use the -s flag to output just a summary of the information.

```
% du -s
1627      .
```

Of course, you can look anywhere on the file system, but the more subdirectories there are, the longer it takes.

3. Error messages with du are possible:

```
% du -s /etc
/etc/shadow: Permission denied
4417      /etc
```

In this example, one of the directories within the /etc directory has a permissions set denying access:

```
% ls -ld /etc/shadow
drwx------   2 root          512 Oct 10 16:34 /etc/shadow/
```

The du command summarizes disk usage only for the files it can read, so regardless of the size of the shadow directory, I'd still have the 4,417 kilobytes size indicated.

4. Although by default du lists only the sizes of directories, it also computes the size of all files. If you're interested in that information, you can, by adding the -a flag, have the program list it for all files.

```
% cd InfoWorld
% du -a
9         ./PIM.review.Z
```

```
5         ./Expert.opinion.Z
4         ./PIMS/proposal.txt.Z
1         ./PIMS/task1.txt.Z
2         ./PIMS/task2.txt.Z
2         ./PIMS/task3.txt.Z
2         ./PIMS/task4.txt.Z
2         ./PIMS/task5.txt.Z
2         ./PIMS/task6.txt.Z
1         ./PIMS/contact.info.Z
14        ./PIMS
28        .
```

The problems of the -a flag for du are similar to those for the -R flag for ls. There may be more files in a directory than you care to view.

5. The -a flag for listing all files overrides the -s flag for summarizing, but without telling you it's doing so. A preferable way would be for the program to note that the two flags are incompatible, as many UNIX programs indicate, but that isn't how du works.

```
% du -s -a
9         ./PIM.review.Z
5         ./Expert.opinion.Z
4         ./PIMS/proposal.txt.Z
1         ./PIMS/task1.txt.Z
2         ./PIMS/task2.txt.Z
2         ./PIMS/task3.txt.Z
2         ./PIMS/task4.txt.Z
2         ./PIMS/task5.txt.Z
2         ./PIMS/task6.txt.Z
1         ./PIMS/contact.info.Z
28        .
```

6. The du command is an exception to the rule that multiple flags can be more succinctly stated as a single multiletter flag. With ls, you'll recall, -a -F -l could be more easily typed as -aFl. The command du does not allow similar shorthand.

```
% du -sa
-sa: No such file or directory
```

JUST A MINUTE

UNIX is nothing if not varied. Some systems will accept du -as, and others will not accept du -a -s. Try yours and see what does and doesn't work.

CAUTION

It isn't a problem that du does not allow multiletter flags, however, because you do not use the -s and -a flags to du at the same time.

Task 4.11: Check Available Disk Space with df

DESCRIPTION
Figuring out how much disk space is available on the overall UNIX system is difficult for everyone except experts. The df command is used for this task, but it doesn't summarize its results—the user must add the column of numbers.

ACTION

1. This is the system's response to the df command:

```
% df
Filesystem              kbytes     used   avail capacity  Mounted
/dev/zd0a                17259    14514    1019     93%    /
/dev/zd8d               185379   143995   22846     86%    /userf
/dev/zd7d               185379    12984  153857      8%    /tmp
/dev/zd3f               385689   307148   39971     88%    /users
/dev/zd3g               367635   232468   98403     70%    /userc
/dev/zd2f               385689   306189   40931     88%    /usere
/dev/zd2g               367635   207234  123637     63%    /userb
/dev/zd1g               301823   223027   48613     82%    /usera
/dev/zd5c               371507   314532   19824     94%    /usr
/dev/zd0h               236820   159641   53497     75%    /usr/src
/dev/zd0g               254987    36844  192644     16%    /var
```

You end up with lots of information, but it isn't easy to add up quickly to find the total space available. Nonetheless, the output offers quite a bit of information.

2. Because I know that my home directory is on the disk /users, I can simply look for that directory in the rightmost column to find out that I'm using the hard disk /dev/zd3f. I can see that there are 385,689KB on the disk, and 88 percent of the disk is used, which means that 307,148KB are used and 39,971KB, or only about 38MB, are unused.

3. Some UNIX systems have relatively few separate computer disks hooked up, making the df output more readable. The df output is explained in Figure 4.5.

```
% df
Filesystem              kbytes     used   avail capacity  Mounted
/dev/sd0a                55735    37414   12748     75%    /
/dev/sd2b               187195   153569   14907     91%    /usr
/dev/sd1a                55688    43089    7031     86%    /utils
```

Figure 4.5.
Understanding df *output.*

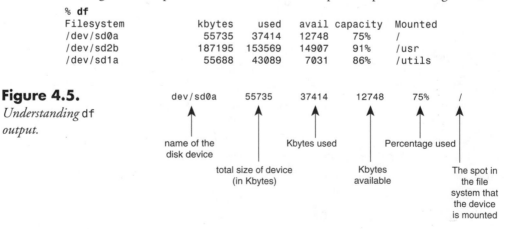

4

You can add the columns to find that the system has a total of about 300MB of disk space (55,735 + 187,195 + 55,688), of which 230MB are used. The remaining space is therefore 33MB, or 16 percent of the total disk size.

SUMMARY Try using the du and df commands on your system to figure out how much disk space is available on both the overall system and the disk you're using for your home directory. Then use du to identify how much space your files and directories are occupying.

Task 4.12: Shrink Big Files with the compress Program

DESCRIPTION Now that you can figure out how much space you're using with the files in your directory, you're ready to learn how to save space without removing any files. UNIX has a built-in program—the compress program—that offers this capability.

ACTION

1. In this simple example, the compress program is given a list of filenames and then compresses each of the files, renaming them with a .z suffix, which indicates that they are compressed.

   ```
   % ls -l LISTS
   -rw-------  1 taylor      106020 Oct 10 13:47 LISTS
   % compress LISTS
   % ls -l LISTS.Z
   -rw-------  1 taylor       44103 Oct 10 13:47 LISTS.Z
   ```

   Compressing the LISTS file has reduced its size from 106KB to a little more than 44KB (a savings of almost 60 percent in disk space). If you expect to have large files on your system that you won't access very often, using the compress program can save lots of disk space.

2. Using compress on bigger files can show even greater savings:

   ```
   % ls -l huge.file
   -rwxrwxrwx  1 root      3727360 Sep 27 14:03 huge.file
   % compress huge.file
   % ls -l huge.file.Z
   -rwxrwxrwx  1 taylor    2121950 Sep 27 14:03 huge.file.Z
   ```

   In this example, it took a powerful Sun computer with no other users exactly 20 seconds to compress huge.file. This single command was able to free over 1.5MB of disk space. If you're using a PC to run UNIX, or if you are on a system with many users (which you can easily ascertain by using the w command), it might take a significant amount of time to compress files.

3. To reverse the operation, use the companion command uncompress, and specify either the current name of the file (that is, with the .Z suffix) or the name of the file before it was compressed (that is, without the .Z suffix).

```
% uncompress LISTS
% ls -l LISTS
-rw-------  1 taylor      106020 Oct 10 13:47 LISTS
```

JUST A MINUTE

Why would you compress files? You would do so to save file space. Before you use any of the compressed files, though, you must uncompress them, so the compress utility is best used with large files you won't need for a while.

4. For information on how well the compress program shrunk your files, you can add a -v flag to the program for verbose output:

```
% compress -v huge.file
huge.file: Compression: 43.15% -- replaced with huge.file.Z
```

SUMMARY Try using the compress program on some of the files in your directory, being careful not to compress any files (particularly preference or dot files) that might be required to run programs.

Summary

Most of this hour was spent learning about the powerful and complex ls command and its many ways of listing files and directories. You also learned how to combine command flags to reduce typing. You learned how to use the touch command to create new files and update the modification time on older files, if needed. The hour continued with a discussion of how to ascertain the amount of disk space you're using and how much space is left, using the du and df commands, respectively. Finally, you learned how the compress command can keep you from running out of space by ensuring that infrequently used files are stored in the minimum space needed.

Workshop

The Workshop summarizes the key terms you learned and poses some questions about the topics presented in this chapter. It also provides you with a preview of what you will learn in the next hour.

Key Terms

access permission   The set of accesses (read, write, and execute) allowed for each of the three classes of users (owner, group, and everyone else) for each file or directory on the system.

block   At its most fundamental, a block is like a sheet of information in the virtual notebook that represents the disk: A disk is typically composed of many tens, or hundreds, of thousands of blocks of information, each 512 bytes in size. You also might read the explanation of **i-node** in the Glossary to learn more about how disks are structured in UNIX.

column-first order   When you have a list of items that are listed in columns and span multiple lines, column-first order is a sorting strategy in which items are sorted so that the items are in alphabetical order down the first column and continuing at the top of the second column, then the third column, and so on. The alternative strategy is **row-first order**.

permission strings   The string that represents the access permissions.

row-first order   In contrast to column-first order, this is when items are sorted in rows so that the first item of each column in a row is in alphabetical order from left to right, then the second line contains the next set of items, and so on.

Questions

1. Try using the du command on different directories to see how much disk space each requires. If you encounter errors with file permissions, use ls -ld to list the permissions of the directory in question.

2. Why would you want all the different types of sorting alternatives available with ls? Can you think of situations in which each would be useful?

3. Use a combination of the ls -t and touch commands to create a few new files. Then update their modification times so that in a most-recently-modified listing of files, the first file you created shows up ahead of the second file you created.

4. Try using the du -s .. command from your home directory. Before you try it, however, what do you think will happen?

5. Use df and bc or dc to figure out the amounts of disk space used and available on your system.

6. Use the compress command to shrink a file in /tmp or your home directory. Use the -v flag to learn how much the file was compressed, and then restore the file to its original condition.

Preview of the Next Hour

The next hour is a bit easier. It offers further explanation of the various information given by the ls command and a discussion of file ownership, including how to change the owner and group of any file or directory. You will learn about the chmod command, which can change the specific set of permissions associated with any file or directory, and the umask command, which can control the modes that new files are given upon creation.

Hour 5

Ownership and Permissions

This hour focuses on teaching the basics of UNIX file permissions. Topics include setting and modifying file permissions with chmod, analyzing file permissions as shown by the ls -l command, and setting up default file permissions with the umask command. Permission is only half the puzzle, however, and you also learn about file ownership and group ownership, and how to change either for any file or directory.

Goals for This Hour

In this hour, you learn how to

- ☐ Understand file permissions settings
- ☐ Understand directory permissions settings
- ☐ Modify file and directory permissions with chmod
- ☐ Set new file permissions with chmod
- ☐ Establish default file and directory permissions with umask

☐ Identify the owner and group for any file or directory
☐ Change the owner of a file or directory
☐ Change the group of a file or directory

The preceding hour contained the first tutorial dealing with the permissions of a file or directory using the -l option with ls. If you haven't read that hour recently, it would help to review the material. In this hour, you learn about another option to ls that tells UNIX to show the group and owner of files or directories. Four more commands are introduced and discussed in detail: chmod for changing the permissions of a file, umask for defining default permissions, chown for changing ownership, and chgrp for changing the group of a file or directory.

As you have seen in examples throughout the book, UNIX treats all directories as files; they have their own size (independent of their contents), their own permissions strings, and more. As a result, unless it's an important difference, from here on I talk about files with the intention of referring to files and directories both. Logic will confirm whether commands can apply to both, or to files only, or to directories only. (For example, you can't edit a directory and you can't store files inside other files.)

Task 5.1: Understand File Permissions Settings

DESCRIPTION   In the last hour you learned a bit about how to interpret the information that ls offers on file permissions when ls is used with the -l flag. Consider the following example.

```
% ls -l
total 403
drwx------   2 taylor          512 Sep 30 10:38 Archives/
drwx------   3 taylor          512 Oct  1 08:23 InfoWorld/
-rw-------   1 taylor       106020 Oct 10 13:47 LISTS
drwx------   2 taylor         1024 Sep 30 10:50 Mail/
drwx------   2 taylor          512 Oct  6 09:36 News/
drwx------   2 taylor          512 Sep 30 10:51 OWL/
-rw-------   1 taylor         4643 Oct 10 14:01 RUMORS.18Sept
drwx------   2 taylor          512 Oct 10 19:09 bin/
-rw-------   1 taylor         3843 Oct 10 16:22 iecc.list
-rw-rw-r--   1 taylor       280232 Oct 10 16:22 mailing.lists
-rw-rw----   1 taylor         1031 Oct  7 15:44 newlists
drwx------   2 taylor          512 Oct 10 19:09 src/
```

The first item of information on each line is what is key here. You learned in the previous hour that the first item is called the permissions string or, more succinctly, permissions. It also is sometimes referred to as the *mode* or *permissions mode* of the file, a mnemonic that can be valuable for remembering how to change permissions.

The permissions can be broken into four parts: type, owner, group, and other permissions. The first character indicates the file type: d is a directory and - is a regular file. There are a number of other types of files in UNIX, each indicated by the first letter of its permissions string, as summarized in Table 5.1. You can safely ignore, however, any file that isn't either a regular file or directory.

5

Table 5.1. The `ls` file type indicators.

Letter	Indicated File Type
d	Directory
b	Block-type special file
c	Character-type special file
l	Symbolic link
p	Pipe
s	Socket
-	Regular file

The next nine letters in the permissions string are broken into three groups of three each—representing the owner, group, and everyone else—as shown in Figure 5.1.

Figure 5.1.

Interpreting file permissions.

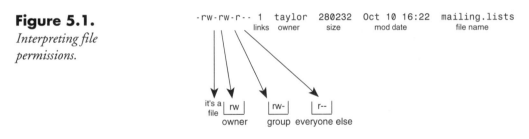

To understand what the permissions actually mean to the computer system, remember that UNIX treats everything as a file. If you install an application, it's just like everything else, with one exception: the system knows that an application is executable. A letter to your Mum is a regular file, but if you were to tell UNIX that it was executable, the system would merrily try to run it as a program (and fail).

There are three primary types of permission for files: read, write, and execute. Read permission enables users to examine the contents of the file with a variety of different programs, but they cannot alter, modify, or delete any information. They can copy the file and then edit the new version, however.

Write permission is the next step up. Users with write access to a file can add information to the file. If you have write permission and read permission for a file, you can edit the file—the read permission enables you to view the contents, and the write permission lets you alter them. With write permission only, you'd be able to add information to the file, but you wouldn't be able to view the contents of the file at any time. Admittedly, write-only permission is unusual in UNIX, but you might see it for log files, which are files that track activity on the system. Imagine if each time anyone logged in to your UNIX system the computer recorded the fact, noting who logged in, where they logged in from, and the current time and date. Armed with that information, you could ascertain who last logged in, who uses dial-up phone lines, and who uses the computer the most. (In fact, there's a UNIX command that does just that. It's called last.)

So far you've learned that you can have files with read-only permission, read-write permission, and write-only permission. The third type of access permission is execute, noted by ls with an x in the third slot of the permissions string.

```
% ls -l bin
total 57
-rwx------  1 taylor        1507 Aug 17 13:27 bounce.msg
-rwxrwx---  1 taylor       32916 Oct 10 19:09 calc
-rwx------  1 taylor       18567 Sep 14 22:14 fixit
-rw-------  1 taylor         334 Oct  1 09:53 punt
-rwx------  1 taylor        3424 Sep 10 22:27 rumor.mill.sh
```

ACTION

1. Try listing the files in the directory /etc on your system, and see if you can identify which are executable files or programs, which are directories, which are symbolic links (denoted with an l as the first character of the permissions string; they're files that point to other files or directories that point to other directories), and which are regular files.

2. Execute permission is slightly different from either read or write permission. If the directory containing the file is in your search path (the value of the environment variable PATH), any file that has execute permission is automatically started each time that filename is entered, regardless of where you are in the file system.

```
% pwd
/users/taylor
% env PATH
/users/taylor/bin:/bin:/usr/bin:/usr/ucb:/usr/local:/usr/local/bin:
% ls -l bin/say.hi
-rwxrwx---  1 taylor           9 Oct 11 13:32 bin/say.hi
% say.hi
hi
```

You can now see the importance of your search PATH. Without a search PATH, the system wouldn't be able to find any commands, and you'd be left with a barely functional system. You can also see the purpose of checking the executable permission status. I'm going to jump ahead a bit to show you one use of the chmod function so that you can see what happens if I remove the execute permission from the say.hi program:

```
% chmod -x bin/say.hi
% ls -l bin/say.hi
-rw-rw----  1 taylor           9 Oct 11 13:32 bin/say.hi
% say.hi
/users/taylor/bin/say.hi: Permission denied.
```

5

This time UNIX searched through my search path, found a file that matched the name of the program I requested, and then ascertained that it wasn't executable. The resultant error message: `Permission denied`.

3. Now try entering `say.hi` on your computer system. You'll get a different error message, `Command not found`, which tells you that UNIX searched all the directories in your search path but couldn't find a match anywhere.

4. Check your `PATH` and find a directory that you can add files in. You'll probably have a `bin` directory in your home directory on the list, as I have `/users/taylor/bin` in my search path. That's a good place to add a file using the `touch` command:

```
% env PATH
/users/taylor/bin:/bin:/usr/bin:/usr/ucb:/usr/local:/usr/local/bin:
% touch bin/my.new.cmd
% ls -l bin
-rw-rw----  1 taylor          0 Oct 11 15:07 my.new.cmd
```

5. Now try to actually execute the command by entering its name directly:

```
% my.new.cmd
/users/taylor/bin/my.new.cmd: Permission denied.
```

JUST A MINUTE

If you're using the C Shell as your command interpreter, it probably won't find the new command you just created. This is because, to speed things up, it keeps an internal table of where different commands are found in your search path. You need to force the program to rebuild its table, and you can do that with the simple command `rehash`. If, when you enter the filename, you don't get permission denied but instead see `Command not found`, enter `rehash` and try again.

5

6. Finally, use `chmod` to add execute permission to the file, and try executing it one more time.

```
% chmod +x bin/my.new.cmd
% ls -l bin/my.new.cmd
-rwxrw----  1 taylor          0 Oct 11 15:07 bin/my.new.cmd
% my.new.cmd
%
```

Voila! You've created your first UNIX command, an achievement even though it doesn't do much. You can now see how the search path and the UNIX philosophy of having applications be identical to regular files, except for the permission, can be invaluable as you learn how to customize your environment.

SUMMARY Execute permission enables the user to run the file as if it were a program. Execute permission is independent of other permissions granted—or denied—so it's perfectly feasible to have a program with read and execute permission, but no write permission. (After all, you wouldn't want others altering the program itself.) You also can have programs with execute permission only. This means that users can run the application, but they can't examine it to see how it works or copy it. (Copying requires the ability to read the file.)

JUST A MINUTE

> Though actual programs with execute-only permission work fine, a special class of programs called *shell scripts* fail. Shell scripts act like a UNIX command-line macro facility, which enables you to save easily a series of commands in a file and then run them as a single program. To work, however, the shell must be able to read the file and execute it, too, so shell scripts always require both read and execute permissions.

There are clearly quite a few permutations on the three different permissions: read, write, and execute. In practice, there are a few that occur most commonly, as listed in Table 5.2.

Table 5.2. The most common file permissions.

Permission	Meaning
- - -	No access is allowed
r - -	Read-only access
r - x	Read and execute access, for programs and shell scripts
rw -	Read and write access, for files
rwx	All access allowed, for programs

These permissions have different meanings when applied to directories, but - - - always indicates that no one can access the file in question.

Interpretation of the following few examples should help:

```
-rw-------   1 taylor        3843 Oct 10 16:22 iecc.list
-rw-rw-r--   1 taylor      280232 Oct 10 16:22 mailing.lists
-rw-rw----   1 taylor        1031 Oct  7 15:44 newlists
-rwxr-x---   1 taylor          64 Oct  9 09:31 the.script
```

The first file, iecc.list, has read and write permission for the owner (taylor) and is off-limits to all other users. The file mailing.lists offers similar access to the file owner (taylor) and to the group but offers read-only access to everyone else on the system. The third file, newlists, provides read and write access to both the file owner and group, but no access to anyone not in the group.

The fourth file on the list, the.script, is a program that can be run by both the owner and group members, read (or copied) by both the owner and group, and written (altered) by the owner. In practice, this probably would be a shell script, as described earlier, and these permissions would enable the owner (taylor) to use an editor to modify the commands therein. Other members of the group could read and use the shell script but would be denied access to change it.

Task 5.2: Directory Permissions Settings

DESCRIPTION Directories are similar to files in how you interpret the permissions strings. The differences occur because of the unique purpose of directories, namely to store other files or directories. I always think of directories as bins or boxes. You can examine the box itself, or you can look at what's inside.

In many ways, UNIX treats directories simply as files in the file system, where the content of the file is a list of the files and directories stored within, rather than a letter, program, or shopping list.

The difference, of course, is that when you operate with directories, you're operating both with the directory itself, and, implicitly, with its contents. By analogy, when you fiddle with a box full of toys, you're not altering just the state of the box itself, but also potentially the toys within.

There are three permissions possible for a directory, just as for a file: read, write, and execute. The easiest is write permission. If a directory has write permission enabled, you can add new items and remove items from the directory. It's like owning the box; you can do what you'd like with the toys inside.

The interaction between read and execute permissions with a directory is confusing. There are two types of operations you perform on a directory: listing the contents of the directory (usually with ls) and examining specific, known files within the directory.

ACTION

1. Start by listing a directory, using the -d flag:

```
% ls -ld testme
dr-x------  2 taylor          512 Oct 11 17:03 testme/
% ls -l testme
total 0
-rw-rw----  1 taylor            0 Oct 11 17:03 file
% ls -l testme/file
-rw-rw----  1 taylor            0 Oct 11 17:03 testme/file
```

For a directory with both read and execute permissions, you can see that it's easy to list the directory, find out the files therein, and list specific files within the directory.

2. Read permission on a directory enables you to read the "table of contents" of the directory but, by itself, does not allow you to examine any of the files therein. By itself, read permission is rather bizarre:

```
% ls -ld testme
dr--------  2 taylor             512 Oct 11 17:03 testme/
% ls -l testme
testme/file not found
total 0
% ls -l testme/file
testme/file not found
```

Notice that the system indicated the name of the file contained in the testme directory. When I tried to list the file explicitly, however, the system couldn't find the file.

3. Compare this with the situation when you have execute permission—which enables you to examine the files within the directory—but you don't have read permission, and you are prevented from viewing the table of contents of the directory itself:

```
% ls -ld testme
d--x------  2 taylor             512 Oct 11 17:03 testme/
% ls -l testme
testme unreadable
% ls -l testme/file
-rw-rw----  1 taylor               0 Oct 11 17:03 testme/file
```

With execute-only permission, you can set up directories so that people who know the names of files contained in the directories can access those files, but people without that knowledge cannot list the directory to learn the filenames.

4. I've actually never seen anyone have a directory in UNIX with execute-only permission, and certainly you would never expect to see one set to read-only. It would be nice if UNIX would warn you if you set a directory to have one permission and not the other. However, UNIX won't do that. So, remember for directories always to be sure that you have both read and execute permission set. Table 5.3 summarizes the most common directory permissions.

Table 5.3. The most common directory permissions.

Permission	Meaning
- - -	No access allowed to directory
r-x	Read-only access, no modification allowed
rwx	All access allowed

5. One interesting permutation of directory permissions is for a directory that's write-only. Unfortunately, the write-only permission doesn't do what you'd hope, that is, enable people to add files to the directory without being able to see what the directory already contains. Instead, it's functionally identical to having it set for no access permission at all.

At the beginning of this hour, I used `ls` to list various files and directories in my home directory:

```
% ls -l
total 403
drwx------   2 taylor          512 Sep 30 10:38 Archives/
drwx------   3 taylor          512 Oct  1 08:23 InfoWorld/
-rw-------   1 taylor       106020 Oct 10 13:47 LISTS
drwx------   2 taylor         1024 Sep 30 10:50 Mail/
drwx------   2 taylor          512 Oct  6 09:36 News/
drwx------   2 taylor          512 Sep 30 10:51 OWL/
-rw-------   1 taylor         4643 Oct 10 14:01 RUMORS.18Sept
drwx------   2 taylor          512 Oct 10 19:09 bin/
-rw-------   1 taylor         3843 Oct 10 16:22 iecc.list
-rw-rw-r--   1 taylor       280232 Oct 10 16:22 mailing.lists
-rw-rw----   1 taylor         1031 Oct  7 15:44 newlists
drwx------   2 taylor          512 Oct 10 19:09 src/
```

Now you can see that all my directories are set so that I have list, examine, and modify (read, execute, and write, respectively) capability for myself, and no access is allowed for anyone else.

6. The very top-level directory is more interesting, with a variety of different directory owners and permissions:

```
% ls -l /
-rw-r--r--    1 root        61440 Nov 29  1991 boot
drwxr-xr-x    4 root        23552 Sep 27 11:31 dev
-r--r--r--    1 root       686753 Aug 27 21:58 dynix
drwxr-xr-x    6 root         3072 Oct 11 16:30 etc
drwxr-xr-x    2 root         8192 Apr 12  1991 lost+found
lrwxr-xr-x    1 root            7 Jul 28  1988 sys -> usr/sys
drwxrwxrwx   65 root        12800 Oct 11 17:33 tmp
drwxr-xr-x  753 root        14848 Oct  5 10:07 usera
drwxr-xr-x  317 root        13312 Oct  5 10:17 userb
drwxr-xr-x  626 root        13312 Oct  8 13:02 userc
drwxr-xr-x  534 root        10752 Sep 30 13:06 users
drwxr-xr-x   34 root         1024 Oct  1 09:10 usr
drwxr-xr-x    5 root         1024 Oct  1 09:20 var
```

Clearly, this machine has a lot of users. Notice that the link count for usera, userb, userc, and users are each in the hundreds. The dev directory has read and execute permission for everyone and write permission for the owner (root). Indeed, all the directories at this level are identical except for tmp, which has read, write, and execute permission for all users on the system.

7. Did you notice the listing for the sys directory buried in that output?

```
lrwxr-xr-x  1 root          7 Jul 28  1988 sys -> usr/sys
```

From the information in Table 5.1, you know that the first letter of the permissions string being an l means that the directory is a symbolic link. The filename shows just the specifics of the link, indicating that sys points to the directory usr/sys. In fact, if you count the number of letters in the name usr/sys, you'll find that it exactly matches the size of the sys link entry, too.

8. Try using ls -l / yourself. You should be able to understand the permissions of any file or directory that you encounter.

SUMMARY Permissions of files and directories will prove easier as you work with UNIX more.

Task 5.3: Modify File and Directory Permissions with chmod

DESCRIPTION Now that you can list directory permissions and understand what they mean, how about learning a UNIX command that lets you change them to meet your needs? You've already had a sneak preview of the command: chmod. The mnemonic is "change mode," and it derives from early UNIX folk talking about permission modes of files. You can remember it by thinking of it as a shortened form of change permission modes.

> To sound like a UNIX expert, pronounce chmod as "ch-mod," "ch" like the beginning of child, and "mod" to rhyme with cod.

JUST A MINUTE

The chmod command enables you to specify permissions in two different ways: symbolically or numerically. Symbolic notation is most commonly used to modify existing permissions, whereas numeric format always replaces any existing permission with the new value specified. In this task, you learn about symbolic notation, and the next task focuses on the powerful numeric format.

Symbolic notation for chmod is a bit like having a menu of different choices, enabling you to pick the combination that best fits your requirements. Figure 5.2 shows the two menus.

Figure 5.2.
The menu of symbolic chmod *values.*

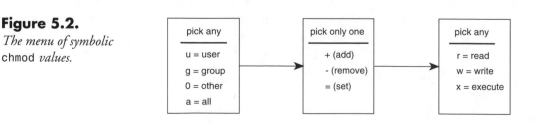

The command chmod is like a smorgasbord where you can choose any combination of items from either the first or last boxes, and stick your choice from the center box between them.

For example, if you wanted to add write permission to the file test for everyone in your group, you would, working backwards from that description, choose g for group, + for add, and w for write. The finished UNIX command would be chmod g+w test.

If you decided to take away read and execute permission for everyone not in your group, you could use chmod o-rx test to accomplish the task.

ACTION

1. Turn to your computer and, using touch and ls, try changing permissions and see what happens. I'll do the same:

```
% touch test
% ls -l test
-rw-rw----  1 taylor          0 Oct 11 18:29 test
```

2. The first modification I want to make is that people in my group should be able to read the file. Because I don't really want them altering it, I'll rescind write permission for group members:

```
% chmod g-w test
% ls -l test
-rw-r-----  1 taylor          0 Oct 11 18:29 test
```

3. But then my boss reminds me that everyone in the group should have all access permissions for everyone in that group. Okay, I'll do so.

```
% chmod g+wx test
% ls -l test
-rw-rwx---  1 taylor          0 Oct 11 18:29 test
```

I also could have done that with chmod g=rwx, of course.

4. Wait a second. This test file is just for my own use, and nobody in my group should be looking at it anyway. I'll change it back.

```
% chmod g-rwx test
% ls -l test
-rw-------  1 taylor          0 Oct 11 18:29 test
```

Great. Now the file is set so that I can read and write it, but nobody else can touch it, read it, modify it, or anything else.

5. If I relented a bit, I could easily add, with one last chmod command, read-only permission for everyone:

```
% chmod a+r test
% ls -l test
-rw-r--r--  1 taylor          0 Oct 11 18:29 test
```

5

SUMMARY Permissions in UNIX are based on a concentric access model from Multics. (In Hour 1, you learned that the name UNIX is also a pun on Multics.) Figure 5.3 illustrates this concept.

Figure 5.3.

The concentric circles of access.

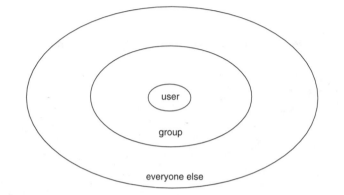

As a result, it's incredibly rare to see a file where the owner doesn't have the most access to a file. It'd be like buying a car and letting everyone but yourself drive it—rather silly. Similarly, members of the group are given better or equal permission to everyone else on the machine. You would never see r--r--rwx as a permissions string.

Experiment a bit more with the various combinations possible with the chmod symbolic notation. How would you change permission on a directory to enable all users to use ls to examine it but to deny them the ability to add or remove files? How about adding write access for the owner but removing it for everyone else?

Task 5.4: Set New File Permissions with chmod

DESCRIPTION The second form of input that chmod accepts is absolute numeric values for permissions. Before you can learn how to use this notation, you have to learn a bit about different numbering systems first.

The numbering system you're familiar with, the one you use to balance your checkbook and check the receipt from the market, is decimal, or base 10. This means that each digit—from right to left—has the value of the digit raised by a power of 10, based on the digit's location in the number. Figure 5.4 shows what the number 5,783 is in decimal.

You can see that in a base-10 numbering system, the value of a number is the sum of the value of each digit multiplied by the numeric base raised to the nth power. The n is the number of spaces the digit is away from the rightmost digit. That is, in the number 5,783, you know that the 7 is worth more than just 7, because it's two spaces away from the rightmost digit (the 3). Therefore, its value is the numeric base (10) raised to the nth power, where n is 2 (it's two spaces away). Ten to the second power equals 100 ($10^2 = 100$), and when you multiply that by 7, sure enough, you find that the 7 is worth 700 in this number.

Figure 5.4.

Interpreting decimal numbers.

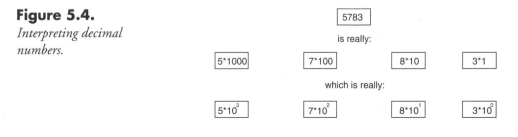

What does all this have to do with the chmod command? At its most fundamental, UNIX permissions are a series of on/off switches. Does the group have write permission? One equals yes, zero equals no. Each digit in a decimal system can have 10 different values. A binary system is one in which each digit can have only two values: on or off, yes or no. Therefore, you can easily and uniquely describe any permissions string as a series of zeroes and ones—as a binary number. Figure 5.5 demonstrates.

Figure 5.5.

Permissions as binary numbers.

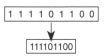

The convention is that if a letter is present, the binary digit is a 1—that permission is permitted—and if no letter is present, the digit is a zero. Thus, r-xr----- can be described as 101100000, and r--r--r-- can be described in binary as 100100100.

You've already learned that the nine-character permissions string is really just a three-character permissions string duplicated thrice for the three different types of user (the owner, group, and everyone else). That means that you can focus on learning how to translate a single tri-character permissions substring into binary and extrapolate for more than one permission. Table 5.3 lists all possible permissions and their binary equivalents.

Table 5.3. Permissions and binary equivalents.

Permissions String	Binary Equivalent
- - -	000
- - x	001
- w -	010
- wx	011
r - -	100
r - x	101
rw -	110
rwx	111

Knowing how to interpret decimal numbers using the rather complex formula presented earlier, you should not be surprised that the decimal equivalent of any binary number can be obtained by the same technique. Figure 5.6 shows how, with the binary equivalent of the r-x permission.

Figure 5.6.

Expressing r-x *as a single digit.*

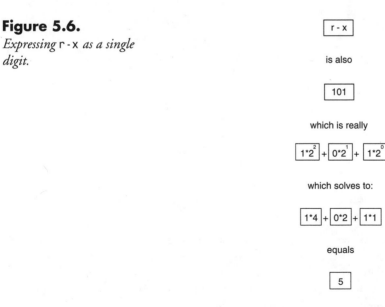

If r-x is equal to 5, it stands to reason that each of the possible three-character permissions has a single-digit equivalent, and Table 5.4 expands Table 5.3 to include the single-digit equivalents.

Table 5.4. Permissions and numeric equivalents.

Permissions String	Binary Equivalent	Decimal Equivalent
- - -	000	0
- -x	001	1
-w-	010	2
-wx	011	3
r--	100	4
r-x	101	5
rw-	110	6
rwx	111	7

The value of having a single digit to describe any of the seven different permission states should be obvious. Using only three digits, you now can fully express any possible combination of permissions for any file or directory in UNIX—one digit for the owner permission, one for group, and one for everyone else. Figure 5.7 shows how to take a full permissions string and translate it into its three-digit numeric equivalent.

Figure 5.7.

Translating a full permissions string into its numeric equivalent.

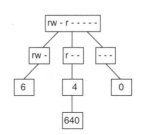

From this illustration, you can see how the permissions string rw-r----- (read and write permission for the owner, read permission for the group, and no access allowed for everyone else) is exactly equivalent to the numeric string 640.

ACTION

1. Try to create numeric strings on your own, using Table 5.4 to help. Turn to your computer and use ls to display some listings. Break each permissions string into three groups of three letters, and figure out the numeric equivalents. Here are some examples from the ls -C -F listing of my home directory:

   ```
   drwx------   2 taylor        512 Sep 30 10:38 Archives/
   ```

   For Archives/, the equivalent numeric permission is 700.

```
-rw-------   1 taylor     106020 Oct 10 13:47 LISTS
```

For LISTS, the equivalent numeric permission is 600.

```
-rw-rw-r--  1 taylor     280232 Oct 10 16:22 mailing.lists
```

For mailing.lists, the equivalent numeric permission is 664.

```
-rw-rw----  1 taylor       1031 Oct  7 15:44 newlists
```

For newlists, the equivalent numeric permission is 660.

SUMMARY There's one last step required before you can try using the numeric permissions strings with chmod. You need to be able to work backwards to determine a permission that you'd like to set, and figure out the numeric equivalent for that permission.

Task 5.5: Calculating Numeric Permissions Strings

DESCRIPTION For example, if you wanted to have a directory set so that you have all access, people in your group can look at the contents but not modify anything, and everyone else is shut out, how would you do it?

All permissions for yourself means you want read+write+execute for owner (or numeric permission 7); read and listing permission for others in the group means read+execute for group (numeric permission 5); and no permission for everyone else, numeric permission 0. Put the three together and you have the answer, 750.

That's the trick of working with chmod in numeric mode. You specify the absolute permissions you want as a three-digit number, and the system sets the permissions on the file or directory appropriately.

The absolute concept is important with this form of chmod. You cannot use the chmod numeric form to add or remove permissions from a file or directory. It is usable only for reassigning the permissions string of a file or directory.

The good news is that, as you learned earlier in this hour, there is a relatively small number of commonly-used file permissions, summarized in Table 5.5.

Table 5.5. Common permissions and their numeric equivalents.

Permission	Numeric	Used With
---------	000	All types
r--------	400	Files
r--r--r--	444	Files
rw-------	600	Files
rw-r--r--	644	Files
rw-rw-r--	664	Files

5

Permission	Numeric	Used With
rw-rw-rw-	666	Files
rwx------	700	Programs and directories
rwxr-x---	750	Programs and directories
rwxr-xr-x	755	Programs and directories

ACTION

1. Turn to your computer and try using the numeric mode of chmod, along with ls, to display the actual permissions to learn for yourself how this works.

   ```
   % touch example
   % ls -l example
   -rw-rw----  1 taylor          0 Oct 12 10:16 example
   ```

   By default, files are created in my directory with mode 660.

2. To take away read and write permission for people in my group, I'd replace the 660 permission with what numeric permissions string? I'd use 600:

   ```
   % chmod 600 example
   % ls -l example
   -rw-------  1 taylor          0 Oct 12 10:16 example
   ```

3. What if I change my mind and want to open the file up for everyone to read or write? I'd use 666:

   ```
   % chmod 666 example
   % ls -l example
   -rw-rw-rw-  1 taylor          0 Oct 12 10:16 example
   ```

4. Finally, pretend that the example is actually a directory. What numeric mode would I specify to enable everyone to use ls in the directory and enable only the owner to add or delete files? I'd use 755:

   ```
   % chmod 755 example
   % ls -l example
   -rwxr-xr-x  1 taylor          0 Oct 12 10:16 example
   ```

SUMMARY You've looked at both the numeric mode and the symbolic mode for defining permissions. Having learned both, which do you prefer?

JUST A MINUTE

Somehow I've never gotten the hang of symbolic mode, so I almost always use the numeric mode for chmod. The only exception is when I want to add or delete simple permissions. Then, I use something like chmod +r test to add read permission. Part of the problem is that I don't think of the user of the file but rather the owner, and specifying o+r causes chmod

> to change permissions for others. It's important, therefore, that you remember that files have users so you remember u for user, and that everyone not in the group is other so you remember o. Otherwise, learn the numeric shortcut!

File permissions and modes are one of the most complex aspects of UNIX. You can tell—it's taken two hours to explain it fully. It's very important that you spend the time really to understand how the permissions strings relate to directory permissions, how to read the output of ls, and how to change modes using both styles of the chmod command. It'll be time well spent.

Task 5.6: Establish Default File and Directory Permissions with the umask Command

DESCRIPTION When I've created files, they've had read+write permissions for the owner and group, but no access allowed for anyone else. When you create files on your system, you might find that the default permissions are different.

The controlling variable behind the default permissions is called the *file creation mask*, or umask for short.

Inexplicably, umask doesn't always list its value as a three-digit number, but you can find its value in the same way you figured out the numeric permissions strings for chmod. For example, when I enter umask, the system indicates that my umask setting is 07. A leading zero has been dropped, so the actual value is 007, a value that British MI6 could no doubt appreciate!

But 007 doesn't mean that the default file is created with read+write+execute for everyone else and no permissions for the owner or group. It means quite the opposite, literally.

The umask command is a filter through which permissions are pushed to ascertain what remains. Figure 5.8 demonstrates how this works.

Think of your mask as a series of boxes: if the value is true, the information can't exude through the box. If the value is false, it can. Your mask is therefore the direct opposite to how you want your permissions to be set. In Figure 5.8, I want to have 770 as the default permission for any new file or directory I create, so I want to specify the exact opposite of that, 007. Sure enough, with this umask value, when I create new files, the default permission allows read and write access to the owner and group, but no access to anyone else.

Figure 5.8.

Interpreting the umask *value.*

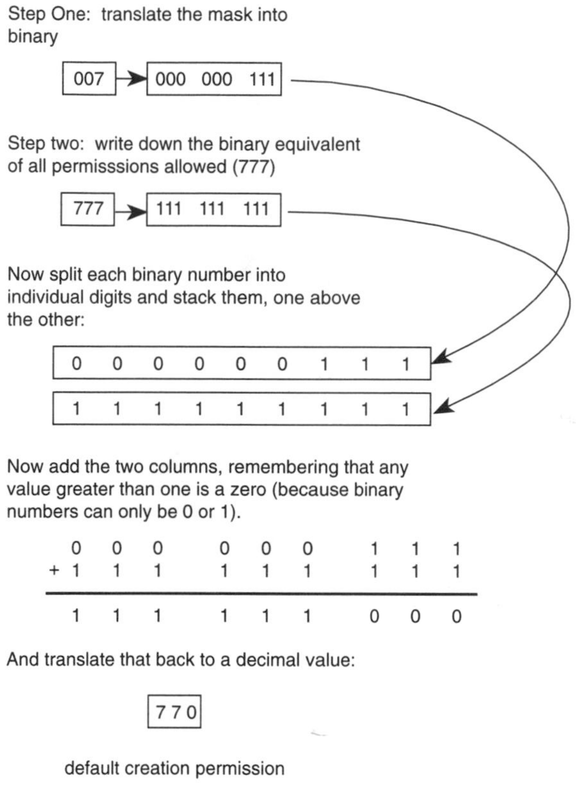

Step One: translate the mask into binary

007 → 000 000 111

Step two: write down the binary equivalent of all permisssions allowed (777)

777 → 111 111 111

Now split each binary number into individual digits and stack them, one above the other:

| 0 | 0 | 0 | 0 | 0 | 0 | 1 | 1 | 1 |

| 1 | 1 | 1 | 1 | 1 | 1 | 1 | 1 | 1 |

Now add the two columns, remembering that any value greater than one is a zero (because binary numbers can only be 0 or 1).

```
    0  0  0     0  0  0     1  1  1
  + 1  1  1     1  1  1     1  1  1
  ─────────────────────────────────
    1  1  1     1  1  1     0  0  0
```

And translate that back to a decimal value:

7 7 0

default creation permission

Things are a bit trickier than that. You've probably already asked yourself, "Why, if I have 007 as my mask (which results in 770 as the default permissions), do my files have 660 as the actual default permission?"

The reason is that UNIX tries to be smart about the execute permission setting. If I create a directory, UNIX knows that execute permission is important, and so it grants it. However, for some files (particularly text files), execute permission doesn't make sense, so UNIX actually masks it out internally.

Another way to look at this is that any time you create a file containing information, the original mask that the system uses to compare against your umask is not 777 (not rwxrwxrwx, to put it another way), but rather 666 (rw-rw-rw-), in recognition of the unlikelihood that you'll want to execute the new file.

The good news is that you now know an easy way to set the execute permission for a file if the system gets it wrong: chmod +x *filename* does the trick.

ACTION

1. Turn to your computer and check your umask setting, then alternate between
   changing its values and creating new files with touch:

   ```
   % umask
   7
   % touch test.07
   % ls -l test.07
   -rw-rw----  1 taylor           0 Oct 12 14:38 test.07
   ```

2. To change the value of your umask, add the numeric value of the desired mask to
   the command line:

   ```
   % umask 077
   ```

   This changes my umask value from 007 (------rwx) to 077 (---rwxrwx). Before you
   look at the following listing, what would you expect this modification to mean?
   Remember, you should read it as the exact opposite of how you want the default
   permissions.

   ```
   % touch test.077
   % ls -l test.077
   -rw-------  1 taylor           0 Oct 12 14:38 test.077
   ```

   Is that what you expected?

3. What would you do if you wanted to have the default permission keep files private
   to just the owner and make them read-only?

   You can work through this problem in reverse. If you want r-x------ as the default
   permission (since the system takes care of whether execute permission is needed,
   based on file type), write down the opposite permission, which is -w-rwxrwx.
   Translate that to a binary number, 010 111 111, and then to a three-digit value,
   277 (010=2, 111=7, 111=7). That's the answer. The value 277 is the correct umask
   value to ensure that files you create are read-only for yourself and off-limits to
   everyone else.

   ```
   % umask 277
   % touch test.277
   % ls -l test.277
   -r--------  1 taylor           0 Oct 12 14:39 test.277
   ```

4. What if you wanted to have files created with the default permission being read-
   only for everyone, read-write for the group, but read-only for the owner? Again,
   work backwards. The desired permission is r-xrwxr-x, so create the opposite value
   (-w-----w-), translate it into binary (010 000 010), and then translate that into a
   three-digit value: 202 (010=2, 000=0, 010=2).

5

As a rule of thumb, it's best to leave the execute permission enabled when building umask values so the system doesn't err when creating directories.

SUMMARY The umask is something set once and left alone. If you've tried various experiments on your computer, remember to restore your umask back to a sensible value to avoid future problems (though each time you log in to the system it's reset to your default value).

In the next hour, you learn how to use the mkdir command to create new directories, and you see how the umask value affects default directory access permissions.

Task 5.7: Identify Owner and Group for Any File or Directory

DESCRIPTION One of the many items of information that the ls command displays when used with the -l flag is the owner of the file or directory. So far, all the files and directories in your home directory have been owned by you, with the probable exception of the ".." directory, which is owned by whomever owns the directory above your home.

In other words, when you enter ls -l, you should see your account name as the owner for every file in the listing.

If you're collaborating with another user, however, there might well be times when you'll want to change the owner of a file or directory once you've created and modified it. The first step in accomplishing this is to identify the owner and group.

Identifying the owner is easy; ls lists that by default. But how do you identify the group of which the file or directory is a part?

ACTION

1. The ls command can show the group membership of any file or directory by the addition of a new command flag, -g. By itself, -g doesn't alter the output of ls, but when used with the -l flag, it adds a column of information to the listing. Try it on your system. Here is an example:

```
% ls -lg /tmp
-rw-r--r--  1 root      root            0 Oct 12 14:52 sh145
drwxr-xr-x  2 shakes    root          512 Oct 12 07:23 shakes/
-rw-------  1 meademd   com435          0 Oct 12 14:46 snd.12
-rw-------  1 dessy     stuprsac     1191 Oct 12 14:57 snd.15
-rw-------  1 steen     utech           1 Oct 12 10:28 snd.17
-rw-r-----  1 jsmith    utech      258908 Oct 12 12:37 sol2
```

5

On many System V-based systems, the output of ls -l always shows user and group. The -g flag actually turns off this display!

Both owners and groups vary for each of the files and directories in this small listing. Notice that files can have different owners while having the same group. (There are two examples here: sh145 and the shakes directory, and snd.17 and sol2.)

2. Directories that have a wide variety of owners are the directories above your own home directory and the tmp directory, as you can see in instruction 1. Examine both on your system and identify both the owner and group of all files. For files in the same group you're in (with the id command, you can find which group or groups you are in) but not owned by you, you'll need to check which of the three permission values to identify your own access privileges?

SUMMARY Files and directories have both owners and groups, although the group is ultimately less important than the owner, particularly where permissions and access are involved.

Task 5.8: Change the Owner of a File or Directory

DESCRIPTION Now that you can ascertain the ownership of a file or directory, it's time to learn about the chown command. This command lets you change the ownership of whatever you specify.

CAUTION

Before you go any further, however, a stern warning: once you've changed the ownership of a file, you cannot restore it to yourself. Only the owner of a file can give away its ownership, so don't use the chown command unless you're absolutely positive you want to!

ACTION

1. The format for changing the ownership of a file is to specify the new owner and then list the files or directory you are giving away:

```
% ls -l test
-rwxrwxrwx  1 taylor            0 Oct 12 15:17 mytest
% chown root test
% ls -l test
-rwxrwxrwx  1 root              0 Oct 12 15:17 mytest
```

This would change the ownership of the file test from me to the user root on the system.

2. If I now try to change the ownership back, it fails:

```
% chown taylor test
chown: test: Not owner
```

Most modern UNIX systems prevent users from changing the ownership of a file due to the inherent dangers. If you try chown, and it returns Command not found or Permission denied, that means you're barred from making any file ownership changes.

3. On one of the systems I use, chown always reports Not owner when I try to change a file regardless of whether I really am the owner or not:

```
% ls -l mytest
-rwxrwxrwx  1 taylor           0 Oct 12 15:17 mytest
% chown root mytest
chown: mytest: Not owner
```

This is needlessly confusing—a message like "you're not allowed to change file ownership" would be better. But, alas, like so much of UNIX, it's up to the user to figure out what's going on.

SUMMARY To change the ownership of a file or directory, you can use the chown command if you have the appropriate access on your system. It's like a huge supertanker, though; you can't change course once underway, so be cautious!

Task 5.9: Change the Group of a File or Directory

DESCRIPTION Changing the group membership of a file or directory is quite analogous to the steps required for changing file ownership. Almost all UNIX systems enable users to use the chgrp command to accomplish this task.

ACTION

5

1. Usage of chgrp is almost identical to chown, too. Specify the name of the group, followed by the list of files or directories to reassign:

```
% ls -lg
-rwxrwxrwx  1 taylor   ci        0 Oct 12 15:17 mytest
% chgrp ftp mytest
% ls -lg
-rwxrwxrwx  1 taylor   ftp       0 Oct 12 15:17 mytest
```

The caveat on this command, however, is that you must be a member of the group you're assigning for the file, or it fails:

```
% ls -lg
-rwxrwxrwx  1 taylor   ftp       0 Oct 12 15:17 mytest
% chgrp root mytest
chgrp: You are not a member of the root group
```

SUMMARY Portions of UNIX are well thought out and offer innovative approaches to common computer problems. File groups and file ownership aren't examples of this, unfortunately. The majority of UNIX users tend to be members of only one group, so they cannot change the group membership or ownership of any file or directory on the system. Instead, users seem to just use chmod to allow full access to files; then they encourage colleagues to copy the files desired, or they simply allow everyone access.

Unlike the other commands you've learned in this book, chown might be one you will not use. It's entirely possible that you'll never need to change the ownership or group membership of any file or directory.

Summary

In this hour, you learned the basics of UNIX file permissions, including how to set and modify file permissions with chmod and how to analyze file permissions as shown by the ls -l command. You also learned about translating between numeric bases (binary and decimal) and how to convert permissions strings into numeric values. Both are foundations for the umask command, which you learned to interpret and alter as desired. Permission is only half the puzzle, however, so you also learned about file ownership, group ownership, and how to change either for any file or directory.

Workshop

The Workshop summarizes the key terms you learned and poses some questions about the topics presented in this chapter. It also provides you with a preview of what you will learn in the next hour.

Key Terms

file creation mask   When files are created in UNIX, they inherit a default set of access permissions. These defaults are under the control of the user and are known as the file creation mask.

mode   A shorthand way of saying permissions mode.

permissions mode   The set of accesses (read, write, and execute) allowed for each of the three classes of users (owner, group, and everyone else) for each file or directory on the system. This is a synonym for access permission.

shell script   A collection of shell commands in a file.

Questions

1. In what situations might the following file permissions be useful?

   ```
   r--rw-r--        r--r--rw-
   rw--w--w-        -w--w--w-
   rwxr-xr-x        r-x--x--x
   ```

2. Translate the six file permissions strings in instruction 1 into their binary and numeric equivalents.

3. Explain what the following umask values would make the default permissions for newly created files:

007	077	777
111	222	733
272	544	754

4. Count the number of groups that are represented by group membership of files in the tmp directory on your system. Use id to see if you're a member of any of them.

5. Which of the following directories could you modify, if the id command listed the following information? Which could you view using the ls command?

   ```
   % id
   uid=19(smith) gid=50(users) groups=50(users)
   % ls -lgF
   drw-r--r--  2 root     users       512 Oct 12 14:52 sh/
   drwxr-xr-x  2 shakes   root        512 Oct 12 07:23 shakes/
   drw-------  2 meademd  com435     1024 Oct 12 14:46 tmp/
   drwxr-x---  3 smith    users       512 Oct 12 12:37 viewer/
   drwx------  3 jin      users       512 Oct 12 12:37 Zot!/
   ```

Preview of the Next Hour

In the next hour, you learn the various UNIX file-manipulation commands, including how to copy files, how to move them to new directories, and how to create new directories. You also learn how to remove files and directories as well as about the dangers of file removal on UNIX.

5

Hour 6

Creating, Moving, Renaming, and Deleting Files and Directories

In this hour, you learn the basic UNIX file-manipulation commands. These commands will explain how to create directories with `mkdir`, remove directories with `rmdir`, use `cp` and `mv` to move files about in the file system, and use `rm` to remove files. The `rm` command has its dangers: you learn that there isn't an "unremove" command in UNIX and how to circumvent the possible dangers that lurk in the program.

Goals for This Hour

In this hour, you learn how to

- [ ] Create new directories using `mkdir`
- [ ] Copy files to new locations using `cp`

☐ Move files to new locations using `mv`

☐ Rename files using `mv`

☐ Remove directories using `rmdir`

☐ Remove files using `rm`

☐ Minimize the danger of using the `rm` command

This hour introduces several tremendously powerful commands that enable you to create a custom file-system hierarchy (or wreak unintentional havoc on your files). As you learn these commands, you also learn hints and ideas on how to best use the UNIX file system to keep your files neat and organized. These simple UNIX commands, all new in this hour, are found not only in all variants of UNIX, both BSD-based and System V-based, but they also can be brought onto DOS through utilities such as the MKS Toolkit from Mortice-Kern Systems.

Task 6.1: Creating New Directories Using `mkdir`

DESCRIPTION One important aspect of UNIX that has been emphasized continually in this book is that the UNIX file system is hierarchical. The UNIX file system includes directories containing files and directories, each of which can contain both files and directories. Your own home directory, however, probably doesn't contain any directories (except ".", and "..", of course), which prevents you from exploiting what I call the virtual file cabinet of the file system.

The command for creating directories is actually one of the least complex and most mnemonic (for UNIX, anyway) in this book: `mkdir`, called "make directory."

Pronounce the `mkdir` command as "make dir."

JUST A MINUTE

ACTION

1. Turn to your computer, move to your home directory, and examine the files and directories there. Here's an example:

```
% cd
% ls
Archives/              OWL/                    rumors.26Oct.Z
InfoWorld/             PubAccessLists.Z        rumors.5Nov.Z
LISTS                  bin/                    src/
Mail/                  educ
News/                  mailing.lists.bitnet.Z
```

2. To create a directory, you need to specify what you'd like to name the directory and where you'd like to locate it in the file system (the default location is your current working directory):

```
% mkdir NEWDIR
% ls
Archives/                News/                    mailing.lists.bitnet.Z
InfoWorld/               OWL/                     rumors.26Oct.Z
LISTS                    PubAccessLists.Z         rumors.5Nov.Z
Mail/                    bin/                     src/
NEWDIR/                  educ
```

3. That's all there is to it. You've created your first UNIX directory, and you can now list it with ls to see what it looks like:

```
% ls -ld NEWDIR
drwxrwx---   2 taylor              24 Nov  5 10:48 NEWDIR/
% ls -la NEWDIR
total 2
drwxrwx---   2 taylor              24 Nov  5 10:48 ./
drwx------  11 taylor            1024 Nov  5 10:48 ../
```

Not surprisingly, the directory is empty other than the two default entries of "." (the directory itself) and ".." (the parent directory, your home directory).

4. Look closely at the permissions of the directory. Remember that the permissions are a result of your umask setting. As you learned in the previous hour, changing the umask setting changes the default directory permissions. Then, when you create a new directory, the new permissions will be in place:

```
% umask
07
% umask 0
% mkdir NEWDIR2
% ls -ld NEWDIR2
drwxrwxrwx  2 taylor              24 Nov  5 10:53 NEWDIR2/
% umask 222
% mkdir NEWDIR3
% ls -ld NEWDIR3
dr-xr-xr-x  2 taylor              24 Nov  5 10:54 NEWDIR3/
```

5. What happens if you try to create a directory with a name that has already been used?

```
% mkdir NEWDIR
mkdir: NEWDIR: File exists
```

6. To create a directory other than your current location, prefix the new directory name with a location:

```
% mkdir /tmp/testme
% ls -l /tmp
-rwx------  1 zhongqi      22724 Nov  4 21:33 /tmp/a.out*
-rw-------  1 xujia        95594 Nov  4 23:10 /tmp/active.10122
-rw-r--r--  1 beast          572 Nov  5 05:59 /tmp/anon1
```

```
-rw-rw----  1 root           0 Nov  5 10:30 /tmp/bar.report
-rw-------  1 qsc            0 Nov  5 00:18 /tmp/lh013813
-rwx------  1 steen      24953 Nov  5 10:40 /tmp/mbox.steen*
-rwx------  1 techman     3711 Nov  5 10:45 /tmp/mbox.techman*
-rw-r--r--  1 root      997536 Nov  5 10:58 /tmp/quotas
-rw-------  1 zhongqi   163579 Nov  4 20:16 /tmp/sp500.1
drwxrwx---  2 taylor        24 Nov  5 10:56 testme/
-rw-r--r--  1 aru           90 Nov  5 02:55 /tmp/trouble21972
```

SUMMARY Like other basic UNIX utilities, mkdir has no command arguments, so it is quite easy to use. There are two things to keep in mind: You must have write permission to the current directory if you're creating a new directory, and you should ensure that the name of the directory is not the same as (or, to avoid confusion, similar to) a directory name that already exists.

Task 6.2: Copying Files to New Locations Using cp

DESCRIPTION One of the most basic operations in any system is moving files, the modern-office computer equivalent of paper shuffling. On a computer, moving files is a simple matter of using one or two commands: you can move a file to a different location, or you can create a copy of the file and move the copy to a different location.

The Macintosh has an interesting strategy for differentiating between moving and copying. If you drag a file to another location that's on the same device (a hard disk, for example), then by default the computer moves the file to that location. If you drag the file to a location on a different device (from a floppy to a hard disk, for instance), the computer automatically copies the file, placing the new, identically named copy on the device.

UNIX lacks this subtlety. Instead, UNIX lets you choose which of the two operations you'd like to perform. The two commands are typically succinct UNIX mnemonics: mv to move files, and cp to copy files. The mv command also serves the dual duty of enabling you to rename files.

JUST A MINUTE

Pronounce cp as "sea pea." When you talk about copying a file, however, say "copy." Similarly, pronounce mv as "em vee," but when you speak of moving a file, say "move."

I find myself using cp more than mv because it offers a slightly safer way to organize files: if I get confused and rename it such that it steps on another file (you'll see what I mean in a moment), I still have original copies of all the files.

6

ACTION

1. The format of a cp command is to specify first the name of the file you want to copy and then the new filename. Both names must be either relative filenames (that is, without a leading slash or other indication of the directory) or absolute filenames. Start out by making a copy of your .login file, naming the new copy login.copy:

```
% cp .login login.copy
% ls -ld .login login.copy
-rw-------  1 taylor        1858 Oct 12 21:20 .login
-rw-------  1 taylor        1858 Nov  5 12:08 login.copy
```

You can see that the new file is identical in size and permissions but that it has a more recent creation date, which certainly makes sense.

2. What happens if you try to copy a directory?

```
% cp . newdir
cp: .: Is a directory (not copied).
```

Generally, UNIX won't permit you to use the cp command to copy directories.

JUST A MINUTE

> I found that this command worked—sort of—on one machine I have used. The system's response to the cp command indicated that something peculiar was happening with the following message:
>
> cp: .: Is a directory (copying as plain file)
>
> But, the system also created newdir as a regular, executable file. You may find that your system reacts in this manner, but you probably do not have any use for it.

3. The cp command is quite powerful, and it can copy many files at once if you specify a directory as the destination rather than specifying a new filename. Further, if you specify a directory destination, the program automatically will create new files and assign them the same names as the original files.

First, you need to create a second file to work with:

```
% cp .cshrc cshrc.copy
```

Now try it yourself. Here is what I did:

```
% cp login.copy cshrc.copy NEWDIR
% ls -l NEWDIR
total 4
-rw-------  1 taylor        1178 Nov  5 12:18 cshrc.copy
-rw-------  1 taylor        1858 Nov  5 12:18 login.copy
```

6

SUMMARY You can use the cp command to copy an original file as a new file or to a specific directory (the format being cp *original-file new-file-or-directory*), and you can copy a bunch of files to a directory (cp *list-of-files new-directory*). Experiment with creating new directories using mkdir and copying the files into the new locations. Use ls to confirm that the originals aren't removed as you go along.

Task 6.3: Moving Files to New Locations Using mv

DESCRIPTION Whereas cp leaves the original file intact, making a sort of electronic equivalent of a photocopy of a paper I may pick up at my desk, mv functions like a more traditional desk: papers are moved from one location to another. Rather than creating multiple copies of the files you're copying, mv physically relocates them from the old directory to the new.

1. You use mv almost the same way that you use cp:

```
% ls -l login.copy
-rw-------  1 taylor        1858 Nov  5 12:08 login.copy
% mv login.copy new.login
% ls -l login.copy new.login
login.copy not found
-rw-------  1 taylor        1858 Nov  5 12:08 new.login
```

2. Also, you move a group of files together using mv almost the same way you do it using cp:

```
% cd NEWDIR
% ls
cshrc.copy   login.copy
% mv cshrc.copy login.copy ..
% ls -l
total 0
% ls ..
Archives/            OWL/                 mailing.lists.bitnet.Z
InfoWorld/           PubAccessLists.Z     new.login
LISTS                bin/                 rumors.26Oct.Z
Mail/                cshrc.copy           rumors.5Nov.Z
NEWDIR/              educ                 src/
News/                login.copy
```

3. Because you can use mv to rename files or directories, you can relocate the new directory NEWDIR. However, you cannot use mv to relocate the dot directory because you're inside it:

```
% mv . new.dot
mv: .: rename: Invalid argument
```

4. Both mv and cp can be dangerous. Carefully consider the following example before trying either mv or cp on your own computer:

```
% ls -l login.copy cshrc.copy
-rw-------  1 taylor        1178 Nov  5 12:38 cshrc.copy
-rw-------  1 taylor        1858 Nov  5 12:37 login.copy
% cp cshrc.copy login.copy
% ls -l .login login.copy cshrc.copy
```

```
-rw------- 1 taylor          1178 Nov  5 12:38 cshrc.copy
-rw------- 1 taylor          1178 Nov  5 12:38 login.copy
```

Without bothering to warn me, UNIX copied the file cshrc.copy over the existing file login.copy. Notice that after the cp operation occurred, both files had the same size and modification dates.

The mv command will cause the same problem:

```
% ls -l cshrc.copy login.copy
-rw------- 1 taylor          1178 Nov  5 12:42 cshrc.copy
-rw------- 1 taylor          1858 Nov  5 12:42 login.copy
% mv cshrc.copy login.copy
% ls -l cshrc.copy login.copy
cshrc.copy not found
-rw------- 1 taylor          1178 Nov  5 12:42 login.copy
```

JUST A MINUTE

> The good news is that you can set up UNIX so it won't overwrite files. The bad news is that for some reason many systems don't default to this behavior. If your system is configured reasonably, when you try either of the two preceding dangerous examples, the system's response is remove login.copy? You can either press the Y key to replace the old file or press Enter to change your mind. If your system cannot be set up to respond this way, you can use the -i flag to both cp and mv to avoid this problem. Later, you learn how to permanently fix this problem with a shell alias.

SUMMARY   Together, mv and cp are the dynamic duo of UNIX file organization. These commands enable you to put the information you want where you want it, leaving duplicates behind if desired.

Task 6.4: Renaming Files with mv

DESCRIPTION   Both the DOS and Macintosh systems have easy ways to rename files. In DOS, you can use RENAME to accomplish the task. On the Mac, you can select the name under the file icon and enter a new filename.

UNIX has neither option. To rename files, you use the mv command, which, in essence, moves the old name to the new name. It's a bit confusing, but it works.

ACTION

1. Rename the file cshrc.copy with your own first name. Here's an example:

```
% ls -l cshrc.copy
-rw------- 1 taylor          1178 Nov  5 13:00 cshrc.copy
% mv cshrc.copy dave
% ls -l dave
-rw------- 1 taylor          1178 Nov  5 13:00 dave
```

6

2. Rename a directory, too:

```
% ls -ld NEWDIR
drwxrwx---  2 taylor          512 Nov  5 12:32 NEWDIR/
% mv NEWDIR New.Sample.Directory
% ls -ld New.Sample.Directory
drwxrwx---  2 taylor          512 Nov  5 12:32 New.Sample.Directory/
```

3. Be careful! Just as moving files with cp and mv can carelessly overwrite existing files, renaming files using mv can overwrite existing files:

```
% mv dave login.copy
```

If you try to use mv to rename a directory with a name that already has been assigned to a file, the command fails:

```
% mv New.Sample.Directory dave
mv: New.Sample.Directory: rename: Not a directory
```

The reverse situation works fine because the file is moved into the directory as expected. It's the subtlety of using the mv command to rename files.

4. If you assign a new directory a name that belongs to an existing directory, some versions of mv will happily overwrite the existing directory and name the new one as requested:

```
% mkdir testdir
% mv New.Sample.Directory testdir
```

SUMMARY Being able to rename files is another important part of building a useful UNIX virtual file cabinet for yourself. There are some major dangers involved, however, so tread carefully and always use ls in conjunction with cp and mv to ensure that in the process you don't overwrite or replace an existing file.

Task 6.5: Removing Directories with rmdir

DESCRIPTION Now that you can create directories with the mkdir command, it's time to learn how to remove directories using the rmdir command.

ACTION

1. With rmdir, you can remove any directory for which you have appropriate permissions:

```
% mkdir test
% ls -l test
total 0
% rmdir test
```

Note that the output of ls shows there are no files in the test directory.

6

2. The `rmdir` command removes only directories that are empty:

```
% mkdir test
% touch test/sample.file
% ls -l test
total 0
-rw-rw----  1 taylor              0 Nov  5 14:00 sample.file
% rmdir test
rmdir: test: Directory not empty
```

To remove a directory, you must first remove all files therein using the `rm` command. In this example, `test` still has files in it.

3. Permissions are important, too. Consider what happens when I try to remove a directory that I don't have permission to touch:

```
% rmdir /tmp
rmdir: /tmp: Permission denied
% ls -l /tmp
drwxrwxrwt 81 root          15872 Nov  5 14:07 /tmp/
```

The permissions of the parent directory, rather than the directory you're trying to remove, are the important consideration.

SUMMARY   There's no way to restore a directory you've removed, so be careful and think through what you're doing. The good news is that, because with `rmdir` you can't remove a directory having anything in it (a second reason the attempt in the preceding example to remove /tmp would have failed), you're reasonably safe from major gaffes. You are not safe, however, with the next command, `rm`, because it will remove anything.

Task 6.6: Removing Files Using `rm`

DESCRIPTION   The `rm` command is the most dangerous command in UNIX. Lacking any sort of archival or restoration feature, the `rm` command removes files permanently. It's like throwing a document into a shredder instead of into a dustbin.

ACTION

1. Removing a file using `rm` is easy. Here's an example:

```
% ls -l login.copy
-rw-------  1 taylor         1178 Nov  5 13:00 login.copy
% rm login.copy
% ls -l login.copy
login.copy not found
```

If you decide that you removed the wrong file and actually wanted to keep the `login.copy` file, it's too late. You're out of luck.

6

2. You can remove more than one file at a time by specifying each of the files to the rm command:

```
% ls
Archives/              PubAccessLists.Z        new.login
InfoWorld/             bin/                    rumors.26Oct.Z
LISTS                  cshrc.copy              rumors.5Nov.Z
Mail/                  educ                    src/
News/                  login.copy              test/
OWL/                   mailing.lists.bitnet.Z  testdir/
% rm cshrc.copy login.copy new.login
% ls
Archives/              OWL/                    rumors.26Oct.Z
InfoWorld/             PubAccessLists.Z        rumors.5Nov.Z
LISTS                  bin/                    src/
Mail/                  educ                    test/
News/                  mailing.lists.bitnet.Z  testdir/
```

3. Fortunately, rm does have a command flag that to some degree helps avoid accidental file removal. When you use the -i flag to rm (the i stands for *interactive* in this case), the system will ask you if you're sure you want to remove the file:

```
% touch testme
% rm -i testme
rm: remove testme? n
% ls testme
testme
% rm -i testme
rm: remove testme? y
% ls testme
testme not found
```

Note that n is *no* and y is *yes*. Delete the file.

4. Another flag that is often useful for rm, but is very dangerous, is the -r flag for recursive deletion of files (a *recursive command* repeatedly invokes itself). When the -r flag to rm is used, UNIX will remove any specified directory along with all its contents:

```
% ls -ld test ; ls -lR test
drwxrwxrwx  3 taylor           512 Nov  5 15:32 test/
total 1
-rw-rw----  1 taylor             0 Nov  5 15:32 alpha
drwxrwx---  2 taylor           512 Nov  5 15:32 test2/

test/test2:
total 0
-rw-rw----  1 taylor             0 Nov  5 15:32 file1
% rm -r test
% ls -ld test
test not found
```

Without any warning or indication that it was going to do something so drastic, entering rm -r test caused not just the test directory, but all files and directories inside it as well, to be removed.

JUST A MINUTE

This latest example demonstrates that you can give several commands in a single UNIX command line. To do this, separate the commands with a semicolon. Instead of giving the commands `ls -ld test` and `ls -1R test` on separate lines, I opted for the more efficient `ls -ld test; ls -1R test`, which uses both commands at once.

SUMMARY The UNIX equivalent of the paper shredder, the `rm` command allows easy removal of files. With the `-r` flag, you can even clean out an entire directory. Nothing can be retrieved after the fact, however, so use great caution.

Task 6.7: Minimizing the Danger of the `rm` Command

DESCRIPTION At this point, you might be wondering why I am making such a big deal of the `rm` command and the fact that it does what it is advertised to do—that is, remove files. The answer is that learning a bit of paranoia now can save you immense grief in the future. It can prevent you from destroying a file full of information you really needed to save.

For DOS, there are commercial programs (Norton Utilities, for instance) that can retrieve accidentally removed files. The trash can on the Macintosh can be clicked open and the files retrieved with ease. If the trash can is emptied after a file is accidentally discarded, a program such as Symantec Utilities for the Macintosh can be used to restore files.

UNIX just doesn't have that capability, though, and files that are removed are gone forever.

The only exception is if you work on a UNIX system that has an automatic, reliable backup schedule. In such a case, you might be able to retrieve from a storage tape an older version of your file (maybe).

That said, there are a few things you can do to lessen the danger of using `rm` and yet give yourself the ability to remove unwanted files.

ACTION

1. You can use a shorthand, a *shell alias*, to attach the `-i` flag automatically to each use of `rm`. To do this, you need to ascertain what type of login shell you're running, which you can do most easily by using the following command. (Don't worry about what it all does right now. You learn about the `grep` command a few hours from now.)

```
% grep taylor /etc/passwd
taylor:?:19989:1412:Dave Taylor:/users/taylor:/bin/csh
```

The last word on the line is what's important. The /etc/passwd file is one of the database files UNIX uses to track accounts. Each line in the file is called a *password entry* or *password file entry*. On my password entry, you can see that the login shell specified is /bin/csh. If you try this and you don't have an identical entry, you should have /bin/sh or /bin/ksh.

2. If your entry is /bin/csh, enter exactly what is shown here:

```
% echo "alias rm /bin/rm -i" >> ~/.cshrc
% source ~/.cshrc
```

Now rm includes the -i flag each time it's used:

```
% touch testme
% rm testme
rm: remove testme? n
```

3. If your entry is /bin/ksh, enter exactly what is shown here, paying particular attention to the two different quotation mark characters used in the example:

```
$ echo 'alias rm="/bin/rm -i"' >> ~/.profile
$ . ~/.profile
```

Now rm includes the -i flag each time it's used.

CAUTION

> One thing to pay special attention to is the difference between the single quote ('), the double quote ("), and the backquote (`). UNIX interprets each differently, although single and double quotes are often interchangeable. The backquotes, also known as grave accents, are more unusual and delineate commands within other commands.

4. If your entry is /bin/sh, you cannot program your system to include the -i flag each time rm is used. The Bourne shell, as sh is known, is the original command shell of UNIX. The Bourne shell lacks an alias feature, a feature that both the Korn shell (ksh) and the C shell (csh) include. As a result, I recommend that you change your login shell to one of these alternatives, if available.

To see what's available, look in the /bin directory on your machine for the specific shells:

```
% ls -l /bin/sh /bin/ksh /bin/csh
-rwxr-xr-x  1 root           102400 Apr  8  1991 /bin/csh*
-rwxr-xr-x  1 root           139264 Jul 26 14:35 /bin/ksh*
-rwxr-xr-x  1 root            28672 Oct 10  1991 /bin/sh*
```

Most of the examples in this book focus on the C Shell because I think it's the easiest of the three shells to use. To change your login shell to csh, you can use the chsh—change login shell—command:

```
% chsh
Changing login shell for taylor.
```

```
Old shell: /bin/sh
New shell: /bin/csh
```

Now you can go back to instruction 2 and set up a C shell alias. This will help you avoid mischief with the rm command.

SUMMARY The best way to avoid trouble with any of these commands is to learn to be just a bit paranoid about them. Before you remove a file, make sure it's the one you want. Before you remove a directory, make doubly sure that it doesn't contain any files you might want. Before you rename a file or directory, double-check to see if renaming it is going to cause any trouble.

Take your time with the commands you learned in this hour, and you should be fine. Even in the worst case, you might have the safety net of a system backup performed by a system administrator, but don't rely on it.

Summary

You now have completed six hours of UNIX instruction, and you are armed with enough commands to cause trouble and make UNIX do what you want it to do. In this hour, you learned the differences between cp and mv for moving files and how to use mv to rename both files and directories. You also learned how to create directories with the mkdir command and how to remove them with the rmdir command. And you learned about the rm command for removing files and directories, and how to avoid getting into too much trouble with it.

Finally, if you were really paying attention, you learned how to identify which login shell you're using (csh, ksh, or sh) and how to change from one to another using the chsh command.

Workshop

The Workshop summarizes the key terms you learned and poses some questions about the topics presented in this chapter. It also provides you with a preview of what you will learn in the next hour.

6

Key Terms

password entry   For each account on the UNIX system, there is an entry in the account database known as the *password file*. This also contains an encrypted copy of the account password. This set of information for an individual account is known as the *password entry*.

recursive command   A command that repeatedly invokes itself.

shell alias   Most UNIX shells have a convenient way for you to create abbreviations for commonly used commands or series of commands, known as shell aliases. For example, if I always found myself typing ls -CF, an alias can let me type just ls and have the shell automatically add the -CF flags each time.

Questions

1. What are the differences between cp and mv?

2. If you were installing a program from a floppy disk onto a hard disk, would you use cp or mv?

3. If you know DOS, this question is for you. Although DOS has a RENAME command, it doesn't have both COPY and MOVE. Which of these two do you think DOS includes? Why?

4. Try using mkdir to create a directory. What happens and why?

5. You've noticed that both rmdir and rm -r can be used to remove directories. Which is safer to use?

6. The rm command has another flag that wasn't discussed in this hour. The -f flag forces removal of files regardless of permission (assuming you're the owner, that is). In combination with the -r flag, this can be amazingly destructive. Why?

Preview of the Next Hour

The seventh hour introduces the useful file command, which indicates the contents of any file in the UNIX file system. With file, you will explore various directories in the UNIX file system to see what it reveals about different system and personal files. Then, when you've found some files worth reading, you will learn about cat, more, and pg, which are different ways of looking at the contents of a file.

Hour 7

Looking into Files

By this point, you've learned a considerable number of UNIX commands and a lot about the operating and file systems. This hour focuses on UNIX tools to help you ascertain what type of files you've been seeing in all the different directories. It then introduces five powerful tools for examining the content of files.

Goals for This Hour

In this hour, you learn how to

- [ ] Use `file` to identify file types
- [ ] Explore UNIX directories with `file`
- [ ] Peek at the first few lines with `head`
- [ ] View the last few lines with `tail`
- [ ] View the contents of files with `cat`
- [ ] View larger files with `more`

This hour begins with a tool to help ensure that the files you're about to view are intended for human perusal and then explores many of the commands available to view the contents of the file in various ways.

Task 7.1: Using `file` to Identify File Types

DESCRIPTION   One of the most undervalued commands in UNIX is `file`, which is often neglected and collecting dust in some corner of the system. The `file` command is a program that can easily offer you a good hint as to the contents of a file by looking at the first few lines.

Unfortunately, there is a problem with the `file` command: It isn't 100 percent accurate. The program relies on a combination of the permissions of a file, the filename, and an analysis of the first few lines of the text. If you had a text file that started out looking like a C program or that had execute permission enabled, `file` might well identify it as an executable program rather than an English text file.

JUST A MINUTE

> You can determine how accurate your version of `file` is by checking the size of its database of file types. You can do this with the UNIX command `wc -l /etc/magic`. The number of entries in the database should be around 100. If you have many less than this number, you're probably going to have trouble. If you have considerably more, you might have a very accurate version of `file` at your fingertips! Remember, however, even if it's relatively small, `file` can still offer invaluable suggestions regarding file content anyway.

ACTION

1. Start by logging in to your account and using the `ls` command to find a file or two to check.

    ```
    % ls -F
    Archives/               OWL/                    rumors.26Oct.Z
    InfoWorld/              PubAccessLists.Z        rumors.5Nov.Z
    LISTS                   bin/                    src/
    Mail/                   educ                    temp/
    News/                   mailing.lists.bitnet.Z
    ```

    Next, simply enter the `file` command, listing each of the files you'd like the program to analyze:

    ```
    % file LISTS educ rumors.26Oct.Z src
    LISTS:  ascii text
    educ:   ascii text
    rumors.26Oct.Z: block compressed 16 bit code data
    src:    directory
    ```

    From this example, you can see that `file` correctly identifies `src` as a directory, offers considerable information on the compressed file `rumors.26Oct.Z`, and tags both `LISTS` and `educ` as plain ASCII text files.

7

JUST A MINUTE

> ASCII is the American Standard Code for Information Interchange and means that the file contains the letters of the English alphabet, punctuation, and numbers, but not much else. There are no multiple typefaces, italics, or underlined passages, and there are no graphics. It's the lowest common denominator of text in UNIX.

2. Now try using the asterisk (*), a UNIX wildcard (explained in Hour 9, "Wildcards and Regular Expressions"), to have the program analyze all files in your home directory:

```
% file *
Global.Software:        English text
Interactive.Unix:       mail folder
Mail:           directory
News:           directory
Src:            directory
bin:            directory
history.usenet.Z:       compressed data block compressed 16 bits
```

The asterisk (*) is a special character in UNIX. Used by itself, it tells the system to replace it with the names of all the files in the current directory.

This time you can begin to see how `file` can help differentiate files. Using this command, I am now reminded that the file `Global.Software` is English text, but `Interactive.Unix` is actually an old electronic mail message (`file` can't differentiate between a single mail message and a multiple-message folder, so it always errs on the side of saying that the file is a mail folder).

3. Mail folders are actually problematical for the `file` command. On one of the systems I use, the `file` command doesn't know what mail messages are, so asking it to analyze mail folders results in a demonstration of how accuracy is related to the size of the `file` database.

On a Sun system, I asked `file` to analyze two mail folders, with the following results:

```
% file Mail/mailbox Mail/sent
Mail/mailbox:   mail folder
Mail/sent: mail folder
```

Those same two files on a Berkeley UNIX system, however, have very different results when analyzed:

```
% file Mail/mailbox Mail/sent Mail/netnews
Mail/mailbox:        ascii text
Mail/sent:      shell commands
Mail/netnews:        English text
```

Not only does the Berkeley version of UNIX not identify the files correctly, it doesn't even misidentify them consistently.

4. Another example of the `file` command's limitations is how it interacts with file permissions. Use `cp` to create a new file and work through this example to see how your `file` command interprets the various changes.

```
% cp .cshrc test
% file test
test: shell commands
% chmod +x test
% file test
test: shell script
```

Adding execute permission to this file caused `file` to identify it as a shell script rather than shell commands.

SUMMARY Don't misinterpret the results of these examples as proof that the `file` command is useless and that you shouldn't use it. Quite the opposite is true. UNIX has neither a specific file-naming convention (DOS has its three-letter filename suffixes) nor indication of file ownership by icon (Macintosh does this with creator information added by each program). As a result, it's vital that you have a tool for helping ascertain file types without actually opening the file.

Why not just look at the contents? The best way to figure out the answer to this question is to display accidentally the contents of an executable file on the screen. You'll see it's quite a mess, loaded with special control characters that can be best described as making your screen go berserk.

Task 7.2: Exploring UNIX Directories with `file`

DESCRIPTION Now that you know how to work with the `file` command, it's time to wander through the UNIX file system, learning more about types of files that tend to be found in specific directories. Your system might vary slightly—it'll certainly have more files in some directories than what I'm showing here in the examples, but you'll quickly see that `file` can offer some valuable insight into the contents of files.

ACTION

1. First things first. Take a look at the files found in the very top level of the file system, in `/` (root):

```
% cd /
% ls -CF
-No _rm_ star   boot        flags/        rhf@        userb/
OLD/            core        gendynix      stand/      userc/
archive/        dev/        lib@          sys@        userd/
ats/            diag@       lost+found/   tftpboot@   usere/
backup/         dynix       mnt/          tmp/        users/
bin@            etc/        net/          usera/      usr/
% file boot core gendynix tftpboot
boot:   SYMMETRY i386 stand alone executable version 1
```

```
core:    core from getty
gendynix:        SYMMETRY i386 stand alone executable not
➥stripped version 1
tftpboot:        symbolic link to /usr/tftpboot
```

This example is from a Sequent computer running DYNIX, the Sequents' version of UNIX, based on Berkeley 4.3 BSD with some AT&T System V extensions. It's the same machine that has such problems identifying mail folders.

Executable binaries are explained in detail by the `file` command on this computer: `boot` is listed as SYMMETRY i386 stand alone executable version 1. The specifics aren't vital to understand: The most important word to see in this output is `executable`, indicating that the file is the result of compiling a program. The format is SYMMETRY i386, version 1, and the file requires no libraries or other files to execute—it's stand-alone.

For `gendynix`, the format is similar, but one snippet of information is added that isn't indicated for `boot`: The executable file hasn't been stripped.

JUST A MINUTE

> Stripping a file doesn't mean that you peel its clothes off, but rather that a variety of information included in most executables to help identify and isolate problems has been removed to save space.

When a program dies unexpectedly in UNIX, the operating system tries to leave a snapshot of the memory that the program was using, to aid in debugging. Wading through these core files can be quite difficult—it's usually reserved for a few experts at each site, but there is still some useful information inside. The best, and simplest, way to check it is with the `file` command. You can see in the preceding listing that `file` recognized the file core as a crashed program memory image and further extracted the name of the program that originally failed, `getty`, causing the program to fail. When this failure happens, UNIX creates an image of the program in memory at the time of failure, which is called a *core dump*.

The fourth of the listings offers an easy way to understand symbolic links, indicated in `ls -CF` output with the special suffix @, as shown in the preceding example with `tftpboot@`. Using `file`, you can see that the file `tftpboot` in the root directory is actually a symbolic link to a file with the same name elsewhere in the file system, `/usr/tftpboot`.

2. There are differences in output formats on different machines. The following example shows what the same command would generate on a Sun Microsystems workstation, examining analogous files:

```
% file boot core kadb tmp
boot:            sparc executable
core:            core file from 'popper'
```

7

```
kadb:              sparc executable not stripped
tmp:               symbolic link to /var/tmp
```

The Sun computer offers the same information but fewer specifics about executable binaries. In this case, Sun workstations are built around SPARC chips (just like PCs are built around Intel chips), so the executables are identified as sparc executable.

3. Are you ready for another directory of weird files? It's time to move into the /lib directory to see what devices are present on your system and what type of files they are.

   Entering ls will demonstrate quickly that there are a lot of files in this directory! The file command can tell you about any of them. On my Sun computer, I asked for information on a few select files, many of which you might also have on yours:

```
% file lib.b lib300.a diffh sendmail
lib.b:             c program text
lib300.a:          archive random library
diffh:             sparc pure dynamically linked executable not stripped
sendmail:          sparc demand paged dynamically linked set-uid executable
```

   The first file, lib.b, demonstrates that the file command works regardless of the name of a file: Standard naming for C program files specifies that they end with the characters .c, as in test.c. So, without file, you might never have suspected that lib.b is a C program. The second file is an actual program library and is identified here as an archive random library, meaning that it's an archive and that the information within can be accessed in random order (by appropriate programs).

   The third file is an executable, demonstrating another way that file can indicate programs on a Sun workstation. The sendmail program is an interesting program: It's an executable, but it has some new information that you haven't seen before. The set-uid indicates that the program is set up so that when anyone runs it, sendmail runs as the user who owns the file, not the user who launched the program. A quick ls can reveal a bit more about this:

```
% ls -l /lib/sendmail
-r-sr-x--x  1 root         155648 Sep 14 09:11 /lib/sendmail*
```

   Notice here that the fourth character of the permissions string is an s rather than the expected x for an executable. Also check the owner of the file in this listing. Combined, the two mean that when anyone runs this program, sendmail actually will set itself to a different user ID (root in this case) and have that set of access permissions. Having sendmail run with root permissions is how you can send electronic mail to someone else without fuss, but you can't view his or her mailbox.

4. Consider now one more directory full of weird files before you start the next task. This time, move into the /dev directory and see what's inside. Again, it's a directory with a lot of files, so don't be surprised if the output scrolls off the screen!

7

Try to identify a few files that are similar in name to the ones I examine here, and see what `file` says about them:

```
% cd /dev
% file MAKEDEV audio spx sr0 tty
MAKEDEV:        executable shell script
audio:          character special (69/0)
spx:            character special (37/35)
sr0:            block special (18/0)
tty:            character special (2/0)
```

UNIX has two different types of devices, or peripherals, that can be attached: those that expect information in chunks and those that are happier working on a byte-by-byte basis. The former are called *block special devices* and the latter *character special devices*. You don't have to worry about the differences, but notice that `file` can differentiate between them: audio, spx, and tty are all character-special-device files, whereas sr0 is a block-special-device file.

The pair of numbers in parentheses following the description of each file are known as the *major number* and *minor number* of the file. The first indicates the type of device, and the second indicates the physical location of the plug, wire, card, or other hardware that is controlled by the specific peripheral.

SUMMARY The good news is that you don't have to worry a bit about what files are in the `/lib`, `/etc`, or any other directory other than your own home directory. There are thousands of happy UNIX folk working busily away each day without ever realizing that these other directories exist, let alone knowing what's in them.

What's important here is that you have learned that the `file` command is quite sophisticated at identifying special UNIX system files of various types. It can be a very helpful tool when you are looking around in the file system and even when you are just trying to remember which files are which in your own directory.

Task 7.3: Peeking at the First Few Lines with head

DESCRIPTION Now that you have the tools needed to move about in the file system, to double check where you are, and to identify the types of different files, it's time to learn about some of the many tools UNIX offers for viewing the contents of files. The first on the list is head, a simple program for viewing the first ten lines of any file on the system.

The head program is more versatile than it sounds: you can use it to view up to the first few hundred lines of a very long file, actually. To specify the number of lines you want to see, you just need to indicate how many as a starting argument, prefixing the number of lines desired with a dash.

JUST A MINUTE

> This command, `head`, is the first of a number of UNIX commands that tend
> to work with their own variant on the regular rules of starting arguments.
> Instead of a typical UNIX command argument of `-133` to specify 33 lines,
> `head` uses `-33` to specify the same information.

ACTION

1. Start by moving back into your home directory and viewing the first few lines of
   your `.cshrc` file:

```
% cd
% head .cshrc
#
# Default user .cshrc file (/bin/csh initialization).

set host=limbo

set path=(. ~/bin /bin /usr/bin /usr/ucb /usr/local /etc
/usr/etc/usr/local/bin /usr/unsup/bin)

# Set up C shell environment:

alias  diff     '/usr/bin/diff -c -w'
```

   The contents of your own `.cshrc` file will doubtless be different, but notice that the
   program lists only the first few lines of the file.

2. To specify a different number of lines, use the `-n` format (where *n* is the number of
   lines). I'll look at just the first four lines of the `.login` file:

```
% head -4 .login
#
# @(#) $Revision: 62.2 $

setenv TERM vt100
```

3. You also can easily check multiple files by specifying them to the program:

```
% head -3 .newsrc /etc/passwd
==> .newsrc <==
misc.forsale.computers.mac: 1-14536
utech.student-orgs! 1
general! 1-546

==> /etc/passwd <==
root:?:0:0: root,,,,:/:/bin/csh
news:?:6:11:USENET News,,,,:/usr/spool/news:/bin/ksh
ingres:*?:7:519:INGRES Manager,,,,:/usr/ingres:/bin/csh
```

4. More importantly, `head`, and other UNIX commands, can work also as part of a
   pipeline, where the output of one program is the input of the next. The special
   symbol for creating UNIX pipelines is the pipe (¦) character. Pipes are read left to

7

right, so you can easily have the output of who, for example, feed into head, offering powerful new possibilities. Perhaps you want to see just the first five people logged in to the computer right now. Try this:

```
% who ¦ head -5
root       console Nov  9 07:31
mccool     ttyaO   Nov 10 14:25
millekl2 ttyaP   Nov 10 14:58
paulwhit ttyaR   Nov 10 14:50
bobweir  ttyaS   Nov 10 14:49
Broken pipe
```

Pipelines are one of the most powerful features of UNIX, and there are many examples of how to use them to best effect throughout the remainder of this book.

5. Here is one last thing. Find an executable, /boot will do fine, and enter head -1 / boot. Watch what happens. Or, if you'd like to preserve your sanity, take it from me that the random junk thrown on your screen is plenty to cause your program to get quite confused and possibly even quit or crash.

The point isn't to have that happen to your screen, but rather to remind you that using file to confirm file type for unfamiliar files can save you lots of grief and frustration!

SUMMARY The simplest of programs for viewing the contents of a file, head, is easy to use, efficient, and works as part of a pipeline, too. The remainder of this hour focuses on other tools in UNIX that offer other ways to view the contents of text and ASCII files.

Task 7.4: Viewing the Last Few Lines with tail

DESCRIPTION The head program shows you the first 10 lines of the file you specify. What would you expect tail to do, then? I hope you guessed the right answer: It shows the last 10 lines of a file. Like head, tail also understands the same format for specifying the number of lines to view.

ACTION

1. Start out viewing the last 12 lines of your .cshrc file:

```
% tail -12 .cshrc

   set noclobber history=100 system=filec
   umask 007

   setprompt
endif

# special aliases:

alias info       ssinfo
alias ssinfo     'echo "connecting..." ; rlogin oasis'
```

2. Next, the last four lines of the file LISTS in my home directory can be shown with the following command line:

```
% tail -5 LISTS
            College of Education
            Arizona State University
            Tempe, AZ 85287-2411
            602-965-2692
```

Don't get too hung up trying to figure out what's inside my files: I'm not even sure myself sometimes.

3. Here's one to think about. You can use head to view the first *n* lines of a file and tail to view the last *n* lines of a file. Can you figure out a way to combine the two so you can see just the tenth, eleventh, and twelfth lines of a file?

```
% head -12 .cshrc ¦ tail -3
alias  diff      '/usr/bin/diff -c -w'
alias  from      'frm -n'
alias  ll        'ls -l'
```

It's easy with UNIX command pipelines!

 SUMMARY Combining the two commands head and tail can give you considerable power in viewing specific slices of a file on the UNIX system. Try combining them in different ways for different effects.

Task 7.5: Viewing the Contents of Files with cat

DESCRIPTION Both head and tail offer the capability to view a piece of a file, either the top or bottom, but neither lets you see the entire file, regardless of length. For this job, the cat program is the right choice.

JUST A MINUTE

> The cat program got its name from its function in the early versions of UNIX; its function was to concatenate (or join together) multiple files. It isn't, unfortunately, homage to feline pets or anything else so exotic!

The cat program also has a valuable secret capability, too: Through use of the -v flag, you can use cat to display any file on the system, executable or otherwise, with all characters that normally would not be printed (or would drive your screen bonkers) displayed in a special format I call *control-key notation*. In control key notation, each character is represented as ^*n*, where *n* is a specific printable letter or symbol. A character with the value of 0 (also referred to as a *null* or *null character*) is displayed as ^@, a character with the value 1 is ^A, a character with the value 2 is ^B, and so on.

Another cat flag that can be useful for certain files is -s, which suppresses multiple blank lines from a file. It isn't immediately obvious how that could help, but there are some files that can have a screen full (or more) of blank lines. To avoid having to watch them all fly past, you can use cat -s to chop 'em all down to a single blank line.

ACTION

1. Move back to your home directory again, and use cat to display the complete contents of your .cshrc file:

```
% cd
% cat .cshrc
#
# Default user .cshrc file (/bin/csh initialization).

set path=(. ~/bin /bin /usr/bin /usr/ucb /usr/local /etc
/usr/etc/usr/local/bin /usr/unsup/bin )

# Set up C shell environment:

alias  diff      '/usr/bin/diff -c -w'
alias  from      'frm -n'
alias  ll        'ls -l'
alias  ls        '/bin/ls -F'
alias  mail      Mail
alias  mailq     '/usr/lib/sendmail -bp'

alias  newaliases 'echo you mean newalias...'

alias  rd        'readmsg $ ¦ page'
alias  rn        '/usr/local/bin/rn -d$HOME -L -M -m -e -S -/'

# and some special stuff if we're in an interactive shell

if ( $?prompt ) then            # shell is interactive.

  alias  cd             'chdir \!* ; setprompt'
  alias  env            'printenv'
  alias  setprompt      'set prompt="$system ($cwd:t) \! : "'

  set noclobber history=100 system=limbo filec
  umask 007

  setprompt
endif

# special aliases:

alias info       ssinfo
alias ssinfo     'echo "connecting..." ; rlogin oasis'
```

Don't be too concerned if the content of your .cshrc file (or mine) doesn't make any sense to you. You are slated to learn about the contents of this file within a few hours, and, yes, it is complex.

You can see that cat is pretty simple to use. If you specify more than one filename to the program, it lists them in the order you specify. You can even list the contents of a file multiple times by specifying the same filename on the command line multiple times.

2. The cat program also can be used as part of a pipeline. Compare the following command with my earlier usage of head and tail:

```
% cat LISTS ¦ tail -5
          College of Education
          Arizona State University
          Tempe, AZ 85287-2411
          602-965-2692
```

3. Now find an executable file, and try cat -v in combination with head to get a glimpse of the contents therein:

```
% cat -v /bin/ls ¦ head -1
M-k"^@^@^@M-^@^@^@^@^P^@^@M-45^@^@^@^@^@^@M-l^P^@^@^@^@^@^@
➥^@^@^@^@^@^@^@^@
^@^@^@^@^@^@^@^@^@^@^@^@^@^@^@^@^@^@^@^@^@^@^@^@^@^@^@^@^@^@
➥^@^@^@^@^@^@^@^@^@
^@^@^@^@^@^@^@^@^@^@^@^@^@^@^@^@^@^@^@^@^@^@^@^@^@^@^@^@^@^@
➥^@^@^@^@^@^@^@^@^@
^@^@^@^@^@^@^@^@^@^@^@^@^@A^@^@^@$Header: crt0.c 1.4 87/04/23
➥$^@^@@(#)Copy
right (C) 1984 XXXXXXX Computer Systems, Inc.  All rights reserved.
➥^@M-^KM-NM-^KM-
tM-^MF^DM-^KM-XM-^K^F@M-^M^DM-^E^@^@^@^@M-^KM-S^AM-BM-^I^U^@M-^@^@
➥^@SM-^?6M-hw^T^@^@M-
^CM-D^HM-^?5^@M-^@^@^@SM-^?6M-h&^@^@^@M-^CM-D^LPM-h)[^@^@YM-tM-^PM-
➥^PM-^PM-k^BM-IM-CUM-
^KM-1M-kM-yM-^PM-^PM-^PM
-k^BM-IM-CUM-^KM-1M-kM-yM-^PM-^PM-^PUM-^KM-1M-^CM-1^XWVSM-^K
➥u^LM-^K]^HKM-^CM-F^DM-hM
-X^V^@^@M-^EM-@u^FM-^?^EM-1M-^L^@^@h^DM-^M^@^@M-hM-P7^@^
➥@YM-^K^E^DM-^M^@^@-^@NM-
m^@M-^I^E^HM-^M^@^@M-^K^E^DM-^M^@^@^E^P^N^@^@M-^I^E^LM-^
➥M^@^@M-^C^E^DM-^M^@^@<M-
G^E^PM-^M^@^@P^@^@^@j^AM-hM-%[^@^@YM-^EM-@tNh^TM-^M^@^@h
➥M-HM-^J^@^@M-h12^@^@M-^C
M-D^HM-G^EM-pM-^L^@^@^A^@^@^@M-8^A^@^@^@M-^I^EM-hM-^L^@^
➥@M-ht^S^@^@M-^MEM-nPj^AM
-h]^V^@^@M-^CM-D^H^OM-?EM-r%^@^L^@^@=^@Broken pipe
```

This is complex and confusing, indeed! What's worse, this isn't the entire first line of the executable. You can see that, because this block of data ends with Broken pipe, which indicates that a lot more was being fed to head than it could process, due to the constraint of having only the first line listed—a line that head defines as no more than 512 characters long.

SUMMARY The cat command is useful for viewing files and is quite easy to use, too. The problem with it is that if the file you choose to view has more than the number of lines on your screen, the file will just fly past you without your having any way to slow it down. That's where the next two commands come in handy: more for stepping through files, and page for paging through files. Both solve this problem, albeit in slightly different ways.

Task 7.6: Viewing Larger Files with more

DESCRIPTION   You can now wander about the file system, find files that might be of interest, check their types with file, and even view them with the cat command, but what if they're longer than the size of your screen? That's the job of the more program, a program that knows how big your screen is and displays the information page by page.

There are three primary flags in more:

- -s   Suppresses multiple blank lines, just like the -s flag to cat
- -d   Forces more to display friendlier prompts at the bottom of each page
- -c   Causes the program to clear the screen before displaying each screen full of text

The program also allows you to start at a specific line in the file by using the curious +*n* notation, where *n* is a specific number. Finally, you can start also at the first occurrence of a specific pattern by specifying that pattern to the program in a format similar to +/*pattern* (patterns are defined in Hour 9).

ACTION

1. View the .cshrc file using more:
```
% more ~/.cshrc
#
# Default user .cshrc file (/bin/csh initialization).

set host=limbo

set path=(. ~/bin /bin /usr/bin /usr/ucb /usr/local /etc
/usr/etc /usr/local/bin /usr/unsup/bin)

# Set up C shell environment:

alias   diff      '/usr/bin/diff -c -w'
alias   from      'frm -n'
alias   ll        'ls -l'
alias   ls        '/bin/ls -F'
alias   mail      Mail
alias   mailq     '/usr/lib/sendmail -bp'

alias   newaliases 'echo you mean newalias...'

alias   rd        'readmsg $ | page'
--More--(51%)
```

7

Unlike previous examples where the program runs until completed, leaving you back on the command line, more is the first *interactive program* you've encountered. When you see the --More--(51%) prompt, the cursor sits at the end of that line, waiting for you to tell it what to do. The more program lets you know how far into the file you've viewed, too; in the example, you've seen about half of the file (51 percent).

At this point, there is quite a variety of commands available. Press the spacebar to see the next screen of information, until you have seen the entire file.

2. Try starting up the program with the twelfth line of the file:

```
% more +12 ~/.cshrc
alias  mailq     '/usr/lib/sendmail -bp'

alias  newaliases 'echo you mean newalias...'

alias  rd         'readmsg $ ¦ page'
alias  rn         '/usr/local/bin/rn -d$HOME -L -M -m -e -S -/'

# and some special stuff if we're in an interactive shell

if ( $?prompt ) then              # shell is interactive.

  alias  cd          'chdir \!* ; setprompt'
  alias  env         'printenv'
  alias  setprompt   'set prompt="$system ($cwd:t) \! : "'

  set noclobber history=100 filec
  umask 007

  setprompt
endif
--More--(82%)
```

3. You can see that about halfway through the .cshrc file there is a line that contains the word newaliases. I can start up more so that the line with this pattern is displayed on the top of the first screenful.

```
% more +/newaliases ~/.cshrc

...skipping
alias  mailq     '/usr/lib/sendmail -bp'

alias  newaliases 'echo you mean newalias...'

alias  rd         'readmsg $ ¦ page'
alias  rn         '/usr/local/bin/rn -d$HOME -L -M -m -e -S -/'

# and some special stuff if we're in an interactive shell

if ( $?prompt ) then              # shell is interactive.
```

```
alias   cd               'chdir \!* ; setprompt'
alias   env              'printenv'
alias   setprompt        'set prompt="$system ($cwd:t) \! : "'

set noclobber history=100 filec
umask 007

setprompt
endif

# special aliases:

alias info       ssinfo
--More--(86%)
```

Actually, notice that the line containing the pattern newaliases shows up as the third line of the first screen, not the first line. That's so you have a bit of context to the matched line, but it can take some getting used to. Also note that more tells us—with the message ...skipping as the very first line—that it's skipping some lines to find the pattern.

4. The range of commands available at the --More-- prompt is quite extensive, as listed in Table 7.1. The sidebar following the table explains what the conventions used in the table mean and how to enter the following commands.

Table 7.1. Commands available within the more program.

Command	Function
[Space]	Press the spacebar to display the next screenful of text.
n[Return]	Display the next n lines (the default is the next line only of text).
h	Display a list of commands available in the more program.
d	Scroll down half a page.
q	Quit the more program.
ns	Skip forward n lines (default is 1).
nf	Skip forward n screenfuls (default is 1).
b or Control-b	Skip backward a screenful of text.
=	Display the current line number.
/pattern	Search for an occurrence of a pattern.
n	Search for the next occurrence of the current pattern.
v	Start the vi editor at the current line.
Control-l	(That's a lowercase L.) Redraw the screen.
:f	Display the current filename and line number.

7

Entering Commands in the more Program

In this table and in the following text, the word space enclosed in brackets [Space] refers to pressing the spacebar as a command. Likewise, [Return] means you should press the Return key as part of the command.

A hyphen in a command—for example Ctrl-b—means that you should hold down the first indicated key while you press the second key. The lowercase-letter commands in the table indicate that you should press the corresponding key, the A key for the a command, for example.

Two characters together, but without a hyphen (:f), mean that you should press the appropriate keys in sequence as you would when typing text.

Finally, entries that have an *n* before the command mean that you can prefix the command with a number, which will let it use that value to modify its action. For example, 3[Return] displays the next three lines of the file and 250s skips the next 250 lines. Typically, pressing Return after typing a command within more is not necessary.

Try some commands on a file of your own. A good file that will have enough lines to make this interesting is /etc/passwd:

```
% more /etc/passwd
root:?:0:0: root:/:/bin/csh
news:?:6:11:USENET News:/usr/spool/news:/bin/ksh
ingres:*?:7:519:INGRES Manager:/usr/ingres:/bin/csh
usrlimit:?:8:800:(1000 user system):/mnt:/bin/false
vanilla:*?:20:805:Vanilla Account:/mnt:/bin/sh
charon:*?:21:807:The Ferryman:/users/tomb:
actmaint:?:23:809: Maintenance:/usr/adm/actmaint:/bin/ksh
pop:*?:26:819:,,,,:/usr/spool/pop:/bin/csh
lp:*?:70:10:System V Lp Admin:/usr/spool/lp:
trouble:*?:97:501:Trouble Report Facility:/usr/trouble:/usr/msh
postmaster:?:98:504:Mail:/usr/local/adm:/bin/csh
aab:?:513:1233:Robert Townsend:/users/aab:/bin/ksh
billing:?:516:1233:Accounting:/users/billing:/bin/csh
aai:?:520:1233:Pete Cheeseman:/users/aai:/bin/csh
--More--(1%) 60s

...skipping 60 lines

cq:?:843:1233:Rob Tillot:/users/cq:/usr/local/bin/tcsh
robb:?:969:1233:Robb:/users/robb:/usr/local/lib/msh
aok:?:970:1233:B Jacobs:/users/aok:/usr/local/lib/msh
went:?:1040:1233:David Math:/users/went:/bin/csh
aru:?:1076:1233:Raffie:/users/aru:/bin/ksh
varney:?:1094:1233:/users/varney:/bin/csh
brandt:?:1096:1233:Eric Brand:/users/brand:/usr/local/bin/tcsh
ask:?:1098:1233:/users/ask:/bin/csh
asn:?:1101:1233:Ketter Wesley:/users/asn:/usr/local/lib/msh
--More--(2%)
```

7

This example isn't exactly what you'll see on your screen because each time you type a command to more, it erases its own prompt and replaces the prompt with the appropriate line of the file. Try pressing [Return] to move down one line, and you'll see what I mean.

Quit more in the middle of viewing this file by typing q.

SUMMARY The more program is one of the best general-purpose programs in UNIX, offering an easy and powerful tool for perusing files. The biggest limitation, however, is that you can't go backward in the file: If you realize that what you are looking for is on the previous page, you have to quit and start the program again.

Summary

Now that you can add this set of commands to your retinue of UNIX expertise, you are most certainly ready to wander about your own computer system, understanding what files are what, where they are, and how to peer inside. You learned about file to ascertain type, head and tail for seeing snippets of files, and cat and more to help easily view files of any size on your screen.

Workshop

The Workshop summarizes the key terms you learned and poses some questions about the topics presented in this chapter. It also provides you with a preview of what you will learn in the next hour.

Key Terms

block special device   A device driver that controls block-oriented peripherals. A hard disk, for example, is a peripheral that works by reading and writing blocks of information (as distinguished from a character special device). See also **character special device**.

character special device   A device driver that controls a character-oriented peripheral. Your keyboard and display are both character-oriented devices, sending and displaying information on a character-by-character basis. See also **block special device**.

control-key notation   A notational convention in UNIX that denotes the use of a control key. There are three common conventions: Ctrl-C, ^c and C-C all denote the Control-c character, produced by pressing the Control key (labeled Control or Ctrl on your keyboard) and, while holding it down, pressing the c key.

core dump   The image of a command when it executed improperly.

interactive program   An interactive UNIX application is one that expects the user to enter information and then responds as appropriate. The ls command is not interactive, but the more program, which displays text a screenful at a time, is interactive.

7

major number   For device drivers, the major number identifies the specific type of device in use to the operating system. This is more easily remembered as the device ID number.

minor number   Once the device driver is identified to the operating system by its major number, the address of the device in the computer itself (that is, which card slot a peripheral card is plugged into) is indicated by its minor number.

null character   Each character in UNIX has a specific value, and any character with a numeric value of zero is known as a null or null character.

pipeline   A series of UNIX commands chained by ¦, the pipe character.

Questions

1. Many people who use UNIX systems tend to stick with file-naming conventions. Indeed, UNIX has many of its own, including .c for C source files, .z for compressed files, and a single dot prefix for dot files. Yet `file` ignores filenames (test it yourself). Why?

2. Use `more` to check some of the possible file types that can be recognized with the `file` command by peeking in the configuration file `/etc/magic`.

3. Do you remember the television game show "Name that Tune?" If so, you'll recall how contestants had to identify a popular song by hearing just the first few notes. The `file` command is similar; the program must guess at the type of the file by checking only the first few characters. Do you think it would be more accurate by checking more of the file, or less accurate? (Think about this one.)

4. How did the `cat` command get its name? Do you find that a helpful mnemonic?

5. Here's an oddity: What will this command do?

   `cat LISTS ¦ more`

6. If you were looking at an absolutely huge file and you were pretty sure that what you wanted was near the bottom, what command would you use, and why?

7. What if the information is near the top?

Preview of the Next Hour

There are lots of special characters in UNIX, as you have doubtless learned by accidentally typing a slash, asterisk, question mark, quote, or just about any other punctuation character. What may surprise you is that they all have different, specific meanings. The next hour explains considerably more about how pipelines work and how programs are used as filters. Among the new commands you will learn are `sort`, `wc`, `nl`, `uniq`, and `spell`. You also will learn a new, immensely helpful flag to `cat` that makes `cat` produce line numbers.

7

Hour 8

Filters and Piping

If you've ever learned a foreign language, you know that the most common approach is to start by building your vocabulary (almost always including the names of the months, for some reason), and then you learn about sentence construction rules. The UNIX command line is a lot like a language. Now you've learned a lot of UNIX words, so it's time to learn how to put them together as sentences using file redirection, filters, and pipes.

Commands to be added to your vocabulary this hour include wc, sort, nl, and uniq. You also learn about the -n flag to the cat command, which forces cat to add line numbers, and how you can use that to help find information within files.

Goals for This Hour

In this hour, you learn

- ☐ The secrets of file redirection
- ☐ How to count words and lines using wc
- ☐ How to remove extraneous lines using uniq
- ☐ How to sort information in a file using sort
- ☐ How to add line numbers to files with cat -n and nl
- ☐ Cool nl tricks and capabilities

This hour begins by focusing on one aspect of constructing powerful custom commands in UNIX by using file redirection. The introduction of some filters, programs that are intended to be used as part of command pipes, follow. Next you learn another aspect of creating your own UNIX commands using pipelines.

Task 8.1: The Secrets of File Redirection

DESCRIPTION So far, all the commands you've learned while teaching yourself UNIX have required you to enter information at the command line, and all have produced output on the screen. But, as Gershwin wrote in *Porgy and Bess*, "it ain't necessarily so." In fact, one of the most powerful features of UNIX is that the input can come from a file as easily as it can come from the keyboard, and the output can be saved to a file as easily as it can be displayed on your screen.

The secret is *file redirection*, the special commands in UNIX that instruct the computer to read from a file, write to a file, or even append information to an existing file. Each of these acts can be accomplished by placing a file-redirection command in a regular command line: < redirects input, > redirects output, and >> redirects output and appends the information to the existing file. A mnemonic for remembering which is which is to remember that, just as in English, UNIX works from left to right, so a character that points to the left (<) changes the input, whereas a character that points right (>) changes the output.

ACTION

1. Log in to your account and create an empty file using the touch command:

    ```
    % touch testme
    ```

2. First, use this empty file to learn how to redirect output. Use ls to list the files in your directory, saving them all to the newly created file:

    ```
    % ls -l testme
    -rw-rw-r--   1 taylor          0 Nov 15 09:11 testme
    % ls -l > testme
    % ls -l testme
    -rw-rw-r--   1 taylor        120 Nov 15 09:12 testme
    ```

    Notice that when you redirected the output, nothing was displayed on the screen; there was no visual confirmation that it worked. But it did, as you can see by the increased size of the new file.

3. Instead of using cat or more to view this file, try using file redirection:

    ```
    % cat < testme
    total 127
    drwx------   2 taylor        512 Nov  6 14:20 Archives/
    drwx------   3 taylor        512 Nov 16 21:55 InfoWorld/
    drwx------   2 taylor       1024 Nov 19 14:14 Mail/
    drwx------   2 taylor        512 Oct  6 09:36 News/
    ```

8

```
drwx------   3 taylor        512 Nov 11 10:48 OWL/
drwx------   2 taylor        512 Oct 13 10:45 bin/
-rw-rw----   1 taylor      57683 Nov 20 20:10 bitnet.lists.Z
-rw-rw----   1 taylor      46195 Nov 20 06:19 drop.text.hqx
-rw-rw----   1 taylor      12556 Nov 16 09:49 keylime.pie
drwx------   2 taylor        512 Oct 13 10:45 src/
drwxrwx---   2 taylor        512 Nov  8 22:20 temp/
-rw-rw----   1 taylor          0 Nov 20 20:21 testme
```

The results are the same as if you had used the `ls` command, but the output file is saved, too. You now can easily print the file or go back to it later to compare the way it looks with the way your files look in the future.

4. Use the `ls` command to add some further information at the bottom of the `testme` file by using >>, the append double-arrow notation:

    `% ls -FC >> testme`

    Recall that the -C flag to `ls` forces the system to list output in multicolumn mode. Try redirecting the output of `ls` -F to a file to see what happens without the -C flag.

5. It's time for a real-life example. You've finished learning UNIX, and your colleagues now consider you an expert. One afternoon, Shala tells you she has a file in her directory, but she isn't sure what it is. She wants to know what it is, but she can't figure out how to get to it. You try the `file` command, and UNIX tells you the file is data. You are a bit puzzled. But then you remember file redirection:

    `% cat -v < mystery.file > visible.mystery.file`

    This command has `cat` -v take its input from the file `mystery.file` and save its output in `visible.mystery.file`. All the nonprinting characters are transformed, and Shala can poke through the file at her leisure.

    Find a file on your system that `file` reports as a data file, and try using the redirection commands to create a version with all characters printable through the use of `cat` -v.

SUMMARY   There is an infinite number of ways that you can combine the various forms of file redirection to create custom commands and to process files in various ways. This hour has really just scratched the surface. Next, you learn about some popular UNIX filters and how they can be combined with file redirection to create new versions of existing files. Also, study the example about Shala's file, which shows the basic steps in all UNIX file-redirection operations: Specify the input to the command, specify the command, and specify where the output should go.

Task 8.2: Counting Words and Lines Using wc

DESCRIPTION   Writers generally talk about the length of their work in terms of number of words, rather than number of pages. In fact, most magazines and newspapers are laid out according to formulas based on multiplying an average-length word by the number of words in an article.

These people are obsessed with counting the words in their articles, but how do they do it? You can bet they don't count each word themselves. If they're using UNIX, they simply use the UNIX wc program, which computes a word count for the file. It also can indicate the number of characters (which ls -l indicates, too) and the number of lines in the file.

ACTION

1. Start by counting the lines, words, and characters in the testme file you created earlier in this hour:

```
% wc testme
        4       12      121
% wc < testme
        4       12      121
% cat testme ¦ wc
        4       12      121
```

All three of these commands offer the same result (which probably seems a bit cryptic now). Why do you need to have three ways of doing the same thing? Later, you learn why this is so helpful. For now, stick to using the first form of the command.

The output is three numbers, which reveal how many lines, words, and characters, respectively, are in the file. You can see that there are 4 lines, 12 words, and 121 characters in testme.

2. You can have wc list any one of these counts, or a combination of two, by using different command flags: -w counts words, -c counts characters, and -l counts lines:

```
% wc -w testme
   12 testme
% wc -l testme
    4 testme
% wc -wl testme
       12        4 testme
% wc -lw testme
        4       12 testme
```

3. Now the fun begins. Here's an easy way to find out how many files you have in your home directory:

```
% ls ¦ wc -l
37
```

The ls command lists each file, one per line (because you didn't use the -c flag). The output of that command is fed to wc, which counts the number of lines it's fed. The result is that you can find out how many files you have (37) in your home directory.

4. How about a quick gauge of how many users are on the system?

```
% who ¦ wc -l
    12
```

5. How many accounts are on your computer?

```
% cat /etc/passwd ¦ wc -l
    3877
```

SUMMARY The wc command is a great example of how the simplest of commands, when combined in a sophisticated pipeline, can be very powerful.

Task 8.3: Removing Extraneous Lines Using `uniq`

DESCRIPTION Sometimes when you're looking at a file, you'll notice that there are many duplicate entries, either blank lines or, perhaps, lines of repeated information. To clean up these files and shrink their size at the same time, you can use the uniq command, which lists each unique line in the file.

Well, it sort of lists each unique line in the file. What uniq really does is compare each line it reads with the previous line. If the lines are the same, uniq does not list the second line. You can use flags with uniq to get more specific results: -u lists only lines that are not repeated, -d lists only lines that are repeated (the exact opposite of -u), and -c adds a count of how many times each line occurred.

ACTION

1. If you use uniq on a file that doesn't have any common lines, uniq has no effect.

```
% uniq testme
Archives/               OWL/                    keylime.pie
InfoWorld/              bin/                    src/
Mail/                   bitnet.mailing-lists.Z  temp/
News/                   drop.text.hqx           testme
```

2. A trick using the cat command is that cat lists the contents of each file sequentially, even if you specify the same file over and over again, so you can easily build a file with lots of lines:

```
% cat testme testme testme > newtest
```

Examine newtest to verify that it contains three copies of testme, one after the other. (Try using wc.)

3. Now you have a file with duplicate lines. Will uniq realize these files have duplicate lines? Use wc to find out:

```
% wc newtest
    12    36    363
% uniq newtest ¦ wc
    12    36    363
```

They're the same. Remember, the uniq command removes duplicate lines only if they're adjacent.

4. Create a file that has duplicate lines:

```
% tail -1 testme > lastline
% cat lastline lastline lastline lastline > newtest2
% cat newtest2
News/                    drop.text.hqx              testme
News/                    drop.text.hqx              testme
News/                    drop.text.hqx              testme
News/                    drop.text.hqx              testme
```

Now you can see what uniq does:

```
% uniq newtest2
News/                    drop.text.hqx              testme
```

5. Obtain a count of the number of occurrences of each line in the file. The -c flag does that job:

```
% uniq -c newtest2
   4 News/                    drop.text.hqx              testme
```

This shows that this line occurs four times in the file. Lines that are unique have no number preface.

6. You also can see what the -d and -u flags do, and how they have exactly opposite actions:

```
% uniq -d newtest2
News/                    drop.text.hqx              testme
% uniq -u newtest2
%
```

Why did the -u flag list no output? The answer is that the -u flag tells uniq to list only those lines that are not repeated in the file. Because the only line in the file is repeated four times, there's nothing to display.

SUMMARY Given this example, you probably think uniq is of marginal value, but you will find that it's not uncommon for files to have many blank lines scattered willy-nilly throughout the text. The uniq command is a fast, easy, and powerful way to clean up such files.

Task 8.4: Sorting Information in a File Using sort

DESCRIPTION Whereas wc is useful at the end of a pipeline of commands, uniq is a *filter*, a program that is really designed to be tucked in the middle of a pipeline. Filters, of course, can be placed anywhere in a line, anywhere that enables them to help direct UNIX to do what you want it to do. The common characteristic of all UNIX filters is that they can read input from standard input, process it in some manner, and list the results in standard output. With file redirection, standard input and output also can be files. To do this, you can either specify the filenames to the command (usually input only) or use the file-redirection symbols you learned earlier in this hour (<, >, and >>).

JUST A MINUTE

Standard input and standard output are two very common expressions in UNIX. When a program is run, the default location for receiving input is called *standard input*. The default location for output is *standard output*. If you are running UNIX from a terminal, standard input and output are your terminal.

There is a third I/O location, *standard error*. By default, this is the same as standard output, but you can re-direct standard error to a different location than standard output. You learn more about I/O redirection later in the book.

One of the most useful filters is sort, a program that reads information and sorts it alphabetically. You can customize the behavior of this program, like all UNIX programs, to ignore the case of words (for example, to sort Big between apple and cat, rather than before—most sorts put all uppercase letters before the lowercase letters), and to reverse the order of a sort (z to a). The program sort also enables you to sort lists of numbers.

Few flags are available for sort, but they are powerful, as shown in Table 8.1.

Table 8.1. Flags for the sort command.

Flag	Function
-b	Ignore leading blanks.
-d	Sort in dictionary order (only letters, digits, and blanks are significant).
-f	Fold uppercase into lowercase; that is, ignore the case of words.
-n	Sort in numerical order.
-r	Reverse order of the sort.

ACTION

1. By default, the ls command sorts the files in a directory in a case-sensitive manner. It first lists those files that begin with uppercase letters and then those that begin with lowercase letters:

```
% ls -1F
Archives/
InfoWorld/
Mail/
News/
OWL/
bin/
bitnet.mailing-lists.Z
drop.text.hqx
```

```
keylime.pie
src/
temp/
testme
```

JUST A MINUTE

> To force `ls` to list output one file per line, you can use the `-1` flag (that's the number one, not a lowercase L).

To sort filenames alphabetically regardless of case, you can use `sort -f`:

```
% ls -1 ¦ sort -f
Archives/
bin/
bitnet.mailing-lists.Z
drop.text.hqx
InfoWorld/
keylime.pie
Mail/
News/
OWL/
src/
temp/
testme
```

2. How about sorting the lines of a file? You can use the `testme` file you created earlier:

```
% sort < testme
Archives/            OWL/                   keylime.pie
InfoWorld/           bin/                   src/
Mail/                bitnet.mailing-lists.Z temp/
News/                drop.text.hqx          testme
```

3. Here's a real-life UNIX example. Of the files in your home directory, which are the largest? The `ls -s` command indicates the size of each file, in blocks, and `sort -n` sorts numerically:

```
% ls -s ¦ sort -n
total 127
    1 Archives/
    1 InfoWorld/
    1 Mail/
    1 News/
    1 OWL/
    1 bin/
    1 src/
    1 temp/
    1 testme
   13 keylime.pie
   46 drop.text.hqx
   64 bitnet.mailing-lists.Z
```

It would be more convenient if the largest files were listed first in the output.
That's where the -r flag to reverse the sort order can be useful:

```
% ls -s ¦ sort -nr
 64 bitnet.mailing-lists.Z
 46 drop.text.hqx
 13 keylime.pie
  1 testme
  1 temp/
  1 src/
  1 bin/
  1 OWL/
  1 News/
  1 Mail/
  1 InfoWorld/
  1 Archives/
total 127
```

4. One more refinement is available to you. Instead of listing all the files, use the head
command, and specify that you want to see only the top five entries:

```
% ls -s ¦ sort -nr ¦ head -5
 64 bitnet.mailing-lists.Z
 46 drop.text.hqx
 13 keylime.pie
  1 testme
  1 temp/
```

That's a powerful and complex UNIX command, yet it is composed of simple and
easy-to-understand components.

SUMMARY Like many of the filters, sort isn't too exciting by itself. As you explore UNIX further
and learn more about how to combine these simple commands to build sophisticated
instructions, you will begin to see their true value.

Task 8.5: Number Lines in Files Using cat -n and nl

DESCRIPTION It often can be helpful to have a line number listed next to each line of a file. It's quite
simple to do with the cat program by specifying the -n flag to number lines in the
file displayed.

On many UNIX systems, there's a considerably better command for numbering lines in a file
and for many other tasks. The command nl, for number lines, is an AT&T System V command. A system that doesn't have the nl command will complain nl: command not found.
If you have this result, experiment with cat -n instead.

Step 2. Action

1. Because one of my own systems did not have the nl command, I moved to one that
had the nl command for this example. I quickly rebuilt the testme file:

```
% ls -l > testme
```

To see line numbers now, cat -n will work fine:

```
% cat -n testme
     1  total 60
     2  -rw-r--r--  1 taylor    1861 Jun  2  1992 Global.Software
     3  -rw-------  1 taylor   22194 Oct  1  1992 Interactive.Unix
     4  drwx------  4 taylor    4096 Nov 13 11:09 Mail/
     5  drwxr-xr-x  2 taylor    4096 Nov 13 11:09 News/
     6  drwxr-xr-x  2 taylor    4096 Nov 13 11:09 Src/
     7  drwxr-xr-x  2 taylor    4096 Nov 13 11:09 bin/
     8  -rw-r--r--  1 taylor   12445 Sep 17 14:56 history.usenet.Z
     9  -rw-r--r--  1 taylor       0 Nov 20 18:16 testme
```

2. The alternative, which does exactly the same thing here, is to try nl without any flags:

```
% nl testme
     1  total 60
     2  -rw-r--r--  1 taylor    1861 Jun  2  1992 Global.Software
     3  -rw-------  1 taylor   22194 Oct  1  1992 Interactive.Unix
     4  drwx------  4 taylor    4096 Nov 13 11:09 Mail/
     5  drwxr-xr-x  2 taylor    4096 Nov 13 11:09 News/
     6  drwxr-xr-x  2 taylor    4096 Nov 13 11:09 Src/
     7  drwxr-xr-x  2 taylor    4096 Nov 13 11:09 bin/
     8  -rw-r--r--  1 taylor   12445 Sep 17 14:56 history.usenet.Z
     9  -rw-r--r--  1 taylor       0 Nov 20 18:16 testme
```

3. Notice that both commands also can number lines fed to them via a command pipeline:

```
% ls -CF | cat -n
     1  Global.Software    News/       history.usenet.Z
     2  Interactive.Unix   Src/        testme
     3  Mail/              bin/        % ls -CF | nl
     1  Global.Software    News/       history.usenet.Z
     2  Interactive.Unix   Src/        testme
     3  Mail/              bin/
```

SUMMARY Like many other UNIX tools, nl and its doppelganger cat -n aren't very thrilling by themselves. As additional members in the set of powerful UNIX tools, however, they can prove tremendously helpful in certain situations. As you soon will see, nl also has some powerful options that can make it a bit more fun.

Task 8.6: Cool nl Tricks and Capabilities

DESCRIPTION A program that prefaces each line with a line number isn't much of an addition to the UNIX command toolbox, so the person who wrote the nl program added some further capabilities. With different command flags, nl can either number all lines (by default it numbers only lines that are not blank) or skip line numbering (which means it's an additional way to display the contents of a file). The best option, though, is that nl can selectively number just those lines that contain a specified pattern.

8

JUST A MINUTE

If you don't have the nl command on your system, I'm afraid you're out of luck in this section. Later in the book, you learn other ways to accomplish these tasks. For now, though, if you don't have nl, skip to the next hour and start to learn about the grep command.

The command flag format for nl is a bit more esoteric than you've seen up to this point. The different approaches to numbering lines with nl are all modifications of the -b flag (for body numbering options). The four flags are -ba, which numbers all lines; -bt, which numbers printable text only; -bn, which results in no numbering; and -bp *pattern*, for numbering lines that contain the specified pattern.

One final option is to insert a different separator between the line number and the line by telling nl to use -s, the separator flag.

ACTION

1. To begin, I'll use a command that you haven't seen before to add a few blank lines to the testme file. The echo command simply writes back to the screen anything specified. Try echo hello.

```
% rm testme
% ls -CF > testme
% echo "" >> testme
% echo "" >> testme
% ls -CF >> testme
% cat testme
Global.Software        News/              history.usenet.Z
Interactive.Unix       Src/               testme
Mail/                  bin/


Global.Software        News/              history.usenet.Z
Interactive.Unix       Src/               testme
Mail/                  bin/
```

JUST A MINUTE

Parts of UNIX are rather poorly designed, as you have already learned. For example, if you use the echo command without arguments, you get no output. However, if you add an empty argument (a set of quotation marks with nothing between them), echo outputs a blank line. It doesn't make much sense, but it works.

2. Now watch what happens when nl uses its default settings to number the lines in testme:

```
% nl testme
     1  Global.Software     News/              history.usenet.Z
     2  Interactive.Unix    Src/               testme
     3  Mail/               bin/


     4  Global.Software     News/              history.usenet.Z
     5  Interactive.Unix    Src/               testme
     6  Mail/               bin/
```

You can accomplish the same thing by specifying nl -bt testme. Try this to verify that your system gives the same results.

3. It's time to use one of the new two-letter command options to number the lines, including the blank lines:

```
% nl -ba testme
     1  Global.Software     News/              history.usenet.Z
     2  Interactive.Unix    Src/               testme
     3  Mail/               bin/
     4
     5
     6  Global.Software     News/              history.usenet.Z
     7  Interactive.Unix    Src/               testme
     8  Mail/               bin/
```

4. If you glance at the contents of my testme file, you can see that two lines contain the word history. To have nl number just those lines, try the -bp pattern-matching option:

```
% nl -bphistory testme
     1  Global.Software     News/              history.usenet.Z
        Interactive.Unix Src/                  testme
        Mail/               bin/


     2  Global.Software     News/              history.usenet.Z
        Interactive.Unix Src/                  testme
        Mail/               bin/
```

Notice that numbering the two lines has caused the rest of the lines to fall out of alignment on the display.

5. This is when the -s, or separator, option comes in handy:

```
% nl -bphistory -s: testme
     1:Global.Software     News/              history.usenet.Z
        Interactive.Unix Src/                  testme
        Mail/               bin/


     2:Global.Software     News/              history.usenet.Z
        Interactive.Unix Src/                  testme
        Mail/               bin/
```

In this case, I specified that instead of using a tab, which is the default separator between the number and line, nl should use a colon. As you can see, the output now lines up again.

Just about anything can be specified as the separator, as sensible or weird as it might be:

```
% nl -s', line is: ' testme
     1, line is: Global.Software          News/
history.
usenet.Z
     2, line is: Interactive.Unix     Src/               testme
     3, line is: Mail/                bin/


     4, line is: Global.Software          News/
history.
usenet.Z
     5, line is: Interactive.Unix     Src/               testme
     6, line is: Mail/                bin/
```

Notice the use of single quotation marks (') in this example. I want to include spaces as part of my pattern, so I need to ensure that the program knows this. If I didn't use the quotation marks, nl would use a comma as the separator and then tell me that it couldn't open a file called line or is:.

SUMMARY The nl command demonstrates that there are plenty of variations on simple commands. When you read earlier that you would learn how to number lines in a file, did you think that this many subtleties were involved?

Summary

You have learned quite a bit in this hour and are continuing down the road to UNIX expertise. You learned about file redirection. You can't go wrong by spending time studying these closely. The concept of using filters and building complex commands by combining simple commands with pipes has been more fully demonstrated here, too. This higher level of UNIX command language is what makes UNIX so powerful and easy to mold.

This hour hasn't skimped on commands, either. It introduced wc for counting lines, words, and characters in a file (or more than one file: try wc * in your home directory). You also learned to use the uniq, sort, and spell commands. You learned about using nl for numbering lines in a file—in a variety of ways—and cat -n as an alternative "poor person's" line-numbering strategy. You also were introduced to the echo command.

By the way, the echo command also can tell you about specific environment variables, just like env or printenv do. Try echo $HOME or echo $PATH to see what happens, and compare the output with env HOME and env PATH.

Workshop

The Workshop summarizes the key terms you learned and poses some questions about the topics presented in this chapter. It also provides you with a preview of what you will learn in the next hour.

Key Terms

file redirection   Most UNIX programs expect to read their input from the user (that is, standard input) and write their output to the screen (standard output). By use of file redirection, however, input can come from a previously created file, and output can be saved to a file instead of being displayed on the screen.

filter   Filters are a particular type of UNIX program that expects to work either with file redirection or as part of a pipeline. These programs read input from standard input, write output to standard output, and often don't have any starting arguments.

standard input   UNIX programs always default to reading information from the user by reading the keyboard and watching what's typed. With file redirection, input can come from a file, and with pipelines, input can be the result of a previous UNIX command.

standard error   This is the same as standard output, but you can redirect standard error to a different location than standard output.

standard output   When processing information, UNIX programs default to displaying the output on the screen itself, also known as standard output. With file redirection, output can easily be saved to a file; with pipelines, output can be sent to other programs.

Questions

1. The placement of file-redirection characters is important to ensure that the command works correctly. Which of the following six commands do you think will work, and why?

   ```
   < file wc                wc file <                wc < file
   cat file ¦ wc            cat < file ¦ wc          wc ¦ cat
   ```

   Now try them and see if you're correct.

2. The wc command can be used for lots of different tasks. Try to imagine a few that would be interesting and helpful to learn (for example, how many users are on the system right now?). Try them on your system.

3. Does the file size listed by wc -c always agree with the file size listed by the ls command? With the size indicated by ls -s? If there is any difference, why?

4. What do you think would happen if you tried to sort a list of words by pretending they're all numbers? Try it with the command `ls -1 | sort -n` to see what happens. Experiment with the variations.

5. Do you spell your filenames correctly? Use `spell` to find out.

Preview of the Next Hour

The next hour introduces wildcards and regular expressions, and tools to use those powerful concepts. You learn how these commands can help you extract data from even the most unwieldy files.

You learn one of the secret UNIX commands for those really in the know, the secret-society, pattern-matching program `grep`. Better yet, you learn how it got its weird and confusing name! You also learn about the `tee` command and the curious-but-helpful << file-redirection command.

Hour 9

Wildcards and Regular Expressions

One of the trickiest aspects of UNIX is the concept of wildcards and regular expressions. Wildcards are a tool that allows you to "guess" at a filename, or to specify a group of filenames easily. Regular expressions are pattern-matching tools that are different, and more powerful, than wildcards.

You'll meet two new commands, sed and grep, that use regular expressions.

Goals for This Hour

In this hour, you learn about

- ☐ Filename wildcards
- ☐ Advanced wildcards
- ☐ Regular expressions
- ☐ Searching files using grep
- ☐ A more powerful grep
- ☐ A fast grep
- ☐ Using the stream editor sed to change output on-the-fly

This hour begins by looking at the two pattern-matching tools frequently found in UNIX. A foray into commands that use these tools immediately follows.

Task 9.1: Filename Wildcards

DESCRIPTION By now you are doubtless tired of typing every letter of each filename into your system for each example. There is a better and easier way! Just as the special card in poker can have any value, UNIX has special characters that the various shells (the command-line interpreter programs) all interpret as *wildcards*. This allows for much easier typing of patterns.

There are two wildcards to learn here: * acts as a match for any number and sequence of characters, and ? acts as a match for any single character. In the broadest sense, a lone * acts as a match for all files in the current directory (in other words, ls * is identical to ls), whereas a single ? acts as a match for all one-character-long filenames in a directory (for instance, ls ?, which will list only those filenames that are one character long). The following examples will make this clear.

ACTION

1. Start by using ls to list your home directory.

```
% ls -CF
Archives/              OWL/                    keylime.pie
InfoWorld/             bin/                    src/
Mail/                  bitnet.mailing-lists.Z  temp/
News/                  drop.text.hqx           testme
```

2. To experiment with wildcards, it's easiest to use the echo command. If you recall, echo repeats anything given to it, but—and here's the secret to its value—the shell interprets anything that is entered before the shell lets echo see it. That is, the * is expanded before the shell hands the arguments over the command.

```
% echo *
Archives InfoWorld Mail News OWL bin bitnet.mailing-lists.Z
drop.text.hqx keylime.pie src temp testme
```

Using the * wildcard enables me to reference easily all files in the directory. This is quite helpful.

3. A wildcard is even more helpful than the example suggests because it can be embedded in the middle of a word or otherwise used to limit the number of matches. To see all files that began with the letter t, use the *:

```
% echo t*
temp testme
Try echo b* to see all your files that start with the letter b.
```

9

4. Variations are possible, too. I could use wildcards to list all files or directories that end with the letter s:

```
% echo *s
Archives News
```

Watch what happens if I try the same command using the ls command rather than the echo command:

```
% ls -CF *s
Archives:
Interleaf.story    Tartan.story.Z        nextstep.txt.Z
Opus.story         interactive.txt.Z     rae.assist.infoworld.Z

News:
mailing.lists.usenet  usenet.1            usenet.alt
```

Using the ls command here makes UNIX think I want it to list two directories, not just the names of the two files. This is where the -d flag to ls could prove helpful to force a listing of the directories rather than of their contents.

5. Notice that, in the News directory, I have three files with the word usenet somewhere in their names. The wildcard pattern usenet* would match two of them, and *usenet would match one. A valuable aspect of the * wildcard is that it can match zero or more characters, so the pattern *usenet* will match all three.

```
% echo News/*usenet*
News/mailing.lists.usenet News/usenet.1 News/usenet.alt
```

Also notice that wildcards can be embedded in a filename or pathname. In this example, I specified that I was interested in files in the News directory.

6. Could you match a single character? To see how this can be helpful, it's time to move into a different directory, OWL on my system.

```
% cd OWL
% ls -CF
Student.config   owl.c        owl.o
WordMap/         owl.data     simple.editor.c
owl*             owl.h        simple.editor.o
```

If I request owl*, which files will be listed?

```
% echo owl*
owl owl.c owl.data owl.h owl.o
```

What do I do if I am interested only in the source, header, and object files, which are here indicated by a .c, .h, or .o suffix. Using a wildcard that matches zero or more letters won't work; I don't want to see owl or owl.data. One possibility would be to use the pattern owl.* (by adding the period, I can eliminate the owl file itself). What I really want, however, is to be able to specify all files that start with the four characters owl. and have exactly one more character. This is a situation in which the ? wildcard works:

```
% echo owl.?
owl.c owl.h owl.o
```

Because no files have exactly one letter following the three letters owl, watch what happens when I specify owl? as the pattern:

```
% echo owl?
echo: No match.
```

This leads to a general observation. If you want to have echo return a question to you, you have to do it carefully because the shell interprets the question mark as a wildcard:

```
% echo are you listening?
echo: No match.
```

To accomplish this, you simply need to surround the entire question with quotation marks:

```
% echo 'are you listening?'
are you listening?
```

SUMMARY It won't surprise you that there are more complex ways of using wildcards to build filename patterns. What likely will surprise you is that the vast majority of UNIX users don't even know about the * and ? wildcards! This knowledge gives you a definite advantage.

Task 9.2: Advanced Filename Wildcards

DESCRIPTION Earlier, you learned about two special wildcard characters that can help you when specifying files for commands in UNIX. The first was the ?, which matches any single character, and the other was the *, which matches zero or more characters. There are more special wildcards for the shell when specifying filenames, and it's time to learn about another of them.

This new notation is known as a *character range*, serving as a wildcard less general than the question mark.

ACTION

1. A pair of square brackets denotes a range of characters, which can be either explicitly listed or indicated as a range with a dash between them. I'll start with a list of files in my current directory:

```
% ls
Archives/     News/        bigfiles     owl.c        src/
InfoWorld/    OWL/         bin/         sample       temp/
Mail/         awkscript    keylime.pie  sample2      tetme
```

9

If I want to see both `bigfiles` and the `bin` directory, I can use b* as a file pattern:

```
% ls -ld b*
-rw-rw----   1 taylor            165 Dec  3 16:42 bigfiles
drwx------   2 taylor            512 Oct 13 10:45 bin/
```

If I want to see all entries that start with a lowercase letter, I can explicitly type each
one:

```
% ls -ld a* b* k* o* s* t*
-rw-rw----   1 taylor            126 Dec  3 16:34 awkscript
-rw-rw----   1 taylor            165 Dec  3 16:42 bigfiles
drwx------   2 taylor            512 Oct 13 10:45 bin/
-rw-rw----   1 taylor          12556 Nov 16 09:49 keylime.pie
-rw-rw----   1 taylor           8729 Dec  2 21:19 owl.c
-rw-rw----   1 taylor            199 Dec  3 16:11 sample
-rw-rw----   1 taylor            207 Dec  3 16:11 sample2
drwx------   2 taylor            512 Oct 13 10:45 src/
drwxrwx---   2 taylor            512 Nov  8 22:20 temp/
-rw-rw----   1 taylor            582 Nov 27 18:29 tetme
```

That's clearly quite awkward. Instead, I can specify a range of characters to match.
I specify the range by listing them all tucked neatly into a pair of square brackets:

```
% ls -ld [abkost]*
-rw-rw----   1 taylor            126 Dec  3 16:34 awkscript
-rw-rw----   1 taylor            165 Dec  3 16:42 bigfiles
drwx------   2 taylor            512 Oct 13 10:45 bin/
-rw-rw----   1 taylor          12556 Nov 16 09:49 keylime.pie
-rw-rw----   1 taylor           8729 Dec  2 21:19 owl.c
-rw-rw----   1 taylor            199 Dec  3 16:11 sample
-rw-rw----   1 taylor            207 Dec  3 16:11 sample2
drwx------   2 taylor            512 Oct 13 10:45 src/
drwxrwx---   2 taylor            512 Nov  8 22:20 temp/
-rw-rw----   1 taylor            582 Nov 27 18:29 tetme
```

In this case, the shell matches all files that start with an a, b, k, o, s, or t. This
notation is still a bit clunky and would be more so if there were more files involved.

2. The ideal is to specify a range of characters by using the hyphen character in the
middle of a range:

```
% ls -ld [a-z]*
-rw-rw----   1 taylor            126 Dec  3 16:34 awkscript
-rw-rw----   1 taylor            165 Dec  3 16:42 bigfiles
drwx------   2 taylor            512 Oct 13 10:45 bin/
-rw-rw----   1 taylor          12556 Nov 16 09:49 keylime.pie
-rw-rw----   1 taylor           8729 Dec  2 21:19 owl.c
-rw-rw----   1 taylor            199 Dec  3 16:11 sample
-rw-rw----   1 taylor            207 Dec  3 16:11 sample2
drwx------   2 taylor            512 Oct 13 10:45 src/
drwxrwx---   2 taylor            512 Nov  8 22:20 temp/
-rw-rw----   1 taylor            582 Nov 27 18:29 tetme
```

In this example, the shell will match any file that begins with a lowercase letter,
ranging from a to z, as specified.

3. Space is critical in all wildcard patterns, too. Watch what happens if I accidentally add a space between the closing bracket of the range specification and the asterisk following:

```
% ls -CFd [a-z] *
Archives/     News/         bigfiles      owl.c         src/
InfoWorld/    OWL/          bin/          sample        temp/
Mail/         awkscript     keylime.pie   sample2       tetme
```

This time, the shell tried to match all files whose names were one character long and lowercase, and then it tried to match all files that matched the asterisk wildcard, which, of course, is all regular files in the directory.

4. The combination of character ranges, single-character wildcards, and multi-character wildcards can be tremendously helpful. If I move to another directory, I can easily search for all files that contain a single digit, dot, or underscore in the name:

```
% cd Mail
% ls -CF
71075.446       emilyc          mailbox          sartin
72303.2166      gordon_hat      manley           sent
bmcinern        harrism         mark             shalini
bob_gull        j=taylor        marmi            siob_n
cennamo         james           marv             steve
dan_some        jeffv           matt_ruby        tai
dataylor        john_welch      mcwillia         taylor
decc            john_prage      netnews.postings v892127
disserli        kcs             raf              wcenter
druby           lehman          rexb             windows
dunlaplm        lenz            rock             xd1f
ean_huts        mac             rustle

% ls *[0-9._]*
71075.446       ean_huts        matt_ruby        xd1f
72303.2166      gordon_hat      netnews.postings
bob_gull        john_welcher    siob_n
dan_some        john_prage      v892127
```

SUMMARY I think that the best way to learn about pervasive features of UNIX such as shell filename wildcards is just to use them. If you flip through this book, you immediately notice that the examples are building on earlier information. This will continue to be the case, and the filename range notation shown here will be used again and again, in combination with the asterisk and question mark, to specify groups of files or directories.

Remember that, if you want to experiment with filename wildcards, you can most easily use the echo command because it dutifully prints the expanded version of any pattern you specify.

Task 9.3: Creating Sophisticated Regular Expressions

DESCRIPTION A regular expression can be as simple as a word to be matched letter for letter, such as *acme*, or as complex as the example in the printers script, `'(^[a-zA-Z]|:wi)'`, which matches all lines that begin with an upper- or lowercase letter or that contain `:wi`.

The language of *regular expressions* is full of punctuation characters and other letters used in unusual ways. It is important to remember that regular expressions are different from shell wildcard patterns. It's unfortunate, but it's true. In the C shell, for example, a* lists any file that starts with the letter a. Regular expressions aren't *left rooted*, which means that you need to specify ^a if you want to match only lines that begin with the letter a. The shell pattern a* matches only filenames that start with the letter a, and the * has a different interpretation completely when used as part of a regular expression: a* is a pattern that matches zero or more occurrences of the letter a. The notation for regular expressions is shown in Table 9.1. The egrep command has additional notation that you will learn shortly.

Table 9.1. Summary of regular-expression notation.

Notation	Meaning
c	Matches the character c
\c	Forces c to be read as the letter *c*, not as another meaning the character might have
^	Beginning of the line
$	End of the line
.	Any single character
[xy]	Any single character in the set specified
[^xy]	Any single character not in the set specified
c*	Zero or more occurrences of character c

The notation isn't as complex as it looks in this table. The most important things to remember about regular expressions are that the * denotes zero or more occurrences of the previous character, and . is any single character. Remember that shell patterns use * to match any set of zero or more characters independent of the previous character, and ? to match a single character.

ACTION

1. The easy searches with `grep` are those that search for specific words without any special regular expression notation:

```
% grep taylor /etc/passwd
taylorj:?:1048:1375:James Taylor:/users/taylorj:/bin/csh
mtaylor:?:769:1375:Mary Taylor:/users/mtaylor:/usr/local/bin/tcsh
dataylor:?:375:518:Dave Taylor:/users/dataylor:/usr/local/lib/msh
taylorjr:?:203:1022:James Taylor:/users/taylorjr:/bin/csh
taylorrj:?:662:1042:Robert Taylor:/users/taylorrj:/bin/csh
taylorm:?:869:1508:Melanie Taylor:/users/taylorm:/bin/csh
taylor:?:1989:1412:Dave Taylor:/users/taylor:/bin/csh
```

   I searched for all entries in the `passwd` file that contain the pattern `taylor`.

2. I've found more matches than I wanted, though. If I'm looking for my own account, I don't want to see all these alternatives. Using the `^` character before the pattern left-roots the pattern:

```
% grep "^taylor" /etc/passwd
taylorj:?:1048:1375:James Taylor:/users/taylorj:/bin/csh
taylorjr:?:203:1022:James Taylor:/users/taylorjr:/bin/csh
taylorrj:?:662:1042:Robert Taylor:/users/taylorrj:/bin/csh
taylorm:?:869:1508:Melanie Taylor:/users/taylorm:/bin/csh
taylor:?:1989:1412:Dave Taylor:/users/taylor:/bin/cshx
```

   Now I want to narrow the search further. I want to specify a pattern that says "show me all lines that start with `taylor`, followed by a character that is not a lowercase letter."

3. To accomplish this, I use the `[^xy]` notation, which indicates an *exclusion set*, or set of characters that cannot match the pattern:

```
% grep "^taylor[^a-z]" /etc/passwd
taylor:?:1989:1412:Dave Taylor:/users/taylor:/bin/csh
```

   It worked! You can specify a set two ways: You can either list each character or use a hyphen to specify a range starting with the character to the left of the hyphen and ending with the character to the right of the hyphen. That is, `a-z` is the range beginning with a and ending with z, and `0-9` includes all digits.

4. To see which accounts were excluded, remove the `^` to search for an *inclusion range*, which is a set of characters of which one must match the pattern:

```
% grep '^taylor[a-z]' /etc/passwd
taylorj:?:1048:1375:James Taylor:/users/taylorj:/bin/csh
taylorjr:?:203:1022:James Taylor:/users/taylorjr:/bin/csh
taylorrj:?:668:1042:Robert Taylor:/users/taylorrj:/bin/csh
taylormx:?:869:1508:Melanie Taylor:/users/taylorm:/bin/csh
```

9

5. To see some other examples, I use head to view the first 10 lines of the password file:

```
% head /etc/passwd
root:?:0:0:root:/:/bin/csh
news:?:6:11:USENET News:/usr/spool/news:/bin/ksh
ingres:*?:7:519:INGRES Manager:/usr/ingres:/bin/csh
usrlimit:?:8:800:(1000 user system):/mnt:/bin/false
vanilla:*?:20:805:Vanilla Account:/mnt:/bin/sh
charon:*?:21:807:The Ferryman:/users/tomb:
actmaint:?:23:809:Maintenance:/usr/adm/actmaint:/bin/ksh
pop:*?:26:819::/usr/spool/pop:/bin/csh
lp:*?:70:10:Lp Admin:/usr/spool/lp:
trouble:*?:97:501:Report Facility:/usr/mrg/trouble:/usr/local/lib/msh
```

Now I'll specify a pattern that tells grep to search for all lines that contain zero or more occurrences of the letter z.

```
% grep 'z*' /etc/passwd ¦ head
root:?:0:0:root:/:/bin/csh
news:?:6:11:USENET News:/usr/spool/news:/bin/ksh
ingres:*?:7:519:INGRES Manager:/usr/ingres:/bin/csh
usrlimit:?:8:800:(1000 user system):/mnt:/bin/false
vanilla:*?:20:805:Vanilla Account:/mnt:/bin/sh
charon:*?:21:807:The Ferryman:/users/tomb:
actmaint:?:23:809:Maintenance:/usr/adm/actmaint:/bin/ksh
pop:*?:26:819::/usr/spool/pop:/bin/csh
lp:*?:70:10:Lp Adminuniverse(att):/usr/spool/lp:
trouble:*?:97:501:Report Facility:/usr/mrg/trouble:/usr/local/lib/msh
Broken pipe
```

The result is identical to the previous command, but it shouldn't be a surprise. Specifying a pattern that matches zero or more occurrences will match every line! Specifying only the lines that have one or more z's produces output that is a bit more odd looking:

```
% grep 'zz*' /etc/passwd ¦ head
marg:?:724:1233:Guyzee:/users/marg:/bin/ksh
axy:?:1272:1233:martinez:/users/axy:/bin/csh
wizard:?:1560:1375:Oz:/users/wizard:/bin/ksh
zhq:?:2377:1318:Zihong:/users/zhq:/bin/csh
mm:?:7152:1233:Michael Kenzie:/users/mm:/bin/ksh
tanzm:?:7368:1140:Zhen Tan:/users/tanzm:/bin/csh
mendozad:?:8176:1233:Don Mendoza:/users/mendozad:/bin/csh
pavz:?:8481:1175:Mary L. Pavzky:/users/pavz:/bin/csh
hurlz:?:9189:1375:Tom Hurley:/users/hurlz:/bin/csh
tulip:?:9222:1375:Liz Richards:/users/tulip:/bin/csh
Broken pipe
```

6. Earlier I found that a couple lines in the /etc/passwd file were for accounts that didn't specify a login shell. Each line in the password file must have a certain number of colons, and the very last character on the line for these accounts will be a colon, an easy grep pattern:

```
% grep ':$' /etc/passwd
charon:*?:21:807:The Ferryman:/users/tomb:
lp:*?:70:10:System V Lp Adminuniverse(att):/usr/spool/lp:
```

7. Consider this. I get a call from my accountant, and I need to find a file containing a message about a $100 outlay of cash to buy some software. I can use grep to search for all files that contain a dollar sign, followed by a one, followed by one or more zeroes:

```
% grep '$100*' * */*
Mail/bob_gale:      Unfortunately, our fees are currently $100 per test
➥drive, budgets
Mail/dan_sommer:We also pay $100 for Test Drives, our very short "First
➥Looks" section. We often
Mail/james:has been dropped, so if I ask for $1000 is that way outta
➥line
Mail/john_spragens:time testing things since it's a $100 test drive: I'm
➥willing to
Mail/john_spragens:      Finally, I'd like to request $200 rather than
➥$100 for
Mail/mac:again: expected pricing will be $10,000 - $16,000 and the
➥BriteLite LX with
Mail/mark:I'm promised $1000 / month for a first
Mail/netnews.postings:  Win Lose or Die, John Gardner (hardback) $10
Mail/netnews.postings:I'd be willing to pay, I dunno, $100 / year for
➥the space? I would
Mail/sent:to panic that they'd want their $10K advance back, but the
➥good news is
Mail/sent:That would be fine.  How about $100 USD for both, to include
➥any
Mail/sent:        Amount: $100.00
```

That's quite a few matches. Notice that among the matches are $1000, $10K, and $10. To match the specific value $100, of course, I can use $100 as the search pattern.

TIME SAVER

> You can use the shell to expand files not just in the current directory, but one level deeper into subdirectories, too: * expands your search beyond files in the current directory, and */* expands your search to all files contained one directory below the current point. If you have lots of files, you might instead see the error arg list too long; that's where the find command proves handy.

This pattern demonstrates the sophistication of UNIX with regular expressions. For example, the $ character is a special character that can be used to indicate the end of a line, but only if it is placed at the very end of the pattern. Because I did not place it at the end of the pattern, the grep program reads it as the $ character itself.

8. Here's one more example. In the old days, when people were tied to typewriters, an accepted convention for writing required that you put two spaces after the period at the end of a sentence even though only one space followed the period of an

abbreviation such as J. D. Salinger. Nowadays, with more text being produced through word processing and desktop publishing, the two-space convention is less accepted, and indeed, when submitting work for publication, I often have to be sure that I don't have two spaces after punctuation lest I get yelled at! The grep command can help ferret out these inappropriate punctuation sequences, fortunately; but the pattern needed is tricky.

To start, I want to see if, anywhere in the file dickens.note, I have used a period followed by a single space:

```
% grep '. ' dickens.note
                         A Tale of Two Cities
                              Preface
When I was acting, with my children and friends, in Mr Wilkie Collins's
drama of The Frozen Deep, I first conceived the main idea of this
story.  A strong desire came upon me then, to
embody it in my own person;
and I traced out in my fancy, the state of mind of which it would
necessitate the presentation
to an observant spectator, with particular
care and interest.
As the idea became familiar to me, it gradually shaped itself into its
present form.  Throughout its execution, it has had complete possession
of me; I have so far verified what
is done and suffered in these pages,
as that I have certainly done and suffered it all myself.
Whenever any reference (however slight) is made here to the condition
of the Danish people before or during the Revolution, it is truly made,
on the faith of the most trustworthy
witnesses.  It has been one of my hopes to add
something to the popular and picturesque means of
understanding that terrible time, though no one can hope
to add anything to the philosophy of Mr Carlyle's wonderful book.
Tavistock House
November 1859
```

What's happening here? The first line doesn't have a period in it, so why does grep say it matches the pattern? In grep, the period is a special character that matches any single character, not specifically the period itself. Therefore, my pattern matches any line that contains a space preceded by any character.

To avoid this interpretation, I must preface the special character with a backslash (\) if I want it to be read as the . character itself:

```
% grep '\. ' dickens.note
story.  A strong desire came upon me then, to
present form.  Throughout its execution, it has had complete posession
witnesses.  It has been one of my hopes to add
```

Ahhh, that's better. Notice that all three of these lines have two spaces after each period.

SUMMARY With the relatively small number of notations available in regular expressions, you can create quite a variety of sophisticated patterns to find information in a file.

Task 9.4: Searching Files Using grep

DESCRIPTION Two commonly used commands are the key to you becoming a power user and becoming comfortable with the capabilities of the system. The ls command is one example, and the grep command is another. The oddly named grep command makes it easy to find lost files or to find files that contain specific text.

JUST A MINUTE

> After laborious research and countless hours debating with UNIX developers, I am reasonably certain that the derivation of the name grep is as follows: Before this command existed, UNIX users would use a crude line-based editor called ed to find matching text. As you know, search patterns in UNIX are called regular expressions. To search throughout a file, the user prefixed the command with global. Once a match was made, the user wanted to have it either listed to the screen with print. To put it all together, the operation was global/*regular expression*/print. That phrase was pretty long, however, so users shortened it to g/re/p. Thereafter, when a command was written, grep seemed to be a natural, if odd and confusing, name.

The grep command not only has a ton of different command options, but it has two variations in UNIX systems, too. These variations are egrep, for specifying more complex patterns (regular expressions), and fgrep, for using file-based lists of words as search patterns.

You could spend the next 100 pages learning all the obscure and weird options to the grep family of commands. When you boil it down, however, you're probably going to use only the simplest patterns and maybe a useful flag or two. Think of it this way: Just because there are more than 500,000 words in the English language (according to the Oxford English Dictionary) doesn't mean that you must learn them all to communicate effectively.

With this in mind, youl learn the basics of grep this hour, but you'll pick up more insight into the program's capabilities and options during the next few hours.

A few of the most important grep command flags are listed in Table 9.2.

Table 9.2. The most helpful grep flags.

Flag	Function
-c	List a count of matching lines only.
-i	Ignore the case of the letters in the pattern.
-l	List filenames of files that match the specified *pattern* only.
-n	Include line numbers.

ACTION

1. Begin by making sure you have a test file to work with. The example shows the `testme` file from the previous `uniq` examples:

```
% cat testme
Archives/              OWL/                    keylime.pie
InfoWorld/             bin/                    src/
Mail/                  bitnet.mailing-lists.Z  temp/
News/                  drop.text.hqx           testme
```

2. The general form of `grep` is to specify the command, any flags you want to add, the pattern, and a filename:

```
% grep bitnet testme
Mail/                  bitnet.mailing-lists.Z  temp/
```

As you can see, `grep` easily pulled out the line in the `testme` file that contained the pattern `bitnet`.

3. Be aware that `grep` finds patterns in a case-sensitive manner:

```
% grep owl testme
%
```

Note that `OWL` was not found because the pattern specified with the `grep` command was all lowercase, `owl`.

But that's where the `-i` flag can be helpful, which causes `grep` to ignore case:

```
% grep -i owl testme
Archives/              OWL/                    keylime.pie
```

4. For the next few examples, I'll move into the `/etc` directory because some files therein there have lots of lines. The `wc` command shows that the file `/etc/passwd` has almost 4,000 lines:

```
% cd /etc
% wc -l /etc/passwd
   3877
```

My account is `taylor`. I'll use `grep` to see my account entry in the password file:

```
% grep taylor /etc/passwd
taylorj:?:1048:1375:James Taylor:/users/taylorj:/bin/csh
mtaylor:?:760:1375:Mary Taylor:/users/mtaylor:/usr/local/bin/tcsh
dataylor:?:375:518:Dave Taylor:/users/dataylor:/usr/local/lib/msh
taylorjr:?:203:1022:James Taylor:/users/taylorjr:/bin/csh
taylorrj:?:668:1042:Robert Taylor:/users/taylorrj:/bin/csh
taylorm:?:862:1508:Melanie Taylor:/users/taylormx:/bin/csh
taylor:?:1989:1412:Dave Taylor:/users/taylor:/bin/csh
```

Try this on your system, too.

9

5. As you can see, many accounts contain the pattern `taylor`.

A smarter way to see how often the `taylor` pattern appears is to use the `-c` flag to `grep`, which will indicate how many case-sensitive matches are in the file before any of them are displayed on the screen:

```
% grep -c taylor /etc/passwd
7
```

The command located seven matches. Count the listing in instruction 4 to confirm this.

6. With 3,877 lines in the `password` file, it could be interesting to see if all the `Taylors` started their accounts at about the same time. (This presumably would mean they all appear in the file at about the same point.) To do this, I'll use the `-n` flag to number the output lines:

```
% grep -n taylor /etc/passwd
319:taylorj:?:1048:1375:James Taylor:/users/taylorj:/bin/csh
1314:mtaylor:?:760:1375:Mary Taylor:/users/mtaylor:/usr/local/bin/tcsh
1419:dataylor:?:375:518:Dave Taylor:/users/dataylor:/usr/local/lib/msh
1547:taylorjr:?:203:1022:James Taylor:/users/taylorjr:/bin/csh
1988:taylorrj:?:668:1042:Robert Taylor:/users/taylorrj:/bin/csh
2133:taylorm:?:8692:1508:Melanie Taylor:/users/taylorm:/bin/csh
3405:taylor:?:1989:1412:Dave Taylor:/users/taylor:/bin/csh
```

This is a great example of a default separator adding incredible confusion to the output of a command. Normally, a line number followed by a colon would be no problem, but in the `passwd` file (which is already littered with colons), it's confusing. Compare this output with the output obtained in instruction 4 with the `grep` command alone to see what's changed.

You can see that my theory about when the Taylors started their accounts was wrong. If proximity in the `passwd` file is an indicator that accounts are assigned at similar times, then no Taylors started their accounts even within the same week.

SUMMARY These examples of how to use `grep` barely scratch the surface of how this powerful and sophisticated command can be used. Explore your own file system using `grep` to search files for specific patterns.

JUST A MINUTE

Armed with wildcards, you now can try the `-l` flag to `grep`, which, as you recall, indicates the names of the files that contain a specified pattern, rather than printing the lines that match the pattern. If I go into my electronic mail archive directory—`Mail`—I can easily, using the command `grep -l -i chicago Mail/*`, search for all files that contain `Chicago`. Try using `grep -l` to search across all files in your home directory for words or patterns.

Task 9.5: For Complex Expressions, Try egrep

DESCRIPTION Sometimes a single regular expression can't locate what you seek. For example, perhaps you're looking for lines that have either one pattern or a second pattern. That's where the egrep command proves helpful. The command gets its name from "expression grep," and it has a notational scheme more powerful than that of grep, as shown in Table 9.3.

9

Table 9.3. Regular expression notation for egrep.

Notation	Meaning
c	Matches the character c
\c	Forces c to be read as the letter c, not as another meaning the character might have
^	Beginning of the line
$	End of the line
.	Any single character
[xy]	Any single character in the set specified
[^xy]	Any single character not in the set specified
c*	Zero or more occurrences of character c
c+	One or more occurrences of character c
c?	Zero or one occurrences of character c
a¦b	Either a or b
(a)	Regular expression

ACTION

1. Now I'll search the password file to demonstrate egrep. A pattern that seemed a bit weird was the one used with grep to search for lines containing one or more occurrences of the letter z: 'zz*'. With egrep, this search is much easier:

```
% egrep 'z+' /etc/passwd ¦ head
marg:?:724:1233:Guyzee:/users/marg:/bin/ksh
axy:?:1272:1233:martinez:/users/axy:/bin/csh
wizard:?:1560:1375:Oz:/users/wizard:/bin/ksh
zhq:?:2377:1318:Zihong:/users/zhq:/bin/csh
mm:?:7152:1233:Michael Kenzie:/users/mm:/bin/ksh
tanzm:?:7368:1140:Zhen Tan:/users/tanzm:/bin/csh
mendozad:?:8176:1233:Don Mendoza:/users/mendozad:/bin/csh
pavz:?:8481:1175:Mary L. Pavzky:/users/pavz:/bin/csh
hurlz:?:9189:1375:Tom Hurley:/users/hurlz:/bin/csh
tulip:?:9222:1375:Liz Richards:/users/tulip:/bin/csh
Broken pipe
```

2. To search for lines that have either a z or a q, I can use the following:

```
% egrep '(z¦q)' /etc/passwd ¦ head
aaq:?:528:1233:Don Kid:/users/aaq:/bin/csh
abq:?:560:1233:K Laws:/users/abq:/bin/csh
marg:?:724:1233:Guyzee:/users/marg:/bin/ksh
ahq:?:752:1233:Andy Smith:/users/ahq:/bin/csh
cq:?:843:1233:Rob Till:/users/cq:/usr/local/bin/tcsh
axy:?:1272:1233:Alan Yeltsin:/users/axy:/bin/csh
helenq:?:1489:1297:Helen Schoy:/users/helenq:/bin/csh
wizard:?:1560:1375:Oz:/users/wizard:/bin/ksh
qsc:?:1609:1375:Enid Grim:/users/qsc:/usr/local/bin/tcsh
zhq:?:2377:1318:Zong Qi:/users/zhq:/bin/csh
Broken pipe
```

3. Now I can visit a complicated `egrep` pattern, and it should make sense to you:

```
% egrep '(^[a-zA-Z]¦:wi)' /etc/printcap ¦ head
aglw:\
        :wi=AG 23:wk=multiple Apple LaserWriter IINT:
aglw1:\
        :wi=AG 23:wk=Apple LaserWriter IINT:
aglw2:\
        :wi=AG 23:wk=Apple LaserWriter IINT:
aglw3:\
        :wi=AG 23:wk=Apple LaserWriter IINT:
aglw4:\
        :wi=AG 23:wk=Apple LaserWriter IINT:
Broken pipe
```

Now you can see that the pattern specified looks either for lines that begin (^) with an upper- or lowercase letter (`[a-zA-Z]`) or for lines that contain the pattern `:wi`.

SUMMARY Any time you want to look for lines that contain more than a single pattern, `egrep` is the best command to use.

Task 9.6: Searching for Multiple Patterns at Once with `fgrep`

DESCRIPTION Sometimes it's helpful to look for many patterns at once. For example, you might want to have a file of patterns and invoke a UNIX command that searches for lines that contain any of the patterns in that file. That's where the `fgrep`, or file-based `grep`, command comes into play. A file of patterns can contain any pattern that `grep` would understand (which means, unfortunately, that you can't use the additional notation available in `egrep`) and is specified with the `-f file` option.

ACTION

1. I use `fgrep` with `wrongwords`, an alias and file that contains a list of words I commonly misuse. Here's how it works:

```
% alias wrongwords fgrep -i -f .wrongwords
% cat .wrongwords
effect
affect
insure
ensure
idea
thought
```

Any time I want to check a file, for example `dickens.note`, to see if it has any of these commonly misused words, I simply enter the following:

```
% wrongwords dickens.note
drama of The Frozen Deep, I first conceived the main idea of this
As the idea became familiar to me, it gradually shaped itself into its
```

I need to determine whether these are ideas or thoughts. It's a subtle distinction I often forget in my writing.

2. Here's another sample file that contains a couple words from `wrongwords`:

```
% cat sample3
At the time I was hoping to insure that the cold weather
would avoid our home, so I, perhaps foolishly, stapled the
weatherstripping along the inside of the sliding glass
door in the back room. I was surprised how much affect it
had on our enjoyment of the room, actually.
```

Can you see the two incorrectly used words in that sentence? The `spell` program can't:

```
% spell sample3
```

The `wrongwords` alias, on the other hand, can detect these words:

```
% wrongwords sample3
At the time I was hoping to insure that the cold weather
door in the back room. I was surprised how much affect it
```

3. This would be a bit more useful if it could show just the individual words matched, rather than the entire sentences. That way I wouldn't have to figure out which words are incorrect. To do this, I can use the `awk` command. It is a powerful command that uses regular expressions, which will be discussed in greater detail in the next chapter. This time the command will use a `for` loop, that is, will repeat the command starting from the initial state (`i=1`) and keep adding one to the counter (`i++`) until the end condition is met (`i>NF`): `'{for (i=1;i<=NF;i++) print $i}'`. Each line seen by `awk` will be printed one word at a time with this command. Remember that `NF` is the number of fields in the current line.

Here is a short example:

```
% echo 'this is a sample sentence' | awk '{for (i=1;i<=NF;i++) print $i}'
this
is
a
sample
sentence
```

4. I could revise my alias, but trying to get the quotation marks correct is a nightmare. It would be much easier to make this a simple shell script instead:

```
% cat bin/wrongwords
# wrongwords - show a list of commonly misused words in the file

cat $* | \
  awk '{for (i=1;i<=NF;i++) print $i}' |\
  fgrep -i -f .wrongwords
```

To make this work correctly, I need to remove the existing alias for wrongwords by using the C shell unalias command, add execute permission to the shell script, and then use rehash to ensure that the C shell can find the command when requested:

```
% unalias wrongwords
% chmod +x bin/wrongwords
% rehash
```

Now it's ready to use:

```
% wrongwords sample3
insure
affect
```

5. The fgrep command also can exclude words from a list. If you have been using the spell command, it's quickly clear that the program doesn't know anything about acronyms or some other correctly spelled words that you might use in your writing. That's where fgrep can be a helpful compatriot. Build a list of words that you commonly use that aren't misspelled but that spell reports as being misspelled:

```
% alias myspell    'spell \!* | fgrep -v -i -f $HOME/.dictionary'
% cat $HOME/.dictionary
BBS
FAX
Taylor
Utech
Zygote
```

Now spell can be more helpful:

```
% spell newsample
FAX
illetterate
Letteracy
letteracy
letterate
Papert
pre
rithmetic
Rs
Taylor
Utech
Zygote
% myspell newsample
illetterate
Letteracy
```

```
letteracy
letterate
Papert
pre
rithmetic
Rs
```

SUMMARY You have now met the entire family of grep commands. For the majority of your searches for information, you can use the grep command itself. Sometimes, though, it's nice to have options, particularly if you decide to customize some of your commands as shown in the scripts and aliases explored in this hour.

Task 9.7: Changing Things En Route with sed

DESCRIPTION I'm willing to bet that when you read about learning some UNIX programming tools in this hour, you got anxious, your palms started to get sweaty, maybe your fingers shook, and the little voice in your head started to say, "It's too late! We can use a pad and paper! We don't need computers at all!"

Don't panic.

If you think about it, you've been programming all along in UNIX. When you enter a command to the shell, you're programming the shell to perform immediately the task specified. When you specify file redirection or build a pipe, you're really writing a small UNIX program that the shell interprets and acts upon. Frankly, when you consider how many different commands you now know and how many different flags there are for each of the commands, you've got quite a set of programming tools under your belt already, so onward!

With the ¦ symbol called a pipe, and commands tied together called pipelines, is it any wonder that the information flowing down a pipeline is called a stream? For example, the command cat test ¦ wc means that the cat command opens the file test and streams it to the wc program, which counts the number of lines, words, and characters therein.

To edit, or modify, the information in a pipeline, then, it seems reasonable to use a stream editor, and that's exactly what the sed command is! In fact, its name comes from its function: *s* for stream, and *ed* for editor.

Here's the bad news. The sed command is built on an old editor called ed, the same editor that's responsible for the grep command. Remember? The global/*regular expression*/ print eventually became grep. A microcosm of UNIX itself, commands to sed are separated by a semicolon.

There are many different sed commands, but, keeping with my promise not to overwhelm you with options and variations that aren't going to be helpful, I'll focus on using sed to substitute one pattern for another and for extracting ranges of lines from a file. The general format of the substitution command is: s/*old*/*new*/*flags*, where *old* and *new* are the patterns you're working with, s is the abbreviation for the substitute command, and the two most helpful flags are g (to replace all occurrences globally on each line) and *n* (to tell sed to replace only the first *n* occurrences of the pattern). By default, lines are listed to the screen, so a sed expression like 10q will cause the program to list the first 10 lines and then quit (making it an alternative to the command head -10). Deletion is similar: the command is prefaced by one or two addresses in the file, reflecting a request to delete either all lines that match the specified address or all in the range of the first to last.

The format of the sed command is sed, followed by the expression in quotes, then, optionally, the name of the file to read for input.

Here are some examples.

ACTION

1. I'll start with an easy example. I'll use grep to extract some lines from the /etc/ passwd file and then replace all colons with a single space. The format of this command is to substitute each occurrence of : with a space, or s/:/ /:

```
% grep taylor /etc/passwd ¦ sed -e 's/:/ /'
taylorj ?:1048:1375:James Taylor:/users/taylorj:/bin/csh
mtaylor ?:769:1375:Mary Taylor:/users/mtaylor:/usr/local/bin/tcsh
dataylor ?:375:518:Dave Taylor,,,,:/users/dataylor:/usr/local/lib/msh
taylorjr ?:203:1022:James Taylor:/users/taylorjr:/bin/csh
taylorrj ?:662:1042:Robert Taylor:/users/taylorrj:/bin/csh
taylorm ?:869:1508:Melanie Taylor:/users/taylorm:/bin/csh
taylor ?:1989:1412:Dave Taylor:/users/taylor:/bin/csh
```

This doesn't quite do what I want because I neglected to append the global instruction to the sed command to ensure that it would replace all occurrences of the pattern on each line. I'll try it again, this time adding a g to the instruction.

```
% grep taylor /etc/passwd ¦ sed -e 's/:/ /g'
taylorj ? 1048 1375 James Taylor /users/taylorj /bin/csh
mtaylor ? 769 1375 Mary Taylor /users/mtaylor /usr/local/bin/tcsh
dataylor ? 375 518 Dave Taylor /users/dataylor /usr/local/lib/msh
taylorjr ? 203 1022 James Taylor /users/taylorjr /bin/csh
taylorrj ? 662 1042 Robert Taylor /users/taylorrj /bin/csh
taylorm ? 869 1508 Melanie Taylor /users/taylorm /bin/csh
taylor ? 1989 1412 Dave Taylor /users/taylor /bin/csh
```

2. A more sophisticated example of substitution with sed would be to modify names, replacing all occurrences of Taylor with Tailor:

```
% grep taylor /etc/passwd ¦ sed -e 's/Taylor/Tailor/g'
taylorj:?:1048:1375:James Tailor:/users/taylorj:/bin/csh
mtaylor:?:769:1375:Mary Tailor:/users/mtaylor:/usr/local/bin/tcsh
dataylor:?:375:518:Dave Tailor:/users/dataylor:/usr/local/lib/msh
taylorjr:?:203:1022:James Tailor:/users/taylorjr:/bin/csh
taylorrj:?:662:1042:Robert Tailor:/users/taylorrj:/bin/csh
taylorm:?:869:1508:Melanie Tailor:/users/taylorm:/bin/csh
taylor:?:1989:1412:Dave Tailor:/users/taylor:/bin/csh
```

9

The colons have returned, which is annoying, so I'll use the fact that a semicolon can separate multiple sed commands on the same line and try it one more time:

```
% grep taylor /etc/passwd ¦ sed -e 's/Taylor/Tailor/g;s/:/ /g'
taylorj ? 1048 1375 James Tailor /users/taylorj /bin/csh
mtaylor ? 769 1375 Mary Tailor /users/mtaylor /usr/local/bin/tcsh
dataylor ? 375 518 Dave Tailor /users/dataylor /usr/local/lib/msh
taylorjr ? 203 1022 James Tailor /users/taylorjr /bin/csh
taylorrj ? 662 1042 Robert Tailor /users/taylorrj /bin/csh
taylorm ? 8692 1508 Melanie Tailor /users/taylorm /bin/csh
taylor ? 1989 1412 Dave Tailor /users/taylor /bin/csh
```

This last sed command can be read as "each time you encounter the pattern Taylor, replace it with Tailor even if it occurs multiple times on each line. Then, each time you encounter a colon, replace it with a space."

3. Another example of using sed might be to rewrite the output of the who command to be a bit more readable. Consider the results of entering who on your system:

```
% who
strawmye ttyAc    Nov 21 19:01
eiyo     ttyAd    Nov 21 17:40
tzhen    ttyAg    Nov 21 19:13
kmkernek ttyAh    Nov 17 23:22
macedot  ttyAj    Nov 21 20:41
rpm      ttyAk    Nov 21 20:40
ypchen   ttyAl    Nov 21 18:20
kodak    ttyAm    Nov 21 20:43
```

The output is a bit confusing; sed can help:

```
% who ¦ sed 's/tty/On Device /;s/Nov/Logged in November/'
strawmye On Device Ac    Logged in November 21 19:01
eiyo     On Device Ad    Logged in November 21 17:40
tzhen    On Device Ag    Logged in November 21 19:13
kmkernek On Device Ah    Logged in November 17 23:22
macedot  On Device Aj    Logged in November 21 20:41
rpm      On Device Ak    Logged in November 21 20:40
ypchen   On Device Al    Logged in November 21 18:20
kodak    On Device Am    Logged in November 21 20:43
```

This time, each occurrence of the letters tty is replaced with the phrase On Device and, similarly, Nov is replaced with Logged in November.

4. The sed command also can be used to delete lines in the stream as it passes. The simplest version is to specify only the command:

```
% who ¦ sed 'd'
%
```

There's no output because the command matches all lines and deletes them. Instead, to delete just the first line, simply preface the d command with that line number:

```
% who ¦ sed '1d'
eiyo     ttyAd    Nov 21 17:40
tzhen    ttyAg    Nov 21 19:13
kmkernek ttyAh    Nov 17 23:22
```

```
macedot  ttyAj   Nov 21 20:41
rpm      ttyAk   Nov 21 20:40
ypchen   ttyAl   Nov 21 18:20
kodak    ttyAm   Nov 21 20:43
```

To delete more than just the one line, specify the first and last lines to delete, separating them with a comma. The following deletes the first three lines:

```
% who ¦ sed '1,3d'
macedot  ttyAj   Nov 21 20:41
rpm      ttyAk   Nov 21 20:40
ypchen   ttyAl   Nov 21 18:20
kodak    ttyAm   Nov 21 20:43
```

5. There's more to deletion than that. You also can specify patterns by surrounding them with slashes, identically to the substitution pattern. To delete the entries in the who output between eiyo and rpm, the following would work:

```
% who ¦ head -15 ¦ sed '/eiyo/,/rpm/d'
root      console Nov  9 07:31
rick      ttyAa   Nov 21 20:58
brunnert  ttyAb   Nov 21 20:56
ypchen    ttyAl   Nov 21 18:20
kodak     ttyAm   Nov 21 20:43
wh        ttyAn   Nov 21 20:33
klingham  ttyAp   Nov 21 19:55
linet2    ttyAq   Nov 21 20:17
mdps      ttyAr   Nov 21 20:11
```

You can use patterns in combination with numbers, too, so if you wanted to delete text from the first line to the line containing kmkernek, here's how you could do it:

```
% who ¦ sed '1,/kmkernek/d'
macedot  ttyAj   Nov 21 20:41
rpm      ttyAk   Nov 21 20:40
ypchen   ttyAl   Nov 21 18:20
kodak    ttyAm   Nov 21 20:43
```

6. Another aspect of sed is that the patterns are actually regular expressions. Don't be intimidated, though. If you understood the * and ? of filename wildcards, you've learned the key basics of regular expressions: Special characters can match zero or more letters in the pattern. Regular expressions are slightly different from shell patterns because regular expressions are more powerful (although more confusing). Instead of using the ? to match a character, use the . character.

Within this context, it's rare that you need to look for patterns sufficiently complex to require a full regular expression, which is definitely good news. The only two characters you want to remember for regular expressions are ^, which is the imaginary character before the first character of each line, and $, which is the imaginary character after the end of each line.

9

> Here are some pronunciation tips. UNIX folk tend to refer to the " as quote, the ' as single quote, and the ` as back quote. The * is star, the . is dot, the ^ is caret or circumflex, the $ is dollar, and the - is dash.

What does this mean? It means that you can use sed to list everyone reported by who that doesn't have s as the first letter of his or her account. You can, perhaps a bit more interestingly, eliminate all blank lines from a file with sed, too. I'll show you by returning to the testme file:

```
% cat testme
Archives/              OWL/                    keylime.pie
InfoWorld/             bin/                    src/
Mail/                  bitnet.mailing-lists.Z  temp/
News/                  drop.text.hqx           testme


Archives/              OWL/                    keylime.pie
InfoWorld/             bin/                    src/
Mail/                  bitnet.mailing-lists.Z  temp/
News/                  drop.text.hqx           testme


Archives/              OWL/                    keylime.pie
InfoWorld/             bin/                    src/
Mail/                  bitnet.mailing-lists.Z  temp/
News/                  drop.text.hqx           testme
```

Now I'll use sed and clean up this output:

```
% sed '/^$/d' < testme
Archives/              OWL/                    keylime.pie
InfoWorld/             bin/                    src/
Mail/                  bitnet.mailing-lists.Z  temp/
News/                  drop.text.hqx           testme
Archives/              OWL/                    keylime.pie
InfoWorld/             bin/                    src/
Mail/                  bitnet.mailing-lists.Z  temp/
News/                  drop.text.hqx           testme
Archives/              OWL/                    keylime.pie
InfoWorld/             bin/                    src/
Mail/                  bitnet.mailing-lists.Z  temp/
News/                  drop.text.hqx           testme
```

7. These commands can be used in combination, of course; to remove all blank lines, all lines that contain the word keylime, and substitute BinHex for each occurrence of hqx, one sed command can be used, albeit a complex one:

```
% cat testme ¦ sed '/^$/d;/keylime/d;s/hqx/BinHex/g'
InfoWorld/             bin/                    src/
Mail/                  bitnet.mailing-lists.Z  temp/
News/                  drop.text.BinHex                    testme
InfoWorld/             bin/                    src/
Mail/                  bitnet.mailing-lists.Z  temp/
```

9

```
News/                    drop.text.BinHex              testme
InfoWorld/               bin/                    src/
Mail/                    bitnet.mailing-lists.Z  temp/
News/                    drop.text.BinHex              testme
```

8. If you've ever spent any time on an electronic network, you've probably seen either electronic mail or articles wherein the author responds to a previous article. Most commonly, each line of the original message is included, each prefixed by >. It turns out that sed is the appropriate tool either to add a prefix to a group of lines or to remove a prefix from lines in a file.

```
% cat << EOF > sample
Hey Tai! I've been looking for a music CD and none of
the shops around here have a clue about it. I was
wondering if you're going to have a chance to get into
Tower Records in the next week or so?
EOF
% sed 's/^/> /' < sample > sample2
% cat sample2
> Hey Tai! I've been looking for a music CD and none of
> the shops around here have a clue about it. I was
> wondering if you're going to have a chance to get into
> Tower Records in the next week or so?
% cat sample2 | sed 's/^> //'
Hey Tai! I've been looking for a music CD and none of
the shops around here have a clue about it. I was
wondering if you're going to have a chance to get into
Tower Records in the next week or so?
```

Recall that the caret (^) signifies the beginning of the line, so the first invocation of sed searches for the beginning of each line and replaces it with "> ", saving the output to the file sample2. The second use of sed—wherein I remove the prefix—does the opposite search, finding all occurrences of "> " that are at the beginning of a line and replacing them with a null pattern (a null pattern is what you have when you have two slash delimiters without anything between them).

SUMMARY I've only scratched the surface of the sed command here. It's one of those commands where the more you learn about it, the more powerful you realize it is. But, paradoxically, the more you learn about it, the more you'll really want a graphical interface to simplify your life, too.

JUST A MINUTE

The only sed command I use is s (substitution). I figure that matching patterns is best done with grep, and it's very rare that I need to delete specific lines from a file anyway. One helpful command I learned while researching this portion of the hour is that sed can be used to delete from the first line of a file to a specified pattern, meaning that it easily can be used to strip headers from an electronic mail message by specifying the pattern 1,/^$/d. Soon, you will learn about e-mail and how this command can be so helpful.

9

Summary

In this hour, you really have had a chance to build on the knowledge you're picking up about UNIX with your introduction to two exciting and powerful UNIX utilities, grep and sed. Finally, what's a poker hand without some new wildcards? Because one-eyed-jacks don't make much sense in UNIX, you instead learned about how to specify ranges of characters in filename patterns, further ensuring that you can type the minimum number of keys for maximum effect.

Workshop

The Workshop summarizes the key terms you learned and poses some questions about the topics presented in this chapter. It also provides you with a preview of what you will learn in the next hour.

Key Terms

exclusion set   A set of characters that the pattern must not contain.

inclusion range   A range of characters that a pattern must include.

left rooted   Patterns that must occur at the beginning of a line.

regular expressions   A convenient notation for specifying complex patterns. Notable special characters are ^ to match the beginning of the line and $ to match the end of the line.

wildcards   Special characters that are interpreted by the UNIX shell or other programs to have meaning other than the letter itself. For example, * is a shell wildcard and creates a pattern that matches zero or more characters. Prefaced with a particular letter, X—x* —this shell pattern will match all files beginning with X.

Questions

1. What wildcard expressions would you use to find the following?

   ☐ All files in the /tmp directory

   ☐ All files that contain a w in that directory

   ☐ All files that start with a b, contain an e, and end with .c

   ☐ All files that either start with test or contain the pattern hi (Notice that it can be more than one pattern.)

2. Create regular expressions to match the following:

   ☐ Lines that contain the words hot and cold

   ☐ Lines that contain the word cat but not cats

   ☐ Lines that begin with a numeral

3. There are two different ways you could have UNIX match all lines that contain the words `hot` and `cold`: one uses grep and one uses pipelines. Show both.

4. Use the `-v` flag with various `grep` commands, and show the command and pattern needed to match lines that:

   ☐ Don't contain `cabana`

   ☐ Don't contain either `jazz` or `funk`

   ☐ Don't contain `jazz`, `funk`, `disco`, `blues`, or `ska`.

5. Use a combination of `ls -1`, `cat -n`, and `grep` to find out the name of the 11th or 24th file in the `/etc` directory on your system.

6. There are two ways to look for lines containing any one of the words `jazz`, `funk`, `disco`, `blues`, and `ska`. Show both of them.

4. What does the following do?

   ```
   sed 's/:/ /;s/ /:/' /etc/passwd ¦ head
   ```

7. What does this one do?

   ```
   sed 's/^/$ /' < testme
   ```

Preview of the Next Hour

In the next hour, you are introduced to some more advanced pipelining commands and the incredibly powerful filter, `awk`.

9

Hour 10

Power Filters and File Redirection

In this hour, you get to put on your programming hat and learn about two powerful commands that can be customized infinitely and used for a wide variety of tasks. The first of them is awk, a program that can let you grab specific columns of information, modify text as it flows past, and even swap the order of columns of information in a file.

The other is the tee program, which enables you to save a copy of the data being transmitted within a pipeline.

Goals for This Hour

In this hour, you learn

- [ ] How to use the wild and weird awk command
- [ ] How to re-route the pipeline with tee

Beginning with last hour, in which you learned the grep command, you are learning about commands that can take months of study to master. One of the commands treated in this hour, awk, has books written just about it, if you can imagine such a thing. I say this to set the scene; this is a complex and very powerful command. By necessity, you learn only some of the easier capabilities of these commands, but don't worry.

Finally, what's a plumbing metaphor without a plumbing-related command or two? UNIX is just the system to have odd command names. The command in question is tee.

Task 10.1: The Wild and Weird awk Command

DESCRIPTION Although the sed command can be helpful for simple editing tasks in a pipeline, for real power, you need to invoke the awk program. The awk program is a programming kit for analyzing and manipulating text files that have words. It's one of the most helpful general purpose filters in UNIX.

JUST A MINUTE

> Of course, you're wondering where awk got its name. The initial guess is that it refers to its awkward syntax, but that's not quite right. The name is derived from the last names of the authors: Aho, Weinberger, and Kernighan.

Similar to sed, awk can take its commands directly, as arguments. You also can write programs to a file and have awk read the file for its instructions. The general approach to using the program is awk '{ commands }'. There are two possible flags to awk: -f file specifies that the instructions should be read from the file file rather than from the command line, and -Fc indicates that the program should consider the letter c as the separator between fields of information, rather than the default of white space (for example, one or more space or tab characters).

ACTION

1. The first awk command to learn is the most generally useful one, too, in my view: It's the print command. Without any arguments, it prints the lines in the file, one by one:

```
% who ¦ awk '{ print }'
root      console Nov  9 07:31
yuenca    ttyAo   Nov 27 17:39
limyx4    ttyAp   Nov 27 16:22
wifey     ttyAx   Nov 27 17:16
tobster   ttyAz   Nov 27 17:59
taylor    ttyqh   Nov 27 17:43   (vax1.umkc.edu)
```

A line of input is broken into specific fields of information, each field being assigned a unique identifier. Field one is $1, field two $2, and so on:

```
% who ¦ awk '{ print $1 }'
root
yuenca
limyx4
wifey
tobster
taylor
```

The good news is that you also can specify any other information to print by surrounding it with double quotes:

```
% who ¦ awk '{ print "User " $1 " is on terminal line " $2 }'
User root is on terminal line console
User yuenca is on terminal line ttyAo
User limyx4 is on terminal line ttyAp
User hawk is on terminal line ttyAw
User wifey is on terminal line ttyAx
user taylor is on terminal line ttyqh
```

CAUTION

> You couldn't use single quotes to surround parameters to the print command because they would conflict with the single quotes surrounding the entire awk program!

2. You can see already that awk can be quite useful. Return now to the /etc/passwd file and see how awk can help you understand the contents:

```
% grep taylor /etc/passwd ¦ awk -F: '{ print $1 " has "$7" as a
➥login shell." }'
User taylorj has /bin/csh as their login shell.
User mtaylor has /usr/local/bin/tcsh as their login shell.
User dataylor has /usr/local/lib/msh as their login shell.
User taylorjr has /bin/csh as their login shell.
User taylorrj has /bin/csh as their login shell.
User taylormx has /bin/csh as their login shell.
User taylor has /bin/csh as their login shell.
```

3. An interesting question that came up while I was working with these examples is how many different login shells are used at my site and which one is most popular. On most systems, you'd be trapped, probably having to write a program to solve this question; but with awk and some other utilities, UNIX gives you all the tools you need:

```
% awk -F: '{print $7}' /etc/passwd ¦ sort ¦ uniq -c
   2
3365 /bin/csh
   1 /bin/false
  84 /bin/ksh
  21 /bin/sh
  11 /usr/local/bin/ksh
 353 /usr/local/bin/tcsh
  45 /usr/local/lib/msh
```

Here I'm using awk to extract just the seventh field of the password file, the home directory, handing them all to the sort program. I then let uniq figure out which ones occur how often and, with -c, report the count of occurrences to me. Try this on your system, too.

4. Sticking with the password file, notice that the names therein are all in first-name-then-last-name format. That is, my account is Dave Taylor,,,,. A common requirement that you might have is to generate a report of system users. You'd like to sort them by name, but by last name. You do it with awk, of course:

```
% grep taylor /etc/passwd ¦ awk -F: '{print $5}'
James Taylor,,,,
Mary Taylor,,,,
Dave Taylor,,,,
James Taylor,,,,
Robert Taylor,,,,
Melanie Taylor,,,,
Dave Taylor,,,,
```

That generates the list of users. Now I'll use sed to remove those annoying commas and awk again to reverse the order of names:

```
% grep taylor /etc/passwd ¦ awk -F: '{print $5}' ¦ sed 's/,//g'
➡¦ awk '{print $2", "$1}'
Taylor, James
Taylor, Mary
Taylor, Dave
Taylor, James
Taylor, Robert
Taylor, Melanie
Taylor, Dave
```

If I feed the output of this command to sort, the names will finally be listed in the order desired:

```
% grep taylor /etc/passwd ¦ awk -F: '{print $5}' ¦ sed 's/,//g'
➡¦ awk '{print $2", "$1}' ¦ sort
Taylor, Dave
Taylor, Dave
Taylor, James
Taylor, James
Taylor, Mary
Taylor, Melanie
Taylor, Robert
```

This is slick. It also illustrates how you can use various UNIX commands incrementally to build up to your desired result.

5. The script earlier that looked for the login shell isn't quite correct. It turns out that if the user wants to have /bin/sh—the Bourne shell—as his or her default shell, the final field can be left blank:

```
joe:?:45:555:Joe-Bob Billiard,,,,:/home/joe:
```

This can be a problem because the blank field will confuse the awk program; awk is just counting fields in the line. The good news is that each line has an associated number of fields, known as the NF variable. Used without a dollar sign, it indicates how many fields are on a line; used with a dollar sign, it's always the value of the last field on the line itself:

```
% who ¦ head -3 ¦ awk '{ print NF }'
5
5
5
% who ¦ head -3 ¦ awk '{ print $NF }'
07:31
16:22
18:21
```

Because I'm interested in the last field in the /etc/passwd file, the best approach for the preceding command would be to use this $NF parameter explicitly:

```
% grep taylor /etc/passwd ¦ awk -F: '{print $NF}' ¦ sort ¦ uniq -c
3365 /bin/csh
   1 /bin/false
  84 /bin/ksh
  21 /bin/sh
  11 /usr/local/bin/ksh
 353 /usr/local/bin/tcsh
  45 /usr/local/lib/msh
```

6. Similar to NF is NR, which keeps track of the number of records (or lines) displayed. Here's a quick way to number a file:

```
% ls -l ¦ awk '{ print NR": "$0 }'
1: total 29
2: drwx------  2 taylor        512 Nov 21 10:39 Archives/
3: drwx------  3 taylor        512 Nov 16 21:55 InfoWorld/
4: drwx------  2 taylor       1024 Nov 27 18:02 Mail/
5: drwx------  2 taylor        512 Oct  6 09:36 News/
6: drwx------  3 taylor        512 Nov 21 12:39 OWL/
7: drwx------  2 taylor        512 Oct 13 10:45 bin/
8: -rw-rw----  1 taylor      12556 Nov 16 09:49 keylime.pie
9: -rw-------  1 taylor      11503 Nov 27 18:05 randy
10: drwx------  2 taylor        512 Oct 13 10:45 src/
11: drwxrwx---  2 taylor        512 Nov  8 22:20 temp/
12: -rw-rw----  1 taylor          0 Nov 27 18:29 testme
```

Here you can see that the zero field of a line is the entire line. This can be useful, too:

```
% who ¦ awk '{ print $2": "$0 }'
ttyAp: limyx4   ttyAp   Nov 27 16:22
ttyAt: ltbei    ttyAt   Nov 27 18:21
ttyAu: woodson  ttyAu   Nov 27 18:19
ttyAv: morning  ttyAv   Nov 27 18:19
ttyAw: hawk     ttyAw   Nov 27 18:12
ttyAx: wifey    ttyAx   Nov 27 17:16
ttyAz: wiwatr   ttyAz   Nov 27 18:22
ttyAA: chong    ttyAA   Nov 27 13:56
ttyAB: ishidahx ttyAB   Nov 27 18:20
```

10

7. Here's another example of awk. I'll modify the output of the `ls -l` command so that I build a quick list of files and their sizes (which isn't what is shown with the `ls -s` command, recall):

```
% ls -lF ¦ awk '{ print $9 "   " $5 }'
rchives/ 512
InfoWorld/ 512
Mail/ 1024
News/ 512
OWL/ 512
bin/ 512
keylime.pie 12556
randy 11503
src/ 512
temp/ 512
testme 582
```

The output is a bit messy, so you should learn about two special character sequences that can be embedded in the quoted arguments to `print`:

\n	Generates a carriage return
\t	Generates a tab character

In any case, the output is in the wrong order, anyway:

```
% ls -lF ¦ awk '{ print $5 "\t" $9 }'
512      Archives/
512      InfoWorld/
1024     Mail/
512      News/
512      OWL/
512      bin/
12556    keylime.pie
11503    randy
512      src/
512      temp/
582      testme
```

Piping the preceding results to `sort -rn` could easily be used to figure out your largest files:

```
% ls -l ¦ awk '{print $5"\t" $9 }' ¦ sort -rn ¦ head -5
12556    keylime.pie
11503    randy
1024     Mail/
582      testme
512      temp/
```

8. The awk program basically looks for a pattern to appear in a line and then, if the pattern is found, executes the instructions that follow the pattern in the awk script. There are two special patterns in awk: BEGIN and END. The instructions that follow BEGIN are executed before any lines of input are read. The instructions that follow END are executed only after all the input has been read.

10

This can be very useful for computing the sum of a series of numbers. For example, I'd like to know the total number of bytes I'm using for all my files:

```
% ls -l | awk '{print $5}'
512
512
1024
512
512
512
12556
11503
512
512
582
```

That generates the list of file sizes, but how do I sum them up? One way is to create a new variable `totalsize` and output its accumulated value after each line:

```
% ls -l | awk '{ totalsize = totalsize + $5; print totalsize }'
512
1024
2048
2560
3072
3584
16140
27643
28155
28667
29249
```

One easy cleanup is to learn that += is a shorthand notation for "add the following value to the variable":

```
% ls -l | awk '{ totalsize += $5; print totalsize }'
512
1024
2048
2560
3072
3584
16140
27643
28155
28667
29249
```

I can use `tail` to get the last line only, of course, and figure out the total size that way:

```
% ls -l | awk '{ totalsize += $5; print totalsize }' | tail -1
29249
```

A better way, however, is to use the END programming block in the awk program:

```
% ls -l | awk '{ totalsize += $4 } END { print totalsize }'
29249
```

One more slight modification and it's done:

```
% ls -l ¦ awk '{ totalsize += $4 } END { print "You have a
➡total of" totalsize " bytes used in files." }'
You have a total of 29249 bytes used in files.
```

9. Here's one further addition that can make this program even more fun:

```
% ls -l ¦ awk '{ totalsize += $5 } END { print "You have a
➡total of" totalsize " bytes used across "NR" files." }'
You have a total of 29249 bytes used across 11 files.
```

An easier way to see all this is to create an awk program file:

```
% cat << EOF > script
        { totalsize += $4 }
END     { print "You have a total of "totalsize        \
        " bytes used across "NR" files."
}
EOF
% ls -l ¦ awk -f script
You have a total of 29249 bytes used across 11 files.
```

10. Here's one last example before I leave awk. Scripts in awk are really programs and have all the flow-control capabilities you'd want (and then some!). One thing you can do within an awk script is to have conditional execution of statements, the if-then condition. The length routine returns the number of characters in the given argument:

```
% awk -F: '{ if (length($1) == 2) print $0 }' /etc/passwd ¦ wc -l
    26
```

Can you tell what this does? First off, notice that it uses the /etc/passwd file for input and has a colon as the field delimiter (the -F:). For each line in the password file, this awk script tests to see whether the length of the first field (the account name) is exactly two characters long. If it is, the entire line from the password file is printed. All lines printed are then read by the wc program, which, because I used the -l flag, reports the total number of lines read.

What this command tells us is that on the machine, there are 26 accounts for which the account name is two characters long.

11. The next logical question is, "How many account names have a length of each possible number of characters?" To find out, I'll use an advanced feature of awk just to tantalize you: I'll have the program build a table to keep track of the count, with one entry per number of characters in the name:

```
% cat << EOF > awkscript
{
        count[length($1)]++
}
END {
        for (i=1; i < 9; i++)
          print "There are " count[i] " accounts with " i " letter names."
}
```

```
EOF
% awk -F: -f awkscript < /etc/passwd
There are 1 accounts with 1 letter names.
There are 26 accounts with 2 letter names.
There are 303 accounts with 3 letter names.
There are 168 accounts with 4 letter names.
There are 368 accounts with 5 letter names.
There are 611 accounts with 6 letter names.
There are 906 accounts with 7 letter names.
There are 1465 accounts with 8 letter names.
```

You can see that longer names are preferred at this site. How about that lone account with a single-letter account name? That's easy to extract with the earlier script:

```
% awk -F: '{ if (length($1) = 1) print $0 }' < /etc/passwd
awk: syntax error near line 1
awk: illegal statement near line 1
```

Oops! I'll try it again with a double equal sign:

```
% awk -F: '{ if (length($1) == 1) print $0 }' < /etc/passwd
z:?:1325:1375:Chris Zed,,,,:/users/z:/bin/csh
```

JUST A MINUTE

> The worst part of awk is its appalling error messages. Try deliberately introducing an error into one of these awk scripts, and you'll learn quickly just how weird it can be! The classic error is syntax error on or near line 1: bailing out.

SUMMARY The awk program is incredibly powerful. The good news is that you can easily use it and you should find it helpful. It is a great addition to your collection of UNIX tools. I use awk almost daily, and 99 percent of those uses are simply to extract specific columns of information or to change the order of entries, as you saw when I reversed first name and last name from the /etc/passwd file.

I easily could fill the rest of this book with instructions on the awk program, teaching you how to write powerful and interesting scripts. Indeed, I could do the same with the sed program, although I think awk has an edge in power and capabilities. The point, though, isn't to learn exhaustively about thousands of command options and thousands of variations, but rather to have the key concepts and utilities at your fingertips, enabling you to build upon that knowledge as you grow more sophisticated with UNIX.

To this goal, I note that awk is a program that has more depth and capabilities than just about any other UNIX utility—short of actually writing programs in C. When you've mastered all the lessons of this book, awk is a fruitful utility to explore further and expand your knowledge.

Task 10.2: Re-routing the Pipeline with `tee`

DESCRIPTION After the substantial sed and awk commands, this next command, tee, should be a nice reprieve. It's simple, can't be programmed, and has only one possible starting flag.

Recall that the ¦ symbol denotes a pipeline and that information traveling from one command to another is considered to be streaming down the pipe. For example, who ¦ sort has the output of the who command streaming down the pipe to the sort command. Imagine it all as some huge, albeit weird, plumbing construction.

With the plumbing metaphor in mind, you can imagine that it is helpful at times to be able to split off the stream to make it travel down two different directions instead of just one. If multiple pipelines really were allowed, neither you nor I ever could figure out what the heck was going on. The simpler goal, however, of saving a copy of the stream in a file as it whizzes past is more manageable, and that's exactly what the tee command can do.

The only option to tee is -a, which appends the output to the specified file, rather than replaces the contents of the file each time.

ACTION

1. At its simplest, tee can grab a copy of the information being shown on the screen:

```
% who ¦ tee who.out
root      console Nov  9 07:31
jeffhtrt  ttyAo   Nov 27 18:39
limyx4    ttyAp   Nov 27 16:22
cherlbud  ttyAq   Nov 27 18:34
garrettj  ttyAr   Nov 27 18:34
coyote    ttyAs   Nov 27 18:34
ltbei     ttyAt   Nov 27 18:21
woodson   ttyAu   Nov 27 18:19
morning   ttyAv   Nov 27 18:19
wifey     ttyAx   Nov 27 17:16
% cat who.out
root      console Nov  9 07:31
jeffhtrt  ttyAo   Nov 27 18:39
limyx4    ttyAp   Nov 27 16:22
cherlbud  ttyAq   Nov 27 18:34
garrettj  ttyAr   Nov 27 18:34
coyote    ttyAs   Nov 27 18:34
ltbei     ttyAt   Nov 27 18:21
woodson   ttyAu   Nov 27 18:19
morning   ttyAv   Nov 27 18:19
wifey     ttyAx   Nov 27 17:16
```

This can be quite useful for saving output.

2. Better, though, is to grab a copy of the information going down a stream in the middle:

```
% ls -l ¦ awk '{ print $5 "\t" $9 }' ¦ sort -rn ¦ tee bigfiles ¦ head -5
12556    keylime.pie
8729     owl.c
1024     Mail/
582      tetme
512      temp/
```

This shows only the five largest files on the screen, but the `bigfiles` file actually has a list of all files, sorted by size:

```
% cat bigfiles
12556    keylime.pie
8729     owl.c
1024     Mail/
582      tetme
512      temp/
512      src/
512      bin/
512      OWL/
512      News/
512      InfoWorld/
512      Archives/
207      sample2
199      sample
126      awkscript
```

SUMMARY The `tee` command is a classic little UNIX utility, where, as stated before, it seems useful but a bit limited in purpose. As you're learning through all the examples in this book, however, from lots of little commands do big, powerful commands grow.

Summary

In this hour, you really have had a chance to build on the knowledge you're picking up about UNIX, with your introduction to an exciting and powerful UNIX utility, `awk`.

Workshop

This Workshop poses some questions about the topics presented in this chapter. It also provides you with a preview of what you will learn in the next hour.

Questions

1. Expand on the plumbing metaphor with UNIX. What program enables you to split the flow into multiple files? What enables you to fit multiple commands into a pipeline? What enables you to put something into the file?

2. Will the following two commands do the same thing?

```
who ¦ awk '{print $1}' ¦ grep taylor
who ¦ grep taylor ¦ awk '{print $1}'
```

3. Will this command do the same as those in the second question?

```
who ¦ awk '{ if ($1 == "taylor") print }'
```

4. Create a simple awk script that will sort lines in a file by the number of words on the line. Pay attention to the NF record in awk itself.

Preview of the Next Hour

Starting with the next hour, you learn about another powerful and popular program in the entire UNIX system, a program so helpful that versions of it exist even on DOS and the Macintosh today. It fills in the missing piece of your UNIX knowledge and, if what's been covered so far focuses on the plumbing analogy, this command finally moves you beyond considering UNIX as a typewriter (a tty). What's the program? It's the vi screen-oriented editor. It's another program that deserves a book or two, but in two hours, you learn the basics of vi and enough additional commands to let you work with the program easily and efficiently.

Hour 11

An Introduction to the vi Editor

If you like primitive tools, you've already figured out that you can use a combination of << and cat to add lines to a file, and you can use sed and file redirection to modify the contents of a file. These tools are rough and awkward, and when it's time either to create new files or to modify existing files, you need a screen-oriented editor. In UNIX, the screen editor of choice is called vi.

There are a number of editors that may be included with your UNIX system, including ed, ex, vi, and emacs. The latter two use the entire screen, a big advantage, and both are powerful editors. You learn about both in these hours. I focus on vi, however, because I believe it's easier and, perhaps more important, it's guaranteed to always be part of UNIX, whereas most vendors omit emacs, forcing you to find it yourself.

The next three hours focus on full-screen editing tools for UNIX. This is the first of two hours in which you learn how to use vi to create and modify files. This hour covers the basics, including how to move around in the file; how to insert and delete characters, words, and lines; and how to search for specific patterns in the text. The next hour gives an introduction to key mapping, default files, and the ways to use the rest of UNIX while within vi. In the last hour, you learn to use an alternate UNIX editor called emacs.

Goals for This Hour

In this hour, you learn

- ☐ How to start and quit vi
- ☐ Simple cursor motion in vi
- ☐ How to move by words and pages
- ☐ How to insert text into the file
- ☐ How to delete text
- ☐ How to search within a file
- ☐ How to have vi start out right
- ☐ The key colon commands in vi

In some ways, an editor is like another operating system living within UNIX; it is so complex that you will need two hours to learn to use vi. If you're used to Windows or Macintosh editors, you'll be unhappy to find that vi doesn't know anything about your mouse. Once you spend some time working with vi, however, I promise it will grow on you. By the end of this hour, you will be able to create and modify files on your UNIX system to your heart's content.

Task 11.1: How To Start and Quit vi

DESCRIPTION You may have noticed that many of the UNIX commands covered so far have one characteristic in common. They all do their work, display their results, and quit. Among the few exceptions are more and pg, where you work within the specific program environment until you have viewed the entire contents of the file being shown or until you quit. The vi editor is another program in this small category of environments, programs that you move in and use until you explicitly tell the program to quit.

JUST A MINUTE Where did vi get its name? It's not quite as interesting as some of the earlier, more colorful command names. The vi command is so named because it's the visual interface to the ex editor. It was written by Bill Joy while he was at the University of California at Berkeley.

11

Before you start vi for the first time, you must learn about two aspects of its behavior. The first is that vi is a *modal* editor. A mode is like an environment. Different modes in vi interpret the same key differently. For example, if you're in *insert mode*, typing a adds an a to the text, whereas in *command mode*, typing a puts you in insert mode; a is the key abbreviation for the append command. If you ever get confused about what mode you're in, press the Escape key on your keyboard. Pressing Escape always returns you to the command mode (and if you're already in command mode, it simply beeps to remind you of that fact).

When you are in command mode, you can manage your document; this includes the capability to change text, rearrange it, and delete it. Insert mode is when you are adding text directly into your document from the keyboard.

JUST A MINUTE

In vi, the Return key is a specific command (meaning move to the beginning of the next line). As a result, you never need to press Return to have vi process your command.

JUST A MINUTE

emacs is a *modeless* editor. In emacs, the a key always adds the letter a to the file. Commands in emacs are all indicated by holding down the Control key while pressing the command key; for example, Control-c deletes a character.

The second important characteristic of vi is that it's a screen-oriented program. It must know what kind of terminal, computer, or system you are using to work with UNIX. This probably won't be a problem for you because most systems are set up so that the default terminal type matches the terminal or communications program you're using. In this hour, you learn how to recognize when vi cannot figure out what terminal you're using and what to do about it.

You can start vi in a number of different ways, and you learn about lots of helpful alternatives later this hour. Right now, you learn the basics. The vi command, by itself, starts the editor, ready for you to create a new file. The vi command with a filename starts vi with the specified file so that you can modify that file immediately.

Let's get started!

ACTION

1. To begin, enter `vi` at the prompt. If all is working well, the screen will clear, the first character on each line will become a tilde (~), and the cursor will be sitting at the top-left corner of the screen:

   `% vi`

JUST A MINUTE

> I'm going to show you only the portion of the screen that is relevant to the command being discussed for vi, rather than show you the entire screen each time. When the full screen is required to explain something, it'll show up. A smooth edge will indicate the edge of the screen, and a jagged edge will indicate that the rest of the display has been omitted.

Type a colon character. Doing so moves the cursor to the bottom of the screen and replaces the last tilde with the colon:

```
~
~
~
~
~
~
~
:_
```

11

Type q and press the Return key, and you should be back at the shell prompt:

```
~
~
~
~
~
~
~
:q
%
```

2. If that operation worked without a problem, skip to the next section, instruction 3. If the operation did not work, you received the unknown-terminal-type error message. You might see this on your screen:

```
% vi
"unknown": Unknown terminal type
I don't know what type of terminal you are on. All I have is "unknown"
[using open mode]
_
```

Alternatively, you might see this:

```
% vi
Visual needs addressible cursor or upline capability
:
```

Don't panic. You can fix this problem. The first step is to get back to the shell prompt. To do this, do exactly what you did in instruction 1: type :q followed by the Return key. You should then see this:

```
% vi
"unknown": Unknown terminal type
I don't know what type of terminal you are on. All I have is "unknown"
[using open mode]
:q
%
```

The problem here is that vi needs to know the type of terminal you're using, but it can't figure that out on its own. Therefore, you need to tell the operating system by setting the TERM environment variable. If you know what kind of terminal you have, use the value associated with the terminal; otherwise, try the default of vt100:

```
% setenv TERM vt100
```

If you have the $ prompt, which means you're using the Bourne shell (sh) or Korn shell (ksh), rather than the C shell (csh), try this:

```
$ TERM=vt100 ; export TERM
```

Either way, you can now try entering vi again, and it should work.

If it does work, append the command (whichever of these two commands was successful for you) to your .login file if you use csh or to .profile if you use sh or ksh. You can do this by entering whichever of the following commands is appropriate for your system:

```
% echo "setenv TERM vt100" >> .login
```

or

```
$ echo "TERM=vt100 ; export TERM" >> .profile
```

This way, the next time you log in, the system will remember what kind of terminal you're using.

JUST A MINUTE

> vi and other screen commands use a UNIX package called curses to control the screen. Like most UNIX applications, curses was not designed for a specific configuration; instead, it was designed to be device-independent. Therefore, to work on a specific device, you need to give it some additional information—in this case, the terminal type.
>
> If vt100 didn't work, it's time to talk with your system administrator about the problem or to call your UNIX vendor to find out what the specific value should be. If you are connected through a modem or other line and you actually are using a terminal emulator or communications package, you might also try using ansi as a TERM setting. If that fails, call the company that makes your software and ask the company what terminal type the communications program is emulating.

3. Great! You have successfully launched vi, seen what it looks like, and even entered the most important command: the quit command. Now create a simple file and start vi so it shows you the contents of the file:

```
% ls -l > demo
% vi demo
```

```
total 29
drwx------   2 taylor        512 Nov 21 10:39 Archives/
drwx------   3 taylor        512 Dec  3 02:03 InfoWorld/
drwx------   2 taylor       1024 Dec  3 01:43 Mail/
drwx------   2 taylor        512 Oct  6 09:36 News/
drwx------   4 taylor        512 Dec  2 22:08 OWL/
-rw-rw----   1 taylor        126 Dec  3 16:34 awkscript
-rw-rw----   1 taylor        165 Dec  3 16:42 bigfiles
drwx------   2 taylor        512 Oct 13 10:45 bin/
-rw-rw----   1 taylor          0 Dec  3 22:26 demo
```

```
-rw-rw----   1 taylor      12556 Nov 16 09:49 keylime.pie
-rw-rw----   1 taylor       8729 Dec  2 21:19 owl.c
-rw-rw----   1 taylor        199 Dec  3 16:11 sample
-rw-rw----   1 taylor        207 Dec  3 16:11 sample2
drwx------   2 taylor        512 Oct 13 10:45 src/
drwxrwx---   2 taylor        512 Nov  8 22:20 temp/
-rw-rw----   1 taylor        582 Nov 27 18:29 tetme
~
~
~
~
~
~
"demo" 17 lines, 846 characters
```

You can see that vi reads the file specified on the command line. In this example, my file is 17 lines long, but my screen can hold 25 lines. To show that some lines lack any text, vi uses the tilde on a line by itself. Finally, note that, at the bottom, the program shows the name of the file, the number of lines it found in the file, and the total number of characters.

Type :q again to quit vi and return to the command line for now. When you type the colon, the cursor will flash down to the bottom line and wait for the q as it did before.

SUMMARY You have learned the most basic command in vi—the :q command—and survived the experience. It's all downhill from here.

Task 11.2: Simple Cursor Motion in vi

DESCRIPTION Getting to a file isn't much good if you can't actually move around in it. Now you will learn how to use the cursor control keys in vi. To move left one character, type h. To move up, type k. To move down, type j, and to move right a single character, type l (lowercase L). You can move left one character by pressing the Backspace key, and you can move to the beginning of the next line with the Return key.

ACTION

1. Launch vi again, specifying the demo file:

   ```
   % vi demo
   ```

```
total 29
drwx------    2 taylor         512 Nov 21 10:39 Archives/
drwx------    3 taylor         512 Dec  3 02:03 InfoWorld/
drwx------    2 taylor        1024 Dec  3 01:43 Mail/
drwx------    2 taylor         512 Oct  6 09:36 News/
drwx------    4 taylor         512 Dec  2 22:08 OWL/
-rw-rw----    1 taylor         126 Dec  3 16:34 awkscript
-rw-rw----    1 taylor         165 Dec  3 16:42 bigfiles
drwx------    2 taylor         512 Oct 13 10:45 bin/
-rw-rw----    1 taylor           0 Dec  3 22:26 demo
-rw-rw----    1 taylor       12556 Nov 16 09:49 keylime.pie
-rw-rw----    1 taylor        8729 Dec  2 21:19 owl.c
-rw-rw----    1 taylor         199 Dec  3 16:11 sample
-rw-rw----    1 taylor         207 Dec  3 16:11 sample2
drwx------    2 taylor         512 Oct 13 10:45 src/
drwxrwx---    2 taylor         512 Nov  8 22:20 temp/
-rw-rw----    1 taylor         582 Nov 27 18:29 tetme
~
~
~
~
~
~
"demo" 17 lines, 846 characters
```

You should see the cursor sitting on top of the t in total on the first line or perhaps flashing underneath the t character. Perhaps you have a flashing-box cursor or one that shows up in a different color. In any case, that's your starting spot in the file.

2. Type h once to try to move left. The cursor stays in the same spot, and vi beeps to remind you that you can't move left any farther on the line. Try the k key to try to move up; the same thing will happen.

   Now try typing j to move down a character:

```
total 29
drwx------    2 taylor         512 Nov 21 10:39 Archives/
drwx------    3 taylor         512 Dec  3 02:03 InfoWorld/
drwx------    2 taylor        1024 Dec  3 01:43 Mail/
```

   Now the cursor is on the d directory indicator of the second line of the file.

   Type k to move back up to the original starting spot.

3. Using the four cursor-control keys—the h, j, k, and l keys—move around in the file for a little bit, until you are comfortable with what's happening on the screen.

Now try using the Backspace and Return keys to see how they help you move around.

4. Move to the middle of a line:

```
total 29
drwx------   2 taylor          512 Nov 21 10:39 Archives/
drwx------   3 taylor          512 Dec  3 02:03 InfoWorld/
drwx------   2 taylor         1024 Dec  3 01:43 Mail/
```

Here, I'm at the middle digit in the file size of the second file in the listing. Here are a couple of new cursor motion keys: The 0 (zero) key moves the cursor to the beginning of the line, and $ moves it to the end of the line. First, I type 0:

```
total 29
drwx------   2 taylor          512 Nov 21 10:39 Archives/
drwx------   3 taylor          512 Dec  3 02:03 InfoWorld/
drwx------   2 taylor         1024 Dec  3 01:43 Mail/
```

Now I type $ to move to the end of the line:

```
total 29
drwx------   2 taylor          512 Nov 21 10:39 Archives/
drwx------   3 taylor          512 Dec  3 02:03 InfoWorld/
drwx------   2 taylor         1024 Dec  3 01:43 Mail/
```

5. If you have arrow keys on your keyboard, try using them to see if they work the same way that the h, j, k, and l keys work. If the arrow keys don't move you about, they might have shifted you into insert mode. If you type characters and they're added to the file, you need to press the Escape key (or Esc, depending on your keyboard) to return to command mode. Let's wrap this up by leaving this edit session. Because vi now knows that you have modified the file, it will try to ensure that you don't quit without saving the changes:

```
~
~
:q
No write since last change (:quit! overrides)
```

Use :q! (shorthand for :quit) to quit without saving the changes.

JUST A MINUTE

In general, if you try to use a colon command in vi and the program complains that it might do something bad, try the command again, followed by an exclamation point. I like to think of this as saying, "Do it anyway!"

Stay in this file for the next task if you'd like, or use :q to quit.

SUMMARY Moving about a file using these six simple key commands is, on a small scale, much like using the entire process of using the vi editor when working with files. Stick with these simple commands until you're comfortable moving around, and you will be well on your way to becoming proficient using vi.

Task 11.3: Moving by Words and Pages

DESCRIPTION Earlier, in the description of the emacs editor, I commented that because it's always in insert mode, all commands must include the Control key. Well, it turns out that vi has its share of control-key commands, commands that require you to hold down the Control key and press another key. In this section, you learn about Ctrl-f, Ctrl-b, Ctrl-u, and Ctrl-d. These move you forward or backward a screen and up or down half a screen of text, respectively.

I toss a few more commands into the pot, too: w moves you forward word by word, b moves you backward word by word, and the uppercase versions of these two commands have very similar, but not identical, functions.

ACTION

1. To see how this works, you need to create a file that is longer than the size of your screen. An easy way to do this is to save the output of a common command to a file over and over until the file is long enough. The system I use has lots of users, so I needed to use the who command just once. You might have to append the output of who to the big.output file a couple times before the file is longer than 24 lines. (You can check using wc, of course.)

```
% who > big.output; wc -l big.output
    40
% vi big.output
```

```
leungtc  ttyrV   Dec  1 18:27   (magenta)
tuyinhwa ttyrX   Dec  3 22:38   (expert)
hollenst ttyrZ   Dec  3 22:14   (dov)
brandt   ttyrb   Nov 28 23:03   (age)
holmes   ttyrj   Dec  3 21:59   (age)
yuxi     ttyrn   Dec  1 14:19   (pc115)
frodo    ttyro   Dec  3 22:01   (mentor)
labeck   ttyrt   Dec  3 22:02   (dov)
chenlx2  ttyru   Dec  3 21:53   (mentor)
leungtc  ttys0   Nov 28 15:11   (gold)
chinese  ttys2   Dec  3 22:53   (excalibur)
cdemmert ttys5   Dec  3 23:00   (mentor)
yuenca   ttys6   Dec  3 23:00   (mentor)
janitor  ttys7   Dec  3 18:18   (age)
mathisbp ttys8   Dec  3 23:17   (dov)
janitor  ttys9   Dec  3 18:18   (age)
cs541    ttysC   Dec  2 15:16   (solaria)
yansong  ttysL   Dec  1 14:44   (math)
mdps     ttysO   Nov 30 19:39   (localhost)
md       ttysU   Dec  2 08:45   (muller)
jac      ttysa   Dec  3 18:18   (localhost)
eichsted ttysb   Dec  3 23:21   (pc1)
sweett   ttysc   Dec  3 22:40   (dov)
"big.output" 40 lines, 1659 characters
```

Because I have only a 25-line display and the output is 40 lines long (you can see that on the status line at the bottom), there is more information in this file than the screen can display at once.

2. To see the next screenful, press Ctrl-f.

I press Control-f and get the following output:

```
eichsted ttysb   Dec  3 23:21   (pc1)
sweett   ttysc   Dec  3 22:40   (dov)
wellman  ttysd   Dec  3 23:01   (dov)
tuttleno ttyse   Dec  3 23:03   (indyvax)
wu       ttysf   Dec  3 23:10   (term01)
daurismj ttysg   Dec  3 23:10   (dov)
cs414    ttysh   Dec  3 23:12   (xds)
cq       ttysi   Dec  3 23:13   (expert)
cdemmert ttysk   Dec  3 22:37   (xsun22)
jrlee    ttysn   Dec  3 22:53   (mac1)
fitzgejs ttyso   Dec  3 23:18   (dov)
doerrhb  ttysp   Dec  3 23:20   (dov)
cdemmert ttysq   Dec  3 23:00   (xsun22)
frazierw ttysr   Dec  3 23:01   (dov)
buckeye  ttyss   Dec  3 23:20   (mac2)
mtaylor  ttyst   Dec  3 23:22   (dov)
look     ttysu   Dec  3 23:12   (age)
```

```
janitor   ttysw   Dec  3 18:29   (age)
ajones    ttysx   Dec  3 23:23   (rass)
~
~
~
~
```

Notice that the entire screen was rewritten and that the familiar tilde characters have popped up again to let me know that I have reached the end of the file.

By default, vi has a two-line overlap when you move from screen to screen. If you look carefully, you can see that both eichsted and sweett show up on both screens of data. This doesn't mean that they appear twice in the file; rather, vi is trying to help me not get lost while I wander through the file.

3. Now, what do you think will happen if I press Control-u?

```
leungtc   ttys0   Nov 28 15:11   (gold)
chinese   ttys2   Dec  3 22:53   (excalibur)
cdemmert  ttys5   Dec  3 23:00   (mentor)
yuenca    ttys6   Dec  3 23:00   (mentor)
janitor   ttys7   Dec  3 18:18   (age)
mathisbp  ttys8   Dec  3 23:17   (dov)
janitor   ttys9   Dec  3 18:18   (age)
cs541     ttysC   Dec  2 15:16   (solaria)
yansong   ttysL   Dec  1 14:44   (math)
mdps      ttysO   Nov 30 19:39   (localhost)
md        ttysU   Dec  2 08:45   (muller)
jac       ttysa   Dec  3 18:18   (localhost)
eichsted  ttysb   Dec  3 23:21   (pc1)
sweett    ttysc   Dec  3 22:40   (dov)
wellman   ttysd   Dec  3 23:01   (dov)
tuttleno  ttyse   Dec  3 23:03   (indyvax)
wu        ttysf   Dec  3 23:10   (term01)
daurismj  ttysg   Dec  3 23:10   (dov)
cs414     ttysh   Dec  3 23:12   (xds)
cq        ttysi   Dec  3 23:13   (expert)
cdemmert  ttysk   Dec  3 22:37   (xsun22)
jrlee     ttysn   Dec  3 22:53   (mac1)
fitzgejs  ttyso   Dec  3 23:18   (dov)
```

The command has moved me up half a screen. Notice where eichsted and sweett are now. Instead of the text being replaced at once, as when I used Control-f, the text was scrolled downward a line at a time, each new line being added as the program went along. The Control-u command might work either way—one line or an entire screen at a time—for you.

4. Now it's time to try moving around in this file word by word. Type w once to see what happens.

```
leungtc  ttys0   Nov 28 15:11   (gold)
chinese  ttys2   Dec  3 22:53   (excalibur)
cdemmert ttys5   Dec  3 23:00   (mentor)
```

Now type w six times more, noting that the cursor stops three times in the field to indicate what time the user logged into the system (15:11 in this listing). Now your cursor should be sitting on the parenthesized field:

```
leungtc  ttys0   Nov 28 15:11   (gold)
chinese  ttys2   Dec  3 22:53   (excalibur)
cdemmert ttys5   Dec  3 23:00   (mentor)
```

5. It's time to move backward. Type b a few times; your cursor moves backward to the beginning of each word.

What happens if you try to move backward and you're already on the first word, or if you try to move forward with the w command and you're already on the last word of the line? Let's find out.

6. Using the various keys you've learned, move back to the beginning of the line that starts with leungtc, which you used in instruction 4:

```
leungtc  ttys0   Nov 28 15:11   (gold)
chinese  ttys2   Dec  3 22:53   (excalibur)
cdemmert ttys5   Dec  3 23:00   (mentor)
```

This time, type W (uppercase W, not lowercase w) to move through this line. Can you see the difference? Notice what happens when you hit the time field and the parenthesized words. Instead of typing w seven times to move to the left parenthesis before gold, you can type W only five times.

7. Try moving backward using the B command. Notice that the B command differs from the b command the same way the W command differs from the w command.

SUMMARY Moving about by words, both forward and backward, being able to zip through half screens or full screens at a time, and being able to zero in on specific spots with the h, j, k, and l cursor-motion keys give you quite a range of motion. Practice using these commands in various combinations to get your cursor to specific characters in your sample file.

Task 11.4: Inserting Text into the File
Using i, a, o, and 0

DESCRIPTION Being able to move around in a file is useful. The real function of an editor, however, is to enable you to easily add and remove—in editor parlance, insert and delete—information. The vi editor has a special insert mode, which you must use in order to add to the contents of the file. There are four different ways to shift into insert mode, and you learn about all of them in this unit.

The first way to switch to insert mode is to type the letter i, which, mnemonically enough, inserts text into the file. The other commands that accomplish more or less the same thing are a, to append text to the file; o, to open up a line below the current line; and 0, to open up a line above the current line.

ACTION

1. For this task, you need to start with a clean file, so quit from the big.output editing session and start vi again, this time specifying a nonexistent file called buckaroo:

   % **vi buckaroo**

```
~
~
~
~
~
~
~
~
~
~
~
~
~
~
~
~
~
~
~
~
"buckaroo" [New file]
```

11

Notice that vi reminds you that this file doesn't exist; the bottom of the screen says New file, instead of indicating the number of lines and characters.

2. Now it's time to try using insert mode. Try to insert a k into the file by typing k once:

```
_
~
~
~
```

The system beeps at you because you haven't moved into insert mode yet, and the k still has its command meaning of moving down a line (and of course, there isn't another line yet).

Type i to move into insert mode, then type k again:

```
k_
~
~
~
```

There you go! You've added a character to the file.

3. Press the Backspace key, which will move the cursor over the letter k:

```
k
~
~
~
```

Now see what happens when you press Escape to leave insert mode and return to the vi command mode:

```
_
~
~
~
```

Notice that the k vanished when you pressed Escape. That's because vi only saves text you've entered to the left of or above the cursor, not the letter the cursor is resting on.

4. Now move back into insert mode by typing i, and enter a few sentences from a favorite book of mine:

JUST A MINUTE

> Movie buffs perhaps will recognize that the text used in this hour comes from the book *Buckaroo Banzai*. The film *The Adventures of Buckaroo Banzai Across the Eighth Dimension* is based on this very fun book.

```
"He's not even here," went the conservation.
"Banzai."
"Where is he?"
"At a hotpsial in El paso."
"What? Why werent' we informed? What's wrong with him?"_
~
~
```

I've deliberately left some typing errors in the text here. Fixing them will demonstrate some important features of the vi editor. If you fixed them as you went along, that's okay, and if you added errors of your own, that's okay, too!

Press Escape to leave insert mode. Press Escape a second time to ensure that it worked; remember that vi beeps to remind you that you're already in command mode.

5. Use the cursor motion keys (h, j, k, and l) to move the cursor to any point on the first line:

```
"He's not even here," went the conservation.
"Banzai."
"Where is he?"
"At the hotpsial in El paso."
"What? Why werent' we informed? What's wrong with him?"
~
~
```

It turns out that I forgot a line of dialog between the line I'm on and the word Banzai. One way to enter the line would be to move to the beginning of the line "Banzai.", insert the new text, and press Return before pressing Escape to quit insert mode. But vi has a special command—o—to open a line immediately below the current line for inserting text. Type o and follow along:

```
"He's not even here," went the conservation.

"Banzai."
"Where is he?"
"At the hotpsial in El paso."
"What? Why werent' we informed? What's wrong with him?"
~
~
```

Now type the missing text:

```
"He's not even here," went the conservation.
"Who?"_
"Banzai."
"Where is he?"
"At the hotpsial in El paso."
"What? Why werent' we informed? What's wrong with him?"
~
~
```

That's it. Press Escape to return to command mode.

6. The problem with the snippet of dialog we're using is that there's no way to figure
    out who is talking. Adding a line above this dialog helps identify the speakers.
    Again, use cursor motion keys to place the cursor on the top line:

```
"He's not _even here," went the conservation.
"Banzai."
"Where is he?"
"At the hotpsial in El paso."
"What? Why werent' we informed? What's wrong with him?"
~
~
```

Now you face a dilemma. You want to open up a line for new text, but you want
the line to be above the current line, not below it. It happens that vi can do that,
too. Instead of using the o command, use its big brother O instead. When I type O,
here's what I see:

```
‾
"He's not even here," went the conservation.
"Banzai."
"Where is he?"
"At the hotpsial in El paso."
"What? Why werent' we informed? What's wrong with him?"
~
~
```

Type the new sentence and then press Escape.

```
I found myself stealing a peek at my own watch and overheard
General Catbird's
aide give him the latest._
"He's not even here," went the conservation.
"Banzai."
"Where is he?"
"At the hotpsial in El paso."
"What? Why werent' we informed? What's wrong with him?"
~
~
```

Now the dialog makes a bit more sense. The conversation, overheard by the narrator, takes place between the general and his aide.

7. I missed a couple of words in one of the lines, so the next task is to insert them. Use the cursor keys to move the cursor to the fifth line, just after the word `Where`:

```
I found myself stealing a peek at my own watch and overheard
General Catbird's
aide give him the latest.
"He's not even here," went the conservation.
"Banzai."
"Where_is he?"
"At the hotpsial in El paso."
"What? Why werent' we informed? What's wrong with him?"
~
~
```

At this juncture, I need to add the words the `hell` to make the sentence a bit stronger (and correct). I can use `i` to insert the text, but then I end up with a trailing space. Instead, I can add text immediately after the current cursor location by using the `a` command to append, or insert, the information. When I type a, the cursor moves one character to the right:

```
I found myself stealing a peek at my own watch and overheard
General Catbird's
aide give him the latest.
"He's not even here," went the conservation.
"Banzai."
"Where is he?"
"At the hotpsial in El paso."
"What? Why werent' we informed? What's wrong with him?"
~
~
```

Here's where vi can be difficult to use. I'm in insert mode, but there's no way for me to know that. When I type the letters I want to add, the screen shows that they are appended, but what if I thought I was in insert mode when I actually was in command mode? One trick I could use to ensure I'm in insert mode is to type the command a second time. If the letter a shows up in the text, I simply would backspace over it; now I would know that I'm in append mode. When I'm done entering the new characters and I'm still in insert mode, here's what my screen looks like:

```
I found myself stealing a peek at my own watch and overheard
General Catbird's
aide give him the latest.
"He's not even here," went the conservation.
"Banzai."
"Where the hell is he?"
"At the hotpsial in El paso."
"What? Why werent' we informed? What's wrong with him?"
~
~
```

Notice that the cursor always stayed on the i in is throughout this operation. Press Escape to return to command mode. Notice that the cursor finally hops off the i and moves left one character.

JUST A MINUTE

To differentiate between the i and a commands, remember that the insert command always adds the new information immediately before the character that the cursor is sitting upon, whereas the append command adds the information immediately to the right of the current cursor position.

11

8. With this in mind, try to fix the apostrophe problem in the word `werent'` on the last line. Move the cursor to the `n` in that word:

```
"Where the hell is he?"
"At the hotpsial in El paso."
"What? Why werent' we informed? What's wrong with him?"
~
```

To add the apostrophe immediately after the current character, do you want to use the insert command (`i`) or the append (`a`) command? If you said "append," give yourself a pat on the back! Type `a` to append the apostrophe:

```
"Where the hell is he?"
"At the hotpsial in El paso."
"What? Why werent' we informed? What's wrong with him?"
~
```

Type `'` once and then press Escape.

9. Quit `vi` using `:q`, and the program reminds you that you haven't saved your changes to this new file:

```
~
~
No write since last change (:quit! overrides)
```

To write the changes, you need a new command, so I'll give you a preview of a set of colon commands you learn later in this hour. Type `:` (the colon character), which moves the cursor to the bottom of the screen.

```
~
~
:_
```

Now type `w` to write out (save) the file, and then press the Return key:

```
~
~
"buckaroo" 8 lines, 272 characters
```

11

It's okay to leave vi now. I'll use :q to quit, and I'm safely back at the command prompt. A quick cat confirms that the tildes were not included in the file itself:

```
% cat buckaroo
I found myself stealing a peek at my own watch and overheard
General Catbird's
aide give him the latest.
"He's not even here," went the conservation.
"Banzai."
"Where the hell is he?"
"At the hotpsial in El paso."
"What? Why weren't' we informed? What's wrong with him?"
%
```

SUMMARY As you can tell, the vi editor is quite powerful, and it has a plethora of commands. Just moving about and inserting text, you have learned 24 commands, as summarized in Table 10.1.

Table 10.1. Summary of vi motion and insertion commands.

Command	Meaning
0	Move to the beginning of the line.
$	Move to the end of the line.
a	Append text—enter into insert mode after the current character.
^b	Back up one screen of text.
B	Back up one space-delimited word.
b	Back up one word.
Backspace	Move left one character.
^d	Move down half a page.
Escape	Leave insert mode and return to command mode.
^f	Move forward one screen of text.
h	Move left one character.
i	Insert text—enter into insert mode before the current character.
j	Move down one line.
k	Move up one line.
l	Move right one character.
O	Open new line for inserting text above the current line.
o	Open new line for inserting text below the current line.
Return	Move to the beginning of the next line.

continues

Table 10.1. continued

Command	Meaning
^u	Move up half a page.
W	Move forward one space-delimited word.
w	Move forward one word.
:w	Write the file to disk.
:q	Quit vi and return to the UNIX system prompt.
:q!	Quit vi and return to the UNIX system prompt, throwing away any changes made to the file.

JUST A MINUTE

In this table, I use the simple shorthand notation introduced in Hour 7, "Looking into Files." UNIX users often use a caret followed by a character instead of the awkward Control-c notation. Therefore, ^f has the same meaning as Control-f. Expressing this operation as ^f does not change the way it's performed: you'd still press and hold down the Control key and then type f. It's just a shorter notation.

You've already learned quite a few commands, but you have barely scratched the surface of the powerful vi command!

Task 11.5: Deleting Text

DESCRIPTION You now have many of the pieces you need to work efficiently with the vi editor, to zip to any point in the file, and to add text wherever you'd like. Now you need to learn how to delete characters, words, and lines.

The simplest form of the delete command is the x command, which functions as though you are writing an *X* over a letter you don't want on a printed page: It deletes the character under the cursor. Type x five times, and you delete five characters. Deleting a line of text this way can be quite tedious, so vi has some alternate commands. (Are you surprised?) One command that many vi users don't know about is the D (for "delete through the end of the line") command. Wherever you are on a line, if you type D, you immediately will delete everything after the cursor to the end of that line of text.

If there's an uppercase D command, you can just bet there's a lowercase d command, too. The d delete command is the first of a set of more sophisticated vi commands that you follow with a second command that indicates what you'd like to do with the command. You already know

11

that w and W move you forward a word in the file; they're known as *addressing commands* in vi. You can follow d with one of these addressing commands to specify what you would like to delete. For example, to delete a word, simply type dw.

TIME SAVER

Sometimes you might get a bit overzealous and delete more than you anticipated. That's not a problem—well, not too much of a problem—because vi remembers the state of the file prior to the most recent action taken. To undo a deletion (or insertion, for that matter), use the u command. To undo a line of changes, use the U command. Be aware that once you've moved off the line in question, the U command is unable to restore it!

ACTION

1. Start vi again with the big.output file you used earlier:

```
leungtc   ttyrV   Dec  1 18:27   (magenta)
tuyinhwa  ttyrX   Dec  3 22:38   (expert)
hollenst  ttyrZ   Dec  3 22:14   (dov)
brandt    ttyrb   Nov 28 23:03   (age)
holmes    ttyrj   Dec  3 21:59   (age)
yuxi      ttyrn   Dec  1 14:19   (pc)
frodo     ttyro   Dec  3 22:01   (mentor)
labeck    ttyrt   Dec  3 22:02   (dov)
chenlx2   ttyru   Dec  3 21:53   (mentor)
leungtc   ttys0   Nov 28 15:11   (gold)
chinese   ttys2   Dec  3 22:53   (excalibur)
cdemmert  ttys5   Dec  3 23:00   (mentor)
yuenca    ttys6   Dec  3 23:00   (mentor)
janitor   ttys7   Dec  3 18:18   (age)
mathisbp  ttys8   Dec  3 23:17   (dov)
janitor   ttys9   Dec  3 18:18   (age)
cs541     ttysC   Dec  2 15:16   (solaria)
yansong   ttysL   Dec  1 14:44   (math)
mdps      ttysO   Nov 30 19:39   (localhost)
md        ttysU   Dec  2 08:45   (muller)
jac       ttysa   Dec  3 18:18   (localhost)
eichsted  ttysb   Dec  3 23:21   (pc1)
sweett    ttysc   Dec  3 22:40   (dov)
"big.output" 40 lines, 1659 characters
```

11

Type x a few times to delete a few characters from the beginning of the file:

```
gtc  ttyrV   Dec  1 18:27    (magenta)
tuyinhwa ttyrX    Dec  3 22:38    (expert)
hollenst ttyrZ    Dec  3 22:14    (dov)
brandt   ttyrb    Nov 28 23:03    (age)
holmes   ttyrj    Dec  3 21:59    (age)
```

Now type u to undo the last deletion:

```
ngtc  ttyrV   Dec  1 18:27    (magenta)
tuyinhwa ttyrX    Dec  3 22:38    (expert)
hollenst ttyrZ    Dec  3 22:14    (dov)
brandt   ttyrb    Nov 28 23:03    (age)
holmes   ttyrj    Dec  3 21:59    (age)
```

If you type u again, what do you think will happen?

```
gtc  ttyrV   Dec  1 18:27    (magenta)
tuyinhwa ttyrX    Dec  3 22:38    (expert)
hollenst ttyrZ    Dec  3 22:14    (dov)
brandt   ttyrb    Nov 28 23:03    (age)
holmes   ttyrj    Dec  3 21:59    (age)
```

The undo command alternates between the last command having happened or not having happened. To explain it a bit better, the undo command is an action unto itself, so the second time you type u, you're undoing the undo command that you just requested. Type u a few more times to convince yourself that this is the case.

2. It's time to make some bigger changes to the file. Type dw twice to delete the current word and the next word in the file. It should look something like this after using the first dw:

```
ttyrV   Dec  1 18:27    (magenta)
tuyinhwa ttyrX    Dec  3 22:38    (expert)
hollenst ttyrZ    Dec  3 22:14    (dov)
brandt   ttyrb    Nov 28 23:03    (age)
holmes   ttyrj    Dec  3 21:59    (age)
```

11

Then it should look like this after using the second dw:

```
Dec  1 18:27   (magenta)
tuyinhwa ttyrX   Dec  3 22:38   (expert)
hollenst ttyrZ   Dec  3 22:14   (dov)
brandt   ttyrb   Nov 28 23:03   (age)
holmes   ttyrj   Dec  3 21:59   (age)
```

Type u. You see that you can undo only the most recent command. At this point, though, because I haven't moved from the line I'm editing, the U, or undo-a-line-of-changes, command, will restore the line to its original splendor:

```
leungtc  ttyrV   Dec  1 18:27   (magenta)
tuyinhwa ttyrX   Dec  3 22:38   (expert)
hollenst ttyrZ   Dec  3 22:14   (dov)
brandt   ttyrb   Nov 28 23:03   (age)
holmes   ttyrj   Dec  3 21:59   (age)
```

3. Well, in the end, I really don't want to see some of these folks. Fortunately, I can change the contents of this file by using the dd command to delete lines. When using one of these two-letter commands, repeating the letter means to apply the command to the entire line. What if I want to delete the entries for chinese and janitor, both of which are visible on this screen?

    The first step is to use the cursor keys to move down to any place on the line for the chinese account, about halfway down the screen:

```
chenlx2  ttyru   Dec  3 21:53   (mentor)
leungtc  ttys0   Nov 28 15:11   (gold)
chinese  ttys2   Dec  3 22:53   (excalibur)
cdemmert ttys5   Dec  3 23:00   (mentor)
yuenca   ttys6   Dec  3 23:00   (mentor)
janitor  ttys7   Dec  3 18:18   (age)
mathisbp ttys8   Dec  3 23:17   (dov)
```

If your cursor isn't somewhere in the middle of this line, move it so that you, too, are not at an edge.

I had planned to remove this line completely, but perhaps I'd rather just remove the date, time, and name of the system (in parentheses) instead. To accomplish this, I don't need to type `dw` a bunch of times or even `x` a lot of times, but rather just `D` to delete through the end of the line:

```
chenlx2  ttyru   Dec  3 21:53   (mentor)
leungtc  ttys0   Nov 28 15:11   (gold)
chinese  ttys2   _
cdemmert ttys5   Dec  3 23:00   (mentor)
yuenca   ttys6   Dec  3 23:00   (mentor)
janitor  ttys7   Dec  3 18:18   (age)
mathisbp ttys8   Dec  3 23:17   (dov)
```

Oh, that's not quite what I wanted to do. No problem; the `undo` command can fix it. Simply typing `u` restores the text I deleted:

```
chenlx2  ttyru   Dec  3 21:53   (mentor)
leungtc  ttys0   Nov 28 15:11   (gold)
chinese  ttys2   Dec  3 22:53   (excalibur)
cdemmert ttys5   Dec  3 23:00   (mentor)
yuenca   ttys6   Dec  3 23:00   (mentor)
janitor  ttys7   Dec  3 18:18   (age)
mathisbp ttys8   Dec  3 23:17   (dov)
```

4. The problem is that I wanted to delete the two entries `chinese` and `janitor` from the file, but I used the wrong command. Instead of using the `D` command, I should use `dd`. Typing `dd` once has these results:

```
Dec  1 18:27    (magenta)
tuyinhwa ttyrX   Dec  3 22:38   (expert)
hollenst ttyrZ   Dec  3 22:14   (dov)
brandt   ttyrb   Nov 28 23:03   (age)
holmes   ttyrj   Dec  3 21:59   (age)
yuxi     ttyrn   Dec  1 14:19   (pc)
frodo    ttyro   Dec  3 22:01   (mentor)
labeck   ttyrt   Dec  3 22:02   (dov)
chenlx2  ttyru   Dec  3 21:53   (mentor)
leungtc  ttys0   Nov 28 15:11   (gold)
cdemmert ttys5   Dec  3 23:00   (mentor)
yuenca   ttys6   Dec  3 23:00   (mentor)
janitor  ttys7   Dec  3 18:18   (age)
mathisbp ttys8   Dec  3 23:17   (dov)
janitor  ttys9   Dec  3 18:18   (age)
cs541    ttysC   Dec  2 15:16   (solaria)
yansong  ttysL   Dec  1 14:44   (math)
mdps     ttys0   Nov 30 19:39   (localhost)
```

11

```
md        ttysU   Dec  2 08:45   (muller)
jac       ttysa   Dec  3 18:18   (localhost)
eichsted  ttysb   Dec  3 23:21   (pc1)
sweett    ttysc   Dec  3 22:40   (dov)
wellman   ttysd   Dec  3 23:01   (dov)
```

Notice that a new line of information has been pulled onto the screen at the bottom to replace the blank line that you removed.

If you try using the u command now, what happens?

I'm almost done. A few presses of the Return key and I'm down to the entry for the janitor account. Using dd removes that line, too:

```
Dec  1 18:27   (magenta)
tuyinhwa ttyrX   Dec  3 22:38   (expert)
hollenst ttyrZ   Dec  3 22:14   (dov)
brandt   ttyrb   Nov 28 23:03   (age)
holmes   ttyrj   Dec  3 21:59   (age)
yuxi     ttyrn   Dec  1 14:19   (pc)
frodo    ttyro   Dec  3 22:01   (mentor)
labeck   ttyrt   Dec  3 22:02   (dov)
chenlx2  ttyru   Dec  3 21:53   (mentor)
leungtc  ttys0   Nov 28 15:11   (gold)
cdemmert ttys5   Dec  3 23:00   (mentor)
yuenca   ttys6   Dec  3 23:00   (mentor)
mathisbp ttys8   Dec  3 23:17   (dov)
janitor  ttys9   Dec  3 18:18   (age)
cs541    ttysC   Dec  2 15:16   (solaria)
yansong  ttysL   Dec  1 14:44   (math)
mdps     ttysO   Nov 30 19:39   (localhost)
md       ttysU   Dec  2 08:45   (muller)
jac      ttysa   Dec  3 18:18   (localhost)
eichsted ttysb   Dec  3 23:21   (pc1)
sweett   ttysc   Dec  3 22:40   (dov)
wellman  ttysd   Dec  3 23:01   (dov)
tuttleno ttyse   Dec  3 23:03   (indyvax)
```

Each line below the one deleted moves up a line to fill in the blank space, and a new line, for tuttleno, moves up from the following screen.

5. Now I want to return to the buckaroo file to remedy some of the horrendous typographical errors! I don't really care whether I save the changes I've just made to this file, so I'm going to use :q! to quit, discarding these changes to the big.output file. Entering vi buckaroo starts vi again:

```
I found myself stealing a peek at my own watch and overheard
General Catbird's
aide give him the latest.
"He's not even here," went the conservation.
"Banzai."
"Where the hell is he?"
"At the hotpsial in El paso."
"What? Why weren't' we informed? What's wrong with him?"
~
~
~
~
~
~
~
~
~
~
~
~
"buckaroo" 8 lines, 272 characters
```

There are a couple of fixes you can make in short order. The first is to change
conservation to conversation on the fourth line. To move there, press the Return
key twice, and then use W to zip forward until the cursor is at the first letter of the
word you're editing:

```
I found myself stealing a peek at my own watch and overheard
General Catbird's
aide give him the latest.
"He's not even here," went the conservation.
"Banzai."
"Where the hell is he?"
```

Then use the dw command:

```
I found myself stealing a peek at my own watch and overheard
General Catbird's
aide give him the latest.
"He's not even here," went the .
"Banzai."
"Where the hell is he?"
```

Now enter insert mode by typing i, type the correct spelling of the word conversation, and then press Escape:

```
I found myself stealing a peek at my own watch and overheard
General Catbird's
aide give him the latest.
"He's not even here," went the conversation.
"Banzai."
"Where the hell is he?"
```

6. That's one fix. Now move down a couple of lines to fix the atrocious misspelling of hospital:

```
"Banzai."
"Where the hell is he?"
"At the hotpsial in El paso."
"What? Why weren't' we informed? What's wrong with him?"
~
```

Again, use dw to delete the word, type i to enter insert mode, type hospital, and then press Escape. Now all is well on the line:

```
"Banzai."
"Where the hell is he?"
"At the hospital in El paso."
"What? Why weren't' we informed? What's wrong with him?"
~
```

Well, almost all is well. The first letter of Paso needs to be capitalized. Move to it by typing w to move forward a few words:

```
"Banzai."
"Where the hell is he?"
"At the hospital in El paso."
"What? Why weren't' we informed? What's wrong with him?"
~
```

11

7. It's time for a secret vi expert command! Instead of typing x to delete the letter, i to enter insert mode, P as the correct letter, and then Escape to return to command mode, there's a much faster way to *transpose case*: the ~ (tilde) command. Type ~ once, and here's what happens:

```
"Banzai."
"Where the hell is he?"
"At the hospital in El Paso."
"What? Why weren't' we informed? What's wrong with him?"
~
```

Cool, isn't it? Back up to the beginning of the word again, using the h command, and type ~ a few times to see what happens. Notice that each time you type ~, the character's case switches—transposes—and the cursor moves to the next character. Type ~ four times, and you should end up with this:

```
"Banzai."
"Where the hell is he?"
"At the hospital in El pASO."
"What? Why weren't' we informed? What's wrong with him?"
~
```

Back up to the beginning of the word and type ~ until the word is correct.

8. One more slight change, and the file is fixed! Move to the last line of the file, to the extra apostrophe in the word weren't', and type x to delete the offending character. The screen should now look like this:

```
I found myself stealing a peek at my own watch and overheard
General Catbird's
aide give him the latest.
"He's not even here," went the conversation.
"Banzai."
"Where the hell is he?"
"At the hospital in El Paso."
"What? Why weren't we informed? What's wrong with him?"
~
~
~
~
~
~
~
~
```

11

```
~
~
~
~
~
~
```

That looks great! It's time to save it for posterity. Use :wq, a shortcut that has vi write out the changes and immediately quit the program:

```
~
~
~
"buckaroo" 8 lines, 271 characters
%
```

SUMMARY Not only have you learned about the variety of deletion options in vi, but you also have learned a few simple shortcut commands: ~ to transpose case and :wq to write out the changes and quit the program all in one step.

You should feel pleased; you're now a productive and knowledgeable vi user, and you can modify files, making easy or tough changes. Go back to your system and experiment further, modifying some of the other files. Be careful, though, not to make changes in any of your dot files (for example, .cshrc), lest you cause trouble that would be difficult to fix!

Task 11.6: Searching Within a File

DESCRIPTION With the addition of two more capabilities, you'll be ready to face down any vi expert, demonstrating your skill and knowledge of the editor, and, much more important, you will be able to really fly through files, moving immediately to the information you desire.

The two new capabilities are for finding specific words or phrases in a file and for moving to a specific line in a file. Similar to searching for patterns in more and page, the /*pattern* command searches forward in the file for a specified pattern, and ?*pattern* searches backward for the specified pattern. To repeat the previous search, use the n command to tell vi to search again, in the same direction, for the next instance of the same pattern.

You can move easily to any specific line in a file, using the G, or go-to-line, command. If you type a number before you type G, the cursor will move to that line in the file. If you type G without a line number, the cursor will zip you to the very last line of the file (by default).

ACTION

1. Start vi again with the big.output file:

```
leungtc   ttyrV   Dec  1 18:27   (magenta)
tuyinhwa  ttyrX   Dec  3 22:38   (expert)
hollenst  ttyrZ   Dec  3 22:14   (dov)
brandt    ttyrb   Nov 28 23:03   (age)
holmes    ttyrj   Dec  3 21:59   (age)
yuxi      ttyrn   Dec  1 14:19   (pc)
frodo     ttyro   Dec  3 22:01   (mentor)
labeck    ttyrt   Dec  3 22:02   (dov)
chenlx2   ttyru   Dec  3 21:53   (mentor)
leungtc   ttys0   Nov 28 15:11   (gold)
chinese   ttys2   Dec  3 22:53   (excalibur)
cdemmert  ttys5   Dec  3 23:00   (mentor)
yuenca    ttys6   Dec  3 23:00   (mentor)
janitor   ttys7   Dec  3 18:18   (age)
mathisbp  ttys8   Dec  3 23:17   (dov)
janitor   ttys9   Dec  3 18:18   (age)
cs541     ttysC   Dec  2 15:16   (solaria)
yansong   ttysL   Dec  1 14:44   (math)
mdps      ttysO   Nov 30 19:39   (localhost)
md        ttysU   Dec  2 08:45   (muller)
jac       ttysa   Dec  3 18:18   (localhost)
eichsted  ttysb   Dec  3 23:21   (pc1)
sweett    ttysc   Dec  3 22:40   (dov)
"big.output" 40 lines, 1659 characters
```

Remember that I used :q! to quit earlier, so my changes were not retained.

To move to the very last line of the file, I type G once and see this:

```
cdemmert  ttysk   Dec  3 22:37   (xsun)
jrlee     ttysn   Dec  3 22:53   (mac1)
fitzgejs  ttyso   Dec  3 23:18   (dov)
doerrhb   ttysp   Dec  3 23:20   (dov)
cdemmert  ttysq   Dec  3 23:00   (xsun)
frazierw  ttysr   Dec  3 23:01   (dov)
buckeye   ttyss   Dec  3 23:20   (mac2)
mtaylor   ttyst   Dec  3 23:22   (dov)
look      ttysu   Dec  3 23:12   (age)
janitor   ttysw   Dec  3 18:29   (age)
ajones    ttysx   Dec  3 23:23   (rassilon)
~
~
~
~
```

```
        ~
        ~
        ~
        ~
        ~
        ~
        ~
```

To move to the third line of the file, I type 3 followed by G:

```
leungtc   ttyrV   Dec  1 18:27   (magenta)
tuyinhwa  ttyrX   Dec  3 22:38   (expert)
hollenst  ttyrZ   Dec  3 22:14   (dov)
brandt    ttyrb   Nov 28 23:03   (age)
holmes    ttyrj   Dec  3 21:59   (age)
yuxi      ttyrn   Dec  1 14:19   (pc)
frodo     ttyro   Dec  3 22:01   (mentor)
labeck    ttyrt   Dec  3 22:02   (dov)
chenlx2   ttyru   Dec  3 21:53   (mentor)
leungtc   ttys0   Nov 28 15:11   (gold)
chinese   ttys2   Dec  3 22:53   (excalibur)
cdemmert  ttys5   Dec  3 23:00   (mentor)
yuenca    ttys6   Dec  3 23:00   (mentor)
janitor   ttys7   Dec  3 18:18   (age)
mathisbp  ttys8   Dec  3 23:17   (dov)
janitor   ttys9   Dec  3 18:18   (age)
cs541     ttysC   Dec  2 15:16   (solaria)
yansong   ttysL   Dec  1 14:44   (math)
mdps      ttysO   Nov 30 19:39   (localhost)
md        ttysU   Dec  2 08:45   (muller)
jac       ttysa   Dec  3 18:18   (localhost)
eichsted  ttysb   Dec  3 23:21   (pc1)
sweett    ttysc   Dec  3 22:40   (dov)
```

Notice that the cursor is on the third line of the file.

2. Now it's time to search. From my previous travels in this file, I know that the very last line is for the account ajones, but instead of using G to move there directly, I can search for the specified pattern by using the / search command.

Typing / immediately moves the cursor to the bottom of the screen:

```
md        ttysU   Dec  2 08:45   (mueller)
jac       ttysa   Dec  3 18:18   (localhost)
eichsted  ttysb   Dec  3 23:21   (pc1)
sweett    ttysc   Dec  3 22:40   (dov)
/_
```

Now I can type in the pattern `ajones`:

```
md        ttysU   Dec  2 08:45   (mueller)
jac       ttysa   Dec  3 18:18   (localhost)
eichsted  ttysb   Dec  3 23:21   (pc1)
sweett    ttysc   Dec  3 22:40   (dov)
/ajones_
```

When I press Return, vi spins through the file and moves me to the first line it finds that contains the specified pattern:

```
cdemmert  ttysk   Dec  3 22:37   (xsun)
jrlee     ttysn   Dec  3 22:53   (mac1)
fitzgejs  ttyso   Dec  3 23:18   (dov)
doerrhb   ttysp   Dec  3 23:20   (dov)
cdemmert  ttysq   Dec  3 23:00   (xsun)
frazierw  ttysr   Dec  3 23:01   (dov)
buckeye   ttyss   Dec  3 23:20   (mac2)
mtaylor   ttyst   Dec  3 23:22   (dov)
look      ttysu   Dec  3 23:12   (age)
janitor   ttysw   Dec  3 18:29   (age)
ajones    ttysx   Dec  3 23:23   (rassilon)
~
~
~
~
~
~
~
~
~
~
~
```

3. If I type n to search for this pattern again, a slash appears at the very bottom line to show that vi understood my request. But the cursor stays exactly where it is, which indicates that this is the only occurrence of the pattern in this file.

4. Looking at this file, I noticed that the account `janitor` has all sorts of sessions running. To search backward for occurrences of the account, I can use the ? command:

```
~
~
?janitor_
```

The first search moves the cursor up one line, which leaves the screen looking almost the same:

```
cdemmert ttysk    Dec  3 22:37    (xsun)
jrlee    ttysn    Dec  3 22:53    (mac1)
fitzgejs ttyso    Dec  3 23:18    (dov)
doerrhb  ttysp    Dec  3 23:20    (dov)
cdemmert ttysq    Dec  3 23:00    (xsun)
frazierw ttysr    Dec  3 23:01    (dov)
buckeye  ttyss    Dec  3 23:20    (mac2)
mtaylor  ttyst    Dec  3 23:22    (dov)
look     ttysu    Dec  3 23:12    (age)
janitor  ttysw    Dec  3 18:29    (age)
ajones   ttysx    Dec  3 23:23    (rassilon)
~
~
~
~
~
~
~
~
~
~
~
?janitor
```

11

Here's where the n, or next search, can come in handy. If I type n this time and there is another occurrence of the pattern in the file, vi moves me directly to the match:

```
yuxi     ttyrn    Dec  1 14:19    (pc)
frodo    ttyro    Dec  3 22:01    (mentor)
labeck   ttyrt    Dec  3 22:02    (dov)
chenlx2  ttyru    Dec  3 21:53    (mentor)
leungtc  ttys0    Nov 28 15:11    (gold)
chinese  ttys2    Dec  3 22:53    (excalibur)
cdemmert ttys5    Dec  3 23:00    (mentor)
yuenca   ttys6    Dec  3 23:00    (mentor)
janitor  ttys7    Dec  3 18:18    (age)
mathisbp ttys8    Dec  3 23:17    (dov)
janitor  ttys9    Dec  3 18:18    (age)
cs541    ttysC    Dec  2 15:16    (solaria)
yansong  ttysL    Dec  1 14:44    (math)
mdps     ttysO    Nov 30 19:39    (localhost)
md       ttysU    Dec  2 08:45    (muller)
jac      ttysa    Dec  3 18:18    (localhost)
eichsted ttysb    Dec  3 23:21    (pc1)
sweett   ttysc    Dec  3 22:40    (dov)
wellman  ttysd    Dec  3 23:01    (dov)
tuttleno ttyse    Dec  3 23:03    (indyvax)
```

```
wu        ttysf    Dec  3 23:10   (term01)
daurismj  ttysg    Dec  3 23:10   (dov)
cs414     ttysh    Dec  3 23:12   (xds)
```

When you're done, quit vi by using :q.

SUMMARY There are not dozens, but hundreds of commands in vi. Rather than overwhelm you with all of them, even in a table, I have opted instead to work with the most basic and important commands. By the time you're done with this hour, your knowledge of vi commands will be substantial, and you will be able to use the editor with little difficulty. The next hour will expand your knowledge with more shortcuts and efficiency commands.

This task focused on searching for patterns, which is a common requirement and helpful feature of any editor. In addition, you learned how to move to the top of the file (1G) and to the bottom of the file (G), as well as anywhere in between.

Task 11.7: How To Start vi Correctly

DESCRIPTION The vi command wouldn't be part of UNIX if it didn't have some startup options available, but there really are only two worth mentioning. The -R flag sets up vi as a read-only file, to ensure that you don't accidentally modify a file. The second option doesn't start with a dash, but with a plus sign: Any command following the plus sign is used as an initial command to the program. This is more useful than it may sound. The command vi +$ sample, for example, starts the editor at the bottom of the file sample, and vi +17 sample starts the editor on the 17th line of sample.

ACTION

1. First, this is the read-only format:

   `% vi -R buckaroo`

```
I found myself stealing a peek at my own watch and overheard
General Catbird's
aide give him the latest.
"He's not even here," went the conversation.
"Banzai."
"Where the hell is he?"
"At the hospital in El Paso."
"What? Why weren't we informed? What's wrong with him?"
~
~
~
~
~
~
```

11

```
    ~
    ~
    ~
    ~
    ~
    ~
    ~
    ~
"buckaroo" [Read only] 8 lines, 271 characters
```

Notice the addition of the [Read only] message on the status line. You can edit the file, but if you try to save the edits with :w, you will see this:

```
    ~
    ~
"buckaroo" File is read only
```

Quit vi with :q!.

2. Next, recall that janitor occurs in many places in the big.output file. I'll start vi on the file line that contains the pattern janitor in the file. This time, notice where the cursor is sitting.

   % **vi +/janitor big.output**

```
brandt    ttyrb   Nov 28 23:03   (age)
holmes    ttyrj   Dec  3 21:59   (age)
yuxi      ttyrn   Dec  1 14:19   (pc)
frodo     ttyro   Dec  3 22:01   (mentor)
labeck    ttyrt   Dec  3 22:02   (dov)
chenlx2   ttyru   Dec  3 21:53   (mentor)
leungtc   ttys0   Nov 28 15:11   (gold)
chinese   ttys2   Dec  3 22:53   (excalibur)
cdemmert  ttys5   Dec  3 23:00   (mentor)
yuenca    ttys6   Dec  3 23:00   (mentor)
janitor   ttys7   Dec  3 18:18   (age)
mathisbp  ttys8   Dec  3 23:17   (dov)
janitor   ttys9   Dec  3 18:18   (age)
cs541     ttysC   Dec  2 15:16   (solaria)
yansong   ttysL   Dec  1 14:44   (math)
mdps      ttysO   Nov 30 19:39   (localhost)
md        ttysU   Dec  2 08:45   (muller)
jac       ttysa   Dec  3 18:18   (localhost)
eichsted  ttysb   Dec  3 23:21   (pc1)
sweett    ttysc   Dec  3 22:40   (dov)
wellman   ttysd   Dec  3 23:01   (dov)
tuttleno  ttyse   Dec  3 23:03   (indyvax)
wu        ttysf   Dec  3 23:10   (term01)
"big.output" 40 lines, 1659 characters
```

11

3. Finally, launch `vi` with the cursor on the third line of the file `buckaroo`:

`% vi +3 buckaroo`

```
I found myself stealing a peek at my own watch and overheard
General Catbird's
aide give him the latest.
"He's not even here," went the conversation.
"Banzai."
"Where the hell is he?"
"At the hospital in El Paso."
"What? Why weren't we informed? What's wrong with him?"
~
~
~
~
~
~
~
~
~
~
~
~
~
"buckaroo" 8 lines, 271 characters
```

Again, notice where the cursor rests.

SUMMARY At times it can be helpful to know these two starting options. In particular, I often use +/*pattern* to start the editor at a specific pattern, but you can use `vi` for years without ever knowing more than just the name of the command itself.

Task 11.8: The Colon Commands in `vi`

DESCRIPTION Without too much explanation, you have learned a couple of colon commands, commands that have a colon as the first character. The colon immediately zooms the cursor to the bottom of the screen for further input. These commands are actually a subset of quite a large range of commands, all part of the `ex` editor on which `vi` is based.

The colon commands that are most helpful are as follows:

Command	Function
`:e` *filename*	Stop editing the current file and edit the specified file.
`:n`	Stop editing the current file and edit the next file specified on the command line.

Command	Function
`:q`	Quit the editor.
`:q!`	Quit regardless of whether any changes have occurred.
`:r `*`filename`*	Include the contents of the specified file at this position in the file that is currently being edited.
`:w`	Save the file to disk.
`:w `*`filename`*	Save the file to disk with the specified filename.

ACTION

1. Start `vi` again, this time specifying more than one file on the command line; `vi` quickly indicates that you want to edit more than one file:

    ```
    % vi buckaroo big.output
    2 files to edit.
    ```

    Then it clears the screen and shows you the first file:

    ```
    I found myself stealing a peek at my own watch and overheard
    General Catbird's
    aide give him the latest.
    "He's not even here," went the conversation.
    "Banzai."
    "Where the hell is he?"
    "At the hospital in El Paso."
    "What? Why weren't we informed? What's wrong with him?"
    ~
    ~
    ~
    ~
    ~
    ~
    ~
    ~
    ~
    ~
    ~
    ~
    ~
    "buckaroo" 8 lines, 271 characters
    ```

11

Using :w results in this:

```
~
~
~
"buckaroo" 8 lines, 271 characters
```

2. Instead, try writing to a different file, using :w newfile:

```
~
~
:w newfile_
```

When you press Return, you see this:

```
~
~
"newfile" [New file] 8 lines, 271 characters
```

3. Now pay attention to where the cursor is in the file. The :r, or read-file, command always includes the contents of the file below the current line. Just before I press Return, then, here's what my screen looks like:

```
I found myself stealing a peek at my own watch and overheard
General Catbird's
aide give him the latest.
"He's not even here," went the conversation.
"Banzai."
"Where the hell is he?"
"At the hospital in El Paso."
"What? Why weren't we informed? What's wrong with him?"
~
~
~
~
~
~
~
~
```

```
~
~
~
~
~
~
:r newfile_
```

Pressing Return yields this:

```
I found myself stealing a peek at my own watch and overheard
General Catbird's
I found myself stealing a peek at my own watch and overheard
General Catbird's
aide give him the latest.
"He's not even here," went the conversation.
"Banzai."
"Where the hell is he?"
"At the hospital in El Paso."
"What? Why weren't we informed? What's wrong with him?"

aide give him the latest.
"He's not even here," went the conversation.
"Banzai."
"Where the hell is he?"
"At the hospital in El Paso."
"What? Why weren't we informed? What's wrong with him?"
~
~
~
~
~
~
```

This can be a helpful way to include files within one another or to build a file that contains lots of other files.

4. Now that I've garbled the file, I want to save it to a new file, buckaroo.confused:

```
~
~
:w buckaroo.confused_
```

When I press Return, I see this:

```
~
~
"buckaroo.confused" [New file] 16 lines, 542 characters
```

JUST A MINUTE

> Older UNIX systems have a 14-character filename limit. If yours does, you will see buckaroo.confu as the saved filename.

5. Now it's time to move to the second file in the list of files given to vi at startup. To do this, I use the :n, or next-file, command:

```
~
~
:n_
```

Pressing Return results in the next file being brought into the editor to replace the first:

```
leungtc  ttyrV   Dec  1 18:27   (magenta)
tuyinhwa ttyrX   Dec  3 22:38   (expert)
hollenst ttyrZ   Dec  3 22:14   (dov)
brandt   ttyrb   Nov 28 23:03   (age)
holmes   ttyrj   Dec  3 21:59   (age)
yuxi     ttyrn   Dec  1 14:19   (pc)
frodo    ttyro   Dec  3 22:01   (mentor)
labeck   ttyrt   Dec  3 22:02   (dov)
chenlx2  ttyru   Dec  3 21:53   (mentor)
leungtc  ttys0   Nov 28 15:11   (gold)
chinese  ttys2   Dec  3 22:53   (excalibur)
cdemmert ttys5   Dec  3 23:00   (mentor)
yuenca   ttys6   Dec  3 23:00   (mentor)
janitor  ttys7   Dec  3 18:18   (age)
mathisbp ttys8   Dec  3 23:17   (dov)
janitor  ttys9   Dec  3 18:18   (age)
cs541    ttysC   Dec  2 15:16   (solaria)
yansong  ttysL   Dec  1 14:44   (math)
mdps     ttysO   Nov 30 19:39   (localhost)
md       ttysU   Dec  2 08:45   (muller)
jac      ttysa   Dec  3 18:18   (localhost)
eichsted ttysb   Dec  3 23:21   (pc1)
sweett   ttysc   Dec  3 22:40   (dov)
"big.output" 40 lines, 1659 characters
```

11

6. In the middle of working on this, I suddenly realize that I need to make a slight change to the recently saved buckaroo.confused file. That's where the :e command comes in handy. Using it, I can edit any other file:

```
~
~
:e buckaroo.confused_
```

I press Return and see this:

```
I found myself stealing a peek at my own watch and overheard
General Catbird's
I found myself stealing a peek at my own watch and overheard
General Catbird's
aide give him the latest.
"He's not even here," went the conversation.
"Banzai."
"Where the hell is he?"
"At the hospital in El Paso."
"What? Why weren't we informed? What's wrong with him?"

aide give him the latest.
"He's not even here," went the conversation.
"Banzai."
"Where the hell is he?"
"At the hospital in El Paso."
"What? Why weren't we informed? What's wrong with him?"
~
~
~
~
~
~
"buckaroo.confused" 16 lines, 542 characters
```

SUMMARY That's it! You now know a considerable amount about one of the most important, and certainly most used, commands in UNIX. There's more to learn (isn't there always?), but you now can edit your files with aplomb!

Summary

Table 10.2 summarizes the basic vi commands you learned in this hour.

Table 10.2. Basic vi commands.

Command	Meaning
0	Move to the beginning of the line.
$	Move to the end of the line.
/pattern	Search forward for the next line using a specified pattern.
?pattern	Search backward for the next line using a specified pattern.
a	Append text—enter into insert mode after the current character.
^b	Back up one screen of text.
B	Back up one space-delimited word.
b	Back up one word.
Backspace	Move left one character.
^d	Move down half a page.
D	Delete through the end of the line.
d	Delete—dw = delete word, dd = delete line.
Escape	Leave insert mode and return to command mode.
^f	Move forward one screen of text.
G	Go to the last line of the file.
nG	Go to the nth line of the file.
h	Move left one character.
i	Insert text—enter into insert mode before the current character.
j	Move down one line.
k	Move up one line.
l	Move right one character.
n	Repeat last search.
O	Open new line for inserting text above the current line.
o	Open new line for inserting text below the current line.
Return	Move to the beginning of the next line.
^u	Move up half a page.
U	Undo—restore current line if changed.

11

Command	Meaning
u	Undo the last change made to the file.
W	Move forward one space-delimited word.
w	Move forward one word.
x	Delete a single character.
:e *file*	Edit a specified file without leaving vi.
:n	Move to the next file in the file list.
:q	Quit vi and return to the UNIX system prompt.
:q!	Quit vi and return to the UNIX system prompt, throwing away any changes made to the file.
:r *file*	Include the contents of the specified file at this position in the file that is currently being edited.
:w *file*	Save the file to disk with this name.
:w	Save the file to disk.

Workshop

The Workshop summarizes the key terms you learned and poses some questions about the topics presented in this chapter. It also provides you with a preview of what you will learn in the next hour.

Key Terms

addressing commands   The set of vi commands that enable you to specify what type of object you want to work with. The d commands serve as an example: dw means delete word, and db means delete the previous word.

colon commands   The vi commands that begin with a colon, usually used for file manipulation.

command mode   The mode in which you can manage your document; this includes the capability to change text, rearrange it, and delete it.

insert mode   The vi mode that lets you enter text directly into a file. The i command starts the insert mode, and Escape exits it.

modal   A modal program has multiple environments, or modes, that offer different capabilities. In a modal program, the Return key, for example, might do different things, depending on which mode you are in.

modeless   A modeless program always interprets a key the same way, regardless of what the user is doing.

transpose case   Switch uppercase letters to lowercase or lowercase to uppercase.

Questions

1. What happens if you try to quit vi using :qw? Before you try it, do you expect it to work?

2. If you're familiar with word processing programs in the Mac or Windows environment, would you describe them as modal or modeless?

3. The d command is an example of a command that understands addressing commands. You know of quite a few. Test them to see if they will all work following d. Make sure you see if you can figure out the command that has the opposite action to the D command.

4. Do each of the following three commands give the same result?

   ```
   D
   d$
   dG
   ```

5. Imagine you're in command mode in the middle of a line that's in the middle of the screen. Describe what would happen if you were to type each of the following:

   ```
   Badluck
   Window
   blad$
   ```

6. What would happen if you were to use the following startup flags?

   ```
   vi +0 test
   vi +/joe/ names
   vi +hhjjhh
   vi +:q testme
   ```

Preview of the Next Hour

The next hour expands your knowledge of the vi editor. It introduces the techniques of using numeric repeat prefixes for commands, changing characters (rather than deleting and inserting), searching and replacing, key mapping to enable arrow keys, and working with UNIX while in vi.

Hour **12**

Advanced vi Tricks, Tools, and Techniques

In the previous hour, you learned some 50 vi commands that enable you to easily move about in files, insert text, delete other text, search for specific patterns, and move from file to file without leaving the program. This hour expands your expertise by showing you some more powerful vi commands. Before you begin this hour, I strongly recommend that you use vi to work with a few files. Make sure you're comfortable with the different modes of the program.

Goals for This Hour

In this hour, you learn how to

- ☐ Use the change and replace commands.
- ☐ Use numeric repeat prefixes.
- ☐ Number lines in the file.
- ☐ Search and replace.

☐ Map keys with the :map command.

☐ Move sentences and paragraphs.

☐ Use the :! command to access UNIX commands.

This may seem like a small list, but there's a lot packed into it. I'll be totally honest: You can do fine in vi without ever reading this hour. You already know how to insert and delete text, save or quit without saving, and you can search for particular patterns, too—even from the command line as you start vi for the first time! On the other hand, vi is like any other complex topic. The more you're willing to study and learn, the more the program will bow to your needs. This means you can accomplish a wider variety of different tasks on a daily basis.

Task 12.1: The Change and Replace Commands

DESCRIPTION In the previous hour, you saw me fix a variety of problems by deleting words and then replacing them with new words. There is, in fact, a much smarter way to do this, and that is by using either the change or the replace command.

Each command has a lowercase and an uppercase version, and each is quite different from the other. The r command replaces the character that the cursor is sitting upon with the next character you type, whereas the R command puts you into *replace mode* so that anything you type overwrites whatever is already on the line until you stop typing. By contrast, C replaces everything on the line with whatever you type. (It's a subtle difference, but I will demonstrate it, so don't fear.) The c command is the most powerful of them all. The change command c works just like the d command does, as described in the previous hour. You can use the c command with any address command, and it will enable you to change text through to that address, whether it's a word, a line, or even the rest of the document.

ACTION

1. Start vi with the buckaroo.confused file.

```
I found myself stealing a peek at my own watch and overheard
General Catbird's
I found myself stealing a peek at my own watch and overheard
General Catbird's
aide give him the latest.
"He's not even here," went the conversation.
"Banzai."
"Where the hell is he?"
"At the hospital in El Paso."
"What? Why weren't we informed? What's wrong with him?"

aide give him the latest.
"He's not even here," went the conversation.
```

```
"Banzai."
"Where the hell is he?"
"At the hospital in El Paso."
"What? Why weren't we informed? What's wrong with him?"

~
~
~
~
~
"buckaroo.confused" 16 lines, 542 characters
```

Without moving the cursor at all, type R. Nothing happens, or so it seems. Now type the words Excerpt from "Buckaroo Banzai", and watch what happens:

```
Excerpt from "Buckaroo Banzai"at my own watch and overheard
General Catbird's
I found myself stealing a peek at my own watch and overheard
General Catbird's
aide give him the latest.
"He's not even here," went the conversation.
```

Now press Escape and notice that what you see on the screen is exactly what's in the file.

2. This isn't, however, quite what I want. I could use either D or d$ to delete through the end of the line, but that's a bit awkward. Instead, I'll use 0 to move back to the beginning of the line. You do so, too:

```
Excerpt from "Buckaroo Banzai" at my own watch and overheard
General Catbird's
I found myself stealing a peek at my own watch and overheard
General Catbird's
aide give him the latest.
"He's not even here," went the conversation.
```

This time, type C to change the contents of the line. Before you type even a single character of the new text, notice what the line now looks like:

```
Excerpt from "Buckaroo Banzai" at my own watch and overheard
General Catbird'$
I found myself stealing a peek at my own watch and overheard
General Catbird's
aide give him the latest.
"He's not even here," went the conversation.
```

Here's where a subtle difference comes into play! Look at the very last character on the current line. Where the s had been, when you pressed c, the program placed a $ instead to show the range of the text to be changed by the command. Press the Tab key once, and then type Excerpt from "Buckaroo Bansai" by Earl MacRauch.

```
        Excerpt from "Buckaroo Bansai" by Earl MacRauchheard General
Catbird'$
I found myself stealing a peek at my own watch and overheard
General Catbird's
aide give him the latest.
"He's not even here," went the conversation.
```

This time, watch what happens when I press Escape:

```
        Excerpt from "Buckaroo Bansai" by Earl MacRauch
I found myself stealing a peek at my own watch and overheard
General Catbird's
aide give him the latest.
"He's not even here," went the conversation.
```

3. I think I made another mistake. The actual title of the book is Buckaroo Banzai with a *z*, but I've spelled it with an *s* instead. This is a chance to try the new r command.

    Use cursor control keys to move the cursor to the offending letter. I'll use b to back up words and then h a few times to move into the middle of the word. My screen now looks like this:

```
        Excerpt from "Buckaroo Bansai" by Earl MacRauch
I found myself stealing a peek at my own watch and overheard
General Catbird's
aide give him the latest.
"He's not even here," went the conversation.
```

Now type r. Again, nothing happens; the cursor doesn't move. Type r again to make sure it worked:

```
        Excerpt from "Buckaroo Banrai" by Earl MacRauch
I found myself stealing a peek at my own watch and overheard
General Catbird's
aide give him the latest.
"He's not even here," went the conversation.
```

That's no good. It replaced the s with an r, which definitely isn't correct. Type rz, and you should have the following:

```
        Excerpt from "Buckaroo Banzai" by Earl MacRauch
I found myself stealing a peek at my own watch and overheard
General Catbird's
aide give him the latest.
"He's not even here," went the conversation.
```

4. Okay, those are the easy ones. Now it's time to see what the c command can do for you. In fact, it's incredibly powerful. You can change just about any range of information from the current point in the file in either direction!

   To start, move to the middle of the file, where the second copy of the passage is located:

```
        Excerpt from "Buckaroo Banzai" by Earl MacRauch
I found myself stealing a peek at my own watch and overheard
General Catbird's
aide give him the latest.
"He's not even here," went the conversation.
"Banzai."
"Where the hell is he?"
"At the hospital in El Paso."
"What? Why weren't we informed? What's wrong with him?"

aide give him the latest.
"He's not even here," went the conversation.
"Banzai."
"Where the hell is he?"
"At the hospital in El Paso."
"What? Why weren't we informed? What's wrong with him?"


~
~
~
~
```

12

```
~
~
~
"buckaroo.confused" 16 lines, 542 characters
```

I think I'll just change the word aide that the cursor is sitting on to The tall beige wall clock opted to instead. First, I type c and note that, like many other commands in vi, nothing happens. Now I type w because I want to change just the first word. The screen should look like this:

```
"At the hospital in El Paso."
"What? Why weren't we informed? What's wrong with him?"

aid$ give him the latest.
"He's not even here," went the conversation.
"Banzai."
```

Again, the program has replaced the last character in the range of the change to a $, so I can eyeball the situation. Now I type The tall beige wall clock opted to. Once I reach the $, the editor stops overwriting characters and starts inserting them instead; the screen now looks like this:

```
"At the hospital in El Paso."
"What? Why weren't we informed? What's wrong with him?"

The tall beige wall clock opted to_give him the latest.
"He's not even here," went the conversation.
"Banzai."
```

Press Escape and you're done (though you can undo the change with the u or U command, of course).

5. Tall and beige or not, this section makes no sense now, so change this entire line by using the $ motion command you learned in the previous hour. First, use 0 to move to the beginning of the line, and then type c$:

```
"At the hospital in El Paso."
"What? Why weren't we informed? What's wrong with him?"

The tall beige wall clock opted to give him the latest$
"He's not even here," went the conversation.
"Banzai."
```

This is working. The last character changed to $. Press Escape, and the entire line is deleted:

```
"At the hospital in El Paso."
"What? Why weren't we informed? What's wrong with him?"


"He's not even here," went the conversation.
"Banzai."
```

6. There are still five lines below the current line. I could delete them and then type in the information I want, but that's primitive. Instead, the c command comes to the rescue. Move down one line, type c5, and press Return. Watch what happens:

```
"At the hospital in El Paso."
"What? Why weren't we informed? What's wrong with him?"

_
~
~
~
~
~
~
~
~
~
~
6 lines changed
```

In general, you always can change the current and next lines by using c followed by a Return (because the Return key is a motion key, too, remember). By prefacing the command with a number, I changed the range from two lines to five.

JUST A MINUTE

You might be asking, "Why two lines?" The answer is subtle. In essence, whenever you use the c command, you change the current line plus any additional lines that might be touched by the command. Pressing Return moves the cursor to the following line; therefore, the current line (starting at the cursor location) through the following line are changed. The command probably should change just to the beginning of the following line, but that's beyond even my control!

Now press Tab four times, type (page 8), and then press the Escape key. The
screen should look like this:

```
"Where the hell is he?"
"At the hospital in El Paso."
"What? Why weren't we informed? What's wrong with him?"


                                        (page 8)

~
~
~
```

7. What if I change my mind? That's where the u command comes in handy. Typing
    u once undoes the last command:

```
            Excerpt from "Buckaroo Banzai" by Earl MacRauch
I found myself stealing a peek at my own watch and overheard
General Catbird's
aide give him the latest.
"He's not even here," went the conversation.
"Banzai."
"Where the hell is,he?"
"At the hospital in El Paso."
"What? Why weren't we informed? What's wrong with him?"

"He's not even here," went the conversation.
"Banzai."
"Where the hell is he?"
"At the hospital in El Paso."
"What? Why weren't we informed? What's wrong with him?"

~
~
~
~
~
~

5 more lines
```

SUMMARY The combination of replace and change commands adds a level of sophistication to
an editor that you might have suspected could only insert or delete. There's much
more to cover in this hour, so don't stop now!

12

Task 12.2: Numeric Repeat Prefixes

DESCRIPTION You have seen two commands that were prefixed by a number to cause a specific action. The G command, in the previous hour, moves you to the very last line of the file, unless you type in a number first. If you type in a number, the G command moves to the specified line number. Similarly, in the previous section, you saw that typing a number before the Return key causes vi to repeat the key the specified number of times.

Numeric repeat prefixes are actually widely available in vi and are the missing piece of your navigational tool set.

ACTION

1. I'll move back to the top of the buckaroo.confused file. This time, I use 1G to move there, rather than a bunch of k keys or other steps. The top of the screen now looks like this:

```
        Excerpt from "Buckaroo Banzai" by Earl MacRauch
I found myself stealing a peek at my own watch and overheard
General Catbird's
aide give him the latest.
"He's not even here," went the conversation.
```

Now I'll move forward 15 words. Instead of typing w 15 times, I'll type 15w.

```
        Excerpt from "Buckaroo Banzai" by Earl MacRauch
I found myself stealing a peek at my own watch and overheard
General Catbird's
aide give him the latest.
"He's not even here," went the conversation.
```

2. Now I'll move down seven lines by typing 7 and pressing Return. I'll use o to give myself a blank line and then press Escape:

```
"Where the hell is he?"
"At the hospital in El Paso."
"What? Why weren't we informed? What's wrong with him?"


_

"He's not even here," went the conversation.
"Banzai."
```

I'd like to have `Go Team Banzai!` on the bottom, and I want to repeat it three times. Can you guess how to do it? I simply type `3i` to move into insert mode and then type `Go Team Banzai!` . The screen looks like this:

```
"Where the hell is he?"
"At the hospital in El Paso."
"What? Why weren't we informed? What's wrong with him?"

Go Team Banzai! _

"He's not even here," went the conversation.
"Banzai."
```

Pressing Escape has a dramatic result:

```
"Where the hell is he?"
"At the hospital in El Paso."
"What? Why weren't we informed? What's wrong with him?"

Go Team Banzai! Go Team Banzai! Go Team Banzai!

"He's not even here," went the conversation.
"Banzai."
```

3. Now I'd like to get rid of all the lines below the current line. There are many different ways to do this, but I'm going to try to guess how many words are present and use a repeat count prefix to `dw` to delete that many words. (Actually, it's not critical I know the number of words, because `vi` will repeat the command only while it makes sense to do so).

I type `75dw`, and the screen instantly looks like this:

```
        Excerpt from "Buckaroo Banzai" by Earl MacRauch
I found myself stealing a peek at my own watch and overheard
General Catbird's
aide give him the latest.
"He's not even here," went the conversation.
"Banzai."
"Where the hell is he?"
"At the hospital in El Paso."
"What? Why weren't we informed? What's wrong with him?"

Go Team Banzai! Go Team Banzai! Go Team Banzai!
```

```
                     ~
                     ~
                     ~
                     ~
                     ~
                     ~
                     ~
                     ~
                     ~
                     ~
                     ~
                     7 lines deleted
```

Try the undo command here to see what happens!

SUMMARY Almost all commands in vi can work with a numeric repeat prefix, even commands that you might not expect to work, such as the i insert command. Remember that a request can be accomplished in many ways. To delete five words, for example, you could use 5dw or d5w. Experiment on your own, and you'll get the idea.

Task 12.3: Numbering Lines in the File

DESCRIPTION It's very helpful to have an editor that works with the entire screen, but sometimes you need to know only what line you're currently on. Further, sometimes it can be very helpful to have all the lines numbered on the screen. With vi, you can do both of these—the former by pressing ^g (remember, that's Control-g) while in command mode, and the latter by using a complex colon command, :set number, followed by Return. To turn off the display of line numbers, simply type :set nonumber and press Return.

ACTION

1. Much as I try to leave this file, I'm still looking at buckaroo.confused in vi. The screen looks like this:

```
          Excerpt from "Buckaroo Banzai" by Earl MacRauch
I found myself stealing a peek at my own watch and overheard
General Catbird's
aide give him the latest.
"He's not even here," went the conversation.
"Banzai."
"Where the hell is he?"
"At the hospital in El Paso."
"What? Why weren't we informed? What's wrong with him?"
```

12

```
Go Team Banzai! Go Team Banzai! Go Team Banzai!
~
~
~
~
~
~
~
~
~
7 lines deleted
```

Can you see where the cursor is? To find out what line number the cursor is on, press ^g, and the information is listed on the status line at the bottom:

```
~
~
~
"buckaroo.confused" [Modified] line 10 of 11, column 1  --90%--
```

There's lots of information here, including the name of the file (buckaroo.confused), an indication that vi thinks I've changed it since I started the program ([Modified]), the current line (10), total lines in the file (11), what column I'm in (1), and, finally, an estimate of how far into the file I am (90%).

2. Eleven lines? Count the display again. There are 12 lines. What's going on? The answer will become clear if I turn on line numbering for the entire file. To do this, I type :, which zips the cursor to the bottom of the screen, where I then enter the :set number command:

```
~
~
~
:set number_
```

Pressing Return causes the screen to change, thus:

```
     1              Excerpt from "Buckaroo Banzai" by Earl MacRauch
     2  I found myself stealing a peek at my own watch and overheard
General Catbird's
     3  aide give him the latest.
     4  "He's not even here," went the conversation.
     5  "Banzai."
     6  "Where the hell is he?"
     7  "At the hospital in El Paso."
     8  "What? Why weren't we informed? What's wrong with him?"
     9
    10  Go Team Banzai! Go Team Banzai! Go Team Banzai!
    11
~
~
~
~
~
~
~
~
~
```

Now you can see how it figures that there are only 11 lines, even though it seems by the screens shown in the book that there are 12 lines.

3. To turn off the line numbering, use the opposite command :set nonumber followed by Return, which restores the screen to how you're used to seeing it.

SUMMARY There are definitely some times when being able to include the number of each line is helpful. One example is if you are using awk (covered in Hour 10, "Power Filters and File Redirection"), and it's complaining about a specific line being in an inappropriate format (usually by saying syntax error, bailing out!, or something similar).

Task 12.4: Search and Replace

DESCRIPTION Though most of vi is easy to learn and use, one command that always causes great trouble for users is the search-and-replace command. The key to understanding this command is to remember that vi is built on the line editor (ex). Instead of trying to figure out some arcane vi command, it's easiest to just drop to the line editor and use a simple colon command—one identical to the command used in sed (as described in Hour 9, "Wildcards and Regular Expressions")—to replace an old pattern with a new one. To replace an existing word on the current line with a new word (the simplest case), use :s/old/new/. If you want to have all occurrences on the current line matched, you need to add the g suffix (just as with sed): :s/old/new/g.

12

To change all occurrences of one word or phrase to another across the entire file, the command is identical to the preceding command, except that you must prefix an indication of the range of lines affected. Recall that $ is the last line in the file and that ranges are specified (in this case, as in sed) by two numbers separated by a comma. It should be no surprise that the command is :1,$ s/*old*/*new*/g.

ACTION

1. You won't be surprised to find that I'm still working with the buckaroo.confused file, so your screen should look very similar to this:

```
        Excerpt from "Buckaroo Banzai" by Earl MacRauch
I found myself stealing a peek at my own watch and overheard
General Catbird's
aide give him the latest.
"He's not even here," went the conversation.
"Banzai."
"Where the hell is he?"
"At the hospital in El Paso."
"What? Why weren't we informed? What's wrong with him?"

Go Team Banzai! Go Team Banzai! Go Team Banzai!

~
~
~
~
~
~
~
~
~
~
~
~
~
~
```

The cursor is on the very first line. I'm going to rename Earl. I type :, the cursor immediately moves to the bottom, and then I type s/Earl/Duke/. Pressing Return produces this:

```
            Excerpt from "Buckaroo Banzai" by Duke MacRauch
I found myself stealing a peek at my own watch and overheard General
Catbird's
aide give him the latest.
"He's not even here," went the conversation.
```

As you can see, this maneuver was simple and effective.

2. I've decided that development psychology is my bag. Now, instead of having this Banzai character, I want my fictional character to be called Bandura. I could use the previous command to change the occurrence on the current line, but I really want to change all occurrences within the file.

This is no problem. I type :1,$ s/Banzai/Bandura/ and press Return. Here's the result:

```
            Excerpt from "Buckaroo Bandura" by Duke MacRauch
I found myself stealing a peek at my own watch and overheard
General Catbird's
aide give him the latest.
"He's not even here," went the conversation.
"Bandura."
"Where the hell is he?"
"At the hospital in El Paso."
"What? Why weren't we informed? What's wrong with him?"

Go Team Bandura! Go Team Banzai! Go Team Banzai!

~
~
~
~
~
~
~
~
~
~
~
~
```

12

The result is not quite right. Because I forgot the trailing g, vi changed only the very first occurrence on each line, leaving the "go team" exhortation rather confusing.

To try again, I type `:1,$ s/Banzai/Bandura/g`, press Return, and the screen changes as desired:

```
                Excerpt from "Buckaroo Bandura" by Duke MacRauch
I found myself stealing a peek at my own watch and overheard
General Catbird's
aide give him the latest.
"He's not even here," went the conversation.
"Bandura."
"Where the hell is he?"
"At the hospital in El Paso."
"What? Why weren't we informed? What's wrong with him?"

Go Team Bandura! Go Team Bandura! Go Team Bandura!

~
~
~
~
~
~
~
~
~
~
7 substitutions
```

Notice that vi also indicates the total number of substitutions in this case.

4. I'll press u to undo the last change.

SUMMARY Search and replace is one area where a windowing system like that of a Macintosh or PC running Windows comes in handy. A windowing system offers different boxes for the old and new patterns; it shows each change and a dialog box asking, "Should I change this one?" Alas, this is UNIX, and it's still designed to run on ASCII terminals.

Task 12.5: Mapping Keys with the `:map` Command

DESCRIPTION As you have worked through the various examples, you might have tried pressing the arrow keys on your keyboard or perhaps a key labeled Ins or Del to insert or delete characters. Odds are that the keys not only didn't work, but instead caused all sorts of weird things to happen!

The good news is that within vi is a facility that enables you to map any key to a specific action. If these key mappings are saved in a file called `.exrc` in your home directory, the mappings will be understood by vi automatically each time you use the program. The format for using the map command is `:map key command-sequence`. (In a nutshell, mapping is a way of

12

associating an action with another action or result. For example, by plugging your computer into the correct wall socket, you could map your action of flipping the light switch on the wall with the result of having your computer turn on.)

JUST A MINUTE

> The use of the filename .exrc is a puzzling remnant of vi having been built on top of the ex editor. Why it couldn't be named .virc I don't know.

You can also save other things in your .exrc file, including the :set number option if you're a nut about seeing line numbers. More interestingly, vi can be taught abbreviations so that each time you type the abbreviation, vi expands it. The format for defining abbreviations is :abbreviate *abbreviation expanded-value*. Finally, any line that begins with a double quote is considered a comment and is ignored.

ACTION

1. It's finally time to leave the buckaroo.confused file and restart vi, this time with the .exrc file in your home directory:

```
% cd
% vi .exrc
```

```
_
~
~
~
~
~
~
~
~
~
~
~
~
~
~
~
~
~
~
~
~
~
".exrc" [New file]
```

Before I actually add any information to this new file, I'm going to define a few abbreviations to make life a bit easier. To do this, I type :, which, as you know, moves the cursor to the bottom of the screen. Then I'm going to define `tyu` as a simple abbreviation for the lengthy phrase `Teach Yourself UNIX in a Few Minutes`:

```
~
~
~

:abbreviate tyu Teach Yourself UNIX in a Few Minutes_
```

Pressing Return moves the cursor back to the top.

2. Now I'll try the abbreviation. Recall that in the `.exrc`, lines beginning with a double quote are comments and are ignored when `vi` starts up. I press `i` to enter insert mode and then type `" Sample .exrc file as shown in tyu`. The screen looks like this:

```
" Sample .exrc file as shown in tyu_
~
~
```

As soon as I type a space or a punctuation character, or press Return, the abbreviation is expanded. In this case, I opt to move to the next line by pressing Return:

```
" Sample .exrc file as shown in Teach Yourself UNIX in a Few Minutes
~
~
~
```

Press Escape to leave the insert mode.

3. This feature can be used also to correct common typos you make. I know that I have a bad habit of typing `teh` instead of `the`. Because `vi` is smart about abbreviation expansion, I can "abbreviate" `the` as `teh` and not get into trouble:

```
~
~

:ab teh the_
```

12

You don't have to type the entire word abbreviation each time. The first two letters, ab, are sufficient for vi to figure out what's going on!

I press Return. Now I can use my typo whenever I want, and the editor will fix it. I can demonstrate this by adding a second comment to this file. Adding a comment is easy because I'm still at the beginning of the second line. When I type i followed by " (subtly different from the example in teh, I get the following result:

```
" Sample .exrc file as shown in Teach Yourself UNIX in a Few Minutes
" (subtly different from the example in the_
~
~
```

If I type another character, instead of pressing the spacebar, vi is smart enough not to expand the abbreviation. Try it yourself. After typing h again, I'll see this:

```
" Sample .exrc file as shown in Teach Yourself UNIX in a Few Minutes
"  (subtly different from the example in tehh_
~
~
```

Because I'm still in insert mode, however, I can backspace and replace the spare h with a space, which instantly fixes the spelling. Finally, I type book) and press Escape to return to command mode.

4. I have one more nifty abbreviation trick before moving to the map command. Type :ab by itself and press Return, and vi shows you a list of the abbreviations currently in effect:

```
~
~
:ab
tyu     tyu     Teach Yourself UNIX in a Few Minutes
teh     teh     the
[Hit any key to continue]  _
```

Okay, now you can move on to key mapping.

12

5. Key mapping is as easy as defining abbreviations except that you must remember one thing: Any control character entered must be prefaced with a ^v so that vi doesn't interpret it immediately. The Escape key is included in this list, too.

To map the Clear key on my keyboard to the D function, which, as you recall, deletes text through the end of the current line, I type :map, followed by a single space:

```
~
~
:map
```

TIME SAVER

Your keyboard might not have a Clear key. If not, please read through the example anyway.

Now I need to type the ^v; otherwise, when I press the Clear key, it will send a series of non-printable characters to the screen, called an *escape sequence* that will confuse vi to no end. I type ^v and see this:

```
~
~
:map ^
```

The cursor is floating over the caret, which indicates that the next character typed should be a control character. Instead of typing any specific character, however, I simply press the Clear key. The result is that it sends the escape sequence, and vi captures it without a problem:

```
~
~
:map ^[OP_
```

Now I type another space, because the key part of the key mapping has been defined, and then type the command to which vi should map the Clear key:

```
~
~
:map ^[OP D_
```

Finally, I press Return, and it's done! To test the key mapping, I'll move back to the very first line, to the phrase Few Minutes:

```
" Sample .exrc file as shown in Teach Yourself UNIX in a Few Minutes
"  (subtly different from the example in the book)
~
~
```

To clear this line, I need only press Clear, and it works.

6. To save this as a permanent key mapping in the .exrc file, I duplicate each keystroke, but this time while in insert mode instead of at the bottom of the screen. The result is a file that now looks like this:

```
" Sample .exrc file as shown in Teach Yourself UNIX in a
"  (subtly different from the example in the book)
:map ^[OP D_
~
~
```

7. Mapping the arrow keys is done the same way, and, in fact, just as typing :ab and then pressing Return shows all abbreviations. Typing :map and then Return demonstrates that I already have my arrow keys mapped to the vi motion keys:

```
~
~
:map
up      ^[[A    k
down    ^[[B    j
left    ^[[D    h
right   ^[[C    l
^[OP    ^[OP    D
[Hit any key to continue] _
```

You can see that sometimes the system can be smart about defining specific keys by name rather than by value, but the end result is the same. I now can use the arrow keys and Clear key, and vi knows what they mean.

8. Now I'll present one final demonstration of what you can do with keyboard mapping. Sometimes when I'm working, I find there's a simple, tedious activity I must do over and over. An example might be surrounding a specific word with quotes to meet a style guideline. This sounds more painful than it need be because a simple key mapping can automate the entire process of quoting the current word.

12

I know that ^a isn't used by vi, so I can map that to the new quote-a-single-word command, making sure that I use either ^v before each control character or Escape. I type the characters :map ^v^a i", and I see this:

```
~

~
:map ^A i"_
```

Now I again press ^v and then the Escape key. To insert a double quote, I need to have vi go into insert mode (the i), type the quote, and then receive an Escape to leave insert mode. The e command moves to the end of the current word, so I type that, followed by the commands needed to append the second double quote. The final map now looks like:

```
~

~
:map ^A i"^[ea"^[_
```

Press Return and it's done. Now move to the beginning of a word and try the new key mapping for ^a.

SUMMARY   There are a variety of customizations you can use with the vi editor, including teaching it about special keys on your keyboard and defining task-specific keys to save time. You can use it to abbreviate commonly used words or phrases to save time or avoid typographical errors. Be cautious when working with the .exrc file, however, because if you enter information that isn't valid, it can be a bit confusing to fix it. Always try the command directly before using it in a special key mapping, and you should stay out of trouble.

Task 12.6: Moving Sentences and Paragraphs

DESCRIPTION   You have learned quite a variety of commands for moving about in files, but there are two more vi movement commands for you to try before you learn about shell escapes in the next unit. So far, movement has been based on screen motion, but vi hasn't particularly known much about the information in the file itself: Type k, and you move up a line, regardless of what kind of file you're viewing.

The vi editor is smarter than that, however. It has a couple of movement commands that are defined by the text you're currently editing. Each of these is simply a punctuation character on your keyboard, but each is quite helpful. The first is), which moves the cursor forward to the beginning of the next sentence in the file. Use the opposite, (, and you can move to the beginning of the current sentence in the file. Also worth experimenting with is }, which moves forward a paragraph in the file, or {, which moves backwards a paragraph.

12

ACTION

1. To try this out, create a new file that has several sentences in a paragraph and a couple of paragraphs. Start vi and type the following text:

```
% cat dickens.note
                    A Tale of Two Cities
                         Preface

When I was acting, with my children and friends, in Mr Wilkie Collins's
drama of The Frozen Deep, I first conceived the main idea of this
story.  A strong desire was upon me then, to
embody it in my own person;
and I traced out in my fancy, the state of mind of which it would
necessitate the presentation
to an observant spectator, with particular
care and interest.

As the idea became familiar to me, it gradually shaped itself into its
present form.  Throughout its execution, it has had complete possession
of me; I have so far verified what
is done and suffered in these pages,
as that I have certainly done and suffered it all myself.

Whenever any reference (however slight) is made here to the condition
of the French people before or during the Revolution, it is truly made,
on the faith of the most trustworthy
witnesses.  It has been one of my hopes to add
something to the popular and picturesque means of
understanding that terrible time, though no one can hope
to add anything to the philosophy of Mr Carlyle's wonderful book.

Tavistock House
November 1859
```

When I start vi on this file, here's what my initial screen looks like:

```
                    A Tale of Two Cities
                         Preface

When I was acting, with my children and friends, in Mr Wilkie Collins's
drama of The Frozen Deep, I first conceived the main idea of this
story.  A strong desire was upon me then, to
embody it in my own person;
and I traced out in my fancy, the state of mind of which it would
necessitate the presentation
to an observant spectator, with particular
care and interest.

As the idea became familiar to me, it gradually shaped itself into its
present form.  Throughout its execution, it has had complete possession
of me; I have so far verified what
is done and suffered in these pages,
as that I have certainly done and suffered it all myself.
```

12

```
Whenever any reference (however slight) is made here to the condition
of the French people before or during the Revolution, it is truly made,
on the faith of the most trustworthy
witnesses.  It has been one of my hopes to add
something to the popular and picturesque means of
"dickens.note" 28 lines, 1122 characters
```

Now I'll move to the beginning of the first paragraph of text by typing /When followed by Return. Now the screen looks like this:

```
                          A Tale of Two Cities
                               Preface

When I was acting, with my children and friends, in Mr Wilkie Collins's
drama of The Frozen Deep, I first conceived the main idea of this
story.  A strong desire was upon me then, to
embody it in my own person;
```

2. Type) once. The cursor moves to the beginning of the next sentence:

```
When I was acting, with my children and friends, in Mr Wilkie Collins's
drama of The Frozen Deep, I first conceived the main idea of this
story.  A strong desire was upon me then, to
embody it in my own person;
and I traced out in my fancy, the state of mind of which it would
necessitate the presentation
```

Try (to move back a sentence. I end up back on the W of When starting the sentence. Repeatedly typing (and) should let you fly back and forth through the file, sentence by sentence. Notice what occurs when you're at the top few lines of the title.

CAUTION

A little experimentation will demonstrate that vi defines a sentence as anything that occurs either at the beginning of a block of text (for example, When I was...) or any word that follows a punctuation character followed by two spaces. This two-space rule is a bit unfortunate because modern typographic conventions have moved away from using two spaces after the end of a sentence. If you use only one space between sentences (as I have for this book), moving by sentence is less helpful.

12

3. I can move back to the opening word of the first paragraph by typing n to repeat the last search pattern. The screen now looks like this:

```
                         A Tale of Two Cities
                              Preface

When I was acting, with my children and friends, in Mr Wilkie Collins's
drama of The Frozen Deep, I first conceived the main idea of this
story.  A strong desire was upon me then, to
embody it in my own person;
and I traced out in my fancy, the state of mind of which it would
necessitate the presentation
to an observant spectator, with particular
care and interest.

As the idea became familiar to me, it gradually shaped itself into its
present form.  Throughout its execution, it has had complete possession
of me; I have so far verified what
is done and suffered in these pages,
as that I have certainly done and suffered it all myself.

Whenever any reference (however slight) is made here to the condition
of the French people before or during the Revolution, it is truly made,
on the faith of the most trustworthy
witnesses.  It has been one of my hopes to add
something to the popular and picturesque means of
"dickens.note" 28 lines, 1122 characters
```

To move to the next paragraph, type } once:

```
                         A Tale of Two Cities
                              Preface

When I was acting, with my children and friends, in Mr Wilkie Collins's
drama of The Frozen Deep, I first conceived the main idea of this
story.  A strong desire was upon me then, to
embody it in my own person;
and I traced out in my fancy, the state of mind of which it would
necessitate the presentation
to an observant spectator, with particular
care and interest.

As the idea became familiar to me, it gradually shaped itself into its
present form.  Throughout its execution, it has had complete possession
of me; I have so far verified what
is done and suffered in these pages,
as that I have certainly done and suffered it all myself.
```

12

```
Whenever any reference (however slight) is made here to the condition
of the French people before or during the Revolution, it is truly made,
on the faith of the most trustworthy
witnesses.  It has been one of my hopes to add
something to the popular and picturesque means of
"dickens.note" 28 lines, 1122 characters
```

Type {, and you move right back to the beginning of the previous paragraph. In fact, you can fly easily back and forth in the file by using sequences of } (or a numeric repeat prefix like 2}) to get there faster.

SUMMARY These two motion commands to move by sentence and to move by paragraph are helpful when working with stories, articles, or letters. Any time you're working with words rather than commands (as in the .exrc file), these commands are worth remembering.

By the way, try d) to delete a sentence, or c} to change an entire paragraph. Recall that you always can undo the changes with u if you haven't done anything else between the two events.

Task 12.7: Access UNIX with !

DESCRIPTION This final task on vi introduces you to one of the most powerful and least-known commands in the editor: the ! escape-to-UNIX command. When prefaced with a colon (:!, for example), it enables you to run UNIX commands without leaving the editor. More powerfully, the ! command in vi itself, just like d and c, accepts address specifications, feeds that portion of text to the command, and replaces that portion with the results of having run that command on the text.

Let's have a look.

ACTION

1. You should still be in the dickens.intro file. I'll start by double-checking what files I have in my home directory. To do this, I type :!, which moves the cursor to the bottom line:

```
of the French people before or during the Revolution, it is truly made,
on the faith of the most trustworthy
witnesses.  It has been one of my hopes to add
something to the popular and picturesque means of
:!_
```

I simply type ls -CF and press Return, as if I were at the % prompt in the command line:

```
of the French people before or during the Revolution, it is truly made,
on the faith of the most trustworthy
witnesses.  It has been one of my hopes to add
something to the popular and picturesque means of
:!ls -CF
Archives/         big.output        dickens.note      src/
InfoWorld/        bigfiles          keylime.pie       temp/
Mail/             bin/              newfile           tetme
News/             buckaroo          owl.c
OWL/              buckaroo.confused sample
awkscript         demo              sample2
[Hit any key to continue] _
```

If I press Return, I'm back in the editor, and I have quickly checked what files I have in my home directory.

2. Now for some real fun, move back to the beginning of the first paragraph and add the text Chuck, here are my current files:. Press Return twice before using the Escape key to return to command mode. My screen now looks like this:

```
                    A Tale of Two Cities
                        Preface

Chuck, here are my current files:

_

When I was acting, with my children and friends, in Mr Wilkie Collins's
drama of The Frozen Deep, I first conceived the main idea of this
story.  A strong desire was upon me then, to
```

Notice that the cursor was moved up a line. I'm now on a blank line, and the line following is also blank.

To feed the current line to the UNIX system and replace it with the output of the command, vi offers an easy shortcut: !!. As soon as I type the second ! (or, more precisely, once vi figures out the desired range specified for this command), the cursor moves to the bottom of the screen and prompts with a single ! character:

```
of the French people before or during the Revolution, it is truly made,
on the faith of the most trustworthy
witnesses. It has been one of my hopes to add
something to the popular and picturesque means of
:!_
```

12

To list all the files in my directory, I can again type ls -CF and press Return. After a second, vi adds the output of that command to the file:

```
                              A Tale of Two Cities
                                   Preface

Chuck, here are my current files:
Archives/              bigfiles              newfile
InfoWorld/             bin/                  owl.c
Mail/                  buckaroo              sample
News/                  buckaroo.confused     sample2
OWL/                   demo                  src/
awkscript              dickens.note          temp/
big.output             keylime.pie           tetme

When I was acting, with my children and friends, in Mr Wilkie Collins's
drama of The Frozen Deep, I first conceived the main idea of this
story.  A strong desire was upon me then, to
embody it in my own person;
and I traced out in my fancy, the state of mind of which it would
necessitate the presentation
to an observant spectator, with particular
care and interest.

As the idea became familiar to me, it gradually shaped itself into its
present form.  Throughout its execution, it has had complete possession
6 more lines
```

Notice that this time the status on the bottom indicates how many lines were added to the file.

Type u to undo this change. Notice that the vi status indicator on the bottom line says there are now six fewer lines.

3. Move back to the W in When. You are now ready to learn one of the commands that I like most in vi. This command gives you the ability to hand a paragraph of text to an arbitrary UNIX command.

This time, I'm going to use a sed command that was first shown in Hour 9 sed 's/ ^/> /', which prefaces each line with >. Ready? This is where the } command comes in handy, too. To accomplish this trick, I type !}, moving the cursor to the bottom of the screen, and then type the sed command as you saw earlier: sed 's/^/ > /'. Pressing Return feeds the lines to sed. The sed command makes the change indicated and replaces those lines with the output of the sed command. Voilà! The screen now looks like this:

```
                        A Tale of Two Cities
                            Preface

Chuck, here are my current files:


> When I was acting, with my children and friends, in Mr Wilkie Collins's
> drama of The Frozen Deep, I first conceived the main idea of this
> story.  A strong desire was upon me then, to
> embody it in my own person;
> and I traced out in my fancy, the state of mind of which it would
> necessitate the presentation
> to an observant spectator, with particular
> care and interest.

As the idea became familiar to me, it gradually shaped itself into its
present form.  Throughout its execution, it has had complete possession
of me; I have so far verified what
is done and suffered in these pages,
as that I have certainly done and suffered it all myself.

Whenever any reference (however slight) is made here to the condition
of the French people before or during the Revolution, it is truly made,
!sed 's/^/> /'
```

4. I hope you're excited to see this command in action! It's a powerful way to interact with UNIX while within vi.

    I'll provide a few more examples of ways to interact with UNIX while within vi. First, I don't really want the prefix to each line, so I'm going to type u to undo the change.

    Instead, I would rather have the system actually tighten up the lines, ensuring that a reasonable number of words occur on each line and that no lines are too long. On the majority of systems, there is a command called either fmt or adjust to accomplish this. To figure out which works on your system, simply use the : ! command, and feed a word or two to the fmt command to see what happens:

```
Whenever any reference (however slight) is made here to the condition
of the French people before or during the Revolution, it is truly made,
:!echo hi ¦ fmt
[No write since last change]
hi
[Hit any key to continue] _
```

In this case, fmt did what I hoped, so I can be sure that the command exists on my system. If your response was command unknown, adjust is a likely synonym. If neither exists, complain to your vendor!

Armed with this new command, you can try another variant of !}, this time by feeding the entire paragraph to the `fmt` command. I'm still at the beginning of the word `When` in the text. So when I type the command !}fmt, the paragraph is cleaned up, and the screen changes to this:

```
                        A Tale of Two Cities
                              Preface

Chuck, here are my current files:


When I was acting, with my children and friends, in Mr Wilkie Collins's
drama of The Frozen Deep, I first conceived the main idea of this
story.  A strong desire was upon me then, to embody it in my own
person; and I traced out in my fancy, the state of mind of which it
would necessitate the presentation to an observant spectator, with
particular care and interest.

As the idea became familiar to me, it gradually shaped itself into its
present form.  Throughout its execution, it has had complete possession
of me; I have so far verified what
is done and suffered in these pages,
as that I have certainly done and suffered it all myself.

Whenever any reference (however slight) is made here to the condition
of the French people before or during the Revolution, it is truly made,
on the faith of the most trustworthy
witnesses.  It has been one of my hopes to add
2 fewer lines
```

Again, `vi` tells us that the number of lines in the file has changed as a result of the command. In this situation, tightening up the paragraph actually reduced it by two display lines, too.

This command is so helpful that I often have it bound to a specific key with the `map` command. A typical way to do this in an `.exrc` might be this:

```
:map ^P !}fmt^M
```

The ^M is what `vi` uses to record a Return. (Recall that you need to use the ^v beforehand.) With this defined in my `.exrc`, I can press ^p to format the current paragraph.

5. I will provide one more example of the ! command before I wrap up this hour. Remember the `awk` command that was introduced in Hour 10? Remember how it can easily be used to extract specific fields of information? This can be tremendously helpful in `vi`. Rather than continue working with the `dickens.intro` file, however, I'll quit `vi` and create a new file containing some output from the `ls` command:

```
% ls -CF
Archives/          big.output       dickens.note    src/
InfoWorld/         bigfiles         keylime.pie     temp/
Mail/              bin/             newfile         tetme
News/              buckaroo         owl.c
OWL/               buckaroo.confused sample
awkscript          demo             sample2
% ls -l a* b* > listing
```

Now I can use vi listing to start the file with the output of the ls command:

```
-rw-rw----   1 taylor        126 Dec  3 16:34 awkscript
-rw-rw----   1 taylor       1659 Dec  3 23:26 big.output
-rw-rw----   1 taylor        165 Dec  3 16:42 bigfiles
-rw-rw----   1 taylor        270 Dec  4 15:09 buckaroo
-rw-rw----   1 taylor        458 Dec  4 23:22 buckaroo.confused
~
~
~
~
~
~
~
~
~
~
~
~
~
~
~
"listing" 5 lines, 282 characters
```

It would be nice to use this as the basis for creating a *shell script* (which is just a series of commands that you might type to the shell directly, all kept neatly in a single file). A shell script can show me both the first and last few lines of each file, with the middle chopped out.

The commands I'd like to have occur for each file entry are these:

```
echo ==== filename ====
head -5 filename; echo ...size bytes...; tail -5 filename
```

I'll do this with a combination of the ! command in vi and the awk program with the awk command:

```
awk '{ print "echo ==== "$8" ===="; print "head "$8; echo
..."$4" bytes...; tail "$8}'
```

With the cursor on the very top line of this file, I can now type !G to pipe the
entire file through the command. The cursor drops to the bottom of the screen,
and then I type the awk script shown previously and press Return. The result is this:

```
echo ==== awkscript ====
head -5 awkscript; echo ...126 bytes...; tail -5 awkscript
echo ==== big.output ====
head -5 big.output; echo ...1659 bytes...; tail -5 big.output
echo ==== bigfiles ====
head -5 bigfiles; echo ...165 bytes...; tail -5 bigfiles
echo ==== buckaroo ====
head -5 buckaroo; echo ...270 bytes...; tail -5 buckaroo
echo ==== buckaroo.confused ====
head -5 buckaroo.confused; echo ...458 bytes...; tail -5 buckaroo.confused~
~
~
~
~
~
~
~
~
~
!awk '{ print "echo ==== "$8" ===="; print "head "$8"; echo
...$4" bytes...; tail "$8}'_
```

If I now quit vi and ask sh to interpret the contents, here's what happens:

```
% chmod +x listing
% sh listing
==== awkscript ====
{
        count[length($1)]++
}
END {
        for (i=1; i < 9; i++)
...126 bytes...
}
END {
        for (i=1; i < 9; i++)
            print "There are " counti " accounts with " i " letter names."
}
==== big.output ====
leungtc  ttyrV   Dec  1 18:27   (magenta)
tuyinhwa ttyrX   Dec  3 22:38   (expert)
hollenst ttyrZ   Dec  3 22:14   (dov)
brandt   ttyrb   Nov 28 23:03   (age)
holmes   ttyrj   Dec  3 21:59   (age)
...1659 bytes...
```

```
buckeye   ttyss    Dec  3 23:20    (mac2)
mtaylor   ttyst    Dec  3 23:22    (dov)
look      ttysu    Dec  3 23:12    (age)
janitor   ttysw    Dec  3 18:29    (age)
ajones    ttysx    Dec  3 23:23    (rassilon)
==== bigfiles ====
12556     keylime.pie
8729      owl.c
1024      Mail/
582       tetme
512       temp/
...165 bytes...
512       Archives/
207       sample2
199       sample
126       awkscript

==== buckaroo ====
I found myself stealing a peek at my own watch and overheard
General Catbird's
aide give him the latest.
"He's not even here," went the conversation.
"Banzai."
"Where the hell is he?"
...270 bytes...
"Banzai."
"Where the hell is he?"
"At the hospital in El Paso."
"What? Why weren't we informed? What's wrong with him?"

==== buckaroo.confused ====
         Excerpt from "Buckaroo Bandura" by Duke MacRauch
I found myself stealing a peek at my own watch and overheard
General Catbird's
aide give him the latest.
"He's not even here," went the conversation.
"Bandura."
...458 bytes...
"At the hospital in El Paso."
"What? Why weren't we informed? What's wrong with him?"

Go Team Bandura! Go Team Bandura! Go Team Bandura!

%
```

SUMMARY Clearly the ! command opens up vi to work with the rest of the UNIX system. There's almost nothing that you can't somehow manage to do within the editor, whether it's add or remove prefixes, clean up text, or even show what happens when you try to run a command or reformat a passage within the current file.

12

Summary of `vi` Commands

A summary of the commands you learned in this hour is shown in Table 12.1.

Table 12.1. Advanced `vi` commands.

Command	Meaning
`!!`*command*	Replace the current line with the output of the specified UNIX command.
`!}`*command*	Replace the current paragraph with the results of piping it through the specified UNIX command or commands.
`(`	Move backward one sentence.
`)`	Move forward one sentence.
`C`	Change text from the point of the cursor through the end of line.
`c`	Change text in the specified range—`cw` changes the following word, whereas `c}` changes the next paragraph.
`e`	Move to the end of the current word.
`^g`	Show the current line number and other information about the file.
`R`	Replace text from the point of the cursor until Escape is pressed.
`r`	Replace the current character with the next pressed.
`^v`	Prevent `vi` from interpreting the next character.
`{`	Move backward one paragraph.
`}`	Move forward one paragraph.
`:!`*command*	Invoke the specified UNIX command.
`:ab` *a bcd*	Define abbreviation *a* for phrase *bcd*.
`:ab`	Show current abbreviations, if any.
`:map` *a bcd*	Map key *a* to the `vi` commands *bcd*.
`:map`	Show current key mappings, if any.
`:s/`*old*`/`*new*`/`	Substitute *new* for the first instance of *old* on the current line.
`:s/`*old*`/`*new*`/g`	Substitute *new* for all occurrences of *old* on the current line.
`:set nonumber`	Turn off line numbering.
`:set number`	Turn on line numbering.

Summary

Clearly, vi is a very complex and sophisticated tool that enables you not only to modify your text files, but also to customize the editor for your keyboard. Just as important, you can access all the power of UNIX while within vi.

Workshop

The Workshop summarizes the key terms you learned and poses some questions about the topics presented in this chapter. It also provides you with a preview of what you will learn in the next hour.

Key Terms

escape sequence   An unprintable sequence of characters that usually specifies that your terminal take a specific action, such as clearing the screen.

key mapping   A facility that enables you to map any key to a specific action.

replace mode   A mode of vi in which any characters you type replace those already in the file.

shell script   A collection of shell commands in a file.

Questions

1. What does the following command do?

   ```
   :1,5 s/kitten/puppy
   ```

2. What do these commands do?

   ```
   15i?ESCh
   i15?ESCh
   i?ESC15h
   ```

3. Try ^g on the first and last lines of a file. Explain why the percentage indicator might not be what you expected.

4. What's the difference between the following four strings:

   ```
   rr
   RrESC
   cwrESC
   CrESC
   ```

5. What key mappings do you have in your version of vi? Do you have labeled keys on your keyboard that could be helpful in vi but aren't defined? If so, define them in your .exrc file using the :map command.

12

6. What do you think the following command will do? Try it and see if you're right.

   `!}ls`

Preview of the Next Hour

With this hour and the previous one, you now know more about vi than the vast majority of people using UNIX today. There's a second popular editor, however, one that is modeless and offers its own interesting possibilities for working with files and the UNIX system. It's called emacs, and if you have it on your system, it's definitely worth a look. In the next hour, you learn about this editor and some of the basics of using it.

Hour 13

An Overview of the emacs Editor

The only screen-oriented editor that's guaranteed to be included with the UNIX system is vi, but that doesn't mean that it's the only good editor available in UNIX! An alternative editor that has become quite popular in the last decade (remember that UNIX is almost 25 years old) is called emacs. This hour teaches you the fundamentals of this very different and quite powerful editing environment.

Goals for This Hour

In this hour, you learn how to

- ☐ Launch emacs and insert text
- ☐ Move around in a file
- ☐ Delete characters and words
- ☐ Search and replace in emacs
- ☐ Use the emacs tutorial and help system
- ☐ Work with other files

Remember what I said in the previous hour, when I introduced the emacs editor: emacs is modeless, so be prepared for an editor that is quite unlike vi. And because it's modeless, there's no insert or command mode. The result is that you have ample opportunity to use the Control key.

JUST A MINUTE

> Over the years, I have tried to become an emacs enthusiast, once even forcing myself to use it for an entire month. I had crib sheets of commands taped up all over my office. At the end of the month, I had attained an editing speed that was about half of my speed in vi, an editor that I've used thousands of times in the past 14 years I've worked in UNIX. I think emacs has a lot going for it, and generally I think that modeless software is better than modal software. The main obstacle I see for emacs, however, is that it's begging for pull-down menus like a Mac or Windows program has. Using Control, Meta, Shift-Meta, and other weird key combinations just isn't as easy to use for me. On the other hand, your approach to editing might be different, and you might not have years of vi experience affecting your choice of editing environments. I encourage you to give emacs a fair shake by working through all the examples I have included. You may find that it matches your working style better than vi.

Task 13.1: Launching emacs and Inserting Text

DESCRIPTION   Starting emacs is as simple as starting any other UNIX program. Simply type the name of the program, followed by any file or files you'd like to work with. The puzzle with emacs is figuring out what it's actually called on your system, if you have it. There are a couple of ways to try to identify emacs; I'll demonstrate these in the "Action 2" section for this task.

Once in emacs, it's important to take a look at your computer keyboard. emacs requires you to use not just the Control key, but another key known as the *Meta key*, a sort of alternative Control key. If you have a key labeled Meta or Alt (for Alternative) on your keyboard, that's the one. If, like me, you don't, simply press Escape every time a Meta key is indicated.

Because there are both Control and Meta keys in emacs, the notation for indicating commands is slightly different. Throughout this book, a control-key sequence has been shown either as Control-f or as ^f. emacs people write this differently, to allow the difference between Control and Meta keys. In emacs notation, ^f is shown as C-f, where C- always means Control. Similarly, M-*x* is the Meta key plus the character specified by *x*. If you don't have a Meta key, the sequence is Escape, followed by *x*. Finally, some arcane commands involve both the Control and Meta keys being pressed (simultaneously with the other key involved). This notation is C-M-*x* and indicates that you need either to press and hold down both the Control and Meta keys while typing *x* or, if you don't have a Meta (or Alt) key, to press Escape followed by C-*x*.

13

With this notation in mind, you leave emacs by pressing C-x C-c (Control-x, followed by Control-c).

ACTION

1. First, see if your system has emacs available. The easiest way to find out is to type emacs at the command line and see what happens.

```
% emacs
emacs: Command not found.
%
```

This is a good indication that emacs isn't available. If your command worked, and you now are in the emacs editor, move down to instruction 2 in this task.

A popular version of emacs is from the Free Software Foundation, and it's called gnu emacs. To see if you have this version, type gnuemacs or gnumacs at the command line.

2. Rather than start with a blank screen, quit the program (C-x C-c) and restart emacs with one of the earlier test files, dickens.note:

```
% gnuemacs dickens.note
```

```
                         A Tale of Two Cities
        _                       Preface

When I was acting, with my children and friends, in Mr Wilkie Collins's
drama of The Frozen Deep, I first conceived the main idea of this
story. A strong desire was upon me then, to
embody it in my own person;
and I traced out in my fancy, the state of mind of which it would
necessitate the presentation
to an observant spectator, with particular
care and interest.

As the idea became familiar to me, it gradually shaped itself into its
present form. Throughout its execution, it has had complete possession
of me; I have so far verified what
is done and suffered in these pages,
as that I have certainly done and suffered it all myself.

Whenever any reference (however slight) is made here to the condition
of the French people before or during the Revolution, it is truly made,
on the faith of the most trustworthy
witnesses. It has been one of my hopes to add
----Emacs: dickens.note          (Fundamental)----Top----------------
```

13

As you can see, it's quite different from the display shown when vi starts up. The status line at the bottom of the display offers useful information as you edit the file at different points, and it also reminds you at all times of the name of the file, a feature that can be surprisingly helpful. emacs can work with different kinds of files, and here you see by the word Fundamental in the status line that emacs is prepared for a regular text file. If you're programming, emacs can offer special features customized for your particular language.

3. Quit emacs by using the C-x C-c sequence, but let a few seconds pass after you press C-x to watch what happens. When I press C-x, the bottom of the screen suddenly changes to this:

```
on the faith of the most trustworthy
witnesses. It has been one of my hopes to add
----Emacs: dickens.note          (Fundamental)----Top----------------
C-x-
```

Confusingly, the cursor remains at the top of the file, but emacs reminds me that I've pressed C-x and that I need to enter a second command once I've decided what to do. I now press C-c, and immediately exit emacs.

SUMMARY Already you can see there are some dramatic differences between emacs and vi. If you're comfortable with multiple key sequences such as C-x C-c to quit, I think you're going to enjoy learning emacs. If not, stick with it anyway. Even if you never use emacs, it's good to know a little bit about it.

JUST A MINUTE

Why learn about a tool you're not going to use? In this case, the answer is that UNIX people tend to be polarized around the question of which editor is better. Indeed, the debate between vi and emacs is referred to as a "religious war" because of the high levels of heat and low levels of actual sensibility of the participants. My position is that different users will find different tools work best for them. If emacs is closer to how you edit files, that's wonderful, and it's great that UNIX offers emacs as an alternative to vi. Ultimately, the question isn't whether one is better than the other, but whether or not you can edit your files more quickly and easily in one or the other.

Task 13.2: How To Move Around in a File

DESCRIPTION Files are composed of characters, words, lines, sentences, and paragraphs, and emacs has commands to help you move about. Most systems have the arrow keys enabled, which helps you avoid worrying about some of the key sequences, but it's best to know them all anyway.

The most basic motions are C-f and C-b, which are used to move the cursor forward and backward one character, respectively. Switch those to the Meta command equivalents, and the cursor will move by words: M-f moves the cursor forward a word, and M-b moves it back a word. Pressing C-n moves the cursor to the next line, C-p to the previous line, C-a to the beginning of the line, and C-e to the end of the line. (The vi equivalents for all of these are l, h, w, and b for moving forward and backward a character or word; j and k for moving up or down a line; and 0 or $ to move to the beginning or end of the current line. Which makes more sense to you?)

To move forward a sentence, you can use M-e, which actually moves the cursor to the end of the sentence. Pressing M-a moves it to the beginning of the sentence. Notice the parallels between Control and Meta commands: C-a moves the cursor to the beginning of the line, and M-a moves it to the beginning of the sentence.

Scrolling within the document is accomplished by using C-v to move forward a screen and M-v to move back a screen. To move forward an actual page (usually 60 lines of text; this is based on a printed page of information), you can use either C-x] or C-x [for forward motion or backward motion, respectively.

Finally, to move to the very top of the file, use M-<, and to move to the bottom, use the M-> command.

ACTION

1. Go back into emacs and locate the cursor. It should be at the very top of the screen:

```
                        A Tale of Two Cities
  _                          Preface

When I was acting, with my children and friends, in Mr Wilkie Collins's
drama of The Frozen Deep, I first conceived the main idea of this
story. A strong desire was upon me then, to
embody it in my own person;
and I traced out in my fancy, the state of mind of which it would
necessitate the presentation
to an observant spectator, with particular
care and interest.
```

13

```
As the idea became familiar to me, it gradually shaped itself into its
present form. Throughout its execution, it has had complete posession
of me; I have so far verified what
is done and suffered in these pages,
as that I have certainly done and suffered it all myself.

Whenever any reference (however slight) is made here to the condition
of the French people before or during the Revolution, it is truly made,
on the faith of the most trustworthy
witnesses. It has been one of my hopes to add
----Emacs: dickens.note              (Fundamental)----Top----------------
```

Move down four lines by using C-n four times. Your cursor should now be sitting on the d of drama:

```
                                    Preface

When I was acting, with my children and friends, in Mr Wilkie Collins's
drama of The Frozen Deep, I first conceived the main idea of this
story. A strong desire was upon me then, to
embody it in my own person;
and I traced out in my fancy, the state of mind of which it would
```

2. Next, move to the end of this sentence by using the M-e command (just like vi, emacs expects two spaces to separate sentences):

```
When I was acting, with my children and friends, in Mr Wilkie Collins's
drama of The Frozen Deep, I first conceived the main idea of this
story._ A strong desire was upon me then, to
embody it in my own person;
and I traced out in my fancy, the state of mind of which it would
```

Now type in the following text: I fought the impulse to write this novel vociferously, but, dear reader, I felt the injustice of the situation too strongly in my breast to deny. Don't press Return or Escape when you're done. The screen should now look similar to this:

```
drama of The Frozen Deep, I first conceived the main idea of this
story. I fought the impulse to write this novel vociferously, but, dear reader,\
 I felt
the injustice of the situation too strongly in my breast to deny_  A strong des\
ire was upon me then, to
embody it in my own person;
```

```
and I traced out in my fancy, the state of mind of which it would
necessitate the presentation
```

You can see that emacs wrapped the line when the line became too long (between the words felt and the), and because the lines are still too long to display, a few of them end with a backslash. The backslash isn't actually a part of the file; with it, emacs is telling me that those lines are longer than I might expect.

3. Now try to move back a few characters by pressing Backspace.

    Uh oh! If your system is like mine, the Backspace key doesn't move the cursor back a character at all. Instead it starts the emacs help system, where you're suddenly confronted with a screen that looks like this:

```
You have typed C-h, the help character. Type a Help option:

A  command-apropos.  Give a substring, and see a list of commands
                (functions interactively callable) that contain
                that substring. See also the  apropos  command.
B  describe-bindings. Display table of all key bindings.
C  describe-key-briefly. Type a command key sequence;
                it prints the function name that sequence runs.
F  describe-function. Type a function name and get documentation of it.
I  info. The  info  documentation reader.
K  describe-key. Type a command key sequence;
                it displays the full documentation.
L  view-lossage. Shows last 100 characters you typed.
M  describe-mode. Print documentation of current major mode,
                which describes the commands peculiar to it.
N  view-emacs-news. Shows emacs news file.
S  describe-syntax. Display contents of syntax table, plus explanations
T  help-with-tutorial. Select the Emacs learn-by-doing tutorial.
V  describe-variable. Type name of a variable;
                it displays the variable's documentation and value.
W  where-is. Type command name; it prints which keystrokes
                invoke that command.
--**-Emacs: *Help*              (Fundamental)----Top----------------
A B C F I K L M N S T V W C-c C-d C-n C-w or Space to scroll: _
```

To escape the help screen (which you learn more about later in this hour), press Escape, and your screen should be restored. Notice that the filename has been changed and is now shown as *Help* instead of the actual file. The status line also shows what file you're viewing, but you aren't always viewing the file you want to work with.

The correct key to move the cursor back a few characters is C-b. Use that to back up, and then use C-f to move forward again to the original cursor location.

13

4. Check that the last few lines of the file haven't changed by using the emacs move-to-end-of-file command M->. (Think of file redirection to remember the file motion commands). Now the screen looks like this:

```
Whenever any reference (however slight) is made here to the condition
of the French people before or during the Revolution, it is truly made,
on the faith of the most trustworthy
witnesses. It has been one of my hopes to add
something to the popular and picturesque means of
understanding that terrible time, though no one can hope
to add anything to the philosophy of Mr Carlyle's wonderful book.

Tavistock House
November 1859

_




--**-Emacs: dickens.note          (Fundamental)----Bot----------------
```

5. Changing the words of Charles Dickens was fun, so save these changes and quit. If you try to quit the program with C-x C-c, emacs reminds you that there are unsaved changes:

```
--**-Emacs: dickens.note          (Fundamental)----Bot----------------
Save file /users/taylor/dickens.note? (y or n) _
```

Typing y saves the changes; n quits without saving the changes; if you instead decide to return to the edit session, Escape will cancel the action entirely. Typing n reminds you a second time that the changes are going to be lost if you don't save them.

```
--**-Emacs: dickens.note          (Fundamental)----Bot----------------
Modified buffers exist; exit anyway? (yes or no) _
```

This time type y and, finally, you're back on the command line.

13

SUMMARY Entering text in emacs is incredibly easy. It's as if the editor is always in insert mode. The price that you pay for this, however, is that just about anything else you do requires Control or Meta sequences; even the Backspace key did something other than what you wanted.

The motion commands are summarized in Table 13.1.

Table 13.1. emacs **motion commands.**

Command	Meaning
M->	Move to the end of file.
M-<	Move to the beginning of file.
C-v	Move forward a screen.
M-v	Move backward a screen.
C-x]	Move forward a page.
C-x [	Move backward a page.
C-n	Move to the next line.
C-p	Move to the previous line.
C-a	Move to the beginning of the line.
C-e	Move to the end of the line.
M-e	Move to the end of the sentence.
M-a	Move to the beginning of the sentence.
C-f	Move forward a character.
C-b	Move backward a character.
M-f	Move forward a word.
M-b	Move backward a word.

Task 13.3: How To Delete Characters and Words

DESCRIPTION Inserting text into an emacs buffer is quite simple, and once you get the hang of it, moving about in the file isn't too bad, either. How about deleting text? The set of Control and Meta commands that enable you to insert text are a precursor to all commands in emacs, and it should come as no surprise that C-d deletes the current character, M-d deletes the next word, M-k deletes the rest of the current sentence, and C-k deletes the rest of the current line. If you have a key on your keyboard labeled DEL, RUBOUT, or Delete, you're in luck, because Delete deletes the previous character, M-Delete deletes the previous word, and C-x Delete deletes the previous sentence.

13

Unfortunately, I have a Delete key, but it's tied to the Backspace function on my system, so every time I press it, it actually sends a C-h sequence to the system, not the DEL sequence. The result is that I cannot use any of these backward-deletion commands.

JUST A MINUTE

> Actually, VersaTerm Pro, the terminal emulation package I use on my Macintosh to connect to the various UNIX systems, is smarter than that. I can tell it whether pressing the Delete key should send a C-h or a DEL function in the keyboard configuration screen. One flip of a toggle, and I'm fully functional in emacs. Unfortunately, it's not always this easy to switch from Backspace to DEL.

ACTION

1. Restart emacs with the dickens.note file, and move the cursor to the middle of the fifth line (remember, C-n moves to the next line, and C-f moves forward a character). It should look like this:

```
                              Preface

When I was acting, with my children and friends, in Mr Wilkie Collins's
drama of The Frozen Deep, I first conceived the main idea of this
story. A strong desire was upon me then, to
embody it in my own person;
and I traced out in my fancy, the state of mind of which it would
necessitate the presentation
to an observant spectator, with particular
```

Notice that my cursor is on the w in was on the fifth line here.

2. Press C-d C-d C-d to remove the word was. Now simply type came to revise the sentence slightly. The screen should now look like this:

```
                              Preface

When I was acting, with my children and friends, in Mr Wilkie Collins's
drama of The Frozen Deep, I first conceived the main idea of this
story. A strong desire came_upon me then, to
embody it in my own person;
and I traced out in my fancy, the state of mind of which it would
necessitate the presentation
to an observant spectator, with particular
```

Now press Delete once to remove the last letter of the new word, and then type e to reinsert it. Instead of backing up a character at a time, I am instead going to use M-Delete to delete the word just added. The word is deleted, but the spaces on either side of the word are retained.

```
                                  Preface

When I was acting, with my children and friends, in Mr Wilkie Collins's
drama of The Frozen Deep, I first conceived the main idea of this
story. A strong desire _upon me then, to
embody it in my own person;
and I traced out in my fancy, the state of mind of which it would
necessitate the presentation
to an observant spectator, with particular
```

I'll try another word to see if I can get this sentence to sound the way I'd prefer. Type crept to see how it reads.

3. On the other hand, it's probably not good to revise classic stories such as *A Tale of Two Cities*, so the best move is for me to delete this entire sentence. If I press C-x Delete, which is an example of a *multi-keystroke command* in emacs, will it do the right thing? Recall that C-x Delete deletes the previous sentence. I press C-x Delete, and the results are helpful, if not completely what I want to accomplish:

JUST A MINUTE

emacs also requires some multistroke commands, where you might press a control sequence and follow it with a second keystroke. Although this allows you to have many commands to control your text, it also means you need to know many commands.

```
                                  Preface

When I was acting, with my children and friends, in Mr Wilkie Collins's
drama of The Frozen Deep, I first conceived the main idea of this
story. _upon me then, to
embody it in my own person;
and I traced out in my fancy, the state of mind of which it would
necessitate the presentation
to an observant spectator, with particular
```

13

That's okay. Now I can delete the second part of the sentence by using the M-k command. Now the screen looks like what I want:

```
When I was acting, with my children and friends, in Mr Wilkie Collins's
drama of The Frozen Deep, I first conceived the main idea of this
story. _

As the idea became familiar to me, it gradually shaped itself into its
present form. Throughout its execution, it has had complete posession
of me; I have so far verified what
```

4. Here's a great feature of emacs! I just realized that deleting sentences is just as wildly inappropriate as changing words, so I want to undo the last two changes. If I were using vi, I'd be stuck, because vi remembers only the last change; but emacs has that beat. With emacs, you can back up as many changes as you'd like, usually until you restore the original file. To step backwards, use C-x u.

The first time I press C-x u, the screen changes to this:

```
When I was acting, with my children and friends, in Mr Wilkie Collins's
drama of The Frozen Deep, I first conceived the main idea of this
story. _upon me then, to
embody it in my own person;
and I traced out in my fancy, the state of mind of which it would
necessitate the presentation
to an observant spectator, with particular
care and interest.

As the idea became familiar to me, it gradually shaped itself into its
present form. Throughout its execution, it has had complete possession
```

The second time I press it, the screen goes back even further in my revision history:

```
When I was acting, with my children and friends, in Mr Wilkie Collins's
drama of The Frozen Deep, I first conceived the main idea of this
story. A strong desire crept_upon me then, to
embody it in my own person;
and I traced out in my fancy, the state of mind of which it would
necessitate the presentation
to an observant spectator, with particular
care and interest.

As the idea became familiar to me, it gradually shaped itself into its
present form. Throughout its execution, it has had complete possession
```

Finally, using C-x u three more times causes the original text to be restored:

```
                          A Tale of Two Cities
                              Preface

When I was acting, with my children and friends, in Mr Wilkie Collins's
drama of The Frozen Deep, I first conceived the main idea of this
story. A strong desire came upon me then, to
embody it in my own person;
and I traced out in my fancy, the state of mind of which it would
necessitate the presentation
to an observant spectator, with particular
care and interest.

As the idea became familiar to me, it gradually shaped itself into its
present form. Throughout its execution, it has had complete posession
of me; I have so far verified what
is done and suffered in these pages,
as that I have certainly done and suffered it all myself.

Whenever any reference (however slight) is made here to the condition
of the French people before or during the Revolution, it is truly made,
on the faith of the most trustworthy
witnesses. It has been one of my hopes to add
--**-Emacs: dickens.note          (Fundamental)----Top----------------
Undo!
```

SUMMARY If you don't have a Delete key, some of the deletion commands will be unavailable to you, regrettably. Generally, though, emacs has as many ways to delete text as vi has, if not more. The best feature, however, is that, unlike vi, emacs remembers edit changes from the beginning of your editing session. You can always back up as far as you want by using the C-x u undo request.

The deletion command keys are summarized in Table 13.2.

Table 13.2. Deletion commands in emacs.

Command	Meaning
Delete	Delete the previous character.
C-d	Delete the current character.
M-Delete	Delete the previous word.
M-d	Delete the next word.
C-x Delete	Delete the previous sentence.
M-k	Delete the rest of the current sentence.
C-k	Delete the rest of the current line.
C-x u	Undo the last edit change.

Task 13.4: Search and Replace in emacs

DESCRIPTION   Because emacs reserves the last line of the screen for its own system prompts, searching and replacing is easier than in vi. Moreover, the system prompts for the fields and asks, for each occurrence, whether to change it. On the other hand, this command isn't a simple key press or two, but rather it is an example of a *named* emacs command. A named emacs command is a command that requires you to type its name, such as query-replace, rather than a command key or two.

Searching forward for a pattern is done by pressing C-s, and searching backward is done with C-r (the mnemonics are search forward or reverse search). To leave the search once you've found what you want, press Escape, and to cancel the search, returning to your starting point, use C-g.

CAUTION

> Unfortunately, you might find that pressing C-s does very strange things to your system. In fact, ^s and ^q often are used as *flow control* on a terminal, and by pressing the C-s key, you're actually telling the terminal emulator to stop sending information until it sees a C-q. Flow control is the protocol used by your computer and terminal to make sure that neither outpaces the other during data transmission. If this happens to you, you need to try to turn off XON/XOFF flow control. Ask your system administrator for help.

Query and replace is really a whole new feature within emacs. To start a query and replace, use M-x query-replace. emacs will prompt for what to do next. Once a match is shown, you can type a variety of different commands to affect what happens: y makes the change; n means to leave it as is but move to the next match; Escape or q quits replace mode; and ! automatically replaces all further occurrences of the pattern without further prompting.

ACTION

1. I'm still looking at the dickens.note file, and I have moved the cursor to the top-left corner by using the M-<. Somewhere in the file is the word Revolution, but I'm not sure where. Worse, every time I press C-s, the terminal freezes up until I press C-q, because of flow control problems. Instead of searching forward, I'll search backward by first moving the cursor to the bottom of the file with M-> and then pressing C-r.

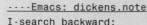

```
----Emacs: dickens.note          (Fundamental)----Bot--------------
I-search backward:
```

As I type each character of the pattern Revolution, the cursor dances backward, matching the pattern as it grows longer and longer, until emacs finds the word I seek:

```
Whenever any reference (however slight) is made here to the condition
of the French people before or during the Revolution, it is truly made,
on the faith of the most trustworthy
witnesses. It has been one of my hopes to add
something to the popular and picturesque means of
understanding that terrible time, though no one can hope
to add anything to the philosophy of Mr Carlyle's wonderful book.

Tavistock House
November 1859




----Emacs: dickens.note          (Fundamental)----Bot----------------
I-search backward: Revol
```

2. Now try the query-replace feature. To begin, I move to the top of the file with M-< and then press M-x, which causes the notation to show up on the bottom status line:

```
of the French people before or during the Revolution, it is truly made,
on the faith of the most trustworthy
witnesses. It has been one of my hopes to add
--**-Emacs: dickens.note          (Fundamental)----Top----------------
M-x _
```

I then type the words query-replace and press Return. emacs understands that I want to find all occurrences of a pattern and replace them with another. emacs changes the prompt to this:

```
of the French people before or during the Revolution, it is truly made,
on the faith of the most trustworthy
witnesses. It has been one of my hopes to add
--**-Emacs: dickens.note          (Fundamental)----Top----------------
Query replace: _
```

13

Now I type in the word that I want to replace. To cause confusion in the file, I think I'll change French to Danish, because maybe *A Tale of Two Cities* really takes place in London and Copenhagen! To do this, I type French and press Return. The prompt again changes to this:

```
of the French people before or during the Revolution, it is truly made,
on the faith of the most trustworthy
witnesses. It has been one of my hopes to add
--**-Emacs: dickens.note          (Fundamental)----Top----------------
Query replace French with: _
```

I type Danish, and again press Return.

```
as that I have certainly done and suffered it all myself.

Whenever any reference (however slight) is made here to the condition
of the French_people before or during the Revolution, it is truly made,
on the faith of the most trustworthy
witnesses. It has been one of my hopes to add
--**-Emacs: dickens.note          (Fundamental)----Top----------------
Query replacing French with Danish:
```

It may not be completely obvious, but emacs has found a match (immediately before the cursor) and is prompting me for what to do next. The choices here are summarized in Table 13.3.

Table 13.3. Options during query and replace.

Command	Meaning
y	Change this occurrence of the pattern.
n	Don't change this occurrence, but look for another.
q	Don't change this occurrence. Leave query-replace completely (you also can use Escape for this function).
!	Change this occurrence and all others in the file.

I opt to make this and all other possible changes in the file, by pressing !, and the screen changes to tell me that there were no more occurrences:

13

```
Whenever any reference (however slight) is made here to the condition
of the Danish_people before or during the Revolution, it is truly made,
on the faith of the most trustworthy
witnesses. It has been one of my hopes to add
--**-Emacs: dickens.note            (Fundamental)----Top---------------
Done
```

SUMMARY Searching in emacs is awkward, particularly due to the flow control problems that you may incur because of your terminal. However, searching and replacing with the query-replace command is fantastic—much better and more powerful than the vi alternative. As I said earlier, your assessment of emacs all depends on what features you prefer.

Task 13.5: Using the emacs Tutorial and Help System

DESCRIPTION Unlike vi and, indeed, unlike most of UNIX, emacs includes its own extensive, built-in documentation and a tutorial to help you learn about how to use the program. As I noted earlier, the entire help system is accessed by pressing C-h. Pressing C-h three times brings up the general help menu screen. There is also an information browser called info (accessed by pressing C-h i) and a tutorial system you can start by pressing C-h t.

emacs enthusiasts insist that the editor is modeless, but in fact it does have modes of its own. You used one just now, the query-replace mode. To obtain help on the current mode that you're working in, you can use C-h m.

ACTION

1. Boldly, I opted to press C-h C-h C-h, and the entire screen is replaced with this:

```
You have typed C-h, the help character. Type a Help option:

A  command-apropos.  Give a substring, and see a list of commands
                (functions interactively callable) that contain
                that substring. See also the  apropos  command.
B  describe-bindings. Display table of all key bindings.
C  describe-key-briefly. Type a command key sequence;
                it prints the function name that sequence runs.
F  describe-function. Type a function name and get documentation of it.
I  info. The  info  documentation reader.
K  describe-key. Type a command key sequence;
                it displays the full documentation.
L  view-lossage. Shows last 100 characters you typed.
```

13

```
M  describe-mode. Print documentation of current major mode,
            which describes the commands peculiar to it.
N  view-emacs-news. Shows emacs news file.
S  describe-syntax. Display contents of syntax table, plus explanations
T  help-with-tutorial. Select the Emacs learn-by-doing tutorial.
V  describe-variable. Type name of a variable;
            it displays the variable's documentation and value.
W  where-is. Type command name; it prints which keystrokes
            invoke that command.
--**-Emacs: *Help*              (Fundamental)----Top----------------
A B C F I K L M N S T V W C-c C-d C-n C-w or Space to scroll: _
```

What to do now? There are actually 17 different options from this point, as shown in Table 13.4.

Table 13.4. emacs **help system command options.**

Command	Meaning
A	List all commands matching the specified word.
B	List all key mappings.
C	Describe any key sequence pressed, instead of doing it.
F	Describe the specified function.
I	Start up the info browser.
K	Fully describe the result of a particular key sequence.
L	Show the last 100 characters you typed.
M	Describe the current mode you're in.
S	List a command syntax table.
T	Start the emacs tutorial.
V	Define and describe the specified variable.
W	Indicate what keystroke invokes a particular function.
C-c	Display emacs copyright and distribution information.
C-d	Display emacs ordering information.
C-n	Display recent emacs changes.
C-w	Display emacs warranty.

2. I choose K and then press M-< to see what that command really does. The first thing that happens after typing K is that the table of help information vanishes, to be replaced by my original text, and then the prompt appears along the bottom:

13

```
of the Danish_people before or during the Revolution, it is truly made,
on the faith of the most trustworthy
witnesses. It has been one of my hopes to add
--**-Emacs: dickens.note              (Fundamental)----Top----------------
Describe key:-
```

Pressing M-< brings up the desired information:

```
                          A Tale of Two Cities
                                Preface

When I was acting, with my children and friends, in Mr Wilkie Collins's
drama of The Frozen Deep, I first conceived the main idea of this
story. A strong desire came upon me then, to
embody it in my own person;
and I traced out in my fancy, the state of mind of which it would
necessitate the presentation
to an observant spectator, with particular
----Emacs: dickens.note~             (Fundamental)----Top----------------
beginning-of-buffer:
Move point to the beginning of the buffer; leave mark at previous
position.
With arg N, put point N/10 of the way from the true beginning.
Don't use this in Lisp programs!
(goto-char (point-min)) is faster and does not set the mark.




----Emacs: *Help*                    (Fundamental)----All----------------
Type C-x 1 to remove help window.
```

A quick C-x 1 removes the help information when I'm done with it.

SUMMARY There is a considerable amount of help available in the emacs editor. If you're interested in learning more about this editor, the online tutorial is a great place to start. Try C-h t to start it, and go from there.

Task 13.6: Working with Other Files

DESCRIPTION By this point, it should be no surprise that there are about a million commands available within the emacs editor, even though it can be a bit tricky to get to them. There are many file-related commands, too, but I'm going to focus on just a few essential commands so you can get around in the program. The emacs help system can offer lots more. (Try using C-h a *file* to find out what functions are offered in your version of the program.)

13

To add the contents of a file to the current edit buffer, use the command C-x i. It will prompt
for a filename. Pressing C-x C-w prompts for a file to write the buffer into, rather than the
default file. To save to the default file, use C-x C-s (that is, if you can; the C-s might again
hang you up, just as it did when you tried to use it for searching). If that doesn't work, you always
can use the alternative C-x s, which also works. To move to another file, use C-x C-f. (emacs
users never specify more than one filename on the command line. They use C-x C-f to move
between files instead). What's nice is that when you use the C-x C-f command, you load the
contents of that file into another buffer, so you can zip quickly between files by using the
C-x b command to switch buffers. emacs allows you to edit several files at once using different
areas of the screen; these areas are called buffers.

ACTION

1. Without leaving emacs, I press C-x C-f to read another file into the buffer. The
   system then prompts me as follows:

```
of the Danish people before or during the Revolution, it is truly made,
on the faith of the most trustworthy
witnesses. It has been one of my hopes to add
----Emacs: dickens.note          (Fundamental)----Top----------------
Find file: ~/ _
```

   I type buckaroo, and the editor opens up a new buffer, moving me to that file:

```
I found myself stealing a peek at my own watch and overhead
General Catbird's
aide give him the latest.
"He's not even here," went the conversation.
"Banzai."
"Where the hell is he?"
"At the hospital in El Paso."
"What? Why weren't we informed? What's wrong with him?"
```

13

```
----Emacs: buckaroo            (Fundamental)----All-----------------
```

2. Now I'll flip back to the other buffer with C-x b. When I enter that command, however, it doesn't automatically move me there. Instead, it offers this prompt:

```
--**-Emacs: buckaroo           (Fundamental)----All-----------------
Switch to buffer: (default dickens.note) _
```

When I type ?, I receive a split screen indicating what the possible answers are:

```
I found myself stealing a peek at my own watch and overhead
General Catbird's
aide give him the latest.
"He's not even here," went the conversation.
"Banzai."
"Where the hell is he?"
"At the hospital in El Paso."
"What? Why weren't we informed? What's wrong with him?"



--**-Emacs: buckaroo           (Fundamental)----All-----------------
Possible completions are:
*Buffer List*                  *Help*
*scratch*                      buckaroo
dickens.note




----Emacs:  *Completions*      (Fundamental)----All-----------------
Switch to buffer: (default dickens.note) _
```

The default is okay, so I press Return and voila! I'm back in the Dickens file. One more C-x b; this time the default is buckaroo, so I again press Return to move back.

3. I'm in the buckaroo file, and I want to see what happens if I read dickens.note into this file. This is done easily. I move the cursor to the end of the file with M->, press

C-x i, and answer dickens.note to the prompt Insert file: ~/. Pressing Return yields the following screen display:

```
I found myself stealing a peek at my own watch and overhead
General Catbird's
aide give him the latest.
"He's not even here," went the conversation.
"Banzai."
"Where the hell is he?"
"At the hospital in El Paso."
"What? Why weren't we informed? What's wrong with him?"

                        A Tale of Two Cities
                        Preface

When I was acting, with my children and friends, in Mr Wilkie Collins's
drama of The Frozen Deep, I first conceived the main idea of this
story. A strong desire came upon me then, to
embody it in my own person;
and I traced out in my fancy, the state of mind of which it would
necessitate the presentation
to an observant spectator, with particular
care and interest.

As the idea became familiar to me, it gradually shaped itself into its
present form. Throughout its execution, it has had complete posession
--**-Emacs: buckaroo              (Fundamental)----Top----------------
```

5. It's time to quit and split. To do this, I press C-x s and wait for an emacs prompt or two. The first one displayed is this:

```
As the idea became familiar to me, it gradually shaped itself into its
present form. Throughout its execution, it has had complete posession
--**-Emacs: buckaroo              (Fundamental)----Top----------------
Save file /users/taylor/buckaroo? (y or n) _
```

I answer y to save this muddled file. It returns me to the top of the file, and a quick C-x C-c drops me back to the system prompt.

SUMMARY One of the more useful facets of emacs that you have learned above is the ability to work with multiple files.

13

Summary

You have now learned quite a bit about the emacs editor. Some capabilities exceed those of the vi editor, and some are considerably more confusing. Which of these editors you choose is up to you, and your choice should be based on your own preferences for working on files. You should spend some time working with the editor you prefer, making sure you can create simple files and modify them without any problems.

Workshop

The Workshop summarizes the key terms you learned and poses some questions about the topics presented in this chapter. It also provides you with a preview of what you will learn in the next hour.

Key Terms

Meta key   Analogous to a Control key, this is labeled either Meta or Alt on your keyboard.

buffer   An area of the screen used to edit a file in emacs.

named emacs command   A command in emacs that requires you to type its name, like query-replace, rather than a command key or two.

key bindings   The emacs term for key mapping.

flow control   The protocol used by your computer and terminal to make sure that neither outpaces the other during data transmission.

XON/XOFF   A particular type of flow control. The receiving end can send an XON (delay transmission) character until it's ready for more information, when it sends an XOFF (resume transmission).

Questions

1. How do you get to the emacs help system?
2. Check your keyboard. If you don't have a Meta or Alt key, what alternative strategy can you use to enter commands such as M-x?
3. What's the command sequence for leaving emacs when you're done?
4. What was the problem I had with the Delete key? How did I solve the problem? What's the alternative delete command if Delete isn't available?

13

5. How do you do global search-and-replace in emacs, and what key do you press to stop the global search-and-replace when you are prompted for confirmation at the very first match?

6. Use the emacs help system to list the emacs copyright information. What's your reaction?

Preview of the Next Hour

The next hour is an in-depth look at the different shells available in UNIX, how to configure them, and how to choose which you'd like to use. You also learn about the contents of the default configuration files for both csh and sh, the two most common shells in UNIX.

Hour 14

Introduction to Command Shells

Welcome to your 14th hour of learning UNIX. You should take a moment to pat yourself on the back. You've come a long way, and you're already quite a sophisticated user. In the past few hours, I've occasionally touched on the differences between the shells, but I haven't really stopped to explain what shells are available, how they differ from one another, and which is the best for your style of interaction. That's what this hour is all about.

Shells, you'll recall, are the command-line interface programs through which you tell the computer what to do. All UNIX systems include C shell (csh) and its predecessor, the Bourne shell (sh). Some also include a newer version of the Bourne shell, called the Korn shell (ksh).

Goals for This Hour

In this hour, you learn

- [ ] What shells are available, and how they differ from one another
- [ ] How to identify which shell you're running

   ☐ How to choose a new shell

   ☐ More about the environment of your shell

   ☐ How to explore csh configuration files

A variety of shells are available in UNIX, but two are quite common: the Bourne shell (sh) and the C shell (csh). You learn about two of the other shells available, the Korn shell (ksh) and the terminal-based C shell (tcsh). Because the C shell is so popular, most of this book focuses on it.

Task 14.1: What Shells Are Available?

DESCRIPTION   If I asked a PC expert how many command interpreters are available for DOS, the immediate answer would be "one, of course." After a few minutes of reflection, however, the answer might be expanded to include The Norton Desktop, DesqView, Windows 95, Windows for Workgroups, and others. This expanded answer reflects the reality that whenever there are different people using a computer, there will evolve different styles of interacting with the machine and different products to meet these needs. Similarly, the Macintosh has several command interpreters. If you decide that you don't like the standard interface, perhaps you will find that At Ease, DiskTop, or Square One works better.

From the very beginning, UNIX has been a programmer's operating system, designed to allow programmers to extend the system easily and gracefully. It should come as no surprise, then, that there are quite a few shells available. Not only that, but any program can serve as a command shell, so you could even start right in emacs if you wanted and then use escapes to UNIX for actual commands. (Don't laugh—I've heard it's done sometimes.)

The original shell was written by Ken Thompson, back in the early UNIX's laboratory days, as part of his design of the UNIX file system. Somewhere along the way, Steven Bourne, also at AT&T, got hold of the shell and started expanding it. By the time UNIX began to be widely distributed, sh was known as the Bourne shell. Characterized by speed and simplicity, it is the default shell for writing shell scripts, but it is rarely used as a command shell for users today.

The next shell was designed by the productive Bill Joy, author of vi. Entranced by the design and features of the C programming language, Joy decided to create a command shell that shared much of the C language structure and that would make it easier to write sophisticated shell scripts: the C shell, or csh. He also expanded the shell concept to add command aliases, command history, and job control. Command aliases allow users to rename and reconfigure commands easily. Command history ensures that users never have to enter commands a second time. Job control enables users to run multiple programs at once. The C shell is by far the most popular shell on all systems I've ever used, and it's the shell that I have been using myself for about 15 years now, since I first logged in to a BSD UNIX system in 1980.

A *command alias* is a shortcut for a command, allowing you to enter a shorter string for the entire command. The *command history* is a mechanism by which the shell remembers commands you have typed and allows you to repeat the command without retyping the whole command. *Job control* is a mechanism that allows you to start, stop, and suspend commands.

In the past few years, another AT&T Labs software wizard, David Korn, has begun distributing another shell on various UNIX platforms. The Korn shell, also known as ksh, is designed to be a superset of the Bourne shell, sharing its configuration files (.profile) and command syntax, but including many of the more powerful features of the C shell, too, including command aliases (albeit in a slightly different format), command history, and job control. This shell is slowly becoming more popular, but it isn't yet widely distributed. You might not have it on your version of UNIX.

Other shells exist in special niches. A modified version of the C shell, a version that incorporates the slick history-editing features of the Korn shell, has appeared: it is called tcsh. Maintained by some engineers at Cornell University, it is 95 percent csh and 5 percent new features. The most important tcsh additions to the C shell are these:

- [ ] emacs-style command-line editing
- [ ] Visual perusal of the command history list
- [ ] Interactive command, file, and identifying files with the first few unique characters
- [ ] Spelling correction of command, file, and user names
- [ ] Automatic logout after an extended idle period
- [ ] The capability to monitor logins, users, or terminals
- [ ] New pre-initialized environment variables $HOST and $HOSTTYPE
- [ ] Support for a meaningful and helpful system status line

Another shell that you might bump into is called the MH shell, or msh, and it's designed around the MH electronic mail program, originally designed at the Rand Corporation. In essence, the MH shell lets you have instant access to any electronic mail that you might encounter. For sites that have security considerations, a restricted version of the Bourne shell is also available, called rsh (ingeniously, it's called the restricted sh shell). Persistent rumors of security problems with rsh suggest that you should double-check before you trust dubious users on your system with rsh as their login shell (The shell you use, by default, when you log in to the system).

Two other variants of the Bourne shell are worth mentioning: jsh is a version of the Bourne shell that includes C shell-style job control features, and bash, also humorously called the "Bourne Again" shell, is a reimplementation of the original shell with many new features and no licensing restrictions.

14

JUST A MINUTE

Licensing restrictions and intellectual property laws occasionally have stymied the growth of UNIX. Although UNIX is unquestionably popular with programmers, these same programmers have a burning desire to see what's inside, to learn about how UNIX works by examining UNIX itself. UNIX is owned by AT&T. Few people are able to view the source legally. Those who do look into UNIX are "tainted": Anything they write in the future might be inspired by proprietary code of AT&T. The situation is fuzzy in many ways, and that's where the Free Software Foundation comes in. The brainchild of Richard Stallman, the FSF is slowly rewriting all the major UNIX utilities and then distributing them with the source, as part of the ambitious GNU project. GNU emacs is one example, and the Bourne Again shell is another.

1. In Hour 9 you learned how to use awk to extract the default login shell of each user on your system and then use sort and uniq to collate the data and present an attractive output, respectively. Armed with the description of all the different shells, you now can take another look:

```
% awk -F: '{print $7}' /etc/passwd ¦ sort ¦ uniq -c
   2
3361 /bin/csh
   1 /bin/false
  85 /bin/ksh
  21 /bin/sh
  11 /usr/local/bin/ksh
 361 /usr/local/bin/tcsh
   7 /usr/local/lib/msh
```

2. You can see that the vast majority of the people on this system use the C shell. To look at it a different way, compute the number of entries in the password file:

```
% wc -l /etc/passwd
        3849
```

Now, what percentage of users have chosen each of these shells? This is a job for bc!

```
% bc
x=3849
scale=4
3361/x*100
87.3200
85/x*100
2.2000
361/x*100
9.3700
^d
```

It's a tad difficult to interpret, but this output says that 87.3 percent of the users have csh as their login shell, another 9.4 percent use the modified tcsh, and only 2.2 percent use ksh. The remaining 1.1 percent use either the Bourne shell or the

MH shell, or they default to the Bourne shell (the two accounts in the preceding output, without any shell indicated).

JUST A MINUTE

The scale=4 command tells bc how many digits to display after the decimal point in numbers. By default, unfortunately, bc displays no digits after the decimal point.

SUMMARY Quite a variety of shells is available, but the most common one on sites I'm familiar with is the C shell. Clearly, the system that I used for this particular set of examples has an overwhelming majority of C shell users: A combined total of 97 percent of the users are working within either the C shell or its descendent tcsh.

Task 14.2: Identifying Your Shell

DESCRIPTION There are many different approaches to identifying which shell you're using. The easiest, however, is just to swoop into the /etc/passwd file to see what your account lists. It's helpful to know some alternatives because the /etc/passwd option isn't always available (some systems don't have an /etc/passwd file in the interest of security).

ACTION

1. One simple technique to identify your shell is to check your prompt. If your prompt contains a %, you probably are using the C shell or modified C shell (tcsh). If your prompt contains $, you could be using the Bourne shell, the Korn shell, or a variant thereof.

2. A much more reliable way to ascertain which shell you're using is to ask the operating system what program you're currently running. The shell variable $$ identifies the process ID of the shell. You can use $$ as a search pattern for grep on the output of ps to see what shell you are using. Here's what happens when I try it:

```
% ps -ef ¦ grep $$
taylor    26905   0.0   0.2   256   144 Ai S          0:03 -csh (csh)
taylor    29751   0.0   0.1    52    28 Ai S          0:00 grep 26905
```

You can see that I'm running the C shell. Using ps in this fashion also matches the grep process (notice that the $$ have expanded to the current shell process identification, 26905). There is a leading dash on the indication of what shell I'm running because that's how the system denotes whether it's my login shell or just a shell that I'm running.

14

3. Another way to find out what shell I'm running is to peek into the /etc/passwd file, which you can do with some sophistication now that awk is no longer a mystery:

```
% awk -F: '{ if ($1 == "taylor") print "your shell is: "$7}' <
➥/etc/passwd
your shell is: /bin/csh
```

4. The best way to figure out what shell you're running, however, is to use chsh. You learn how to use chsh in the following task.

SUMMARY Once you've identified your shell, you can contemplate choosing a different one.

Task 14.3: How To Choose a New Shell

DESCRIPTION In the past, the only way to switch login shells on many systems was to ask the system administrator to edit the /etc/passwd file directly. This usually meant waiting until the system administrator had time. The good news is that there's now a simple program (on almost all UNIX systems) to change login shells—it's chsh, or change shell. It has no starting flags or options, does not require that any files be specified, and can be used regardless of your location in the file system. Simply type chsh and press Return.

ACTION

1. The first step is to identify what shells are available for use. By convention, all shells have sh somewhere in their names, and they are located in /bin:

```
% ls -1F /bin/*sh*
-rwsr-xr-x  3 root         49152 Apr 23  1992 /bin/chsh*
-rwxr-xr-x  1 root        102400 Apr  8  1991 /bin/csh*
-rwxr-xr-x  1 root        139264 Jul 26 14:35 /bin/ksh*
-rwxr-xr-x  1 root         28672 Oct 10  1991 /bin/sh*
```

The chsh command enables you to change your login shell, as you will learn. The most common shells are csh, ksh, and sh.

On one of the machines I use, some shells are also stored in the /usr/local/bin directory:

```
% ls -1F /usr/local/bin/*sh*
lrwxr-xr-x  1 root             8 Jul 26 14:46 /usr/local/bin/ksh ->
➥/bin/ksh*
-rwxr-xr-x  1 root        266240 Jan 19  1993 /usr/local/bin/tcsh*
```

You can see that there's an entry in /usr/local/bin for the ksh shell but that it's actually just a link pointing to the file in the /bin directory.

2. You might find quite a few more matches to these simple ls commands. On another, very different system, I tried the same two commands and found the following:

```
% ls -CF /bin/*sh*
/bin/chsh*          /bin/ksh*          /bin/shelltool@    /bin/tcsh*
/bin/csh*           /bin/sh*           /bin/shift_lines@  /bin/ypchsh*
% ls -CF /usr/local/bin/*sh*
/usr/local/bin/bash*          /usr/local/bin/showpicture*
/usr/local/bin/bash112*       /usr/local/bin/sun-audio-file.csh*
/usr/local/bin/ircflush@      /usr/local/bin/sun-to-mime.csh*
/usr/local/bin/mush^          /usr/local/bin/tcsh*
/usr/local/bin/mush.old*      /usr/local/bin/tcsh603*
/usr/local/bin/mush725*       /usr/local/bin/unshar*
/usr/local/bin/ntcsh*         /usr/local/bin/unship*
/usr/local/bin/shar*          /usr/local/bin/uupath.sh*
/usr/local/bin/ship*          /usr/local/bin/vsh*
/usr/local/bin/showaudio*     /usr/local/bin/zsh*
/usr/local/bin/showexternal*  /usr/local/bin/zsh210*
/usr/local/bin/shownonascii*  /usr/local/bin/zsh231*
/usr/local/bin/showpartial*
```

Two more shells show up here: vsh and zsh. The visual shell, vsh, is an interface much like the Norton Desktop on DOS. Watch what happens to my screen when I launch it by typing vsh:

```
   Directory: /u1/taylor  User: taylor                        Page 2 / 2

   a    .tin/
   b    Global.Software
   c    Interactive.Unix
   d    Mail/
   e    News/
   f    Src/
   g    bin/
   h    history.usenet.Z
   i    testme




   _
```

14

If you have vsh on your system, you might be interested in experimenting with this very different shell.

The zsh shell is another command shell, one written by Paul Falstad of Princeton University. The Bourne Again shell, bash, also appears in the listing, as does the mush program, which is an electronic mail package.

3. Needless to say, many shells are available! To change my login shell to any of these alternate shells, or even just to verify what shell I'm running, I can use the change shell command:

```
% chsh
Changing login shell for taylor.
Old shell: /bin/csh
New shell: _
```

At this point, the program shows me that I currently have /bin/csh as my login shell and asks me to specify an alternative shell. I'll try to confuse it by requesting that emacs become my login shell:

```
% chsh
Changing login shell for taylor.
Old shell: /bin/csh
New shell: /usr/local/bin/gnuemacs
/usr/local/bin/gnuemacs is unacceptable as a new shell.
```

4. The program has some knowledge of valid shell names, and it requires you to specify one. Unfortunately, it doesn't divulge that information, so typing ? to find what's available results in the program complaining that ? is unacceptable as a new shell.

You can, however, peek into the file that chsh uses to confirm which programs are valid shells. It's called /etc/shells and looks like this:

```
% cat /etc/shells
/bin/ksh
/bin/sh
/bin/csh
/usr/local/bin/ksh
/usr/local/bin/tcsh
```

I'll change my shell from /bin/csh to /usr/local/bin/tcsh:

```
% chsh
Changing login shell for taylor
Old shell: /bin/csh
New shell: /usr/local/bin/tcsh
```

Notice that, in typical UNIX style, there is no actual confirmation that anything was done. I conclude that, because I did not get any error messages, the program worked. Fortunately, I easily can check by either using chsh again or redoing the awk program with a C shell history command:

```
% !awk
awk -F: '{ if ($1 == "taylor") print "your shell is: "$7}' < /etc/passwd
your shell is: /usr/local/bin/tcsh
```

14

In the next hour, you learn more about the powerful C shell command-history mechanism.

JUST A MINUTE

Because of the overwhelming popularity of the C shell, the next few hours focus on the C shell. To get the most out of those hours, I strongly recommend that you use the C shell.

5. A quick reinvocation of the chsh command changes my shell back to /bin/csh:

```
% chsh
Changing login shell for taylor
Old shell: /usr/local/bin/tcsh
New shell: /bin/csh
```

JUST A MINUTE

If you can't change your login shell, perhaps because of not having chsh, you always can enter the C shell after you log in by typing csh.

SUMMARY It's easy to change your login shell. You can try different ones until you find the one that best suits your style of interaction. For the most part, though, shells all have the same basic syntax and use the same commands: ls -l does the same thing in any shell. The differences, then, really come into play when you use the more sophisticated capabilities, including programming the shell (with shell scripts), customizing its features through command aliases, and saving on keystrokes using a history mechanism. That's where the C shell has an edge and why it's so popular. It's easy, straightforward, and has powerful aliasing, history, and job-control capabilities, as you learn in the next hour.

Task 14.4: Learning the Shell Environment

DESCRIPTION Earlier in this book, you used the env or printenv command to find out the various characteristics of your working environment. Now it's time to use this command again to look more closely at the C shell environment and define each of the variables therein.

ACTION

1. To start out, I enter env to list the various aspects of my working environment. Do the same on your system, and, although your environment will not be identical to mine, there should be considerable similarity between the two.

```
% env ¦ cat -n
1   HOME=/users/taylor
2   SHELL=/bin/csh
3   TERM=vt100
```

14

```
 4  USER=taylor
 5  PATH=.:/users/taylor/bin:/bin:/usr/bin:/usr/ucb:/usr/local:/etc:
➡ /usr/etc:/usr/local/bin:/usr/unsup/bin:
 6  MAIL=/usr/spool/mail/taylor
 7  LOGNAME=taylor
 8  EDITOR=/ucb/bin/vi
 9  NAME=Dave Taylor
10  EXINIT=:set ignorecase
11  RNINIT=-hmessage -hreference -hdate-r -hsender -hsummary -hreply
➡ -hdistr -hlines -hline -hfollow -hnews -hkey -hresent -hreturn -hto
➡ -hx-original -hx-sun -hx-note -horiginator -hnntp
12  SUBJLINE=%t -- %s
13  ORGANIZATION=Educational Computing group, School of Education
```

This probably initially seems pretty overwhelming. What are all these things, and why on earth should they matter? They matter because it's important for you to learn exactly how your own environment is set up so that you can change things if you desire. As you soon will be able to recognize, I have modified much of my system's environment so that the C shell does what I want it to do, rather than what its default would tell it to do.

2. When I log in to the system, the system defines some environment variables, indicating where my home directory is located, what shell I'm running, and so on. These variables are listed in Table 14.1.

Table 14.1. Default variables set by UNIX upon login.

Variable	Description
HOME	This is my home directory, obtained from the fourth field of the password file. Try the command `grep $USER /etc/passwd ¦ awk -F: '{print $6}'` to see what your home directory is set to, or just use env HOME or echo $HOME. This is not only the directory that I start in, but it's also the directory that cd moves me back to when I don't specify a different directory. My HOME variable is /users/taylor.
SHELL	When UNIX programs, such as vi, process the ! command to execute UNIX commands, they check this variable to see which shell I'm using. If I were to type :! followed by Return in vi, the program would create a new C shell for me. If I had SHELL=/bin/sh, vi would start up a Bourne shell. My SHELL variable is set to /bin/csh.
TERM	By default, your terminal is defined by the value of this environment variable, which starts out as unknown. (Recall that when you first were learning about vi, the program would complain unknown: terminal not known.) Many sites know what kind of terminals are using which lines, however, so this variable is often set to the correct value before you even see it. If it isn't set, you can define it to the appropriate value within your .login file. (You will learn to do this later in the hour.)

Variable	Description
	My TERM is set to vt100, for a Digital Equipment Corporation Visual Terminal model 100, which is probably the most commonly emulated terminal in communications packages.
USER	Programs can quickly look up your user ID and match it with an account name. However, predefining your account name as an environment setting saves time. That's exactly what USER, and its companion LOGNAME, are—timesavers. My USER is set to taylor.
PATH	A few hours ago, you learned that the UNIX shell finds a command by searching from directory to directory until it finds a match. The environment variable that defines which directories to search and the order in which to search them is the PATH variable. Rather than keep the default settings, I've added a number of directories to my search path, which is now as follows:

```
.:/users/taylor/bin:/bin:/usr/bin:/usr/ucb:/usr/local:/etc
:/usr/etc:/usr/local/bin:/usr/unsup/bin:
```

I have told the shell always to look first for commands in the current directory (.), then in my bin directory (/users/taylor/bin), and then in the standard system directories (/bin, /usr/bin, /usr/ucb, /usr/local). If the commands are not found in any of those areas, the shell should try looking in some unusual directories (/etc, /usr/etc, /usr/local/bin). If the shell still has not found my command, it should check in a weird directory specific to my site: /usr/unsup/bin for unsupported software, /usr/unsup/elm for programs related to the Elm Mail System, and /usr/local/wwb for the AT&T Writers Workbench programs.

CAUTION

I admit it; using . as the first entry in the PATH variable is a security hazard. Why? Imagine this: A devious chap has written a program that will do bad things to my directory when I invoke that bad program. But how will he make me invoke it? The easiest way is to give the bad program the same name as a standard UNIX utility, such as ls, and leave it in a commonly accessed directory, such as /tmp. So what happens? Imagine that the . (current directory) is the first entry in my PATH, and I change directories to /tmp to check something. While I'm in /tmp, I enter ls without thinking, and voilà! I've run the bad program without knowing it. Having the . at the end of the search path would avoid all this because then the default ls command is the correct version. I have it because I often do want to override the standard commands with new ones that I'm working on (an admittedly foolish practice).

14

continues

Table 14.1. continued

Variable	Description
MAIL	One of the most exciting and enjoyable aspects of UNIX is its powerful and incredibly well-connected electronic mail capability. A variety of programs can be used to check for new mail, to read mail, and to send mail messages. Most of these programs need to know where my default incoming mailbox is located, which is what the MAIL environment variable defines. My MAIL is set to /usr/spool/mail/taylor.
LOGNAME	LOGNAME is a synonym for USER. My LOGNAME is set to taylor.

JUST A MINUTE

Having both LOGNAME and USER defined in my environment demonstrates how far UNIX has progressed since the competition and jostling between the Berkeley and AT&T versions (BSD and SVR3, respectively) of UNIX. Back when I started working with UNIX, if I was on a BSD system, the account name would be defined as LOGNAME, and if I used an SVR3 system, the account name would be defined as USER. Programs had to check for both, which was frustrating. Over time, each system has begun to use both terms (instead of using the solution that you and I might think is most obvious, which is to agree on a single word).

Variable	Description
NAME	In addition to wanting to know the name of the current account, some programs, such as many electronic mail and printing programs, need to ascertain my full, human name. The NAME variable contains this information for the environment. It's obtained from the /etc/passwd file. You can check yours with the command grep $USER /etc/passwd	awk -F: '{print $5}'. You can change your NAME variable, if desired, using the chfn, or change-full-name, command. My NAME is set to Dave Taylor.

3. A glance back at the output of the env command reveals that there are more variables in my environment than are listed in Table 14.1. That's because you can define anything you want in the environment. Certain programs can read many environment variables that customize their behavior.

   Many UNIX programs allow you to enter text directly, and then they spin off into an editor, if needed. Others start your favorite editor for entering information. Both types of programs use the EDITOR environment variable to identify which editor to use. I have mine set to /usr/ucb/vi.

You learned earlier that vi can have default information stored in the .exrc file, but the program also can read configuration information from the environment variable EXINIT. To make all my pattern searches *case insensitive* (that is, searching for precision will match Precision), I set the appropriate vi variable in the EXINIT. Mine is set to :set ignorecase. If you want line numbers to show up always, you could easily have your EXINIT set to :set number.

Another program that I use frequently is rn, or read Netnews. If electronic mail is the electronic equivalent of letters and magazines that you receive through the postal service, Netnews is the electronic equivalent of a super bulletin board. The difference is that there are thousands of different boards, and any time a note is tacked onto any board, copies of the note shoot to other UNIX systems throughout the world. For now, you can see that I have three environment variables all defined for the rn program: RNINIT, my personal rn configuration options; SUBJLINE, indicating the format for displaying summary subject lines of new messages; and ORGANIZATION, indicating exactly what organization I'm associated with on this system. They are set as shown earlier.

SUMMARY There are many possible environment variables that you can define for yourself. Most large UNIX programs have environment variables of their own, allowing you to tailor the program's behavior to your needs and preferences. UNIX itself has quite a few environment variables, too. Until you're an expert, however, I recommend that you stick with viewing these variables and ensuring that they have reasonable values, rather than changing them. Particularly focus on the set of variables defined in Table 14.1. If they're wrong, it could be trouble; whereas, if other environment variables are wrong, it's probably not going to be too much trouble.

Task 14.5: Exploring csh **Configuration Files**

DESCRIPTION The C shell uses two files to configure itself, and, although neither of them need to be present, both probably can be found in your home directory: .login and .cshrc. The difference between them is subtle but very important. The .login file is read only once, when you log in, and the .cshrc file is read every time a C shell is started. As a result, if you're working in vi and you enter :!ls, vi carries out the command by starting up a new shell and then feeding the command to that shell. Therefore, new csh shells started from within programs such as vi won't see key shell configurations that are started in .login.

This split between two configuration files isn't too bad, actually, because many modifications to the environment are automatically included in all subshells (a shell other than the login shell) invoked. To be specific, all environment variables are pervasive, but any C shell command aliases are lost and, therefore, must be defined in the .cshrc file to be available upon all occurrences of csh. You learn more about command aliases in the C shell in the next hour.

14

ACTION

1. To begin, I use `cat` to list the contents of my `.login` file. Remember that any line beginning with a # is a comment and is ignored.

```
% cat .login
#
# @(#) $Revision: 62.2 $

setenv TERM vt100

stty erase "^H" kill "^U" intr "^C" eof "^D"
stty crtbs crterase             # special DYNIX stuff for bs processing

# shell vars

set noclobber history=100 savehist=50 filec

# set up some global environment variables...

setenv EXINIT ":set ignorecase"

# Some RN related variables...

setenv RNINIT        "-hmessage -hreference -hdate-r -hsender -hsummary
-hreply -hdistr -hlines -hline -hfollow -hnews -hkey -hresent -hreturn
-hto -hx-original -hx-sun -hx-note -horiginator -hnntp"
setenv SUBJLINE      "%t — %s"
setenv ORGANIZATION      "Educational Computing group, School of Education
"

setenv NAME "Dave Taylor"

newmail

mesg y
```

This is pretty straightforward, once you remove all the comments. Three different kinds of environmental configuration commands are shown: `setenv`, `stty`, and `set`. The `setenv` command defines environment variables; indeed, you can see that many of the variables shown in the previous unit are defined in my `.login` file.

I can use `stty` commands to set specific configuration options related to my terminal (`stty` stands for "set tty driver options"). I use this to ensure that ^h is erase (backspace), ^u is a convenient shortcut allowing me to kill an entire line, and ^c sends an interrupt to a running program. I indicate the end of a file (EOF) with ^d. The second line of the preceding output example indicates that my CRT is capable of backspacing and erasing characters on the display.

14

Here's more arcane UNIX nomenclature: CRT (as used in `stty crtbs` or cathode-ray tube) is the technology used in the screen of a standard terminal. Terminal is not accurate anymore, however, because the command `stty crtbs` also works on my LCD (liquid-crystal diode, if you must know) laptop.

Finally, the `set` commands are configuration options for the C shell. I have told the C shell to warn me before it overwrites existing files with file redirection (`noclobber`), to remember the last 100 commands (`history=100`), and to remember 50 of those even if I log out and log back in (`savehist=50`). I also want the C shell to try, if possible, to complete filenames for me, hence the `filec` addition. Notice that there are two different types of settings: on/off options (such as `noclobber` and `filec`) and options to which I must assign a specific numeric value (such as `history` and `savehist`).

The two commands at the very end of the `.login` file are invoked as though I'd entered them on the command line. The `newmail` variable watches for new electronic mail (in the mailbox defined by the environment variable `MAIL`, in fact) and tells me when it arrives. The `mesg y` variable makes sure that I have my terminal configured so that other folks can beep me or say hello using `write` or `talk`, two communication tools discussed in Hour 20, "Communicating with Others."

2. How about the other file—the one that's read by the C shell each time a shell is started?

```
% cat .cshrc
#
# Default user .cshrc file (/bin/csh initialization).

set path=(. ~/bin /bin /usr/bin /usr/ucb /usr/local /etc /usr/etc
/usr/local/bin /usr/unsup/bin /

# Define a bunch of C shell aliases

alias   diff      '/usr/bin/diff -c -w'
alias   env       'printenv'
alias   from      'frm -n'
alias   info       ssinfo
alias   library   'echo " "; echo " " ; echo "remember: ^J is ENTER";
tn3270 lib
alias   ll        'ls -l'
alias   ls        '/bin/ls -F'
alias   mail       Mail
alias   mailq     '/usr/lib/sendmail -bp'
alias   newaliases 'echo you mean newalias...'
```

```
alias  rd        'readmsg $ ¦ page'
alias  rn        '/usr/local/bin/rn -d$HOME -L -M -m -e -S -/'
alias  ssinfo    'echo "connecting..." ; rlogin oasis'

# and some special stuff if we're in an interactive shell

if ( $?prompt ) then              # shell is interactive.

  alias  cd        'chdir \!* ; setprompt'
  alias  setprompt 'set prompt="$system ($cwd:t) \! : "'

  set noclobber history=100 system=mentor filec
  umask 007

  setprompt
endif
```

Again, any line that begins with a # is considered a comment. There are, therefore, two primary types of commands in this script: the C shell environment modification (set) and the command alias (alias). The first defines the PATH I want to use, although in a format slightly different from the colon-separated list shown by env. The csh command always ensures that the environment variable and shell variable match, and so, although I opt to change the path here as a set, I could just as easily use setenv PATH.

You learn all about aliases in the next hour, but for now you should know that the format is alias *word command* (or *commands*) to execute. When I enter ls, for example, you can see that the shell has that aliased to /bin/ls -F, which saves me from having to type the -F flag each time.

The C shell also has conditional statements and a variety of other commands to indicate what commands to run. Here I'm using the if (*expression*) then to define a set of commands that should be used only when the shell is interactive (that is, I'm going to be able to enter commands). An example of a noninteractive shell is the shell vi uses to create a listing when I enter !!ls within the editor. The $?*prompt* variable is true if there is a prompt defined for the shell (that is, if it's interactive). If not, the variable is false, and the shell zips to the endif before resuming execution of the commands.

If it is an interactive shell, however, I create a few further aliases and again define some C shell configuration options, to ensure that the options are always set in subshells. The umask value is set, and I then invoke setprompt, which is a command alias that runs the command set prompt="$system ($cwd:t) \! : ".

SUMMARY If you're thinking that there is a variety of ways to configure the shell, you are correct. You can have an incredibly diverse set of commands in both your .login and .cshrc files, enabling you to customize many aspects of the C shell and the UNIX environment. If you use either the Bourne shell or the Korn shell, the configuration information is kept in a similar file called .profile.

14

Summary

Armed with the information learned in this hour about shells and shell environments, explore your own environment; examine your `.login` and `.cshrc` files, too.

Workshop

The Workshop summarizes the key terms you learned and poses some questions about the topics presented in this chapter. It also provides you with a preview of what you will learn in the next hour.

Key Terms

command alias   A shorthand command mapping, with which you can define new command names that are aliases of other commands or sequences of commands. This is helpful for renaming commands so that you can remember them, or for having certain flags added by default.

command history   A mechanism the shell uses to remember what commands you have entered already, and to allow you to repeat them without having to type the entire command again.

job control   A mechanism for managing the various programs that are running. Job control enables you to push programs into the background and pull them back into the foreground as desired.

login shell   The shell you use, by default, when you log in to the system.

subshell   A shell other than the login shell.

Questions

1. Draw lines to connect the original shells with their newer variants:

   ```
   sh
   ksh
   tcsh
   csh
   ```

2. What does `chsh` do? What about `chfn`?
3. What shell are you running? What shells are your friends on the system running?
4. What's the difference between the `.login` and the `.cshrc` files?
5. What's the `sh` equivalent of the `csh` `.login` file?
6. What aliases do you think could prove helpful for your daily UNIX interaction?

14

Preview of the Next Hour

I hope this hour has whetted your appetite for learning more about the C shell! In the next hour, you learn how to really customize the shell and make your interaction with UNIX quite a bit easier. Topics include how to create command aliases, how to use the history mechanism, and how to create simple shell scripts when aliases just don't suffice.

14

Hour **15**

Getting the Most Out of the C Shell

The previous hour gave you an overview of the different shells available in UNIX. There are quite a few, but the C shell—originally from Berkeley, California—is the most popular shell at most sites. In this hour, you learn all about the C shell and how to use it to your best advantage. You also learn some valuable tips about working with the Korn shell, a popular alternative to C shell. The goal is for you to be able to customize your UNIX environment to fit your working style.

Goals for This Hour

In this hour, you learn

☐ How to turn on the C shell and Korn shell history mechanism

☐ How to use csh history and ksh history to cut down on typing

☐ About command aliases in the C and Korn shells

☐ Some power aliases for csh

☐ How to set custom prompts

☐ How to create simple shell scripts

This hour focuses on two key facets of the C and Korn shells: the history mechanism and the command alias capability. I guarantee that within a few minutes of learning about these two functions, it will be clear that you couldn't have survived as happily in UNIX without them. There are three ways to ensure that you don't enter commands more than once: csh history enables you to repeat previous commands without re-entering them, an alias enables you to name one command as another, and shell scripts enable you to toss a bunch of commands into a file to be used as a single command. You learn the basics about building shell scripts in this hour.

One of the fun parts of UNIX is that you can customize the prompt that greets you each time you use the system. There's no need to be trapped with a boring % prompt anymore!

Task 15.1: The C Shell and Korn Shell History Mechanisms

DESCRIPTION   If you went through school in the United States, you doubtless have heard the aphorism "Those who do not study history are doomed to repeat it." UNIX stands this concept on its head. For UNIX, the aphorism is best stated, "Those who are aware of their history can easily repeat it."

Both the C shell and the Korn shell build a table of commands as you enter them and assign them a command number. Each time you log in, the first command you enter is command 1, and the command number is incremented for each subsequent command that you enter. You can review or repeat any previous command easily with just a few keystrokes.

To review your history in the C shell, enter history at the csh prompt. Odds are that nothing will happen, though, because by default csh remembers only the very last command. To have it begin building a list of commands, you must turn on this feature through an environment setting set history=n, where n is the number of commands you'd like it to recall.

By contrast, ksh has a default history list size of 128 commands, plenty for anyone. To review your history in ksh, you also can use the history command. Actually, though, it's an alias, and the real command is the more cryptic fc -l. In Korn shell, you don't need to make any changes; the history mechanism is ready to use immediately.

ACTION

1. Log in to your system so that you have a C shell prompt. If you're currently in the Bourne shell, this would be a great time to use chsh to change shells.

15

15

```
% history

%
```

The shell indicates that it has no history. Sir Winston Churchill doubtless would shake his head and mutter under his breath, "To have become such a sophisticated operating system yet never to have studied history!"

2. I need to turn on the shell history mechanism, so I will enter the following command:

```
% set history=100
```

Still there is no feedback, but I can check the status of all the shell parameters by entering set at the csh prompt:

```
% set
argv    ()
cwd     /users/taylor
filec
history 100
home    /users/taylor
host    limbo
noclobber
path    (. /users/taylor/bin /bin /usr/bin /usr/ucb /usr/local /etc
/usr/etc /usr/local/bin /usr/unsup/bin
savehist        50
shell   /bin/csh
status  0
system  limbo
term    unknown
user    taylor
```

3. To take a break, I use w to see who is logged on and what they're doing, ls to check my files again, and date to see if my watch is working:

```
% w | head
  11:41am  up 17:59,  103 users,   load average: 0.54, 0.53, 0.49
User      tty       login@ idle    JCPU    PCPU  what
root      console   6:02pm 12:13       1       1  -csh
taylor    ttyAf     11:40am            5       2  w
bev       ttyAg     9:25am    14    1:09       3  -csh
rekunkel  ttyAh     11:37am            4       3  rlogin ccn
gabh      ttyAi     10:41am    6      46      16  talk dorits
af5       ttyAj     8:27am    21      33       1  -ksh
techman   ttyAk     9:47am           25       7  gopher
tuccie    ttyAl     11:37am            1       1  mail
Broken pipe
% ls
Archives/       OWL/              buckaroo.confused  sample
InfoWorld/      awkscript         dickens.note       sample2
Mail/           bin/              keylime.pie        src/
News/           buckaroo          owl.c              temp/
% date
Tue Dec  7 11:41:29 EST 1993
```

Notice that at the end of the w command output, the system noted Broken pipe. This is nothing to be anxious about; it's just an indication that there was lots more in the pipeline when the program quit. You can see that head read only the first 10 lines. The first line of the w output shows that there are 103 users on the system, which means that head ignored 94 lines of output. Unlike real plumbing, fortunately, this broken pipe doesn't allow the spare data to spill onto the basement floor!

4. Now, when I enter history, the shell remembers the previous commands, presenting them all in a neat, numbered list:

```
% history
     1   set history=100
     2   w ¦ head
     3   ls
     4   date
     5   history
```

5. To turn this on permanently, add the set history command to your .cshrc. If you want the shell to remember commands even if you log out and log back in, also specify the setting savehist. I choose to do this by entering vi +$ .cshrc and adding the following line:

```
    set noclobber system=limbo filec
    umask 007

    setprompt
endif

set history=100 savehist=50 _
~
~
```

If you glance back at the output of the set command, you can see that I already have both of these parameters set: 100 commands will remain in the history list while I'm working, and 50 commands will be retained for the next time I log in. What's particularly helpful is that any time I specify a number n for either history list, the shell actually saves the most recent n commands, so I have the most recent 100 commands for review while I'm using the system, and the 50 most recent commands remembered when I log in later.

Make this change to your .cshrc file, log out, and log in again to ensure that your history mechanism is set up correctly.

SUMMARY Like much of UNIX, turning on the history mechanism of the C shell is quite easy once you learn the trick. In this case, simply remember that you need to specify a set history value to have the shell begin remembering what's going on with your interaction. In Korn shell, you don't need to make any changes; it's ready to use immediately.

Task 15.2: Using History to Cut Down on Typing

DESCRIPTION There are three main mechanisms for working with the history list. You can specify a previous command by its command number, by the first word of the command, or, if you're working with the most recently executed command, by a special notation that easily fixes any mistakes you might have made as you typed it.

Every history command begins with an exclamation point. If the 33rd command you entered was the who command, for example, you can execute it by referring to its command number: enter !33 at the command line. You can execute it also by entering one or more characters of the command: !w, !wh, or !who: You must enter enough characters to uniquely identify it in the history list.

To edit a previous command, type a caret, the pattern you want to change, another caret, and the correct pattern. If you just entered awk -F, '{print $2}' and realize that you meant to type a colon, not a comma, as the field delimiter, ^,^: will do the trick.

A very useful shorthand is !!, which repeats the most recently executed command. Two other history references are valuable to know: !$ expands to the last word of the previous line (which makes sense because $ always refers to the end of something, whether it be a line, the file, or, in this case, a command), and !* expands to all the words in the previous command except the very first. So, for example, if I entered the command ls /usr /etc /dev and then immediately entered the command echo !*, the second command would be expanded automatically to echo /usr /etc /dev.

Korn shell offers all of this and more. You can repeat commands by number by specifying rn, where n is the command number (for example, r33). You can also repeat by name with rname, as in rwho to repeat the most recent who command. Much more useful is the ksh capability to edit directly a command with the familiar vi or EMACS command keys, without leaving the command line. Without any arguments, r will repeat the previous command.

ACTION

1. First, I need to spend a few minutes building up a history list by running various commands:

```
% w ¦ head
 11:58am  up 18:14,  81 users,  load average: 0.54, 0.44, 0.38
User     tty       login@ idle   JCPU   PCPU  what
```

```
root       console   6:02pm 12:30     1        1    -csh
hopkins    ttyAe     11:49am          4        4    telnet whip.isca.uiowa.edu
taylor     ttyAf     11:40am          8        2    wbev       ttyAg      9:25am
31    1:09       3   -csh
af5        ttyAj     8:27am   37      33       1    -ksh
techman    ttyAk     9:47am    4      1:11      4    elm
tuccie     ttyAl     11:37am          2        1    mail
trice      ttyAm     8:16am  1:21      5        2    -csh
Broken pipe
% date
Tue Dec  7 11:58:19 EST 1993
% ls
Archives/          OWL/              buckaroo.confused  sample
InfoWorld/         awkscript         dickens.note       sample2
Mail/              bin/              keylime.pie        src/
News/              buckaroo          owl.c              temp/
% cat buckaroo
I found myself stealing a peek at my own watch and overheard General
Catbird's
aide give him the latest.
"He's not even here," went the conversation.
"Who?"
"Banzai."
"Where the hell is he?"
"At the hospital in El Paso."
"What? Why weren't we informed? What's wrong with him?"
%
```

2. Now I will check my history list to see what commands were squirreled away for later:

```
% history
    51   set history=100
    52   history
    53   w ¦ head
    54   date
    55   ls
    56   cat buckaroo
    57   history
```

JUST A MINUTE

I already have my history mechanism turned on, so my commands begin numbering with 51 rather than with 1. Your system might be different. Regardless of what the command numbers are, they'll work!

3. To repeat the date command, I can specify its command number:

```
% !54
date
Tue Dec  7 12:04:08 EST 1993
```

Notice that the shell shows the command I've entered as command number 54. The ksh equivalent here would be r 54.

15

4. A second way to accomplish this repeat, a way that is much easier, is to specify the first letter of the command:

```
% !w
w ¦ head
 12:05pm  up 18:23,  87 users,  load average: 0.40, 0.39, 0.33
 User      tty       login@ idle   JCPU   PCPU  what
 root      console   6:02pm 12:37     1      1  -csh
 lloyds    ttyAb     12:05pm          1      1  mail windberg
 lusk      ttyAc     12:03pm          3      2  gopher
 hopkins   ttyAe     11:49am          8      8  telnet whip.isca.uiowa.edu
 taylor    ttyAf     11:40am    1    14      3  w
 bev       ttyAg      9:25am   38  1:09      3  -csh
 libphar   ttyAh     12:03pm          3      3  elm
 dgrove    ttyAi     12:02pm          5      2  more inbox/16
 Broken pipe
```

5. Now glance at the history list:

```
% history
    51   set history=100
    52   history
    53   w ¦ head
    54   date
    55   ls
    56   cat buckaroo
    57   history
    58   date
    59   w ¦ head
    60   history
```

Commands expanded by the history mechanism are stored as the expanded command, not as the history command that actually was entered. Thus, this is an exception to the earlier rule that the history mechanism always shows what was previously entered. It's an eminently helpful exception!

History commands are quite helpful for people working on a software program. The most common cycle for programmers to repeat is edit-compile-run, over and over again. The commands UNIX programmers use most often probably will look something like vi test.c, cc -o test test.c, and test, to edit, compile, and run the program, respectively. Using the C shell history mechanism, a programmer easily can enter !v to edit the file, !c to compile it, then !t to test it. As your commands become longer and more complex, this function proves more and more helpful.

6. It's time to experiment a bit with file wildcards.

```
% ls
Archives          awkscript         dickens.note      src
InfoWorld         bin               keylime.pie       temp
Mail              buckaroo          owl.c
News              buckaroo.confused sample
OWL               cshrc             sample2x
```

Oops! I meant to specify the -F flag to ls. I can use !! to repeat the command, then I can add the flag:

```
% !! -F
ls -F
Archives/         awkscript         dickens.note      src/
InfoWorld/        bin/              keylime.pie       temp/
Mail/             buckaroo          owl.c
News/             buckaroo.confused sample
OWL/              cshrc             sample2
```

JUST A MINUTE

The general idea of all these history mechanisms is that you specify a pattern that is replaced by the appropriate command in the history list. So, you could enter echo !! to have the system echo the last command, and it would end up echoing twice. Try it.

JUST A MINUTE

Korn shell users will find that echo !! produces !! and that the ksh repeat-last-command of r also will fail. If your last command was echo r, the result will be r. Further, there is no analogous shorthand to the convenient !! -F in csh. On the other hand, if FCEDIT is set to vi or EMACS, you can pop into the editor to change the command by typing fc.

I want to figure out a pattern or two that will let me specify both buckaroo files, the dickens file, and sample2, but not sample. This is a fine example of where the echo command can be helpful:

```
% echo b* d* s*
bin buckaroo buckaroo.confused dickens.note sample sample2 src
```

That's not quite it. I'll try again:

```
% echo bu* d* sa*
buckaroo buckaroo.confused dickens.note sample sample2
```

That's closer. Now I just need to remove the sample file:

```
% echo bu* d* sa*2
buckaroo buckaroo.confused dickens.note sample2
```

That's it. Now I want to compute the number of lines in each of these files. If I use the csh history mechanism, I can avoid having to enter the filenames again:

```
% wc -l !*
wc -l bu* d* sa*2
      36 buckaroo
      11 buckaroo.confused
      28 dickens.note
```

15

```
    4 sample2
   79 total
```

Notice that the !* expanded to the entire previous command *except the very first word.*

7. What happens if I use !$ instead?

```
% wc -l !$
wc -l sa*2
        4 sample2
```

8. In the middle of doing all this, I became curious about how many people on my system have first names that are four letters long. Is this impossible to compute? Not with UNIX!

The first step is to extract the full names from the /etc/passwd file:

```
% awk -F: '{ print $5 }'
```

The system does not respond. I forgot to specify the filename!

```
% !! < /etc/passwd
awk -F: '{print $5}' < /etc/passwd
limbo root,,,,
USENET News,,,,
INGRES Manager,,,,
(1000 user system) DO NOT,,,,
Vanilla Account,,,,
The Ferryman,,,,
```

I can use ^c to stop this output, because I've seen enough to know that it's what I want. Next, I use awk again to pull just the first names out of this list:

```
% !! ¦ awk '{print $1}'
awk -F: '{print $5}' < /etc/passwd ¦ awk '{print $1}'
root
USENET
INGRES
(1000
Vanilla
The
Account
^c
%
```

It looks okay. Now the final step: I need to revise this awk script to look at the length of each name, and output the name only if it's four letters long:

```
% !-2 ¦ awk '{ if (lng($1) == 4) print $0 }'
awk -F: '{print $5}' < /etc/passwd ¦ awk '{ if (lng($1) == 4) print $0 }'
```

I got no output at all! The reason is that I mistyped length and lng. Fortunately, to fix this is simplicity itself with C shell history commands. Remember, the format is
^old^new:

```
% ^lng^length
awk -F: '{print $5}' < /etc/passwd ¦ awk '{ if (length($1) == 4) print $0
```

```
}'
,,,,
Paul Town,,,,
Pete Cheese,,,,
John Smith,,,,
Dana Tott,,,,
Dick Ply,,,,
Mike Moliak,,,,
Bill Born,,,,
Dale Tott,,,,
Bill Rison,,,,
Gary Flint,,,,
Doug Sherwood,,,,
Ruth Raffy,,,,
Dave Sean,,,,
^c
%
```

That's very close. I just need to pipe the output of this command to `wc`:

```
% !! ¦ wc -1
awk -F: '{print $5}' < /etc/passwd ¦ awk '{ if (length($1) == 4) print
$0 }' ¦ wc -1
       723
```

9. If you are using Korn shell, here's where it shines! Make sure that the environment variable EDITOR is set to your preferred editor:

```
$ echo $EDITOR
vi
$
```

Now, any time you're entering a command, you can press the Escape key and be in ksh history-edit command mode. The usual vi commands work, including h and l to move left and right; i and Escape to enter and leave insert mode; w, W, b, and B to zip about by words; and 0 and $ to move to the beginning or end of the line.

Much more useful are k and j, which replace the current command with the previous or next, enabling you to zip through the history list.

If I'd just entered who and then ls, to append ¦ wc -1 to the who command, I could press the Escape key:

`$_`

Now each time I type k, I will see the previous command. Typing k once reveals this:

`$ls`

Typing k as second time reveals this:

`$who`

That's the right command, so $ moves the cursor to the end of the line:

`$who`

15

Typing a appends, at which point I can add ¦ wc -1 like this:

```
$who ¦ wc -1
```

Pressing Return results in ksh actually executing the command:

```
$ who ¦ wc -1
     130
$_
```

SUMMARY The history mechanisms of the shells are wonderful timesavers when you're working with files. I find myself using the csh !! and !*word* mechanisms daily either to build up complex commands (such as the previous example, in which I built up a very complex command, step by step) or to repeat the most recently used edit commands. Table 15.1 summarizes the different csh history mechanisms available. I encourage you to learn and use them. They soon will become second nature and will save you lots of typing.

Table 15.1. C shell history commands.

Command	Function
!!	Repeat the previous command.
!$	Repeat the last word of the previous command.
!*	Repeat all but the first word of the previous command.
^a^b	Replace *a* with *b* in the previous command.
!*n*	Repeat command *n* from the history list.

Task 15.3: Command Aliases

DESCRIPTION If you think the history mechanism has the potential to save you typing, you just haven't learned about the command-alias mechanism in the Korn and C shells. Using aliases, you easily can define new commands that do whatever you'd like, or even redefine existing commands to work differently, have different default flags, or more!

The general format for using the alias mechanism in csh is alias *word command-sequence*, and in ksh it is alias *word=commands*. If you enter alias without any specified words, the output shows a list of aliases you have defined. If you enter alias *word* in csh, the output lists the current alias, if there is one, for the specified word.

ACTION

1. One of the most helpful aliases you can create specifies certain flags to ls so that each time you enter ls, the output will look as though you used the flags with the command. I like to have the -FC flags set.

```
% ls
Archives            awkscript           dickens.note        src
InfoWorld           bin                 keylime.pie         temp
Mail                buckaroo            owl.c
News                buckaroo.confused   sample
OWL                 cshrc               sample2
```

Now I'll try to create a C shell alias and try it again:

```
% alias ls 'ls -CF'
% ls
Archives/           awkscript           dickens.note        src/
InfoWorld/          bin/                keylime.pie         temp/
Mail/               buckaroo            owl.c
News/               buckaroo.confused   sample
OWL/                cshrc               sample2
```

This is very helpful!

The ksh equivalent would be alias ls = 'ls -CF'.

2. If you're coming from the DOS world, you might have found some of the UNIX file commands confusing. In DOS, for example, you use DIR to list directories, REN to rename files, COPY to copy them, and so on. With aliases, you can recreate all those commands, mapping them to specific UNIX equivalents:

```
% alias DIR 'ls -lF'
% alias REN 'mv'
% alias COPY 'cp -i'
% alias DEL 'rm -i'
% DIR
total 33
drwx------  2 taylor      512 Nov 21 10:39 Archives/
drwx------  3 taylor      512 Dec  3 02:03 InfoWorld/
drwx------  2 taylor     1024 Dec  3 01:43 Mail/
drwx------  2 taylor      512 Oct  6 09:36 News/
drwx------  4 taylor      532 Dec  6 18:31 OWL/
-rw-rw----  1 taylor      126 Dec  3 16:34 awkscript
drwx------  2 taylor      512 Oct 13 10:45 bin/
-rw-rw----  1 taylor     1393 Dec  5 18:48 buckaroo
-rw-rw----  1 taylor      458 Dec  4 23:22 buckaroo.confused
-rw-------  1 taylor     1339 Dec  2 10:30 cshrc
-rw-rw----  1 taylor     1123 Dec  5 18:16 dickens.note
-rw-rw----  1 taylor    12556 Nov 16 09:49 keylime.pie
-rw-rw----  1 taylor     8729 Dec  2 21:19 owl.c
-rw-rw----  1 taylor      199 Dec  3 16:11 sample
-rw-rw----  1 taylor      207 Dec  3 16:11 sample2
drwx------  2 taylor      512 Oct 13 10:45 src/
drwxrwx---  2 taylor      512 Nov  8 22:20 temp/
% COPY sample newsample
%
```

3. To see what aliases have been defined, use the alias command:

```
% alias
COPY    cp -i
DEL     rm -i
```

15

15

```
DIR      ls -lF
REN      mv
ls       ls -CF
```

4. You could improve the alias for DIR by having the output of ls fed directly into the more program so that a directory listing with a lot of output will automatically pause at the end of each page. To redefine an alias, just define it again:

```
% alias DIR 'ls -lF ¦ more'
```

To confirm that the alias is set as you desire, try this:

```
% alias DIR
DIR      ls -lF ¦ more
```

JUST A MINUTE

> If you're just defining one command with an alias, you don't really need to use the quotation marks around the command argument. But what would happen if you entered alias DIR ls -lF ¦ more? The alias would be set to ls -lF, and the output of the alias command would be fed to the more program, which is quite different from what you desired. Therefore, it's just good form to use the quotation marks and a good habit to get into.

SUMMARY Aliases are a great addition to any command shell, and with the arcane UNIX commands, they also can be used to define full-word commands as synonyms. For example, if you decide you'd like the simplicity of remembering only the command move to move a file somewhere else, you could add the new alias alias move mv to your .cshrc file if you're using C shell or alias move=mv to your .profile if you prefer Korn shell, and the shell would include a new command.

Task 15.4: Some Power Aliases

DESCRIPTION Because I have used the C shell for many years, I have created a variety of different aliases to help me work efficiently. A few of the best are shown in this section.

ACTION

1. To see what aliases I have defined, I can use the same command I used earlier:

```
% alias
cd       chdir !* ; setprompt
diff     /usr/bin/diff -c -w
env      printenv
from     frm -n
info     ssinfo
library  echo " "; echo " " ; echo "remember: ^J is ENTER"; tn3270 lib
ll       ls -l
```

```
ls       /bin/ls -F
mail     Mail
mailq    /usr/lib/sendmail -bp
netcom   echo Netcom login: taylor;rlogin netcom.com
newaliases      echo you mean newalias...
rd       readmsg $ ¦ page
rn       /usr/local/bin/rn -d$HOME -L -M -m -e -S -/
setprompt       set prompt="$system ($cwd:t) ! : "
ssinfo   echo "connecting..." ; rlogin oasis
sunworld        echo SunWorld login: taylor;rlogin sunworld.com
```

Recall that each of these aliases started out in my .cshrc file surrounded by single quote marks:

```
% grep alias .cshrc
alias   diff       '/usr/bin/diff -c -w'
alias   from       'frm -n'
alias   ll         'ls -l'
alias   ls         '/bin/ls -F'
alias   mail       Mail
alias   mailq      '/usr/lib/sendmail -bp'
alias   netcom     'echo Netcom login: taylor;rlogin netcom.com'
alias   sunworld   'echo SunWorld login: taylor;rlogin sunworld.com'
alias   newaliases 'echo you mean newalias...'
alias   rd         'readmsg $ ¦ page'
alias   rn         '/usr/local/bin/rn -d$HOME -L -M -m -e -S -/'
alias   cd              'chdir \!* ; setprompt'
alias   env             'printenv'
alias   setprompt       'set prompt="$system ($cwd:t) \! : "'
# special aliases:
alias info      ssinfo
alias ssinfo    'echo "connecting..." ; rlogin oasis'
alias library   'echo " "; echo " " ; echo "remember: ^J is ENTER";
tn3270 lib'
```

Also notice that the shell always keeps an alphabetically sorted list of aliases, regardless of the order in which they were defined.

2. Most of these aliases are easy to understand. For example, the first alias, diff, ensures that the command diff always has the default flags -c and -w. If I enter from, I want the system to invoke frm -n; if I enter ll, I want the system to invoke ls -l, and so on.

   Some commands can cause trouble if entered, so creating an alias for each of those commands is a good way to stay out of trouble. For example, I have an alias for newaliases; if I accidentally enter that command, the system gently reminds me that I probably meant to use the newalias command:

```
% newaliases
you mean newalias...
```

3. I have created aliases for connecting to accounts on other systems. I like to name each alias after the system to which I'm connecting (for example, netcom, sunworld):

```
% alias netcom
echo Netcom login: taylor;rlogin netcom.com
% alias sunworld
echo SunWorld login: taylor;rlogin sunworld.com
```

CAUTION

You can't enter alias netcom sunworld to list the netcom and sunworld aliases because that command means to replace the alias for netcom with the command sunworld.

Separating commands with a semicolon is the UNIX way of having multiple commands on a single line, so when I enter the alias netcom, for example, it's as if I'd entered all these commands one after another:

```
echo Netcom login: taylor
rlogin netcom.com
```

4. Two aliases worth examining more closely are those for the cd and setprompt commands. As you learn in a few moments, you can set your shell prompt to be just about any characters you'd like. (Hang on for just a paragraph or two, and you will learn all about what's occurring in the next example!) I like to have my prompt indicate where in the file system I'm currently working. To ensure that the prompt is always up to date, I simply alias the cd command so that each time I change directories, the prompt is recalculated.

```
% alias cd
chdir !* ; setprompt
% alias setprompt
set prompt="$system ($cwd:t) ! : "
```

JUST A MINUTE

The chdir command does the same thing as cd and is intended for use within aliases as shown. So if you find chdir easier to remember than cd, you can use it instead.

SUMMARY Aliases are what makes both the C shell and Korn shell such great command interfaces. I can, and do, easily customize the set of commands and the default flags (look at all the options I set as default values for the rn command). I even turn off some commands that I don't want to enter accidentally. Let your imagination run wild with aliases. If you decide you really like one and you're using csh, add the alias to your .cshrc so it's permanent (.profile if you're using ksh). If you want to turn off an alias, you can use the unalias command, and it's gone until you log in again. For example, unalias netcom would temporarily remove from the shell the netcom alias shown earlier.

Task 15.5: Setting Custom Prompts

DESCRIPTION Up to this point, the command prompt I've seen is a boring %. It turns out that the C shell lets you set your prompt to just about any possible value, with `set prompt="value"`.

The Korn shell equivalent is even easier: `PS1="value"`. Note that `PS1` must be all uppercase for this to work.

ACTION

1. I'm getting tired of UNIX being so inhospitable. Fortunately, I easily can change how it responds to me:

```
% set prompt="Yes, master? "
Yes, master?
```

That's more fun!

The `ksh` equivalent is `PS1="Yes, master? "`

2. There are a lot of things you can tuck away in your prompt that can be of great help. The first useful variable is `cwd`, which holds the current working directory:

```
Yes, master? set prompt="In $cwd, oh master: "
In /users/taylor, oh master:
```

What happens if I change directories?

```
In /users/taylor, oh master: cd /
In /users/taylor, oh master: pwd
/
In /users/taylor, oh master:
```

This is not so good. Now you can see why it's necessary to alias `cd` to maintain the prompt.

3. Some special ! values can be added to the prompt definition, as shown in Table 15.2.

Table 15.2. Special values for the system prompt.

Value	Expands to
`cmd`	The results of executing `cmd`.
\!	The current command number.
$var	The value of var.
$var:t	The tail (last word) of the value of var.

Here are a few examples of other C shell prompts and what happens when you use them:

```
In /, oh master: set prompt="(\!) % "
(132) %
```

The ksh equivalent is PS1="(\!) $ ".

The number in parentheses is the command number, as used by the C shell history mechanism:

```
(132) % echo hi
hi
(133) % ls News
mailing.lists.usenet   usenet.1                 usenet.alt
(134) % !132
echo hi
hi
(135) %
```

Every time I log in, I automatically set the variable system to the name of the current computer:

```
(135) % set prompt="$system (\!) % "
limbo (136) %
```

I like to include in my prompt the *basename* of the current directory, as shown in the following example. Basename means the closest directory name, so the basename of /usr/home/taylor is taylor, for example. Also, I replace the percent sign with a colon, which is a bit easier to read. There is a slight problem, however; having a : instead of % means that I have to remember I'm in C shell (or Korn shell, as the case may be).

```
limbo (136) % set prompt="$system ($cwd:t) \! : "
limbo (taylor) 137 :
```

4. Now I glance back at the aliases for setprompt and cd, with all these things in mind:

```
limbo (taylor) 139 : alias cd
chdir !* ; setprompt
limbo (taylor) 140 : alias setprompt
set prompt="$system ($cwd:t) ! : "
limbo (taylor) 141 :
```

You can see that the setprompt alias defines the C shell prompt as $system ($cwd:t) ! : ", although the actual line in the .cshrc file includes the backslash (as expected):

```
limbo (taylor) 141 : grep prompt= .cshrc
  alias  setprompt       'set prompt="$system ($cwd:t) \! : "'
limbo (taylor) 142 :
```

Each time I change directories, I use the combined commands of the cd alias (chdir !*) to change the current directory, and then I use setprompt to compute the new prompt.

TIME SAVER

The !* notation in a shell alias expands to all the words you specify after the alias word on the command line. For example, if you have an alias for dir that is "echo !* ; ls !*", entering dir /home actually executes echo /home followed by ls /home.

SUMMARY Experiment and find a set of variables that can help you customize your UNIX prompt. I strongly recommend that you use command numbers to familiarize yourself with the history mechanism.

Task 15.6: Creating Simple Shell Scripts

DESCRIPTION The command-alias capability is a helpful way to cut down on entering short commands time and again, but what if you have a series of 5 or 10 commands that you often enter in sequence? That's where shell scripts can help. At their simplest, shell scripts are a series of shell commands that appears in a file in exactly the order in which they'll be entered. If you change the permissions of the file to add execute permission, you can enter the name of the file as if it were just another UNIX command.

ACTION

1. It's amazing how pervasive shell scripts are in UNIX. A listing of /bin and /usr/ucb on one system reveals that 13 and 17 commands in these files, respectively, are actually shell scripts:

```
limbo (taylor) 33: cd /bin
limbo (bin) 34 : file * ¦ grep script
68k:      executable shell script
false:    executable shell script
i386:     executable shell script
ns32000:        executable shell script
pblock:   executable shell script
pdp11:    executable shell script
true:     executable shell script
u370:     executable shell script
u3b:      executable shell script
u3b10:    executable shell script
u3b2:     executable shell script
u3b5:     executable shell script
vax:      executable shell script
limbo (bin) 38 : cd /usr/ucb
limbo (ucb) 39 : file * ¦ grep script
msgs:     executable shell script
print:    executable c-shell script
```

```
script: SYMMETRY i386 executable (0 @ 0) version 1
tarmail:        shell script
trman:  executable shell script
uncompressdir:  shell script
untarmail:      shell script
vgrind: executable c-shell script
vpq:    executable c-shell script
vpr:    executable c-shell script
vprint: executable c-shell script
vprm:   executable c-shell script
vtroff: executable c-shell script
which:  executable c-shell script
zcmp:   shell script
zdiff:  shell script
zmore:  shell script
```

Shell scripts can be quite short. The script /bin/true is only one line: exit 0. The
script /bin/false contains the opposite command, and it contains only one line:
exit 1. The helpful script print is also just one line: lpr -p $*. Most of the others,
however, are too complex to explain here.

2. Instead of examining these confusing scripts, I'll move to my own bin directory
   and consider a script or two that I have there:

```
limbo (ucb) 42 : cd
limbo (taylor) 43 : cd bin
limbo (bin) 44 : file *
bounce.msg:     executable shell script
calc:   SYMMETRY i386 executable (0 @ 0) not stripped version 1
fixit:  SYMMETRY i386 executable (0 @ 0) not stripped version 1
massage:        SYMMETRY i386 executable (0 @ 0) not stripped version 1
punt:   shell script
rumor.mill.sh:  shell script
say.hi: ascii text
limbo (bin) 45 : cat -n punt
     1  : Use /bin/sh
     2
     3  # Punt: punt a news article from within "rn" to yourself.
     4
     5  trap "/bin/rm -f /tmp/punt.$$" 0 1 9 15
     6
     7  SENDTO=taylor@netcom.com
     8
     9  cat - > /tmp/punt.$$
    10
    11  if [ "$1" != "" ] ; then
    12    ADDRESS=$1
    13  else
    14    ADDRESS=$SENDTO
    15  fi
    16
    17  /usr/lib/sendmail $ADDRESS < /tmp/punt.$$
    18
    19  echo Punted a 'wc -l </tmp/punt.$$' line news article to $ADDRESS
    20
    21  exit 0
    22
```

This script is intended to be part of a pipeline, and it will send a copy of the stream of information either to the default address (SENDTO) or to a specified person ($1 is the first argument given to the script in this case). As shown earlier in the discussion of system prompts, any text that appears in backquotes is interpreted as a command and is executed, and the results of that command are added in its place in the subsequent command. In this case, the echo command on line 19 computes the number of lines in the specified file, and that number is then included in the output, which typically looks like this: Punted a 17 line news article.

JUST A MINUTE

Notice that the very first character of this file is a colon. It turns out that the C shell interprets scripts only if the very first character of the script is a #. Otherwise, it lets the Bourne shell (sh) run the commands, as in this case.

3. That's all well and interesting, but I want to create a new shell script. The first step is to make sure that I'm creating the script in a directory that is included in my search path (otherwise, I won't be able to use the script as a command):

```
limbo (bin) 46 : pwd
/users/taylor/bin
limbo (bin) 47 : echo $PATH
.:/users/taylor/bin:/bin:/usr/bin:/usr/ucb:/usr/local:/etc:/usr/etc:
/usr/local/bin:/usr/unsup/bin (bin) 48 :
```

Here's a very simple shell script that shows how shell scripts can be of assistance:

```
limbo (bin) 86 : cat new.script
# sample shell script

echo searching for shell scripts
pwd
echo " "

file * ¦ grep script ¦ sed 's/:/ /' ¦ awk '{print $1}'

exit 0
```

This script lists the names of all files in the current directory that it identifies as shell scripts:

```
limbo (bin) 88 : chmod +x new.script
limbo (bin) 89 : new.script
searching for shell scripts
/users/taylor/bin

bounce.msg
locate
new.script
punt
rumor.mill.sh
```

To confirm that the new command works, look at what `file` reports about this
same directory:

```
limbo (bin) 90 : file *
bounce.msg:     executable shell script
calc:   SYMMETRY i386 executable (0 @ 0) not stripped version 1
fixit:  SYMMETRY i386 executable (0 @ 0) not stripped version 1
locate: shell script
massage:        SYMMETRY i386 executable (0 @ 0) not stripped version 1
new.script:     commands text
punt:   shell script
rumor.mill.sh:  shell script
say.hi: ascii text
limbo (bin) 91 :
```

4. A more interesting script is one that can search through all the directories in my
   PATH, looking for any occurrences of a specified filename:

```
limbo (bin) 92 : cat locate
# locate - find copies of a file
#
# this should be run by the C shell

set name=$1

foreach directory (`echo $PATH | sed 's/:/ /g'`)
  if ( -f $directory/$name) then
    ls -l $directory/$name
  endif
end
```

The `foreach` loop is evaluated from the inside out. Because of the backquotes, my
PATH is echoed to `sed`, which removes the colons separating the directories. Then
the C shell goes through the `foreach` loop once for each directory in my PATH,
setting the variable `directory` to the subsequent value. Each time through the loop,
the `-f` test checks for the existence of the file: If the file exists in that directory,
`ls -l` lists some information about it.

> Pay careful attention to the backquotes and single quotes in this script.

JUST A MINUTE

Here is `locate` at work:

```
limbo (bin) 93 : locate ls
-rwxr-xr-x  1 root          32768 May 29   1990 /bin/ls*
limbo (bin) 94 : locate vi
-rwxr-xr-t  7 root         163840 Nov 29   1990 /usr/ucb/vi*
limbo (bin) 95 :
```

SUMMARY It really would take an entire book (or two!) to describe fully all the ins and outs of shell scripts. The main idea here, however, is that if you use a lot of commands repetitively, you should make them into a command alias (if they're short) or drop them all into a shell script. In shell scripts, as in awk, $1 is always the first argument, $2 the second, and so on.

Summary

This hour introduced you to many of the most powerful aspects of UNIX command shells. Practice creating aliases and working with the history list to minimize your typing. Also, find a prompt you like and set it in your .cshrc or .profile (for csh and ksh, respectively) so it will be the default.

Workshop

The Workshop summarizes the key terms you learned and poses some questions about the topics presented in this chapter. It also provides you with a preview of what you will learn in the next hour.

Key Terms

basename The closest directory name. For example, the basename of /usr/home/taylor is taylor.

command number The unique number by which the shell indexes all commands. You can place this number in your prompt using \! and use it with the history mechanism as !command-number.

Questions

1. How do you tell the C shell that you want it to remember the last 30 commands during a session and to remember the last 10 commands across login sessions?

2. Assume that you get the following output from entering history:

```
1    ls -CF
2    who ¦ grep dunlaplm
3    wc -l < test
4    cat test
5    history
```

   What would be the result of entering each of the following history commands?

   ```
   !2    !w    !wh    echo !1
   ```

3. Some UNIX systems won't enable you to do the following. What danger do you see lurking in this alias?

   ```
   alias who    who -a
   ```

4. Which of the following aliases do you think would be useful?

```
alias alias who
alias ls cp
alias copy cp -i
alias logout vi
alias vi logout
alias bye logout
```

5. Set your prompt to the following value. Remember that 33 should be replaced with the appropriate command number each time.

```
#33 - I know lots about UNIX. For example:
```

6. Find and examine two shell scripts that are found in either the /bin or /usr/bin directories on your system. Remember, any line beginning with a # is a comment.

Preview of the Next Hour

In the next hour, you learn how to get even more out of your shell. You learn about shell programming and how to create shell programs on-the-fly.

Hour 16

Basic Shell Programming

In the previous hour, you learned about a few of the options available to you when you use a command shell. These shells are how you enter commands for UNIX. What most people don't realize when they first start using UNIX is that these shells are also programming languages and that you can write your own shell programs.

Goals for This Hour

In this hour, you learn all about

- [ ] Shell variables
- [ ] Shell arithmetic
- [ ] Comparison functions
- [ ] Conditional expressions
- [ ] Looping expressions

Because shells are really just interpreted languages, any sequence of commands you wish to run can be placed in a file and run regularly. This is a shell program. Most UNIX experts write their shell programs for the Bourne shell (/bin/sh) because that shell is standard on every UNIX platform. Earlier in this book, I illustrated examples by using the C shell, because I feel this is a better interface for the user. Because I'm programming the Bourne shell, the command prompt is slightly different; it's $ rather than %.

JUST A MINUTE

> I strongly urge you to look at the shells you have available. The best shell to use is the one that makes you the most productive.

Task 16.1: Shell Variables

DESCRIPTION Programming languages usually include variables, and the shell naturally does, too. Variables are just tags to identify values that may change as a program is used. In the shell, these variables can take a single value and are always interpreted as strings. Even numeric values are strings to the shell.

JUST A MINUTE

> The C shell and Korn shell both support arrays and have means of representing numeric values.

You can use any string-manipulation command, such as sed or cut, to change a shell variable.

ACTION

Here is an example of setting the value of a shell variable:

```
$ color=blue
```

This sets the variable color to the string blue. One can output the value of any variable with the echo command:

```
$ echo $color
blue
```

This also indicates how to reference a shell variable: It must be preceded by the dollar sign ($). This can cause some problems. If you are using a shell variable as a prefix and want to immediately append text, you might think this would work:

```
$ leaning='anti-'
$ echo Joe is basically $leaningtaxes
```

The output here is just Joe is basically. The shell does not know to differentiate between the variables $leaning and $leaningtaxes. Because there is no value assigned to $leaningtaxes, the output is a NULL string. To solve this problem, enclose the variable in curly braces.

```
$ echo Joe is basically ${leaning}taxes
Joe is basically anti-taxes
```

If leaning is undefined, the output might not make sense. It would be Joe is basically taxes. Fortunately, the shell provides a means to have a default value if a variable is undefined:

```
$ echo Joe is basically ${leaning:-pro }taxes
Joe is basically pro taxes
```

If leaning is undefined, the : - syntax tells the shell to use the following string, including the space character, instead of leaving the output blank. This does not assign a new value to the variable. If you need to use the variable repeatedly, you might want to assign a new value to it, if it is undefined. The = character does this:

```
$ echo Joe is basically ${leaning=pro }taxes and ${leaning}spending.
Joe is basically pro taxes and pro spending.
```

The first interpretation of the variable finds it undefined, so the shell assigns 'pro ' to the variable and outputs that. The second time the variable is interpreted, it has the value 'pro '.

Variables often are assigned by the read command. This assigns an individual word to a specified variable, with the last variable in the list being assigned the remaining words.

```
$ read city state message
Morristown, New Jersey Hi Mom!
$ echo $city is city
Morristown, is city
$ echo $state is state
New is state
$ echo $message is message
Jersey Hi Mom! is message
```

As you can see, only New is assigned to state. The best way around this is to escape the space with a backslash:

```
$ read city state message
Morristown, New\ Jersey Hi Mom!
$ echo $city is city
Morristown, is city
$ echo $state is state
New Jersey is state
$ echo $message is message
Hi Mom! is message
```

This can be a bit tricky at first.

16

The other common way to assign variables is from command-line arguments. The shell has built-in variables to access the command line. If you've written a script to copy files and named it `copy-files`, you might want to list all the files on the command line:

```
$ copy-files file1 file2 file3
```

The program would access these arguments as $1, $2, and $3:

```
cp $1 destination
cp $2 destination
cp $3 destination
```

The $0 variable is a special case for looking at the command name, and $* lists all the command-line variables.

SUMMARY The standard data in any shell program is the variable. These variables can be assigned in several ways, directly assigned, read in from a user's typing, or by the command line. The shell also provides means to provide some default manipulation of variables.

Task 16.2: Shell Arithmetic

DESCRIPTION Although the shell treats variables as strings, there are methods to perform some basic mathematics on shell variables. Again, the C shell and the Korn shell provide more extensive mathematical capabilities.

ACTION

If a shell is assigned a numeric value, you can perform some basic arithmetic on the value using the command `expr`. This command takes several arguments to perform arithmetic:

```
$ expr 1 + 1
2
```

Arguments must be separated by spaces, and present, for the `expr` command to work. If a variable is undefined or does not have a value assigned to it (sometimes called *zero length*), the result is a syntax error. Here is where the `:-` syntax is particularly helpful:

```
$ expr $undef + 1
expr: syntax error
$ expr ${undef:-0} + 1
1
```

Normal default values of 0 and 1 are useful. When adding 0 to a number, you get the same number. Similarly, multiplying or dividing by 1 also doesn't change the value of the number.

`expr` also supports subtraction, multiplication, integer division, and remainders. These are illustrated here:

```
$ expr 11 - 5
6
```

```
$ expr 11 '*' 5
55
$ expr 11 / 5
2
$ expr 11 % 5
1
```

Note that I had to include the asterisk in single quotes. If I didn't do that, the shell would expand it to be the list of files in the current directory, and the expr program wouldn't understand that.

You can assign the results of the arithmetic to other variables by enclosing the command in backquotes:

```
$ newvalue='expr ${oldvalue:-0) + 1'
```

If *oldvalue* is assigned, it is incremented by 1. If not, *newvalue* is set to 1. This is useful when looping through data for a number of iterations.

The expr command also can work with complex arithmetic. You can write an expression to add two numbers and then multiply by a third number. Normally, you would need to worry about operator precedence, but expr is not that sophisticated. Instead, you just group the operations in parentheses:

```
$ expr \( 11 + 5 \) * 6
2
```

This first adds 11 and 5, then multiplies the result by 6. Because the parentheses are important shell characters, I need to escape them with backslashes.

 SUMMARY The expr is a very useful command for performing arithmetic in the Bourne shell. Strings must be numbers, or there will be errors, and the results of the expr command can be assigned to other variables.

JUST A MINUTE

> The expr command is much more powerful than described here; it includes the capability to perform logical operations and perform operations on strings. For more information, check the man page.

Task 16.3: Comparison Functions

DESCRIPTION Often, when writing a program, you may want the actions taken to be dependent on certain values. A simple example is the rm -i command, where the -i flag tells rm to prompt you before deleting a file. Type y, and a file is deleted. Type n, and it remains. The shell also has similar options. These next two tasks cover how to use those options.

ACTION

Just as `expr` is a powerful program for solving arithmetic expressions and performing operations on strings, the `test` command can be used to perform comparisons. `test` will perform comparisons on strings, as well as numeric values. Always, `test` will return 1 if the condition is true and 0 if it is false. It is standard for UNIX shells to use these values as true and false.

There are three types of operations for which `test` is used. There are numeric comparisons, string comparisons, and status tests for the file system. First up are the numeric comparisons.

Because the shell treats the less-than and greater-than symbols as redirection characters, they can't be used within the `test` command. Instead, I have a series of two letter flags, as described in Table 16.1. These flags are always placed between the two arguments:

```
test 3 -eq 4
```

This example would return false because 3 and 4 are not equal.

Table 16.1. Test operators.

Comparison Flag	Meaning
-eq	True if the numbers are equal
-ne	True if the numbers are not equal
-lt	True if the first number is less than the second number
-le	True if the first number is less than or equal to the second number
-gt	True if the first number is greater than the second number
-ge	True if the first number is greater than or equal to the second number

You can use the result of `expr`, or any other command that returns a numeric value, in `test`. There is also a special expression in `test`, `-l` *string*, that returns the length of a string. So, you can write the following tests:

```
test 'expr $value % 10' -eq -l $string
test 'wc -l filename' -ge 10000
```

The first test determines if the last digit of `$value` (the remainder of a division by 10) is the same as the length of `$string`. The second takes a count of the number of lines in a file and is true if there are 10,000 lines or more present.

The second type of comparison is on strings. The first two are unary, which means they apply to only one string:

```
test -z $string
test -n $string
```

The first test is true if the string is of zero length. If the string is undefined, this is true, too. The second is true if the string has some content.

The next two tests compare strings with each other. The simple equals sign and the exclamation point (commonly used to switch between true and false in UNIX) are used for these comparisons:

```
test alphabet = Alphabet
test alphabet != Alphabet
```

The first is false; the second is true.

JUST A MINUTE

When comparing string variables, you may see something like

```
test X$string1 = X$string2
```

The presence of the X prevents a null string from confusing test. If string1 is null and string2 is string, you'd expand to

```
test X = Xstring
```

Without the X, the test would be expanded to

```
test = string
```

This is a syntax error. The other option is to enclose the string in double quotes:

```
test "$string1" = "$string2"
```

That expands to this

```
test "" = "string"
```

The final test operators work on the file system. They are single flags, listed in Table 16.2, followed by a path.

Table 16.2. File system unary flags.

Option	Meaning
-G	True if the file exists and is owned by the same group as the process.
-L	True if the file exists and points to another file (symbolic link).

continues

Table 16.2. continued

Option	Meaning
-o	True if the file exists and is owned by the same user as the process.
-S	True if the file exists and is a file used for communications between programs (socket).
-b	True if the file exists and is a symbol identifying a physical device used for input and output in large chunks of data, such as a hard disk, (block special device).
-c	True if the file exists and is a symbol identifying a physical device used for input and output in single characters, such as a terminal (character special device).
-d	True if the file is a directory.
-e	True if the file exists.
-f	True if the file exists and is a regular file.
-g	True if the file exists and runs in a specific group.
-k	True if the file exists and is set to remain in memory after execution. This makes a program a faster starter, at the cost of overall system performance.
-p	True if the file exists and is a named pipe.
-r	True if the file exists and is readable.
-s	True if the file exists and has data.
-u	True if the file exists and runs as a specific user.
-w	True if the file exists and is writable.
-x	True if the file exists and is executable.

A sample test would be:

```
test -d $HOME/bin
```

This checks to see if you have a directory named bin in your home directory. The most common flags you see in shell programs are the -f flag and the -d flag. The others are used only in unusual situations.

The file system also has three binary comparisons. The -ef test determines whether the two files are the same. (When you create a link between files, this is true.) The -nt flag is true if the first file is newer than the second, and the -ot flag is true if the first file is older than the second. You might see a test in a looping statement like:

```
test file1 -ot file2
```

This test compares the two files and is true if *file1* is older than *file2*. If you are waiting for data to appear in *file1*, you might use this test to cause a shell program to wait for the first file to appear.

You can negate test commands with the exclamation point or combined with -a for *and* and -o for *or*. You can make arbitrarily long conditions, at the cost of readability:

```
test $var -eq 0 -a ! -e file
```

This checks to see if the value of $var is zero and if *file* exists.

The test command also has a second form. Instead of explicitly calling test, the condition is surrounded by square brackets:

```
[ -f file ]
```

Doing this makes shell programs more readable.

SUMMARY One of the most-used commands in shell programming is the test command. It is essential to understanding the next two tasks, conditional expressions and loops.

Task 16.4: Conditional Expressions

DESCRIPTION Sometimes, when writing a program, you want to perform an action only when another action returns the value true. Shell programming enables you to do this by way of the if command, the case command, and two special command separators.

ACTION

The if command is the most commonly seen conditional command. It takes the form:

```
if
    command-block
then
    command-block
fi
```

A *command-block* is a sequence of one or more shell commands. The first command-block is always executed. The return value of the last statement executed is used to determine if the second block is executed. The most commonly used command at the end of the first command-block is the test command.

```
if
    [ -f $file ]
then
    echo $file is a regular file
fi
```

This `if` statement notifies the user that a file is a regular file. If the file is not a regular file (such as a directory), you don't see output.

Sometimes, you may want output regardless of the situation. In the preceding case, you may be interested in the status of the file even if it is not a regular file. The `if` command can expand with the `else` keyword to provide that second option.

```
if
    [ -f $file ]
then
    echo $file is a regular file
else
    echo $file is not a regular file
fi
```

This statement provides output regardless of the status of the file.

For these simple tests and output, the shell provides a second, quicker means of executing the `if` statement. If the two commands are joined by `&&`, the second command is executed if the first command is true. If the commands are joined by `¦¦`, the second command is executed if the first is false. The preceding command, therefore, would look like:

```
[ -f $file ] && echo $file is a regular file
[ -f $file ] ¦¦ echo $file is not a regular file
```

This shorthand is very useful but can be confusing for a novice. If you accidentally place a space between the characters, you have a wildly different command; the `&` will run the first command at the same time as the `echo`, and the `¦` will pipe the output of the test (none) to the `echo`.

If you want even more information, your `if` statement can have more than two options. You need multiple tests and the `elif` keyword:

```
if
    [ -f $file ]
then
    echo $file is a regular file
elif
    [ -d $file ]
then
    echo $file is a directory
else
    echo $file is not a regular file or a directory.
fi
```

This command first tests to see whether the file is a regular file; if not, it checks to see whether it is a directory, and if it is neither, it gives output. You can expand any `if` statement with an unlimited number of `elif` branches.

16

At some point, though, the code will become confusing. When you have many possible branches, you should use the case command. The syntax is more complicated than for if:

```
case string in
pattern) command-block ;;
pattern) command-block ;;
...
esac
```

If you were looking for possible values for a variable, you could use case:

```
echo What do you want:
read var remainder
case $var in
house) echo The price must be very high;;
car) echo The price must be high;;
popsicle) echo The price must be low;;
*) echo I do not know the price;;
esac
```

This case statement follows an input request and gives the user a rough idea of the price. A case list can contain any number of items.

The pattern-matching algorithms used are for wildcards.

SUMMARY There are two basic conditional expressions and a third shortcut. You can test a condition and perform alternative actions by using if statements and their shortcuts. Or, you can compare strings and perform any number of actions by using the case statement.

Task 16.5: Looping Expressions

DESCRIPTION If you want to run the same set of commands many times instead of writing them out once for each time, you are better off using looping commands. There are two types of loops, the determinate loop and the indeterminate loop.

A *determinate* loop is one where you know exactly how many times you want to execute the commands before you enter the loop. Stepping through a list of files is a good example; you may not know the exact number of files, but once you do, you can start the loop for those files.

An *indeterminate* loop is one where you need to keep executing a command-block until a condition is no longer true. You might be either waiting for something or performing a series of modifications to reach a goal.

ACTION

The usual command for a determinate loop is the `for` command. It has the following syntax:

```
for var in list
do
    command-block
done
```

You can build any list you like. It could be a sequence of numbers or the output of a command. Earlier, I mentioned looping through a list of files. This is performed with the following loop:

```
for var in 'ls'
do
    if
        [ -f $var ]
    then
        echo $var is a regular file
    fi
done
```

This provides a list of all the regular files. You should note that the variable `var` can be used inside the `for` loop. When you are stepping through a list of files, this can be advantageous; you have the name of the file provided to you by the variable `var`.

A nice trick that can be performed in a shell program is to step through the list of command-line arguments. The `for` loop provides a neat mechanism; if the `'in list'` part is omitted from the command, the `for` loop steps through the list of command-line arguments.

```
j=0
for i
do
    j='expr $j + 1'
    echo $i is argument $j
done
```

This command steps through the command-line arguments and identifies where they are in the order of arguments.

In both cases, when you enter the `for` loop, you know how many times you need to run the loop. If you look at the case where you are waiting for something to happen, though, you need to use a different loop. The `while` loop is the solution for this problem.

In Task 16.3, I mentioned the case where you might want to wait on the arrival of a file. This echoes a real-world situation I recently faced. We were processing a daemon's log file, but we did not know exactly when it would be placed in our directory. We tried to set up the job to run after the file arrived, but this still ran into problems.

Using the while loop, we solved the problem. At the end of the execution of our script, we created a checkpoint file. At the beginning, if the checkpoint file was newer than the log file, we'd wait. Programmatically, that is:

```
while
    [ checkpoint -nt logfile ]
do
    sleep 60
done
```

This program would wait one minute between checks. If the new logfile had not been written, the program would go back to sleep for a minute.

You can use while loops also in a determinate manner. In the case where you are not concerned with a variable's value but know a count of times to run a command-block, you can use a counter to increment through the number:

```
i=0
while
    [ $i -lt 100 ]
do
    i='expr "$i" + 1'
    commands
done
```

This is certainly easier than listing 100 items in a list!

SUMMARY The shell provides two convenient mechanisms for running a group of commands repeatedly. These loop commands are useful from both the command line and a program.

Summary

In this hour, you just skimmed the basics of shell programming. You were introduced to the control structures of the shell and two important commands. There is a lot more you can learn about shell programming; *Teach Yourself Shell Programming* (Sams Publishing) is one place you can look. If you are interested in the C shell, *Teach Yourself the UNIX C Shell* (Sams Publishing) is another resource.

Workshop

The Workshop summarizes the key terms you learned and poses some questions about the topics presented in this chapter. It also provides you with a preview of what you will learn in the next hour.

Key Terms

command-block   A list of one or more shell commands that are grouped in a conditional or looping statement.

conditional expression   This is an expression that returns either true or false.

determinate loop   A loop where the number of times the loop is run can be known before starting the loop.

expression   This is a command that returns a value.

indeterminate loop   A loop where the number of times the loop is run is not known before starting the loop.

loop   This is a sequence of commands that is repeatedly executed while a condition is true.

variables   These are names to label data that may change during the execution of a program.

zero-length variable   A variable that does not have a value assigned to it.

Questions

1. How would you read in an address in a shell program? How would you read in a name?
2. If you read in the number of people who read a newspaper and the number of people who subscribe to a particular paper, how would you determine the ratio of subscribers to readers?
3. How do you know if a file has data?
4. How do you wait for data to be placed in a file?

Preview of the Next Hour

In the next hour, you are introduced to managing processes in UNIX. You learn how to start a background job, how to switch between foreground and background, and how to terminate a command.

16

Hour **17**

Job Control

In this hour you will learn about how UNIX handles jobs, and how you can manipulate them. Commands you will learn include `jobs` and `ps`, to see what processes are running; `fg` and `bg`, to move jobs back and forth between the foreground and background; and `kill`, to terminate jobs that you no longer want around.

Goals for This Hour

In this hour, you learn

- [ ] About job control in the shell: stopping jobs
- [ ] How to put jobs in the background and bring them back to the foreground
- [ ] How to find out what tasks are running by using `jobs` and `ps`
- [ ] How to terminate errant processes by using `kill`

Throughout this book, I've indicated that my focus is on the most important and valuable flags and options for the commands covered. That's all well and good, but how do you find out about the other alternatives that might actually work better for your use?

This hour presents an explanation of a UNIX philosophical puzzle: What is a running program? To learn the answer, you are introduced to ps and jobs, for controlling processes; fg and bg, to move your own processes back and forth between the foreground and background; and the quasi-omnipotent kill command, for stopping programs in their proverbial tracks.

Task 17.1: Job Control in the Shell: Stopping Jobs

DESCRIPTION Whether you're requesting a man page, listing files with ls, starting vi, or running just about any UNIX command, you're starting one or more processes. In UNIX, any program that's running is a *process*. You can have multiple processes running at once. The pipeline ls -l ¦ sort ¦ more invokes three processes: ls, sort, and more. Processes in both the C and Korn shells are also known as *jobs*, and the program that you're running is known as the *current job*.

Any job or process can have a variety of different states, with "running" being the most typical state. In both shells, you can stop a job by pressing ^z. To restart it, enter fg when you are ready.

ACTION

1. Earlier I was perusing the man page entry for sort. I had reached the bottom of the first screen:

```
% man sort

SORT(1)              DYNIX Programmer's Manual          SORT(1)

NAME
     sort - sort or merge files

SYNOPSIS
     sort [ -mubdfinrtx ] [ +pos1 [ -pos2 ] ] ... [ -o name ] [
     -T directory ] [ name ] ...

DESCRIPTION
     Sort sorts lines of all the named files together and writes
     the result on the standard output.  The name '-' means the
     standard input.  If no input files are named, the standard
     input is sorted.

     The default sort key is an entire line.  Default ordering is
     lexicographic by bytes in machine collating sequence.  The
     ordering is affected globally by the following options, one
     or more of which may appear.

     b    Ignore leading blanks (spaces and tabs) in field com-
--More-- _
```

17

I'd like to try using the `-b` flag mentioned at the bottom of this screen, but I want to read the rest of the man page, too. Instead of typing q to quit, then starting the man program again later, I can stop the program. I press ^z, and see this:

```
        ordering is affected globally by the following options, one
or more of which may appear.

    b      Ignore leading blanks (spaces and tabs) in field com-
--More--
Stopped
%
```

At this point, I can do whatever I'd like:

```
% ls -s ¦ sort -b ¦ head -4
   1 Archives/
   1 InfoWorld/
   1 Mail/
   1 News/
   1 OWL/
```

2. I can resume at any time. I enter fg, the program reminds me where I was, and man (which is actually the more program invoked by man) returns to its prompt:

```
% fg
man sort
--More-- _
%
```

3. Screen-oriented programs are even smarter about stopping and starting jobs. For example, `vi` refreshes the entire screen when you return from it having been stopped. If I were in vi working on the dickens.note file, the screen would look like this:

```
                    A Tale of Two Cities
                        Preface

When I was acting, with my children and friends, in Mr Wilkie Collins's
drama of The Frozen Deep, I first conceived the main idea of this
story.  A strong desire came upon me then, to
embody it in my own person;
and I traced out in my fancy, the state of mind of which it would
necessitate the presentation
to an observant spectator, with particular
care and interest.

As the idea became familiar to me, it gradually shaped itself into its
present form.  Throughout its execution, it has had complete possession
of me; I have so far verified what
is done and suffered in these pages,
as that I have certainly done and suffered it all myself.
```

```
Whenever any reference (however slight) is made here to the condition
of the Danish people before or during the Revolution, it is truly made,
on the faith of the most trustworthy
witnesses.  It has been one of my hopes to add
something to the popular and picturesque means of
"dickens.note" 28 lines, 1123 characters
```

Pressing ^z would result in this:

```
witnesses.  It has been one of my hopes to add
something to the popular and picturesque means of
"dickens.note" 28 lines, 1123 characters

Stopped
%  _
```

I can check to see if someone is logged in and then return to vi with the fg command.

```
% who ¦ grep marv
% fg
```

```
                        A Tale of Two Cities
                             Preface

When I was acting, with my children and friends, in Mr Wilkie Collins's
drama of The Frozen Deep, I first conceived the main idea of this
story.  A strong desire came upon me then, to
embody it in my own person;
and I traced out in my fancy, the state of mind of which it would
necessitate the presentation
to an observant spectator, with particular
care and interest.

As the idea became familiar to me, it gradually shaped itself into its
present form.  Throughout its execution, it has had complete posession
of me; I have so far verified what
is done and suffered in these pages,
as that I have certainly done and suffered it all myself.

Whenever any reference (however slight) is made here to the condition
of the Danish people before or during the Revolution, it is truly made,
on the faith of the most trustworthy
witnesses.  It has been one of my hopes to add
something to the popular and picturesque means of
"dickens.note" 28 lines, 1123 characters
```

SUMMARY There are many aspects to processes and jobs in UNIX, particularly regarding the level of control offered by the shell. The rest of this hour explains how to exploit these capabilities to make your work easier and faster.

Task 17.2: Foreground/Background and UNIX Programs

DESCRIPTION Now that you know how to suspend programs in their tracks, it's time to learn how to have them keep running in the background (by using the bg command) while you're doing something else and how to have programs instantly go into the background (by using the & notation).

In the first hour, you learned that one of the distinguishing characteristics of UNIX is that it's a true multitasking operating system. It is capable of running hundreds of programs at the same time. The best part is that you're not limited to just one process! If you want to save a couple man pages to a file, for example, you can run those processes in the background while you are working on something else.

Once a job is stopped, you can enter fg to start it up again as the program you're working with. (The fg command takes its name from *foreground*, which refers to the program that your display and keyboard are working with.) If the process will continue without any output to the screen and without any requirement for input, you can use bg to move it into the *background*, where it runs until it is done. If the program needs to write to the screen or read from the keyboard, the system will stop its execution automatically and inform you. You then can use fg to bring the program into the foreground to continue running.

TIME SAVER

If you find that background jobs are just writing information to your screen, try the stty tostop command to fix the problem.

You can use job control also to start up a couple programs and then use the fg command, with the job ID as an argument to start the one you want to work with. Not entering the job ID will bring the most recently stopped job back to the foreground. If your system takes a long time to start up big applications (such as emacs or vi), this could save you lots of time.

JUST A MINUTE

Although a job may be stopped, it still consumes resources, so you should be careful not to have too many stopped programs around, in deference to the other users of your machine.

A different strategy is to start a program in the background, letting UNIX manage it. If the program needs some input or output, it stops, just like processes you've put into the background with bg after they've already started running. To have a program (or pipeline!) automatically start in the background, simply type an & at the end of the command line.

ACTION

1. Here's an example of a command that processes files without needing any input or offering any output:

    ```
    % awk -F: '{print $1" = "$5}' < /etc/passwd ¦ \
    awk -F, '{print $1}'¦ \
    awk '{ if (NF > 2) print $0 }' ¦ \
    sort > who.is.who
    ```

    After about 20 seconds, the % prompt returns; it takes that long to feed the password file through the three-part awk filter, sort the entire output, and save it to the file who.is.who.

CAUTION

> When you're working with long commands, it's useful to know that you always can move to the next line—even in the middle of entering something—by ending the current line with a single backslash. Note that the backslash must be the *very last character* on the line!

With this new file, I easily can look up an account to see the full name of that user:

```
% alias lookup 'grep -i \!* who.is.who'
% who ¦ head
root      console Dec  6 18:02
maritanj  ttyAa   Dec  8 21:20
efb       ttyAb   Dec  8 12:12
wifey     ttyAc   Dec  8 19:41
phamtu    ttyAe   Dec  8 21:14
curts     ttyAf   Dec  8 21:14
seifert   ttyAg   Dec  8 21:11
taylor    ttyAh   Dec  8 21:09
halcyon   ttyAi   Dec  8 18:34
jamilrr   ttyAj   Dec  8 20:25
Broken pipe
% lookup maritanj
maritanj = Jorge Maritan
% lookup efb
efb = Edward F. Billiard
%
```

2. To have this process run in the background, I can stop the process immediately after I start it, by using ^z:

```
% !awk
awk -F: '{print $1" = "$5}' < /etc/passwd | awk -F, '{print $1}'
➡| awk '{ if (NF > 2) print $0 }' | sort > who.is.who
Stopped
%
```

JUST A MINUTE

> Notice that the command I repeated using the history mechanism was listed as being all on a single line!

At this point, bg will continue the program, running it in the background:

```
% bg
[1]     awk -F: {print $1" = "$5} < /etc/passwd | awk -F, {print $1}
➡| awk { if (NF > 2) print $0 } | sort > who.is.who &
%
```

The number in square brackets is this job's *control number* in the shell. In a moment, you learn why this is a handy number to note.

On some systems a completed background job will notify you immediately that it's done, but on most systems, after a completed background job has finished running, it waits until you press Return to get a new system prompt before it lets you know. After about 30 or 40 seconds, I press Return and see this:

```
%
[1]     Done                    awk -F:
{print $1" = "$5} < /etc/passwd | awk -F,
{print $1} | awk { if (NF > 2) print $0 } | sort > who.is.who
%
```

3. Alternatively, a better strategy for moving a program into the background is to move the process to the background automatically by adding an & to the very end:

```
% !awk &
awk -F: '{print $1" = "$5}' < /etc/passwd | awk -F, '{print $1}'
➡| awk '{ if (NF > 2) print $0 }' | sort > ! who.is.who &
[1] 27556 27557 27558 27559
%
```

This is more interesting. This command is shown with a control number of 1, but the four numbers listed after that are the actual process ID numbers of each piece of the pipeline: 27556 is the first awk process, 27557 is the second awk process, 27558 is the third awk process, and 27559 is the sort program.

Again, when complete, pressing Return lets me know:

```
%
[1]     Done                    awk -F: {print $1" = "$5} < /etc/passwd |
➡awk -F, {print $1} | awk { if (NF > 2) print $0 } | sort > who.is.who
%
```

4. What happens if I try to automatically move to the background a program that has input or output?

```
% vi &
[1] 28258
%
```

This looks fine. Pressing Return indicates otherwise, though:

```
%
[1]   + Stopped (tty output) vi
%
```

You can see that this program has stopped because of some information (output) that it wants to display. If the program expected input, the message would be `Stopped (tty input)` *program name*.

I can use `fg` to bring this program into the foreground and work with it, or even just to quit `vi`.

SUMMARY Because so much of the UNIX design focuses on running streams of data through filters and saving the output to a file, there are a number of commands that you could be running in the background, freeing you up to do other work in the meantime. Remember also that you can put in the background jobs that take a fair amount of processing time and then display information on the screen. When it's time to write something to the screen, the program will stop automatically until you enter `fg` to pull it into the foreground again.

Task 17.3: Finding Out What Tasks Are Running

DESCRIPTION There are two ways to keep tabs on what programs are flying around in the UNIX operating system. The easier way, `jobs`, shows what processes you've stopped and moved into the background in the shell. Enter `jobs`, and `csh` (or `ksh`) tells you what programs, if any, are stopped or running.

The alternative is a complex command called `ps`, which shows the processor status for the entire computer. The processor is another name for the computer itself. Fortunately, without any arguments, it shows the active or stopped programs associated with your terminal only. The `ps` program actually has more flags even than `ls`, I think. The vast majority of them, however, are never going to be of value to you or any normal UNIX user. Worse, the flags are very different between BSD systems and System V. The ones that are most helpful are summarized in Table 17.1.

Table 17.1. Useful flags to the `ps` command, BSD-style.

Flag	Meaning
-a	Shows all processes associated with terminals attached to the system.
-g	Shows all interesting processes on the system (that is, all processes other than those required by the operating system).

17

Flag	Meaning
-l	Gives the long listing format for each line.
-t *xx*	Lists only processes associated with the specified tty*xx*.
-u	Produces user-oriented output.
-w	Uses wide output format. If repeated (-ww), it will show as much of each command as possible.
-x	Shows all processes in the system.

The -a, -g, and -x flags each affect how much information is displayed by ps. To use either the -g or -x command, you also must use the -a command. On most machines, -ax yields considerably more output than -ag. The most commonly used flags (and flag combinations) are -u, to have only your processes listed in a friendly format; -aux, to see everything on the machine (you almost always want to pipe this to grep or more, lest you be overrun with hundreds of lines of information); and -wt*xx*, to show all the processes associated with tty*xx*, in wide format.

Just a Minute

The ps program varies from System V to Berkeley UNIX more than any other command. Fortunately, the two or three most common flags are similar across the two systems. To explore more about the ps command on your system, you should start by reading the man page.

Action

1. To begin, I'm going to start vi in the background:

```
% vi dickens.note &
[1] 4352
%
```

I'll start that awk job again, too:

```
% !awk
awk -F: '{print $1" = "$5}' < /etc/passwd ¦ awk -F, '{print $1}'
➡¦ awk '{ if (NF > 2) print $0 }' ¦ sort > ! who.is.who &
[2] 4532 4534 4536 4537
%
```

The jobs command will show what processes I have running:

```
% jobs
[1]  + Stopped (tty output) vi dickens.note
[2]  - Running              awk -F: {print $1" = "$5} < /etc/passwd ¦ awk -
F,
{print $1} ¦ awk { if (NF > 2) print $0 } ¦ sort > who.is.who
%
```

2. Now that you know the job numbers (the numbers in square brackets here), you easily can move specific jobs into the foreground or the background by specifying the job number prefixed by %. To show what I mean, I'll put a couple more vi jobs in the background:

```
% vi buckaroo.confused &
[2] 13056
% vi awkscript csh.man cheryl mbox &
[3] 13144
%
```

Now I'll use the jobs command to see what's running:

```
% jobs
[1]    Stopped (tty output) vi dickens.note
[2]  - Stopped (tty output) vi buckaroo.confused
[3]  + Stopped (tty output) vi awkscript csh.man cheryl mbox
%
```

JUST A MINUTE

> Notice that the awk job finished.

To edit the buckaroo.confused note, I need only to enter fg %2 to pull the file into the foreground. To terminate all these processes (something you learn more about later in this hour), I can use the kill command:

```
% kill %1 %2 %3
%
```

Nothing happened. Or did it? Pressing Return reveals what occurred in the operating system:

```
%
[3]  - Done              vi awkscript csh.man cheryl mbox
[2]  - Done              vi buckaroo.confused
[1]  + Done              vi dickens.note
%
```

3. Restart the awk command with !awk. Contrast the output of jobs with the output of the Berkeley (BSD) ps command:

```
% ps
  PID TT STAT   TIME COMMAND
 4352 Ah T      0:00 vi dickens.note
 4532 Ah R      0:03 awk - : {print $1"
 4534 Ah R      0:02 awk - , {print $1}
 4536 Ah S      0:01 - k { if (NF > 2) print $0 } (awk)
 4537 Ah S      0:00 sort
 4579 Ah R      0:00 ps
%
```

17

You can see here that there really are four unique processes running for that pipeline: three awk processes and one sort process. In addition, vi and ps are listed as running. Note that my login shell (csh) isn't in this listing.

Figure 17.1 explains each field, and Table 17.2 lists possible values for the STAT program status column.

Figure 17.1.
The ps default process output.

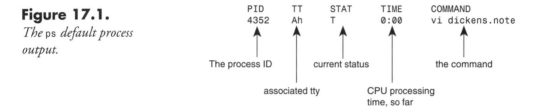

Table 17.2. Possible process status values.

Value	Meaning
R	Running
S	Sleeping (20 seconds or less)
I	Idle (sleeping more than 20 seconds)
T	Stopped
Z	Zombie process

There are other process states, but they rarely show up for most users. A *zombie process* is one that has ended but hasn't freed up its resources. Usually, it takes a second or two for the system to completely recover all memory used by a program. Sometimes, zombies are stuck in the process table for one reason or other. UNIX folk refer to this as a *wedged process*, which stays around until the system is rebooted. Sometimes it's listed as <defunct> in process listings. Any process that is preceded by a sleep command is noted as sleeping.

4. Adding some flags can change the output of ps quite dramatically:

```
% ps -x
  PID TT STAT  TIME COMMAND
 4352 Ah T     0:00 vi dickens.note
 6171 Ah R     0:02 awk - : {print $1"
 6172 Ah R     0:01 awk - , {print $1}
 6173 Ah S     0:01 - k { if (NF > 2) print $0 } (awk)
 6174 Ah S     0:00 sort
 6177 Ah R     0:00 ps -x
19189 Ah S     0:06 -csh (csh)
19649 Ah I     0:02 newmail
%
```

Two new processes show up here: `-csh` (the shell) which is—finally—my login shell, and `newmail`, a program that automatically starts up in the background when I log in to the system (it's located at the end of my `.login`).

JUST A MINUTE

> The shell process is shown with a leading dash to indicate that it's a login shell. Any other copies of `csh` that I run won't have that leading dash. That's one way the C shell knows not to read through the `.login` file every time it's run.

5. To see more about what's happening, I add yet another flag, `-u`, to expand the output on the display:

```
% ps -xu
USER      PID  %CPU %MEM  SZ  RSS TT STAT ENG   TIME COMMAND
taylor   7011  10.4  0.2 184  100 Ah R     6   0:02 awk - : {print $1"
taylor   7012   6.3  0.1 160   92 Ah S         0:01 awk - , {print $1}
taylor   7013   5.9  0.1 160   92 Ah R     3   0:01 - k { if (NF > 2)
print
taylor  19189   1.1  0.2 256  148 Ah S         0:07 -csh (csh)
taylor   7014   1.0  0.1 316   64 Ah S         0:00 sort
taylor   7022   0.1  0.2 180  116 Ah R     0   0:00 ps -xu
taylor   4352   0.0  0.3 452  168 Ah T         0:00 vi dickens.note
taylor  19649   0.0  0.1 124   60 Ah I         0:02 newmail
%
```

Figure 17.2 explains these fields.

Figure 17.2.

The `-u` *user-oriented output of* ps.

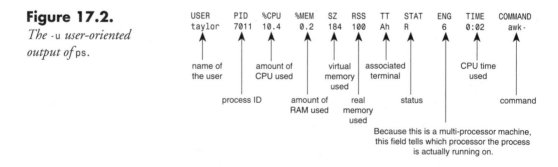

6. I won't show the output from the `-aux` flags, but you should look at the number of lines produced by both the `-ag` and `-ax` flags:

```
% ps -ag ¦ wc -l
    377
% ps -ag ¦ head
  PID TT STAT   TIME COMMAND
 1403 co IW    0:01 -csh (csh)
 2200 p3 IW    0:18 server
```

```
 6076 p6 I        0:13 rlogin sage -l hirschna
 6082 p6 I        0:11 rlogin sage -l hirschna
25341 p8 IW       0:06 -tcsh (tcsh)
  681 pa IW       0:05 -tcsh (tcsh)
10994 pa IW       2:10 ghostview pop5.ps
11794 pa IW       0:12 pwlookup
13861 pa I        0:56 gs
Broken pipe
%
```

You can see here that each process is owned by a specific terminal but that these processes are all idle (that is, they've been sleeping for more than 20 seconds). This probably means that these users have turned away for a little while. Look back at the output generated by ps -xu, and you will see that newmail is also idle. That's because the program runs in a loop: It sleeps for five minutes, checks for new mail, goes back to sleep again, and so on. Processes that have the W after the I in the status column are processes that have been moved out of main memory and are swapped out to disk. This is not a problem, and the users might not even realize anything has happened; the only symptom of this is that when the users wake up their programs, the programs will take an additional second or two to return.

What is the output from ps -ax?

```
% ps -ax | wc -l
     765
% ps -ax | head
  PID TT STAT   TIME COMMAND
    0 ?  D      8:58 swapper
    1 ?  S     14:45 (init)
    2 ?  D     20:43 pagedaemon
   27 ?  I      0:00 rpc.rquotad
   59 ?  S      6:36 /etc/syslogd -m480
   70 ?  I      0:02 /etc/portmap
   74 ?  IW     0:00 (biod)
   75 ?  IW     0:00 (biod)
   76 ?  IW     0:00 (biod)
Broken pipe
%
```

These are some of the "guts" of the UNIX operating system. Notice that none of these processes are actually associated with a terminal. Also notice that some of these processes have incredibly low process ID numbers! Any one-digit process ID is a program that is a part of the core UNIX system and must be running for UNIX to be alive. Any two-digit process is also started by the system itself but is probably optional. The D status for some of these processes indicates that they're waiting for disk resources of some sort. Finally, note how much time these processes have taken. I venture that you will never have a process that takes 20 minutes of CPU time—ever!

17

7. On a Sun workstation, the output of the ps commands is a bit different:

```
% ps
  PID TT STAT   TIME COMMAND
 8172 qb S      0:00 -csh (csh)
 8182 qb T      0:00 vi
 8186 qb R      0:00 ps
%
```

In many ways, though, these different workstations have very similar output from the ps commands. For example, compare this Sequent output from ps -xu to the ps -xu output on the Sun that I already showed:

```
% ps -xu
USER       PID %CPU %MEM   SZ  RSS TT STAT START   TIME COMMAND
taylor    8191  7.7  0.4  284  536 qb R   19:16   0:00 ps -xu
taylor    8182  0.0  0.4  140  432 qb T   19:16   0:00 vi
taylor    8172  0.0  0.3   68  400 qb S   19:16   0:00 -csh (csh)
taylor    8180  0.0  0.1   52  144 qb S   19:16   0:00 newmail
%
```

The ENG column of the previous examples is replaced by a START column on the Sun workstation. The numbers in the ENG column indicate the exact time that the processes were started on the computer.

SUMMARY UNIX works with processes. Your login shell, the edit session you run, and even the ls program listing your files are all processes in the operating system. This means that you can work with processes. You can stop programs temporarily to do something else, restart them as you choose, and even look at all the programs you're running at any time, including otherwise hidden processes such as your login shell itself.

Task 17.4: Terminating Processes with `kill`

DESCRIPTION Now that you know how to create multiple processes, tuck some into the background, and find stray processes, you need some way to permanently stop them from running, as needed. The command to accomplish this in UNIX is `kill`. For the most part, to use `kill`, you specify the process ID numbers of those programs you want to terminate. Both the C shell and Korn shell have a convenient shorthand that you've already seen: the percent–job-number notation.

There are a variety of different signals that the `kill` command can send to a process. To specify a job control action, you need to specify to `kill` one of a variety of different signals. Table 17.3 lists signals you can use with `kill`.

Table 17.3. Some signals to use with `kill`.

Number	Name	Meaning
1	SIGHUP	Hang up
2	SIGINT	Interrupt

17

Number	Name	Meaning
9	SIGKILL	kill (cannot be caught or ignored)
15	SIGTERM	Software termination signal from kill

There are over 30 different signals that UNIX knows about, but Table 17.3 lists the ones that are most helpful. The SIGHUP signal is what's sent to every process you are running just before you hang up (log out of the system). SIGINT is the signal sent when you press ^c; many programs respond in specific ways when this signal is received. SIGKILL is "The Terminator" of the UNIX signals: Programs cannot ignore it and cannot process it. The process is terminated immediately, without even a chance to clean up after itself. SIGTERM is the more graceful alternative: It requests an immediate termination of the program, but it allows the program an opportunity to remove temporary files it might have created.

By default, kill sends a SIGTERM to the processes specified. You can specify other signals, however, by using either the number or the name of the signal (minus the SIG prefix, that is). On many systems, you also can specify the -1 flag *to* kill to see what signals are available.

CAUTION

> The kill command should be used with caution. It can get you into a lot of trouble. For example, do you want to log out rather suddenly? To do that, find the process ID of your login shell and terminate it. Learn to use kill, but learn to use it cautiously.

ACTION

1. The simplest way to use the kill command is from the shell. First, start a job in the background:

```
% vi &
[1] 6016
%
```

I can terminate this process now by using either kill %1 or kill 6016, but if I try both of them, the second will fail because the first already will have terminated the process:

```
% kill %1
% kill 6016
6016: No such process
[1]    Done                    vi
%
```

Just as if I had dropped a process into the background and it instantly stopped because it needed to produce output, the kill process also had no feedback and took a second or two to occur. In the interim, I entered the second `kill` command, which then output the error message `No such process`. Following that, I get an indication from the shell itself that the job ended.

2. Using the `ps` command, I can find that pesky `newmail` program that's always running in the background:

```
% ps -ux ¦ grep newmail
taylor    6899   0.1  0.1   52   28 Av S          0:00 grep newmail
taylor   25817   0.0  0.1  124   60 Av I          0:01 newmail
%
```

I want to send that process a hang-up signal (`SIGHUP`):

```
% kill -HUP 25817
% !ps
ps -ux ¦ grep newmail
taylor    7220   0.0  0.1   52   28 Av S          0:00 grep newmail
%
```

Because the `newmail` program isn't in this listing, I can't conclude that the `SIGHUP` signal stopped `newmail`.

JUST A MINUTE

> Because `kill` tells you if a process cannot be found, the typical UNIX solution to finding out if the command worked is to enter `!!` immediately to repeat the `kill` command a second time. If `kill` worked, you see `No such process`.

3. Some processes are pesky and can resist the less powerful signals `SIGTERM` and `SIGHUP`. (In UNIX, this is called "catching" a signal. In some processes, you need to send and catch signals to perform certain actions.) That's when you need to use what I call "The Big Guns," or `SIGKILL`. You see this referred to sometimes as the terminate-with-extreme-prejudice command; the format is `kill -9 processID`, and it's not for the faint of heart!

    I strongly recommend that you just let `kill` send the `SIGTERM` signal and see if that does the job. If it doesn't, try `SIGHUP`, and if that also fails, use `SIGKILL` as a last resort.

4. What happens if you try to use `kill` on jobs that aren't yours? Fortunately, it doesn't work:

```
% ps -aux ¦ head -5
USER        PID  %CPU %MEM   SZ  RSS TT STAT ENG   TIME COMMAND
news       7460  97.7  0.4  336  252 ?  R N    4   4:33 sort -u
➥ /tmp/nnsubj6735a
phaedrus   8693  18.1  1.1 1260  720 rm S           0:03 nn
root       8741  14.4  0.4  416  252 ?  R      9    0:03 nntpd
root       8696  13.9  0.4  416  252 ?  S           0:03 nntpd
```

```
Broken pipe
% kill 7460
7460: Not owner
%
```

5. Finally, if you forget and leave stopped jobs in the background and try to log out, here's what happens:

```
% logout
There are stopped jobs.
%
```

You must either use fg to bring each job into the foreground and terminate them normally, or use kill to terminate each of the jobs, then log out.

SUMMARY In this task, you have been introduced to the kill command and some of the signals associated with it.

Summary

Although the file is the underlying unit in the UNIX file system, including all directories, the most fundamental piece of UNIX is the process. In this hour, you learned how to have background processes, how to stop and restart processes, and how to use kill to quit any errant program—running or not.

Workshop

The Workshop summarizes the key terms you learned and poses some questions about the topics presented in this chapter. It also provides you with a preview of what you will learn in the next hour.

Key Terms

control number   A unique number that the C shell assigns to each background job for easy reference and for using with other commands, such as fg and kill.

current job   The job that is currently running on the terminal and keyboard (it's the program you're actually running and working within).

foreground job   A synonym for current job.

errant process   A process that is not performing the job you expected it to perform.

job   A synonym for process.

kill   Terminate a process.

login shell   The shell process that started when you logged in to the system. This is usually where you're working when you're logged in to UNIX.

process   A program stopped or running within the UNIX operating system. Also known as a job.

signals   Special messages that can be sent to stopped or running processes.

stop a job   Stop the running program without terminating it.

wedged process   A process that is stuck in memory and can't free up its resources even though it has ceased running. This is rare, but annoying.

zombie   A terminated process that has not been cleaned up by the parent process.

Questions

1. Start a program, such as vi, and use ^z to stop it. Now terminate the process using kill.

2. Start vi again, stop it, and put it in the background. Work on something else, and then return vi to the foreground.

3. Use ps to check the status of processes to see what processes you have running that aren't shown on jobs. Why might ps and jobs list different processes?

Preview of the Next Hour

The next hour focuses on the many facets of printing and generating hard copy on the UNIX system. It's not as easy as you might think, so stay tuned!

Printing in the UNIX Environment

One of the greatest shortcomings of UNIX is printing. Generating printouts is a sufficiently common task that it should be fairly easy to accomplish. However, in this one area of UNIX, there has been continual conflict between the System V and BSD groups, to the detriment of all.

This hour focuses on some of the most common UNIX commands for working with printers. It is a primer on how to find out what printers are hooked up to your system, how to send output to a printer, how to check that your print requests are in the queue for printing, and how to remove your print requests from the queue if you change your mind for any reason.

Goals for This Hour

In this hour, you learn how to

- [ ] Find local printers with printers
- [ ] Send a print job to a printer with lpr or lp
- [ ] Format print jobs with pr
- [ ] Work with the print queue by using lpq, lprm

Various techniques can minimize the complexity of printing in UNIX, the best of which is to create an alias called print that has all the default configuration information you want. If you define PRINTER as an environment variable, most of the UNIX print utilities will default to the printer you specify as the value of the PRINTER environment variable, for example, when searching print queues for jobs. The queue, or list, is where all print jobs are placed for processing by the specific printer.

JUST A MINUTE

The differing "philosophies" of BSD and System V have caused problems in the area of printing. In a nutshell, because UNIX systems are always networked (that is, hooked together with high-speed data-communications lines), the most valuable feature of a printing tool would be allowing the user to choose to print on any of the many printers attached. For this to work, each machine with an attached printer must be listening for requests from other machines. The root of the BSD versus System V problem is that the two listen for different requests. A System V machine can't send a print job to a printer attached to a BSD machine, and vice versa.

Task 18.1: Find Local Printers with printers

DESCRIPTION   Of the many problems with printing in UNIX, none is more grievous than trying to figure out the names of all the different printers available, what kinds of printers they are, and where they're located. A complicated configuration file—/etc/printcap—contains all this information, but it's definitely not easy to read. So what do you do?

JUST A MINUTE

Some systems have an lpstat command, which lists printers available on the system. I find the output of this command difficult to read, hence my inclusion of the printers script here. If you find the output acceptable (see the next task in this hour for a sample), you can skip this first unit, although you still might want to spend a few minutes looking at the printers script anyway.

I will present a simple 20-line shell script, printers, that reads through the /etc/printcap file and creates an attractive and easily read listing of all printers configured on your system. This hour presents the script and shows it at work on a few different computer systems. I encourage you to enter this script and place it in your own bin directory ($HOME/bin should be in your PATH for this to work).

ACTION

1. To start, take a quick look at the contents of the /etc/printcap file:

```
% head -23 /etc/printcap
# $Header: /usr/msrc/usr/etc/printcap/RCS/printcap,v 1.235 93/11/04
➥10:55:21 mm
Exp Locker: mm $
aglw\ag\Iwag:\
        :dr=/usr/local/lib/lp/lpmq:\
        :gc=cc:\
        :lf=/usr/spool/lpr/aglw/logfile:\
        :lo=/usr/spool/lpr/aglw/lock:lp=/dev/null:\
        :mj#25:mx#3000:nd=/usr/local/lib/lp/lpnc:\
        :pf=gnpt:\
        :rm=server.utech.edu:rw:sd=/usr/spool/lpr/aglw:sh:\
        :gf=/usr/local/bin/psplot:\
        :nf=/usr/local/lib/devps/devps:\
        :qo=age:mq=aglw1,aglw2,aglw3,aglw4:mu:\
        :wi=AG 23:wk=multiple Apple LaserWriter IINT:
aglw1:\
        :dr=/usr/local/lib/lp/lwp.sh:\
        :gc=cc:\
        :lf=/usr/spool/lpr/aglw1/logfile:\
        :lo=/usr/spool/lpr/aglw1/lock:lp=/dev/null:\
        :mj#25:mx#3000:nd=/usr/local/lib/lp/lpnc:\
        :pf=gnpt:\
        :rm=server.utech.edu:rw:sd=/usr/spool/lpr/aglw1:sh:\
        :gf=/usr/local/bin/psplot:\
        :nf=/usr/local/lib/devps/devps:\
        :wi=AG 23:wk=Apple LaserWriter IINT:
```

I won't go into exhaustive detail about the meaning of each field in this listing. It suffices to say that the first line in each entry lists the name of the printer, a ¦ character, and any other possible names for the printer. Each field following the printer name is surrounded by colons and has a two-letter field name (for example, dr, nf), followed by the value of that particular field or setting. The fields of interest are the printer name; the wi field, which indicates the location of the printer; and the wk field, which indicates the type of printer.

2. There are no UNIX utilities to keep you from having to slog through this configuration file. I have written a short, yet powerful, C shell script called printers to list the desired information in a readable format. Notice the use of a here document to create the awk script and the multiple-line pipeline at the end of the script that does all the actual work.

```
% cat bin/printers
# printers - create a simple list of printers from the /etc/printcap
#            file on the system.
#
# From
# Teach Yourself UNIX in 24 Hours
```

```
set printcap=/etc/printcap
set awkscript=/tmp/awkscript.$$

/bin/rm -f $awkscript

cat << 'EOF' > $awkscript
NF == 2 { split($1, words, "|");
          prname=words[1]
        }
NF > 2  { printf("%-10s %s\n", prname, $0) }
'EOF'

egrep '(^[a-zA-Z]|:wi)' $printcap | \
  sed 's/:/ /g' | \
  awk -f $awkscript | \
  sed 's/wi=//;s/wk=/(/;s/ $)/' | \
  more

/bin/rm -f $awkscript

  exit 0
```

Some of this script is beyond what you have learned in this book about commands and scripts. In particular, the awk script, although only four lines long, shows some of the more powerful features of the program. Enter this as shown, and be careful to match the quotes and slash characters.

3. Once you've entered this script, enter the following:

% chmod +x bin/printers

That will ensure that it's an executable script. Next, you need to inform the C shell, using the rehash command, that you have added a new command to the search path. Then you can try your new shell script:

```
% rehash
% printers | head -15
aglw           AG 23 (multiple Apple LaserWriter IINT)
aglw1          AG 23 (Apple LaserWriter IINT)
aglw2          AG 23 (Apple LaserWriter IINT)
aglw3          AG 23 (Apple LaserWriter IINT)
aglw4          AG 23 (Apple LaserWriter IINT)
alpslw         LIB 111 (Apple LaserWriter IINTX)
bio            COM B117 (DataPrinter (self-service))
cary           CQuad (NE-B7) (IBM 4019 Laser Printer)
cslw           CS 2249 (Apple LaserWriter IIg)
cs115lw        CS 115 (IBM 4019 LaserPrinter (for CS180))
cs115lw2       CS 115 (IBM 4019 LaserPrinter (for CS180))
csg40lw        CS G040 (IBM 4019 LaserPrinter )
csg50lw        CS G050 (IBM 4019 LaserPrinter )
cslp1          CS G73 (C.Itoh, white paper (self-service))
eng130ci       ENG 130 (C.Itoh, white paper (self-service))
Broken pipe
```

18

You can use this script also to find printers of a certain type or in a specific location, if the descriptions in your /etc/printcap file are configured in the correct manner:

```
% printers ¦ grep -i plotter
knoxhp      KNOX 316A (Hewlett Packard 7550+ Plotter)
ccp         MATH G109 (CALCOMP 1073 Plotter)
cvp         MATH G109 (VERSATEC V-80 Plotter)
% printers ¦ grep -i math
lwg186      MATH G186 (Apple LaserWriter IINT(private))
mathci      MATH B9 (C.Itoh, white paper (self-service))
mathlw      MATH 734 (multiple Apple LaserWriter IINT)
mathlw1     MATH 734 (Apple LaserWriter IINT)
mathlw2     MATH 734 (Apple LaserWriter IINT)
mathlw3     MATH 734 (Apple LaserWriter IINT)
cci         MATH G109 (C.Itoh, 3 hole white paper)
ccp         MATH G109 (CALCOMP 1073 Plotter)
cil         MATH G109 (IBM 4019 Laser Printer)
cvp         MATH G109 (VERSATEC V-80 Plotter)
```

4. You now should be able to choose a printer that's most convenient for your location. Set the environment variable PRINTER to that value. You also might want to tuck that into the last line of your .login file so that next time you log in, the system will remember your printer selection.

```
% setenv PRINTER mathlw
% vi .login
```

JUST A MINUTE

> If your printer is not responding to what you set the PRINTER variable to, try using the LPDEST variable, especially on System V.

```
setenv NAME "Dave Taylor"
setenv BIN  "889"

newmail

mesg y
setenv PRINTER mathlw
~
~
```

SUMMARY The first, and perhaps biggest, hurdle for printing on UNIX has been solved: figuring out what the system calls the printer you're interested in using. Not only do you now have a new command, printers, for your UNIX system, but you can see how you can customize UNIX to meet your needs by creating aliases and shell scripts.

Task 18.2: Printing Files with `lpr` or `lp`

DESCRIPTION Now that you have identified the name of the printer to use, how about sending information to the printer? If you are on a BSD system, the command to do this is `lpr`. You can print the results of a pipe command by adding `lpr` at the end of the pipeline, or you can print files directly by specifying them to the program. You can even use < to redirect input.

If you're using a System V version of UNIX, you will need to use the `lp` command instead. As you read through this hour, you will see the differences between `lpr` and `lp` indicated. Note how the philosophies of the two vary.

The flags available for `lpr` and `lp` are numerous, and the most valuable ones are listed in Tables 18.1 and Table 18.2.

Table 18.1. Useful flags for `lpr`.

Flag	Meaning
-h	Do not print the header page.
-i	Indent the entire file eight spaces before printing.
-L	Print in landscape (sideways) mode, if the printer is capable of doing so.
-Ppr	Send the print job to printer `pr`.
-R	Print pages in reverse order.

Table 18.2. Useful flags for `lp`.

Flag	Meaning
-d*ptr*	Send the print job to the printer named *ptr*.
-P*n*	Print only page *n*.
-t*title*	Use *title* as the cover page title, where *title* is any string.

ACTION

1. Here's a demonstration of what happens if you try to use `lp` or `lpr` without specifying a printer and without having the PRINTER environment variable set. First, use the unsetenv command to remove environment variable definitions:

```
% unsetenv PRINTER
% who ¦ lpr
lpr: No printer specified
Broken pipe
```

18

Some systems default to a printer named lp in this situation, so if you don't get an error message, that's what happened. If you have lpstat (a command for checking the status of a printer), the -d flag will result in lpstat listing your default printer.

To specify a printer, use the -P flag with lpr or the -d flag with lp, followed immediately by the name of the printer:

```
% who ¦ lpr -Pmathlw
```

Specifying a printer with the -P flag (or -d with lp) always will override the environment variable specified in PRINTER; therefore, you can specify the default printer with PRINTER and specify other printers as needed without any further work.

Notice that I printed the output of the who command but received absolutely no information from the lpr command regarding what printer it was sent to, the print job number, or any other information.

To make life easier, I'm going to redefine PRINTER:

```
% setenv PRINTER mathlw
```

2. To find out what's in the print queue, I can use lpstat -p*printer* on System V or the lpq -P*printer* command:

```
% lpq -Pmathlw

mathlw@server.utech.edu:    driver not active
           Printing is disabled.

Pos  User      Bin   Size  Jobname
---  ----      ---   ----  -------
  1  KOSHIHWE  0104  008   KOSHIHWE0104a
  2  KOSHIHWE  0104  008   KOSHIHWE0104b
  3  KOSHIHWE  0104  008   KOSHIHWE0104c
  4  kleimanj  0317  032   kleimanj0317a
  5  zeta      0042  008   zeta0042a
  6  jharger   0167  008   jharger0167a
  7  jharger   0167  008   jharger0167b
  8  ssinfo    0353  000   ssinfo0353a
  9  fuelling  0216  024   fuelling0216a
 10  zeta      0042  152   zeta0042b
 11  tkjared   0142  012   tkjared0142a
 12  SUJATHA   0043  016   SUJATHA0043a
 13  SUJATHA   0043  024   SUJATHA0043b
 14  SUJATHA   0043  044   SUJATHA0043c
 15  bee       0785  012   bee0785a
 16  bee       0785  056   bee0785b
 17  bee       0785  028   bee0785c
 18  ssinfo    0353  004   ssinfo0353b
 19  ssinfo    0353  000   ssinfo0353c
 20  ssinfo    0353  000   ssinfo0353d
 21  ssinfo    0353  004   ssinfo0353e
 22  stacysm2  0321  000   stacysm20321a
```

18

```
23  ssinfo    0353   000  ssinfo0353f
24  taylor    0889   000  taylor0889a
```

```
mathlw: waiting to be transmitted to server.utech.edu
```

```
The queue is empty.
```

Quite a few print jobs are waiting to be sent, but it's not obvious why the printer is disabled. The output of the lpq and lpstat commands are explained in detail later in this hour.

3. To print the file dickens.note in landscape mode, without a header page, indented eight spaces, and in reverse order, I can use the following flags:

```
% lpr -hiLR < dickens.note
```

If I did this often, a C shell alias could be helpful:

```
% alias lpr...'lpr -hiLR'
```

On a System V machine, you also could create the alias alias lpr 'lp', though none of these particular options are available with lp.

If you find yourself printing to a couple different printers quite often, you easily can define a few shell aliases to create printer-specific print commands:

```
% alias mathprint    'lpr -Pmathlw'
% alias libprint     'lpr -Plibrary'
% alias edprint      'lpr -Pedlw'
```

On System V machines, the name would be this:

```
% alias mathprint    'lp -dmathlw'
% alias libprint     'lp -dlibrary'
% alias edprint      'lp -dedlw'
```

4. Some systems have a command lpinfo that also offers information about printers:

```
% lpinfo mathlw
mathlw: server.utech.edu; MATH 734; multiple Apple LaserWriter IINT
```

To find out more information about the printer, you can specify the -v flag:

```
% lpinfo -v mathlw
mathlw description:
        driver: /usr/local/lib/lp/lpmq
        printer control group: cc
        graphic filter: /usr/local/bin/psplot
        log file: /usr/spool/lpr/mathlw/logfile
        lock file: /usr/spool/lpr/mathlw/lock
        hardware line: /dev/null
        maximum job count per user = 25
        subqueue list: mathlw1,mathlw2,mathlw3
        maximum print file blocks = 3000
        make unique via bin change
```

```
network driver: /usr/local/lib/lp/lpnc
ditroff filter: /usr/local/lib/devps/devps
print formats: graphics, ditroff, use pr, troff
queue ordering: age
host attachment: server.utech.edu
spooling directory: /usr/spool/lpr/mathlw
location: MATH 734
description: multiple Apple LaserWriter IINT
```

5. The lpinfo command also can show you a list of what printers are available, but I find the output format considerably more difficult to understand than lpstat:

```
% lpinfo -a ¦ head -15
aglw:    server.utech.edu; AG 23; multiple Apple LaserWriter IINT
aglw1:        server.utech.edu; AG 23; Apple LaserWriter IINT
aglw2:        server.utech.edu; AG 23; Apple LaserWriter IINT
aglw3:        server.utech.edu; AG 23; Apple LaserWriter IINT
aglw4:        server.utech.edu; AG 23; Apple LaserWriter IINT
alpslw: sentinel.utech.edu; LIB 111; Apple LaserWriter IINTX
bio:    ace.utech.edu; COM B117; DataPrinter (self-service)
cary:    franklin.utech.edu; CQuad (NE-B7); IBM 4019 Laser Printer
cslw: server.utech.edu; CS 2249; Apple LaserWriter IIg
cs115lw:      expert.utech.edu; CS 115; IBM 4019 LaserPrinter (for CS180)
cs115lw2:     expert.utech.edu; CS 115; IBM 4019 LaserPrinter (for CS180)
csg40lw:      franklin.utech.edu; CS G040; IBM 4019 LaserPrinter
csg50lw:      franklin.utech.edu; CS G050; IBM 4019 LaserPrinter
cslp1: expert.utech.edu; CS G73; C.Itoh, white paper (self-service)
eng130ci:     age.utech.edu; ENG 130; C.Itoh, white paper (self-service)
Broken pipe
```

If you find this output readable, you're undoubtedly becoming a real UNIX expert!

SUMMARY The output of the printers command specifies the location of the printer that printed the file. I need to go to another building to pick up my hard copy. (The location is specified in the output of the printers command.)

Task 18.3: Formatting Print Jobs with pr

DESCRIPTION The printout I generated looked good, but boring. I would like to have a running header on each page that specifies the name of the file and the page number. I'd also like to have a bit more control over some other formatting characteristics. This is exactly where the pr command comes in handy. Not intended just for printing, pr is a general pagination and formatting command that can be used to display information on the screen. Even better, pr is available on both BSD and System V UNIX.

The pr program is loaded with options, most of which are quite useful at times. For example, -2 makes the output two columns, which is useful for printing results of the who command in landscape mode! The most useful options are presented in Table 18.3.

18

Table 18.3. Useful flags in pr.

Flag	Meaning
-n	Produce *n*-column output per page.
+n	Begin printing on the *n*th page.
-f	Don't print the page header and footer information.
-h*hdr*	Use *hdr* as the head of each page.
-w*n*	Set the page width to *n* characters (for landscape mode).
-m	Print all files at once, one per column.

JUST A MINUTE

On some UNIX systems, the -f flag to pr causes the program to put form feeds at the bottom of each printed page. To suppress the header and footer, use -t.

ACTION

1. My printout of the who command showed me that my choice of paper was poor. In a 128-character-wide landscape printout, I actually was using only the first 30 characters or so of each line. Instead, I can use pr to print in two-column mode:

```
% who ¦ pr -2 ¦ more

Dec  9 13:48 1993    Page 1


root      console Dec 6 18:02    ab        ttypk  Dec 9 07:57  (nova)
princess  ttyaV   Dec 9 13:44    dutch     ttypl  Dec 8 13:36  (dov)
tempus    ttyaW   Dec 9 13:43    malman    ttypm  Dec 9 13:07  (dov)
enatsuex  ttyaY   Dec 9 13:41    bakasmg   ttypq  Dec 9 13:09  (age)
coxt      ttyaZ   Dec 9 13:35    dodsondt  ttyps  Dec 8 11:37  (age)
scfarley  ttyAa   Dec 9 13:36    md        ttypv  Dec 8 08:23  (kraft)
nancy     ttyAb   Dec 9 13:12    rothenba  ttypw  Dec 9 13:15  (trinetra)
rick      ttyAc   Dec 9 13:12    xuxiufan  ttypy  Dec 9 13:16  (ector)
fitzte    ttyAd   Dec 9 13:47    nashrm    ttyq3  Dec 9 13:04  (pc115)
maluong   ttyAe   Dec 9 13:46    dls       ttyq5  Dec 9 13:06  (dialup01)
af5       ttyAg   Dec 9 09:12    myounce   ttyq8  Dec 9 02:14  (limbo)
zjin      ttyAh   Dec 9 13:44    liyan     ttyq9  Dec 9 13:11  (volt)
herbert1  ttyAi   Dec 9 13:29    daffnelr  ttyqA  Dec 9 13:36  (localhost)
ebranson  ttyAj   Dec 9 13:44    mm        ttyqB  Dec 9 10:32  (mm)
billiam   ttyAk   Dec 9 13:36    jlapham   ttyqC  Dec 9 12:46  (mac18)
linet2    ttyAm   Dec 9 11:04    chuicc    ttyqE  Dec 9 13:38  (icarus)
--More--
```

18

Notice that the pr program not only made this a two-column listing, but it also added a page header that indicates the current date and page number.

2. The header still doesn't contain any information about the command name, which is what would really be helpful. Fortunately, I easily can add the header information I want by using pr:

```
% who ¦ pr -h "(output of the who command)" -2 ¦ more


Dec  9 13:50 1993   (output of the who command) Page 1


root       console Dec 6 18:02    ab       ttypk   Dec 9 07:57  (nova)
princess ttyaV   Dec 9 13:44    dutch    ttypl   Dec 8 13:36  (dov)
tempus   ttyaW   Dec 9 13:43    malman   ttypm   Dec 9 13:07  (dov)
enatsuex ttyaY   Dec 9 13:41    bakasmg  ttypq   Dec 9 13:09  (age)
coxt     ttyaZ   Dec 9 13:35    dodsondt ttyps   Dec 8 11:37  (age)
scfarley ttyaa   Dec 9 13:36    md       ttypv   Dec 8 08:23  (kraft)
nancy    ttyAb   Dec 9 13:12    rothenba ttypw   Dec 9 13:15  (trinetra)
rick     ttyAc   Dec 9 13:12    xuxiufan ttypy   Dec 9 13:16  (ector)
fitzte   ttyAd   Dec 9 13:47    dls      ttyq5   Dec 9 13:06  (dialup01)
maluong  ttyAe   Dec 9 13:46    myounce  ttyq8   Dec 9 02:14  (limbo)
maritanj ttyAf   Dec 9 13:49    liyan    ttyq9   Dec 9 13:11  (volt)
af5      ttyAg   Dec 9 09:12    daffnelr ttyqA   Dec 9 13:36  (localhost)
zjin     ttyAh   Dec 9 13:48    mm       ttyqB   Dec 9 10:32  (mm)
herbert1 ttyAi   Dec 9 13:29    jlapham  ttyqC   Dec 9 12:46  (mac18)
ebranson ttyAj   Dec 9 13:44    chuicc   ttyqE   Dec 9 13:38  (icarus)
--More--
```

That's much better.

3. I might want to compare the contents of two different directories. Remember that the -1 flag to ls forces the ls program to list the output one filename per line, so I can create a couple of files in this format easily:

```
% ls -1 src > src.listing
% ls -1 /tmp > tmp.listing
```

These files look like this:

```
% head src.listing tmp.listing
==> src.listing <==
calc-help
calc.c
fixit.c
info.c
info.o

==> tmp.listing <==
Erik/
GIri/
Garry/
MmIsAlive
```

18

```
Re01759
Re13201
Sting/
VR001187
VR002540
VR002678
```

Now I will use pr to build a two-column output:

```
% pr -m src.listing tmp.listing ¦ head -15


Dec  9 13:53 1993   Page 1


calc-help                        Erik/
calc.c                           GIri/
fixit.c                          Garry/
info.c                           MmIsAlive
info.o                           Re01759
massage.c                        Re13201
                                 Sting/
                                 VR001187
                                 VR002540
Broken pipe
```

4. This would be more helpful if I could turn off the blank lines automatically included at the top of each listing page, which is a job for the -f flag (or -t, if your version of pr was -f for form feeds):

```
% ^pr^pr -f
pr -f -m src.listing tmp.listing ¦ head -15
Dec  9 13:56 1993   Page 1


calc-help                        Erik/
calc.c                           GIri/
fixit.c                          Garry/
info.c                           MmIsAlive
info.o                           Re01759
massage.c                        Re13201           ¦
                                 Sting/
                                 VR001187
                                 VR002540
                                 VR002678
                                 VR002982
                                 VR004477
Broken pipe
```

5. It looks good. Now it's time to print by piping the output of the pr command to the lpr command:

```
% !pr ¦ lpr
pr -f -m src.listing tmp.listing ¦ head -15 ¦ lpr
```

18

SUMMARY The pr command can be used to ensure that your printouts are always clean and readable. Again, it's a perfect place to create an alias: `alias print 'pr ¦ lpr'` or `alias print 'pr ¦ lp'`. Even without any flags, pr automatically adds page numbers to the top of each page.

Task 18.4: Working with the Print Queue

DESCRIPTION On a personal computer, you might be used to having your printer directly connected to your system, so anything you print using PRT: (on DOS) or File | Print (on the Mac) instantly prints. Unfortunately, UNIX doesn't grant you the luxury of using your own personal printer. Instead, it handles print requests in a print queue, a managed list of files to print. When you send a file to a printer with lpr or lp, the request is added to a queue of files waiting to print. Your request goes to the bottom of the list, and any subsequent print requests are added below yours. Your print request gradually moves up to the top of the list and prints, without interrupting the print requests of those folks ahead of you.

Sometimes it can be frustrating to wait for a printout. However, there are some advantages to using a queuing system over simply allowing users to share a single printer. The greatest is that you can use the lprm command to change your mind and remove print requests from the queue before they waste paper. The lprm command works with the *print job name*, which you can learn by checking the print queue, using lpq. Both lprm and lpq either can use the default PRINTER setting or can have printers specified with -Pprinter. The lpq command also can limit output to just your jobs by adding your account name to the command.

If your system doesn't have lprm, use the cancel command to remove entries from the print queue. The lpstat command is also the System V replacement for the lpq command, though many sites alias lpq = lpstat to make life a bit easier.

To use cancel, you need to specify the name of the printer and the job ID, as shown in the lpstat output. If I had print request ID 37 on printer hardcopy, I could cancel the print request with the command cancel hardcopy -37.

18

ACTION

1. A glance at the mathlw queue shows that there are a lot of files waiting to print:

   ```
   % lpq

   mathlw@server.utech.edu:   driver not active
           Printing is disabled.

   Pos  User      Bin   Size  Jobname
   ---  ----      ---   ----  -------
     1  KOSHIHWE  0104  008   KOSHIHWE0104a
     2  KOSHIHWE  0104  008   KOSHIHWE0104b
     3  KOSHIHWE  0104  008   KOSHIHWE0104c
   ```

```
 4   kleimanj   0317   032   kleimanj0317a
 5   zeta       0042   008   zeta0042a
 6   jharger    0167   008   jharger0167a
 7   jharger    0167   008   jharger0167b
 8   ssinfo     0353   000   ssinfo0353a
 9   fuelling   0216   024   fuelling0216a
10   zeta       0042   152   zeta0042b
11   tkjared    0142   012   tkjared0142a
12   SUJATHA    0043   016   SUJATHA0043a
13   SUJATHA    0043   024   SUJATHA0043b
14   SUJATHA    0043   044   SUJATHA0043c
15   bee        0785   012   bee0785a
16   bee        0785   056   bee0785b
17   bee        0785   028   bee0785c
18   info       0353   004   info0353b
19   info       0353   000   info0353c
20   info       0353   000   info0353d
21   info       0353   004   info0353e
22   stacysm2   0321   000   stacysm20321a
23   info       0353   000   info0353f
24   taylor     0889   000   taylor0889a
```

```
mathlw: waiting to be transmitted to server.utech.edu
```

```
The queue is empty.
```

My print job is job number 24, with the print job name taylor0889a. Figure 18.1 explains the different fields in the queue listing.

Figure 18.1.

The lpq *output format explained.*

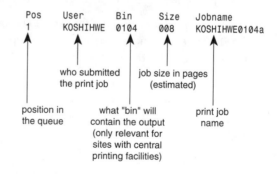

The printer is also turned off. You can see at the top of the lpq output that telltale message driver not active Printing is disabled. Obviously, if the printer is disabled, it's rather futile to wait for a printout.

2. To limit the output to just those print jobs that are mine, I specify my account name:

```
% lpq taylor
mathlw@server.utech.edu:  driver not active
          Printing is disabled.
```

18

```
Pos  User      Bin   Size  Jobname
---  ----      ---   ----  -------
  1  taylor    0889  004   taylor0889a

mathlw: waiting to be transmitted to server.utech.edu

The queue is empty.
```

3. To check the status of another printer, I can specify the printer with the `-P` flag:

```
% lpq -Pb280il

b280il@franklin.utech.edu:        driver not active

The queue is empty.

b280il:     waiting to be transmitted to franklin.utech.edu

The queue is empty.
```

That's better. The queue is empty.

4. To remove my print job from the `mathlw` print queue, I simply specify the print job name from the `lpq` output:

```
% lprm taylor0889a
```

UNIX carries out my command without giving me confirmation that it has done so, but a quick check with `lpq` shows me what's up:

```
% lpq taylor
mathlw@server.utech.edu:   driver not active
        Printing is disabled.

The queue is empty.

mathlw: waiting to be transmitted to server.utech.edu

The queue is empty.
```

JUST A MINUTE

I wish the default for the `lpq` command would show only print jobs that I have in the queue, and I could use the `-a` flag to show all print jobs queued. Furthermore, instead of incorrectly saying `The queue is empty`, `lpq` should report something more useful, like there are 23 other print jobs in the queue.

5. Now I resubmit the print job request, this time to the `b280il` printer:

```
% !pr -Pb280il
pr -f -m src.listing tmp.listing ¦ head -15 ¦ lpr -Pb280il
```

Uh oh! I don't want that `head -15` cutting off the information in the printout.

```
% lpq -Pb280il
b280il@franklin.utech.edu:        driver active; no job printing

Pos  User      Bin   Size  Jobname
---  ----      ---   ----  -------
  1  nfsuser   0058  268   nfsuser0058a
  2  nfsuser   0054  012   nfsuser0054a
  3  taylor    0889  000   taylor0889a

b280il:    waiting to be transmitted to franklin.utech.edu
```

The queue is empty.

To remove my print request, I use lprm:

```
% lprm taylor0889a
"taylor0889a" not located.
```

I've made a second mistake! I need to specify the printer.

```
% lprm -Pb280il taylor0889a
```

Now I can fix the original command and print the files correctly:

```
% pr -f -m src.listing tmp.listing ¦ lpr -Pb280il
```

SUMMARY   UNIX offers some printing abilities that you might not be accustomed to working with, particularly the ability to change your mind and stop a print job before it touches paper. You can see that it's a good idea to set the PRINTER environment variable to your favorite printer so that you can save yourself from struggling to enter weird printer names each time you print a file.

Summary

A few judiciously defined aliases can save you a lot of frustration down the road. Choose your favorite printer, define the PRINTER environment variable to point to that printer, and give yourself an alias like print to include all the default options you like for your printouts. You might consider creating an alias pq to show your own print requests queued for your favorite printer. (This is easy to do. Use alias pq 'lpq $LOGNAME' or alias pq 'lpstat -u $LOGNAME'.) You also could show only your print requests, if any, by tucking a grep into the command: alias pq 'lpq ¦ grep $LOGNAME'.

Workshop

The Workshop summarizes the key terms you learned and poses some questions about the topics presented in this chapter. It also provides you with a preview of what you will learn in the next hour.

18

Key Terms

print job name   The unique name assigned to a print job by the `lpr` or `lp` command.

print queue   The queue, or list, in which all print jobs are placed for processing by the specific printer.

Questions

1. Use the `lpinfo -a` or `printers` command to find out what printers are available on your system. Which command is easier to use? How many are available?

2. Is your `PRINTER` variable already set to a printer? Is it the printer you would choose?

3. Use `man -k` to see what commands you have on your system that work with the printers and print queues. Use `man` to peruse them.

4. Show three ways to print the file `dickens.note` with `lpr`.

5. Add a print job to the queue and then remove it with `lprm`. What happened?

6. How would you use `pr` to add `A Tale of Two Cities` as a running title across each printout page of the file `dickens.note`? How would you start the printout on the second page of the file?

Preview of the Next Hour

In the next hour, you learn about the `find` command, with its unique command flags and its partner `xargs`. This command enables you to search the UNIX file system for files that meet specific criteria, and `xargs` enables you to perform actions on those files.

18

Hour 19

Searching for Information and Files

One of the greatest challenges in UNIX is to find the files you want, when you want them. Even the best organization in the world, with mnemonic subdirectories and carefully named files, can break down and leave you saying to yourself, "I know it's somewhere, and I remember that it contains a bid for Acme Acres Construction to get that contract; but for the life of me, I just can't remember where it is!"

Goals for This Hour

In this hour, you learn about

☐ The find command and its weird options

☐ How to use find with xargs

In this hour, you learn sophisticated ways to find specific information on the UNIX system. The powerful find command and its partner, xargs, are the contents of this hour.

Task 19.1: The `find` Command and Its Weird Options

DESCRIPTION The `grep` family can help you find files by their content. There are a lot of other ways to look for things in UNIX, and that's where the `find` command can help. This command has a notation that is completely different from all other UNIX commands: It has full-word options rather than single-letter options. Instead of `-n` *pattern* to match filenames, for example, `find` uses `-name` *pattern*.

The general format for this command is to specify the starting point for a search through the file system, followed by any actions desired. The list of possible options, or flags, is shown in Table 19.1.

Table 19.1. Useful options for the `find` command.

Option	Meaning
`-atime` *n*	True if file was accessed *n* days ago.
`-ctime` *n*	True if the file was created *n* days ago.
`-exec` *command*	Execute *command*.
`-mtime` *n*	True if file was modified *n* days ago.
`-name` *pattern*	True if filename matches *pattern*.
`-print`	Print names of files found.
`-type` *c*	True if file is of type *c* (as shown in Table 19.2).
`-user` *name*	True if file is owned by user *name*.

The `find` command checks the specified options, going from left to right, once for each file or directory encountered. Further, `find` with any of the time-oriented commands can search for files more recent than, older than, or exactly the same age as a specified date, with the specifications *-n*, *+n*, and *n*, respectively. Some examples will make this clear.

ACTION

1. At its simplest, `find` can be used to create a list of all files and directories below the current directory:

```
% find . -print
.
./OWL
./OWL/owl.h
./OWL/owl
./OWL/owl.c
```

19

```
./OWL/simple.editor.c
./OWL/ask.c
./OWL/simple.editor.o
./OWL/owl.o
./OWL/Doc
./OWL/Doc/Student.config
./OWL/handout.c
./OWL/owl.question
./OWL/WordMap
./OWL/WordMap/a.out
./OWL/WordMap/lots-of-lines
./OWL/WordMap/msw-to-txt.c

lots and lots of output removed

./src/info.o
./src/massage.c
./keylime.pie
./csh.man
./sample
./sample2
./awkscript
./dickens.note
./newsample
./.sh-history
./mbox
./cheryl
./temp
./temp/zmail
./temp/attach.msg
./.profile
./buckaroo
./sample3
./buckaroo.confused
./deleteme
./dead.letter
./who.is.who
./src.listing
./tmp.listing
./.wrongwords
./papert.article
```

2. To limit the output to just those files that are C source files (those that have a .c suffix), I can use the -name option before the -print option:

```
% find . -name "*.c" -print
./OWL/owl.c
./OWL/simple.editor.c
./OWL/ask.c
./OWL/handout.c
./OWL/WordMap/msw-to-txt.c
./OWL/WordMap/newtest.c
./OWL/feedback.c
./OWL/define.c
./OWL/spell.c
./OWL/submit.c
./OWL/utils.c
```

```
./OWL/parse.c
./OWL/sendmail.c
./owl.c
./src/calc.c
./src/info.c
./src/fixit.c
./src/massage.c
```

Using the -name option before the -print option can be very handy.

3. To find just those files that have been modified in the last seven days, I can use -mtime with the argument -7 (include the hyphen):

```
% find . -mtime -7 -name "*.c" -print
./OWL/owl.c
./OWL/simple.editor.c
./OWL/ask.c
./OWL/utils.c
./OWL/sendmail.c
```

If I use just the number 7 (without a hyphen), I will match only those files that were modified exactly seven days ago:

```
% find . -mtime 7 -name "*.c" -print
%
```

To find those C source files that I haven't touched for at least 30 days, I use +30:

```
% find . -mtime +30 -name "*.c" -print
./OWL/WordMap/msw-to-txt.c
./OWL/WordMap/newtest.c
./src/calc.c
./src/info.c
./src/fixit.c
./src/massage.c
```

4. With find, I now have a tool for looking across vast portions of the file system for specific file types, filenames, and so on.

To look across the /bin and /usr directory trees for filenames that contain the pattern cp, I can use the following command:

```
% find /bin /usr -name "*cp*" -print
/usr/diag/sysdcp
/usr/spool/news/alt/bbs/pcbuucp
/usr/spool/news/alt/sys/amiga/uucp
/usr/spool/news/comp/mail/uucp
/usr/spool/news/comp/os/cpm
/usr/spool/news/comp/protocols/tcp-ip
/usr/spool/uucp
find: cannot open <"/usr/spool/nqs">
/usr/spool/lpr/mathcp
/usr/spool/mail/cpotter
/usr/spool/mail/mcpherso
/usr/spool/erpcd/support/acp-config
/usr/spool/erpcd/support/acp-portinfo
/usr/local/bin/cnews/input/recpnews
/usr/local/bin/cppstdin
```

```
/usr/local/lib/libXdmcp.a
/usr/local/lib/gcc-lib/i386-sequent-bsd4.2/2.4.5/include
➥/netinet/tcp.h
/usr/local/lib/gcc-lib/i386-sequent-bsd4.2/2.4.5/include
➥/netinet/tcp-var.h
/usr/local/lib/gcc-lib/i386-sequent-bsd4.2/2.4.5/cpp
/usr/local/etc/tcpd
/usr/local/etc/acp-restrict
/usr/local/etc/acp-logfile
/usr/local/man/man1/cccp.1
/usr/man/man1/RCS/rcp.1c,v
/usr/man/man1/RCS/cpp.1,v
/usr/man/man1/RCS/cp.1,v
/usr/man/man1/RCS/uucp.1c,v
/usr/man/man1/cpplot.1l
/usr/man/man1/cpio.1u
/usr/man/man1/cp.1
/usr/man/man1/cpp.1
/usr/man/man1/rcp.1c
/usr/man/man1/macptopbm.1u
/usr/man/man1/pbmtomacp.1u
/usr/man/man3/RCS/p-cpus-online.3p,v
/usr/man/man3/RCS/cpus-online.3p,v
/usr/man/man3/RCS/getrpcport.3r,v
/usr/man/man3/cpus-online.3p
/usr/man/man3/getrpcport.3r
/usr/man/man3/p-cpus-online.3p
/usr/man/man3/unitcp.3f
/usr/man/man3/strcpy.3
/usr/man/man3/strncpy.3
/usr/man/man4/RCS/tcp.4p,v
/usr/man/man4/tcp.4p
/usr/man/man8/tcpd.8l
/usr/man/cat3f/%unitcp.3f.Z
/usr/man/cat3f/unitcp.3f.Z
/usr/unsup/bin/cpio
/usr/unsup/gnu/man/man1/cccp.1
/usr/news/cpulimits
/usr/doc/local/form/cp
/usr/doc/local/form/cpio
/usr/doc/local/form/rcp
/usr/doc/uucp
```

JUST A MINUTE

> This type of search can take a long time on a busy system. When I ran this command on my system, it took almost an hour to complete!

5. To find a list of the directories I've created in my home directory, I can use the -type specifier with one of the values shown in Table 19.2. Here's one example:

```
% find . -type d -print
.
./OWL
./OWL/Doc
```

```
./OWL/WordMap
./.elm
./Archives
./InfoWorld
./InfoWorld/PIMS
./Mail
./News
./bin
./src
./temp
%
```

Table 19.2. Helpful `find -type` **file types.**

Letter	Meaning
d	Directory
f	File
l	Link

6. To find more information about each of these directories, I can use the `-exec`
   option to `find`. Unfortunately, I cannot simply enter the command: The `exec`
   option must be used with `{}`, which will be replaced by the matched filename, and
   `\;` at the end of the command. (If the `\` is left out, the C shell will interpret the `;` as
   the end of the `find` command.) You also must ensure that there is a space between
   the `{}` and the `\:`.

```
% find . -type d -exec ls -ld {} \;
drwx------ 11 taylor          1024 Dec 10 14:13 .
drwx------  4 taylor           532 Dec  6 18:31 ./OWL
drwxrwx---  2 taylor           512 Dec  2 21:18 ./OWL/Doc
drwxrwx---  2 taylor           512 Nov  7 11:52 ./OWL/WordMap
drwx------  2 taylor           512 Dec 10 13:30 ./.elm
drwx------  2 taylor           512 Nov 21 10:39 ./Archives
drwx------  3 taylor           512 Dec  3 02:03 ./InfoWorld
drwx------  2 taylor           512 Sep 30 10:38 ./InfoWorld/PIMS
drwx------  2 taylor          1024 Dec  9 11:42 ./Mail
drwx------  2 taylor           512 Oct  6 09:36 ./News
drwx------  2 taylor           512 Dec 10 13:58 ./bin
drwx------  2 taylor           512 Oct 13 10:45 ./src
drwxrwx---  2 taylor           512 Nov  8 22:20 ./temp
```

7. The `find` command is commonly used to remove core files that are more than a
   few days old. These core files, as you recall, are copies of the actual memory image
   of a running program when the program dies unexpectedly. They can be huge, so
   occasionally trimming them is wise:

```
% find . -name core -ctime +4 -exec /bin/rm -f {} \;
%
```

There's no output from this command because I didn't use the `-print` at the end of
the command.

19

Summary The find command is a powerful command in UNIX. It helps you find files by owner, type, filename, and other attributes. The most awkward part of the command is the required elements of the -exec option, and that's where the xargs command helps immensely.

Task 19.2: Using find with xargs

Description You can use find to search for files, and you can use grep to search within files, but what if you want to search a combination? That's where xargs is helpful.

Action

1. A few days ago, I was working on a file that was computing character mappings of files. I'd like to find it again, but I don't remember either the filename or where the file is located.

   First off, what happens if I use find and have the -exec argument call grep to find files containing a specific pattern?

```
% find . -type f -exec grep -i mapping {} \;
typedef struct mappings {
map-entry character-mapping[] = {
int         long-mappings = FALSE;
        case 'l': long-mappings = TRUE;
          if (long-mappings)
      /** do a short mapping **/
      /** do a long mapping **/
      /** Look up the specified character in the mapping database **/
      while ((character-mapping[pointer].key < ch) &&
            (character-mapping[pointer].key > 0))
      if (character-mapping[pointer].key == ch)
        return ( (map-entry *) &character-mapping[pointer]);
# map,uucp-map    = The UUCP Mapping Project = nca-maps@apple.com
grep -i "character*mapping" * */* */*/*
to print PostScript files produced by a mapping application that
➥runs on the
bionet.genome.chromosomes        Mapping and sequencing of
➥eucaryote chromosomes.
./bin/my.new.cmd: Permission denied
typedef struct mappings {
map-entry character-mapping[] = {
int         long-mappings = FALSE;
        case 'l': long-mappings = TRUE;
          if (long-mappings)
      /** do a short mapping **/
      /** do a long mapping **/
      /** Look up the specified character in the mapping database **/
      while ((character-mapping[pointer].key < ch) &&
            (character-mapping[pointer].key > 0))
      if (character-mapping[pointer].key == ch)
        return ( (map-entry *) &character-mapping[pointer]);
or lower case values. The table mapping upper to
```

   The output is interesting, but it doesn't contain any filenames!

19

2. A second, smarter strategy would be to use the -l flag to grep so that grep specifies only the matched filename:

```
% find . -type f -exec grep -l -i mapping {} \;
./OWL/WordMap/msw-to-txt.c
././.elm/aliases.text
./Mail/mark
./News/usenet.alt
./bin/my.new.cmd: Permission denied
./src/fixit.c
./temp/attach.msg
```

3. That's a step in the right direction, but the problem with this approach is that each time find matches a file, it invokes grep, which is a very resource-intensive strategy. Instead, you use the xargs to read the output of find and build calls to grep (remember that each time a file is seen, the grep program will check through it) that specify a lot of files at once. This way, grep is called only four or five times even though it might check through 200 or 300 files. By default, xargs always tacks the list of filenames to the end of the specified command, so using it is as easy as can be:

```
% find . -type f -print ¦ xargs grep -l -i mapping
./OWL/WordMap/msw-to-txt.c
././.elm/aliases.text
./Mail/mark
./News/usenet.alt
./bin/my.new.cmd: Permission denied
./src/fixit.c
./temp/attach.msg
```

This gave the same output, but it was a lot faster.

4. What's nice about this approach to working with find is that because grep is getting multiple filenames, it will automatically include the filename of any file that contains a match when grep shows the matching line. Removing the -l flag results in exactly what I want:

```
% ^-l^
find . -type f -print ¦ xargs grep -i mapping
./OWL/WordMap/msw-to-txt.c:typedef struct mappings {
./OWL/WordMap/msw-to-txt.c:map-entry character-mapping[] = {
./OWL/WordMap/msw-to-txt.c:int          long-mappings = FALSE;
./OWL/WordMap/msw-to-txt.c:      case 'l': long-mappings = TRUE;
./OWL/WordMap/msw-to-txt.c:        if (long-mappings)
./OWL/WordMap/msw-to-txt.c:    /** do a short mapping **/
./OWL/WordMap/msw-to-txt.c:    /** do a long mapping **/
./OWL/WordMap/msw-to-txt.c:    /** Look up the specified character in
➥the mapping database **/
./OWL/WordMap/msw-to-txt.c:    while ((character-mapping[pointer].key
➥< ch) &&
./OWL/WordMap/msw-to-txt.c:
➥(character-mapping[pointer].key > 0))
./OWL/WordMap/msw-to-txt.c:
```

```
→if (character-mapping[pointer].key == ch)
./OWL/WordMap/msw-to-txt.c:        return ( (map-entry *)
→&character-mapping[pointer]);
././.elm/aliases.text:# map,uucp-map      = The UUCP Mapping Project
→  = nca-maps@apple.com
././.history:grep -i "character*mapping" * */* */*/*
././.history:find . -type f -exec grep -i mapping {} \;
./Mail/mark:to print PostScript files produced by a mapping
→application that runs on the
./News/usenet.alt:bionet.genome.chromosomes        Mapping and sequencing
→of eucaryote chromosomes.
./bin/my.new.cmd: Permission denied
./src/fixit.c:typedef struct mappings {
./src/fixit.c:map-entry character-mapping[] = {
./src/fixit.c:int          long-mappings = FALSE;
./src/fixit.c:    case 'l': long-mappings = TRUE;
./src/fixit.c:     if (long-mappings)
./src/fixit.c: /** do a short mapping **/
./src/fixit.c: /** do a long mapping **/
./src/fixit.c: /** Look up the specified character in the
→mapping database **/
./src/fixit.c: while ((character-mapping[pointer].key < ch) &&
./src/fixit.c:          (character-mapping[pointer].key > 0))
./src/fixit.c: if (character-mapping[pointer].key == ch)
./src/fixit.c:    return ( (map-entry *) &character-mapping[pointer]);
./temp/attach.msg:or lower case values. The table mapping upper to
```

SUMMARY When used in combination, find, grep, and xargs are a potent team to help find files lost or misplaced anywhere in the UNIX file system. I encourage you to experiment further with these important commands to find ways they can help you work with UNIX.

Summary

The find command is one of the more potent commands in UNIX. It has a lot of esoteric options, and to get the full power out of find, xargs, and grep, you need to experiment.

Workshop

This Workshop poses some questions about the topics presented in this chapter. It also provides you with a preview of what you will learn in the next hour.

Questions

1. Use find and wc -l to count how many files you have. Be sure to include the -type f option so that you don't include directories in the count.

2. Use the necessary commands to list the following:

☐ All filenames that contain abc

☐ All files that contain abc

19

Preview of the Next Hour

The next hour introduces you to techniques to communicate with other users.

Hour 20

Communicating with Others

It's time to learn about what's probably the single most exciting aspect of the operating system: the ability to communicate with other users on your computer, both interactively and through electronically transmitted mail, *e-mail.*

Goals for This Hour

In this hour, you learn about

- [ ] Enabling messages using `mesg`
- [ ] Writing to other users with `write`
- [ ] Reading electronic mail with `mailx`
- [ ] Sending electronic mail with `mailx`
- [ ] The smarter alternative for sending mail, `elm`

Of all the places in UNIX where there is variety, most of it surely is found in electronic mail, or e-mail. At least 15 different programs are available from various vendors to accomplish two tasks: to read mail from and send mail to other folks. In this hour, you learn about the standard electronic mail system, Berkeley Mail. I also take a little time to whet your appetite by showing you the Elm Mail System, a full-screen alternative mail program that's widely distributed.

JUST A MINUTE

> There's a much bigger world than the machine you're on; it's called the Internet. You learn lots about how to use this valuable system in these closing hours of *Teach Yourself UNIX in 24 Hours*.

Task 20.1: Enabling Messages Using mesg

DESCRIPTION   Earlier you learned that all peripherals hooked up to UNIX are controlled by device drivers and that each device driver has an associated /dev file. If you want to talk with other users on the system, you need to ensure that they can communicate with you, too. (This pertains only to write, however; e-mail works regardless of the mesg setting.)

ACTION

1. To find out through what device I'm connected to the system, I can use the UNIX command tty:

```
% tty
/dev/ttyAo
```

The tty device is just another UNIX file, so I can look at it as I'd look at any other file:

```
% ls -l /dev/ttyAo
crw---x--- 1 taylor     21,  71 Dec  8 10:34 /dev/ttyAo*
```

Notice that I own the file and that I have write permission, but others do not.

2. To enable other users to communicate with me directly, I need to ensure that they can run programs that can write to my terminal. That is, I need to give them write permission to my tty device. Instead of using the chmod command—tracking down what line I'm on and all that—I use a simple alternative, mesg. To turn messages on—allowing other users to communicate with me—I specify the y flag to mesg:

```
% mesg y
% ls -l `tty`
crw-rwx--- 1 taylor     21,  71 Dec  8 10:33 /dev/ttyAo*
```

To disable messages (perhaps if I'm busy and don't want to be bothered), I can use the n flag, which says that no, I don't want messages:

20

```
% mesg n
% ls -l `tty`
crw---x--- 1 taylor    21,  71 Dec  8 10:34 /dev/ttyAo*
```

3. At any point, you can double-check your current terminal write permission by entering mesg without any flags. The output is succinct, but it tells you what you want to know:

```
% mesg
is n
```

TIME SAVER

> To see the settings of your tty, use the backquotes with the tty command, as shown in the preceding examples.

SUMMARY Don't tell anyone this secret. Once you have write permission to someone else's terminal, you can redirect the output of commands to their tty device as easily as to any other file in UNIX. In fact, that's how the write command works: It opens the other person's tty device for writing, and each line you enter is also written to the other person's screen. I note this simply so you can see why the permissions of your /dev/tty line are so important, not so you can go wild and start tormenting your fellow UNIX users!

Task 20.2: Writing to Other Users with write

DESCRIPTION Now that you can allow others to write to your terminal as well as prevent them from writing to it, it's time to find out how to write to theirs and what you can do with that capability. The command for interacting directly with other users is the write command. It's a relatively simple command. When you start write, you specify the other user with whom you want to communicate, and write starts up for you only, and then it "pages" the other user to let him or her know that you're interested in communicating.

Once you're in the program, each line that you type is sent to the other person as soon as you press Return. Until they respond by using write on their system to respond, however, they can't send any messages to you. Electronic etiquette suggests that you connect and then you wait without typing until the other user connects with you. Then you can have a conversation!

To connect with someone, you just need to specify the person's account name to write. If the user is logged in more than once, write will try to choose the most recently used line, but it isn't always successful. Using w is a good strategy. Simply look at the idle time on each connection to identify which line the person is actually using. Once you identify the connection, you can invoke write with the user's account name and the tty line you desire.

20

ACTION

1. I always start out by ensuring that I've turned on `mesg` to ensure that others can write to my terminal. Otherwise, the chap at the other end is going to be pretty darn frustrated trying to talk with me!

   ```
   % mesg
   is y
   ```

2. The best way to find out whether your friend is on the system is to use `who`, piping the output into the `grep` program.

   ```
   % who ¦ grep marv
   marv     ttyAx    Dec  8 10:30
   ```

   He's logged in on `tty` line `/dev/ttyAx` (simply add `/dev/` before the line indicated by `who`). I can use `ls` to see whether he has his messages turned on:

   ```
   % ls -l /dev/ttyAx
   crw-rwx---  1 marv     21,  71 Dec  8 10:33 /dev/ttyAx*
   ```

3. To ask him to join a `write` session, I simply enter the following:

   ```
   % write marv
   ```

   What he sees on his screen is the following:

   ```
   Message from taylor@netcom.com on ttyAo at 10:38 ...
   _
   ```

4. Now I must wait until he responds, which should take only a few seconds. He types `write taylor`, and then I see:

   ```
   Message from marv@netcom.com on ttyAx at 10:40 ...
   ```

   We're both connected. Etiquette suggests I wait for his initial hello, which appears on my screen without preamble:

   ```
   Hi Dave! -o
   _
   ```

   I can enter lines to him, and he can enter lines to me. When I'm done with my communication, I press `^d` to end it, and he does the same:

   ```
   Okay, I'll talk with you tomorrow. -oo
   See ya! -oo
   ^d
   EOF
   ```

   A single press of Return gets me back to the system prompt, `%`.

Because it's so easy for people to step all over each other's communication in write, a simple protocol is borrowed from radio communication: When you're done with a transmission (one or more lines of text, in this case), you should indicate "over," or -o. Then, the other person types and sends you information, ending with an -o. When you're done with the conversation, end with an "over and out," or -oo. It makes life a lot more pleasant!

SUMMARY Like many things in life, the write command is simple—it has almost no options and precious little sophistication—yet it is valuable and enjoyable. If you have a quick question for someone who is logged in, or if you just want to ask your buddy if he's ready to have lunch, this is the best way to do it.

Task 20.3: Reading Electronic Mail with `mailx`

DESCRIPTION The write command is helpful for those situations when your friend or colleague is logged in to the computer at the same time you are, but what do you do if the person is not logged in and you want to leave a note? What if you want a friend to receive a copy of a note you're sending to, say, your boss?

That's where electronic mail moves into the spotlight. Of all the capabilities of UNIX, one of the most popular is undoubtedly this capability to send electronic mail to another user—even on another computer system—with a few keystrokes. In this section, you learn how to work with other users on your own computer, and later in this hour you learn how to send mail to folks who are on different computers, even in different countries.

A variety of programs for reading mail can be used on UNIX systems, but the two most common are mail and Mail. (The latter is also often called mailx on SVR4 systems.) Because of the similarity of the names, the former is known as "mail" and the latter as either "cap mail" ("cap" for the uppercase M) or "Berkeley Mail." I refer to "Mail" either as Berkeley Mail or as its AT&T name, mailx. You should never use mail to read or write mail if Berkeley Mail is available to you because Berkeley Mail is much easier to use. I will focus on using Berkeley Mail.

To envision electronic mail, imagine that you have a butler who is friendly with the local post office. You can hand him mail with only the name of the recipient written on the envelope, and the butler will make sure it's delivered. If new mail arrives, the butler discreetly lets you know about it, so you can then display the messages, one by one, and read them. Furthermore, your butler organizes your old mail in a big filing cabinet, filing each message by any criteria you request.

That's almost exactly how Berkeley Mail works. To send mail, you simply state on the command line the account name of the recipient, indicate a subject, enter the message itself, and poof! Your message is sent through the system and arrives at the recipient's terminal

20

posthaste. When mail arrives for you, the C shell or one of a variety of utilities, such as `biff` or `newmail`, can notify you. Each time you log in, the system checks for electronic mail, and if you have any, the system will say `You have mail` or `You have new mail`. You can save mail in files called *mail folders*.

Berkeley Mail has many command options, both flags that you can specify when you invoke the program from the command line and commands used within the program. Fortunately, you always can enter help while you're in the program to review these options. The most noteworthy flags are `-s` *subject*, which enables you to specify the subject of the message on the command line, and `-f` *mailfolder*, which enables you to specify a mail folder to read rather than the default (which is your incoming mailbox).

The most valuable commands to use within the program are summarized in Table 20.1.

Table 20.1. Berkeley Mail command summary.

Command	Meaning
delete *msgs*	Mark the specified messages for deletion.
headers	Display the current page of *headers* (the cryptic lines of information at the very top of an e-mail message; I explain them a bit later in this lesson). Add a + to see the next page, or a - to see the previous page.
help	Display a summary of Berkeley Mail commands.
mail *address*	Send mail to the specified address.
print *msgs*	Show the specified message or messages.
quit	Leave the Berkeley Mail program.
reply	Respond to the current message.
save *folder*	Save the current message to the specified mail folder.
undelete *msgs*	Undelete the messages that you've specified for deletion using the `delete` command.

ACTION

1. I have lots of electronic mail in my mailbox. When I logged in to the system today, the shell indicated that I had new mail. To find out what the new messages are, I use `mailx` (though I also could have typed `Mail` because they're synonymous on my machine):

```
% mailx
Mail version 5.2 6/21/85.  Type ? for help.
```

```
"/usr/spool/mail/taylor": 9 messages 5 new
      1 disserli Mon Nov 22 19:40  54/2749 "Re: Are you out there somewhe"
  >N  2 Laura.Ramsey Tue Nov 30 16:47  46/1705 "I've got an idea..."
   N  3 ljw      Fri Dec  3 22:57  130/2712 "Re: Attachments to XALT mail"
   N  4 sartin   Sun Dec  5 15:15  15/341 "I need your address"
   N  5 rustle   Tue Dec  7 15:43  29/955 "flash cards"
      6 harrism  Tue Dec  7 16:13  58/2756 "Re: Writing Lab OWL project ("
      7 CBUTCHER Tue Dec  7 17:00  19/575 "Computer Based GRE's"
      8 harrism  Tue Dec  7 21:46  210/10636 "Various writing environments"
   N  9 v892127  Wed Dec  8 07:09  38/1558 "Re: Have you picked up the co"
  & _
```

I have lots of information here. On the very first line, the program identifies itself as Mail version 5.2, built June 21, 1985. Tucked away in that top corner is the reminder that I can type ? at any point to get help on the commands.

The second line tells me what mailbox I'm reading. In this case, I'm looking at the default mailbox for my incoming mail, which is /usr/spool/mail/taylor. On your system, you might find your mailbox in this directory, or you might find it in a directory similarly named /usr/mail. Either way, you don't have to worry about where it's located because Berkeley Mail can find it automatically.

The third through eleventh lines list mail messages that I have received from various people. The format is N in the first column if I haven't seen the piece of mail before, a unique index number (the first item in each listing is one), the account that sent the message, the date and time the message was sent, the number of lines and characters in the message, and the subject of the message, if known. Figure 20.1 illustrates this more clearly.

Figure 20.1.

Understanding the message display in mailx.

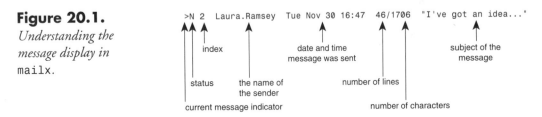

2. To read a specific message, I need enter only the index number of that message:

```
& 7
Message  7:
From: CBUTCHER Tue Dec  7 17:00:28 1993
From: Cheryl <CBUTCHER>
Subject:       Computer Based GRE's
To: Dave Taylor <TAYLOR>

I've scheduled to take the computer based GRE's in Indy on Jan. 6th.
Call me crazy but someone's got to do it.  I'll let you know how it goes.

Do you know anyone else that has taken the GRE's this way?  I figure
there's a paper in it somewhere.......
```

20

```
If you have that handout from seminar in a file, could you please send it
to me?

Thanks.

&  _
```

This message is from my friend Cheryl Butcher. Collectively, the first set of lines in the message—each a single word, a colon, and some information or other—is the *header* of the message, or the electronic equivalent of the postmark and envelope. The header always will include `From:`, `Subject:`, and `To:`, specifying the name and electronic address of the sender, the subject of the message, and the list of recipients.

3. To respond to this message, I enter `reply`:

```
& reply
To: CBUTCHER
Subject: RE: Computer Based GRE's

_
```

Anything I now enter will be sent back to Cheryl:

```
Hi. I am very interested in hearing about your reaction to the
computer-based GRE test. I'm sure you're correct that there is
a paper there, but wouldn't it be best to work with ETS on the
project?

I'll dig around and find those handouts soonest.

Happy holidays!

Dave
```

To end the message, I either press ^d on its own line or use the shorthand . by itself:

```
.
Cc: _
```

Berkeley Mail is now asking me to specify any other people I might like to receive *carbon copies* of this message. Entering an account name or two here will allow the designated people to see a copy of this message to Cheryl. Because I don't want anyone else to read this message, I press Return, which sends the message and returns me to the & prompt:

```
& _
```

4. I now can use the `headers` command to see what is the current message (the one I just read). It's the message indicated by the >. (Look at Figure 20.1 if you're having trouble finding it.)

```
& headers
       1 disserli Mon Nov 22 19:40  54/2749 "Re: Are you out there somewhe"
       2 Laura.Ramsey Tue Nov 30 16:47  46/1705 "I've got an idea..."
  N  3 ljw       Fri Dec  3 22:57  130/2712 "Re: Attachments to XALT mail"
  N  4 sartin    Sun Dec  5 15:15  15/341 "I need your address"
  N  5 rustle    Tue Dec  7 15:43  29/955 "flash cards"
       6 harrism  Tue Dec  7 16:13  58/2756 "Re: Writing Lab OWL project ("
  >  7 CBUTCHER  Tue Dec  7 17:00  19/575 "Computer Based GRE's"
       8 harrism  Tue Dec  7 21:46  210/10636 "Various writing environments"
  N  9 v892127   Wed Dec  8 07:09  38/1558 "Re: Have you picked up the co"
& _
```

To save Cheryl's message in a folder, I use the save command:

```
& save cheryl
"cheryl" [New file] 19/575
& _
```

5. Now that I'm done with this message, I can mark it for deletion with the delete command:

```
& delete 7
& _
```

Notice that after I enter headers, Cheryl's message vanishes from the list:

```
& headers
       1 disserli Mon Nov 22 19:40  54/2749 "Re: Are you out there somewhe"
       2 Laura.Ramsey Tue Nov 30 16:47  46/1705 "I've got an idea..."
  N  3 ljw       Fri Dec  3 22:57  130/2712 "Re: Attachments to XALT mail"
  N  4 sartin    Sun Dec  5 15:15  15/341 "I need your address"
  N  5 rustle    Tue Dec  7 15:43  29/955 "flash cards"
       6 harrism  Tue Dec  7 16:13  58/2756 "Re: Writing Lab OWL project ("
  >  8 harrism  Tue Dec  7 21:46  210/10636 "Various writing environments"
  N  9 v892127   Wed Dec  8 07:09  38/1558 "Re: Have you picked up the co"
& _
```

Look closely at the list, and you will see that it hasn't completely forgotten the message; the program hides message 7 from this list. I could still read the message by using print 7, and I could use undelete 7 to pull it off the deletion list.

JUST A MINUTE

Deleted messages in Berkeley Mail are actually marked for future deletion and aren't removed until you quit the program. Once you quit, however, there's no going back. A deleted message is gone. While you're within the program, you can delete and undelete to your heart's content.

6. Now I want to delete both messages from harrism (numbers 6 and 8):

```
& delete 6 8
```

Now the list of messages in my mailbox is starting to look pretty short:

```
& h
       1 disserli Mon Nov 22 19:40  54/2749 "Re: Are you out there somewhe"
       2 Laura.Ramsey Tue Nov 30 16:47  46/1705 "I've got an idea..."
```

20

```
N  3 ljw        Fri Dec  3 22:57  130/2712 "Re: Attachments to XALT mail"
N  4 sartin     Sun Dec  5 15:15  15/341 "I need your address"
N  5 rustle     Tue Dec  7 15:43  29/955 "flash cards"
>N 9 v892127    Wed Dec  8 07:09  38/1558 "Re: Have you picked up the co"
& _
```

TIME SAVER

Most commands in Berkeley Mail can be abbreviated to just their first letters, which cuts down on typing.

7. You can save a group of messages to a file by specifying the numbers between the save command and the folder name:

```
& save 6 8 harris
6: Inappropriate message
```

Oops. I deleted messages 6 and 8. I must undelete them before I can proceed:

```
& undelete 6 8
& save 6 8 harris
"harris" [New file] 268/13392
```

8. Use the quit command to get out of this program:

```
& quit
Saved 1 message in mbox
Held 6 messages in /usr/spool/mail/taylor
%
```

The messages that I viewed and didn't delete are moved out of my incoming mailbox to the file mbox. The messages that I saved and the messages I marked for deletion are silently removed, and all remaining messages are retained in /usr/spool/mail/taylor.

JUST A MINUTE

The biggest complaint I have with Berkeley Mail is that it does all this activity silently. I don't like the fact that saved messages are deleted automatically from the incoming mailbox when I quit and that—more importantly—messages I've read are tossed automatically into another folder. To ensure that messages you've read aren't moved into mbox when you quit, you can use the preserve command, which you can use with a list of numbers, the same way you can use other Berkeley Mail commands. Any message with which you use preserve will remain in your incoming mailbox.

SUMMARY   Once you get the hang of it, Berkeley Mail offers quite a lot of power, enabling you to read through your electronic mail, save it, and respond as needed with ease. The program has considerably more commands than shown here, so further study is helpful.

Task 20.4: Sending Mail with `mailx`

DESCRIPTION Now you know how to read your electronic mail using Berkeley Mail (aka `mailx`), and you know how to send mail from within the program. How do you send messages and files to people from the command line? It's quite simple. You even can specify the message subject with the `-s` starting flag.

ACTION

1. To send a message to someone, enter the name of the command, followed by the recipient's account name:

```
% mail marv
Subject: Interested in lunch tomorrow?
_
```

I now can enter as many lines of information as I want, ending, as within the Berkeley Mail program itself, with either ^d or .:

```
I'm going to be in town tomorrow and would like to
rustle up some Chinese food. What's your schedule
look like?

Dave
.
Cc: _
```

Again, I'm offered the option of copying someone else, but—again—I opt not to do so. Pressing Return sends the message.

2. To send a file to someone, combine file redirection with the use of the `-s` flag:

```
% mail -s "here's the contents of sample.file" marv < sample.file
```

The file was sent without any fuss.

3. Even though Berkeley Mail gives you no indication, several commands are available for use while entering the text of a message, and all can be listed with ~?:

```
% mail dunlaplm
Subject: Good morning!
~?
-----------------------------------------------------------
The following ~ escapes are defined:
~~               Quote a single tilde
~b users         Add users to "blind" cc list
~c users         Add users to cc list
~d               Read in dead.letter
~e               Edit the message buffer
~h               Prompt for to list, subject and cc list
~m messages      Read in messages, right shifted by a tab
~p               Print the message buffer
~r file          Read a file into the message buffer
~s subject       Set subject
```

20

```
~t users        Add users to to list
~v              Invoke display editor on message
~w file         Write message onto file.
~?              Print this message
~!command       Invoke the shell
~¦command       Pipe the message through the command
- - - - - - - - - - - - - - - - - - - - - - - - - - - - - - - - - - - - - - - - -

-
```

The ones most important to remember are ~v, to start up vi in the message; ~r, to read in a file; ~h, to edit the message headers; ~!, to invoke a shell command; and ~p, to show the message that's been entered so far:

```
    I wanted to wish you a cheery good morning!  You asked about
the contents of that one file, so here it is:
~!ls
Archives/       bin/             deleteme         sample
InfoWorld/      buckaroo         dickens.note     sample2
Mail/           buckaroo.confused keylime.pie     src/
News/           cheryl           mbox             temp/
OWL/            csh.man          newsample
awkscript       dead.letter      owl.c
!
```

The output of the command isn't included in the message, as is shown if you use the ~p command:

```
~p
- - - - - - -
Message contains:
To: taylor
Subject: Good morning!


Linda,

    I wanted to wish you a cheery good morning!  You asked about
the contents of that one file, so here it is:
(continue)

-
```

4. To read in a file, use the ~r command:

```
~r dickens.note
"dickens.note" 28/1123
```

Here, the contents of the file are included in the note, but mailx didn't list the contents to the screen. Again, using ~p will list the current message:

```
- - - - - - -
Message contains:
To: taylor
Subject: Good morning!


Linda,

    I wanted to wish you a cheery good morning!  You asked about
the contents of that one file, so here it is:
```

```
                         A Tale of Two Cities
                              Preface

When I was acting, with my children and friends, in Mr Wilkie Collins's
drama of The Frozen Deep, I first conceived the main idea of this
story.  A strong desire came upon me then, to
embody it in my own person;
and I traced out in my fancy, the state of mind of which it would
necessitate the presentation
to an observant spectator, with particular
care and interest.

As the idea became familiar to me, it gradually shaped itself into its
present form.  Throughout its execution, it has had complete possession
of me; I have so far verified what
is done and suffered in these pages,
as that I have certainly done and suffered it all myself.

Whenever any reference (however slight) is made here to the condition
of the Danish people before or during the Revolution, it is truly made,
on the faith of the most trustworthy
witnesses.  It has been one of my hopes to add
something to the popular and picturesque means of
understanding that terrible time, though no one can hope
to add anything to the philosophy of Mr Carlyle's wonderful book.

Tavistock House
November 1859
(continue)
```

5. I can fine-tune the headers using the ~h command:

```
~h
To: dunlaplm_
```

Pressing Return leaves it as is, and pressing Backspace lets me change it as desired. A Return moves to the next header in the list:

```
Subject: Good morning!
```

Pressing Return a few more times gives me the opportunity to change other headers in the message:

```
Cc:
Bcc:
(continue)
```

The Cc: header allows me to specify other people to receive this message. The Bcc: is what's known as a *blind carbon copy*, an invisible copy of the message. If I send a message to dunlaplm and a carbon copy to cbutcher, each can see that the other received a copy because the message will have To: dunlaplm as a header and also will list the other's name after Cc:. If I want to send a copy to someone without any of the other parties knowing about it, that's where a blind carbon copy can be helpful. Specifying someone on the Bcc: list means that that person receives a copy of the message, but his or her name doesn't show up on any header in the message itself.

20

6. Finally, I use ^d to end the message.

```
^d
Cc:
%
```

SUMMARY All so-called *tilde commands* (so named because they all begin with the ~, or tilde, character) are available when you send mail from the command line. They also are available when you send mail while within the Berkeley Mail program.

Task 20.5: The Smarter Electronic Mail Alternative, elm

DESCRIPTION Just as line editors pale compared to screen editors such as vi, so does Berkeley Mail when compared to the Elm Mail System, or elm. Although it's not available on all UNIX systems, the Elm Mail System is widely distributed, and if you don't have it on your system, your system's vendor should be able to help out.

The basic premise of elm is that the user should be able to focus on the message, not the medium. Emphasis is placed on showing human information. The best way to show how it works is to go straight into it!

JUST A MINUTE

I'm probably just a bit biased about elm because I am the author of the program. The widespread acceptance of the design, however, suggests that I'm not alone in having sought a friendlier alternative to Berkeley Mail.

Another mailer with a very similar user interface is Pine. If you have access to both Elm and Pine, however, I recommend that you pick Elm because it lets you work with your mail in a much more efficient manner.

ACTION

1. To start up the Elm Mail System, enter elm:

```
% elm
```

The screen clears and is replaced with this:

```
Mailbox is '/usr/spool/mail/taylor' with 15 messages [ELM 2.3 PL11]

-->  1   Dec 8   v892127@nooteboom. (52)   Re: Have you picked up the com
     2   Dec 7   Mickey Harris     (214)   Various writing environments
     3   Dec 7   Cheryl            (24)    Computer Based GRE's
     4   Dec 7   Mickey Harris     (69)    Re: Writing Lab OWL project
     5   Dec 7   Russell Holt      (37)    flash cards
```

```
      6   Dec 7   Bill McInerney      (121)  New Additions to U.S. Dept
      7   Dec 5   Mickey Harris        (29)  Re: OWL non-stuff
      8   Dec 5   Rob Sartin           (31)  I need your address
      9   Dec 4   J=TAYLOR@MA@168ARG   (28)  Note to say HI!
OU  10   Dec 3   Linda Wei           (143)  Re: Attachments to XALT


     You can use any of the following commands by pressing the first char
   d)elete or u)ndelete mail, m)ail a message, r)eply or f)orward, q)uit
     To read a message, press <return>.  j=move down, k=move up, ?=help

Command: _
```

The current message is indicated by the arrow (or, on some screens, the entire message line appears in inverse video). Whenever possible, elm shows the name of the person who sent the message (for example, Mickey Harris rather than mharris as in Berkeley Mail), indicates the number of lines in the message (in parentheses), and shows the subject of the message.

The last few lines on the screen indicate the options available at this point. Notice that j and k move the cursor up and down the list, just as they move up and down lines in vi.

2. To read a message, use the j key to zip down to the appropriate message and press Return. You then will see this:

```
Message 3/15  From Cheryl                       Dec 7 '93 at 4:57 pm est
                        Computer Based GRE's


I've scheduled to take the computer based GRE's in Indy on Jan. 6th.
Call me crazy but someone's got to do it.  I'll let you know how it
goes.

Do you know anyone else that has taken the GRE's this way?  I figure
there's a paper in it somewhere.....

If you have that handout from seminar in a file, could you please
send it to me?

Thanks.




Command ('i' to return to index): _
```

At this point, you can use j to read the next message directly, r to reply, or i to return to the table of contents.

3. I realized that I said something in my message to Cheryl that was incorrect. I can type r here to reply to her message. Typing r causes the last few lines of the screen to be replaced with this:

```
-----------------------------------------------------------------------
Command: Reply to message                    Copy message? (y/n) n
```

To include the text of the message in your response, type y. I don't want to, so I press Return:

```
-----------------------------------------------------------------------
Command: Reply to message     To: CBUTCHER (Cheryl)
Subject of message: Re: Computer Based GRE's_
```

Now you can see the address to which the response will be sent, the name of the recipient (in parentheses), and the subject of the message. (The elm command automatically adds the Re prefix to the subject.) The cursor sits at the end of the subject line so you can change the subject if you wish. It's fine, so I again press Return:

```
-----------------------------------------------------------------------
Command: Reply to message     To: CBUTCHER(Cheryl)
Subject of message: Re: Computer Based GRE's
Copies To: _
```

No copies are needed, so I again press Return. The bottom of the screen now looks like this:

```
-----------------------------------------------------------------------
Command: Reply to message     To: CBUTCHER(Cheryl)
Subject of message: Re: Computer Based GRE's
Copies to:

Enter message.  Type Elm commands on lines by themselves.
Commands include:  ^D or '.' to end, ~p to list, ~? for help.


_
```

Notice that ~p and ~? are available. In fact, all the tilde commands available in Berkeley Mail also are available in the Elm Mail System.

I enter the message, and end with a .:

```
Just a reminder that we have that seminar tomorrow
afternoon too. See ya there?   -- Dave
.
```

Ending the message calls up this:

```
Please choose one of the following options by parenthesized letter: s
         e)dit message, edit h)eaders, s)end it, or f)orget it.
```

I press Return once more, and the message is sent.

4. I type i to return to the index page and q to quit.

SUMMARY There's a lot more that the Elm Mail System can do to simplify your electronic mail interaction. If elm is available on your system, I encourage you to check it out further, and if you don't, try calling your vendor or a user group to see if someone else can arrange for you to have a copy. Like the Free Software Foundation applications, elm is free. With it you even get the source so you can see how things are done internally if you're so inclined.

Summary

For awhile, you've known that there are other users on your computer system, and you've even learned how to find out what they're doing (with the w command). Now you know how to communicate with them, too!

Here's a word of advice: It can be frustrating and annoying to be pestered by unknown folk, so I recommend that you begin by sending mail to yourself and then to just your friends on the system. After some practice, you'll learn how net etiquette works and what is or isn't appropriate for write or mail.

TIME SAVER

You can learn a lot more about network etiquette by visiting my online Network Etiquette Primer at http://www.intuitive.com/tyu24/netiq.html.

20

Workshop

The Workshop summarizes the key terms you learned and poses some questions about the topics presented in this chapter. It also provides you with a preview of what you will learn in the next hour.

Key Terms

blind carbon copy   An exact copy of a message, sent without the awareness of the original recipient.

carbon copy   An exact copy of a message sent to other people. Each recipient can see the names of all other recipients on the distribution list.

e-mail   Electronically transmitted and received mail or messages.

mail folder   A file containing one or more e-mail messages.

mail header   The `To:`, `From:`, `Subject:`, and other lines at the very beginning of an e-mail message. All lines up to the first blank line are considered headers.

mailbox   A synonym for mail folder.

preserve   Ensure that a message doesn't move out of your incoming mailbox even though you've read it.

starting flag   Parameters that you specify on the command line when you invoke the program.

tilde command   A command beginning with ~ in Berkeley Mail or the Elm Mail System.

undelete   Restore a deleted message to its original state.

Questions

1. Use `tty` to identify your terminal device name, and then use `ls` to look at its current permissions. Do you have messages enabled or disabled? Confirm with the `mesg` command.

2. Try using the `write` command by writing to yourself; or, if you have a friend on the system, try using `write` to say hi and see whether the person knows how to respond. If he or she doesn't respond in about 30 seconds, you might want to enter `To respond to me, type **write joe** at the command line!` (filling in your account name in place of `joe`).

3. Send yourself a message using `mailx`.

4. Now use Berkeley Mail to read your new message, and then save it to a file, delete it, undelete it, and save it to a mail folder.

5. Start Berkeley Mail so that it reads in the newly created mail folder rather than in your default mailbox. What's different?

6. If `elm` is available to you, try using it to read your mail. Do you like this mail program or Berkeley Mail better? Why?

Preview of the Next Hour

In the next hour, you learn about the World Wide Web and how to use Netscape Navigator to access Web sites throughout the world.

20

Hour **21**

Using Netscape To See the World Wide Web

In the previous hour, you learned how to communicate across the Internet with other users via `talk` and `mail`. This hour introduces you to the World Wide Web, the most commonly recognized part of the Internet.

Goals for This Hour

In this hour, you learn

- ☐ The basics of the Internet
- ☐ How to start your browser
- ☐ How to find some sites
- ☐ How to customize your browser

The Internet and its predecessors have been around for as long as, or even longer than UNIX. Originally, the Defense Advanced Research Projects Agency, DARPA, decided to build a computer network for national defense. The National Science Foundation also encouraged and funded a network of computers for academic research. As scientists became aware of UNIX, many of these network applications were ported. Because the UNIX operating system was itself designed to be portable between machine architectures, UNIX quickly became the operating system of choice for networking, and it became the backbone of what is now called the Internet.

The most common way to access the Internet today is through a Web browser. The two most common browsers are Netscape's Navigator and Microsoft's Internet Explorer.

Although Microsoft makes a version of its browser for UNIX, Navigator is by far the most popular UNIX browser.

This hour introduces you to the World Wide Web using Netscape Navigator.

Introduction to the Internet

The Internet is a very interesting organization of computers. When most people hear the word *Internet*, they immediately think of the World Wide Web and Web browsers. The Internet is really a lot more than that.

The first use of the Internet's predecessors was to transfer data from one machine to another, primarily for either defense-related applications (such as missile targeting, code breaking, and the like) or scientific research. Early in the Internet's life, the capability to send messages between users was added. This has since developed into what is now called *electronic mail*, or *e-mail*. E-mail messages were exchanged initially back in the late 1960's.

Two subsequent additions were the capabilities to transfer files and to remotely access machines. These capabilities, defined as *protocols*, have evolved into FTP (for transferring files) and Telnet (for remotely accessing machines). Protocols are the underlying methods on the Internet that enable two different machines to exchange information. The UNIX tools that implement these protocols are described in greater detail in the next hour.

In the late 1970s, two graduate students, Tom Truscott at Duke University and Steve Bellovin at the University of North Carolina, developed a means to transmit general-purpose messages between the two campuses. This has since evolved into Netnews, which is essentially a bulletin board system (BBS) where messages are not stored on a single machine but are shared between all the machines that contact the BBS.

The 1980s saw the addition of the Internet Relay Chat (IRC) protocol. These are text messages shared instantly with other people subscribed to a discussion. This is where you can take part in real-time communication with others.

Another protocol was introduced by the University of Minnesota, and in homage to the university's mascot, it is naturally called Gopher. This was a means of making files available to browsers anywhere on the Web. Details on using gopher are in Hour 22, "Internet E-Mail, Netnews, and IRC."

21

All of these remained primarily text oriented. Sure, there is a standard, called *MIME* (multimedia Internet mail extension), for sending pictures, sounds, and other non-text files via e-mail and Netnews, but its use is still rather restricted. Even so, MIME requires the translation of the images into a form of text that is again translated at the receiving end. There was still a need for a method to transmit sound, images, movies, and other data via the Internet. These problems have been addressed in the World Wide Web.

Underneath the Web is a protocol called HTTP, for *hyper-text transfer protocol.* This protocol allows for the transmission of non-text files for images, as well as text for pages. HTTP is the underpinnings of Web communications.

On the presentation level is a language called HTML, for *hypertext markup language.* This is an interpreted mark-up language that specifies layout and presentation of information. The file that you create will not look like the file displayed. A markup language is one where the formatting instructions of a document are actually text that is interspersed (and visible) throughout the document, and you don't see the effects of them until the document is interpreted by a printer or browser. In WYSIWYG word processors, such as Word, the formatting instructions are in the document, but you don't see them.

Web browsers, however, go far beyond using HTTP. You can specify in HTML different links (special sections of a document that you can use to access other documents), using a fairly large number of protocols. Mail, Netnews, FTP, Telnet, Gopher, and HTTP all are supported by most browsers. This tends to make the browser a universal tool for accessing many of the resources on the Internet.

Task 21.1: Starting Your Browser

DESCRIPTION   This section introduces you to the basics of Netscape Navigator. Navigator has many command-line options, but the primary methods you learn here are for surfing the Net, starting at a specific site, or examining your own local files.

ACTION   Before you get started with Navigator, you need to be running the X Window System, which I refer to as "X." X is the standard graphical interface for most UNIX systems and usually can be started with the command `startx`. On my system, you won't even need to do that because once you log in, you are already running X. If you can move your mouse on a UNIX system, odds are you have the X Window System installed.

If you can't run X, talk with your system administrator or your software provider. You'll be amazed how much better UNIX looks when you have a graphical interface to help out!

The next step is to enter the command `netscape` at the shell prompt. This first either brings up a license agreement, as shown in Figure 21.1 (if this is the first time you've run Navigator), or just brings up the main browser window. After a short period of time (long enough for you to read all the legal mumbo-jumbo), this window is replaced by the Netscape home page (see Figure 21.2).

21

Figure 21.1.

The Navigator license agreement.

Netscape is licensed software. Its use is subject to the
terms and conditions of the license agreement below.

BY CLICKING ON THE "ACCEPT" BUTTON OR OPENING THE PACKAGE, YOU ARE
CONSENTING TO BE BOUND BY THIS AGREEMENT. IF YOU DO NOT AGREE TO ALL
OF THE TERMS OF THIS AGREEMENT, CLICK THE "DO NOT ACCEPT" BUTTON AND
THE INSTALLATION PROCESS WILL NOT CONTINUE OR RETURN THE PRODUCT TO
THE PLACE OF PURCHASE FOR A FULL REFUND.

NETSCAPE NAVIGATOR END USER LICENSE AGREEMENT
REDISTRIBUTION NOT PERMITTED

This Agreement has 3 parts. Part I applies if you have not purchased
a license to the accompanying software (the "Software"). Part II
applies if you have purchased a license to the Software. Part III
applies to all license grants. If you initially acquired a copy of
the Software without purchasing a license and you wish to purchase a
license, contact Netscape Communications Corporation ("Netscape") on
the Internet at http://home.netscape.com.

If you accept the terms of this license agreement,
press 'Accept.' Otherwise press 'Do Not Accept.'

Accept   Do Not Accept

Figure 21.2.

The Netscape home page.

File   Edit   View   Go   Bookmarks   Options   Directory   Window   Help

Back   Forward   Home   Edit   Reload   Images   Open   Print   Find   Stop

Netsite: http://home.netscape.com/   N

What's New? What's Cool? Destinations   Net Search   People   Software

WELCOME TO
NETSCAPE
YOUR GUIDE TO NAVIGATING THE NET

GUIDE TO | COMPANY & | INTRANET | DEVEDGE | GENERAL | ASSISTANCE | ONE STOP
INTERNET | PRODUCTS | SOLUTIONS | ONLINE | STORE | | SOFTWARE

NETSCAPE ANNOUNCES INCREASED Q1 REVENUES

APRIL 26-28, 1997   GET THE LATEST NETSCAPE SOFTWARE

Netscape reports revenues of $120 million for
the first quarter ending March 31, 1997, marking   Pull down to select product
a 114 percent increase over revenues for the
same period in 1996.

• Netscape outlines its vision for a new type of   Need JavaScript?
                                                       Download Navigator.

Document: Done.

JUST A MINUTE

If Navigator doesn't start for you, it may not be installed. Read about
ftp in the next hour, and then ftp a copy of Navigator from
ftp.netscape.com and install it. Be certain to get the right Navigator
for your hardware.

If you have problems doing this, talk with your system administrator.

21

JUST A MINUTE

> You may not end up on the Netscape home page. This is entirely dependent on the configuration set up by the software provider. For example, on BSDI UNIX (a BSD product for Intel Computers distributed by Berkeley Systems Design, Inc.), the default home page is `http://www.bsdi.com`, their corporate home page. You can change your default starting page pretty easily from the Preferences section of the program.

When you reach this window, you can click on the text that is underlined in blue (these are the hypertext links on the Web page), or you can click on buttons displayed on the Web page or buttons displayed by the browser itself to go to new locations.

A good place to start is the What's New page (see Figure 21.3). Click on the What's New? button in your browser to get a listing of new sites.

Figure 21.3.

Netscape's What's New site.

Being interested in wildlife, I'll click on the "Arabian Wildlife Online" link to visit that site, as shown in Figure 21.4.

You can continue from there to explore other sites.

Another means of starting Navigator is by specifying a URL on the command line. This starts Navigator at the specified location:

```
% netscape http://www.internetmall.com
```

21

Figure 21.4.

The Arabian Wildlife Online Web site.

This particular command sends you to the largest location for shopping on the Internet, as shown in Figure 21.5, and you can explore the different stores from there. If you want to see how people are making money on the Net, this is a good place to start!

Figure 21.5.

Shop 'til you drop at The Internet Mall.

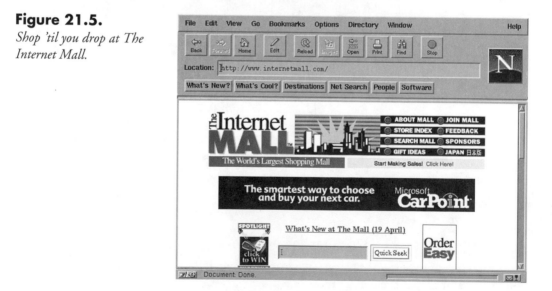

The last method to start Navigator is by specifying a local file on the command line. If the file is HTML, it will be loaded, and you will see it displayed in the browser. (This is a good method for testing pages you are writing without making them publicly available.) If the file is text, it is displayed purely as text, and if it's a graphic of either type XBM (an X bitmap format), GIF (Graphics Interchange Format, probably the most common form of graphics on the Web), or JPEG (Joint Photographic Experts Group, a high-color format), the graphic will be displayed against a gray background in the browser.

I've been working on a site called Raptor World and recently wrote the page describing the bald eagle (see Figure 21.6). I could check and see how it looks simply by typing netscape followed by the name of the file, baea.html:

```
% netscape baea.html
```

Figure 21.6.

You also can view local files with Netscape.

| File | Edit | View | Go | Bookmarks | Options | Directory | Window | | Help |

Back Forward Home Edit Reload Images Open Print Find Stop

Location: file:/home/james/html/raptor/species/baea.html

What's New? What's Cool? Destinations Net Search People Software

Bald Eagle

Name
    Bald Eagle
Latin Name
    haliaeetus leucocephalus
Also known as
    ○ American Eagle
    ○ Fishing Eagle
    ○ Washington Eagle
Description
    The bald eagle is the second largest raptor in North America, trailing only the California Condor. The image of an adult bird is well known to anyone growing up in the United States; the white head and white tail, with the dark brown body is a familiar image.

You may note the strange graphic under the title, "Bald Eagle." This is a placeholder for a picture that I plan to add later. It isn't there yet, so the browser doesn't know what to place there. This and other changes need to be made to the page before I bring up the page online.

If you find a site you are interested in visiting, you can pull down the Bookmark menu and add the site to your list of *bookmarks*. Bookmarks are sites that you have decided are interesting and that you want to save for easy recall. Then, you can later pull down that menu and go straight to that site.

SUMMARY There are three simple methods for getting started with Navigator. You can first visit your default home page and surf the Web from there, you can go to a specific location as your starting point, or you can use Navigator to examine files on your home system.

Task 21.2: Finding Some Sites

DESCRIPTION One of the biggest weaknesses in the Web is the lack of organization. People who write Web pages try to keep their own sites organized, but the volume of information out there is large, and finding the information you want can be difficult.

ACTION Here, I set out with a plan. I'm a fan of Duke basketball, so I want to find out as much information about the team as there is available. There are several sites that have search engines to find information on the Web. One of the oldest is Yahoo!, http://www.yahoo.com/, so let's start there. Yahoo! is shown in Figure 21.7.

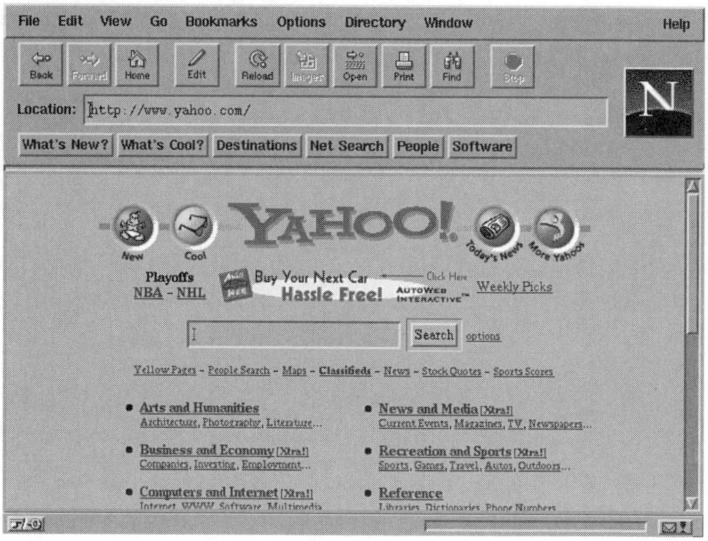

Figure 21.7.

Despite the weird name, Yahoo! is very serious about searching the Web.

The most likely search location is Sports, under Recreation and Sports. So, I'll click on that and see what information is there (see Figure 21.8).

As you can see, basketball is listed—with over 2,600 links! If I click on that link, I see the screen displayed in Figure 21.9.

Figure 21.8.
Use Yahoo!'s tree structure to drill down to the topic you want.

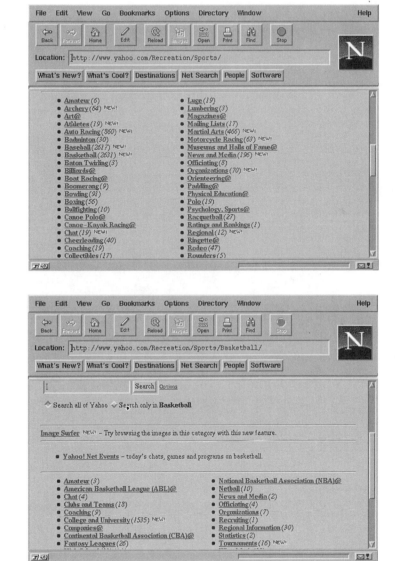

Figure 21.9.
Each topic breaks down into more diverse sub-topics.

The next stop is obviously College and University, which takes me to Figure 21.10.

21

Figure 21.10.
Finally, the goal is close at hand.

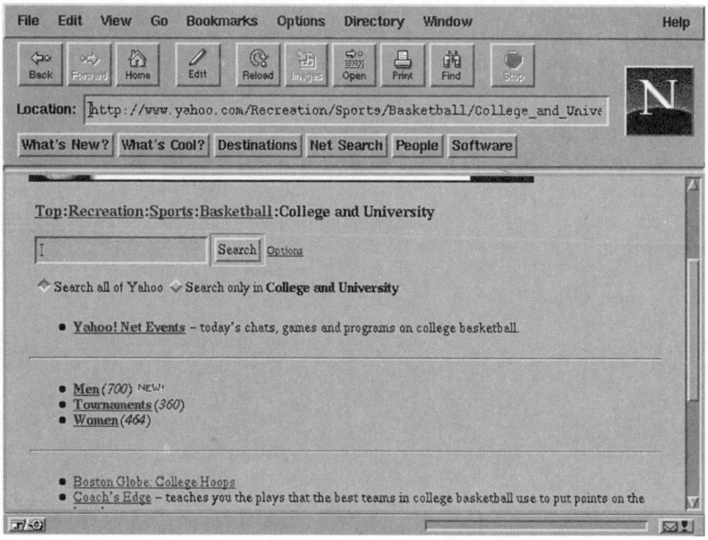

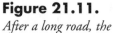

And from there to Men, then Teams, which reveals what's in Figure 21.11.

Figure 21.11.
After a long road, the goal is reached.

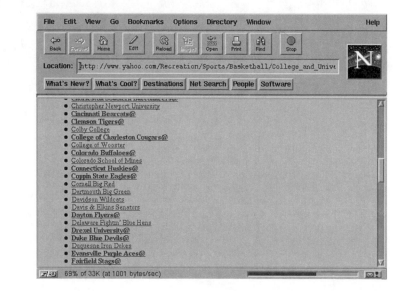

Finally! I see Duke Blue Devils listed. If I click this, I find there are seven links (see Figure 21.12).

Figure 21.12.

Many links are cross-referenced under different topics.

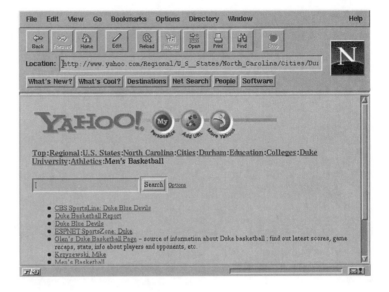

As shown in Figure 21.12, the title has changed to refer to all Duke athletics. Most of the pages refer to basketball. The most interesting page looks like Duke Basketball Report (see Figure 21.13), so I'll click there.

Figure 21.13.

Welcome to North Carolina.

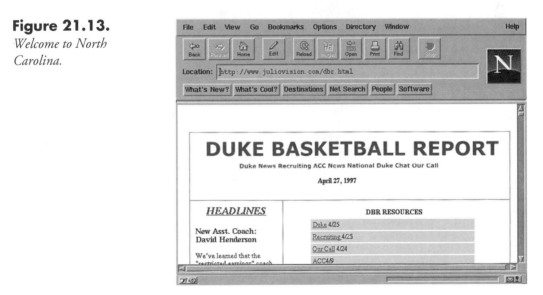

This page is good, so I'll set a bookmark to it. To do this, pull down the Bookmarks menu from the title bar and select Add Bookmark.

Another search method is to use a site that has a Web crawler to index pages. *Web crawlers* are specialized programs that search out Web sites and attempt to index them.

AltaVista is one such Web crawler. So, I first go to their home page, `http://www.altavista.digital.com/` (see Figure 21.14).

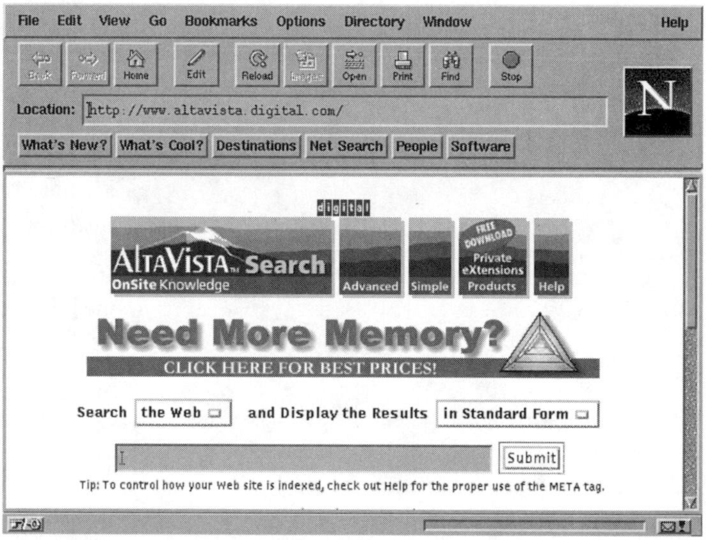

Figure 21.14.

The AltaVista home page.

This is a search system, so I enter Duke basketball in the Submit box. This produces a much longer list of sites (see Figure 21.15), but on the first page, I see 10 sites, including the Duke Basketball Report I just bookmarked.

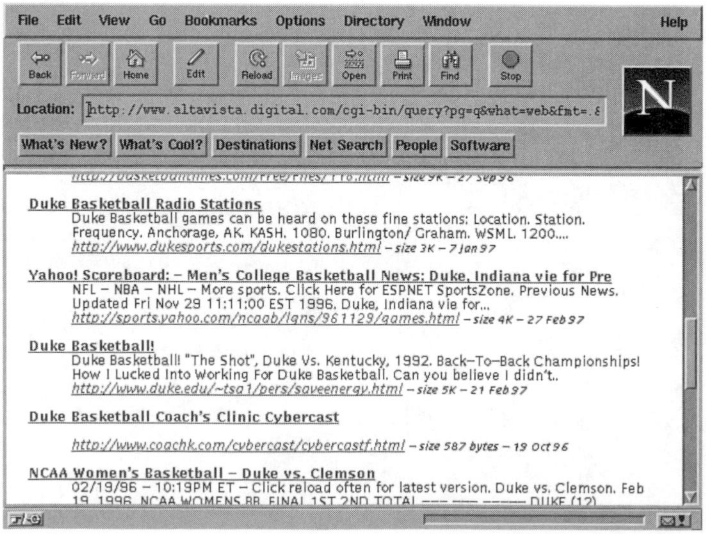

Figure 21.15.

The search results.

I can search over this list and find other places that aren't registered with Yahoo!. I am particularly interested in the page with "The Shot." So, I click on that page and find a set of pictures from Duke's recent history. One is of the exultation after Christian Laettner hit the shot to beat Kentucky in overtime in 1992, and one is of the back-to-back NCAA championship banners. A great site.

SUMMARY Finding information on the Web can be tricky, but many sites exist that attempt to catalog Web sites. Of the several starting points, Yahoo! and AltaVista provide copious volumes of data.

Task 21.3: Customizing Your Browser

DESCRIPTION Once you've been using Navigator for a while, you may want to change how it appears. Fortunately, Navigator is quite customizable, by using the Options menu.

After you have started Navigator, click on the Options button on the menu bar. At the top of the menu are five areas for customization. The one I'll look at today is General Preferences.

There are five tabs under General Preferences that provide areas for customization: Appearance, Fonts, Applications, Helpers, and Images, as shown in Figure 21.16. Under Appearance, you can change your default home page. Because I liked that Duke Basketball Report page, I can enter it. By clicking OK, I make that my default home page.

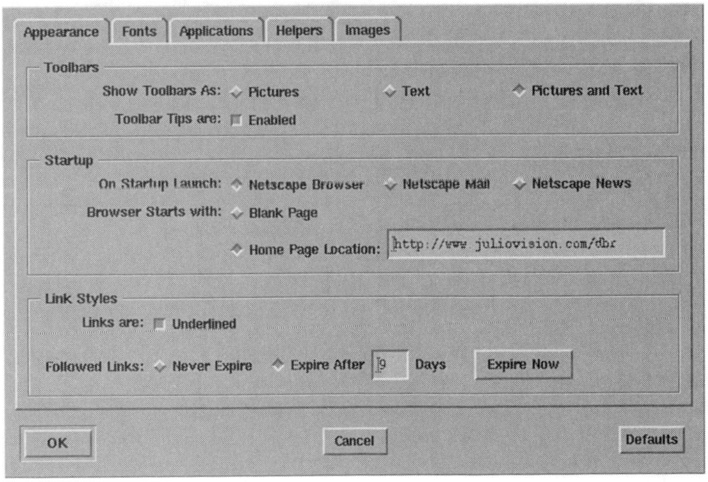

Figure 21.16.
Navigator's General Preferences window.

Under Fonts (see Figure 21.17), I find a list of different fonts available and in different sizes. Here, I've changed the font size to be a bit larger and to use New Century Schoolbook as my typeface. When I look at my home page with this new font setting, it looks like Figure 21.18.

21

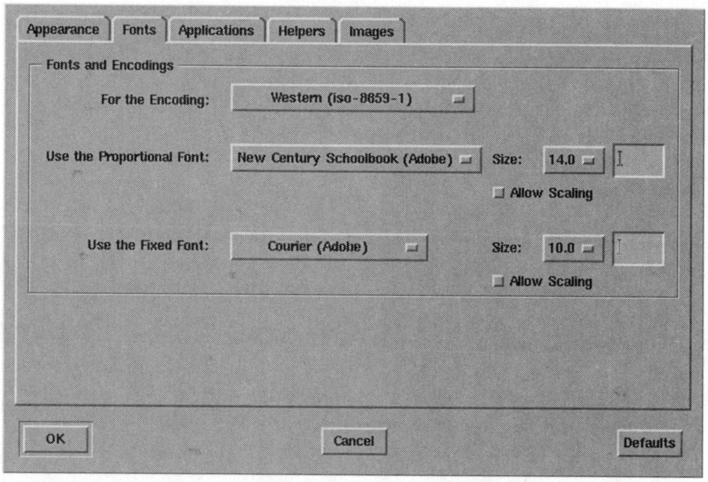

Figure 21.17.
Changing your font settings.

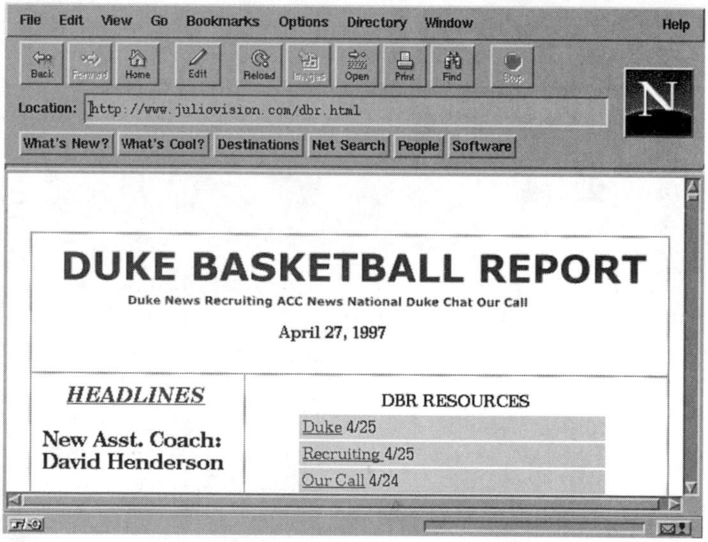

Figure 21.18.
Customize the look of every Web page you visit.

The next option is for Applications (see Figure 21.19). These are the commands started by Navigator when a protocol is requested. I'll leave these intact. If you have a different UNIX configuration than the default, you may want to change them. Check with your administrator.

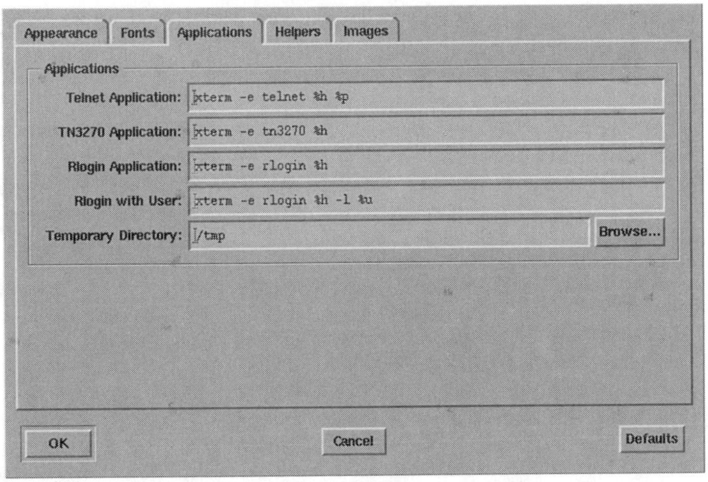

Figure 21.19.

*You can use any applica-
tion to view sites out on
the Net.*

Helpers (shown in Figure 21.20) are tools to interpret MIME input, the mechanism by which Web servers send different types of Web page elements such as graphics, audio, and so on. I would recommend extreme caution before you modify any of these settings lest you end up being unable to display common Web page elements.

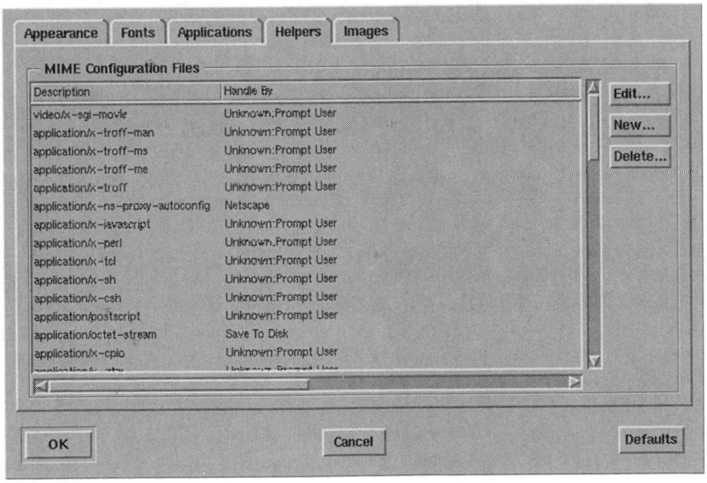

Figure 21.20.

*The list of helper
applications.*

The last tab under General Preferences is Images, shown in Figure 21.21. These define how images are displayed; because I'd rather not see an incomplete image, I click Display Images After Loading.

21

Figure 21.21.
Set up how images are displayed.

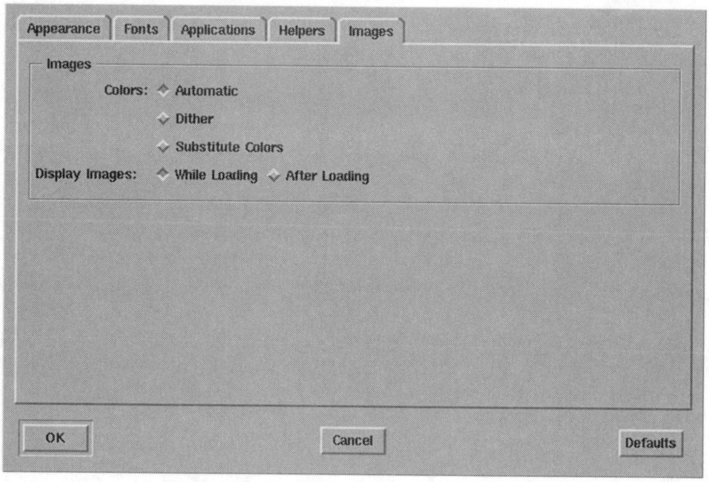

SUMMARY   Navigator is fully customizable from the Options menu on your browser. Although normally it is set up for the standard UNIX configuration, if you have differences from the norm, you will need to customize Navigator.

Summary

This hour introduced you to the basics of Netscape Navigator and the World Wide Web. Now you know how to start and use Navigator to access resources on the Internet and how to find resources through different search engines.

Workshop

The Workshop summarizes the key terms you learned and poses some questions about the topics presented in this chapter. It also provides you with a preview of what you will learn in the next hour.

Key Terms

bookmarks   A listing of favorite sites for quick retrieval.

browser   A program designed to load hypertext pages and follow hyperlinks.

hyperlinks   Specifications within a document that include instructions for loading a different document.

surfing   A style of interacting with the World Wide Web, usually for pleasure, where you follow hyperlinks from Web site to Web site.

21

URL The specification for a document on the World Wide Web. Usually, it includes a protocol, machine name, and filename.

World Wide Web A collection of sites that provide hypertext documents on the Internet.

Questions
1. How would you find sites about General Custer?
2. Where is Sagarmatha National Park?
3. How would you change your default home page?

Preview of the Next Hour
In the next hour, we look at different Internet tools, including Internet e-mail and Netnews.

21

Hour 22

Internet E-Mail, Netnews, and IRC

I thought you might enjoy a guided tour of some of the more astounding resources on the Internet, a global network of UNIX and other computer systems—all connected by high-speed links. Most of these resources require you to have an account on a machine that's connected to the Internet, but a surprising number of them have electronic mail alternatives, too, so you won't be completely in the cold even if you don't have an account. If you don't have access to the Internet, I encourage you to read this final hour just to get a feel for the astounding amount and variety of information and services already available on the fastest growing network in the world.

Goals for This Hour

In this hour, you learn about

- [ ] Sending e-mail to Internet users
- [ ] Talking with remote Internet users
- [ ] Searching databases with WAIS

    ☐ Having the whole world with `gopher`

    ☐ All the news that's fit or otherwise

This hour is intended to offer a quick and enjoyable overview of the many services available through the Internet. From finding that long-lost archive to looking for a book at a library overseas, the range of information available undoubtedly will astound you!

Task 22.1: Sending E-Mail to Internet Users

DESCRIPTION The most common use of the Internet is probably to send electronic mail between individuals and to mailing lists. What's really a boon is that everyone, from New York to Los Angeles, Japan to Germany, South Africa to India, has an address that's very similar, and you've already seen it shown here! The notation is *user@host.domain*, where *user* is the account name or full name, *host* is the name of the user's machine, and *domain* is the user's location in the world.

By reading the host and domain information from right to left (from the outside in, really), you can decode information about someone by looking at the person's e-mail address. My address at a system called Netcom, for example, is `taylor@netcom2.netcom.com`, which, reading right to left, tells you that I'm at a commercial site (`com`), with a company by the name of Netcom (`netcom`), and the name of the computer I'm using is `netcom2`. My account on Netcom is `taylor`.

There are lots of top-level domains, and the most common are shown in Table 22.1.

Table 22.1. Common top-level Internet domains.

Domain	Type of Site or Network
edu	Educational sites
com	Commercial businesses
mil	Military or defense systems
net	Alternative networks accessible via Internet
org	Nonprofit organizations
us	United States systems not otherwise classified

ACTION

1. To send mail to someone on the Internet is easy because the C shell doesn't view the @ as a special character. If you'd like to send me a message, for example, you could use this:

```
% mailx taylor@netcom.com
Subject: _
```

Enter the message and end it with a ^d as you would in any e-mail message. It is immediately sent to me!

> I encourage you to drop me a note if you're so inclined, letting me know how you're enjoying this book, any problems you might have encountered, and any commands you were puzzled by that might be easier with a bit more explanation. If nothing else, just say hi!

2. Although electronic mail addresses always follow the same format, they can vary quite a bit. To give you an idea of the variation, I used grep to extract the From: addresses of some mail I've recently received:

```
% grep '^From:' /usr/spool/mail/taylor
From: Steve Frampton <frampton@vicuna.ocunix.on.ca>
From: Joanna Tsang <tsang@futon.SFSU.EDU>
From: "Debra Isserlis" <disserli@us.oracle.com>
From: "Jay Munro [PC Mag]" <72241.554@CompuServe.COM>
From: ljw@ras.amdahl.com (Linda Wei)
From: Cheryl <CBUTCHER@VM.CC.PURDUE.EDU>
From: harrism@mace.utech.edu (Mickey Harris)
From: v892127@nooteboom.si.hhs.nl
From: "ean houts" <ean_houts@ccgate.infoworld.com>
From: harrism@mace.utech.edu (Mickey Harris)
From: "Barbara Maxwell" <maxwell@sales.synergy.com>
From: steve@xalt.com (Steve Mansour)
From: abhasin@itsmail1.hamilton.edu (Aditya Bhasin)
From: gopher@scorpio.kent.edu
From: marv@netcom.com (Marvin Raab)
```

The national convention for the From: line in electronic mail clearly varies. There are three basic notations you see in this line: just an address, such as the one from gopher@scorpio.kent.edu; an address with the name in parentheses, such as the message from Linda Wei about halfway down the list; and a line with the person's name followed by his or her e-mail address in angle brackets, such as the first listed line.

Notice the various sites from which I've received electronic mail in the past few days: SFSU.EDU is San Francisco State University, oracle.com is Oracle Corporation in California, PURDUE.EDU is Purdue University, CompuServe.COM is the CompuServe network, ccgate.infoworld.com is *InfoWorld* magazine's Macintosh network running cc:Mail, xalt.com is from XALT Corporation, and kent.edu is Kent State University. The message from v892127@nooteboom.si.hhs.nl is from an educational institution in The Netherlands!

To decode these addresses, you need to have a lot of information, some excellent guesses, a glance at an Organization: line that might appear in the messages, or, if you're on a system with all the latest software, an invocation of the netinfo command to explain the site you're curious about.

SUMMARY Sending electronic mail back and forth with users throughout the world is one of the most exciting and fun parts of learning UNIX. I often read magazine articles, for example, in which the author lists an electronic mail address. It's a simple task to zip out a message if I have questions or kudos on the piece. Many magazines, from the *Utne Reader* to *MacWorld*, even list electronic mail addresses for the editorial staff. Even reporters from *The Wall Street Journal* and the *New York Times* are on the Internet now.

Task 22.2: Talking with Remote Internet Users

DESCRIPTION To see who is logged in to a remote system, you can use a command called finger, which by default will show you a summary of who is on the local machine. Add a user name to the command, and it will show information about the specified account. Specify a user on a remote system, and you can find out if that user is logged in. Specify just the remote site, and it shows you who is logged in at the current moment. To check on a local account, use finger *accountname*. To make it a remote system, append the hostname: finger *account@host.domain*. To check all users on a remote site, use finger *@host.domain*.

Once you've ascertained that a friend is logged in to a local or remote system, you can use the talk program to chat with the person live across the Internet. As opposed to the primitive line-oriented mode of write, talk is a full-screen program that enables both of you to type at the same time. Your screen always shows the other person's typing on the bottom half of your screen.

ACTION

1. A quick glance at the output of who shows that there are a lot of people currently logged in to the local system:

```
% finger
Login       Name                TTY Idle    When      Location
root        root                *co 1:13 Mon 18:02
taylor      Dave Taylor         aV       Mon 16:49
kippje      Jeff Kip            Ab       Mon 16:41
adamr       Adam Coy            *Ae      Mon 18:36
daffnelr    Lawrence Daff       sK       Mon 12:45  (dov27)
tsa         Earl the Unctuous Aardva sL 42 Mon 12:48 (expert)
daffnelr    Lawrence Daff       *sM      Mon 12:49  (localhost)
ben         Ben Moon            sN  8:42 Mon 09:16  (corona)
ben         Ben Moon            sR  8:47 Mon 09:22  (corona)
marteldr    David Martel        *sY    7d Mon 18:41 (limbo)
gerlema     David Geman         sb       Mon 18:38  (mac19)
mk          Michael Kenzie      *sc 2:48 Mon 08:07  (mk)
mzabel      Mary Zabeliski      *sf      Mon 18:45  (sun1)
fritzg      Geoff Fritzen       sh    9 Mon 18:45   (pc43)
brynta      Bryan Ayerson       *si      Mon 18:46  (limbo)
deckersl    Sharon Deck         sk    3 Mon 18:51   (xds31)
```

22

2. To learn more about the account mk, I can specify that account name to the finger program:

```
% finger mk

Login name: mk           (messages off) Real name: Michael Kenzie
Office: Math 204                         Home phone:
Directory: /users/mk                     Shell: /bin/ksh
Universe: universe(ucb)
Member of groups: utech root actadmin source
On since Dec 13 08:07:12 on ttysc from mk
2 hours 50 minutes Idle Time
No unread mail on this host.
Plan:
```

You can see that this is full of information. Notice that Michael is currently logged in to the system (the output says On since Dec 13 08:07:12 on ttysc).

3. To see who is logged in to the USENIX Association main computer in Berkeley, California, I can use this:

```
% finger @usenix.org
[usenix.org]
Login    Name              TTY Idle    When     Where
pmui     Peter Mui         co   2d Tue 10:10
ah       Alain Henon       Z5      Mon 15:58     remote # 5408955 Dia
toni     Toni Veglia       p1   3d Thu 17:09     exec
diane    Diane DeMartini   p3    9 Mon 08:41     mac2.usenix.ORG
mis      Mark Seiden       p4   3d Thu 21:46     seiden.com
mis      Mark Seiden       p5   2d Fri 15:18     msbnext.internex
scott    Scott Seebass     p6   3d Tue 14:54     biohazard
lilia    Lilia Carol Scott p7 1:12 Mon 08:39     thing1
mis      Mark Seiden       p8   3d Thu 22:09     seiden.com
toni     Toni Veglia       pa   3d Mon 10:38     exec
ellie    Ellie Young       q1 1:00 Mon 10:33     boss:0.0
scott    Scott Seebass     q2  18: Wed 15:36     biohazard
ellie    Ellie Young       q3 1:01 Mon 10:33     boss:0.0
mis      Mark Seiden       q6   1d Fri 11:28     seiden.com
```

Here you can see that lots of folks are logged in, but that almost everyone has a lot of idle time. A d suffix indicates the number of days idle. So, you can see that Peter Mui's account has been idle for two days.

JUST A MINUTE

To find out what the weather is like in the greater San Francisco area, try finger weather@rogue.llnl.gov, which will connect you to the Lawrence Livermore National Laboratories in Walnut Creek, California.

4. To learn more information about a specific user on a remote site, specify the name of the user and the name of the user's system:

```
% finger ellie@usenix.org
[usenix.org]
```

```
Login name: ellie                    In real life: Ellie Young
Directory: /staff/ellie              Shell: /bin/csh
On since Dec 13 10:33:57 on ttyq1 from boss:0.0
1 hour 3 minutes Idle Time
Mail last read Mon Dec 13 15:05:08 1993
No Plan.
```

You can see that Ellie has been logged in since December 13 but has had over an hour of idle time.

5. To talk with someone on a remote system, use finger to verify that the person is logged in, not off doing something else (which is what a high idle time usually suggests), use talk:

```
% finger marv@netcom.com
Login name: marv                     In real life: Marvin Raab
Directory: /u1/marv                  Shell: /bin/csh
Logged in since Mon Dec  6 15:22 on ttys8
5 seconds idle time
Mail last read Mon Dec 13 15:22:22 1993
No Plan.
% talk marv@netcom.com
```

```
[Waiting for your party to respond]




----------------------------------------------------------------------
```

On the remote system, here's what Marvin sees:

```
Message for marv(ttyaV) from Talk-Daemon@limbo.utech.edu at 18:55 ...
talk: connection requested by taylor@limbo.utech.edu.
talk: respond with: "talk taylor@limbo.utech.edu"
```

Once he responds, the screen looks like this:

22

```
[Connected]
_




- - - - - - - - - - - - - - - - - - - - - - - - - - - - - - - - - - - - - - - - - -
Hi Dave! What's going on?
```

Notice that the cursor is in the top pane. Anything I enter will be sent along to Marvin, character by character, so we can interactively chat and even type at the same time without our words getting jumbled. When I'm done, I simply press ^C to quit the program.

SUMMARY The finger program offers further information about users on your own and remote systems, and using it is an essential first step in talking with your friends on the Internet via talk. Try entering taylor@netcom.com, and if I'm logged in, what the heck! Try using talk to say hi interactively!

Task 22.3: Searching Databases with WAIS

DESCRIPTION The next stop on your tour of Internet information resources is the Wide Area Information Server, or WAIS. The WAIS system is a collection of databases accessible through a single search or query, and it was developed as a joint research project of Apple Computer, Dow Jones News Service, and Thinking Machines, Inc. You can access WAIS by using telnet to connect to a system called quake.think.com at Thinking Machines, Inc., in Boston.

WAIS is a database of databases. As of this writing, there are over 500 databases accessible for conducting searches and queries through the WAIS system. The range of information is astounding—from databases of acronyms to the CIA World Factbook, from White House press releases to cold fusion. The program is reasonably friendly to use, though it takes a bit of experience to be comfortable doing searches.

ACTION

1. To connect to the WAIS system, use `telnet` to connect to `quake.think.com`, and log in as `wais`.

JUST A MINUTE

You can find an alternative WAIS server at the address `wais.com` if `quake.think.com` is unavailable.

```
% telnet quake.think.com
Trying...
Connected to quake.think.com.
Escape character is '^]'.

SunOS UNIX (quake.think.com)
login: wais
Last login: Wed Dec 15 11:13:56 from alexia.lis.uiuc.
SunOS Release 4.1.3 (SUN4C-STANDARD) #9: Wed Oct 27 18:18:30 EDT 1993
Welcome to swais.
Please type user identifier (optional, i.e user@host): taylor@netcom.com
TERM = (vt100)
Starting swais (this may take a little while)...
```

After a few seconds, the screen clears and is replaced by this:

```
SWAIS                          Source Selection              Sources: 510
  #         Server                            Source                  Cost
001: [          archie.au] aarnet-resource-guide               Free
002: [ndadsb.gsfc.nasa.gov] AAS_jobs                           Free
003: [ndadsb.gsfc.nasa.gov] AAS_meeting                        Free
004: [       munin.ub2.lu.se] academic_email_conf              Free
005: [wraith.cs.uow.edu.au] acronyms                           Free
006: [     archive.orst.edu] aeronautics                       Free
007: [ ftp.cs.colorado.edu] aftp-cs-colorado-edu               Free
008: [nostromo.oes.orst.ed] agricultural-market-news           Free
009: [     archive.orst.edu] alt.drugs                         Free
010: [     wais.oit.unc.edu] alt.gopher                        Free
011: [       sunsite.unc.edu] alt.sys.sun                      Free
012: [     wais.oit.unc.edu] alt.wais                          Free
013: [alfred.ccs.carleton.] amiga-slip                         Free
014: [       munin.ub2.lu.se] amiga_fish_contents              Free
015: [   coombs.anu.edu.au] ANU-Aboriginal-EconPolicies  $0.00/minute
016: [   coombs.anu.edu.au] ANU-Aboriginal-Studies       $0.00/minute
017: [   coombs.anu.edu.au] ANU-Ancient-DNA-L            $0.00/minute
018: [   coombs.anu.edu.au] ANU-Ancient-DNA-Studies      $0.00/minute
Keywords:
<space> selects, w for keywords, arrows move, <return> searches, q quits, or ? _
```

You can see here a table of contents of the different databases available for searching through WAIS. Although they're all free of charge at this point, it is entirely possible that at some point in the future some of these databases will have costs associated with them.

Type J and K to move up and down a screen at a time, respectively, and j and k to move up and down a single source. To add a database to a search, type . to select it. An asterisk will show up just before the name of the system that holds the database selected. Type q to quit.

2. To find out more about a particular database, use the v command for version information. When I choose that option for acronyms, here's what I find out:

```
Name:          acronyms.src
Directory:     /sources/
Maintainer:    steve@wraith.cs.uow.edu.au
Selected:      Yes
Cost:          Free
Server:        wraith.cs.uow.edu.au (Accessed)
Service:       210
Database:      acronyms
Description:
Server created with WAIS release 8 b5 on Oct 23 10:49:48 1992 by
steve@wraith.cs.uow.edu.au
        A public domain database of acronyms and abbreviations maintained
        by Dave Sill (de5@ornl.gov).
The files of type one_line used in the index were:
   /shr/lib/wais/wais-sources/acronyms
(END)
```

3. I'm interested in how many acronyms have the word *mail* in them, so I choose the acronym database by pressing the spacebar (an asterisk appears to show that the database has been selected). Then I use w to specify a keyword, in this case mail. A quick search, and the screen now looks like this:

```
SWAIS                          Search Results            Item
  #    Score    Source                   Title           Lines
001:  [1000] (       acronyms) EMAIL  - Electronic MAIL, "E-MAIL"        1
002:  [ 333] (       acronyms) ECOM   - Electronic Computer Originated Ma 1
003:  [ 333] (       acronyms) EMA    - Electronic Mail Association      1
004:  [ 333] (       acronyms) IMAP   - Interactive Mail Access Protocol 1
005:  [ 333] (       acronyms) IMAP3  - Interactive Mail Access Protocol  1
006:  [ 333] (       acronyms) MIME   - Multipurpose Internet Mail Extens 1
007:  [ 333] (       acronyms) MO     - Mail Order        1
008:  [ 333] (       acronyms) MTA    - Mail Transfer Agent    1
009:  [ 333] (       acronyms) MUA    - Mail User Agent    1
010:  [ 333] (       acronyms) MX     - Mail eXchange      1
011:  [ 333] (       acronyms) PBM    - Play By Mail game      1
012:  [ 333] (       acronyms) PEM    - Privacy Enhanced Mail  1
013:  [ 333] (       acronyms) RMS    - Royal Mail Ship        1
```

```
014:    [ 333] (          acronyms)  SMTP   - Simple Mail Transfer Protocol         1
015:    [ 333] (          acronyms)  USM    - United States Mail           1
016:    [ 333] (          acronyms)  VMS    - Voice Mail System         1


<space> selects, arrows move, w for keywords, s for sources, ? for help _
```

4. Here's another way this can be helpful: WAIS lists a database of recipes, and I've been looking for a good oatmeal cookie recipe for quite a while. I can search the recipe database by returning to the main WAIS screen and then entering /rec to move to that particular database:

```
SWAIS                         Source Selection              Sources: 510
   #         Server                     Source                     Cost
397:  [    munin.ub2.lu.se]  rec.gardens                     Free
398:  [  wais.wu-wien.ac.at]  rec.music.early                 Free
399:  [    wais.oit.unc.edu]  rec.pets                        Free
400:  [    wais.oit.unc.edu]  recipes                         Free
401:  [bloch.informatik.uni]  reports-abstracts               Free
402:  [       gopher.uv.es]  Research-in-Surgery             Free
403:  [       wais.cic.net]  rfc-index                       Free
404:  [      ds.internic.net]  rfcs                            Free
405:  [         ns.ripe.net]  ripe-database                   Free
406:  [         ns.ripe.net]  ripe-internet-drafts            Free
407:  [         ns.ripe.net]  ripe-rfc                        Free
408:  [ cmns-moon.think.com]  risks-digest                    Free
409:  [       wais.cic.net]  roget-thesaurus                 Free
410:  [    mpcc3.rpms.ac.uk]  RPMS-pathology                  Free
411:  [ cmns-moon.think.com]  RSInetwork                      Free
412:  [    uniwa.uwa.oz.au]  s-archive                       Free
413:  [athena3.cent.saitama]  saitama-jp                      Free
414:  [RANGERSMITH.SDSC.EDU]  Salk_Genome_Center              Free

<space> selects, w for keywords, arrows move, <return> searches, q quits, or ? _
```

CAUTION

One problem I consistently have with the WAIS programs is that I can't use my Backspace key to erase previous search words. The trick to getting around this is to use ^u to erase the entire line of keywords!

I choose the recipes database, again by pressing the spacebar, then search for keywords cookie and oatmeal to see what kind of oatmeal cookie recipes are available. It indicates 18 matches, sorted in order of the "quality" of the match— the more each keyword occurs, the better the hit. The first number in square brackets indicates the "quality" of the match, with 1,000 being the best possible score. This time, however, the recipe I'm looking for appears to be the lowest-rated in the list:

```
SWAIS                          Search Results                    Item
  #     Score    Source                 Title                    Lines
001:   [1000] (        recipes)  shafer@rig Re: COLLECTION BAKERY Pumpkin   186
002:   [ 957] (        recipes)  shafer@rig Re: COLLECTION BAKERY VEG Bis  1038
003:   [ 696] (        recipes)  Anne Louis Re: BREAD: Bread Recipes Coll  1101
004:   [ 522] (        recipes)  darsie@eec Re: Re: world-wide cookie rec   130
005:   [ 522] (        recipes)  kyoung@prs Re: Diabetic Cookie Recipes      91
006:   [ 522] (        recipes)  the1edr@ca Re: 3 Recipes for Oatmeal Pea   122
007:   [ 435] (        recipes)  WHITEJER@c Re: Re: REQUEST Cookie dough     53
008:   [ 391] (        recipes)  julie@eddi Re: Re: REQUEST Cookie dough     47
009:   [ 348] (        recipes)  anne@csrux Re: Re: REQUEST Cookie dough     53
010:   [ 348] (        recipes)  arielle@ta Re: Appetizers (Long)          1591
011:   [ 348] (        recipes)  kyoung@prs Re: Diabetic Cookie Recipes C    77
012:   [ 348] (        recipes)  arielle@ta Re: Muffins 5                   717
013:   [ 348] (        recipes)  arielle@ta Re: Appetizers                 1590
014:   [ 304] (        recipes)  springer@k Re: Re: REQUEST Cookie dough     44
015:   [ 304] (        recipes)  kyoung@prs Re: Diabetic Treats Cont'd.     109
016:   [ 261] (        recipes)  arielle@ta Re: RECIPE: Ice Cream Sandwic    63
017:   [ 261] (        recipes)  arielle@ta Re: REQUEST Cookie dough for     22
018:   [ 261] (        recipes)  laura@hobb Re: Oatmeal Rasin Cookies (ca    31

<space> selects, arrows move, w for keywords, s for sources, ? for help _
```

To read recipe number 18, I can enter 18 to retrieve the recipe itself:

```
Getting "laura@hobb Re: Oatmeal Rasin Cookies (cake like)" from recipes.src...
Newsgroups: rec.food.recipes
From: laura@hobb.mystery.edu (Laura Smith)
Subject: Oatmeal Rasin Cookies (cake like)
Apparently-To: rec-food-recipes@uunet.uu.net
Organization: The Mystery University
Date: Tue, 22 Dec 1992 15:33:33 GMT
Approved: arielle@taronga.com
Lines: 18


Hi,

      My father was over helping me bake cookies this year for christmas.
He got to talking about an oatmeal cookie that his mother used to make.
These cookies were almost like little individual oatmeal rasin cakes
Unfortunately.. he never got the recipe written down.... I'd really like to
find a recipe and surprise him with them.

--More-- _
```

Voilà! I can sit at my UNIX system and dig up just about anything on the Internet, even cookie recipes!

SUMMARY Of the different services on the Internet, the WAIS system is the one I find the most promising, yet least useful. There are lots of problems with the system, but it's evolving at such a fast pace that I encourage you to try it for yourself. By the time you read this, the program undoubtedly will have changed a fair bit.

Task 22.4: Having the Whole World with gopher

DESCRIPTION At this point, you're probably wondering how people are actually supposed to choose from and navigate all these different services—and rightfully so! A team of programmers at the University of Minnesota wondered just that. They realized that what they wanted was a "go-for," a program that would "go for things." Conveniently the gopher is their school mascot, so the gopher program was born.

Of all the different systems on the Internet, gopher is undoubtedly the easiest to use. It has a simple, menu-based interface that enables you to step through information sources, seamlessly switching from machine to machine throughout the Internet. The program offers some helpful customization, too: As you travel through what's called *gopherspace*, you can mark interesting locations with a bookmark (simply press a at the item), then zoom straight to your list of bookmarks with the v key, to view your bookmarks. If you have bookmarks, gopher -b will start you up with your bookmark page; otherwise, it will display the default gopher introductory page, which varies quite a bit from site to site.

TIME SAVER

> If you don't have the gopher program on your system, you can log in as gopher at consultant.micro.umn.edu, gopher.uiuc.edu, or panda.uiowa.edu. Use telnet to connect.

ACTION

1. I enter gopher at the command line of my account at the UTech University, and the screen is rewritten:

```
                    Internet Gopher Information Client v1.12S

                    Root gopher server: thorplus.utech.edu

    -->  1.  About UTech University.
         2.  About THOR+ the UTech University Libraries Gopher Site.
         3.  Other Information Servers at UTech University/
```

22

```
     4.  Other information Servers on the Internet/
     5.  Thor+ Suggestion Form <TEL>
     6.  Administrivia/
     7.  E-Mail & Telephone Directory for Utech & World Wide/
     8.  Library Catalogs and Gophers/
     9.  University Libraries/
    10.  Weather Reports and Maps/
    11.  Interesting items on the Net (12/7/93)/
    12.  Current Contents On Diskette/
    13.  Instructions for searching Directories of all UTech Gophers .
    14.  Search Directories of all UTech Gophers (experimental) <?>
    15.  *************Explore Internet Teleconference********/
 Press ? for Help, q to Quit, u to go up a menu              Page: 1/1
```

2. By contrast, if I were logged in to the Whole Earth 'lectronic Link (well) computer in San Francisco, I'd get a completely different first screen:

```
                  Internet Gopher Information Client v1.11

                  Root gopher server: gopher2.tc.umn.edu

   -->  1.  Information About Gopher/
        2.  Computer Information/
        3.  Discussion Groups/
        4.  Fun & Games/
        5.  Internet file server (ftp) sites/
        6.  Libraries/
        7.  News/
        8.  Other Gopher and Information Servers/
        9.  Phone Books/
       10.  Search Gopher Titles at the University of Minnesota <?>
       11.  Search lots of places at the University of Minnesota  <?>
       12.  University of Minnesota Campus Information/



  Press ? for Help, q to Quit, u to go up a menu           Page: 1/1
```

3. The sixth entry—Libraries/—sounds interesting, and because it ends with a slash, I can tell that it will move me to another set of menu choices in gopher. The two lines that end with <?> will actually invoke a program (probably to connect me to the University of Minnesota), and lines that end with a dot are files and can be viewed by choosing them.

To move to a specific location, I can enter its number or use j and k to move up and down, just like in vi. Pressing Return chooses the specific item, so I press j five times to move down five items (the arrow moves so that it points to item 6), then I press Return, which changes the screen:

```
                  Internet Gopher Information Client v1.11

                                  Libraries

      --> 1.  Electronic Books/
          2.  Electronic Journal collection from CICnet/
          3.  Information from the U.S. Federal Government/
          4.  Library Catalogs via Telnet/
          5.  Library of Congress Records/
          6.  Newspapers, Magazines, and Newsletters /
          7.  Reference Works/




      Press ? for Help, q to Quit, u to go up a menu          Page: 1/1
```

4. Electronic books sound interesting, but reference works could be even more
   interesting, so I type 7, which instantly moves the arrow to the last item, and then I
   press Return:

```
                  Internet Gopher Information Client v1.11

                               Reference Works

      --> 1.  ACM SIGGRAPH Online Bibliography Project/
          2.  American English Dictionary (from the UK) <?>
          3.  CIA World Fact Book 1991/
          4.  Current Contents/
          5.  ERIC-archive.
          6.  ERIC-archive Search <?>
          7.  Periodic Table of Elements/
          8.  Roget's Thesaurus (Published 1911)/
          9.  The Hacker's Dictionary/
          10. U.S. Geographic Names Database/
          11. U.S. Telephone Area Codes/
          12. US-State-Department-Travel-Advisories/
          13. Webster's Dictionary/

      Press ? for Help, q to Quit, u to go up a menu          Page: 1/1
```

5. The entry for U.S. State Department travel advisories looks valuable, so I'll add it
   to my bookmark collection:

22

22

```
      7.  Periodic Table of Elements/
*************************************************************************
*                                                                       *
* Name for this bookmark?   US-State-Department-Travel-Advisories        *
*                                                                       *
*            [Cancel ^G] [Accept - Enter] *
*                                                                       *
*************************************************************************
```

The default name works fine, so I press Return to move into the choice, then I
see three choices: 1. Search US-State-Department-Travel-Advisories <?>, 2.
Current-Advisories/, and 3. FTP-Archive/. I opt to see what's current, and
type 2:

```
                    Internet Gopher Information Client v1.11

                              Current-Advisories

    -->   1.  afghanistan.
          2.  albania.
          3.  algeria.
          4.  andorra.
          5.  angola.
          6.  antigua-&-barbuda.
          7.  argentina.
          8.  armenia.
          9.  australia.
         10.  austria.
         11.  azerbaijan.
         12.  bahamas.
         13.  bahrain.
         14.  bangladesh.
         15.  barbados.
         16.  belarus.
         17.  belgium.
         18.  belize.

Press ? for Help, q to Quit, u to go up a menu            Page: 1/13
```

Notice that this time the bottom-right corner indicates that this is page 1 of 13, so
there's a lot more information. To move to the next page of information, use the +
key; to move to the previous page, use -. I have visited Belize, so I'd be interested
to see whether there are any current travel advisories on the country. I choose 18,
and the following information is displayed on my screen:

```
STATE DEPARTMENT TRAVEL INFORMATION - Belize
============================================================
Belize - Consular Information Sheet May 27, 1993

Country Description:  Belize is a developing country.  Its tourism facilities
vary in quality.
Entry Requirements:  A passport, a return/onward ticket, and sufficient funds
are required for travel to Belize.  U. S. citizens who stay less than three
months do not need visas.  However, for visits exceeding one month, travelers
must obtain permits from immigration authorities in Belize.  For further
information, travelers may contact the Embassy of Belize at 2535 Massachusetts
Avenue N.W., Washington, D.C. 20008, tel. (202) 332-9636, the Belize Consulate
in Miami, or the Belize Mission to the U.N. in New York.

Medical Facilities:  Medical care is limited.  Doctors and hospitals often
expect immediate cash payment for health services.

U.S. medical insurance is not always valid outside the United States.  In some
cases, supplemental medical insurance with specific overseas coverage has
proved useful.  For additional health
--More--(9%)[Hit space to continue, Del to abort] _
```

This is only nine percent of the information, so there's a lot more to view. Fortunately, I can electronically mail this file to myself when I've finished viewing it, by selecting the m, or mail file, command at the end-of-listing prompt.

JUST A MINUTE

Gopher notation usually has a nested series of lines indicating the actual text that you'd find on a line of gopher output, so this search would be written much more succinctly as:

```
Libraries/
  Reference Works/
    US-State-Department-Travel-Advisories/
      Current Advisories
        belize.
```

I quit by typing q at any prompt in the gopher system.

7. Back at the university, I have heard that there are electronic books available via gopher. I am particularly interested in *Paradise Lost*, a book I read years ago. After a bit of nosing about, I found it through the following gopherspace path:

```
Other Information Servers on the Internet/
  Academic Resources on the Internet (by Subject)/
    Electronic Journals & Texts/
      Project Gutenberg: Clearinghouse for Machine Readable Texts/
        etext92/
          AAINDEX.NEW.
```

The AAINDEX.NEW file produced a list of books available through this clearinghouse for electronic books. Skipping the introductory matter, I find that the following books are currently online:

```
(Books from earlier years will available in 1992)
(but not yet:  to be announced, don't ask yet!!!)
1971 Declaration-Independence                          (whenxxxx.xxx)
1972 Bill of Rights                                    (billxxxx.xxx)
1973 U.S. Constitution                                 (constxxx.xxx)
1974-1982 The Bible                                    (biblexxx.xxx)
1983-1990 Complete Shakespeare                         (shakesxx.xxx)
(Watch for these entries to be moved below later.
The Bible mentioned above is a different edition from the one we just post
for Easter, 1992)
Books currently available on mrcnext (do a dir):
(These 1991 etexts are now in> cd /etext/etext91)
Jan 1991 Alice in Wonderland                           (alice29x.xxx)
Feb 1991 Through the Looking Glass                     (lglass16.xxx)
Mar 1991 The Hunting of the Snark                      (snark12x.xxx)
Apr 1991 1990 CIA World Factbook                       (world11x.xxx)
May 1991 Moby Dick (From OBI)*                         (mobyxxxx.xxx)
Jun 1991 Peter Pan (for US only)**                     (peter14a.xxx)
Jul 1991 The Book of Mormon                            (mormon11.xxx)
Aug 1991 The Federalist Papers                         (feder11x.xxx)
Sep 1991 The Song of Hiawatha                          (hisong10.xxx)
Oct 1991 Paradise Lost                                 (plboss10.xxx)
Nov 1991 Aesop's Fables                                (aesop10x.xxx)
Dec 1991 Roget's Thesaurus                             (roget11x.xxx)
*Moby Dick is missing Hour 72
**Please do not download Peter Pan outside the US
(These 1992 etext releases in> cd /etext/etext92)
Jan 1992 Frederick Douglass                            (duglas10.xxx)
Jan 1992 O Pioneers!  Willa Cather                     (opion10x.xxx)
Feb 1992 1991 CIA World Factbook                       (world91a.xxx)
Feb 1992 Paradise Lost (Raben)                         (plrabn10.xxx)
Mar 1992 Far From the Madding Crowd                    (crowd13x.xxx)
Mar 1992 Aesop's Fables (Advantage)                    (aesopa10.xxx)
Apr 1992 Data From the 1990 Census                     (uscen901.xxx)
Apr 1992 New Etext of Bible (KJV)                      (bible10x.xxx)
May 1992 Sophocles' Oedipus Trilogy                    (oedip10x.xxx)
May 1992*Herland (not yet in place                     (hrlnd10x.xxx)
```

There are more resources than this, but here you can see that if you're interested in obtaining a copy of *Paradise Lost*, you can use gopher to find the book and have it sent via Internet to your home account—in a matter of a few steps!

SUMMARY The gopher system offers a wide variety of capabilities, as you can see, and the connectivity is astounding. One aid to finding information in gopherspace is a search program called veronica, with which you can specify one or more words that you think might show up in the one-line menu listings. Overall, I find it enjoyable just to wander about and see what's available. At any point, you can type u to return to a previous menu, so you can wander to your heart's content.

JUST A MINUTE

> I'm not making this up: veronica stands for *very easy rodent-oriented net-wise index to computerized archives.*

Task 22.5: Visiting Libraries Around the World

DESCRIPTION As it turns out, I've written another book, one called *Global Software.* How about joining me as I travel through the Internet to various libraries to see what universities have my book?

ACTION

1. The first library I visit is the National Library in Venezuela (Biblioteca Nacional). With gopher, the library computer is only seven steps away from the very top!

```
Libraries/
Library Catalogs via Telnet/
Library Catalogs from Other Institutions/
Catalogs Listed by Location/
Americas/
Venezuela/
Biblioteca Nacional <TEL>
```

Once I log in as biblio, the screen looks like this:

```
                                              Catalogo Bib. Nacional
                                                      Introduccion
----------------------------------------------------------------------
                     Bienvenido al Catalogo Automatizado
                              S A I B I N

      Use los siguientes comandos:        Para buscar por:


                           A=          Autor
                           T=          Titulo
                           M=          Materia
                           K=          Palabra clave
                           C=          Cota
      Ud. puede iniciar una busqueda desde cualquier pantalla
      Para mayor informacion de busqueda en el Catalogo, presione <ENTER>.
      Para ver informacion sobre las BASES DE DATOS, escriba NOTI y
      presione <ENTER>.
      Ademas de LUIN, ud. puede usar el comando LUC2 donde encontrara
```

22

```
-------------------------------------------- + Pag. 1 de 4 -------
                 INGRESE COMANDO BUSQUEDA            <F8>  AVAnza pag.
                 NOTicia


  Prox. Comando: _
```

Fortunately, my Spanish is sufficient to figure this out.... I use t= to search by title
(the command is T=GLOBAL SOFTWARE) for my book *Global Software.*

```
  Solicitud de Busqueda: T=GLOBAL SOFTWARE            Catalogo Bib. Nacional
  Resultados de Busqueda: 0 Entradas Encontadas   No existen Entradas por Titulo
  ------------------------------------------------------------------------
                   No se encontraron Entradas de Titulo

  Las posibles razones para este mensaje son:

  1.  Material no esta en la base de datos (Busque en el fichero.)
  2.  Material no pertenece a la Biblioteca (Consulte al personal de referencia)
  3.  Comando o termino(s)  incorrecto. (Pruebe con otro comando o cambie el
        termino de busqueda.)

      Verifique en la busqueda lo siguiente:
      --Asegurese de que estan correctamente escritos. Si no esta seguro del ti-
        tulo completo o de como se escribe acortelo al final.
      --Omita todos los articulos (a, en, el).
      --Elimine los signos de puntuacion.
  Recuerde:  Ud. puede revisar su busqueda editandola en la linea de comandos).
  -------------------------------------------- Pag. 1 de 1 --------------
  COMenzar          REVisa busquedas realizadas
  OTRas opciones


  Prox. Comando: _
```

Ay caramba! Mi libro no está en al biblioteca national. Qué es la vida!

That is, there isn't a copy of my book in the library. Such is life. I can use salir (to
leave) to log out and return to gopher.

2. My next library to visit is to Australia. To get there, I need to back up a few levels
    in gopher and travel down a different path: Asia and Pacific/ lead to Australia/,
    where I can choose the Queensland University of Technology/:

```
                                              Q U T


            L A T E S T   N E W S                L I B R A R Y


                                        EXCELLENCE IN INFORMATION SERVICES

                                        *************************************
                                        *              OPTIONS              *
                                        *************************************
                                        *                                   *
                                        * 1.     Library Catalogue          *
                                        * 2.     Library Opening Hours       *
                                        * 3.     Logoff                      *
                                        *                                   *
                                        *                                   *
                                        *************************************

                                        or press <HELP>, then <RETURN>
```

This looks likely, so I choose 1:

```
                      L I B R A R Y   C A T A L O G U E

****************************************************************************
*                             MAIN MENU                                   *
****************************************************************************
                    1.   Titles
                    2.   Personal Authors
                    3.   Subjects
                    4.   Series Titles
                    5.   Corporate Authors & Conferences
                    6.   Keyword search across files 1-5
                    7.   Call Numbers
                    8.   Publishers
                    9.   Limited Access Collection - Subject
                   10.   Limited Access Collection - Lecturer
****************************************************************************
*      3 most important keys are:                                         *
*      <ENTER> to activate all commands                                   *
*      <HELP> or <shift and ?> then <ENTER> for advice                    *
*      Full stop <.> then <ENTER> to backtrack or terminate a search.*
****************************************************************************

                                                Please select _
```

I want to select by title, so again I type 1:

```
                    S E A R C H   T E X T   E N T R Y
****************************************************************************
                       TITLE ALPHABETIC BROWSING
****************************************************************************

Please type in some text that you think may occur at the start of a
title of a work that you are attempting to find.

For example, you could type   ECONOMICS AND DEMOGRAPHY    or
                               ECONOMICS AND              or
                               ECON

And remember to use the help key if you need more information.



  Please enter your search text...
****************************************************************************
> global software
```

I press Return to get the news:

```
B R O W S E              H E A D I N G   S E L E C T I O N

        Search text: GLOBAL SOFTWARE
Headings retrieved: 100
                                                            More pages
** TITLES ****************************************************************

  No.  Works
   1.     1   Global simulation models : a comparative study
==> GLOBAL SOFTWARE
   2.     1   Global solutions : innovative approaches to world
              problems: selections from The Futurist
   3.     1   Global sourcing strategy : R&D, manufacturing, and
              marketing interfaces
   4.     1   Global stakes : the future of high technology in America
   5.     2   Global status of mangrove ecosystems
   6.     1   Global stock market reforms
   7.     1   Global Strategic Management : Impact on New Frontiers....
   8.     1   Global strategic management perspectives
****************************************************************************
Next Page            Gather Headings            Keyword Search
Previous Page        List Chosen Headings
Top of List
                                            SELECT _
```

Nope, it's not there either, but the book *Global Status of Mangrove Ecosystems*
sounds quite interesting. Next time I'm on this computer system, I should look up
the reference to learn more about mangrove ecosystems.

3. I'll try one more university before I give up hope! I'll check the various libraries of the University of California. Again, the process is to step back in the gopher tree and select `Americas/`, `United States/`, `California/`, `University of California (MELVYL) <TEL>/`:

```
                    Welcome to the University of California's

                          MELVYL* LIBRARY SYSTEM


        -------------------- =>> SYSTEM NEWS <<= ----------------------



        ------------------------------------------------------------------

        (c)1984. *Registered TM of The Regents of the University of California.
        ==================================================================
        OPTIONS:  Choose option, or type command to enter the CATALOG database.

           HELP          - For help in getting started.

          [return]       - Press RETURN to choose a database for searching.

           START <db>    - Type START <db name> to begin searching in a database.
        -> only _
```

First, I can use the shortcut of entering START CAT to start with a catalog of all University of California library holdings:

```
                    Welcome to the MELVYL CATALOG Database

           Contents:    As of 12/15/93, approximately 7,563,498 titles
                        representing 11,761,300 holdings for materials in the
                        University ofCalifornia libraries and the California
                        State Library.

           Coverage:    All publication dates but incomplete for some libraries.

                              --=>> NEWS <<=--



        ------------------------------------------------------------------
        OPTIONS:     Type an option and press RETURN, or type any command.

           HELP       - For help in getting started.
```

```
    E GUIDE     -  For a brief guide to using the Catalog database.

    START       -  To start over or change databases.
    END         -  To end your session.
 CAT-> _
```

Did you see the number at the top of that screen? This database lists over 7.5 million different books, representing over 11 million holdings. That's quite impressive.

4. To save time again, I use the find command, specifying a title word: FIND TW GLOBAL SOFTWARE, which results in nine matches:

```
CAT-> f tw global software

   Search request: F TW GLOBAL SOFTWARE
   Search result:  9 records at all libraries

   Type D to display results, or type HELP.

CAT-> _
```

Typing D displays the first page of matches:

```
Search request: F TW GLOBAL SOFTWARE
Search result:  9 records at all libraries

Type HELP for other display options.

1. Clapes, Anthony Lawrence.
     Softwars : legal battles for control of global software industry /
   Anthony Lawrence Clapes.  Westport, Conn. : Quorum Books, 1993.
        HAST   5th Stks   K1443.C6 C56 1993
        UCB    Bus&Econ   K1443.C6 C56 1993
        UCB    Law Lib    K89 .C48
        UCI    Main Lib   K1443.C6 C56 1993
        UCLA   College    K 1443 C6 C56 1993
        UCSC   McHenry    K1443.C6C56 1993
        UCSD   Central    K1443.C6 C56 1993

2. A computer software system for the generation of global ocean tides
   including self-gravitation and crustal loading effects,
 by ronald h estes.1977.
        UCSD   Scripps    FICHE XSX 1 N77-23709 Floor 1 Microform


Press RETURN to see the next screen.
CAT->
```

I step forward a page or two:

```
Search request: F TW GLOBAL SOFTWARE
Search result:  9 records at all libraries

Type HELP for other display options.

5. Taylor, Dave, 1962-
     Global software : developing applications for the international
   market, Dave Taylor.  New York : Springer-Verlag, c1992.
      UCB    Engin      QA76.76.D47 T39 1992
      UCI    Main Lib   QA76.76.D47 T39 1992
      UCSC   Science    QA76.76.D47T39 1992

6. United States. General Accounting Office.
     Air Force Global Weather Central initiates positive action to
   assess adequacy of software inventory : report to the Secretary
 of the Air Force by the U.S. General Accounting Office.  Washington,
 D.C. : The Office, [1983].
      UCR    Rivera     GA 1.13:IMTEC-84-4 Govt.Pub Microfiche US
      UCSD   Central    GA 1.13:IMTEC-84-4 Documents Fiche
      CSL    Main Lib   GA 1.13:IMTEC-84-4 Govt Pubs


Press RETURN to see next screen. Type PS to see previous screen.
CAT-> _
```

Aha! You can see that there are copies of my book at the University of California at Berkeley (UCB), at Irvine (UCI), and at Santa Cruz (UCSC).

SUMMARY There are hundreds, if not thousands, of libraries connected to the Internet. If a reference book exists, you should be able to find a reference citation.

Task 22.6: All the News That's Fit or Otherwise

DESCRIPTION No discussion of the Internet would be complete without a brief foray into the largest, most active, and most varied discussion forum in the world—the Usenet. Imagine a bulletin board on the wall. Imagine that as people pass it, they glance at what's there, and if they have something to add, they stick their note up, too. Now (and here's the big leap), imagine that there are thousands of bulletin boards in this building, and that there are actually tens of thousands of buildings throughout the world, each with its own "identical" copy of the bulletin boards. Got it? That's Usenet.

Usenet was created in 1979, when two graduate students at Duke University, Tom Truscott and Jim Ellis, hooked their computer to another computer at the University of North Carolina. In 1980, there were two sites with Usenet. Today, at the very end of 1993, there are an estimated 120,000 sites on Usenet, representing over 4.2 million participants.

22

22

A true experiment in free speech and barely controlled anarchy, the range of discussions, called newsgroups, is astonishing. It covers everything from computer modem protocols (`comp.dcom.modem`) to Macintosh programming (`comp.sys.mac.programmer`), topics of relevance to single men and women (`soc.singles`), abortion (`talk.abortion`) to the wonderful TV show "Mystery Science Theater 3000" (`alt.tv.mst3k`). Whatever your interest, there's a group on the Net that talks about just what you're thinking about!

JUST A MINUTE

> A *protocol* is a language that different systems use to speak to each other so that they can interoperate. A modem protocol is the language that your modem uses to interact with your computer. Sound exciting?

The difficulty with Usenet is that the majority of tools designed to help read the volumes of information actually do precious little to help. The first puzzle is to find the groups that you'd like to read, and although almost all Usenet sites have a succinct database of what each group discusses, little Usenet software actually knows about it. Here is a very simple C shell alias that will help out:

```
alias findgroup _grep -i \!* /usr/local/lib/news/newsgroups_
```

At your site, this file might be available also as `/usr/lib/news/newsgroups`. Newsgroups are organized into seven primary hierarchies: `comp` groups are computer and programming related, `sci` groups discuss scientific issues, `misc` groups cover miscellaneous topics, `rec` are recreational, `talk` groups are for controversial and often heated discussion groups, `soc` are social groups, and `news` are groups containing news of the world or at least news of the network itself.

One final hierarchy worth mentioning is the `alt.*` set of groups that are the spot for semi-disorganized anarchy on the Net: Essentially anyone can create an `alt` group with ease, so, as you might expect, these groups are the most varied. Some examples are the excellent `alt.activism` for political activists and `alt.books.technical` for discussion of computer books (like this very book!), juvenile groups such as `alt.binaries.sounds-armpit.noises` for, one presumes, audio files that contain sounds of armpit noises, and `alt.elvis.sighting` for those elusive sightings of The King. If you can't quite tear yourself away from your video game system long enough even to eat, perhaps reading `alt.get.a.life.nintendo.addicts` will help.

One problem with the `alt` groups is that it's much more difficult to find out what's out there. Because there is considerably less control and organization, the convenient one-line descriptions in the newsgroups file don't contain descriptions of these alternative groups. Really, the best solution is to search through your `.newsrc` itself for key words or abbreviations. To find `alt` groups that discuss Disney, for example, I could try `grep disney .newsrc ¦ grep _^alt_` to find `alt.fan.disney.afternoon`.

Once you've found a group to read, it's time to choose from among the many possible packages. Perhaps the most popular is rn, or read news, written by Larry Wall. Another alternative, nn, offers a more screen-oriented view from Kim Storm, and a third possibility, patterned after the Elm Mail System, is tin, designed and written by Iain Lea.

JUST A MINUTE

Of the many programs available for reading netnews, I prefer tin, but because rn is so prevalent, I will use it in this hour. I nonetheless encourage you to use a local copy of tin if it's available. Remember also that you always can use archie to find a local copy. (I talk about archie in the next hour.)

The rn program not only has more options than you can shake a stick at, but it actually has more options than even a tree full of sticks could cover! Table 22.2 lists a small number of its particularly useful options.

Table 22.2. The most useful rn starting options.

Option	Meaning
-/	Set SAVEDIR, so that articles you save are stored in a subdirectory of ~/News named after the group, with the article name corresponding to its numeric identifier on the system.
-c	Check for news and indicate if any has arrived.
-e	Make each page of an article start at the top of the screen.
-h*hdr*	Suppress the header *hdr* in news articles.
-L	Leave information on screen as long as possible.
-M	Force mailbox format for all saved files.
-m	Use inverse video for highlighted information.
-N	Force normal, non-mailbox format for all saved files.
-r	Restart within the last newsgroup read during the previous session.
-S	Use subject search mode when possible.

JUST A MINUTE

That's a lot of options! My alias for starting up the rn program is rn -L -M -m -e -S -/.

Did I mention the RNINIT environment variable yet? In addition to using starting options, the rn program also can read a variety of different options from environment variables. Indeed, any option that is specified at the command line also can be specified in the RNINIT variable. As a result, my RNINIT is this:

```
% echo $RNINIT
-hmessage -hreference -hdate-r -hsender -hsummary -hreply -hdistr -hlines
 -hline -hfollow -hnews -hkey -hresent -hreturn -hto -hx-original -hx-sun
-hx-note -horiginator -hnntp
```

This causes the program to suppress the display of all the specified headers in individual news articles. There are just so many options that it's overwhelming. Let's go into the program and see what it looks like!

ACTION

1. First, I use the alias findgroup to identify a few newsgroups I'd like to read:

```
% findgroup mac
biz.dec.ip           IP networking on DEC machines.
vmsnet.internals     VMS internals, MACRO-32, Bliss, gatewayed to MACRO32 list.
gnu.emacs.announce   Announcements about GNU Emacs. (Moderated)
gnu.emacs.bug        GNU Emacs bug reports and suggested fixes. (Moderated)
gnu.emacs.gnews      News reading under GNU Emacs using Weemba's Gnews.
gnu.emacs.gnus       News reading under GNU Emacs using GNUS (in English).
gnu.emacs.help       User queries and answers.
gnu.emacs.sources    ONLY (please!) C and Lisp source code for GNU Emacs.
gnu.emacs.vm.bug     Bug reports on the Emacs VM mail package.
gnu.emacs.vm.info    Information about the Emacs VM mail package.
gnu.emacs.vms        VMS port of GNU Emacs.
gnu.epoch.misc       The Epoch X11 extensions to Emacs.
comp.binaries.acorn Binary-only postings for Acorn machines. (Moderated)
comp.binaries.mac   Encoded Macintosh programs in binary. (Moderated)
comp.emacs           EMACS editors of different flavors.
comp.lang.forth.mac     The CSI MacForth programming environment.
comp.lang.lisp.mcl      Discussing Apple's Macintosh Common Lisp.
comp.org.acm            Topics about the Association for Computing Machinery.
comp.os.mach            The MACH OS from CMU & other places.
comp.os.msdos.misc      Miscellaneous topics about MS-DOS machines.
comp.os.msdos.programmer   Programming MS-DOS machines.
comp.os.os2.programmer  Programming OS/2 machines.
comp.sources.mac        Software for the Apple Macintosh. (Moderated)
comp.sys.mac.advocacy   The Macintosh computer family compared to others.
comp.sys.mac.announce   Important notices for Macintosh users. (Moderated)
comp.sys.mac.apps       Discussions of Macintosh applications.
comp.sys.mac.comm       Discussion of Macintosh communications.
comp.sys.mac.databases  Database systems for the Apple Macintosh.
comp.sys.mac.digest     Apple Macintosh: info&uses, no programs. (Moderated)
comp.sys.mac.games      Discussions of games on the Macintosh.
comp.sys.mac.hardware   Macintosh hardware issues & discussions.
comp.sys.mac.hypercard  The Macintosh Hypercard: info & uses.
comp.sys.mac.misc       General discussions about the Apple Macintosh.
```

```
comp.sys.mac.oop.macapp3  Version 3 of the MacApp object oriented system.
comp.sys.mac.oop.misc    Object oriented programming issues on the Mac.
comp.sys.mac.programmer  Discussion by people programming the Apple Macintosh.
comp.sys.mac.system      Discussions of Macintosh system software.
comp.sys.mac.wanted      Postings of "I want XYZ for my Mac."
comp.sys.sgi.graphics    Graphics packages and issues on SGI machines.
comp.sys.sgi.misc        General discussion about Silicon Graphics's machines.
comp.text.tex            Discussion about the TeX and LaTeX systems & macros.
comp.unix.aux            The version of UNIX for Apple Macintosh II computers.
misc.forsale.computers.mac      Apple Macintosh related computer items.
rec.games.diplomacy      The conquest game Diplomacy.
sci.nanotech             Self-reproducing molecular-scale machines. (Moderated)
```

Remember that these are only groups that have the word mac in them. The group
comp.sys.mac.announce sounds like it might be interesting. Now, to find a few
more:

```
% findgroup writing
comp.edu.composition Writing instruction in computer-based classrooms.
misc.writing         Discussion of writing in all of its forms.
% findgroup education
k12.ed.art           Art curriculum in K-12 education.
k12.ed.business      Business education curriculum in grades K-12.
k12.ed.health-pe Health and Physical Education curriculum in grades K-12.
k12.ed.life-skills   Home Economics and Career education in grades K-12.
k12.ed.math          Mathematics curriculum in K-12 education.
k12.ed.music     Music and Performing Arts curriculum in K-12 education.
k12.ed.science       Science curriculum in K-12 education.
k12.ed.soc-studies Social Studies and History curriculum in K-12 education.
k12.ed.special    K-12 education for students w/ handicaps or special needs.
k12.ed.tag           K-12 education for talented and gifted students.
k12.ed.tech      Industrial Arts and vocational education in grades K-12.
k12.lang.art         Language Arts curriculum in K-12 education.
comp.ai.edu          Applications of Artificial Intelligence to Education.
comp.edu             Computer science education.
misc.education       Discussion of the educational system.
sci.edu              The science of education.
% findgroup movies
rec.arts.movies         Discussions of movies and movie making.
rec.arts.movies.reviews Reviews of movies. (Moderated)
rec.arts.sf.movies      Discussing SF motion pictures.
rec.arts.startrek.current      New Star Trek shows, movies and books.
% findgroup film
rec.arts.startrek.reviews      Reviews of Star Trek books, episodes, films, &c
(Moderated)
```

Now I have a list of groups to check out: comp.sys.mac.announce, misc.writing,
sci.edu, and rec.arts.movies.

2. It's time to start up the rn program so I can read these groups:

```
% rn
                      *** NEWS NEWS ***

Welcome to version 4.4 of rn (patch level 4).  This version corrects
many bugs of the previous version and has some enhancements you may
find useful.  Type "man rn" for more information.
```

22

```
If you find problems with this program, report them with trouble(1L).

This particular message comes from /usr/local/lib/rn/newsnews.  You
will only see it once.

[Type space to continue] _
```

Because I haven't used the program before, this first time out will have all sorts of information:

```
Trying to set up a .newsrc file--running newsetup...

Creating /users/taylor/.newsrc to be used by news programs.
Done.
```

If you have never used the news system before, you may find the articles in news.announce.newusers to be helpful. There is also a manual entry for rn.

To get rid of newsgroups you aren't interested in, use the u command.

```
Type h for help at any time while running rn.
(Revising soft pointers--be patient.)
Unread news in general                              1 article
Unread news in news.admin.misc                    88 articles
Unread news in news.admin.policy                  68 articles
Unread news in news.admin.technical                6 articles
Unread news in news.announce.conferences          26 articles
etc.
etc.

Finding new newsgroups:

********   1 unread article in general--read now? [ynq] _
```

CAUTION

One of the worst aspects of rn is that, by default, it subscribes you to over 2,400 newsgroups the first time you enter the program. Fortunately, the fix is easy.

3. Now that I'm a member of a few thousand groups, I want to get out of some! The fastest way for me to fix the problem is to quit rn (type q), then use vi to edit my personal Usenet database file, called .newsrc, which resides in my home directory. This file contains a list of all newsgroups, with each group followed by a special character and an indication of which articles I have already seen:

```
% head .newsrc
general: 1-699
news.admin: 1-26982
news.admin.misc: 1-6329
news.admin.policy: 1-8171
news.admin.technical: 1-445
```

```
news.announce.conferences: 1-5326
news.announce.important:
news.announce.newgroups:
news.announce.newusers:
news.answers:
```

To unsubscribe and have no groups included, I simply replace the colon on each line with an exclamation point. A group that isn't subscribed looks like this: `news.admin!` `1-26982`. You can use `:1,$s/:/!/` in `vi` to unsubscribe quickly to all groups. I suggest, however, that you make sure that you do read the group `general` on your system.

4. Now, I start `rn` a second time, and here's what I see:

```
% rn
Unread news in general                                          1 article

*******    1 unread article in general--read now? [ynq] _
```

Instead of answering yes or no to this question, I can go to the groups I'd previously chosen to read, using the `g` *groupname* command:

```
    1 unread article in general--read now? [ynq] g comp.sys.mac.announce
Newsgroup comp.sys.mac.announce is currently unsubscribed to--
➥resubscribe? [yn]
```

It's not surprising that I am not subscribed: I just unsubscribed from almost everything. Joining the group sounds good, so I type y, and the screen changes:

```
0 unread articles in comp.sys.mac.announce--read now? [ynq] _
```

There are no articles pending in this newsgroup, as can be seen by the `0` `unread` message. That's good news—I then can add the other three groups by saying `n` here, because I do not want to read this group, then using the `g` command with each of the other groups specified.

The first time I choose `n`, however, the prompt changes to a new line:

```
End of newsgroups--what next? [qnp] _
```

I can enter the `g` *newsgroup* here just as easily.

5. Imagine it's a couple days later when I log in to my computer and again enter `rn` to see if there's any news. Unsurprisingly, quite a few articles have arrived since I signed up for the groups:

```
% rn
Unread news in general                                          1 article
Unread news in sci.edu                                         28 articles
Unread news in misc.writing                                    81 articles

1 unread article in general--read now? [ynq] _
```

I start by saying `n`, then `y` when it asks about the newsgroup `sci.edu`. The screen changes:

```
Article 4695 (27 more) in sci.edu:
From: choy@cs.usask.ca (Henry Choy)
Subject: Re: Automation and the Need for Education
Date: 9 Dec 1993 22:00:10 GMT
Organization: University of Saskatchewan
NNTP-Posting-Host: sparkle.usask.ca
X-Newsreader: TIN [version 1.2 PL0]

Alberto Moreira (acm@kpc.com) wrote:
:       Computers can't do anything by themselves - they are raw
:       metal.  But the computer program running in a computer is
:       a transliteration of a human creator's thought processes.
:       When you play chess against a computer, you're not playing
:       against the computer; you're playing against the individuals
:       who designed Sargon, Deep Thought, or whatever chess program
:       you're battling.
In a way this is so, but the designers of these programs are working in
the way they were taught to play chess :)
Consider a chess program that is free to consider different evaluation
techniques, and other whatnot procedures and measures concocted with
some element of randomness. This program behaves
--MORE--(46%) _
```

There's a lot of information contained in the first few lines, as shown in Figure 22.1. Also, the lines that begin with a colon are *quoted text* from a previous article in the group, the one written by Alberto Moreira. All lines not beginning with a colon are the thoughts of Henry Choy, the author of this particular article.

Figure 22.1.

Information on rn *article display screen.*

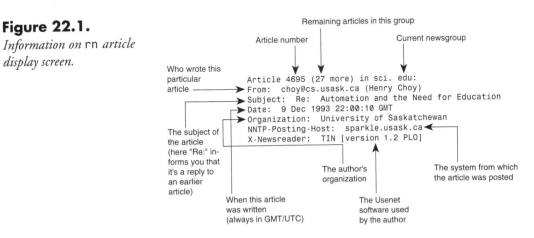

6. While reading a particular article, I can choose from a variety of different commands that I can enter to perform different actions, most notably q to quit reading this particular article, n to move to the next article, k to mark this article and all of a similar subject as read (so that I don't see them), ^s (or space) to read the next article with the same subject in this group, R to reply to the author via electronic mail, and F to follow up this article with thoughts and reactions of my own. One particularly helpful command is =, which offers a table of contents for this group, showing all articles I have not yet read.

TIME SAVER

> One little-known fact about rn is that you can define exactly what is shown in the = table of contents screen with the SUBJLINE environment variable. I have mine set to %t -- %s, which produces a list with both the author and subject indicated.

When I enter =, here's what happens:

```
 4696 office@interact.nl -- INTERACTIVE LEARNING (INTERACT 2)
 4697 yifanhan@helix.nih.gov -- Academic tenure in Australia and
other countries
 4698 cberry@tajo.edu -- Grade Point Averages: What's the point?
 4699 markline@henson.cc.wwu.edu -- Grade Point Averages: What's the
point?
 4700 cravener@uhunix.uhcc.Hawaii.Edu -- Grade Point Averages: What's
the point?
 4701 jbirch@crc.sd68.nanaimo.bc.ca -- Looking for U of A - John Lind...
 4702 hrubin@snap.stat.purdue.edu -- Grade Point Averages: What's the
point?
 4703 hrubin@snap.stat.purdue.edu -- Academic tenure in Australia and
other countries4704 chem@uwpg02.uwinnipeg.ca -- TOSHIBA/NSTA contest info
 4705 mpriestley@vnet.IBM.COM -- Grade Point Averages: What's the point?
 4706 acm@kpc.com -- Grade Point Averages: What's the point?
 4707 acm@kpc.com -- Grade Point Averages: What's the point?
 4708 rablatch@unix.amherst.edu -- Academic tenure in Australia and
other countries
 4709 elkassas@eb.ele.tue.nl -- Q: TV use in education!
 4710 cravener@uhunix.uhcc.Hawaii.Edu -- Grade Point Averages: What's the
point?
 4711 nata@aoibs.msk.su -- Subscription to Russian literature magazine in
English and in Russian!
 4712 reiser@ils.nwu.EDU -- PhD & MA Programs in Learning Sciences at
Northwestern
 4713 gaturner@npmo.pc.ingr.com -- Help needed on paper
[Type space to continue] _
```

There are more articles waiting to be read than can fit on the screen (hence the Type space to continue at the bottom). Here, I can type q to zip back to the bottom of the article I was reading (then M to mail a response to the author, perhaps) or enter a specific article number to read that article. Article 4704, titled TOSHIBA/NSTA contest info, sounds pretty interesting, so I'll enter 4704 and move directly to that article:

```
Article 4704 (23 more) in sci.edu:
From: chem@uwpg02.uwinnipeg.ca
Subject: TOSHIBA/NSTA contest info
Date: 13 DEC 93 02:31:15 CST
Organization: University of Winnipeg
NNTP-Posting-Host: uwpg02.uwinnipeg.ca

Hi. I was wondering if anyone had sample material
regarding the NSTA/TOSHIBA explorovision contest.
SPecifically, sample storyboards and written reports.
Thanks for any info. M. Carroll U of Wpg
internet:  chem@uwpg02.uwinnipeg.ca
End of article 4704 (of 4719)--what next? [^Nnpq]_
```

At this point, again, I could use R to reply, F to post a follow-on article of my own, or any of the other commands. It seems like a good time to quit Usenet for now, so I type q and move to the next group in the list:

```
End of article 4704 (of 4719)--what next? [^Nnpq]

********  81 unread articles in misc.writing--read now? [ynq] _
```

Another q, and I'm back at my C shell prompt.

7. Just for comparison, here's what tin looks like when I launch it on the list of newsgroups that I actually read on an approximately daily basis:

```
                    Group Selection (18)                    h=help


     1    396  misc.forsale.computers.mac   Apple Macintosh related comput
     2         news.announce.important      General announcements of inter
     3         news.announce.newusers       Explanatory postings for new u
     4         comp.binaries.mac            Encoded Macintosh programs in
     5     16  comp.org.sug                 Talk about/for the The Sun Use
     6         comp.org.usenix              USENIX Association events and
     7         comp.sys.mac.announce        Important notices for Macintos
     8      2  comp.sys.sun.announce        Sun announcements and Sunergy
     9         rec.arts.movies.reviews      Reviews of movies. (Moderated)
    10     38  rec.food.recipes             Recipes for interesting food a
    11    447  alt.books.reviews            "If you want to know how it tu
    12    158  alt.education.distance        Learning over nets etc.
    13    110  alt.education.research
    14    603  alt.folklore.herbs
    15     37  misc.education               Discussion of the educational
    16     20  misc.education.language.english
```

```
          <n>=set current to n, TAB=next unread, /=search pattern, c)atchup,
        g)oto, j=line down, k=line up, h)elp, m)ove, q)uit, r=toggle all/unread,
          s)ubscribe, S)ub pattern, u)nsubscribe, U)nsub pattern, y)ank in/out

        _
```

Many of these groups have no articles pending, but you can see (on the second number on the line) that the group misc.forsale.computers.mac has 396 new articles, comp.org.sug has 16, and so on. To read the currently highlighted group, I press Return.

```
              misc.forsale.computers.mac (318T 391A 0K 0H R)              h=help

**     1  + 2  Group Purchase:  SCSI Hard Drives          David La Croix    **
    2  +       BernulliMD150+5(150)carts!$750NEW!         Donn Lasher
    3  +       MUST SELL:  Macintosh external AppleCD 150  Seung Jong Lee
    4  + 4     Mac Centris 650 Forsale                    M Torricelli
    5  + 2     IBM/Tandberg TDC3600/250Mb SCSI Tape Drives asg@world.std.com
    6  +       FOR SALE: Symantec C++ 6.0.1               FDMWINK@UCF1VM.BIT
    7  +       SCSI stuff for sale                        Victor Mark Kalyuz
    8  +       Computer Accessaries for Sale              Qian Zhang
    9  +       DOS 6.0 FOR SALE                           Qian Zhang
   10  +       Performa 600 (Max IIVx NOT!)               Steve Fouts
   11  + 2     WANTED: color '040 mac used.               753mackie@gw.wmich
   12  +       Ashlar Vellum 2D and 3D for sale           robert dornbusch
   13  +       Cheap ImageWriter II for sale $95 (shipping Prachya Chalermwat
   14  +       PB 140                                     Jeffrey Ello
   15  +       Apple CD150 CD_ROM, new $199.00            Victor Mark Kalyuz
   16  +       LCII 8/80 - Gotta sell soon.               Anthony S. Kim

  <n>=set current to n, TAB=next unread, /=search pattern, ^K)ill/select,
a)uthor search, c)atchup, j=line down, k=line up, K=mark read, l)ist thread,
 ¦=pipe, m)ail, o=print, q)uit, r=toggle all/unread, s)ave, t)ag, w=post


        _
```

I press Enter again, and I can read the specific article, or use q to quit. I think I've had enough Usenet for one day, so I quit and again return to my C shell prompt.

SUMMARY   Usenet is a complex, wild, and almost organization-free set of thousands of newsgroups distributed to over 100,000 systems and read by millions of users throughout the world. Between Mac, PC, Amiga, UNIX, and VMS, there are at least 20 different programs available just for reading the vast volumes of information that flow past each day. If you have access to a Mac or a PC, or even a UNIX system running the X Window System, there are some attractive programs available for reading the Net. If not, I'm a fan of tin and also have used rn for many years; both will serve you well once you learn them. Certainly, for any of these programs, start out with the included documentation, or at least read through the (usually quite long) man pages.

Gopher and e-mail are even more wild, but they're all very useful pieces of the Internet and UNIX pie, and, if I had to point to a single program as the "killer application" of the Net, it'd be e-mail. My advice, after almost 17 years of being involved with the UNIX and Internet communities, is that you can't go wrong by becoming extremely comfortable with your favorite e-mail program, and ditto for Usenet.

Workshop

The Workshop summarizes the key terms you learned and poses some questions about the topics presented in this chapter. It also provides you with a preview of what you will learn in the next hour.

Key Terms

domain naming   Domain naming is the addressing scheme for hosts on the Internet. The domain name is the information after the hostname on the right side of the @ in an address. For example, joe@mutt.cornell.edu has a domain name cornell.edu and a full domain name mutt.cornell.edu.

gopherspace   The information space through which gopher travels while you're using the program.

newsgroup   A Usenet group focused on a particular subject or topic of conversation.

protocol   An agreed-upon language for transfer of information between two computers.

quoted text   A portion of a previous article that is included in the current article to give context, particularly in disagreeing with or amplifying specific thoughts.

Questions

1. Use finger to see whether there's anyone logged in at one of the systems in the list, and then use it to find out more information about a person on that list of users.

2. If you have a friend on your system or another system, use talk to say hello.

3. Using archie, find one or two archive sites that have a copy of the tin newsreading program.

4. What does the acronym LISP stand for? Use the WAIS system to find out.

5. Check in to the library at Stanford University with gopher and see whether it has a copy of this book yet.

6. Enter the `findgroup` alias and find the groups that discuss the following:
   plant biology
   laser printers
   UNIX questions
   anthropology

7. Using `rn` or another news reader, check in to one of the groups you just found, and see whether there are any new articles. Based on information in this hour, how many systems do you think get this group?

Preview of the Next Hour

In the next hour, you continue with the tour of the Internet. You learn how to use `archie`, `ftp`, and `telnet`.

22

Hour **23**

Using `telnet` and `ftp`

In this hour, you pick up where you left off, with a tour of Internet facilities.

Goals for This Hour

In this hour, you learn about

- ☐ Connecting to remote Internet sites
- ☐ Copying files from other Internet sites
- ☐ Finding archives with `archie`
- ☐ A few interesting `telnet` sites

This hour is intended to offer a quick and enjoyable overview of the many services available through the Internet. From finding that long-lost archive to exploring hotels available overseas, the range of information available will undoubtedly astound you!

Task 23.1: Connecting to Remote Internet Sites

DESCRIPTION   The really fun part of UNIX, and one reason that it's grown dramatically in the last few years, is that it's the most connected operating system in the world. The variety of different services available for users of a networked UNIX machine is staggering. Not only can you use all the commands explained in this hour, but you can use some additional services, such as gopher and archie, that are on the cutting edge of information services and that will be explained in the final hour.

At its simplest, the connectivity all relies on very high-speed wires coming out of the back of the computer you're on and connecting to other computers. Unlike the telephone-based connections of UUCP, this line is always alive and is much, much faster, able to stream literally megabytes of information in under a minute. The big network itself, the Internet, evolved from an earlier network called the ARPAnet, funded by the Advanced Research Projects Agency of the U.S. Government in the 1970s and into the 1980s. Somewhere along the way, it began to grow beyond the vision and capabilities of the original design and began being known as the ARPA Internet. In the last few years, the government (and particularly the National Science Foundation) has begun to withdraw from its overseer role, and as a result, the system is now known as the Internet.

If you've heard of the Information Highway (which is now being called the Information Superhighway), you've also heard about the Internet, which is the existing roadway that is growing to become this high-speed thoroughfare of information. In fact, next time a friend mentions the Information Highway, you can say that you've already experienced some of it by working on the Internet.

There are three main tasks that the Internet can help you with: using remote systems, sending mail to remote users, and working with remote file systems. In addition, you can find out who is logged on to any system on the Internet and use the talk program to talk with some-one else.

If you know that the remote site is a UNIX system, the easiest way to log in to that site is to use the rlogin command, which has the awkward notation of rlogin *host* -l *account*. If you aren't sure about the system, use telnet, which is the universal program for connecting to remote computer systems. Unlike any of the other programs you've learned so far, telnet actually works either as a simple program you can invoke from the command line, or as a sophisticated environment for connecting to various systems.

ACTION

1. First off, I'll use rlogin to connect to a remote system and see if I have a file there:
   ```
   % rlogin netcom.com
   Password:_
   ```

23

By default, `rlogin` assumes that your account on the remote system has the same name as your account on your home system. If you forget to use the `-l account` option, just press Return here, and it prompts for an account name:

```
% rlogin netcom.com
Password:
Login incorrect
login: taylor
Password:_
```

Once I enter my password, I'm logged in to the remote system:

```
Last login: Mon Dec 13 09:38:35 from utech

SunOS Release 4.1.3 (NETCOM) #1: Wed Sep 23 05:06:55 PDT 1996

NETCOM On-line Communication Services, Inc.

    >>>>
    >>>>    Washington DC:  Additional modems have been added.
    >>>>    Santa Cruz:  Additional modems have been added.
    >>>>
    >>>>    Elm has been updated to version 2.4 (PL 21).  Users
    >>>>    using elm with aliases should run the
    >>>>    "/usr/local/bin/newalias" program.
    >>>>

%
```

Using `ls` tells me what I want to know:

```
netcom % ls
Global.Software    News/        history.usenet.Z
Interactive.Unix   Src/         login
Mail/              bin/         testme
netcom %
```

2. The `rlogin` command offers a shorthand notation for logging out of the remote system; instead of `logout`, you can simply enter `~.`. To stop the `rlogin` session, use `~^z`. No other tilde commands are available in `rlogin`.

   I choose to log out the normal way:

```
netcom % logout
Connection closed
%
```

   Now I'm back on the original computer system.

3. The alternate way to connect to a remote computer is to use `telnet`. The easiest way to use this command is the same way you use `rlogin`. At the command prompt, specify the name of the system to which you want to connect:

```
% telnet netcom.com
Trying...
Connected to netcom.com.
Escape character is '^]'.
```

```
SunOS UNIX (netcom)

login: _
```

Notice that this way is much more like having a terminal connected to this system. I can log in, enter my password, and then have a new login session on the remote system as if I were sitting in that computer room working away.

4. Instead, though, I'm going to use the ^] control character to switch into the telnet program itself:

```
SunOS UNIX (netcom)
login: ^]
telnet > _
```

Now I enter help to see what the options are:

```
telnet> help
Commands may be abbreviated.  Commands are:

close           close current connection
display         display operating parameters
mode            try to enter line-by-line or character-at-a-time mode
open            connect to a site
quit            exit telnet
send            transmit special characters ('send ?' for more)
set             set operating parameters ('set ?' for more)
status          print status information
toggle          toggle operating parameters ('toggle ?' for more)
z               suspend telnet
?               print help information
telnet>  _
```

There are lots of possible commands. I choose to return to my connection to Netcom, however, so I just press Return, and I'm back at the login prompt. If I don't enter anything quickly enough, the remote system automatically drops the connection:

```
login: Login timed out after 60 seconds
Connection closed by foreign host.
%
```

To log out of the remote system, the best strategy is simply to exit the telnet session, which will drop the line automatically. If that doesn't work, the ^] sequence followed by either quit or close will do the trick.

5. To start out directly in the telnet command mode, simply enter the command without specifying a remote host:

```
% telnet
telnet> _
```

From here, connecting to the remote host is also quite simple:

```
telnet> open netcom.com
Trying...
```

```
Connected to netcom.com.
Escape character is '^]'.


SunOS UNIX (netcom)

login: _
```

Again, I use ^] and close to close the connection.

SUMMARY Both the rlogin and telnet commands are useful in different situations, but I find myself using the rlogin command more often because it sends much of the current environment along to the remote system. So if I have my system set for a specific type of terminal (that is, the TERM variable is set to a specific value), that value is automatically copied into the new environment of the remote system, which saves lots of hassle.

Task 23.2: Copying Files from Other Internet Sites

DESCRIPTION The main program used to copy files on the Internet is ftp, which is named after the protocol it implements, the *file transfer protocol*. Like much of UNIX, ftp can take a while to master, particularly because no effort has been made to make it at all user-friendly. Nonetheless, it functions very similarly to the telnet command; you either enter ftp to start the program and then specify the system with which you'd like to connect, or you specify the name of the system on the command line. Either way, you are then prompted for an account and password; then you are dropped into the ftp prompt with the connection open and waiting.

Many sites talk about having anonymous ftp capabilities. Systems allowing this connection indicate that you don't need your own computer account on that machine to be able to connect and copy files from their archives. To use these systems, enter ftp as the account name, and then enter your own e-mail address as the password (that is, I'd enter ftp and then taylor@netcom.com as the password). The most important commands available in ftp are summarized in Table 23.1. The most important one to remember is bye, which you use when you're done.

Table 23.1. Valuable ftp commands.

Command	Meaning
ascii	Set ftp to transfer a text (ASCII) file.
binary	Set ftp to transfer a binary file, probably a program or database of information.
bye	Quit the ftp program.
cd dir	Change the remote directory to dir.
close	Close the current connection.

continues

Table 23.1. continued

Command	Meaning
dir	Print a listing of files in the current remote directory.
get	Transfer a file from the remote system to your local system.
lcd *dir*	Change the current directory on the local system to *dir* or to your home directory if no argument is given.
ls	List the files in the current remote directory.
mget	Multiple get—get files with a wildcard matching capability.
mput	Multiple put—put files with a wildcard matching capability.
open	Open a connection to the specified remote machine.
prompt	Control whether or not to ask for confirmation of each file transferred if using mget or mput.
put	Put a file onto the remote system from the local system.
pwd	Show the present working directory on the remote.

ACTION

1. To start out, I want to pick up a file from netcom that I saw earlier when I used rlogin to look at the remote system. To start ftp, I use the short notation of specifying the host at the command line:

```
% ftp netcom.com
Connected to netcom.com.
220 netcom FTP server (Version 2.1 Fri Apr 9 13:43 PDT 1996) ready.
Name (netcom.com:taylor): _
```

By default, ftp assumes that I want to use the same account name, which in this case I do, so I press Return, and then enter my password:

```
Name (netcom.com:taylor):
331 Password required for taylor.
Password:
230 User taylor logged in.
ftp> _
```

2. Now I'm at the ftp program prompt, and any of the commands shown in Table 23.1 will work here. To start, I use dir and ls to list my files in different formats:

```
ftp> dir
200 PORT command successful.
150 Opening ASCII mode data connection for /bin/ls.
total 140
-rwxr-xr-x  1 taylor   users0      4941 Oct  4  1991 .Pnews.header
-rwx------  1 taylor   daemon       987 Sep 20  1992 .accinfo
-rw-r--r--  1 taylor   users0      2103 Sep 30 19:17 .article
-rw-r--r--  1 taylor   users0       752 Apr 17  1992 .cshrc
-rw-r--r--  1 taylor   users0      1749 Jun  8  1993 .delgroups
```

23

```
drwx------   2 taylor    daemon     4096 Dec  6 14:25 .elm
-rw-r--r--   1 taylor    users0       28 Nov  5 09:50 .forward
-rw-------   1 taylor    users0        0 Jun  9 1993 .ircmotd
-rw-r--r--   1 taylor    users0     1237 Dec 13 09:40 .login
-rw-r--r--   1 taylor    users0        6 Aug  6 1991 .logout
-rw-r--r--   1 taylor    users0      538 Dec  6 14:32 .newsrc
-rw-r--r--   1 taylor    users0      537 Dec  6 14:30 .oldnewsrc
-rw-r--r--   1 taylor    users0     1610 Feb 17 1992 .plan
-rw-r--r--   1 taylor    users0        0 Aug  6 1991 .pnewsexpert
-rw-r--r--   1 taylor    users0       45 Feb  2 1993 .rnlast
-rw-r--r--   1 taylor    users0        6 Feb  8 1993 .rnlock
-rw-r--r--   1 taylor    users0    16767 Jan 27 1993 .rnsoft
-rw-r--r--   1 taylor    users0      114 Apr  6 1992 .sig
drwxr-xr-x   4 taylor    users0     4096 Nov 13 11:09 .tin
-rw-r--r--   1 taylor    users0     1861 Jun  2 1992 Global.Software
-rw-------   1 taylor    users0    22194 Oct  1 1992 Interactive.Unix
drwx------   4 taylor    users0     4096 Nov 13 11:09 Mail
drwxr-xr-x   2 taylor    users0     4096 Nov 13 11:09 News
drwxr-xr-x   2 taylor    users0     4096 Nov 13 11:09 Src
drwxr-xr-x   2 taylor    users0     4096 Nov 13 11:09 bin
-rw-r--r--   1 taylor    users0    12445 Sep 17 14:56 history.usenet.Z
-rw-r--r--   1 taylor    users0     1237 Oct 18 20:55 login
-rw-r--r--   1 taylor    users0      174 Nov 20 19:21 testme
226 Transfer complete.
1792 bytes received in 3.1 seconds (0.56 Kbytes/s)
ftp> ls
200 PORT command successful.
150 Opening ASCII mode data connection for file list.
.cshrc
.login
.elm
Mail
News
.logout
.newsrc
.rnlast
.rnsoft
bin
.tin
Global.Software
.sig
.oldnewsrc
.pnewsexpert
.plan
.Pnews.header
history.usenet.Z
.rnlock
Src
.ircmotd
.article
.delgroups
.accinfo
.forward
Interactive.Unix
testme
login
226 Transfer complete.
269 bytes received in 0.02 seconds (13 Kbytes/s)
ftp>
```

As you can see, ftp can be long-winded.

JUST A MINUTE

> One trick for using the ls command within ftp is that if you specify a set of command flags as a second word, it works fine. Specify a third argument, however, and it saves the output of the command into a local file by that name; so ls -l -C would create a file called -C on your system with the output of the ls -l command.

Because you can supply some flags to the ls command, I always use -CF to force the output to list in multiple columns and show directories, which makes the output readable:

```
ftp> ls -CF
200 PORT command successful.
150 Opening ASCII mode data connection for /bin/ls.
.Pnews.header*          .newsrc                 Interactive.Unix
.accinfo*               .oldnewsrc              Mail/
.article                .plan                   News/
.cshrc                  .pnewsexpert            Src/
.delgroups              .rnlast                 bin/
.elm/                   .rnlock                 history.usenet.Z
.forward                .rnsoft                 login
.ircmotd                .sig                    testme
.login                  .tin/
.logout                 Global.Software
226 Transfer complete.
remote: -CF
287 bytes received in 0.05 seconds (5.6 Kbytes/s)
ftp>
```

3. To transfer the file login from the remote system, I can use the get command:

```
ftp> get
(remote-file) login
(local-file) login.netcom
200 PORT command successful.
150 Opening ASCII mode data connection for login (1237 bytes).
226 Transfer complete.
local: login.netcom remote: login
1281 bytes received in 0.22 seconds (5.7 Kbytes/s)
ftp>
```

4. Alternatively, I could use mget and specify a wildcard pattern similar to one I'd give the shell:

```
ftp> mget log*
mget login? y
200 PORT command successful.
150 Opening ASCII mode data connection for login (1237 bytes).
226 Transfer complete.
local: login remote: login
1281 bytes received in 0.03 seconds (42 Kbytes/s)
ftp>
```

23

There was only one match, so the transfer was easy. Entering anything other than y at the mget login? prompt would have resulted in the file not being transferred.

That was easily accomplished. Now I will look on another system in the anonymous FTP directory to see what's available.

5. To disconnect, I enter close so that I don't leave the ftp program:

```
ftp> close
221 Goodbye
ftp>
```

There are hundreds of information servers on the Internet, offering an astounding variety of information, from weather service maps to the full text of *The Bible* and *Alice in Wonderland* to the source listings of thousands of different programs.

In this example, I want to look at the anonymous FTP archive at the Massachusetts Institute of Technology's Artificial Intelligence Laboratory. The host is called ftp.ai.mit.edu:

```
ftp> open ftp.ai.mit.edu
Connected to mini-wheats.ai.mit.edu.
220 mini-wheats FTP server (Version 2.1b Wed Aug 25 09:20 EDT 1993)

Name (ftp.ai.mit.edu:taylor): ftp
331 Guest login ok, send your complete e-mail address as password.
Password:
230-
230-
230-Welcome to the MIT Artificial Intelligence Laboratory. If you are
230-interested in Artificial Intelligence Laboratory publications please
230-ftp to publications.ai.mit.edu.
230-
230-
230-
230 Guest login ok, access restrictions apply.
ftp>
```

Now I can use ls -CF to look around:

```
ftp> ls -CF
200 PORT command successful.
150 Opening ASCII mode data connection for /bin/ls.
.message        bin/          etc/            pub/
ai-pubs/        dev/          incoming/       usr/
226 Transfer complete.
remote: -CF
58 bytes received in 0.39 seconds (0.15 Kbytes/s)
ftp>
```

It looks like there might be something of interest in the pub directory (a directory by this name usually contains public information). I use cd to change to that directory, then ls -CF to see what's available there:

```
ftp> cd pub
250 CWD command successful.
ftp> ls -CF
```

```
200 PORT command successful.
150 Opening ASCII mode data connection for /bin/ls.
6.824/                             medical-white-paper.ps.Z*
Address:                           memtr
BL.tar.Z                           minsky/
GA/                                misc/
ICv2.45.sit.hqx                    mit1345.tar
Iterate/                           mobile-dist-telecomp/
MC132p_structures.cif              mobot-survey.text
MSV_array.cif                      mr-sd-mapped.ps
MSV_structures.cif                 mr-sd.ps
Peng_Wu_Thesis.ps.Z                mtm/
README                             ontic/
TS/                                patches.c
aal                                pdp8-lovers-archive
adage/                             pgs-th.ps.Z
ai3/                               pinouts/
aimr/                              poker/
akcl.Z                             psabalone.tar.Z
alan@                              pset32new.c
aop/                               publications/
ariel/                             qobi/
autoclass/                         ra.ps
bson/                              rbl-94.archive
cki/                               refer-to-bibtex/
clmath.tar                         sanger-figures/
cube-lovers/                       sanger-papers/
cva/                               sanger.mackey.tar.Z
cwitty/                            sanger.mackey.tar.gz
dam/                               scheme-libraries/
doc/                               screamer/
dssa/                              screamer.tar.Z
dssa.ps                            screamer3.04/
eel/                               screen/
ellens@                            series/
engine/                            square-dancing/
fax/                               squash-ladder
hebrew/                            surf-hippo/
incoming@                          swill
iter-man.ps                        swillcoxswillcoxswillcoxAddress:
iterate.lisp                       systems/
iterate.tar.Z                      tandems@
jupiter/                           tbs/
lemacs/                            texture.tiff
linalg.shar                        tgif.tar.Z
lisp3/                             transition-space.lisp
logtalk.uue.Z                      turing_option
loop-macro.tar                     turing_option.ps
lptrs/                             users/
ltalk*                             viola-fbr.ps.Z
lyskom-0.33.1.english.el.Z         vis/
maddog/                            who-line-gc-thermometer.lisp@
medical-white-paper.dvi            x3j13/
226 Transfer complete.
remote: -CF
1388 bytes received in 3.4 seconds (0.4 Kbytes/s)
ftp>
```

23

6. A README file is usually a good thing to start with. A handy ftp trick is that you can copy files directly to your screen by using /dev/tty as the local filename, or you can even pipe them to programs by using the pipe symbol as the first character:

```
ftp> get README |more
200 PORT command successful.
150 Opening ASCII mode data connection for README (186 bytes).
This file will be expanded eventually.


If you've been looking at directories of specific users, such as 'ian'
or 'ellens', those directories have been moved into the users
directory.

226 Transfer complete.
local: |more remote: README
193 bytes received in 0.55 seconds (0.34 Kbytes/s)
ftp>
```

In this case, the README file is not incredibly helpful.

7. It's time to split and check another FTP archive, this time one at Apple Computer (ftp.apple.com):

```
ftp> close
221 Goodbye.
ftp> open ftp.apple.com
Connected to bric-a-brac.apple.com.
220 bric-a-brac.apple.com FTP server (IG Version 5.93 (from BU,
from UUNET 5.51) Sun Nov 21 14:24:29 PST 1993) ready.
Name (ftp.apple.com:taylor): ftp
331 Guest login ok, send ident as password.
Password:
230 Guest login ok, access restrictions apply.
ftp>
```

Again, ls -CF shows what files are available:

```
ftp> ls -CF
200 PORT command successful.
150 Opening ASCII mode data connection for /bin/ls.
.cshrc       alug/      boot/     echt90/    public/
.login       apda/      cdrom/    etc/       shlib/
.logout      apple/     dev/      pie/       software/
README       bin/       dts/      pub/
226 Transfer complete.
remote: -CF
143 bytes received in 0.01 seconds (14 Kbytes/s)
ftp>
```

Use the |more trick to see what the README file has to say:

```
ftp> get README |more
200 PORT command successful.
150 Opening ASCII mode data connection for README (424 bytes).
This is the top level of our FTP server.
```

```
If you're an authorized person, and you want to have a directory on the
top level, please contact Erik Fair <ftp@apple.com>, (408) 974-1779,
and explain why you want one, and what you're going to use it for.
Otherwise, please make your stuff available in the "public" directory.

There are no writeable directories for anonymous FTP on this server; it
cannot be used as a drop box.
226 Transfer complete.
local: ¦more remote: README
433 bytes received in 0.21 seconds (2.01 Kbytes/s)
ftp>
```

8. There's a new Macintosh application available on this system in dts/mac/hacks that I've been interested in seeing. I can move directly there with cd, confirming that I'm where I think I am with pwd:

```
ftp> cd dts/mac/hacks
250 CWD command successful.
ftp> pwd
257 "/dts/mac/hacks" is current directory.
ftp> ls -CF
200 PORT command successful.
150 Opening ASCII mode data connection for /bin/ls.
aetracker-3-0.hqx*                    mountalias-1-0.hqx*
applicon-2-1.hqx*                     newswatcher.hqx*
appmenu-3-5.hqx*                      okey-dokey-1-0-1.hqx*
bison-flex.hqx*                       oscar.hqx*
colorfinder.hqx*                      piston.hqx*
darkside-of-the-mac-4-1.hqx*          snake.hqx*
dropper.hqx*                          switchapp-1-1.hqx*
escape-dammit-0-4.hqx*                system-picker-1-0.hqx*
extensions-manager-2-0-1.hqx*         thread-manager-exten-1-2.hqx*
flipper.hqx*                          trashman-4-0-2.hqx*
folder-icon-maker-1-1.hqx*            understudy.hqx*
fsid.hqx*                             unlockfolder.hqx*
im-mac-1-0b26w.hqx*                   virtual-controllers.hqx*
lockdisk-1-0.hqx*                     xferit-1-4.hqx*
226 Transfer complete.
remote: -CF
559 bytes received in 0.14 seconds (3.9 Kbytes/s)
ftp>
```

Notice that there's an asterisk following the names of these files. This indicates, as you know from the -F flag to ls, that it's a binary file. Therefore, I need to specify to ftp that it should transfer the file in binary mode, by entering binary:

```
ftp> binary
200 Type set to I.
ftp>
```

I check to see how big the file is, then I can use get to transfer it and drop the connection with bye:

```
ftp> dir colorfinder.hqx
200 PORT command successful.
150 Opening ASCII mode data connection for /bin/ls.
```

23

```
-rw-r-xr-x  1 mjohnson archivis    43442 May 24  1991 colorfinder.hqx
226 Transfer complete.
remote: colorfinder.hqx
71 bytes received in 0 seconds (0.069 Kbytes/s)
ftp> get colorfinder.hqx
200 PORT command successful.
150 Opening BINARY data connection for colorfinder.hqx (43442 bytes).
226 Transfer complete.
local: colorfinder.hqx remote: colorfinder.hqx
43442 bytes received in 2.09 seconds (20 Kbytes/s)
ftp> bye
221 CUL8R.
%
```

Now that I'm back at the command prompt, I can use `ls` again to confirm that I've received both the `colorfinder.hqx` and `login.netcom` files:

```
% ls
Archives/           bin/                keylime.pie         sample3
InfoWorld/          buckaroo            login.netcom        src/
Mail/               buckaroo.confused   newsample           src.listing
News/               cheryl              papert.article      temp/
OWL/                colorfinder.hqx     sample              tmp.listing
awkscript           dickens.note        sample2             who.is.who
%
```

 The FTP system is a terrific way to obtain information from the Internet. Thousands of systems offer various services via anonymous FTP, too. Table 23.2 lists a few of the most interesting ones.

Table 23.2. Some interesting FTP archives.

Site	Institution and Available Information
aenas.mit.edu	Massachusetts Institute of Technology Free Software Foundation site. Files: GNU EMACS
aisun1.ai.uga.edu	University of Georgia. Files: LISP, PROLOG, natural language processing, MS-DOS utilities
archive.nevada.edu	University of Nevada. Files: U.S. Constitution and supporting documents, religious texts, the *Bible*
brownvm.brown.edu	Brown University. Files: Mac
cc.sfu.ca	San Francisco University. Files: MS-DOS, Mac
clvax1.cl.msu.edu	Michigan State University. Files: MS Windows
cs.rice.edu	Rice University. Files: Sun-Spots, Amiga, ispell, ofiles
cscihp.ecst.csuchico.edu	California State University, Chico. Files: online chemistry manual
cu.nih.gov	U.S. National Institute of Health

continues

Table 23.2. continued

Site	Institution and Available Information
`deja-vu.aiss.uiuc.edu`	University of Illinois Champaign-Urbana. Files: Rush Limbaugh transcripts, Monty Python, humor, song lyrics, movie scripts, urban legends
`f.ms.uky.edu`	University of Kentucky. Files: Mac, MS-DOS, UNIX, Amiga, NeXT, 386BSD, AppleII, GNU, RFCs, various Usenet archives
`ftp.apple.com`	Apple Computer. Files: Apple (Mac, II, IIgs) product information, software, developer support
`ftp.cica.indiana.edu`	Indiana University. Files: UNIX, MS-DOS, NeXT updates, MS Windows 3.*x* archive
`ftp.csc.liv.ac.uk`	Liverpool University Computer Science Department. Files: Ports to HP-UX machines (especially Series 700), including X11R4 clients, GNU, recreational software, text editors, system administrator tools
`ftp.eff.org`	Electronic Frontier Foundation.
`gatekeeper.dec.com`	Digital Equipment Corporation, Palo Alto, California. Files: X11, recipes, cron, map, Modula-3
`hobiecat.cs.caltech.edu`	California Institute of Technology. Files: GNU (Free Software Foundation)
`hpcvaaz.cv.hp.com`	Hewlett-Packard, Corvallis, Oregon. Files: Motif, archives
`info.umd.edu`	University of Maryland. Files: government-related, books, economics, MS-DOS, Novell, Mac
`midgard.ucsc.edu`	University of California, Santa Cruz. Files: amoeba, U.S. Constitution
`nnsc.nsf.net`	National Science Foundation Network. Files: Network information, Internet Resource Guide
`nssdca.gsfc.nasa.gov`	NASA. Files: Hubble space telescope images
`sciences.sdsu.edu`	San Diego State University. Files: sounds
`sparkyfs.erg.sri.com`	SRI International Files: improving the security of your UNIX system
`tesla.ee.cornell.edu`	Cornell University. Files: `tcsh`
`vax.ftp.com`	FTP software. Files: FTP-related programs
`watsun.cc.columbia.edu`	Columbia University. Files: kermit
`wsmr-simtel20.army.mil`	U.S. Army—White Sands Missile Range. Files: MS-DOS, UNIX, CPM, Mac

There's no question that the interface to `ftp` is awkward, however, and there are a couple of different programs that have tried to address this problem, as you learn in the last hour in this book.

There's no way here to fully cover all the information available on the Internet, so if you're excited by these possibilities, I strongly recommend that you obtain a copy of the book *Navigating the Internet* by Mark Gibbs and Richard Smith. It's a terrific introduction to the many services available on the Internet, including `gopher`, `archie`, the World Wide Web, `telnet`, and `ftp`. Those that aren't covered in this hour are shown in the last hour of this book, however; so you at least will have seen most of these important Internet information-related commands.

Task 23.3: Finding Archives with `archie`

DESCRIPTION If you spent any time at all looking at the list of FTP archives in the previous task, you already realize that just obtaining a list of files available in one system can be quite a chore. Yet, computers are ideally suited to serve as their own navigational aides, as they easily work with large and complex databases.

The `archie` system was developed at McGill University in Canada. It is a huge database of all files and directories available on all registered FTP sites in the world. That's quite a bit: Over 2.5 million different files are in the database!

Nonetheless, `archie` is a fairly simple-minded program, and there's only so much information you can glean by being able to analyze just file and directory names. For example, if I have a program called "Wallpaper Demo for the Mac" and save it in a file `wallpaper.demo.MAC`, odds are pretty good that people who search for Macintosh demonstration programs could find it. What if I decided that was too many letters and instead named it `wp.mac`? It's much less likely that folks would know what the file contains.

There are a few options worth knowing before using `archie`, most notably that the format of the program itself is `archie` *search-string*. By default, the program lists only exact matches to the pattern, but `-c` forces it to match on either upper- or lowercase letters, depending on the pattern; `-e` forces exact matches (this is the system default, but some sites have other default actions—it's up to your local system administrator); `-s` considers the search pattern as a possible substring; `-r` searches for the specified regular expressions; and `-l` lists the results in a format suitable for use with other programs (such as `fget`). One final option is of interest: The `-L` option lists all `archie` servers known to the program.

CAUTION

If you don't have the `archie` program on your system, don't despair! You can use `telnet` to connect to `archie.rutgers.edu`, `archie.sura.net`, or `archie.unl.edu` to interact with the `archie` databases directly (although

> this isn't necessarily faster than using the archie program if you have it on your system!). Finally, if you aren't on the Internet at all, you can send electronic mail to archie at any of the three systems listed. Use prog *search-string*, and ensure that the last line of your message is quit so it knows when to stop reading your mail for commands.

ACTION

1. To start out, I want to see what archie servers are known by my version of archie:

    ```
    % archie -L
    Known archie servers:
            archie.ans.net (USA [NY])
            archie.rutgers.edu (USA [NJ])
            archie.sura.net (USA [MD])
            archie.unl.edu (USA [NE])
            archie.mcgill.ca (Canada)
            archie.funet.fi (Finland/Mainland Europe)
            archie.au (Australia)
            archie.doc.ic.ac.uk (Great Britain/Ireland)
            archie.wide.ad.jp (Japan)
            archie.ncu.edu.tw (Taiwan)
     * archie.sura.net is the default Archie server.
     * For the most up-to-date list, write to an Archie server and give it
       the command `servers'.
    ```

    Notice the third line from the end: My default archie server is archie.sura.net. The other servers listed can be accessed but aren't checked directly. Usually, it doesn't matter which server is used because the information available through different servers is mostly identical. If you just know something's out there but can't find it, check a few different servers with archie -h *servername*.

2. To search for a specific program, I simply can enter the name of the program. I'm interested in finding a UNIX program called newmail:

    ```
    % archie newmail

    Host plaza.aarnet.edu.au

        Location: /usenet/comp.sources.unix/volume25
                FILE -r--r--r--      15049  Dec 20 1991  newmail

    Host gum.isi.edu

        Location: /share/pub/vmh/bin
                FILE -rwxr-xr-x        104  Jul  9 18:26  newmail

    Host venera.isi.edu

        Location: /pub/vmh/bin
                FILE -rwxr-xr-x        104  Jul  9 11:26  newmail
    ```

23

```
Host pith.uoregon.edu

    Location: /pub/Solaris2.x/bin
          FILE -rwxr-xr-x        46952   Oct 27 12:09  newmail
    Location: /pub/Sun4/bin
          FILE -rwxr-xr-x        65536   Oct 27 12:10  newmail


Host ee.utah.edu

    Location: /screen/bin
          FILE -rwxr-xr-x        57344   Oct 11 1992   newmail
```

You can see that plaza.aarnet.edu.au (an educational facility in Australia—you can tell because of the .au suffix), gum.isi.edu, venera.isi.edu, pith.uoregon.edu, and ee.utah.edu all have one or more programs called newmail. There's no way, however, to ascertain from this listing whether it's the program I'm seeking.

3. The same list can be produced in a more succinct format by using the -1 command:

```
% archie -1 newmail
199112200000000Z   15049 plaza.aarnet.edu.au /usenet/comp.sources.unix/
➥v25/newmail
19930709182600Z      104 gum.isi.edu /share/pub/vmh/bin/newmail
19930709112600Z      104 venera.isi.edu /pub/vmh/bin/newmail
19931027120900Z    46952 pith.uoregon.edu /pub/Solaris2.x/bin/newmail
19931027121000Z    65536 pith.uoregon.edu /pub/Sun4/bin/newmail
199210110000000Z   57344 ee.utah.edu /screen/bin/newmail
```

4. To search for all files that have something, anything, to do with mail (which is going to generate a lot of output!), I can use the -s option:

```
% archie -s mail ¦ more

Host plaza.aarnet.edu.au

    Location: /usenet/comp.sources.unix/volume7
      DIRECTORY drwxr-xr-x         512  Jan 16 1993   smail


Host metro.ucc.su.oz.au

    Location: /pub/netinfo/sendmail
          FILE -rw-r--r--        12410   Jul  9 1992   sendmail.cf
    Location: /pub/netinfo/sendmail/sendmail.mu
          FILE -rw-r--r--        15745   Oct 10 1990   sendmail.cf


Host brolga.cc.uq.oz.au

    Location: /comp.sources.unix/volume7
      DIRECTORY drwxr-xr-x         512  Dec  1 1987   smail


Host cs.ubc.ca

    Location: /mirror3/386BSD/386bsd-0.1/filesystem/etc
          FILE -rw-r--r--        17933   Jul  8 1992   sendmail.cf
--More-- _
```

It turns out that there are 95 matches, mostly comprising either sendmail.cf, smail, or Rnmail.

5. The `archie` system also has a relatively limited database of descriptions called the *software description database*, which you can check by directly connecting to a remote archie system with `telnet`:

```
% telnet archie.unl.edu
Trying...
Connected to crcnis2.unl.edu.
Escape character is '^]'.


SunOS UNIX (crcnis2)

login: archie
Last login: Wed Dec 15 10:47:17 from INS.INFONET.NET
SunOS Release 4.1.2 (CRCNIS2) #1: Wed Dec 16 12:10:12 EST 1992


too many archie users... try again later
Connection closed by foreign host.
```

As you can see, sometimes there are already too many people using the system for you to log in and access their server.

6. I try an alternate site, `archie.internic.net`, the Internet Network Information Center, and connect:

```
% telnet archie.internic.net
Trying...
Connected to ds.internic.net.
Escape character is '^]'.
            InterNIC Directory and Database Services

Welcome to InterNIC Directory and Database Services provided by AT&T.
These services are partially supported through a cooperative agreement
with the National Science Foundation.

First time users may login as guest with no password to receive help.

Your comments and suggestions for improvement are welcome, and can be
mailed to admin@ds.internic.net.

AT&T MAKES NO WARRANTY OR GUARANTEE, OR PROMISE, EXPRESS OR IMPLIED,
CONCERNING THE  CONTENT OR  ACCURACY OF THE  DIRECTORY  ENTRIES AND
DATABASE  FILES  STORED  AND  MAINTAINED  BY  AT&T.  AT&T EXPRESSLY
DISCLAIMS AND EXCLUDES ALL EXPRESS WARANTIES AND IMPLIED WARRANTIES
OF MERCHANTABILITY AND FITNESS FOR A PARTICULAR PURPOSE.


SunOS UNIX (ds)
login: _
```

Any time you're logging into an `archie` system, using the `archie` login is a good bet:

```
login: archie

**********************************************************************

             Welcome to the InterNIC Directory and Database Server.

**********************************************************************

# Message of the day from the localhost Prospero server:

      Welcome to Archie  server for the
      InterNIC Directory and Database Services.

# Bunyip Information Systems, 1993

# Terminal type set to `vt100 24 80'.
# `erase' character is `^?'.
# `search' (type string) has the value `sub'.
archie>
```

Now try the whatis command to search the software description database for mail
and generate a staggering number of matches.

JUST A MINUTE

In fact, there were many more matches than shown here. About 80
matches were made to *Request for Comment* documents available through
the Network Information Center.

```
archie> whatis mail
NMail                   Novice Mail
answer                  vacation(1) replacement. Answer mail while you're away
batchmail               Convert batched news articles to a format suitable for
exchanging via electronic mail
bencode-bdecode         Binary-to-ASCII encoding scheme for mail
brkdig                  Break mailing list digest into USENET messages
bsmtp                   Batch SMTP (Simple Mail Transfer Protocol)
cfc                     "Compile" sendmail.cf files into EASE language
cheap-fax               El-cheapo E-mail to Fax for sendmail
ck                      Check mailboxes for new mail
ckmail                  Check a user's mail and report the "from" lines
clr-queue               Clean out the sendmail mail queue and send the results to
the system administrator
clr.queue               sendmail clean-up script
cms-unix                Transfer files (and files of mail data) between UNIX and
CMS (or MVS) systems
cobwebs                 Check for old or unusually large mailboxes
cryptmail               Send and receive encrypted mail
deliver                 Mail delivery agent which uses shell scripts as its
configuration files
distantbiff             Monitor distant mailboxes
dmail                   Mail reading and sending program whic supports folders
and various methods of grouping messages by subject, address etc
dnamail                 Send DECNET mail to/from a Sun running Sunlink/DNI
```

```
ease                    Ease, a language for writing sendmail.cf files
elm                     Elm (user agent) mail system
faces                   Visual mail/print monitor
fido-usenet-gw          Implement a gateway between UUCP/Usenet/Mail and Fidonet
from                    Mail summary generator
gate                    Simple mail->news->mail gateway suite
gatech                  GaTech Sendmail files
ida-sendmail            Enable sendmail to have direct access to dbm(3) files
and Sun Yellow Pages, separate envelope/header rewriting rulesets, and
multi-token class matches
junkmail                Delete outdated mail automatically
labels                  Program to make mailing labels
lmail                   A local mail delivery program
m                       The more/mail/make/man thing
mail-s                  Mail transmission with subject and suppression
mail.fixes              Patches to BSD4.2 mail (SysV mailx?)
maildigest              Construct a ARPA-style digest from a file of mail messages
mailias                 "decode" mail aliases from your .mailrc and tell you who
things are going to
mailsplit               Send files and/or directories via electronic mail using
"tar", "compress", etc
mailwatcher             A Simple Mailwatcher
malias                  Expand .mailrc aliases
mep102b                 Mail Extensions Package. Handles things like
automatically tossing mail from people you don't want to hear from, logging
incoming mail, and so on
mh-rn-interface         Method of interfacing the Rand MH mail handler with
the "rn" USENET news reading program
ml                      Sort mail by Subject into separate files
mn                      Mail summary/tally utility
mp                      Mail pretty printer (aka mail->postscript)
mp23                    A PostScript pretty printer for mail etc
mq                      Display mail queue and "from" output
mq-from                 PD replacements for mailq(1) and from(1) commands
msg                     Screen oriented mail User agent
mush                    Mail user's shell
mverify                 Mail alias/user verification
na-digest               Archive of mailings to NA distribution list  (argonne)
netdata                 Transfer data (and mail) between SysV and CMS
newsmail                Mail news articles to users automagically
nmail                   Do UUCP mail routing using the output of the
pathalias(1) program
pc-mail-nfs             pc-mail over nfs
pcmail                   Turn a PC into a (non-routing) UUCP node (DOS, PC unix)
pmdc                    A "personal mail daemon" which filters mail much like GNU
Emacs does but without the overhead of Emacs and LISP
procmail                Mail processing package
returnmail              PD vacation(1). Answer your mail while you're away
rmail-uucp              Domain Capable rmail for UUCP sites
round-robin             Mail round-robiner
savemap.nawk            A safe comp.mail.maps saver
sendmail-qref           A sendmail quick reference card
sendmail.ms             Sendmail reference card (troff -ms)
showhook.mh             MH Mail patch to allow actions when mail is read
```

```
      sm-smtp              Sendmail replacement for smail sites
      smail                A smart mailer and UUCP path router
      smsmtp               SMTP server/client implementation for System V and the
      SMAIL program
      smtp_send            SMTP SEND command for Sendmail
      soundmail            Sound mail
      sunmailwatch         A mail watcher for SUNwindows
      tar-untar-mail       Sending tar(1) files through mail
      uumail               Routing program to use the pathalias(1) database
      uumailclean          Clean-up backlogged UUCP mail
      ux-maze              UX-Maze Mail Based File Server
      vacation             PD vacation(1) replacement for Berkeley systems not
      running sendmail
      vmail                Screen-based mail handler
      watch                A SysV program to display mail, time/date, and users on/off
      wrap                 Line wrap per for BIT/EARNnet mailings
      xbiff                Noification of new mail under X11
      xmail                Mail front end for X11
      xmh                  X11 front end to the mh(1) mail agent
      xwatch               Replacement for xbiff and the mailbox widget(X11)
      archie>
```

Now that the search is done, it's time to log out:

```
archie> quit
# Bye.
Connection closed by foreign host.
%
```

7. To find where one of these programs is located, I can again use the local `archie` program:

```
% archie mverify

Host ftp.germany.eu.net

      Location: /pub/mail
         DIRECTORY drwxr-xr-x          512 Jul  7 15:15  mverify
```

It looks like the only host that has the program is in Germany!

SUMMARY With the capability to search the software description database, `archie` is a powerful package for finding programs and information on the Internet. Remember that it's still limited by the ways that people might phrase or describe things as well as file-naming conventions on each server.

Task 23.4: A Few Interesting `telnet` Sites

DESCRIPTION Two tasks on which I spend too much time are purchasing compact discs and books. With the Internet, I can do both without leaving the privacy of my own computer desk! Although these are commercial services, I illustrate them here to demonstrate the incredible breadth of services available only on the Internet.

ACTION

1. The first place to search is the Compact Disk Connection, an electronic record store available through a system called Holonet:

```
% telnet orac.holonet.net
Trying...
Connected to orac.holonet.net.
Escape character is '^]'.


HoloNet(SM) -- A service of IAT

HoloNet Member Name (Non-members type "guest"): _
```

To log in to the CD Connection, I enter cdc:

```
HoloNet Member Name (Non-members type "guest"): cdc
Last login: Wed Dec 15 13:04:18 from intrepid.ece.uc.

- - - - - - - - - - - - - - - - - - - - - - -
HoloNet Services Gateway
- - - - - - - - - - - - - - - - - - - - - - -

The HoloNet Services Gateway provides access to electronic services
through HoloNet.  Use of this service is subject to HoloNet Terms
and Conditions.

The Compact Disc Connection is an independent service not affiliated
with Information Access Technologies, Inc.

Control-C to abort connect
Waiting for the Compact Disc Connection.....................
Connected to CD Connection.
Escape character is '^]'.



                    Welcome to the

            **  Compact Disc Connection  **

        Dealing Exclusively in the Online Sale of

                  * Compact Discs *

                  and Featuring:

+=.=.=.=.=.=.=.=.=.=.=.=.=.=.=.=.=.=.=.=.=.=.=.=.=.=.=.=+
¦ FREE access from the Internet & from 75 Cities, NOW!  ¦
+=.=.=.=.=.=.=.=.=.=.=.=.=.=.=.=.=.=.=.=.=.=.=.=.=.=.=.=+

            - More Than 75,000 CDs Online -
```

```
                    - Discount Prices -

              We accept VISA and MasterCard

   *** CDC News *****************************************************

   Want to know the status of your latest order?  See the (C)heck order
   status feature just added to the CDC Database Menu...

   COMPACT DISC EUROPE, a Florida-based import company, is now online!
   Looking for imports that aren't in our catalog?  Dial into their
   online database of more than 100,000 imports from Europe and Japan
   at: 408 730-8138.  Any speed up to 9600, 8N1.  Voice: 305 481-8984.

   And speaking of imports, all

       PHANTOM IMPORTS
       ALEX IMPORTS

   in our catalog are on sale now!  See (S)ales at the Main Menu...

   ****************************************************************

 ** CDC Main Menu **

   (C)Ds            Enter CD database.
   (I)nformation    Display CDC policies and general information.
   (N)umbers        Display free modem access telephone numbers.
   (O)verseas       Display details of shipping to overseas destinations.
   (A)ll-Music      Display details of the All-Music Guide.
   (G)olden Ears    Display details of the Golden Ears Society.
   (S)ales          Display details of current sales.
   (F)ree CDs       Display details of the free Adventures-in-Music.
   (T)op Selling    Display Top Selling/Grammy Award Winning CDs.
   (D)irectory      Display the directory of CD labels and manufacturers.
   (P)ausing        Toggle pausing/no pausing of scrolling displays.
   (B)rief          Toggle brief/full menu displays.
   (M)essage        Leave a message to the management.
   (R)etrieve       Retrieve messages from the management to you.
   (Q)uit           Sign off & hang up.

=> Your command: C
```

I want to search the CD database, so I enter C:

```
** CDC Database Menu **

   (S)earch         Search database and select CDs.
   (R)eview         Review CDs you've selected.
   (O)rder          Order CDs you've selected.
   (C)heck Status   Check the status of your recent orders.
   (P)assword       Change the password to your CDC account.
   (Q)uit           Return to the Main Menu.

=> Your command: S
```

I use the S key to request a search:

```
** CDC Search Menu **

   (A)rtist     Search by artist or composer's last name, e.g., Mozart, Dylan.
   (S)ong       Search by song or track title, e.g., Star Spangled Banner.
   (T)itle      Search by CD title, e.g., Woodstock.
   (P)erformer  Search for performers of classical music, e.g. Berlin Phil.
   (M)anuf'er   Search by manufacturer's label, e.g., CBS
   (N)umber     Search by manufacturer's catalog number, e.g., 422 493-2.
   (C)ategory   Search by category of music, e.g., classical, rock.
   (L)imits     Set limits for release date, music type, or Golden Ears ratings.
   (1)-line     Toggle 1 or 2-line CD displays.
   (E)xample    Display an example CD and an explanation of its components.
   (Q)uit       Return to the Database Menu.

=> Your command: A
```

Then I search by artist:

```
** CDC Search by Artist **

Enter the first few letters of the artist/composer's name (last, first),
or enter =STRING to search all positions in the artist name for STRING,
or press ENTER to repeat the previous search:
or enter a Q to quit: coltrane,j

   MCA42001    +COLTRANE*JOHN            AFRICA/BRASS VOL.1 & 2     10/1
   $10.58       MCA  9/88  1:07

   PAB20101    COLTRANE*JOHN             AFRO BLUE IMPRESSIONS
   $18.99       PABLO  12/93

   CAP99175    +COLTRANE*JOHN            ART OF JOHN COLTRANE         9/1 ***
   $12.02       CAPITOL  8/92

   oRi415      COLTRANE*JOHN             BAHIA                           **
   $10.50      &ORIGINAL JAZZ CLASSICS  2/90  WILBUR HARDEN, RED GARLAND,
   PAUL

   MCA5885     +COLTRANE*JOHN            BALLADS                    8.7/3 **
   $10.79      &MCA  5/88  :32

   ATL1541     +COLTRANE*JOHN            BEST OF                         ***
   $10.74       ATLANTIC  9/90  :41

   PAB2405417+COLTRANE*JOHN              BEST OF                          **
   $10.59      &PABLO  9/92
```

```
=> Enter a CD selector, a Q, or a ? for help: mca42001

=> Selected:

*MCA42001   +COLTRANE*JOHN           AFRICA/BRASS VOL.1 & 2          10/1
  $10.58      MCA  9/88  1:07

=> 1 item(s) selected.  $10.58

=> Enter a CD selector, a Q, or a ? for help:_
```

That's the CD I want. I easily could choose to buy it here and enter my VISA or MasterCard number when prompted, and the disc would be mailed to me within a week or so. For some cryptic reason, I decide I don't need this album, and I quit the program.

2. Now that I've exercised such self-restraint in avoiding the purchase of the Coltrane album, how about buying a book or two? To connect to Book Stacks Unlimited in Cleveland, Ohio, I use telnet books.com:

```
% telnet books.com
Trying...
Connected to books.com.
Escape character is '^]'.




Book Stacks Unlimited, Inc.
Cleveland, Ohio  USA


The On-Line Bookstore


Modem    : (216)861-0469
Internet : telnet books.com




Enter your FULL Name (e.g SALLY M. SMITH) :
```

I have an account, so follow me as I step through the book database, find a book, and ensure that it's the correct choice.

```
Type P to Pause, S to Stop listing


                   BOOK STACKS UNLIMITED, INC.
                   >>>>   NEWS   <<<<


   1 - Internet Connection Is Now Available.

   2 - Biblio-Tech -- The December Book.

   3 - Helpful Information for Internet Callers.
       NOTE: TELNET must be in character mode to echo keystrokes.

   4 - Biblio-Tech. The Online Book Discussion Group.

   99 - Recent Enhancements (Updated 10/23/93).

   Press Enter to proceed to the Main Menu.

   Type File # to View
   <L>ist Files Again
   <ENTER> To Exit :
```

```
   *****************************************
   *       Book Stacks Unlimited, Inc.     *
   *              MAIN MENU                 *
   *****************************************


         <B>ook Store

         <M>essages

         <N>ews/Notes

         <S>uggestions/Comments

         <F>iles/Magazines

         <U>tilities

         <H>elp

         <G>oodBye

   Command: B
```

23

```
**********************************************************
*                   The Book Store                       *
*                  273,481 Titles                        *
**********************************************************

  <A>uthor Search          <R>eview Your Selections

  <T>itle Search           <O>rder (when done)

  <K>eyWord Title Search   <C>heck Order Status

  <I>SBN Search

  <S>ubject Search \ Just Published


-------------------------------------------------------
       <P>revious Menu    <H>elp    <G>oodbye

Command: T
```

```
SEARCH DATABASE BY TITLE

Enter the first word(s) of the TITLE.

Omit leading 'A', 'AN','THE'. The first few letters are enough.
Only the first 20 characters will be used.

<ENTER> Previous Menu, <?> Help, <ENTER>: tale of two cities
```

```
# TITLE    AUTHOR                         PUB/BINDING/BK MARKS/PRICE
-------------------------------------------------------------------
1 A Tale of Two Cities
        Dickens, Charles                 07/90 Paperback  S/O $  7.95
2 A Tale of Two Cities
        Dickens, Charles/Woodcock, George 06/85 Paperback  S/O $  4.95
3 A Tale of Two Cities
        Dickens, Charles                 05/90 Paperback   12 $  4.99
4 Tale of Two Cities
        Dickens, Charles                 08/91 Paperback    6 $  2.95
5 A Tale of Two Cities
        Dickens, Charles                 12/92 Paperback   12 $  4.99
6 A Tale of Two Cities
        Dickens, Charles                 09/89 Paperback    6 $  2.50
7 Tale of Two Cities (Longman Classics, Stage 2)
        Dickens, Charles                 05/91 Paperback  S/O $  7.25
```

23

```
8 A Tale of Two Cities (World Classics)
         Dickens, Charles                11/88 Paperback  S/O $  4.95
9 A Tale of Two Cities (Courage Classics)
         Dickens, Charles                03/92 Hardcover  S/O $  5.98

<F>orward, <B>ackward, <P>revious Menu, <1-9> View Book # : 7
```

```
YOU HAVE SELECTED THE FOLLOWING TITLE:

Author  : Dickens, Charles

Title   : Tale of Two Cities (Longman Classics, Stage 2)


ISBN    : 0582030471
Volume  :
Subject : General Fiction
Dewey # :
Publisher: Addison Wesley (Longman)
Date Pub : 05/91
Binding  : Paperback
Edition  :
Bookmarks: S/O
Price    : $  7.25

How many copies would you like?, <ENTER> To Exit :
```

Again, I decide not to buy, and back out using the P (previous menu) option until I can use G to say goodbye.

SUMMARY These are but two of hundreds of commercial services available on the Internet. One of the best places to learn about the entire range of services available is to read Scott Yanoff's List of Internet Services, available from anonymous FTP on csd4.csd.uwm.edu. If you're using fget, enter fget csd4.csd.uwm.edu:/pub/inet.services.txt.

This wraps up the tour of Internet navigational packages and Usenet. In these last two hours, you have learned about archie and gopher, and you have traveled with me to library computers in Australia and Venezuela, and even watched over my shoulder as I almost ordered a John Coltrane CD and a recent edition of *A Tale of Two Cities*. And then there's the wonderful world of the Usenet!

The Internet is an amazing resource, and it's growing dramatically each day. By the time you read this, the size of the WAIS database list, the number of archie files in that database, and the number of Usenet newsgroups will have expanded even further. If there's an Information Highway in your future, the Internet is most certainly going to be a key part of it, and you can't go wrong by spending some time learning more about it!

23

Workshop

The Workshop summarizes the key terms you learned and poses some questions about the topics presented in this chapter. It also provides you with a preview of what you will learn in the next hour.

Key Terms

anonymous FTP   A system set up to respond to `ftp` queries that does not require you to have an account on the system.

bookmark   A saved `gopher` menu item through which you easily can build your own custom `gopher` information screens.

Request for Comment   An official UNIX design specification, also known as an RFC.

search string   The pattern specified in a search.

Questions

1. Use `telnet` and `rlogin` to log in to one of the sites shown in Table 23.3. You don't have an account, so drop the connection once you see a `login:` prompt.

2. Use `ftp` to connect to `ftp.eff.org` and see what files the Electronic Frontier Foundation has made available to anonymous FTP users. Copy one onto your system, and read through it to see what you think about the organization itself.

3. Using `archie`, find one or two archive sites that have a copy of the `tin` newsreading program.

Preview of the Next Hour

This completes your tour of the Internet. In your final hour, you are introduced to the basics of C, the primary programming language for UNIX.

Hour **24**

Programming in C for UNIX

This hour introduces you to the basics of the C programming language. C is the most commonly used language for programming UNIX systems. Other common languages are C++ and Perl, but C is the oldest, and many concepts are derived from there. This chapter introduces a lot of concepts. I assume that you have some basic math and programming skills, but even if you don't, I encourage you to skim through the material to learn about some of the foundations of the UNIX system and how programmers can extend it in many different directions. With any luck, you'll have your interest piqued and decide to learn how to get the computer to jump through hoops for you by writing your own programs.

Goals for This Hour

In this hour, you learn to write your first program and about the following:

☐ Basic data types and operators

☐ Expressions

- ☐ Conditional statements
- ☐ Looping statements
- ☐ Functions
- ☐ Arrays
- ☐ Pointers
- ☐ Structures

First, you learn a simple program and how to make it run. After that, you learn the different data types and how to manipulate the data. Control flow follows, where you learn how to make your program execute alternate statements. You'll wind up with some of the more advanced topics in C programming.

Task 24.1: Your First Program

DESCRIPTION   Historically, the first program written is called the "Hello, World" program because it simply outputs that sentence. However, with the recent discovery of life on meteoroids from Mars, and the suspicion that the oceans of Europa may also support life, we should instead be greeting the universe.

ACTION

The first program is actually very simple:

```
#include <stdio.h>

main()
{
printf("Hello, universe!\n");
}
```

Six simple lines; the first is an `include` line. This is a pre-processor instruction that tells the compiler that when you build this program, it should include the contents of the named file in addition to the code in this file. When included in <>, the compiler looks in the standard directory, /usr/include. If the filename is quoted (as in `#include "test.h"`) it looks in the current directory for the specified file.

JUST A MINUTE

A compiler is a special program found on any development system. It reads in your program (source code), checks to make certain that it is correct, and creates an executable program.

24

The file being included, stdio.h, is a header file that defines the standard input and output functions. The .h is a naming convention indicating that the file is a header and is meant to be used with the #include statements. Other common names used in C are .c for the source file and .o for an intermediate object file.

The main is the program header. Every program, no matter how big or how small, must have a main included. This must be followed by a curly brace, {, and any number of statements, followed by a closing curly brace. This is the actual program. In our example, the main has two parentheses following. C treats main as a normal function (described later). You can pass arguments to main from a command line.

The statement is printf("Hello, universe!\n");. This calls the printf function, which takes a string, possibly with some arguments, and places the contents of the string on the output. Within the string, there is a pair of characters that you may not understand, \n. The backslash is a C convention indicating that a special character follows. Table 24.1 lists the special C characters.

Table 24.1. Special C characters.

Character	Meaning
\a	Bell character, which causes your terminal to beep
\b	Backspace
\f	New page
\n	New line
\r	Return
\t	Tab
\v	Vertical tab
\\	Backslash
\?	Question mark
\'	Single quote
\"	Double quote
\ooo	Octal number (o is a digit between 0 and 7)
\xhh	Hexadecimal number (h is a digit between 0 and f, where a is 10, b is 11, c is 12, d is 13, e is 14, and f is 15)

This is a very simple program. Once you've written it, you need to save it to a file. Let's call that file hello.c. Once the file is saved, you can use the cc command to build the program.

```
% cc hello.c
```

This creates a file called a.out, which is an executable file. You can run a.out directly, or you can use the mv command to give it a new name. Alternatively, you can add the -o option to the cc command:

```
% cc -o hello hello.c
```

When you run the program, the output is

```
% hello
Hello, universe!
```

Of course, there are many different ways to write this program, but this is the most basic and direct way to output a line of information to the screen.

SUMMARY This is only the beginning of learning C. This program only outputs a single string.

Task 24.2: Basic Data Types and Operators

DESCRIPTION Data in C programs can be kept in many forms. The basic data types are character, integer, and floating point. These can be modified with standard operators, such as addition and multiplication. Shell programs allow only for strings and arrays; with C, you have more options.

ACTION Each C type is built from three basic data types. You can have a single character, which is type char. The character is the amount of space needed to store a single character. In languages that use the Roman alphabet, such as English, letters, digits, and punctuation symbols are encoded in ASCII, which require seven bits to translate. Because bytes are eight bits, and are a fairly universal data size, a character is allowed eight bits, or one byte.

Other languages use all eight bits. French and Spanish need accents on vowels, and modifiers on consonants. These character sets therefore use the full eight bits. Russian has an entirely different character set, as does Greek, but because there are similarly small numbers of characters, these char variables also are just one byte.

It is when one looks at non-European languages that the single byte causes a problem. Japanese, Chinese, and other languages use a vastly larger number of characters in their script. To accommodate this, in areas where it is needed, the char type is two, or even three, bytes. These are sometimes called *extended characters*.

For the remainder of this book, English and ASCII characters are assumed, so one byte per character is assumed.

The second type of variable is the *integer variable*. This is basically a counter, which can be positive or negative. Usually, the integer is four bytes long, which gives it a range of −2147483648 to 2147483647. All operations on an integer are integer operations, as described in Hour 16, "Basic Shell Programming." The type of an integer is int.

The third type of variable is a *floating-point variable*. This is how you would include fractional, or irrational numbers. If you needed to list a radio station frequency, such as for 88.5 KQED, it would need a floating-point number. Results of uneven division can use floating point. The type of a real number is `float`.

One weakness of floating point is rounding. Floating-point numbers have a limited precision, the end result being a slow, gradual rounding error. If you perform many calculations, this rounding error can grow to be significant.

> A good example of this is your hand-held calculator. Enter the number 2, then take the square root. You should see something like 1.414. Now, square that number. On your calculator, you may see 1.999998. This is the result of rounding error.

A lot of math still can be performed by integers. Programs that handle money often use integers for the total number of cents, because this eliminates rounding error. Answers then are presented as cents divided by 100 (dollars) and the remainder (cents).

These basic variables can be further modified. Integers can be modified with the adjectives `long` and `short`. A `long` integer may use eight bytes and is architecture dependent. On an eight-byte system, the range is then −9223372036854775808 to 9223372036854775807. If you were to spell out that longest number, it would be nine quintillion, two hundred and twenty-three quadrillion, three hundred and seventy-two trillion, thirty-six billion, eight hundred and fifty-four million, seven hundred and seventy-five thousand, eight hundred and seven. A formidable sum in any language.

A `short` integer is usually half the size of a regular integer but is also machine dependent. If your machine has two-byte short integers, the range is −32768 to 32767.

> Many C compilers allow you to omit the `int` when declaring `short` and `long` integers.

The next pair of modifiers is `signed` and `unsigned`. `Signed` is usually assumed; so `unsigned` is the important modifier.

Normally, an integer is considered to have a sign, so of the 32 bits available, one bit, usually the first bit of the 32, acts as a sign flag. If the first bit is set to 1, you take the complement of the number and treat it as the negative number of the same absolute value.

For example, if your bits are

00000000000000001011010010101111

the number you have is 46255. But, if your bits were

10000000000000001011010010101111

The number would be −2147437392.

You could set the integer to unsigned, and then the value would be 2147529903. This extends the top end of the range of integers, at the cost of losing the ability to go negative.

Characters also can be unsigned. Because you can use characters for arithmetic (characters are just bit patterns, as are integers), you also can make them unsigned. This is useful for times when you need only a small range of values; an unsigned character has a range of 0 to 255.

JUST A MINUTE

> A good example of this is in IP addresses. These addresses are a sequence of four numbers between 0 and 255. Many standard libraries store these as arrays of four characters.

As with long and short, the int is not necessary for defining an unsigned integer.

The last modifier is for floating-point numbers. The additional type double is for a double-precision floating-point number. Most UNIX functions now default to double precision if floating point is used.

All variable declarations must go after the opening curly brace. You can define any number of variables, separated by commas, that you wish to use in a program. So, you'll see:

```
int counter;
unsigned long mytaxes;
short myworth,your-worth;
double ratio;
char flag;
```

This declares six variables of five different types.

There are many different operators in UNIX that can be used on any variable. Table 24.2 lists the unary operators first.

Table 24.2. Unary operators.

Operator	Meaning
++var	Increment the variable *var* before using it.
var++	Increment *var* after using it.

Operator	Meaning
--var	Decrement *var* before using it.
var--	Decrement *var* after using it.
-var	Negate the value of *var*.
+var	Use the positive value.
!var	Use the inverse value (for example, 10011100 becomes 01100011).

The increment and decrement operators add or subtract one unit from the value of *var*. The unit for integers and characters is 1, for floating point, it is 1.0. This increment or decrement can have greater meaning for pointers, where it steps to the next member of an array.

Table 24.3 lists the binary operators.

Table 24.3. Binary operators.

Operator	Meaning
a=b	*a* is given the value of *b*
a*b	Multiply *a* and *b*
a/b	Divide *a* by *b*
a%b	The remainder of the division of *a* and *b*
a+b	The sum of *a* and *b*
a-b	The difference of *a* and *b*
a<<b	The value of *a* shifted *b* bits to the left
a>>b	The value of *a* shifted *b* bits to the right
a<b	The result of the comparison of *a* less than *b*
a<=b	The result of the comparison
a>b	The result of the comparison
a>=b	The result of the comparison
a==b	The result of the comparison
a&b	The bitwise AND operation of *a* and *b*
a^b	The bitwise XOR operation
a¦b	The bitwise OR operation
a&&b	The logical AND of *a* and *b*
a¦¦b	The logical OR of *a* and *b*

24

Some of these may not make sense at first glance. *Bitwise shifts* are sometimes useful in different UNIX functions. The same result can be obtained with multiplying the variable by two for a one-bit shift left, or dividing by two for a one-bit shift right. For example, the number 1234 is represented in binary as 0...10011010010. If you do a two-bit left shift, you get 0...1001101001000. This is 4936. A one-bit right shift yields 0...1001101001. This is 617.

The bitwise operators are more interesting. The result is a bit-by-bit comparison of equivalent bits.

	AND	OR	XOR
	1 0	1 0	1 0
1	1 0	1 1	0 1
0	0 0	1 0	1 0

So, if you had two characters, 10110110 and 01101010, the results would be

AND	00100010
OR	11111110
XOR	11011100

JUST A MINUTE

> These are useful for managing flags in a function. You can use AND and OR operations to combine flags for the desired effect. Flags are single bits that, when set, indicate a specific action must be performed. You can use separate variables for each flag, but it is cleaner to include them all in a single variable.

You assign a value to a variable with a simple equals sign.

```
{
int a;
float b;
char c;

a=1;
b=3.1415;
c='c';
```

Note that a single character must be enclosed in single quotes. Later in this chapter, when you look at strings, those need to be enclosed in double quotes. Each of the preceding operators creates an expression. Assignment statements are also expressions. An assignment statement must have a single variable on the left ' " "and any expression or value on the right. This can create some unusual assignments, illustrated here:

```
A=b=c=d=1;
A=((b+c)*d)<=((f/e)<<2);
```

Because an assignment is an expression, you can assign multiple variables the same value, as the first line illustrates. There, the variables A, b, c, and d are all assigned the value 1. The second line is more complicated. First, you add b and c, and then multiply by d. Then, you divide f by e, and do a left bitwise shift of two places. Then, you compare the two values, and if the first is less than or equal to the second, you assign 1 to A; otherwise, you assign 0.

There is a shorthand for many assignments. If you have a=a+4; as a statement, this can be reduced to a+=4;. Any operation where the results of the operation are assigned to one of the operands can be so abbreviated. So, you can perform a bitwise OR with a¦=b;, and you can multiply with a*=b;.

SUMMARY Now you know the basic statements, where you can assign the results of an expression to a variable. You have also learned the different variable types, and a bit about their use.

Task 24.3: Conditional Statements

24

DESCRIPTION *Conditional statements* enable you to take different actions as the result of the evaluation of an expression.

ACTION Any manipulation of a variable in C is considered an *expression;* even the simple assignment is an expression that can be evaluated to a specific value. Furthermore, the results of any expression can be used in a subsequent expression.

You can use an if statement to test an expression and perform an action. The syntax is

```
if (expr) statement-block;
```

You optionally can have an else clause:

```
else statement-block;
```

A *statement-block* is either a single statement followed by a semicolon or a listing of statements surrounded by curly braces.

So, if you wanted to test a specific value to see if it is greater than 1000000, you easily could do this:

```
if (value>1000000) printf("I am rich\n");
```

The else statement can give an alternate answer:

```
if (value>1000000) printf("I am rich\n");
else printf("I have to go to work today.\n");
```

Each expression tested evaluates to a true or false value. C uses 0 for false and 1 for true. However, C also has expanded this to allow any non-zero value to be true. Because zero also is the value NULL, as used when reads fail, you can have

```
if (fgets(stdin,buffer,1024))
    {
    /* Manipulate the input */
    }
```

fgets is a means of reading a line of input, stdin is the standard input file (usually your terminal), and buffer is an array of characters.

One weakness of the if statement is that, with else, the parsing can be tricky. Consider this case:

```
if (a<b) if (c<d) { /* Do something */ }
else { /* Do something else */ }
```

This is a perfectly valid statement in C but is very ambiguous. Is the else clause to be executed if a<b and c>=d? Or is it executed only if a>=b? This depends on the compiler, but it usually will default to the highest valid unmatched condition, that is, if a>=b. If you meant the former, though, you can force that result by putting the second if, with the else, in a statement-block:

```
if (a<b)
    {
    if (c<d)
        {
        /* Do something */
        }
    else
        {
        /* Do something else */
        }
    }
```

You similarly can force the other interpretation with:

```
if (a<b)
    {
    if (c<d)
        {
        /* Do something */
        }
    }
else
    {
    /* Do something else */
    }
```

An alternative forcing is to have an empty block with {} symbols and nothing within:

```
if (a<b)
    if (c<d)
        {
        /* Do something */
        }
    else {}
else
    {
    /* Do something else */
    }
```

There is a very convenient shorthand for simple if statements in C. This is the ?: notation. It takes three expressions and executes the second if the first is true; otherwise, it executes the third. Think of this as *condition*?*true-action*:*false-action*.

A useful form of this is the "plural" statement:

```
printf("%d apple%c",count,(count>1)?"s":"");
```

Here, the comparison is used in the print statement. If there is more than one apple (count>1), the string "s" is appended to apple. You'll find this shorthand in many C programs.

A second type of conditional is the switch statement. This allows for the evaluation of multiple options. The syntax is

```
switch(expression)
    {
case const: statements;
case const: statements;
...
default:
    }
```

The expression can evaluate to any value, and it is then compared with the constant values of each case.

JUST A MINUTE

> If this expression evaluates to a string, using strings in cases won't work; a returned string is just a memory address.

If you were testing input for one of three values as an answer to a question that you output to confirm an action from the user, you'd use this sequence of instructions:

```
switch(c=getchar())
    {
case 'y':
case 'Y':printf("The answer is Yes.\n"); break;
case 'n':
case 'N':printf("Alas, the answer is no.\n"); break;
case 'm':
case 'M':printf("The answer is maybe?\n");break;
default:printf("I do not understand the answer.\n");
    }
```

Note the use of break; after each statement. This indicates that you have finished the execution of this switch block and want to drop to the subsequent code section. Normally, the case statements are just labels, so the program resumes execution from that location.

This drop-through can have its uses; if you want to do the same thing for every valid case but also want to say something in a special case, you can do it:

```
switch(c=getchar())
    {
case 'Y':printf("No need to shout.\n");
case 'y':printf("That's an affirmative.\n");break;
    }
```

Both y and Y will get the message That's an affirmative., but only Y will see No need to shout.

SUMMARY Conditional statements add the power to execute alternative statements.

Task 24.4: Looping Statements

DESCRIPTION There are times when you want to be repetitive. The for, while, and do statements are ideal in this case.

 ACTION The first looping statement is the while loop. These loops test a condition, and while the condition is true, they execute the following code. The syntax is

```
while (expr) statement
```

The statement can be a null statement, if desired. To step through white space in an array of characters, you might use

```
while (str[i++]==' ');
```

While is particularly useful for an indeterminate loop. You just keep executing the statement until the condition is false.

A special case is the infinite loop. You will see this in certain types of programs that wait for events:

```
while(1)
    {
    /* Get event */
    /* Action */
    }
```

The only way to end this program is when the action calls for an exit because the condition 1 is always true

The second kind of loop is the for loop. It takes three expressions, an initialization, a test, and an increment. As long as the test is true, the statement block is executed. The syntax is

```
for(expr1;expr2;expr3) statement;
```

This is exactly the same as:

```
expr1;
while(expr2)
    {
    statement;
    expr3;
    }
```

The choice of loop is up to you.

For loops are particularly useful for stepping through arrays or in any situation where the test is related to an initialization.

For example, you could count the number of characters in an array with:

```
for (i=0; c[i] != 0; i++);
```

You need to remember that an array ends with a character with the value 0, so any real character is true.

None of the conditions needs to be present. A loop for(;;) is an infinite loop.

The third loop is the do loop. It is the same as the while loop, except the test comes after executing the statement block:

```
do
    statement
while (expr);
```

This forces at least one execution of the statement.

You can exit a loop regardless of the condition with a break; statement. This causes you to execute the first statement following the loop. Breaks can occur anywhere in the loop.

You can restart the loop with continue;. In a while loop, continue forces the testing of the condition, then another run through the loop. With a for loop, continue forces the increment expression to be run, then the test, before starting the statement block. With do, the test is executed, then the loop may be restarted.

SUMMARY There are three basic types of loops in C, each usable in different circumstances.

Task 24.5: Functions

DESCRIPTION You can create a more modular program with functions, instead of attempting to include all your statements under main. If you have a piece of code that needs to be executed in different areas of the program, by making it a function, you have a smaller program with the same power.

ACTION There are two types of functions available in C. Strictly speaking, only one is a function; the other is called a macro replacement. Functions start off with a header, this defines the function and its arguments. The complete function syntax is

```
type name(arglist) { statements }
```

The type can be any; it defines the type of variable returned by the function. In addition to the three basic types, there is a fourth, special type, called void. This is used if there is to be no return.

The argument list is a comma-separated list of variables, with a type specified. Even if multiple variables are of the same type, they each need the specifier.

The statements can be any statements at all. In this case, I have a converter from centigrade to Fahrenheit.

```
double fahrenheit(double ctemp)
{
return (ctemp*1.8+32.0);
}
```

This is actually a fairly simple function. The variable ctemp is multiplied by 1.8 (9/5), and has 32 added. You then can include the function in a program.

```
main()
{
printf("The temperature in Fahrenheit when it is");
printf(" 23.3 centigrade is %4.1f\n",
    fahrenheit(23.3));
}
```

Turns out to be a rather balmy 73.9 degrees. Another, more interesting function is one that returns the difference between a centigrade and a Fahrenheit temperature in either centigrade or Fahrenheit:

```
double temperature-difference(double ctemp,double ftemp,char corf)
{
double cftemp;
double difference;

cftemp=ctemp*1.8+32;
difference=(cftemp>ftemp)?cftemp-ftemp:ftemp-cftemp;
return ((corf)?(difference-32)/1.8:difference);
}
```

This is a fairly complicated function. It takes three arguments, a centigrade temperature, a Fahrenheit temperature, and a flag. If the flag is true, the function returns the difference in centigrade. If false, the return is in Fahrenheit.

The function first converts the centigrade temperature into Fahrenheit. It then tests the difference; the test makes sure the difference is always positive. Then, it returns the difference, converted back to centigrade, if needed.

24

The macro is not really a function, but it can be used like one. A macro is a command to the C compiler to replace one piece of text with another. It must occur before the replacement in the file, and it often looks like:

```
#define    CENTIGRADE    1
#define    FAHRENHEIT    0
```

So, any place where CENTIGRADE is used, 1 is replaced. For the preceding difference function, that is quite convenient and much easier to read, too:

```
diff=temperature-difference(centigrade,fahrenheit,CENTIGRADE);
```

This is more clear than:

```
diff=temperature-difference(centigrade,fahrenheit,1);
```

You can specify an argument to the macro, too. Any number can be specified. In this example, I've replaced the conversion of centigrade to Fahrenheit with a macro:

```
#define    fahrenheit(X)    X*1.8+32
```

Now, when a program that calls Fahrenheit is compiled, instead of including a function call, this text—with the X replaced with a value—is substituted and compiled.

SUMMARY You have just had a brief introduction to functions. These are C constructs to group statements that are repeated and which can take arguments and return data.

Task 24.6: Arrays

DESCRIPTION You can associate a group of data items by using arrays.

ACTION Arrays are the means in C where you can declare a list of related objects. The most common type of array is comprised of characters, but arrays of integers and floats are not uncommon.

To declare an array, after you declare the name, follow it by the number of elements:

```
char string[100];
```

This declares that string is an array of 100 characters. The name is not chosen randomly, though. A string, in C, is just an array of characters and can be manipulated as such.

When you access arrays, the first element of the array is always 0. For users of other languages, you may have seen the first element start with 1. That is not the case here. So, an array of size 100 has elements numbered 0 to 99.

Another good example of an array is this prime-number builder:

```
#include <stdio.h>

main()
{
int primes[25];
int counter=1;
int start=3;
int prime;
int i;

primes[0]=2;
printf("2");
while (counter<25)
    {
    prime=1;
    for(i=0;i<counter&&prime;i++)
        if (!(start%primes[i])) prime=0;
    if (prime)
        {
        printf(" %d",start);
        primes[counter++]=start;
        }
    start++;
    }
printf("\n");
}
```

This program builds an array of prime numbers and then uses it to determine further primes. The output is

```
% primes
2 3 5 7 11 13 17 19 23 29 31 37 41 43 47 53 59 61 67 71 73 79 83 89 97x
```

SUMMARY In this task, you were introduced to arrays. Arrays provide a means of relating common data. The most common use is to create a string, which is just an array of characters.

Task 24.7: Pointers

DESCRIPTION Each variable in a C program has a given location in memory. That location, or address, can be assigned to a pointer.

ACTION To understand pointers, you first need to understand how memory is organized. Every time you declare a variable, a piece of memory is allocated in a given size, and is labeled with your variable name. Any time you access that name, the value of the data at that location is provided.

So, when you declare

```
int i;
```

24

a piece of memory the size of an integer is allocated for you to use. In the program, this piece of memory is tracked with the name 'i'.

Suppose, though, you want to know the address of that piece of memory. You can take it with the unary & operator. The value assigned must be a pointer:

```
int i;
int *pointertoint;
```

The asterisk indicates that the variable pointertoint is not an integer, but an address of an integer. Later, you can assign it the address of i with:

```
pointertoint= &i;
```

You then can access that value with (*pointertoint).

This is particularly useful in functions. When you call a function, the arguments you pass to the function remain intact, even after you execute the function. This is called "call by value." So, if you had a function swap and passed it a and b, you'd see this:

```
void swap(int a,int b)
{
int c;

c=a;
a=b;
b=c;
return;
}

main()
{
int a,b;
a=4;
b=2;
printf("%d %d\n",a,b);
swap(a,b);
printf("%d %d\n",a,b);
}
```

Here is an example of the output:

```
% cc -o swapper swapper.c
% swapper
4 2
4 2
```

The swap function did not swap the values. If you want them to change, you need to pass an address and do some pointer arithmetic:

```
void swap(int *a, int *b)
{
int c;
```

24

```
c=(*a);
(*a)=(*b);
(*b)=c;
return;
}

main()
{
int a,b;
a=4;
b=2;
printf("%d %d\n",a,b);
swap(&a,&b);
printf("%d %d\n",a,b);
}
```

Here is an example of the output of the modified program:

```
% cc -o swapper swapper.c
% swapper
4 2
2 4
%
```

By passing the addresses, you can assign the new value to the address in memory of the variables. This is called "call by reference."

Interestingly, pointers and arrays are very closely related. When you declare an array, the memory is allocated for you for all the elements, contiguously. Then, you access this array by an index. You can assign the address of the first member to a pointer as usual:

```
int array[10];
int *point;

point=&array[0];
```

Now, when you increment the pointer, it increments by the size of the array members. So, point+1 now points to the second array member. In fact, *(point+i) is the same as array[i]. The declaration of an array just declares a pointer to that location, and array offsets are calculated as increments to that pointer.

SUMMARY Pointers are an interesting way to access and pass data in a manageable fashion between functions. Instead of using the value in memory, a pointer is the address of the memory. This allows the passing of addresses between functions and the modification of values within functions.

Task 24.8: Structures

DESCRIPTION *Structures* are groupings of unlike data types into a single object. This object can be referenced directly, and the members of the structure can be similarly referenced.

24

ACTION Suppose you wanted to manage a student's academic record. You'd expect to find in there a name, an identification number, and perhaps a GPA. You easily could create this structure:

```
struct academic {
    char name[100];
    int id;
    double gpa;
    };
```

The structure created here is called academic, and it has three fields: a name, which is a string; id, an integer; and gpa, a double-precision floating-point number. Now, I can use this in a program:

```
Char *getname(void)
{
static char buffer[1024];

printf("Enter a name: ");
fgets(buffer,1024,stdin);
while(strlen(buffer)<1)
        {
        printf("No name entered, please try again: ");
        fgets(buffer,1024,stdin);
        }
return buffer;
}

double getgpa(void)
{
static float gpa;

printf("Enter the GPA: ");
scanf("%f",&gpa);
while ((gpa<0.0)||(gpa>4.0))
        {
        printf("The GPA must be between 0 and 4: ");
        scanf("%f",&gpa);
        }
return gpa;
}

main()
{
struct academic {
    char name[100];
    int id;
    double gpa;
    } students[20];
int i;

for(i=0;i<20;i++)
    {
    students[i].id=i;
    strcpy(students[i].name,getname());
    students[i].gpa=getgpa();
    }
}
```

24

This program creates 20 student records. You can assume that `getname` and `getgpa` prompt for name and GPA information, so they are entered manually. You can access members of a structure with the `.` notation, and you can make arrays of structures.

Structures also can have pointers, but the means of accessing the members of a structure are slightly different. Although you could, perhaps, use `(*students).id`, the mechanism `students->id` looks a bit better.

The `->` symbol tells the program that you are using a pointer to reference a part of memory, and you need the specific offset into memory to find a field.

Another type of a structure is the union. In this case, only one member of a union can be accessed at any time. Structures can be viewed as a collection of fields, all included in the data. Unions are means of providing access to only one piece of data, but that data can be interpreted in different fashions.

Unions are not commonly used in early programs, but you may see a union when examining programs.

SUMMARY You now have a grasp of how data in a C program can be related by structures and how to declare a structure.

Summary

This completes a basic walk-through of the C programming language. C is an enormous topic, and there are many books on the subject. The definitive book, if you want to learn more about C, is *The C Programming Language* by the original authors of C, Brian Kernighan and Dennis Ritchie. Of all the programming books James has acquired and read over the years, his C programming language book is the only book always available to him; his copy is a dog-eared third printing of the first edition published back in 1978.

Where To Go Next

This marks the end of your journey. In 24 hours, you've learned considerably more about UNIX than most people ever learn, and I hope you've had fun along the way. Just like any large body of information, particularly one that evolves daily, there's still a lot more to learn. To get from here to there, I have a few suggestions.

To learn more about the Internet, I again recommend the enjoyable and valuable *Navigating the Internet* by Mark Gibbs and Richard Smith. I've read it a couple of times, and each time I find something new and amusing. If nothing else, you will learn what the words *aalii* and *zymurgy* mean, which is a potential boon next time you play Scrabble.

To learn more about C programming, read *Teach Yourself C in 21 Days* by Peter Aitken and Bradley Jones and the official language definition, *The C Programming Language* by Brian Kernighan and Dennis Ritchie. Your UNIX vendor also should have supplied information on C programming tools available with your system.

If you want to become a true UNIX power user, I recommend *UNIX Unleashed*, from Sams Publishing. It is stuffed full of interesting and valuable information about the many UNIX commands on your system.

There are some valuable documents available on the Internet, too: Scott Yanoff has an Internet Services List that can be quite informative. Visit it online for yourself at `http://www.spectracom.com/islist/`. In addition to the list of Usenet newsgroups that you can access with the `findgroup` alias shown earlier, there are thousands of electronic mailing lists. You can obtain a very large listing of all groups by obtaining the file `rtfm.mit.edu:/pub/usenet/news.answers/mail/mailing-lists`. Finally, a list of some of the more fun information servers on the Internet can be obtained as `cerebus.cor.epa.gov:/pub/bigfun`.

Finally, don't forget that your UNIX system has lots of documentation and information, and most of it's online! For any command you find yourself using frequently, the man page entry might well show you new ways to combine things, to work with starting options and files, and more. Always look for an EXAMPLES section at the end of the document, and don't forget that you can print it by using `man cmd ¦ lpr` at the command line.

Have fun, and enjoy UNIX! It's the most powerful operating system you can work with, and it's only as easy or complex as you let it be. Tame the beast and study what's in this book and other books on the subject, and you'll grow to appreciate the system.

Visit the official Web site for this book, too, to get any last-minute updates and pointers to tons more useful and interesting UNIX information online. It's at `http://www.intuitive.com/tyu24`.

Workshop

The Workshop summarizes the key terms you learned and poses some questions about the topics presented in this chapter.

Key Terms

bitwise operator   An operator that works directly on the bits, without changing neighboring bits.

bitwise shift   Changing the location of the bits in memory.

compiler   A program that takes source code and makes it executable.

expression   A C language construct that has a value.

extended characters   A means of displaying non-Latin characters, such as Japanese, Chinese, or Arabic characters.

Questions

1. How would you create the galaxy? How would you greet the solar system?
2. Which types are best for these variables: Social Security number? Eye color? Name?
3. Which loop is better for stepping through elements in an array?
4. How would you build a structure for a driver's license record?

Glossary

absolute filename   Any filename that begins with a leading slash (/); these always uniquely describe a single file in the file system.

access permission   The set of accesses (read, write, and execute) allowed for each of the three classes of users (owner, group, and everyone else) for each file or directory on the system.

account name   This is the official one-word name by which the UNIX system knows you: mine is `taylor`. (See also **account** in Hour 1.)

account   This is the official one-word name by which the UNIX system knows you. Mine is `taylor`.

addressing commands   The set of `vi` commands that enable you to specify what type of object you want to work with. The `d` commands serve as an example: `dw` means delete word, and `db` means delete the previous word.

anonymous FTP   A system set up to respond to `ftp` queries that does not require you to have an account on the system.

arguments   Not any type of domestic dispute, arguments are the set of options and filenames specified to UNIX commands. When you use a command such as `vi test.c`, all words other than the command name itself (`vi`) are arguments, or parameters to the program.

basename   The closest directory name. For example, the basename of `/usr/home/taylor` is `taylor`.

binary   A file format that is intended for the computer to work with directly rather than for humans to peruse. See also **executable**.

bitwise operator   An operator that works directly on the bits, without changing neighboring bits.

bitwise shift   Changing the location of the bits in memory.

blind carbon copy   An exact copy of a message, sent without the awareness of the original recipient.

block special device   A device driver that controls block-oriented peripherals. A hard disk, for example, is a peripheral that works by reading and writing blocks of information (as distinguished from a character special device). See also **character special device**.

block   At its most fundamental, a block is like a sheet of information in the virtual notebook that represents the disk: a disk is typically composed of many tens, or hundreds, of thousands of blocks of information, each 512 bytes in size. See also **i-node** to learn more about how disks are structured in UNIX.

bookmark   A saved `gopher` menu item through which you easily can build your own custom `gopher` information screens.

bookmarks   A listing of favorite sites for quick retrieval.

browser   A program designed to load hypertext pages and follow hyperlinks.

buffer   An area of the screen used to edit a file in emacs.

carbon copy   An exact copy of a message sent to other people. Each recipient can see the names of all other recipients on the distribution list.

character special device   A device driver that controls a character-oriented peripheral. Your keyboard and display are both character-oriented devices, sending and displaying information on a character-by-character basis. See also **block special device**.

colon commands   The vi commands that begin with a colon, usually used for file manipulation.

column-first order   When you have a list of items that are listed in columns and span multiple lines, column-first order is a sorting strategy in which items are sorted so that the items are in alphabetical order down the first column and continuing at the top of the second column, then the third column, and so on. The alternative strategy is **row-first order**.

command alias   A shorthand command mapping, with which you can define new command names that are aliases of other commands or sequences of commands. This is helpful for renaming commands so that you can remember them, or for having certain flags added by default.

command block   A list of one or more shell commands that are grouped in a conditional or looping statement.

command history   A mechanism the shell uses to remember what commands you have entered already, and to enable you to repeat them without having to type the entire command again.

command mode   The mode in which you can manage your document; this includes the capability to change text, rearrange it, and delete it.

command number   The unique number by which the shell indexes all commands. You can place this number in your prompt using \! and use it with the history mechanism as !command-number.

command   Each program in UNIX is also known as a command: the two words are interchangeable.

compiler   A compiler is a program that takes source code and makes it executable.

conditional expression   This is an expression that returns either true or false.

control-key notation   A notational convention in UNIX that denotes the use of a control key. There are three common conventions: Ctrl-C, ^c, and C-C all denote the Control-c character, produced by pressing the Control key (labeled Control or Ctrl on your keyboard) and, while holding it down, pressing the c key.

control number   A unique number that the C shell assigns to each background job for easy reference and for using with other commands, such as `fg` and `kill`.

core dump   The image of a command when it executed improperly.

current job   The job that is currently running on the terminal and keyboard (it's the program you're actually running and working within).

determinant loop   A loop where the number of times the loop is run can be known before starting the loop.

device driver   All peripherals attached to the computer are called devices in UNIX, and each has a control program always associated with it, called a *device driver*. Examples are the device drivers for the display, keyboard, mouse, and all hard disks.

directory   A type of UNIX file used to group other files. Files and directories can be placed inside other directories, to build a hierarchical system.

directory separator character   On a hierarchical file system, there must be some way to specify which items are directories and which is the actual filename itself. This becomes particularly true when you're working with absolute filenames. In UNIX, the directory separator character is the slash (/), so a filename like `/tmp/testme` is easily interpreted as a file called `testme` in a directory called `tmp`.

domain name   UNIX systems on the Internet, or any other network, are assigned a domain within which they exist. This is typically the company (for example, `sun.com` for Sun Microsystems) or institution (for example, `lsu.edu` for Louisiana State University). The domain name is always the entire host address, except the host name itself. (See also **host name**.)

dot   A shorthand notation for the current directory.

dot dot   A shorthand notation for the directory one level higher up in the hierarchical file system from the current location.

dot file   A configuration file used by one or more programs. These files are called dot files because the first letter of the filename is a dot, as in `.profile` or `.login`. Because they're dot files, the `ls` command doesn't list them by default, making them also hidden files in UNIX. See also **hidden file**.

dynamic linking   Although most UNIX systems require all necessary utilities and library routines (such as the routines for reading information from the keyboard and displaying it to the screen) to be plugged into a program when it's built (known in UNIX parlance as *static linking*), some of the more sophisticated systems can delay this inclusion until you actually need to run the program. In this case, the utilities and libraries are linked when you start the program, and this is called *dynamic linking*.

e-mail   Electronically transmitted and received mail or messages.

errant process   A process that is not performing the job you expected it to perform.

escape sequence   An unprintable sequence of characters that usually specifies that your terminal take a specific action, such as clearing the screen.

exclusion set   A set of characters that the pattern must not contain.

executable   A file that has been set up so that UNIX can run it as a program. This is also shorthand for a binary file. You also sometimes see the phrase *binary executable*, which is the same thing! See also **binary**.

expression   A C language construct that had a value. A command that returns a value.

extended characters   A means of displaying non-Latin characters, such as Japanese, Chinese, or Arabic characters.

file-creation mask   When files are created in UNIX, they inherit a default set of access permissions. These defaults are under the control of the user and are known as the file-creation mask.

file redirection   Most UNIX programs expect to read their input from the user (that is, standard input) and write their output to the screen (standard output). By use of file redirection, however, input can come from a previously created file, and output can be saved to a file instead of being displayed on the screen.

filter   Filters are a particular type of UNIX program that expects to work either with file redirection or as part of a pipeline. These programs read input from standard input, write output to standard output, and often don't have any starting arguments.

flags   Arguments given to a UNIX command that are intended to alter its behavior are called *flags*. They're always prefaced by a single dash. As an example, the command line `ls -l /tmp` has `ls` as the command itself, `-l` as the flag to the command, and `/tmp` as the argument.

flow control   The protocol used by your computer and terminal to make sure that neither outpaces the other during data transmission.

foreground job   A synonym for current job.

heuristic   A set of well-defined steps or a procedure for accomplishing a specific task.

hidden file   By default, the UNIX file-listing command `ls` shows only files whose first letter isn't a dot (that is, those files that aren't dot files). All dot files, therefore, are hidden files, and you can safely ignore them without any problems. Later, you learn how to view these hidden files. See also **dot file**.

home directory   This is your private directory, and is also where you start out when you log in to the system.

host name   UNIX computers all have unique names assigned by the local administration team. The computers I use are `limbo`, `well`, `netcom`, and `mentor`, for example. Enter `hostname` to see what your system is called.

hyperlinks   Specifications within a document that include instructions for loading a different document.

i-list   See **i-node**.

i-node   The UNIX file system is like a huge notebook full of sheets of information. Each file is like an index tab, indicating where the file starts in the notebook and how many sheets are used. The tabs are called i-nodes, and the list of tabs (the index to the notebook) is the i-list.

inclusion range   A range of characters that a pattern must include.

indeterminant loop   A loop where the number of times the loop is run is not known before starting the loop.

insert mode   The `vi` mode that lets you enter text directly into a file. The `i` command starts the insert mode, and Escape exits it.

interactive program   An interactive UNIX application is one that expects the user to enter information and then responds as appropriate. The `ls` command is not interactive, but the `more` program, which displays text a screenful at a time, is interactive.

job   A synonym for process.

job control   A mechanism for managing the various programs that are running. Job control enables you to push programs into the background and pull them back into the foreground as desired.

kernel   The underlying core of the UNIX operating system itself. This is akin to the concrete foundation under a modern skyscraper.

key bindings   The `emacs` term for key mapping.

key mapping   A facility that enables you to map any key to a specific action.

kill   Terminate a process.

left rooted   Patterns that must occur at the beginning of a line.

login shell   The shell you use, by default, when you log in to the system.

login   A synonym for account name, this also can refer to the actual process of connecting to the UNIX system and entering your account name and password to your account.

loop   This is a sequence of commands that are repeatedly executed while a condition is true.

mail folder   A file containing one or more e-mail messages.

mail header   The To:, From:, Subject:, and other lines at the very beginning of an e-mail message. All lines up to the first blank line are considered headers.

mailbox   A synonym for mail folder.

major number   For device drivers, the major number identifies the specific type of device in use to the operating system. This is more easily remembered as the device ID number.

man page   Each standard UNIX command comes with some basic online documentation that describes its function. This online documentation for a command is called a man page. Usually, the man page lists the command-line flags and some error conditions.

Meta key   Analogous to a Control key, this is labeled either Meta or Alt on your keyboard.

minor number   Once the device driver is identified to the operating system by its major number, the address of the device in the computer itself (that is, which card slot a peripheral card is plugged into) is indicated by its minor number.

modal   A modal program has multiple environments, or modes, that offer different capabilities. In a modal program, the Return key, for example, might do different things, depending on which mode you were in.

mode   A shorthand way of saying permissions mode.

modeless   A modeless program always interprets a key the same way, regardless of what the user is doing.

multitasking   A multitasking computer is one that actually can run more than one program, or task, at a time. By contrast, most personal computers lock you into a single program that you must exit before you launch another.

multiuser   Computers intended to have more than a single person working on them simultaneously are designed to support multiple users, hence the term *multiuser*. By contrast, personal computers are almost always single-user because someone else can't be running a program or editing a file while you are using the computer for your own work.

named emacs command   A command in emacs that requires you to type its name, like query-replace, rather than a command key or two.

null character   Each character in UNIX has a specific value, and any character with a numeric value of zero is known as a null or null character.

password entry   For each account on the UNIX system, there is an entry in the account database known as the *password file*. This also contains an encrypted copy of the account password. This set of information for an individual account is known as the *password entry*.

pathname   UNIX is split into a wide variety of different directories and subdirectories, often across multiple hard disks and even multiple computers. So that the system needn't search laboriously through the entire mess each time you request a program, the set of directories you reference are stored as your search path, and the location of any specific command is known as its *pathname*.

permission strings   The string that represents the access permissions.

permissions mode   The set of accesses (read, write, and execute) allowed for each of the three classes of users (owner, group, and everyone else) for each file or directory on the system. This is a synonym for access permission.

pipeline   A series of UNIX commands chained by |, the pipe character.

preference file   These are what dot files (hidden files) really are: they contain your individual preferences for many of the UNIX commands you use.

preserve   Ensure that a message doesn't move out of your incoming mailbox even though you've read it.

print job name   The unique name assigned to a print job by the lpr or lp command.

print queue   The queue, or list, in which all print jobs are placed for processing by the specific printer.

process   A program stopped or running within the UNIX operating system. Also known as a job.

recursive command   A command that repeatedly invokes itself.

regular expressions   A convenient notation for specifying complex patterns. Notable special characters are ^ to match the beginning of the line and $ to match the end of the line.

relative filename   Any filename that does not begin with a slash (/) is a filename whose exact meaning depends on where you are in the file system. For example, the file test might exist in both your home directory and in the root directory: /test is an absolute filename and leaves no question which version is being used, but test could refer to either copy, depending on your current directory.

replace mode   A mode of vi in which any characters you type replace those already in the file.

Request for Comment   An official UNIX design specification, also known as an RFC.

root directory   The directory at the very top of the file system hierarchy, also known as *slash*.

row-first order   In contrast to column-first order, this is when items are sorted in rows so that the first item of each column in a row is in alphabetical order from left to right, then the second line contains the next set of items, and so on.

search path   A list of directories used to find a command. When a user enters a command ls, the shell looks in each directory in the search path to find a file ls, either until it is found or the list is exhausted.

search string   The pattern specified in a search.

shell   To interact with UNIX, you type in commands to the command-line interpreter, which is known in UNIX as the *shell*, or *command shell*. It's the underlying environment in which you work with the UNIX system.

shell alias   Most UNIX shells have a convenient way for you to create abbreviations for commonly used commands or series of commands, known as shell aliases. For example, if I always found myself typing ls -CF, an alias can let me type just ls and have the shell automatically add the -CF flags each time.

shell script   A collection of shell commands in a file.

signals   Special messages that can be sent to stopped or running processes.

slash   The root directory.

standard error   This is the same as standard output, but you can re-direct standard error to a different location than standard output.

standard input   UNIX programs always default to reading information from the user by reading the keyboard and watching what's typed. With file redirection, input can come from a file, and with pipelines, input can be the result of a previous UNIX command.

standard output   When processing information, UNIX programs default to displaying the output on the screen itself, also known as standard output. With file redirection, output can easily be saved to a file; with pipelines, output can be sent to other programs.

starting flag   Parameters that you specify on the command line when you invoke the program.

stop a job   Stop the running program without terminating it.

subshell   A shell other than the login shell.

surfing   A style of interacting with the World Wide Web, usually for pleasure, where you follow hyperlinks from Web site to Web site.

symbolic link   A file that contains a pointer to another file rather than contents of its own. This can also be a directory that points to another directory rather than having files of its own. A useful way to have multiple names for a single program or allow multiple people to share a single copy of a file.

tilde command   A command beginning with ~ in Berkeley Mail or the Elm Mail System.

transpose case   Switch uppercase letters to lowercase or lowercase to uppercase.

undelete   Restore a deleted message to its original state.

URL   The specification for a document on the World Wide Web. Usually, it includes a protocol, machine name, and filename.

user environment   A set of values that describe the user's current location and modify the behavior of commands.

user ID   A synonym for account name.

variables   These are names to label data that may change during the execution of a program.

wedged process   A process that is stuck in memory and can't free up its resources even though it has ceased running. This is rare, but annoying.

wildcards   Special characters that are interpreted by the UNIX shell or other programs to have meaning other than the letter itself. For example, * is a shell wildcard and creates a pattern that matches zero or more characters. Prefaced with a particular letter, X—x* —this shell pattern will match all files beginning with X.

working directory   The directory where the user is working.

World Wide Web   A collection of sites that provide hypertext documents on the Internet.

XON/XOFF   A particular type of flow control. The receiving end can send an XON (delay transmission) character until it's ready for more information, when it sends an XOFF (resume transmission).

zero-length variable   A variable that does not have a value assigned to it.

zombie   A terminated process that has not been cleaned up by the parent process.

INDEX

Symbols

" (double quote), 124
' (single quote), 124
  nl command, 157
! (exclamation point), domain
  names, 28
! command
  emacs editor, 296
  vi editor, 270-277
    awk command (creating shell
      scripts), 274-277
    fmt command (tightening
      paragraph lines), 273-274
    ls-CF command output,
      adding to files, 271-272
    paragraphs, assigning to
      UNIX commands, 272-273
!! command (C shell history
  commands), 333
!$ command (C shell history
  commands), 333

!* command (C shell history
  commands), 333
!* notation (aliases), 340
!n command (C shell history
  commands), 333
$ command (vi editor), 219
$ motion command (vi editor),
  250-251
$ notation (egrep command), 175
$ prompt, 24
% (percent sign), 24
& symbol (moving background
  processes), 367
(command (vi editor), 268
) command (vi editor), 268
* (asterisk) wildcard, 129
  filename wildcards, 162-164
    echo command, 162
    limiting number of matches,
      162-164
  regular expressions, 167
+ (vi editor), 234

+= notation, 193
-? flag, 14, 16
-1 flag (ls command), 68, 77, 152
. notation (egrep command), 175
./ls command, 56
/ (filenames), 46
/ command (vi editor), 268
/ search command (vi editor),
  231-232
= command, 141
= command (rn program), 474
? command (vi editor), 232-233
? wildcard (filename wildcards),
  162-164
  echo command, 162
@ (filenames), 46
[^xy] notation (egrep command),
  175
\" character (C programming
  language), 511
\' character (C programming
  language), 511

\? character (C programming language), 511
\\ character (C programming language), 511
^ notation (egrep command), 175
{ command (vi editor), 270
~ command (vi editor), 228
24-hour time, 31

A

\a character (C programming language), 511
a command (vi editor), 216-219
A command (emacs help system), 298
-a flag, 54
    du command, 80-81
    ls command, 68, 77
        dot files, listing, 67
    ps command, 368
(a) notation (egrep command), 175
^a^b command (C shell history commands), 333
a|b notation (egrep command), 175
abbreviations (.exrc file)
    defining, 262
    expanding, 262-263
    listing abbreviations in effect, 263
absolute filenames, 51-52, 60
absolute numeric values (permissions), 98
access permission, 84
account names, 22, 40
accounts, 6
    passwords, changing, 25
acronym database, 451-452
addresses, decoding, 445
addressing commands (vi editor), 243
adjust command, 273
-ag flag (ps command), 372-373
agenda program (hidden files), 55
alias command, 334-335
    man pages, scrolling, 14
alias feature, 124
aliases, 67, 335-337
    !* notation, 340
    cd (customizing prompts), 339-340
    cd command, 337
    chdir command, 337

connecting to accounts on other systems, 336-337
    defining, 335
    printer-specific print commands, 386
    setprompt (customizing prompts), 339-340
    setprompt command, 337
alt newsgroups, 467
AltaVista Web site, 436-437
American Standard Code for Information Interchange (ASCII), 129
American Telephone and Telegraph (AT&T), 3
anonymous FTP, 507
anonymous ftp capabilities (Web sites), 483
AnswerBook, 17
append command (vi editor), 216-218
Apple Computer FTP archive, 489-490
apropos command, 8
    man page, 12
archie program, 493-499
    archie servers, 494
    interacting with archie databases, 493-494
    Internet Network Information Center, 496
        logging in, 496-497
        whatis command (mail searches), 497-499
    program searches, 494-495
        -l command, 495
        -s command, 495
    software description database, 496
archive random library file, 132
archives, finding with archie system, 493-499
    archie servers, 494
    Internet Network Information Center, 496-499
    searching specific programs, 494-495
    software description database, 496
arguments, 35
    command-line arguments
        assigning variables, 350
        for command, 358

arithmetic functions (variables), 350-351
ARPAnet, 480
arrays (C programming language), 523-524
arrow keys, mapping (vi editor), 265
ASCII, 129
ascii command (ftp program), 483
assigning variables
    command-line arguments, 350
    read command, 349
assignment statements (C programming language), 516-517
asterisk wildcard, 129
    filename wildcards, 162-164
        echo command, 162
    regular expressions, 167
at sign (@), filenames, 46
-atime n flag (find command), 398
autoexec.bat (DOS file), 50
awk command, 177, 188-195, 370
    awk program files, creating, 194
    BEGIN pattern, 192
    END pattern, 192-194
    error messages, 195
    -f flag, 188
    -Fc flag, 188
    if-then condition, 194
    interacting with ! command (vi editor), 274-277
    login shells, 189
    modifying output of ls command, 192
    NF variable, 190-191
    NR variable, 191
    print command, 188-189
    sorting data, 190
    tables, building, 194-195
awk filters, 366
awk script (finding local printers), 381-382
-ax flag (ps command), 373

B

\b character (C programming language), 511
^b command (vi editor), 219
b command, 141
    vi editor, 219

B command
  emacs help system, 298
  vi editor, 219
-b flag
  sort command, 151
  test command, 354
b key command (vi editor), 211
B programming language, 5
background processes, 365-368
  & symbol (moving automatically), 367
  files, processing, 366
  input/output, 368
  job ID, 365
  logging out, 377
  starting automatically, 366
  z command, 367
Backspace command (vi editor), 219
base-8 numbering system, 38
basename, 339, 344
bc command (infix calculator), 36-38
  options, 37
BEGIN pattern (awk command), 192
Berkeley Fast File System, 5
Berkeley Mail, 411-416
  command options, 412
  delete command, 415-416
  forwarding messages, 414
  headers command, 414-415
  index numbers, 413-414
  message display, 412-413
  message headers, 414
  quit command, 416
  responding to messages, 414
  save command, 415
    groups of messages, 416
  sending mail, 417-420
    ~h command, 419
    ~p command, 418
    ~r command, 418
    tilde commands, 417-418
Berkeley Systems Design Web site, 429
Berkeley UNIX systems (mail folders), 129
bg command (background processes), 365, 367
bin directory, 46
binary, 60
  permission conventions, 99

binary command (ftp program), 483
binary comparisons (file system), 354
binary format, 46
binary operators (C programming language), 515
bitwise operators, 529
  C programming language, 516
bitwise shift, 529
blind carbon copy, 424
block special devices, 133, 143
blocks, 66, 85
Book Stacks Unlimited telnet site, 503-506
Bookmark menu (Netscape Navigator), 431
bookmarks, 507
  gopher program, 454, 456-457
boot file, 49
Bourne shell, 2, 306
  $ prompt, 24
  alias feature, 124
  Bourne Again shell, 307
  jsh shell, 307
  restricted sh shell, 307
break; statement (exiting loops), 521
browsers, *see* **Netscape Navigator**
BSD, 2
buffers, 303
  emacs editor, 300-302
    moving between buffers, 301
    reading files into buffers, 300
bye command (ftp program), 483

C

C command
  emacs help system, 298
  change commands, 246-248
c command (change commands), 246
  ranges of text, changing, 249-252
-C flag (ls command), 68, 77
-c flag
  grep command, 172, 174
  more program, 139
  test command, 354
  uniq command, 150
\c notation (egrep command), 175
c notation (egrep command), 175

c* notation (egrep command), 175
c+ notation (egrep command), 175
c? notation (egrep command), 175
C programming language
  arrays, 523-524
  compiler, 510
  conditional statements, 517-520
    if statement, 517-519
    switch statement, 519-520
  functions, 521-523
    macro replacements, 523
  looping statements, 520-521
    do loop, 521
    for loop, 520-521
    while loop, 520
  pointers, 524-526
  printf function, 511
  sample program, 510-512
  special C characters, 511
  structures, 526-528
    union structures, 528
  variables, 512-517
    binary operators, 515
    bitwise operators, 516
    character sets, 512
    character variable, 512, 514
    floating-point variables, 513
    integer variable, 512-514
    unary operators, 514-515
    values, assigning, 516-517
C shell, 2, 306
  aliases, 335-337
    !* notation, 340
    cd command, 337
    chdir command, 337
    connecting to accounts on other systems, 336-337
    setprompt command, 337
  command-alias mechanism, 333-335
    alias command, 334-335
    defining an alias, 335
    DOS commands, re-creating, 334
    general format, 333
    ls command flags, 333-334
  configuration files, 317-320
    .cshrc file, 319-320
    .login file, 317-319
  environment, 313-317
    variables, 314-317
  history commands, 333

history list, 327-333
    building, 327-328
    command numbers, 328
    csh history mechanism,
        330-331
    echo command, 330
    file wildcards, 329-330
    filename searches, 331-332
    repeating commands,
        328-329
history mechanism, 324-327
    reviewing histories, 324
    set history command, 326
    shell parameters, checking
        status, 325
    starting, 325
    w command output, 325
jobs (processes)
    fg command, 362, 364
    running in background,
        365-368
    screen-oriented programs,
        363-364
    stopping, 362-365
search path, 91
setting custom prompts, 338-340
    cd alias, 339-340
    cwd variable, 338
    setprompt alias, 339-340
    values, 338
tcsh shell, 307
C shell environment modification
    command, 320
C shell unalias command, 178
C-a command (emacs editor), 289
C-b command (emacs editor),
    287, 289
C-c command (emacs help system),
    298
C-d command (emacs editor), 293
C-d command (emacs help system),
    298
C-e command (emacs editor), 289
C-f command (emacs editor),
    287, 289
C-h command (emacs editor), 287
C-k command (emacs editor), 293
C-n command (emacs editor),
    286, 289
C-n command (emacs help system),
    298
C-p command (emacs editor), 289
C-v command (emacs editor), 289

C-w command (emacs help
    system), 298
C-x [command (emacs editor), 289
C-x] command (emacs editor), 289
C-x Delete command (emacs
    editor), 293
C-x u command (emacs editor),
    293
cal command, 33
calculators, 36
    bc infix, 36, 38
    dc postfix, 38-39
    RPN, 36
    sine, 38
calendar, displaying, 33
cancel command (print queues),
    391
cap mail, 411
carbon copy, 424
case, transposing (vi editor), 228
case command, 357
cat program
    numbering file lines (-n flag),
        153-154
    pipelines, 138
    -s flag, 136-137
    -v flag, 136
    viewing file contents, 136-139
catching signals, 376
cd alias (customizing prompts),
    339-340
cd command, 58
    aliases, 337
cd dir command (ftp program),
    483
cdrom directory, 49
-CF flag (ls command), 486
change command, 246-252
    lines, changing contents, 247-248
    ranges of text, changing, 249-252
change shell (chsh) command,
    310, 312-313
character range (filename
    wildcards), 164-166
character sets, 512
character special devices, 133, 143
character variable, 512
    unsigned variable, 514
chdir command (aliases), 337
chgrp command, 109-110
chmod command
    modifying permissions, 96-98
    numeric permissions strings, 102

    setting new permissions, 98-102
    symbolic notation, 96
chmod function, 90
chown command, 108-109
chsh (change shell) command,
    124, 312-313
Clear key, mapping, 264
clock
    24-hour time, 31
    displaying time, 33
close command (ftp program), 483
colon commands (vi editor),
    236-241, 243
    :e command, 241
    :n command, 240
    :r command, 238-239
    :w command, 238
column-first order, 85
comma-separated lists, 68
command alias command, 320
command aliases, 306-307, 321
command history, 321
    command shells, 306-307
command mode (vi editor), 243
command number, 344
command prompts, see prompts
command shells, see shells
command-alias mechanisms
    (shells), 333-335
    alias command, 334-335
    defining an alias, 335
    DOS commands, re-creating, 334
    general format, 333
    ls command flags, 333-334
command-blocks, 355, 360
command-line arguments
    assigning variables, 350
    for command, 358
command-line interfaces, 2
command-line systems, 6
command.com (DOS file), 50
commands
    ! (emacs editor), 296
    ! (vi editor), 270-277
        awk command (creating shell
            scripts), 274-277
        fmt command (tightening
            paragraph lines), 273-274
        ls-CF command output,
            adding to files, 271-272
        paragraphs, assigning to
            UNIX commands, 272-273
    !! (C shell history commands),
        333

!$ (C shell history commands), 333
!* (C shell history commands), 333
!n (C shell history commands), 333
$ (vi editor), 219
   lines of text, changing, 250-251
((vi editor), 268
) (vi editor), 268
./ls, 56
/ (vi editor), 268
/ search command (vi editor), 231-232
=, 141
   rn program, 474
? (vi editor), 232-233
{ (vi editor), 270
a (vi editor), 219
A (emacs help system), 298
^a^b (C shell history commands), 333
addressing commands (vi editor), 243
adjust, 273
alias, 334-335
append (vi editor), 216-218
apropos, 8
arguments, 35
ascii (ftp program), 483
awk, 177, 188-195, 370
   awk program files, creating, 194
   BEGIN pattern, 192
   END pattern, 192-194
   error messages, 195
   -f flag, 188
   -Fc flag, 188
   if-then condition, 194
   interacting with ! command (vi editor), 274-277
   login shells, 189
   modifying output of ls command, 192
   NF variable, 190-191
   NR variable, 191
   print command, 188-189
   sorting data, 190
   tables, building, 194-195
^b (vi editor), 219
b, 141
   vi editor, 219

B
   emacs help system, 298
   vi editor, 219
Backspace (vi editor), 219
bc (infix calculator), 36, 38
bg (background processes), 365, 367
binary (ftp program), 483
bye (ftp program), 483
C (change commands), 246
   lines, changing contents, 247-248
c (change commands), 246
   ranges of text, changing, 249-252
C (emacs help system), 298
C shell environment modification, 320
C shell unalias, 178
C-a (emacs editor), 289
C-b (emacs editor), 287, 289
C-c (emacs help system), 298
C-d (emacs help system), 298
C-e (emacs editor), 289
C-f (emacs editor), 287, 289
C-h command (emacs editor), 287
C-k (emacs editor), 293
C-n (emacs editor), 286, 289
C-n (emacs help system), 298
C-p (emacs editor), 289
C-v (emacs editor), 289
C-w (emacs help system), 298
C-x [(emacs editor), 289
C-x] (emacs editor), 289
C-x Delete (emacs editor), 293
C-x u (emacs editor), 293
cal, 33
cancel (print queues), 391
case, 357
cd, 58
   aliases, 337
cd dir (ftp program), 483
change, 246-252
   lines, changing contents, 247-248
   ranges of text, changing, 249-252
change shell (chsh), 312-313
chdir (aliases), 337
chgrp, 109-110
chmod
   modifying permissions, 96-98
   symbolic notation, 96

chown, 108-109
chsh, 124
close (ftp program), 483
colon commands (vi editor), 236-241, 243
   :e command, 241
   :n command, 240
   :r command, 238-239
   :w command, 238
command alias, 320
Control-l, 141
cp, 7, 116-117
^d (vi editor), 219
d, 141
   vi editor, 220-221
D (vi editor), 220
date, 33
dc (postfix calculator), 38-39
dc -l math, 47
dd (vi editor), 224-225
delete (mailx), 415-416
df, 82-83
dir (ftp program), 484
   remote directory files, listing, 484-485
disk (man page), 10
du
   -a flag, 80-81
   disk space usage, checking, 79-81
   multi-letter flags, 81
dw (vi editor), 222-223
:e (vi editor), 241
:e filename (vi editor), 236
echo, 58, 155
   filename wildcard characters, 162
   history lists, 330
egrep, 175-176
   notations, 175
emacs motion commands, 289
entering in more program, 142
env, 57, 313-314
Escape (vi editor), 219
exit, 24
expr (arithmetic functions), 350-351
:f, 141
^f (vi editor), 219
F (emacs help system), 298
fdformat (man page), 12
fg
   starting jobs, 365
   stopping jobs, 362, 364

fgrep, 176-179
  awk command, 177
  excluding words from lists,
    178-179
  wrongwords file, 176-178
file
  asterisk wildcard, 129
  core dumps, 131
  determining accuracy of, 128
  file permissions, 130
  identifying file types,
    128-130
  mail folders, 129
  symbolic links, 131
file-redirection, 146-147
file-related commands (emacs
  editor), 299-302
  moving between buffers, 301
  reading files into buffers, 300
find, 398-403
  core files, removing, 402-403
  -exec flag, 402-403
  filename searches, 400-401
  flags, 398
  -l flag, 404
  listing files/directories,
    398-399
  -mtime n flag, 400
  -name flag, 399-400
  -type specifier, 401-402
  xargs command, 403-405
fmt (tightening paragraph lines),
  273-274
for, 358
^g (vi editor), 256
g (rn program), 472
G (vi editor), 229-231
get
  ftp program, 484
  transferring login file, 486
grep, 172-174
  -c flag, 172, 174
  character searches, 169-170
  general form, 173
  -i flag, 172-173
  inclusion range searches, 168
  -l flag, 172, 174
  letter searches, 169
  -n flag, 172, 174
  punctuation sequence
    searches, 170-171
  specific word searches, 168
~h (mailx), 419

h, 141
  vi editor, 219
headers (mailx), 414-415
help, 14, 16-17
history, 329
  C shell, 333
  exclamation points, 327
  repeating commands, 327
i (vi editor), 219
I (emacs help system), 298
id, 30
if, 355-356
insert (vi editor), 216-217
j (vi editor), 219
jobs, 369
k (vi editor), 219
K (emacs help system), 298
kill, 370, 374-377
  hang-up signal (SIGHUP),
    376
  kill signal (SIGKILL), 376
  repeating, 376
  signals, 374-375
-l (archie program), 495
l (vi editor), 219
L (emacs help system), 298
lcd dir (ftp program), 484
lp
  flags, 384
  printing files, 384-387
lpinfo, 386-387
lpq (print queues), 391
lpr
  flags, 384
  printing files, 384-387
lprm (print queues), 391
ls, see ls command
ls -C -F, 60
ls -C -F /, 46
M (emacs help system), 298
M-< (emacs editor), 289
M-> (emacs editor), 288, 289
M-a (emacs editor), 289
M-b (emacs editor), 289
M-d (emacs editor), 293
M-Delete (emacs editor), 293
M-e (emacs editor), 286, 289
M-f (emacs editor), 289
M-k (emacs editor), 293
M-v (emacs editor), 289
map (vi editor)
  arrow keys, mapping, 265
  Clear key, mapping, 264

  control characters, 264
  saving key mappings, 265
mesg, enabling messages,
  408-409
mget
  ftp program, 484
  wildcard patterns, specifying,
    486
mkdir, 114-116
  man page, 9
-More- prompt, 141
mput (ftp program), 484
mv, 116
  moving files, 118-119
  renaming files, 119-120
:n (vi editor), 236, 240
n, 141
  emacs editor, 296
  vi editor, 232-234
n[Return], 141
named emacs command,
  294, 303
netinfo, 445
nf, 141
nl
  -bp pattern-matching
    option, 156
  command flag format, 155
  default settings, 156
  numbering file lines, 153-157
  quotation marks, 157
  -s flag, 156-157
ns, 141
numeric repeat prefixes
  (vi editor), 253-255
O (vi editor), 215-216, 219
o (vi editor), 214-215, 219
open (ftp program), 484
overview, 2
~p (mailx), 418
passwd, 25
/pattern, 141
pr
  -f flag, 390
  flags, 388
  formatting print jobs,
    387-391
  piping output to lpr
    command, 390-391
print, 188-189
printenv, 57
prompt (ftp program), 484

ps, 368-374
   -ag flag, 372-373
   -ax flag, 373
   flags, 368-369
   Sequent workstation
     output, 374
   Sun workstation output, 374
   -u flag, 372
punctuation in, 28
put (ftp program), 484
pwd, 58
   ftp program, 484
:q (vi editor), 220, 237
:q! (vi editor), 230, 237
q, 141
   emacs editor, 296
quit (mailx), 416
:r (vi editor), 238-239
~r (mailx), 418
R (replace commands), 246
r (replace commands), 246
   characters, changing,
     248-249
:r filename (vi editor), 237
read (assigning variables), 349
rehash, 91
   printers script, 382
replace, 246-252
   characters, changing,
     248-249
Return (vi editor), 219
rlogin
   logging in to remote systems,
     480-481
   logging out of remote
     systems, 481
rm, 121, 123
   precautions with, 123-125
rmdir, 120-121
-s (archie program), 495
S (emacs help system), 298
save (mailx), 415
   groups of commands, 416
search-and-replace (vi editor),
   257-260
   changing all occurrences,
     259-260
   words, changing, 258-259
sed, 179-184
   assigning paragraphs to
     UNIX commands, 272-273
   deleting lines in streams,
     181-182

g flag, 180
   multiple sed commands,
     separating, 181
   prefixes, adding/removing,
     184
   regular expressions, 182-183
   rewriting output of who
     command, 181
   substituting patterns, 180
semicolon, 123
set (configuration options), 319
set history, 326
:set number (vi editor), 256
setprompt, aliases, 337
several on one command
   line, 123
sort
   file information, sorting,
     150-153
   filenames, sorting alphabeti-
     cally, 152
   flags, 151
   lines of a file, sorting, 152
   man page, 13
[Space], 141
spacing in, 28
spell, 178-179
stty (configuration options), 318
stty tostop, 365
substitute, 179-180
T (emacs help system), 298
tee (re-routing pipelines),
   196-197
telnet
   connecting to remote archie
     system, 496
   remote system connections,
     481-483
test, 351-355
   file system status tests,
     353-355
   numeric comparisons, 352
   string comparisons, 353
   test operators, 352
   unary flags (file systems),
     353-354
time, 33
touch, 91
   files, creating, 78-79
tty, 408-409
^u (vi editor), 220
u (vi editor), 221-222, 252
umask, 104, 106-107

uncompress, 84
undo (emacs editor), 292-293
uniq, 149-150
users, 31
v, 141
   WAIS, databases, 451
V (emacs help system), 298
vi (starting vi editor), 201
:w (vi editor), 220, 237-238
W
   emacs help system, 298
   vi editor, 220
w, 32
   vi editor, 220
:w filename (vi editor), 237
wc -l /etc/magic, 128
whatis (archie program), 497-499
who, 31
   rewriting output with sed
     command, 181
whoami, 28
wq (vi editor), 229
write, 409-411
x (vi editor), 220
xargs, 403-405
y (emacs editor), 296
z (background processes), 367
see also programs
communicating with users
   enabling messages (mesg
     command), 408-409
   write command, 409-411
   see also e-mail
**Compact Disk Connection telnet
site, 500-503**
**comparison functions (test
command), 351-355**
   file system status tests, 353-355
   numeric comparisons, 352
   string comparisons, 353
   test operators, 352
compilers, 510, 529
complex expressions, 175-176
compress program, 83-84
computing sums, 193
concentric circles of access, 98
conditional expressions, 360
   case command, 357
   if command, 355-356
conditional statements, 517-520
   if statement, 517-519
   switch statement, 519-520
config.sys (DOS file), 50

configuration files
C shell, 317-320
.cshrc file, 319-320
.login file, 317-319
printers, /etc/printcap file, 380-381
connections
device drivers, tty command, 408-409
remote Internet sites, 480-483
logging in, 481
logging out (rlogin command), 481
rlogin command, 480
telnet command, 481-483
continue; statement (restarting loops), 521
control key notation, 136, 143
control number, 377
Control-f command (vi editor), 209-210
control-key commands (vi editor), 208-209
b key (moving around files word by word), 211
Control-f command, 209-210
Control-u command, 210
w key (moving around files word by word), 211
Control-l command, 141
Control-u command (vi editor), 210
copying
files (cp command), 116-117
Internet files (ftp program), 483-493
anonymous ftp capabilities, 483
Apple Computer FTP archive, 489-490
binary files, 490-491
to computer screen, 489
FTP archives, 491-492
ftp commands, 483-484
MIT AI Laboratory (anonymous FTP archive), 487-488
remote directory files, listing, 484-486
starting ftp, 484
transferring login file, 486
core dumps, 131, 143
core files, removing with find command, 402-403

counting words/lines (wc program), 147-149
cp command, 7, 116-117
csh (command shell), 306
configuration files, 317-320
.cshrc file, 319-320
.login file, 317-319
csh history mechanism, 330-331
.cshrc file
apropos command, 8
C shell configuration files, 319-320
displaying contents, 137
viewing with more program, 139
-ctime n flag (find command), 398
Ctrl-c, 37
Ctrl-d, 37
CTSS operating system, 4
current job, 377
cursor control keys (vi editor), 205-208
cursors, command prompts, 24
customizing
Netscape Navigator (General Preferences), 437-440
Appearance tab, 437
Applications tab, 438
Fonts tab, 437
Helpers tab, 439
Images tab, 439
prompts, 338-340
cd alias, 339-340
cwd variable, 338
setprompt alias, 339-340
values, 338

D

^d command (vi editor), 219
d command, 141
vi editor, 220-221
D command (vi editor), 220
-d flag, 93
lp command, 385
ls command, 78
listing directories, 71
more program, 139
sort command, 151
test command, 354
uniq command, 150
d suffix, 447

databases
acronyms, 451-452
recipes, 452-453
searching with WAIS, 449-454
software description database (archie program), 496
v command, 451
date, displaying, 33
date command, 33
dc -l math command, 47
dc command (postfix calculator), 38-39
dd command (vi editor), 224-225
DEC
PDP-11, 4
PDP-7, 4
default environment variables, 314-316
HOME, 314
LOGNAME, 316
MAIL, 316
NAME, 316
PATH, 315
SHELL, 314
TERM, 314-315
USER, 315
default login shells, viewing, 308-309
defining
abbreviations (.exrc file), 262
aliases, 355
delete command (mailx), 415-416
deleting
directories (rmdir command), 120-121
files (rm command), 121, 123
precautions, 123-125
text
dd command, 224-225
dw command, 222-223
editing typos, 225-227
emacs editor, 289-293
u command, 221-222
vi editor, 220-229
deletion commands (emacs editor), 293
determinate loops, 357, 360
/dev directory, 47, 132-133
device drivers, 47, 60
block special devices, 133, 143
character special devices, 133, 143

major number, 144
minor number, 144
tty command, 408-409
df command, 82-83
diag directory, 49
dir command (ftp program), 484
remote directory files, listing, 484-485
directories, 60
absolute filenames, 51-52
bin, 46
cdrom, 49
changing (cd command), 58
copying (cp command), 117
/dev directory, 47, 132-133
diag, 49
etc, 47
file system
/dev directory, 132-133
/lib directory, 132
core dumps, 131
symbolic links, 131
top level, 130-131
group
changing (chgrp command), 109-110
identifying, 107-108
home, 49
/lib directory, 47, 132
listing (ls command), 69-71
lost+found, 48
mnt, 48
net, 49
new (mkdir command), 114-116
owner
changing (chown command), 108-109
identifying, 107-108
pcfs, 49
relative filenames, 51-52
removing (rmdir command), 120-121
renaming (mv command), 120
root, 45
searching, 56
sizes, indicating (ls command), 65-66
blocks occupied, 66
sys, 48
tftpboot, 49
tmp, 48
usr, 48

directory permissions, 93-96
execute, 93-94
execute-only, 94
modifying (chmod command), 96-98
read, 93-94
write-only, 95
directory separator characters, 50, 61
directory trees, listing recursively (ls command), 73-74
disk command (man page), 10
disk space
available disk space, checking (df command), 82-83
usage, checking (du command), 79-81
do loop, 521
domain names, 29, 40
! (exclamation point), 28
domain naming, 477
domain-based naming scheme, 29
domains (e-mail addresses), 444-445
top-level domains, 444
DOS commands, re-creating, 334
dot files, 61
listing, 67
see also hidden files
double quote ("), 124
-dptr flag (lp command), 384
drctry permissions, setting new (chmod command), 98, 100, 102
du command
-a flag, 80-81
disk space usage, checking, 79-81
multi-letter flags, 81
Duke Basketball Report Web site, 435
dw command (vi editor), 222-223
dynamic linking, 48, 61
DYNIX, 9, 22
dynix file, 49

E

:e command (vi editor), 241
:e filename command (vi editor), 236
-e flag (test command), 354

e-mail, 424, 426
addresses, 444-445
decoding, 445
top-level domains, 444
d suffix, 447
Elm Mail System, 420-423
reading messages, 421
replying to messages, 422-423
starting, 420-421
finger command, 446
From: line (basic notations), 445
gopher files, electronic mailing of, 458
mailx
command options, 412
delete command, 415-416
forwarding messages, 414
~h command, 419
headers command, 414-415
index numbers, 413-414
message display, 412-413
message headers, 414
~p command, 418
quit command, 416
~r command (reading in files), 418
reading messages, 411-416
responding to messages, 414
save command, 415-416
sending mail, 417-420
tilde commands, 417-418
netinfo command, 445
sending to Internet users, 444-446
addresses, 444-445
echo command, 58, 155
filename wildcard characters, 162
history lists, 330
echoing passwords, 23
editing typos (vi editor), 225-227
tilde (~) command, 228
EDITOR environment variable, 332
-ef flag (test command), 354
egrep command, 175-176
notations, 175
electronic books, accessing (gopher program), 458-459
electronic mail, *see* e-mail
Elm Mail System, 420-423
reading messages, 421
replying to messages, 422-423
starting, 420-421

elm program (hidden files), 54
emacs editor, 201
  buffers, 300-302
    moving between buffers, 301
    reading files into, 300
  deleting text, 289-293
    restoring deleted text, 293
    sentences, removing, 291-292
    undo command, 292-293
    words, removing, 290-291
  deletion commands, 293
  file-related commands, 299-302
    moving between buffers, 301
    reading files into buffers, 300
  GNU EMACS, 283
  Help options (C-h command), 287
  help system, 297-299
    options, 297-298
  motion commands, 289
  moving around in files, 285-289
    C-b command, 287
    C-f command, 287
    C-n command, 286
    M-> command, 288
    M-e command, 286
  notation for indicating commands, 282-283
  quiting, 283
  saving file changes, 288
  searching and replacing, 294-297
    backward searches, 294-295
    query-replace feature, 294-296
  starting, 282-284
  undo command, 292-293
END pattern (awk command), 192-194
env command, 57, 313-314
environment variables, 314-317
  EDITOR, 332
  EXINIT, 317
  HOME, 314
  LOGNAME, 316
  MAIL, 316
  NAME, 316
  PATH, 315
  PRINTER, 383, 385
  SHELL, 314
  TERM, 314-315
  USER, 315

environment variables (rn program)
  RNINIT, 469
  SUBJLINE, 474
-eq flag (test command), 352
errant processes, 377
error messages (awk command), 195
Escape command (vi editor), 219
escape sequence, 279
etc directory, 47
/etc/passwd file, 142-143
/etc/printcap file, 380-381
  finding specified printers, 383
/etc/shells file, 312
exclamation point (domain names), 28
exclusion set, 185
-exec flags (find command), 398, 402-403
executables, 46, 61
execute permissions
  directory, 93-94
  file, 90-91
execute-only permission (directory), 94
EXINIT variable (environment variables), 317
exit command, 24
expanding abbreviations (.exrc file), 262-263
expr command (arithmetic functions), 350-351
expressions, 360, 530
  C programming language, 517-520
    if statement, 517-519
    switch statement, 519-520
  conditional, *see* conditional expressions
.exrc file (vi editor), 260-264
  defining abbreviations, 262
  expanding abbreviations, 262-263
  listing abbreviations in effect, 263
  saving key mappings, 265
extended characters, 530
external media (mnt and sys directories), 48

F

\f character (C programming language), 511
:f command, 141
^f command (vi editor), 219
F command (emacs help system), 298
-F flag (ls command), 68, 78
  filename suffixes, appending, 67
-f flag
  awk command, 188
  pr command, 388, 390
  sort command, 151
  test command, 354
-Fc flag (awk command), 188
fdformat command (man page), 12
fg command
  starting jobs, 365
  stopping jobs, 362, 364
fgrep command, 176-179
  awk command, 177
  excluding words from lists, 178-179
  wrongwords file, 176-178
file command
  core dumps, 131
  determining accuracy of, 128
  identifying file types, 128-130
    asterisk wildcard, 129
    file permissions, 130
    mail folders, 129
  symbolic links, 131
file permissions, 88, 90-93
  binary equivalents, 100
  file command, 130
  modifying (chmod command), 96-98
  numeric equivalents, 101-103
  setting new (chmod command), 98-102
file redirection, 146-147, 158
  viewing files, 146-147
file system, 45-46, 130-133
  bin directory, 46
  binary comparisons, 354
  cd command, 58
  cdrom directory, 49
  core dumps, 131
  /dev directory, 47, 132-133

diag directory, 49
directory separator characters, 50
echo command, 58
env command, 57
etc directory, 47
hidden files, 52-53
home directory, 49
HOME variable, 57
/lib directory, 47, 132
lost+found directory, 48
Macintosh, differences, 50
mnt directory, 48
net directory, 49
PATH variable, 57
PC, differences, 50
pcfs directory, 49
pwd command, 58
status tests (test command),
    353-355
        unary flags, 353-354
symbolic links, 131
sys directory, 48
tftpboot directory, 49
tmp directory, 48
top level, 130-131
usr directory, 48
file systems
    Berkeley Fast File System, 5
    Thompson, 4
**file types (identifying with file
command), 128-130**
    asterisk wildcard, 129
    file permissions, 130
    mail folders, 129
**file wildcards, history lists,
329-330**
**file-related commands (emacs
editor), 299-302**
    moving between buffers, 301
    reading files into buffers, 300
filenames, 46
    absolute vs relative, 51-52
    rc suffix, 54
    searching with find command,
        400-401
    sorting alphabetically, 152
    suffixes, appending (ls com-
        mand), 67
    wildcards, 162-166
        character range, 164-166
        echo command, 162
        limiting number of matches,
            162-164
        spaces, 166

files
    aliases, 67
    archive random library, 132
    autoexec.bat (DOS file), 50
    awk command, 177
    boot, 49
    changes, saving (emacs editor),
        288
    command.com (DOS file), 50
    compress program, 83-84
    config.sys (DOS file), 50
    configuration files (C shell),
        317-320
            .cshrc file, 319-320
            .login file, 317-319
    contents, viewing (cat program),
        136-139
    copying (cp command), 116-117
    creating with touch command,
        78-79
    .cshrc file
        C shell configuration files,
            319-320
        displaying contents, 137
        viewing with more
            command, 139
    deleting text (vi editor), 220-229
        dd command, 224-225
        dw command, 222-223
        editing typos, 225-227
        u command, 221-222
    dot files, listing, 67
    dynix, 49
    /etc/passwd file, 142-143
    /etc/printcap, 380-381
        finding specified printers, 383
    /etc/shells, 312
    execute permission, 90
    .exrc file (vi editor), 260-264
        defining abbreviations, 262
        expanding abbreviations,
            262-263
        listing abbreviations in
            effect, 263
        saving key mappings, 265
    filenames
        suffixes, appending (ls
            command), 67
        wildcards, 162-166
    formats, binary, 46
    group
        changing (chgrp command),
            109-110
        identifying, 107-108

header files, 511
hidden, 52-53
inserting text with vi editor,
    212-220
        append (a) command,
            216-218
        insert (i) command, 216-217
        O command, 215-216
        o command, 214-215
Internet files (ftp program),
    483-493
        anonymous ftp capabilities,
            483
        Apple Computer FTP
            archive, 489-490
        binary files, 490-491
        to computer screen, 489
        FTP archives, 491-492
        ftp commands, 483-484
        MIT AI Laboratory
            (anonymous FTP archive),
            487-488
        remote directory files, listing,
            484-486
        starting ftp, 484
        transferring login file, 486
large files, viewing (more
    program), 139-143
lib.b file, 132
listing
    comma-separated lists, 68
    ls command, 65
log, write-only permissions, 89
.login file
    C shell configuration files,
        317-319
cp command, 117
moving (mv command), 118-119
moving around in
    emacs editor, 285-289
    vi editor, 205-211
numbering, awk command (NR
    variable), 191
numbering lines, 153-154
    cat program, 153-154
    nl command, 153-157
    vi editor, 255-257
owner
    changing (chown command),
        108-109
    identifying, 107-108
preference, 52
printing, 384-387

aliases, 386
    print queue, 385-386,
        391-394
    printer information, 386-387
    specifying printers, 384-385
removing (rm command),
    121-123
    precautions, 123-125
removing extraneous lines (uniq
    command), 149-150
        common lines, 149
        duplicate lines, 149-150
renaming (mv command),
    119-120
saving (vi editor), 218
searching
    find command, *see* find
        command
    searching and replacing
        (emacs editor), 294-297
    vi editor, 229-234
sizes, indicating (ls command),
    65-66
    blocks occupied, 66
sorting
    changing sort order (ls
        command), 71-73
    sorting information (sort
        command), 150-153
stripping, 131
symbolic links, 68
text, deleting, 289-293
text files (awk command),
    188-195
unix, 49
viewing
    file lines, 133-136
    file redirection, 146-147
vmunix, 49
word counts (wc program),
    147-149
wrongwords file, 176-178
filters, 158
    file information, sorting, 150-153
    filenames, sorting alphabetically,
        152
    lines of a file, sorting, 152
find command, 398-403
    core files, removing, 402-403
    -exec flag, 402-403
    filename searches, 400-401
    flags, 398
    -l flag, 404

listing files/directories, 398-399
-mtime n flag, 400
-name flag, 399-400
-type specifier, 401-402
xargs command, 403-405
findgroup alias (rn program),
    469-470
finger command, 446
finger program (hidden files), 55
flags, 40
    -?, 14, 16
    -1 (ls command), 68, 77, 152
    -a, 54
        du command, 80-81
        ls command, 67-68, 77
        ps command, 368
    -ag (ps command), 372-373
    -atime n (find command), 398
    -ax (ps command), 373
    -b
        sort command, 151
        test command, 354
    -C (ls command), 68, 77
    -c
        grep command, 172-174
        more program, 139
        test command, 354
        uniq command, 150
    -CF (ls command), 486
    combining, 68-69
    -ctime n (find command), 398
    -d, 93
        lp command, 385
        ls command, 71, 78
        more program, 139
        sort command, 151
        test command, 354
        uniq command, 150
    -dptr (lp command), 384
    -e (test command), 354
    -ef (test command), 354
    -eq (test command), 352
    -exec (find command), 403
    exec command, 398
    -F (ls command), 67-68, 78
    -f
        awk command, 188
        pr command, 388-390
        sort command, 151
        test command, 354
    -Fc (awk command), 188
    find command, 398
    -G (test command), 353

-g
    ls command, 107
    ps command, 368
    test command, 354
g (sed command), 180
-ge (test command), 352
-gt (test command), 352
-h, 14, 16
    lpr command, 384
-hhdr (pr command), 388
-i
    grep command, 172-173
    lpr command, 384
    rm command, 122
-k, 7
    stest command, 354
-L
    lpr command, 384
    test command, 353
-l
    find command, 404
    grep command, 172-174
    ls command, 107
    kill command, 375
    ls command, 74-78
    ps command, 369
-l math, 38
-le (test command), 352
-lt (test command), 352
-m
    ls command, 68, 78
    pr command, 388
-mtime n (find command),
    398-400
multi-letter flags (du command),
    81
+n (pr command), 388
-n
    cat program, 153-154
    grep command, 172-174
    pr command, 388
    sort command, 151-152
n (mesg command), 408-409
-name (find command), 399-400
-name pattern (find command),
    398
-ne (test command), 352
-nt (test command), 354
-O (test command), 354
-ot (test command), 354
-P
    lpr command, 385
    print queues, 393

-p
  mkdir command, 10
  test command, 354
-Pn (lp command), 384
-Ppr (lpr command), 384
-print (find command), 398
-R
  lpr command, 384
  ls command, 73-74, 78
  vi editor, 234
-r
  ls command, 72, 78
  rm command, 122
  sort command, 151-153
  test command, 354
-S (test command), 354
-s
  cat program, 136-137
  ls command, 65-68, 78
  more program, 139
  nl command, 156-157
  sending mail (mailx), 417
  test command, 354
sort command, 151
-t (ls command), 72, 78
-t xx (ps command), 369
-ttitle (lp command), 384
-type c (find command), 398
-u
  ps command, 369, 372
  test command, 354
  uniq command, 150
-user name (find command), 398
-v
  cat program, 136
  lpinfo command, 386-387
-w
  ps command, 369
  test command, 354
-wn (pr command), 388
-x
  ls command, 71-72, 78
  ps command, 369
  test command, 354
  y (mesg command), 408
floating-point variables, 513
  modifiers, 514
floppy device driver, 47
floppy disks (man page), 10
flow control, 294, 303
fmt command (tightening
  paragraph lines), 273-274
folders, 45
  mail folders, file command, 129

for command, 358
for loop, 520-521
foreach loop, 343
foreground job, 377
formats, binary, 46
formatting print jobs (pr
  command), 387-391
  comparing directory contents,
    389-390
  header information, adding, 389
  two-column mode, 388
FORTRAN, 5
forwarding e-mail messages
  (mailx), 414
Free Software Foundation (FSF),
  308
From: line, basic notations, 445
FTP, 426
FTP archives
  Apple Computer FTP archive,
    489-490
  MIT Artificial Intelligence
    Laboratory, 487
    pub directory, 487-488
  Table 23.2, 491-492
ftp program
  anonymous FTP archive,
    487-490
    Apple Computer FTP
      archive, 489-490
    MIT Artificial Intelligence
      Laboratory, 487-488
  binary mode (transferring files),
    490-491
  commands, 483-484
  copying Internet files, 483-493
    anonymous ftp capabilities,
      483
    to computer screen, 489
  dir command, 484-485
    flags, 486
  FTP archives, 491-492
  get command, 486
  ls command, 484-485
    flags, 486
  mget command, 486
  remote directory files, listing,
    484-486
  starting, 484
  transferring login file, 486
function libraries, 47
functions (C programming
  language), 521-523
  macro replacements, 523

G

^g command (vi editor), 256
G command (vi editor), 229-231
g command (rn program), 472
-G flag (test command), 353
-g flag
  ls command, 107
  ps command, 368
  sed command, 180
  test command, 354
-ge flag (test command), 352
GECOS (GE computer operating
  system), 4
get command
  ftp program, 484
  transferring login file, 486
gid (group ID), 30
GNU EMACS, 283
go-to-line command (vi editor),
  229-231
gopher program, 454-460
  bookmarks, adding, 456-457
  electronic books, accessing,
    458-459
  electronic mailing of files, 458
  gopherspace, 478
  introduction screen, 454-455
  library searches, 460-466
    National Library in
      Venezuela, 460-461
    Queensland University of
      Technology, 461-463
    University of California,
      464-466
  logging on, 454-455
  navigating, 455-458
  notation, 458
Gopher protocol, 426
grep command, 172-174
  -c flag, 172-174
  general form, 173
  -i flag, 172-173
  -l flag, 172-174
  -n flag, 172-174
  searching
    character searches, 168-170
    inclusion ranges, 168
    letter searches, 169
    punctuation sequences,
      170-171
    specific words, 168

grep program, xargs command,
403-405
groups
directories, identifying, 107-108
files
changing (chgrp command),
109-110
identifying, 107-108
group ID, 30
id command, 30
permissions, 98
-gt flag (test command), 352

H

~h command (mailx), 419
h command, 141
vi editor, 219
-h flag, 14-16
lpr command, 384
hang-up signal (kill command),
376
hard disks, mnt and sys
directories, 48
head program
pipelines, 134-135
viewing file lines, 133-135
multiple files, checking, 134
-n format, 134
header files, 511
headers (e-mail messages), 414
headers command (mailx), 414-415
help
bc command, 37
help command, 14-17
man pages, 7-14
Help options (emacs editor), 287
help systems (emacs editor),
297-299
options, 297-298
heuristics, 40
passwd command, 26
Hewlett-Packard, 5
-hhdr flag (pr command), 388
hidden files, 52-53, 61
history commands, 329
C shell, 333
exclamation points, 327
repeating commands, 327
history lists (shells), 327-333
building, 327-328
command numbers, 328

csh history mechanism, 330-331
echo command, 330
file wildcards, 329-330
filename searches, 331-332
ksh history-edit command mode,
332-333
repeating commands, 328-329
history mechanisms (shells),
324-327
reviewing histories, 324
set history command, 326
shell parameters, checking status,
325
starting, 325
w command output, 325
HoloNet Services Gateway, 500
home directory, 49, 61
HOME variable, 57
cd command, 59
environment variables, 314
host name, 40
HTML (hypertext markup
language), 427
HTTP (hyper-text transfer
protocol), 427
hyperlinks, 440

I

i command (vi editor), 216-219
I command (emacs help system),
298
-i flag
grep command, 172-173
lpr command, 384
rm command, 122
I value (process status values), 371
i-list, 4
i-nodes, 4
id command, 30
if command, 355-356
if statements, 517-519
if-then condition (awk command),
194
inclusion range, 185
indeterminate loops, 357, 360
infinite loops, 520
infix calculators, 36-38
infix notation, 36
Information Highway, 480
information servers list Web
site, 529

initial passwords, 23
input (standard input), 151
insert command (vi editor),
216-219
insert mode (vi editor), 213, 243
insertion commands (vi editor),
219-220
integer variable, 512
modifiers, 513-514
interactive program, 143
interactive shells, 320
interfaces (command-line), 2
Internet, 426-440
copying files (ftp program),
483-493
anonymous ftp capabilities,
483
Apple Computer FTP
archive, 489-490
binary files, 490-491
to computer screen, 489
FTP archives, 491-492
ftp commands, 483-484
MIT AI Laboratory
(anonymous FTP archive),
487-488
remote directory files, listing,
484-486
starting ftp, 484
transferring login file, 486
domain naming, 478
e-mail
addresses, 444-445
d suffix, 447
finger command, 446
From: line, 445
netinfo command, 445
sending to Internet users,
444-446
top-level domains, 444
see also e-mail
gopher program, 454-460
bookmarks, adding, 456-457
electronic books, accessing,
458-459
electronic mailing of
files, 458
introduction screen, 454-455
library searches, 460-466
logging on, 454-455
navigating, 455-458
notation, 458

Netscape Navigator
Bookmark menu, 431
customizing, 437-440
local files, specifying
(command line), 430-431
starting, 427-431
URLs, specifying (command line), 429-430
What's New? button, 429
newsgroups, *see* newsgroups
protocols, 426-427
remote sites (connecting to), 480-483
logging in to, 481
logging out, 481
rlogin command, 480
telnet commands, 481-483
users, talk system, 446-449
Scott Yanoff's List of Internet Services, 506
searching Web sites, 432-437
AltaVista (Web crawler), 436-437
Yahoo! (search engine), 432-435
telnet sites, 499-506
Book Stacks Unlimited, 503-506
Compact Disk Connection, 500-503
Usenet, 466-467
database of newsgroups (C shell alias), 467
WAIS (Wide Area Information Services), 449
accessing, 449-451
Web sites, *see* Web sites
Internet Network Information Center, 496
logging in, 496-497
whatis command (mail searches), 497-499
Internet Relay Chat (IRC) protocol, 426
Internet Services List Web site, 529
ls command
-g flag, 107-108
-l flag, 107

J

j command (vi editor), 219
job control, 321
command shells, 306-307
job ID, 365
jobs, 377
print jobs, formatting (pr command), 387-391
comparing directory contents, 389-390
header information, adding, 389
two-column mode, 388
running in background, 365-368
& symbol (moving automatically), 367
automatic starts, 366
files, processing, 366
input/output, 368
job ID, 365
z command, 367
stopping, 362-365
fg command, 362-364
screen-oriented programs, 363-364
terminating (kill command), 374-377
hang-up signal (SIGHUP), 376
kill signal (SIGKILL), 376
logging out, 377
specifying signals to kill command, 374-375
tracking (ps command), 368-374
-ag flag, 372-373
-ax flag, 373
BSD-style flags, 368-369
status values, 371
-u flag, 372
zombie process, 371
see also processes
jobs command, 369
jsh (command shell), 307
Julian calendar, 34

K

k command (vi editor), 219
K command (emacs help system), 298
-k flag, 7
test command, 354
kernel, 61
lost+found directory, 48
Kernighan, Brian, 3
key bindings, 303
keys
b key (moving around files word by word), 211
control-key commands (vi editors), 208, 209
Control-f command, 209-210
Control-u command, 210
cursor control keys (vi editor), 205-208
mapping, 279
arrow keys, mapping, 265
Clear key, 264
control characters, 264
.exrc file, 260-264
saving key mappings, 265
w key (moving around files word by word), 211
keyword searches (-k flag), 7
kill command, 370, 374-377
repeating, 376
signals, 374-375
hang-up signal (SIGHUP), 376
kill signal (SIGKILL), 376
Korn shell, 2, 307
$ prompt, 24
aliases, 335-337
!* notation, 340
cd command, 337
chdir command, 337
connecting to accounts on other systems, 336-337
setprompt command, 337
command-alias mechanism, 333-335
alias command, 334-335
defining an alias, 335
DOS commands, re-creating, 334

general format, 333
ls command flags, 333-334
history list, 327-333
building, 327-328
command numbers, 328
csh history mechanism,
330-331
echo command, 330
file wildcards, 329-330
filename searches, 331-332
ksh history-edit command
mode, 332-333
repeating commands,
328-329
history mechanism, 324-327
reviewing histories, 324
set history command, 326
shell parameters, checking
status, 325
starting, 325
w command output, 325
jobs (processes)
fg command, 362-364
running in background,
365-368
screen-oriented programs,
363-364
stopping, 362-365
setting custom prompts, 338-340
cd alias, 339-340
cwd variable, 338
setprompt alias, 339-340
values, 338
ksh (command shell), 307
ksh history-edit command mode
(Korn shell), 332-333

L

-l command (archie program), 495
l command (vi editor), 219
L command (emacs help system),
298
-L flag
lpr command, 384
test command, 353
-l flag
find command, 404
grep command, 172-174
ls command, 107
kill command, 375
ls command, 74-78
ps command, 369

-l math flag, 38
lcd dir command (ftp program),
484
-le flag (test command), 352
left rooted patterns, 185
/lib directory, 47, 132
lib.b file, 132
libraries
math, 47
searching with gopher program,
460-466
National Library in
Venezuela, 460-461
Queensland University of
Technology, 461-463
University of California,
464-466
line numbering, 153-154
cat program, 153-154
nl command, 153-157
-bp pattern-matching
option, 156
command flag format, 155
default settings, 156
quotation marks, 157
-s flag, 156-157
vi editor, 255-257
listing
directories (ls command), 69-71
directory trees, listing recursively,
73-74
dot files, 67
files, 65
local printers, finding with printer
script, 380-383
log files, write-only permissions, 89
logging in, 22
remote systems
rlogin command, 480-481
telnet command, 481-482
logging out
background processes, 377
exit command, 24
remote systems
rlogin command, 481
telnet command, 482
.login file (C shell configuration
files), 317-319
login shells, 321, 372, 378
awk command, 189
choosing new shells, 310-313
available shells, identifying,
310-311
change shell command,
312-313

valid shells, confirming, 312
visual shell, 311
identifying system's shell,
309-310
viewing default login shells,
308-309
LOGNAME variable (environment
variables), 316
long directory listings (ls
command), 75-78
long integers (C programming
language), 513
long listing format (ls command)
directories, 75-78
files, 74
looping expressions, 357-359
for command, 358
while loop, 358-359
looping statements, 520-521
do loop, 521
for loop, 520-521
while loop, 520
loops, 360
foreach loop, 343
lost+found directory, 48
lp command
flags, 384
printing files, 384-387
aliases, 386
print queue, 385-386
printer information, 386-387
specifying printers, 384-385
lpinfo command, 386-387
lpq command (print queues), 391
lpr command
flags, 384
printing files, 384-387
aliases, 386
print queue, 385-386
printer information, 386-387
specifying printers, 384-385
lprm command (print queues), 391
ls -C -F command, 60
ls -C -F / command, 46
./ls command, 56
ls command, 53, 64-65
-1 flag, 68, 77
-a flag, 68, 77
-g flag, 107
dot files, listing, 67
-C flag, 68, 77
combining flags, 68-69
-d flag, 78
listing directories, 71

directories, listing, 69-71
directory trees, listing recursively, 73-74
-F flag, 68, 78
    filename suffixes, appending, 67
file type indicators, 89
files
    dot files, listing, 67
    listing, 65
    sizes, indicating, 65-66
flags, 77-78
ftp program, 484
    remote directory files, listing, 484-486
-l flag, 74-78
long listing format
    directories, 75-78
    files, 74
-m flag, 68, 78
    comma-separated lists, 68
mkdir command, 118
modifying output with awk command, 192
numeric permissions strings, 103
permissions, changing, 97
-R flag, 78
    directory trees, listing recursively, 73-74
-r flag, 72, 78
rm command, 120
-s flag, 68, 78
    blocks occupied by files, 66
    file size, indicating, 65-66
sort order, changing, 71-73
-t flag, 72, 78
-x flag, 71-72, 78
-lt flag (test command), 352
Lukasiewicz, Jan, 36

M

M command (emacs help system), 298
-m flag
    ls command, 68, 78
        comma-separated lists, 68
    pr command, 388
M-< command (emacs editor), 289
M-> command (emacs editor), 288-289
M-a command (emacs editor), 289

M-b command (emacs editor), 289
M-d command (emacs editor), 293
M-Delete command (emacs editor), 293
M-e command (emacs editor), 286, 289
M-f command (emacs editor), 289
M-k command (emacs editor), 293
M-v command (emacs editor), 289
Macintosh
    directory delineator, 51
    file system, 50
    hidden files, 53
    moving files, 116
    Preferences folder, 52
    System Folder, 45
Macintosh interface, 2
macro replacements (C programming language), 523
mail, 411
mail folders, 424
    file command, 129
mail headers, 424
MAIL variable (environment variables), 316
mailbox, 424
mailx
    command options, 412
    delete command, 415-416
    forwarding messages, 414
    headers, 414
    headers command, 414-415
    index numbers, 413-414
    message display, 412-413
    quit command, 416
    reading e-mail, 411-416
    responding to messages, 414
    save command, 415
        groups of messages, 416
    sending mail, 417-420
        ~h command, 419
        ~p command, 418
        ~r command, 418
        tilde commands, 417-418
major number (device drivers), 144
man pages, 7-14
    apropos command, 12
    fdformat command, 12
    mkdir command, 9
    more program, 14
    sort command, 13
    System V organization, 8

map command (vi editor)
    arrow keys, mapping, 265
    Clear key, mapping, 264
    control characters, 264
    saving key mappings, 265
mapping keys (vi editor)
    arrow keys, 265
    Clear key, 264
    control characters, 264
    .exrc file, 260-264
        defining abbreviations, 262
        expanding abbreviations, 262-263
        listing abbreviations in effect, 263
        saving key mappings, 265
math functions (sine), 38
math library, 47
mathematical functions (variables), 350-351
mathlw queue, 391-392
McIlroy, 4
mesg command (enabling messages), 408-409
mesg y variable, 319
messages, remove login.copy?, 119
Meta key, 282, 303
mget command
    ftp program, 484
    specifying wildcard patterns, 486
MH shell, 307
MIME (multimedia Internet mail extension), 427
minor number (device drivers), 144
MIT, 3
MIT Artificial Intelligence Laboratory (anonymous FTP archive), 487
    pub directory, 487-488
mkdir command, 114-116
    man page, 9
    -p flag, 10
mnt directory, 48
modal editors, 201
modal programs, 243
modeless editors, 201
modeless programs, 244
modem protocols, 467
modes (vi editor), 201
modifiers
    character variable, 514
    floating-point variable, 514
    integer variable, 513-514

more program
   entering commands, 142
   man command, 14
   viewing large files, 139-143
      /etc/passwd file, 142-143
-More- prompt commands, 141
Motif, 5
motion commands
   emacs editor, 289
   vi editor, 219-220
moving
   files (mv command), 118-119
   sentences and paragraphs (vi
      editor), 266-270
      (command, 268
) command, 268
      / command, 268
      { command, 270
mput command (ftp program), 484
MS-DOS interface, 2
msh (command shell), 307
-mtime n flag (find command),
   398-400
multi-letter flags (du
   command), 81
multichoice system, 2
Multics, 3
multitasking, 2
multiuser systems, 2, 5-6
mv command, 116
   directories, renaming, 120
   files
      moving, 118-119
      renaming, 119-120

N

\n character (C programming
   language), 511
:n command (vi editor), 236, 240
n command, 141
   emacs editor, 296
   vi editor, 232-234
+n flag (pr command), 388
-n flag
   cat program (numbering file
      lines), 153-154
   grep command, 172-174
   pr command, 388
   sort command, 151-152
n flag (mesg command), 408-409
-n format (head command), 134

n[Return] command, 141
-name flag (find command),
   399-400
-name pattern flag (find command), 398
NAME variable (environment
   variables), 316
named emacs command, 294, 303
naming directories, 115
National Library in Venezuela, 460
navigating
   file system, 58
   gopher program, 455-458
Navigator (Netscape)
   Bookmark menu, 431
   customizing (General Prefer-
      ences), 437-440
      Appearance tab, 437
      Applications tab, 438
      Fonts tab, 437
      Helpers tab, 439
      Images tab, 439
   starting, 427-431
      local files, specifying
         (command line), 430-431
      troubleshooting, 428
      URLs, specifying (command
         line), 429-430
      What's New? button, 429
      X Window System, 427
-ne flag (test command), 352
net directory, 49
netinfo command, 445
Netnews, 426
Netscape Navigator
   Bookmark menu, 431
   customizing, 437-440
   customizing (General Prefer-
      ences)
      Appearance tab, 437
      Applications tab, 438
      Fonts tab, 437
      Helpers tab, 439
      Images tab, 439
   starting, 427-431
      local files, specifying
         (command line), 430-431
      troubleshooting, 428
      URLs, specifying (command
         line), 429-430
      What's New? button, 429
      X Window System, 427
networks (multiusers), 29
newmail variable, 319

newsgroups, 467, 478
   alt newsgroups, 467
   hierarchies, 467
   rn program, 468
      findgroup alias, 469-470
      RNINIT environment
         variable, 469
      start up, 470-471
      starting options, 468
      SUBJLINE environment
         variable, 474
   rn program (newsgroups)
      = command, 474
      g command, 472
      reading articles, 472-475
      unsubscribing from
         newsgroups, 471-472
   tin program, 475-476
next search command (vi editor),
   232-234
next-file command (vi editor), 240
nf command, 141
NF variable (awk command),
   190-191
nl command
   -bp pattern-matching
      option, 156
   command flag format, 155
   default settings, 156
   numbering file lines, 153-157
   quotation marks, 157
   -s flag, 156-157
noninteractive shells, 320
Norton Utilities (rescuing DOS
   files), 123
notations
   !* notation (aliases), 340
   += notation, 193
   egrep command, 175
   gopher program, 458
   math notations, 36
   regular expressions, 167
   RPN, 36
NR variable (awk command), 191
ns command, 141
-nt flag (test command), 354
null characters, 144
numbering files
   awk command (NR
      variable), 191
   numbering lines (files), 153-154
      cat program, 153-154
      nl command, 153-157
      vi editor, 255-257

numbering systems, 38
numbers, computing sums, 193
numeric comparisons (test command), 352
numeric equivalents (permissions), 100
numeric permissions strings, calculating, 102-104
numeric repeat prefixes (vi editor), 253-255

O

O command (vi editor), 215-216, 219
o command (vi editor), 214-215, 219
-O flag (test command), 354
\ooo character (C programming language), 511
open command (ftp program), 484
Open Desktop, 5
OpenWindows, 5
operating systems (CTSS), 4
operators (C programming language)
    binary operators, 515
    bitwise operators, 516
    unary operators, 514-515
-ot flag (test command), 354
output
    redirecting, 146-147
    standard output, 151
output formats (Sun Microsystems workstation), 131-132

P

p (dc command), 38
~p command (mailx), 418
-P flag
    lpr command, 385
    print queues, 393
-p flag
    mkdir command, 10
    test command, 354
paragraphs
    assigning to UNIX commands (vi editor), 272-273

moving (vi editor), 266-270
    (command, 268
) command, 268
    / command, 268
    { command, 270
    tightening lines (fmt command), 273-274
passwd command, 25
password entry, 124-125
passwords, 6
    changing (passwd command), 25
    choosing, 26-27
    initial, 23
PATH variable, 57
    environment variables, 315
pathnames, absence of, 4
/pattern command, 141
PC
    directory delineator, 51
    file system, 50
pcfs directory, 49
PDP-7, 4
PDP-11, 4
percent sign (%), 24
permission strings, 74-75, 85
permissions, 92-93
    absolute numeric values, 98
    binary convention, 99
    binary equivalents, 100
    concentric circles of access, 98
    default (umask command), 104, 106-107
    deleting directories, 120-121
    directory, 93-96
        execute, 93-94
        execute-only, 94
        read, 93-94
        write-only, 95
    file, 91
    files, 88-90
        execute, 90-91
        read, 89
        write, 89
    modifying (chmod command), 96-98
    numeric equivalents, 100-103
    numeric strings, calculating, 102-104
    parts, 88
    setting new (chmod command), 98-102
pipe (|) character, 134-135

pipelines, 134-135, 144
    cat program, 138
    re-routing with tee command, 196-197
plus sign (vi editor), 234
-Pn flag (lp command), 384
pointers (C programming language), 524-526
postfix calculators, 38-39
postfix notation, 36
-Ppr flag (lpr command), 384
pr command
    -f flag, 390
    flags, 388
    formatting print jobs, 387-391
        comparing directory contents, 389-390
        header information, adding, 389
        piping output to lpr command, 390-391
        two-column mode, 388
preference files, 52, 61
prefixes, adding/removing with sed command, 184
print command, 188-189
-print flag (find command), 398
print job name, 395
print jobs
    formatting (pr command), 387-391
        comparing directory contents, 389-390
        header information, adding, 389
        two-column mode, 388
    removing from print queues, 393
print queue, 385-386, 391-394
    limiting output, 392-393
    mathlw queue, 391-392
    print requests
        removing, 394
        resubmitting, 393-394
    printer status, checking, 393
    removing print jobs, 393
printenv command, 57
printer configuration files, /etc/printcap file, 380-381
PRINTER environment variable, 383-385

printers script (finding local printers), 380-383
  awk script, creating, 381-382
  PRINTER environment variable, 383
  rehash command, 382
printf function (C programming language), 511
printing files, 384-387
  aliases, 386
  print queue, 385-386, 391-394
  printer information, 386-387
  specifying printers, 384-385
procedural libraries, 47
processes, 378
  errant processes, 377
  running in background, 365-368
    & symbol (moving automatically), 367
    automatic starts, 366
    files, processing, 366
    input/output, 368
    job ID, 365
    z command, 367
  stopping, 362-365
    fg command, 362-364
    screen-oriented programs, 363-364
  terminating (kill command), 374-377
    hang-up signal (SIGHUP), 376
    kill signal (SIGKILL), 376
    logging out, 377
    specifying signals to kill command, 374-375
  tracking (ps command), 368-374
    -ag flag, 372-373
    -ax flag, 373
    BSD-style flags, 368-369
    status values, 371
    -u flag, 372
    zombie process, 371
  wedged processes, 378
  zombies, 378
  see also jobs
programming languages, 5
programs
  archie, *see* archie program
  cat
    -n flag, 153-154
    numbering file lines, 153-154

  pipelines, 138
  -s flag, 136-137
  -v flag, 136
  viewing file contents, 136-139
ftp, *see* ftp program
head
  -n format, 134
  pipelines, 134-135
  viewing file lines, 133-135
more
  entering commands, 142
  /etc/passwd file, 142-143
  viewing large files, 139-143
tail, viewing file lines, 135-136
vi editor, 200-205
  colon commands, 236-241
  control-key commands, 208-209
  cursor control keys, 205-208
  deleting text, 220-229
  insert mode, 213
  modes, 201
  motion and insertion commands, 219-220
  read-only format, 234-235
  saving files, 218
  searching files, 229-234
  starting, 202-203
  startup options, 234-236
  TERM environment variable, setting, 203-204
  text, inserting into files, 212-220
  transposing case (~command), 228
  unknown-terminal-type error message, 203
  viewing file contents, 204-205
  wq command, 229
wc, 147-149
see also commands
prompt command (ftp program), 484
prompts
  $, 24
  setting custom prompts, 338-340
    cd alias, 339-340
    cwd variable, 338

    setprompt alias, 339-340
    values, 338
protocols, 467, 478
  Internet, 426-427
ps command, 368-374
  -ag flag, 372-373
  -ax flag, 373
  flags (BSD-style), 368-369
  Sequent workstation output, 374
  Sun workstation output, 374
  -u flag, 372
punctuation in commands, 28
punctuation sequences, searching, 170-171
put command (ftp program), 484
pwd command, 58
  ftp program, 484

Q

:q command (vi editor), 220, 237
q command, 141
  emacs editor, 296
:q! command (vi editor), 220, 237
Queensland University of Technology, 461
query-replace feature (emacs editor), 294-296
  options, 296
question mark (filename wildcards), 162-164
  echo command, 162
  limiting number of matches, 162-164
queuing systems (printing), 391-394
  limiting output, 392-393
  mathlw queue, 391-392
  print requests
    removing, 394
    resubmitting, 393-394
  printer status, checking, 393
  removing print jobs, 393
quit command (mailx), 416
quiting emacs editor, 283
quotation marks (nl command), 157
quoted text, 478

R

\r character (C programming language), 511
:r command (vi editor), 238-239
~r command (mailx), 418
R command (replace commands), 246
r command (replace commands), 246
  characters, changing, 248-249
:r filename command (vi editor), 237
-R flag
  lpr command, 384
  ls command, 78
    directory trees, listing recursively, 73-74
  vi editor, 234
-r flag
  ls command, 72, 78
  rm command, 122
  sort command, 151-153
  test command, 354
R value (process status values), 371
rc suffix, 54
re-routing pipelines (tee command), 196-197
read command, assigning variables, 349
read Netnews (rn) program, 317
read permissions
  directory, 93-94
  file, 89
read-file command (vi editor), 238-239
read-only format (vi editor), 234-235
reading e-mail
  Elm Mail System, 421
  mailx, 411-416
    command options, 412
    delete command, 415-416
    headers, 414
    headers command, 414-415
    index numbers, 413-414
    message display, 412-413
    quit command, 416
    save command, 415-416
recipes, databases, 452-453
recursive command, 125
redirecting files, 146-147

regular expressions, 167, 185
  notations, 167
  sed command, 182-183
rehash command, 91
  printers script, 382
relative filenames, 51-52, 61
remote Internet sites
  connections, 480-483
    logging in, 481
    logging out, 481
    rlogin command, 480
    telnet command, 481-483
  users, learning information, 447-448
remote system
  d suffix, 447
  Internet, talk system, 446-449
  users, talking with, 448
removable cartridge drives, 48
remove login.copy? message, 119
removing, see deleting
renaming
  directories (mv command), 120
  files (mv command), 119-120
repeating commands (vi editor), 253-255
replace command, 246-252
  characters, changing, 248-249
replace mode (vi editor), 279
Request for Comment, 507
responding to e-mail
  Elm Mail System, 422-423
  mailx, 414
restoring deleted text (emacs editor), 293
restricted sh shell, 307
Return command (vi editor), 219
Return key (vi editor), 201
Ritchie, Dennis, 3
rlogin command, 480-481
rm command, 121-123
  precautions with, 123-125
rmdir command, 120-121
rn program (newsgroups), 317, 468
  findgroup alias, 469-470
  g command, 472
  reading articles, 472-475
    = command, 474
  RNINIT environment variable, 469
  start up, 470-471
  starting options, 468

SUBJLINE environment variable, 474
  unsubscribing from newsgroups, 471-472
RNINIT environment variable (rn program), 469
root directory, 45, 62
row-first order, 85
RPN (reverse Polish notation), 36
rsh (command shell), 307

S

-s command (archie program), 495
S command (emacs help system), 298
-S flag (test command), 354
-s flag
  cat program, 136-137
  ls command, 68, 78
    blocks occupied by files, 66
    file size, indicating, 65-66
  more program, 139
  nl command, 156-157
  sending mail (mailx), 417
  test command, 354
S value (process status values), 371
save command (mailx), 415
  groups of messages, 416
saving
  file changes (emacs editor), 288
  files (vi editor), 218
  key mappings, 265
SCO, 2
Scott Yanoff's List of Internet Services, 506
screen-oriented programs, stopping/starting jobs, 363-364
scripts (shell scripts), 340-344
  creating, 342-343
  filename searches, 343-344
  printers
    awk script, creating, 381-382
    finding local printers, 380-383
    PRINTER environment variable, 383
    rehash command, 382
scrolling man pages (alias command), 14
search path, 62

search-and-replace command (vi editor), 257-260
changing
all occurrences within files, 259-260
words, 258-259
searches
databases, searching with WAIS, 449-454
directories, 56
egrep command, 175-176
notation, 175
expanding file searches, 170
fgrep command
awk command, 177
excluding words from lists, 178-179
multiple patterns, 176-179
wrongwords file, 176-178
filename wildcards, 162-166
character range, 164-166
echo command, 162
limiting number of matches, 162-164
spaces, 166
find command, 398-403
core files, removing, 402-403
-exec flag, 402-403
filename searches, 400-401
flags, 398
-l flag, 404
listing files/directories, 398-399
-mtime n flag, 400
-name flag, 399-400
-type specifier, 401-402
xargs command, 403-405
grep command, 172-174
-c flag, 174
character searches, 169-170
general form, 173-174
-i flag, 173
inclusion range searches, 168
-l flag, 174
letter searches, 169
-n flag, 174
punctuation sequences, 170-171
specific word searches, 168
library searches (gopher program), 460-466
National Library in Venezuela, 460-461

Queensland University of Technology, 461-463
University of California, 464-466
PATH directories (shell scripts), 343-344
PATH variable, 90
regular expressions, 167
searching and replacing (emacs editor), 294-297
backward searches, 294-295
query-replace feature, 294-296
vi editor, 229-234
? command, 232-233
/ search command, 231-232
G command, 229-231
n command, 232-234
Web sites, 432-437
AltaVista (Web crawler), 436-437
Yahoo! (search engine), 432-435
xargs command, 403-405
searching and replacing
emacs editor, 294-297
backward searches, 294-295
query-replace feature, 294-296
security
passwords, 26-27
permission strings, 74-75
sed command, 179-184
assigning paragraphs to UNIX commands (vi editor), 272-273
deleting lines in streams, 181-182
g flag, 180
prefixes, adding/removing, 184
regular expressions, 182-183
rewriting output of who command, 181
substituting patterns, 180
modifying names, 180
multiple sed commands, separating, 181
sending e-mail (mailx), 417-420
~h command, 419
~p command, 418
~r command (reading in files), 418
tilde commands, 417-418
sendmail program, 132

sentences, moving (vi editor), 266-270
(command, 268
) command, 268
/ command, 268
{ command, 270
separator flag (nl command), 156-157
Sequent computers, 131
Sequent workstation, ps command output, 374
set commands (configuration options), 319
set history command, 326
:set number command (vi editor), 256
setprompt alias (customizing prompts), 339-340
setprompt command, aliases, 337
shell alias, 126
restoring deleted files, 123
shell scripts, 92, 279, 340-344
creating, 342-343
filename searches, 343-344
printers
awk script, creating, 381-382
finding local printers, 380-383
PRINTER environment variable, 383
rehash command, 382
SHELL variable (environment variables), 314
shells, 6, 306-309
Bourne shell, 306-307
Bourne Again shell, 307
jsh shell, 307
restricted sh shell, 307
C shell, *see* C shell
case command (conditional expressions), 357
changing (chsh command), 124
choosing new shells, 310-313
available shells, identifying, 310-311
change shell (chsh) command, 312-313
valid shells, confirming, 312
visual shell (vsh), 311
command aliases, 306-307
command history, 306-307
default login shells, viewing, 308-309

environment, 313-317
  variables, 314-317
expanding file searches, 170
identifying system's shell,
  309-310
if command (conditional
  expressions), 355-356
interactive shells, 320
job control, 306-307
jobs, *see* jobs
Korn shell, *see* Korn shell
login shells, 372
looping expressions, 357-359
  for command, 358
  while loop, 358-359
noninteractive shells, 320
test command (comparison
  functions), 351-355
  file system status tests,
    353-355
  numeric comparisons, 352
  string comparisons, 353
  test operators, 352
  unary flags (file systems),
    353-354
variables, 348-350
  arithmetic functions (expr
    command), 350-351
  assigning, 349-350
  setting values, 348-349
visual (vsh) shell, 311
**short integers (C programming
  language), 513**
signals, 378
  catching, 376
**signed modifier (C programming
  language), 513**
sine (bc command), 38
single quote ('), 124
slash (/), 62
  filenames, 46
slash directory, 45, 62
**software description database
  (archie program), 496**
Solaris, 2
sort command
  filenames, sorting alphabetically,
    152
  flags, 151
  lines of a file, sorting, 152
  man page, 13
  -n flag, 152
  -r flag, 153
  sorting file information, 150-153

sorting
  data (awk command), 190
  files, changing sort order (ls
    command), 71-73
[Space] command, 141
spacing in commands, 28
spell command, 178-179
standard error, 151, 158
standard input, 151, 158
standard output, 151, 158
starting emacs editor, 282-284
starting flag, 424
startup options (vi editor), 234-236
  plus sign (+), 234
  -R flag, 234
statements
  break; (exiting loops), 521
  conditional, 517-520
    if statement, 517-519
    switch statement, 519-520
  continue; (restarting loops), 521
  if, 517-519
  looping, 520-521
    do loop, 521
    for loop, 520-521
    while loop, 520
  switch, 519-520
**stream editor (sed command),
  179-184**
  deleting lines in streams, 181-182
  g flag, 180
  multiple sed commands,
    separating, 181
  prefixes, adding/removing, 184
  regular expressions, 182-183
  rewriting output of who
    command, 181
  substitute command, 180
**streams, deleting lines with sed
  command, 181-182**
**string comparisons (test com-
  mand), 353**
stripping files, 131
**structures (C programming
  language), 526-528**
  union structures, 528
**stty commands (configuration
  options), 318**
stty tostop command, 365
**subdirectories, beginning of
  UNIX, 4**
**SUBJLINE environment variable
  (rn program), 474**

subshell, 321
substitute command, 179-180
Sun Microsystems, 5
  workstation, output formats,
    131-132
Sun system mail folders, 129
**Sun workstation (ps command
  output), 374**
surfing, 440
switch statements, 519-520
**Symantec Utilities (Macintosh),
  123**
symbolic links, 46, 62, 68, 131
**symbolic notation (chmod
  command), 96**
SYMMETRY i386, 131
sys directory, 48
**system administrator, initial
  passwords, 23**
**system prompts, setting custom
  prompts, 338-340**
  cd alias, 339-340
  cwd variable, 338
  setprompt alias, 339-340
  values, 338
System V
  man page organization, 8
  System V Release 4, 2

T

**\t character (C programming
  language), 511**
**T command (emacs help system),
  298**
-t flag (ls command), 72, 78
T value (process status values), 371
-t xx flag (ps command), 369
**tables, building with awk
  command, 194-195**
**tail program, viewing file lines,
  135-136**
talk system (Internet), 446-449
tcsh (command shell), 307
**tee command, re-routing pipelines,
  196-197**
Telnet, 426
telnet command, 480
  connecting to remote systems,
    481-482
    archie system, 496
    logging out, 482
    options, 482

telnet sites, 499-506
    Book Stacks Unlimited, 503-506
    Compact Disk Connection,
    500-506
TERM environment variable,
314-315
    setting (vi editor), 203-204
terminating processes (kill
command), 374-377
    logging out, 377
    specifying signals to kill
    command, 374-375
        hang-up signal (SIGHUP),
        376
        kill signal (SIGKILL), 376
test command, 351-355
    file system status tests, 353-355
    numeric comparisons, 352
    string comparisons, 353
    test operators, 352
    unary flags (file systems),
    353-354
text
    change command, 246-252
        lines, changing contents,
        247-248
        ranges of text, changing,
        249-252
    deleting
        emacs editor, 289-293
    deleting (vi editor), 220-229
        dd command, 224-225
        dw command, 222-223
        editing typos, 225-227
        u command, 221-222
    inserting into files (vi editor),
    212-220
        append (a) command,
        216-218
        insert (i) command, 216-217
        O command, 215-216
        o command, 214-215
    moving sentences and paragraphs
    (vi editor), 266-270
        (command, 268
) command, 268
        / command, 268
        { command, 270
    paragraphs, see paragraphs
    replace command, 246-252
        characters, changing,
        248-249

restoring deleted text (emacs
    editor), 293
transposing case (vi editor), 228
text files
    awk command, 188-195
        awk program files,
        creating, 194
        BEGIN pattern, 192
        END pattern, 192-194
        if-then condition, 194
        login shells, 189
        modifying output of ls
        command, 192
        NF variable, 190-191
        NR variable, 191
        print command, 188-189
        sorting data, 190
        tables, building, 194-195
    numbering, awk command
    (NR variable), 191
tftpboot directory, 49
Thompson file system, 4
Thompson, Ken, 3
tilde commands
    mailx, 417-418
    vi editor, 228
time
    24-hour time, 31
    displaying, 33
time command, 33
tin program (newsgroups),
475-476
TMG programming language, 5
tmp directory, 48
top-level Internet domains, 444
touch command, 91
    files, creating, 78-79
    permissions, changing, 97
transposing case (vi editor), 228
troubleshooting
    starting Netscape Navigator, 428
-ttitle flag (lp command), 384
tty, 29
tty command, 408-409
tty devices, 408-409
-type c flag (find command), 398
-type specifier (find command),
401-402
typos, editing (vi editor), 225-227
    tilde (~) command, 228

U

^u command (vi editor), 220
u command (vi editor),
221-222, 252
-u flag
    ps command, 369, 372
    test command, 354
    uniq command, 150
U.S. State Department travel
    advisories (gopher program),
    456-458
uid, 30
umask command, default
    permissions, 104-107
unary operators (C programming
    language), 514-515
uncompress command, 84
undo command, 221-222
    emacs editor, 292-293
undoing last command
    (vi editor), 252
union structures, 528
uniq command, removing
    extraneous lines, 149-150
    -c flag, 150
    common lines, 149
    -d flag, 150
    duplicate lines, 149-150
    -u flag, 150
University of California
    libraries, 464
Unix file, 49
Unix information Web site, 529
UNIXWare, 2
unknown-terminal-type error
    message (vi editor), 203
unsigned modifier (C program-
    ming language), 513-514
unsubscribing from newsgroups
    (rn program), 471-472
URL, 441
Usenet, 466-467
    database of newsgroups (C shell
    alias), 467
Usenet newsgroups list Web
    site, 529
user accounts, 6
user environment, 56, 62
    viewing, 57

user ID, 30, 40
  id command, 30
-user name flag (find command), 398
USER variable (environment variables), 315
users command, 31
usr directory, 48
utilities, whatis, 12

V

\w character (C programming language), 511
v command, 141
  WAIS databases, 451
V command (emacs help system), 298
-v flag
  cat program, 136
  lpinfo command, 386-387
values
  assigning to variables (C programming language), 516-517
  process status values, 371
  setting custom prompts, 338
variables, 360
  C programming language, 512-517
    addresses, assigning to pointers, 524-526
    binary operators, 515
    bitwise operators, 516
    character sets, 512
    character variable, 512-514
    floating-point variables, 513-514
    integer variable, 512-514
    unary operators, 514-515
    values, assigning, 516-517
  cwd (customizing prompts), 338
  environment variables, 314-317
    EDITOR, 332
    EXINIT, 317
    HOME, 57, 314
    LOGNAME, 316
    MAIL, 316
    NAME, 316
    PATH, 57, 315
    RNINIT (rn program), 469

SHELL, 314
SUBJLINE (rn program), 474
TERM, 314-315
USER, 315
shell variables, 348-350
  arithmetic functions (expr command), 350-351
  assigning, 349-350
  setting values, 348-349
veronica, 460
VersaTerm Pro, 290
versions
  BSD, 2
  DYNIX, 9
  SCO, 2
  Solaris, 2
  System V Release 4, 2
  UNIXWare, 2
vi command, 201
vi editor, 200-205
  $ motion command, 250-251
  addressing commands (vi editor), 243
  advanced commands (Table 11.1), 278
  b key (moving around files word by word), 211
  change command, 246-252
    lines, changing contents, 247-248
    ranges of text, changing, 249-252
  colon commands, 236-243
    :e command, 241
    :n command, 240
    :r command, 238-239
    :w command, 238
  command mode, 243
  control-key commands, 208-209
    Control-f command, 209-210
    Control-u command, 210
  cursor control keys, 205-208
  deleting text, 220-229
    dd command, 224-225
    dw command, 222-223
    editing typos, 225-227
    u command, 221-222
  .exrc file, 260-264
    defining abbreviations, 262
    expanding abbreviations, 262-263

listing abbreviations in effect, 263
    saving key mappings, 265
  insert mode, 213, 243
  inserting text into files, 212-220
    append (a) command, 216-218
    insert (i) command, 216-217
    O command, 215-216
    o command, 214-215
  map command
    arrow keys, mapping, 265
    Clear key, mapping, 264
    control characters, 264
    saving key mappings, 265
  modes, 201
  motion and insertion commands, 219-220
  moving sentences and paragraphs, 266-270
    (command, 268
) command, 268
    / command, 268
    { command, 270
  numbering file lines, 255-257
  numeric repeat prefixes, 253-255
  read-only format, 234-235
  replace command, 246-252
    characters, changing, 248-249
  replace mode, 279
  saving files, 218
  search-and-replace command, 257-260
    changing all occurrences, 259-260
    words, changing, 258-259
  searching files, 229-234
    / search command, 231-232
    ? command, 232-233
    G command, 229-231
    n command, 232-234
  starting, 201-203
  startup options, 234-236
    plus sign (+), 234
    -R flag, 234
  TERM environment variable, setting, 203-204
  transposing case (~ command), 228
  undoing last command (u command), 252

UNIX interaction (! command), 270-277
  awk command (creating shell scripts), 274-277
  fmt command (tightening paragraph lines), 273-274
  ls-CF command output, adding to files, 271-272
  paragraphs, assigning to UNIX commands, 272-273
unknown-terminal-type error message, 203
viewing file contents, 204-205
w key (moving around files word by word), 211
wq command, 229

viewing
  file contents, cat program, 136-139
  file lines
    head program, 133-135
    tail program, 135-136
  files, file redirection, 146-147
  large files, more program, 139-143
visual (vsh) shell, 311
vmunix file, 49
vsh (command shell), 311

W

:w command (vi editor), 220, 237-238
w command, 32
  vi editor, 220
W command
  emacs help system, 298
  vi editor, 220
:w filename command (vi editor), 237
-w flag
  ps command, 369
  test command, 354
w key command (vi editor), 211
WAIS (Wide Area Information Server), 449
  accessing, 449-451
  databases
    acronyms, 451-452
    recipes, 452-453
    searching, 449-454
    v command, 451
  keywords, erasing, 452

wc -l /etc/magic command, 128
wc program, 147-149
Web crawlers, 436
Web sites
  AltaVista, 436-437
  Berkeley Systems Design, 429
  copying files (ftp program), 483-493
    anonymous ftp capabilities, 483
    Apple Computer FTP archive, 489-490
    binary files, 490-491
    to computer screen, 489
    FTP archives, 491-492
    ftp commands, 483-484
    MIT AI Laboratory (anonymous FTP archive), 487-488
    remote directory files, listing, 484-486
    starting ftp, 484
    transferring login file, 486
  Duke Basketball Report, 435
  FTP archives, 491-492
  information servers list, 529
  Internet Services List, 529
  searching, 432-437
    AltaVista (Web crawler), 436-437
    Yahoo! (search engine), 432-435
  Unix information, 529
  Usenet newsgroups list, 529
  Yahoo!, 432-435
wedged process, 378
whatis command (archie program), 497-499
whatis database, 7
whatis utility, 12
What's New? button (Netscape Navigator), 429
while loops, 358-359, 520
who command, 31
  rewriting output with sed command, 181
whoami command, 28
Wide Area Information Server, *see* **WAIS**
wildcards, 185
  asterisk, 129
  file wildcards, history lists, 329-330

  filename wildcards, 162-166
    character range, 164-166
    echo command, 162
    limiting number of matches, 162-164
    spaces, 166
-wn flag (pr command), 388
word counts (wc program), 147-149
working directories, 62
World Wide Web, 441
  HTTP (hyper-text transfer protocol), 427
wq command (vi editor), 229
write command, 409-411
write permissions
  files, 89
  mkdir command, 116
  tty devices, 408-409
write-only permission (directory), 95
wrongwords file, 176-178

X-Y-Z

x command (vi editor), 220
-x flag
  ls command, 71-72, 78
  ps command, 369
  test command, 354
X Window System, 5, 427
  calculators, 39
  tftpboot directory, 49
xargs command, 403-405
\xhh character (C programming language), 511
XON/XOFF flow control, 303
[^xy] notation (egrep command), 175
[xy] notation (egrep command), 175

y command (emacs editor), 296
y flag (mesg command), 408
Yahoo! Web site, 432-435

z command (background processes), 367
Z value (process status values), 371
zero-length variables, 360
zombie, 378
  processes, 371

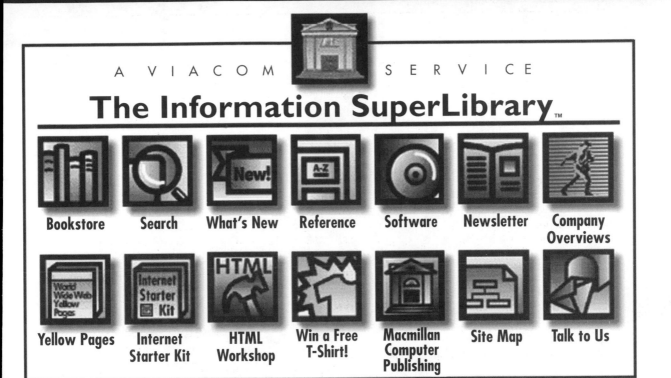

Teach Yourself Microsoft Office 97 in 24 Hours

Greg Perry

An estimated 22 million people use Microsoft Office, and with the new features of Office 97, most of them will want the upgrade. To address that market, Sams has published a mass-market version of its best-selling *Teach Yourself* series. This book shows readers how to use the most widely requested features of Office 97. This entry-level title includes many illustrations, screen shots, and a step-by-step plan to learning Office 97. One of the tasks you learn is how to create documents in Word that include hypertext links to files created with one of the other Office products.

Price: $19.99 USA/$28.95 CDN　　　*User level: New–Casual–Accomplished*
ISBN: 0-672-31009-0　　　　　　　*450 pages*

Teach Yourself the Internet in 24 Hours

Noel Estabrook

This book is the quickest way for users to learn everything they really need to know about the Internet—in just 24 one-hour lessons! It provides extensive coverage of finding access, browsing the Web, using e-mail and newsgroups, performing real-time communication, locating interesting information, and more—for Windows and Macintosh. A support site for the book is available on the Sams Web site—providing links to sites mentioned in the book, easy access to Internet shareware products, and updated material.

Price: $19.99 USA/$28.95 CDN　　　*User level: New–Casual*
ISBN: 1-57521-236-6　　　　　　　*300 pages*

Teach Yourself HTML 3.2 in 24 Hours

Dick Oliver

In just 24 one-hour lessons, you learn everything you need to know to create effective, eye-catching Web pages—from HTML basics, formatting text, and working with graphics to using an HTML editor, publishing to a Web server, and adding interactivity to Web pages. A support site is available on the Sams Web site—providing links to sites mentioned in the book, easy access to Web-publishing shareware products, and continuously updated material.

Price: $19.99 USA/$28.95 CDN　　　*User level: New–Casual*
ISBN: 1-57521-235-8　　　　　　　*300 pages*

Teach Yourself Java 1.1 Programming in 24 Hours

Rogers Cadenhead

This book is the quickest way to learn everything you need to know to create powerful Java applets! Using short, one-hour chapters, you master the basics of programming, work with graphics, and learn how to add interactivity to your own Web pages. The CD-ROM includes the Sun Java Developer's Kit, Microsoft's Internet Explorer 3.0, and additional third-party utilities. A support site for the book is available on the Sams Web site— providing links to sites mentioned in the book, easy access to Java development shareware products, and continuously updated material.

Price: $24.99 USA/$35.95 CDN　　　*User level: Casual–Accomplished*
ISBN: 1-57521-270-6　　　　　　　*350 pages*

Teach Yourself Windows 95 in 24 Hours, Second Edition

Greg Perry

With learning divided into 24 one-hour lessons, this easy-to-follow tutorial can be used by individuals, in seminars, for training sessions, and in classrooms. Whether users are just starting out or are migrating from previous versions of Windows, this is a must-have resource to get them up and running quickly and easily. It is loaded with "quick-start" chapters, "Do and Don't" tips, Question & Answer sections, quizzes, and exercises to help users master the concepts with ease.

Price: $19.99 USA/$28.95 CDN　　　*User level: New–Casual*
ISBN: 0-672-31006-6　　　　　　　*550 pages*

Teach Yourself Access 97 in 24 Hours

Tim Buchanan, Craig Eddy, & Rob Newman

As organizations and end users continue to upgrade to NT Workstation and Windows 95, a surge in 32-bit productivity applications, including Microsoft Office 97, is expected. Using an easy-to-follow approach, this book teaches the fundamentals of a key component in the Microsoft Office 97 package, Access 97. You learn how to use and manipulate existing databases, create databases with wizards, and build databases from scratch in 24 one-hour lessons.

Price: $19.99 USA/$28.95 CDN　　　*User level: New–Casual*
ISBN: 0-672-31027-9　　　　　　　*400 pages*

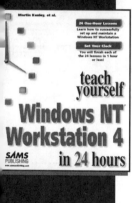

Teach Yourself Windows NT Workstation 4 in 24 Hours

Martin Kenley et al.

This beginner-level book shows users how to use the Windows 95-like environment of Windows NT Workstation. Many corporations soon may be migrating to this powerful new crash-proof Windows operating system. This book shows end-users, not system administrators, the differences between Windows 3.1 and Windows NT Workstation 4, and it teaches users how to install, configure, and use Windows NT Workstation 4.

Price: $19.99 USA/$28.95 CAN　　　*User level: New–Casual*
ISBN: 0-672-31011-2　　　　　　　*400 pages*

Teach Yourself Visual Basic 5 in 24 Hours

Greg Perry

This is the perfect starter kit for beginning Visual Basic programmers! Using step-by-step instructions and task-oriented examples, this hands-on guide teaches you how to use Visual Basic and Visual Basic Control Creation, explains what ActiveXs are and how to build them, and shows you how to increase your marketability in the competitive world of programming. With just 24 one-hour lessons, you will master the basics of this powerful language. The CD-ROM contains the Publisher's Edition of *Visual Basic for Control Creation*, sample applications, and ActiveX controls, as well as downloadable ActiveX samples from Microsoft.

Price: $19.99 USA/$28.95 CAN　　　*User level: New–Casual–Accomplished*
ISBN: 0-672-31064-3　　　　　　　*450 pages*

Add to Your Sams Library Today with the Best Boo
Programming, Operating Systems, and New Techno

The easiest way to order is to pick up the phone and o

1-800-428-5331

between 9:00 a.m. and 5:00 p.m. EST.
For faster service please have your credit card availab

ISBN	Quantity	Description of Item	Unit Cost
0-672-31009-0		Teach Yourself Microsoft Office 97 in 24 Hours	$19.99
1-57521-236-6		Teach Yourself the Internet in 24 Hours	$19.99
1-57521-235-8		Teach Yourself HTML 3.2 in 24 Hours	$19.99
1-57521-270-6		Teach Yourself Java 1.1 Programming in 24 Hours (Book/CD-ROM)	$24.99
0-672-31006-6		Teach Yourself Windows 95 in 24 Hours, Second Edition	$19.99
0-672-31027-9		Teach Yourself Access 97 in 24 Hours	$19.99
0-672-31011-2		Teach Yourself Windows NT Workstation 4 in 24 Hours	$19.99
0-672-31064-3		Teach Yourself Visual Basic 5 in 24 Hours (Book/CD-ROM)	$19.99
		Shipping and Handling: See information below.	
		TOTAL	

❏ 3 ½" Disk

❏ 5 ¼" Disk

Shipping and Handling: $4.00 for the first book, and $1.75 for each additional book. Floppy disk: add $1.75 for s
handling. If you need to have it NOW, we can ship product to you in 24 hours for an additional charge of ap
$18.00, and you will receive your item overnight or in two days. Overseas shipping and handling adds $2.00 p
$8.00 for up to three disks. Prices subject to change. Call for availability and pricing information on latest editior

201 W. 103rd Street, Indianapolis, Indiana 46290

1-800-428-5331 — Orders   1-800-835-3202 — FAX   1-800-858-7674 — Customer Service

Book ISBN 0-672-

MACMILLAN COMPUTER PUBLISHING USA

A VIACOM COMPANY

Technical Support:

If you need assistance with the information in this book or with a CD/Disk
accompanying the book, please access the Knowledge Base on our Web
site at **http://www.superlibrary.com/general/support**. Our most
Frequently Asked Questions are answered there. If you do not find the
answer to your questions on our Web site, you may contact Macmillan
Technical Support **(317) 581-3833** or e-mail us at **support@mcp.com**.

diff | lp -damsra20